Take The Long Way Home

First Edition
Printed by Gauvin in Quebec, Canada

Edited by Andy Brown for Conundrum Press

Library and Archives Canada Cataloguing in Publication

Title: Take the long way home / by Jon Claytor.
Names: Claytor, Jon, author, artist.
Identifiers: Canadiana 20220147280 | ISBN 9781772620702 (softcover)
Subjects: LCSH: Claytor, Jon—Comic books, strips, etc. | LCSH: Claytor, Jon—Travel—Canada—Comic
books, strips, etc. | LCSH: Claytor, Jon—Family—Comic books, strips, etc. | LCSH: Artists—Canada—Biography—Comic books, strips, etc. | LCSH: Recovering alcoholics—Canada—Biography—Comic books,
strips, etc. | CSH: Authors, Canadian (English)—Biography—Comic books, strips, etc. | LCGFT:
Autobiographical comics. | LCGFT: Graphic novels.
Classification: LCC PN6733.C56 T35 2022 | DDC 741.5/971—dc23

Conundrum Press
Wolfville, Nova Scotia, Canada
www.conundrumpress.com

Conundrum Press acknowledges the financial support of the Canada Council for the Arts, the government of Canada, and the province of Nova Scotia toward their publishing program.

Canada Council for the Arts
Conseil des Arts du Canada

NOVA SCOTIA

Take The Long Way Home

By

Jon Claytor

In the fall of 2019 I was offered a chance to do an artist residency in Prince Rupert B.C. I decided to drive there from Halifax and back and make a comic about the trip. I was a bit of a mess and I hoped I might straighten things out a little. This is the story of that trip.

Let's start
in
Halifax
saying
goodbye
to
My dad

1

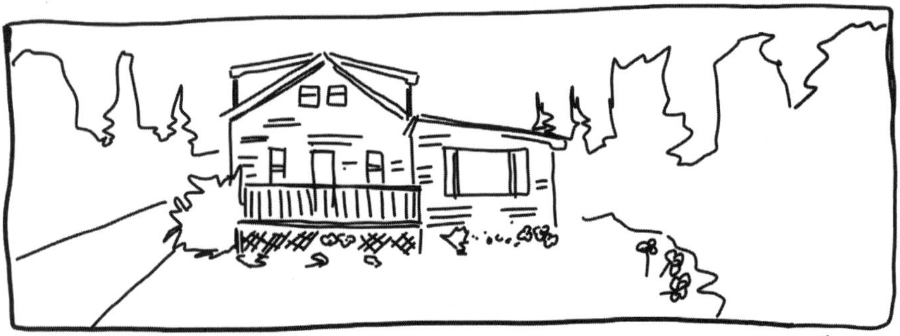

I love visiting my dad and Nora's small blue house in Ketch Harbour.

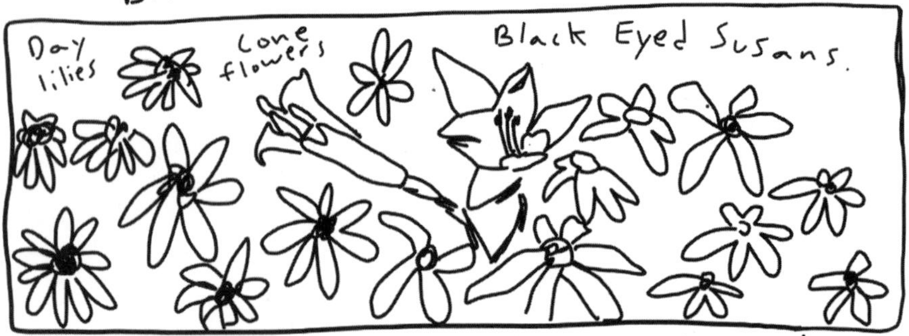
Day lilies
Cone flowers
Black Eyed Susans.

A tour of the flowers is very important.

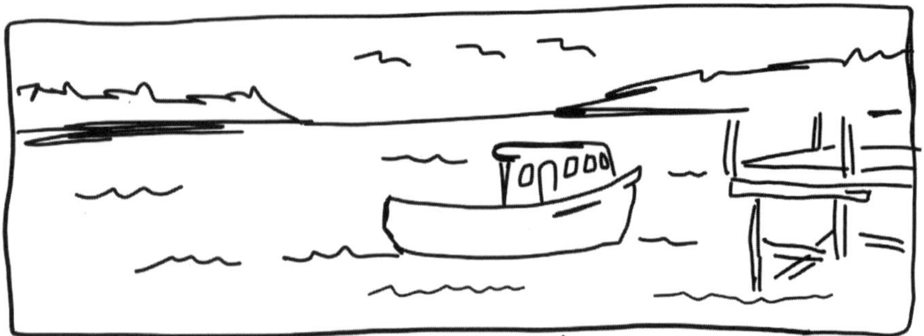

And always a quick walk down by the water.

47 years old and I still go to my dad for advice.

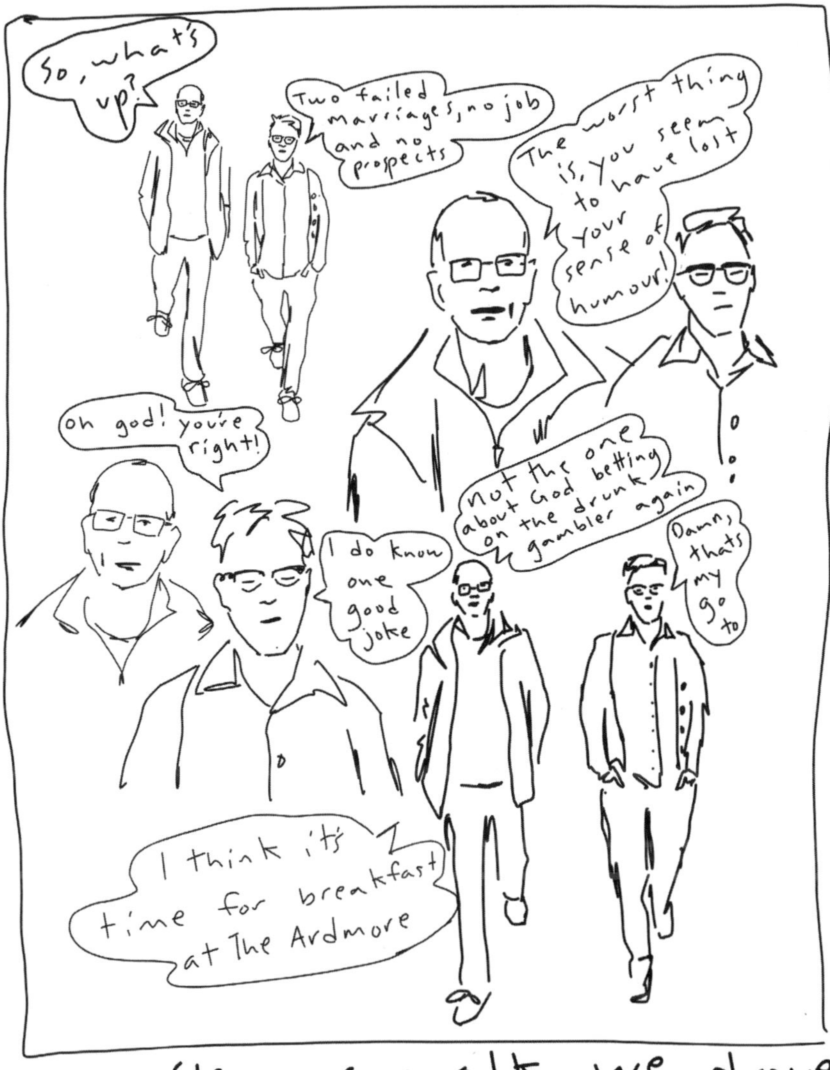
So, what's up?
Two failed marriages, no job and no prospects
The worst thing is, you seem to have lost your sense of humour!
Oh god! you're right!
not the one about God betting on the drunk gambler again
I do know one good joke
Damn, thats my go to
I think it's time for breakfast at The Ardmore

So after our walk we drove down to Quinpool.

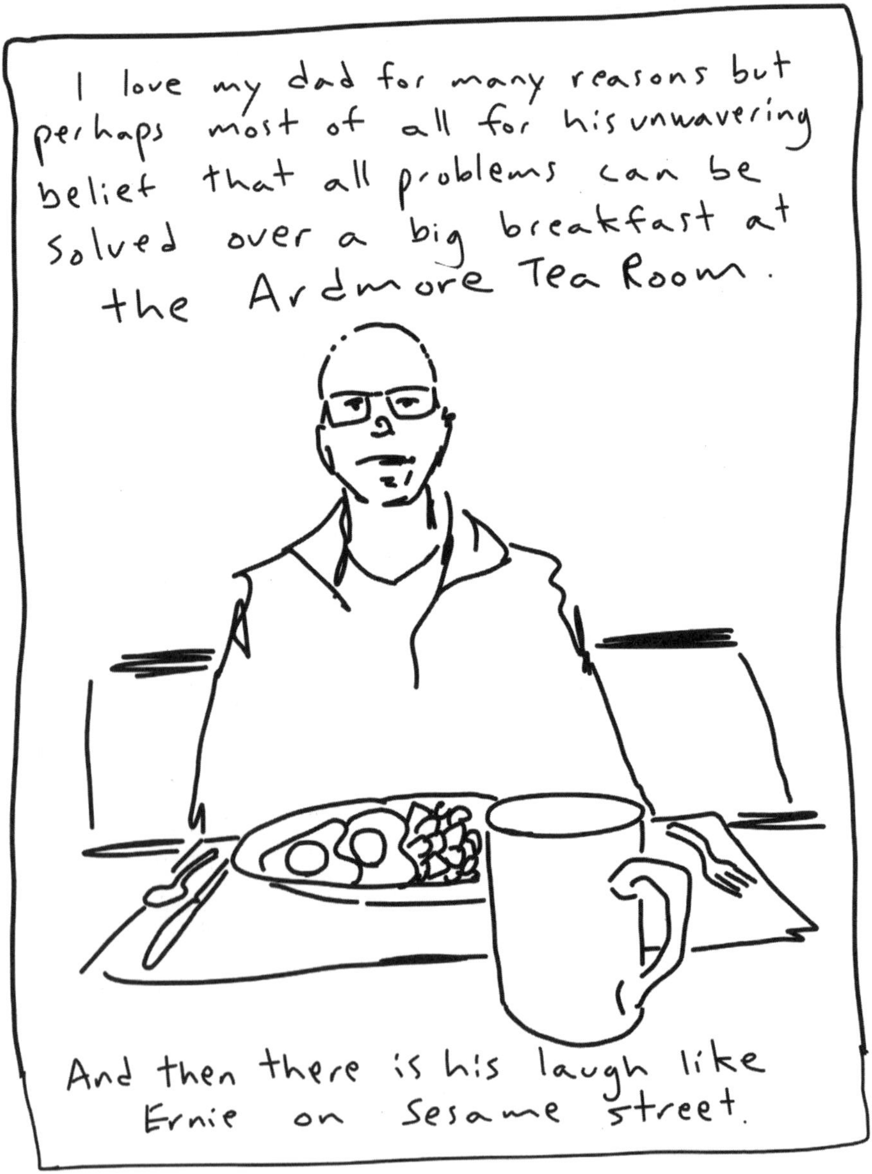
I love my dad for many reasons but perhaps most of all for his unwavering belief that all problems can be solved over a big breakfast at the Ardmore Tea Room.
And then there is his laugh like Ernie on Sesame street.

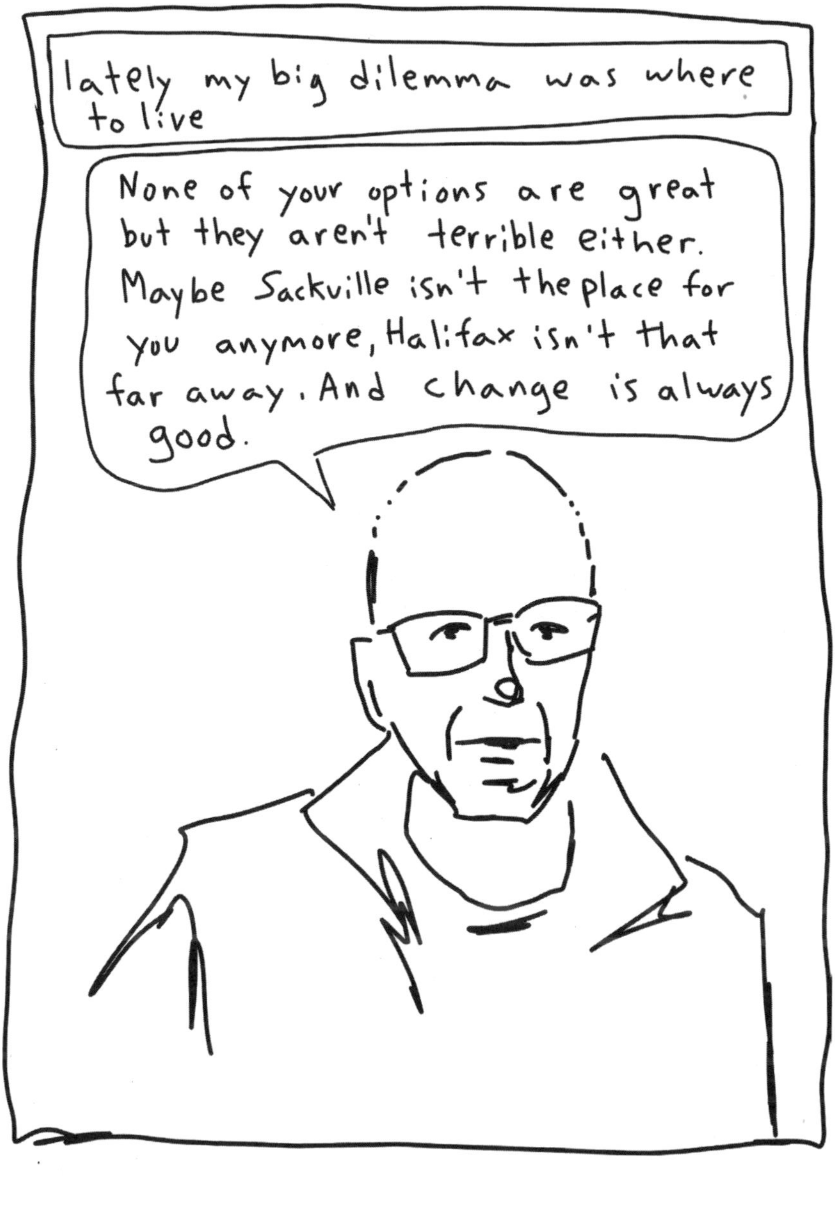
lately my big dilemma was where to live
None of your options are great but they aren't terrible either. Maybe Sackville isn't the place for you anymore, Halifax isn't that far away. And change is always good.

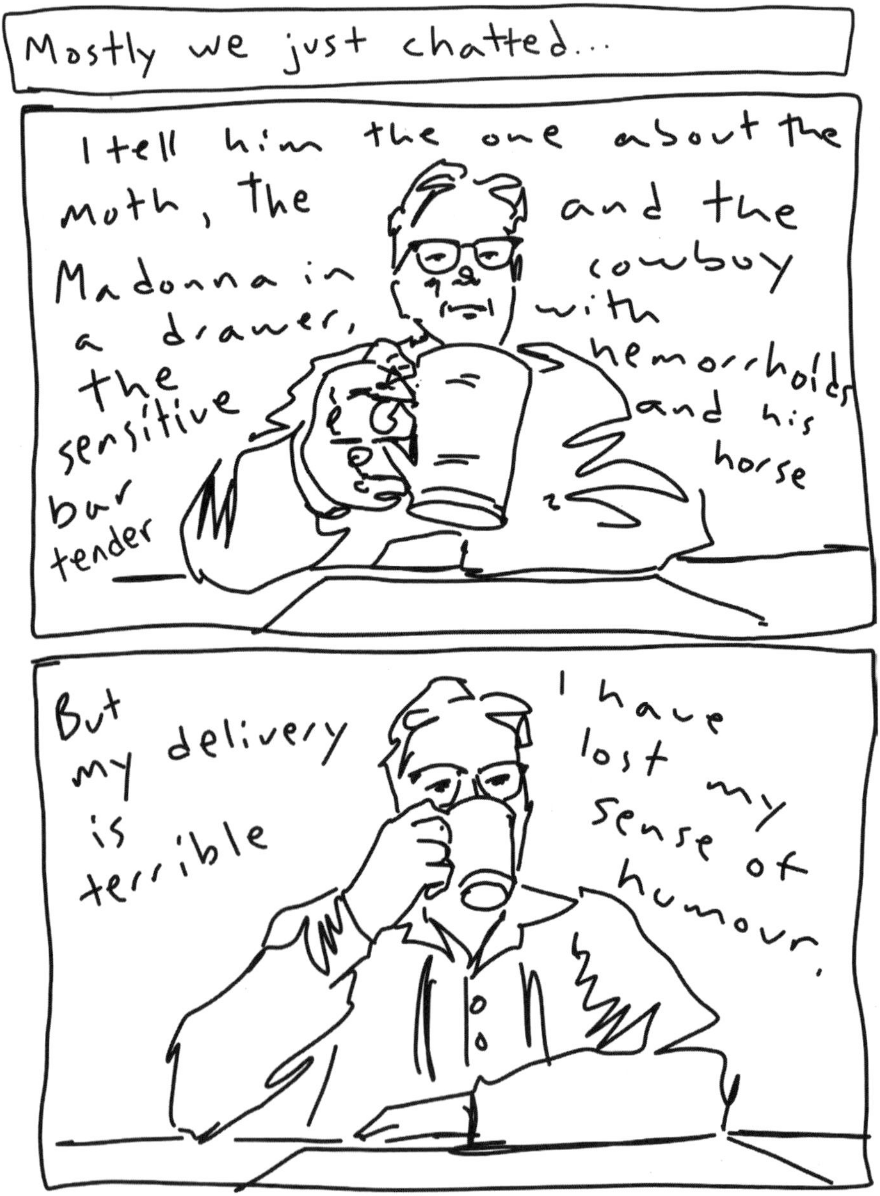
Mostly we just chatted...
I tell him the one about the moth, the Madonna in a drawer, the sensitive bar tender
and the cowboy with hemorrhoids and his horse
But my delivery is terrible
I have lost my sense of humour.

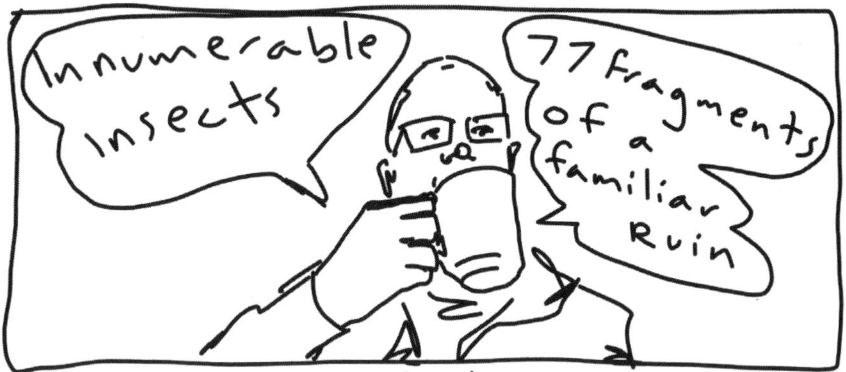
Innumerable insects
77 fragments of a familiar Ruin

He tells me about the books he's reading. Poetry and science. This is a man with answers. And data to back them up.

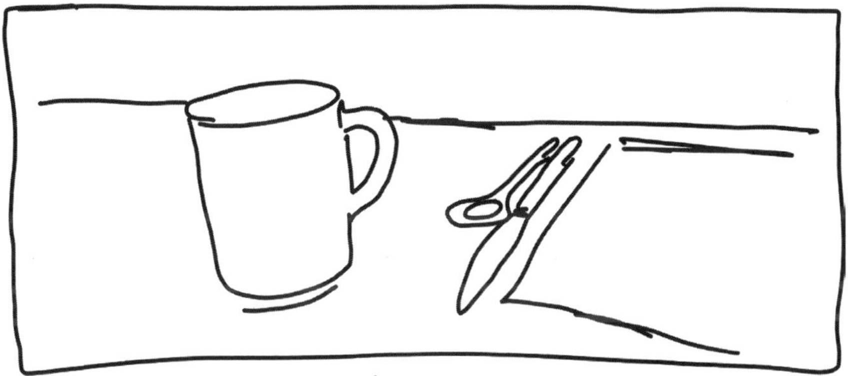

we sit in silence too. A silence made comfortable by coffee.

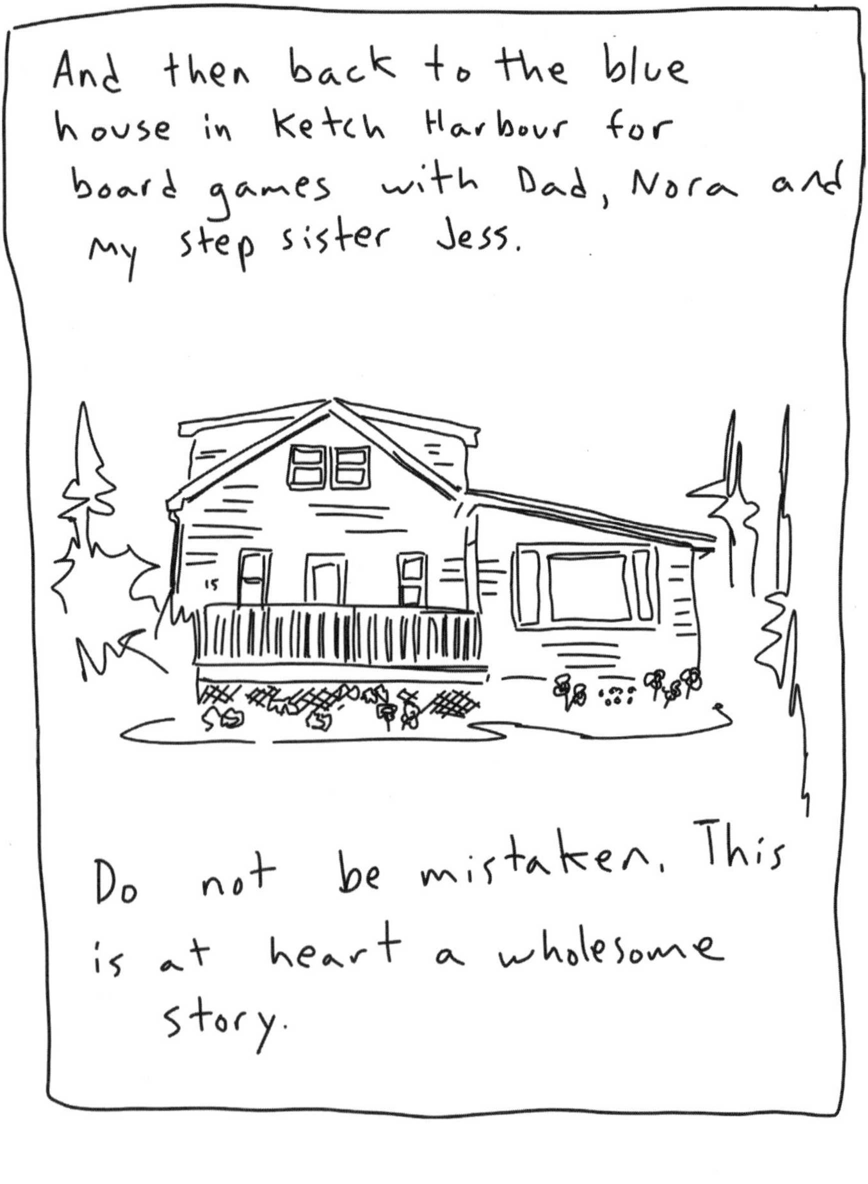
And then back to the blue house in Ketch Harbour for board games with Dad, Nora and my step sister Jess.
Do not be mistaken. This is at heart a wholesome story.

2

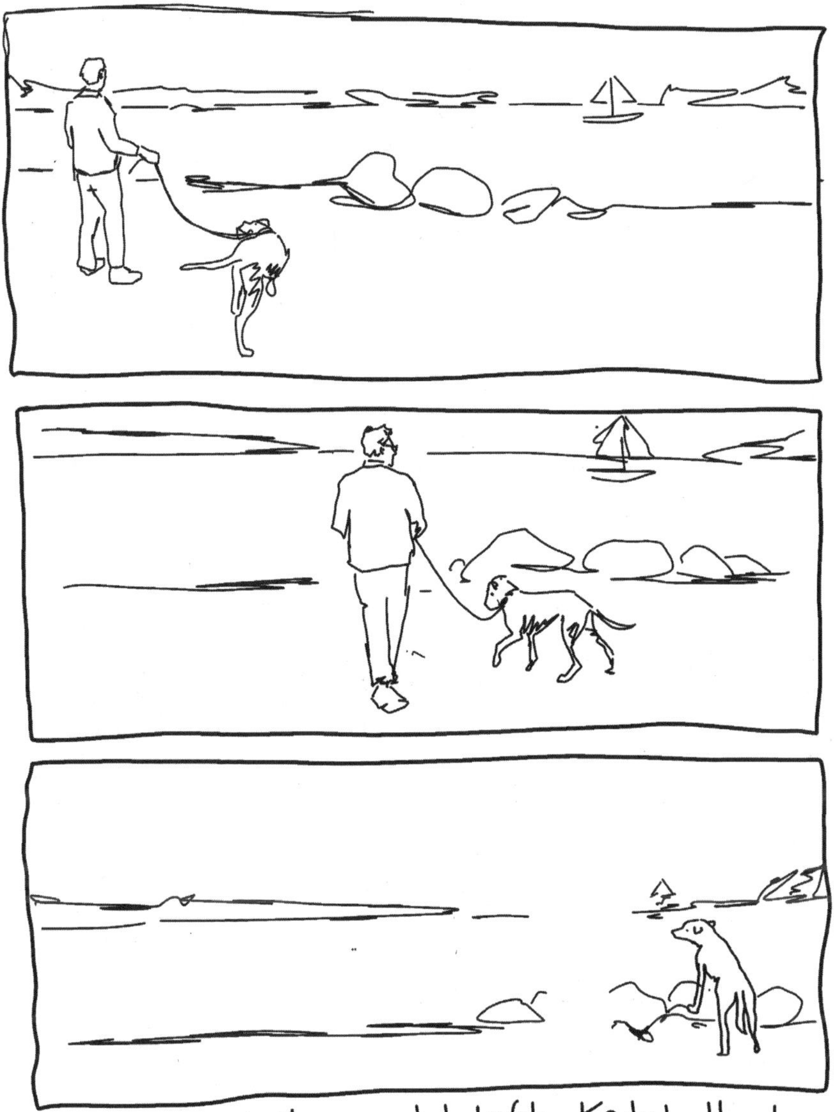

Before Stella and I left Ketch Harbour we walked down to the water.

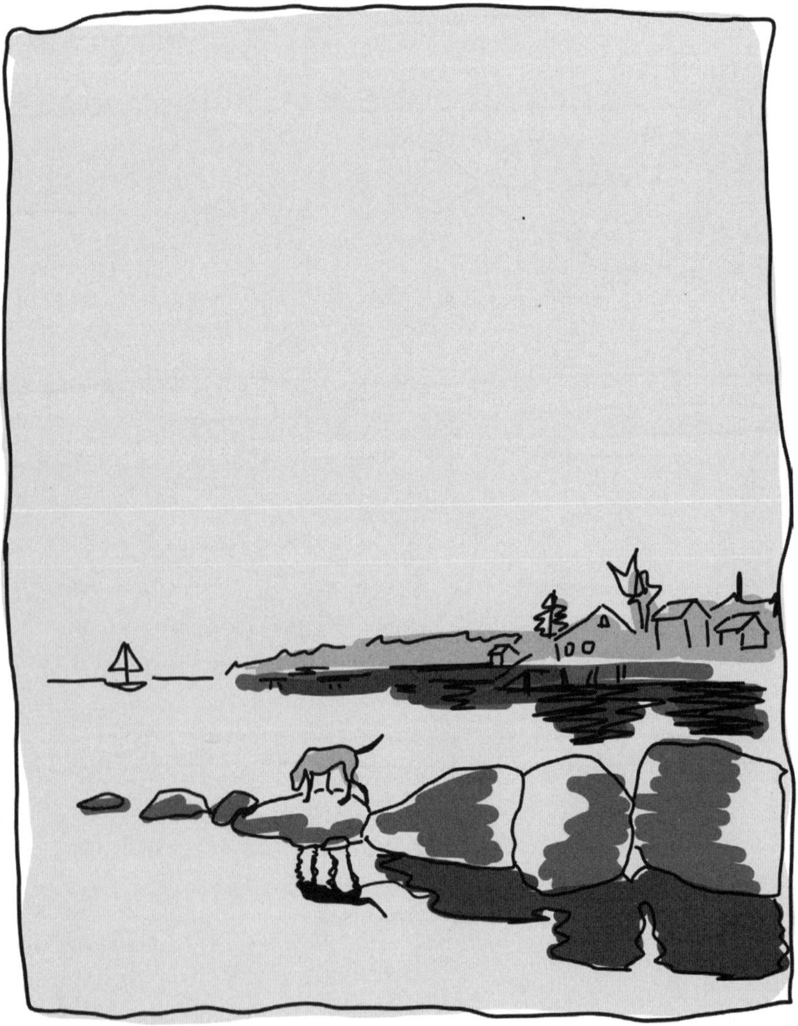

of course, stella had to go as far as possible.

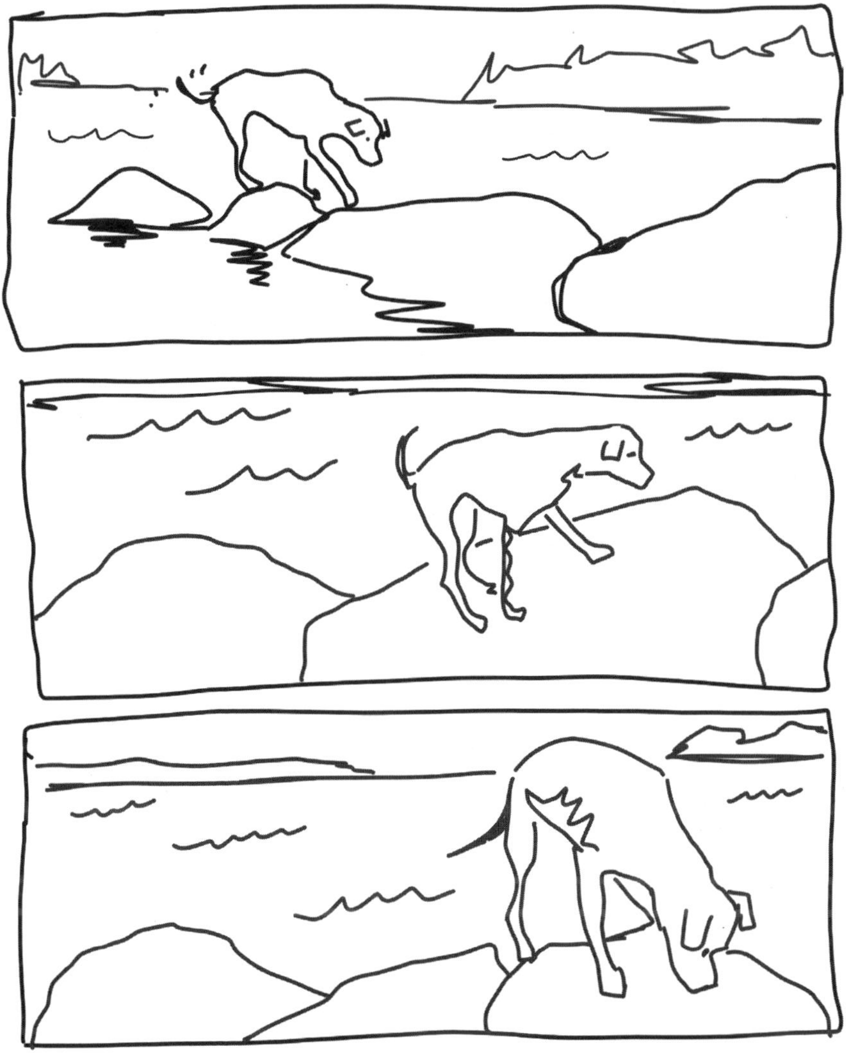

She seemed to have something on her mind.

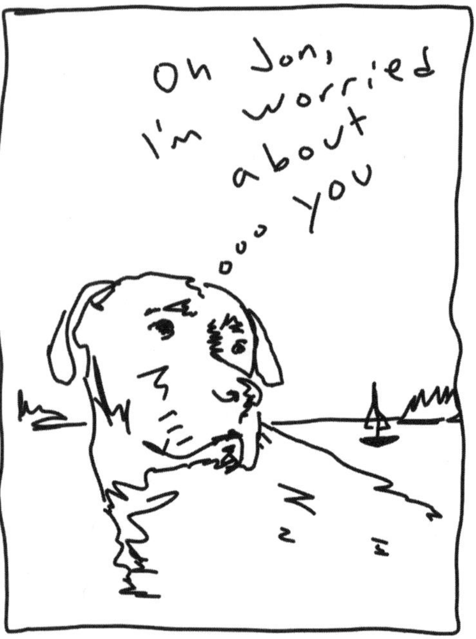
Oh Jon, I'm worried about you

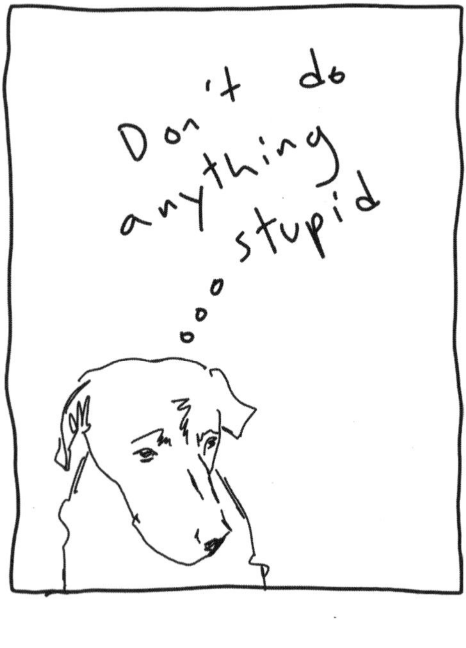
Don't do anything stupid

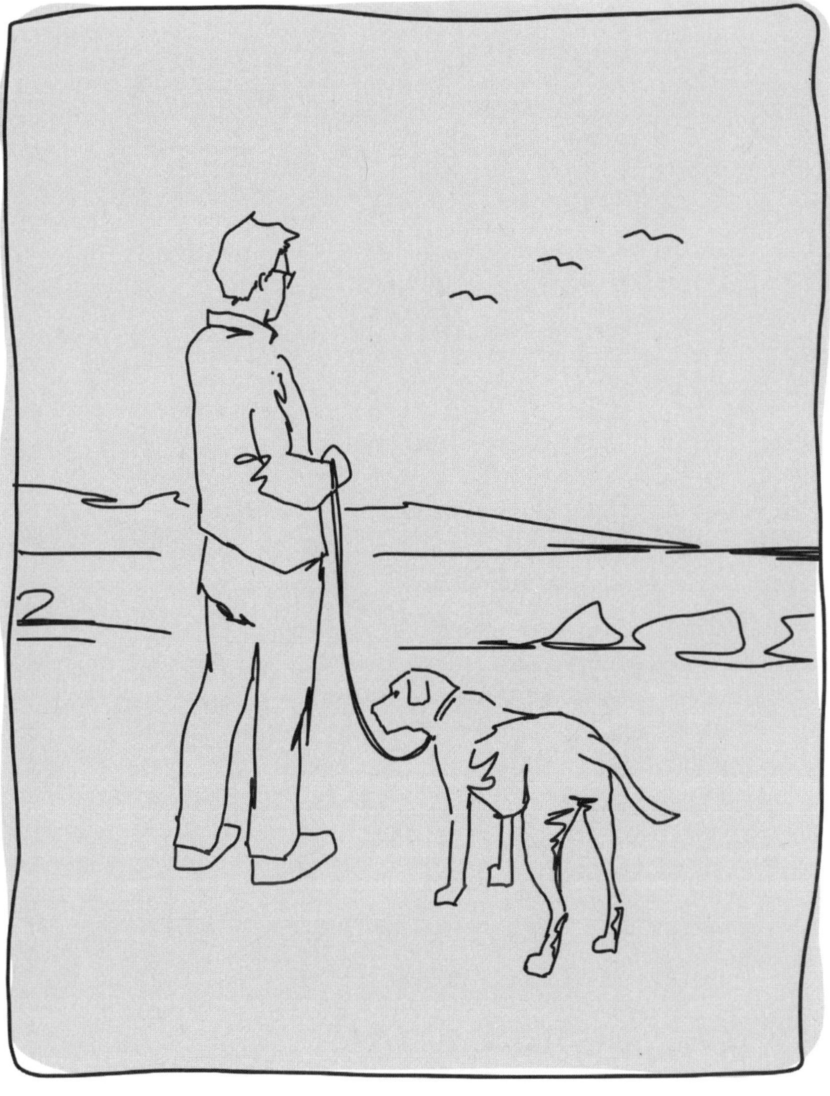

3

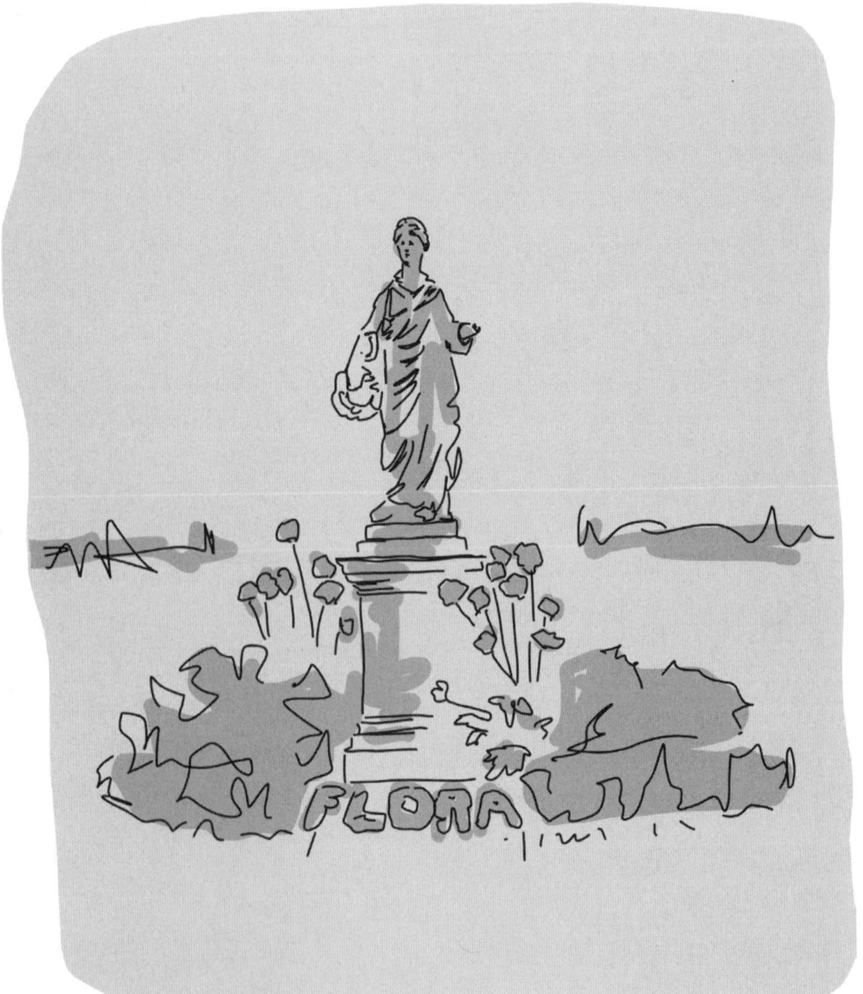
FLORA

Eleanor said to meet her at the Public Gardens, our favourite place to walk.

The dahlias were in bloom and you could easily overhear them gossiping about each other and being a bit nasty.

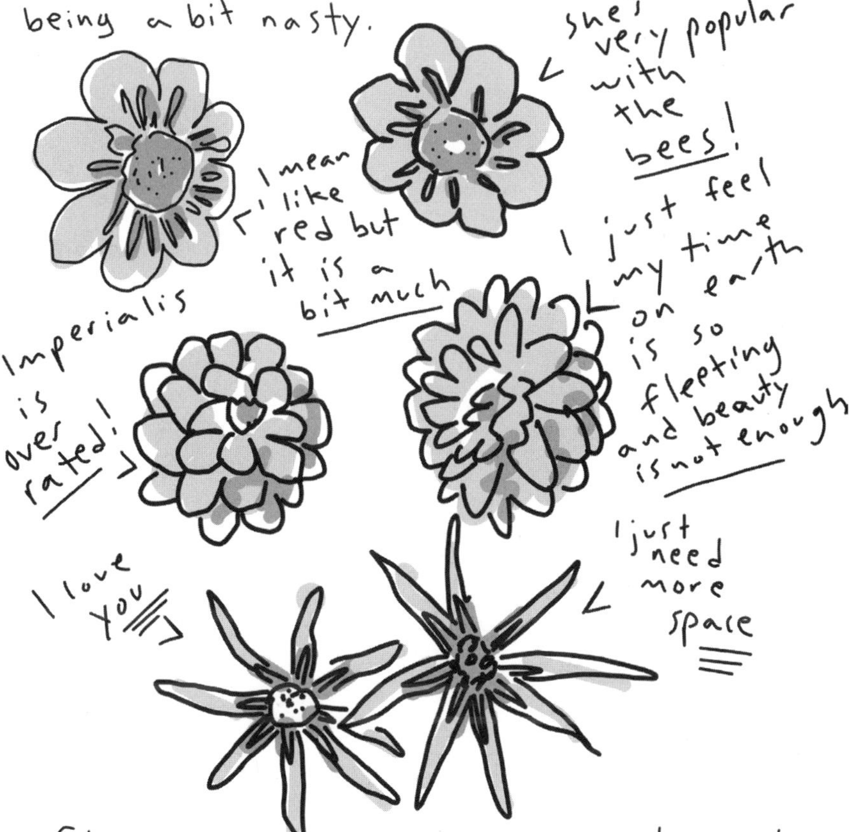
she's very popular with the bees!
I mean I like red but it is a bit much
I just feel my time on earth is so fleeting and beauty is not enough
Imperialis is over rated!
I love you
I just need more space

flowers can be so mean to each other but it can't be easy to be so beautiful.

I found her by the pond.

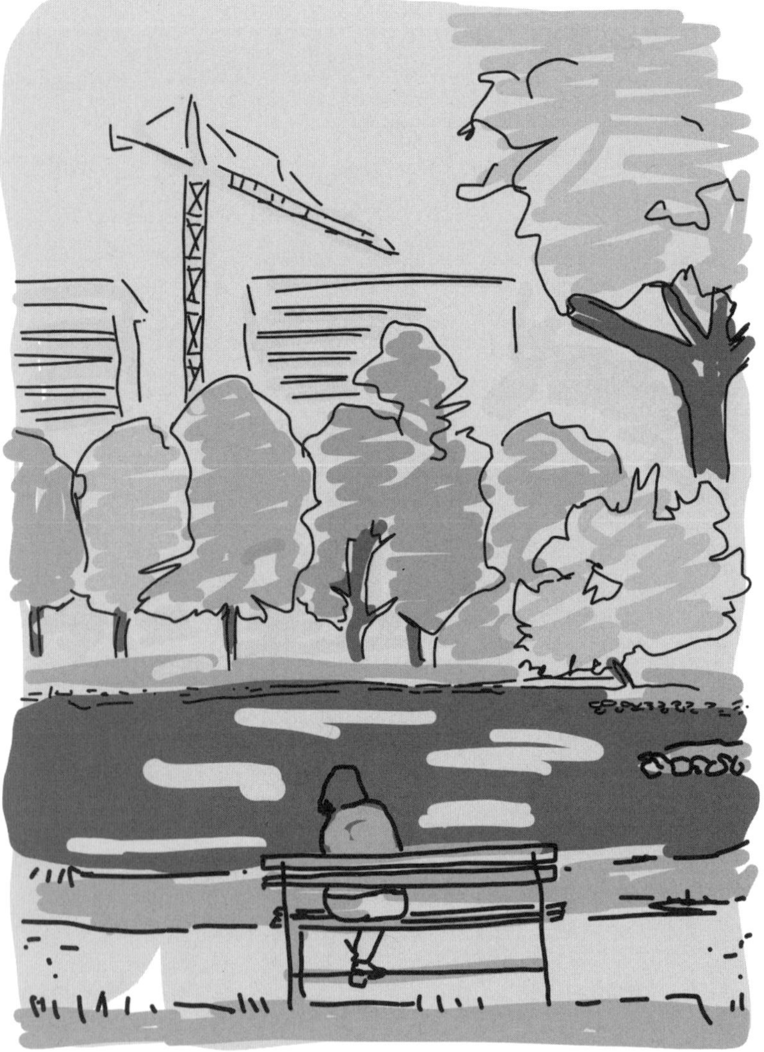

She was quietly watching the city change which is kinda her thing.

A duck strolled over to tell us what she thought of humanity.

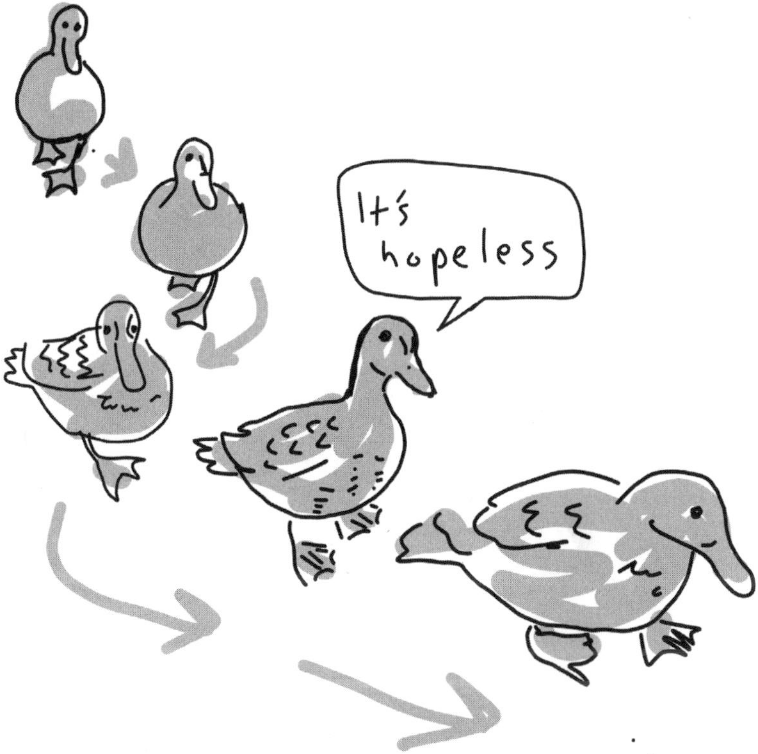
It's hopeless

But then again maybe she was being more specific.

we went for coffee on Dresden Row

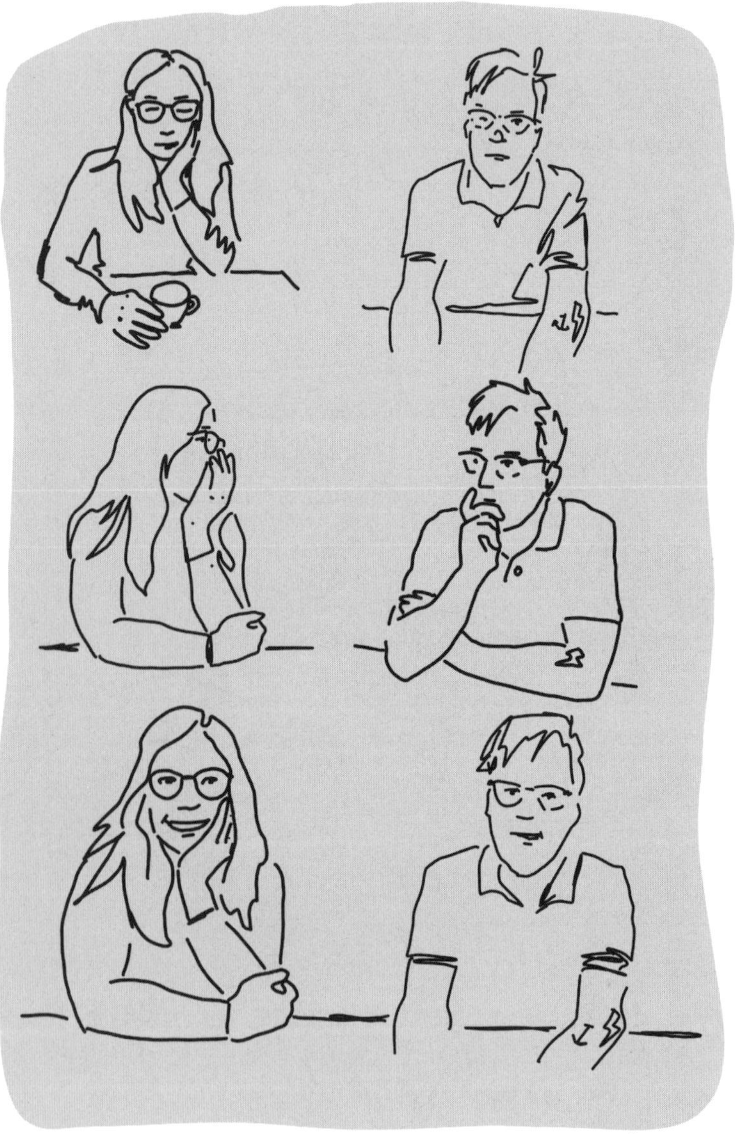

and we talked about everything

And we talked about nothing.

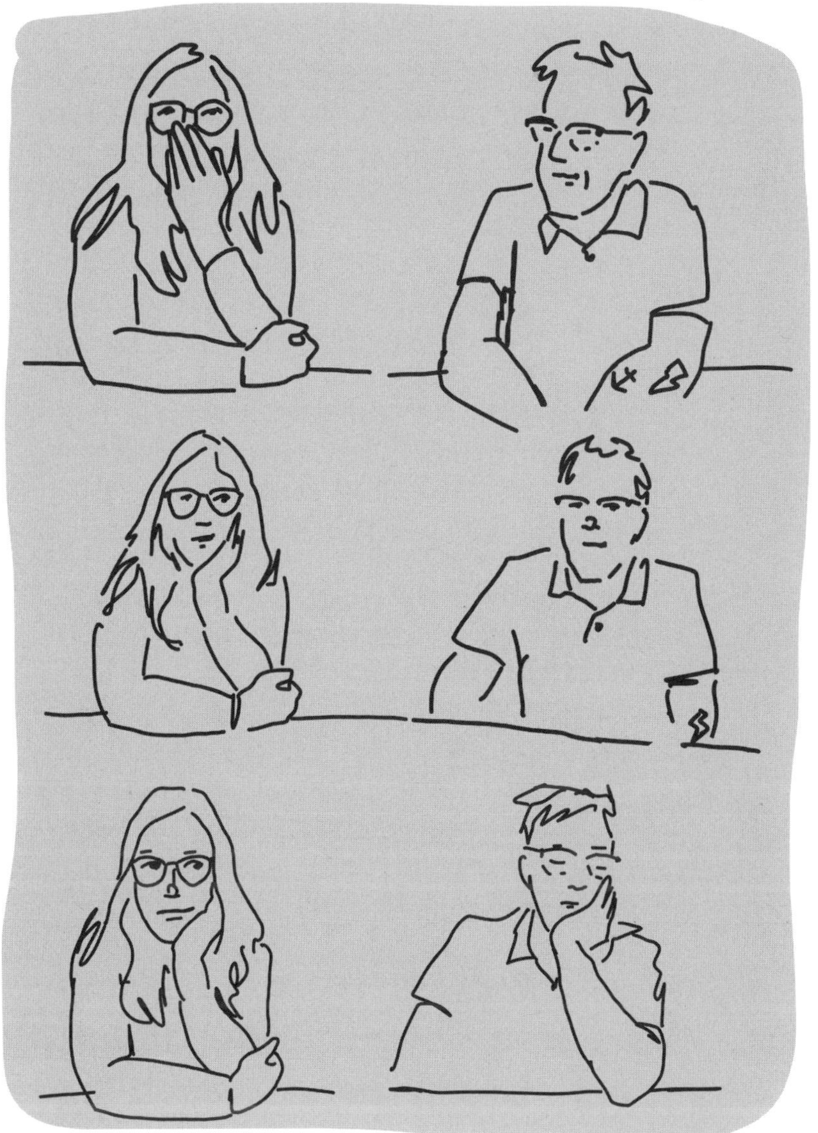

And then it was time to say goodbye

Our relationship was messy, which was all my fault. I was much older than Eleanor and should have known better, more on that later.

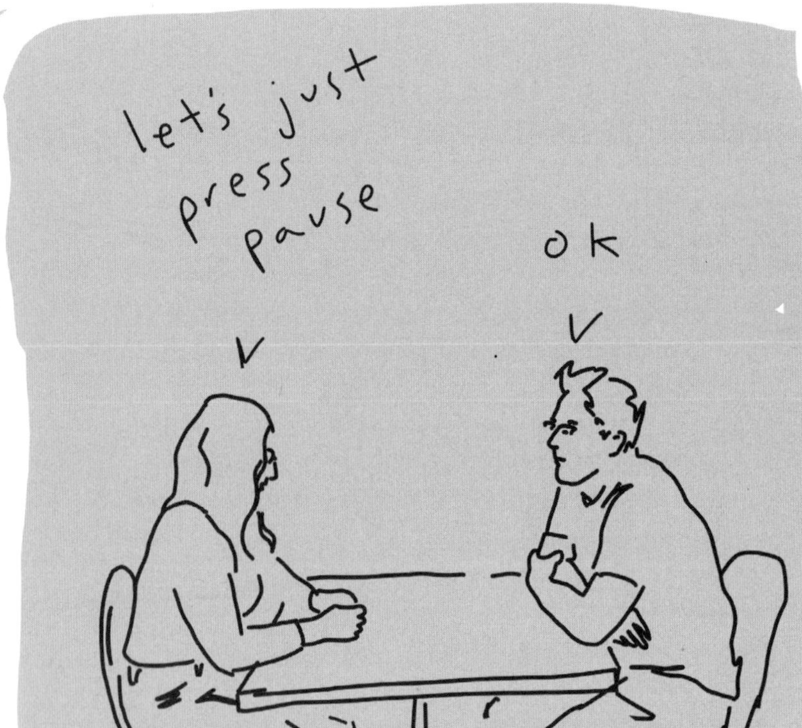
let's just press pause
ok

Finally, we had made a decision. I don't think either of us thought it would be a permanent pause.

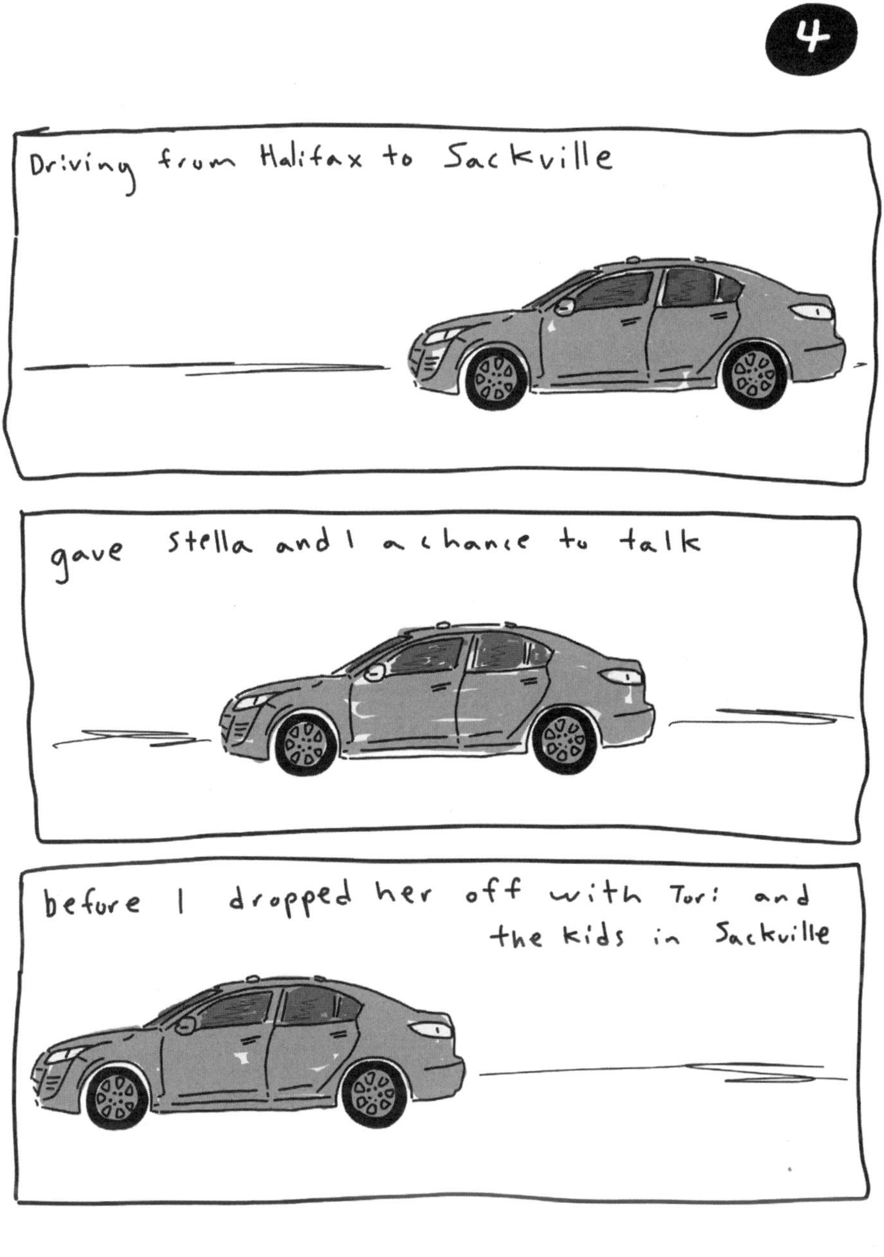
4
Driving from Halifax to Sackville
gave Stella and I a chance to talk
before I dropped her off with Tori and the kids in Sackville

we stopped for some water
and fresh air. I wished I could
bring her all the way on this trip

with me but she would miss the
kids too much and she hates to
travel. I can relate to that
feeling. She's a good girl.

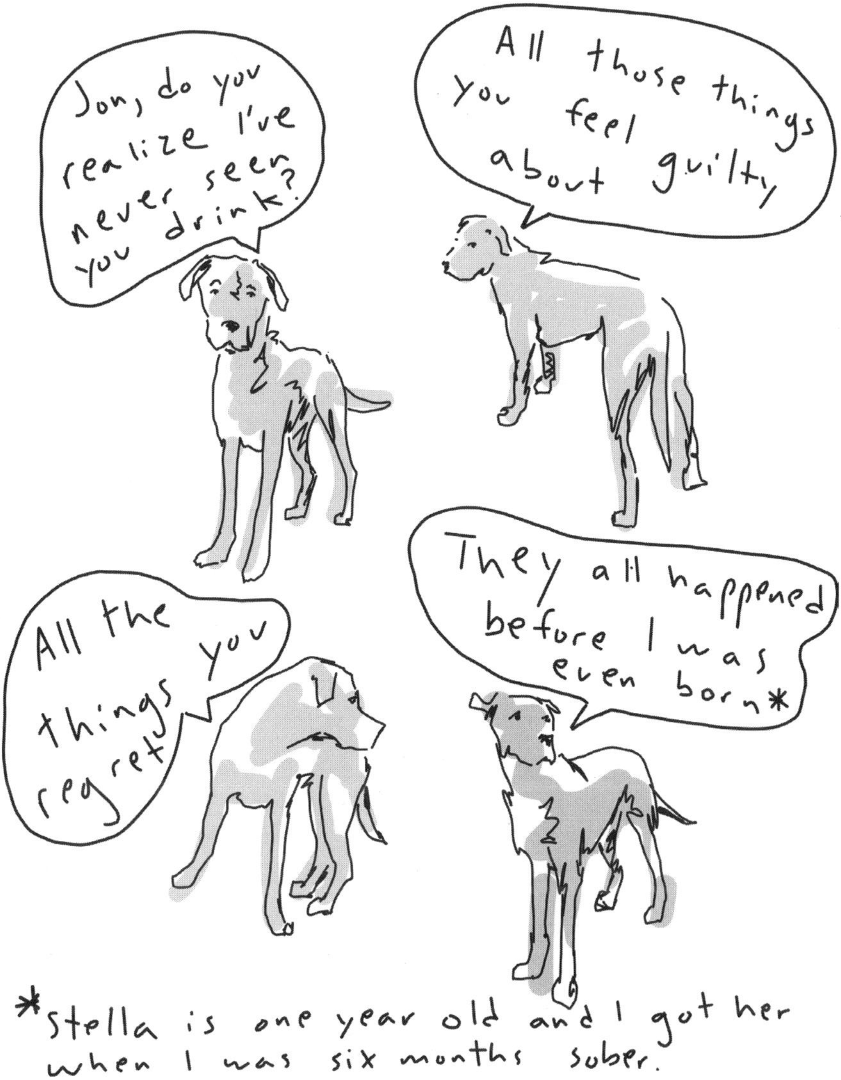
Jon, do you realize I've never seen you drink?
All those things you feel guilty about
All the things you regret
They all happened before I was even born*
*Stella is one year old and I got her when I was six months sober.

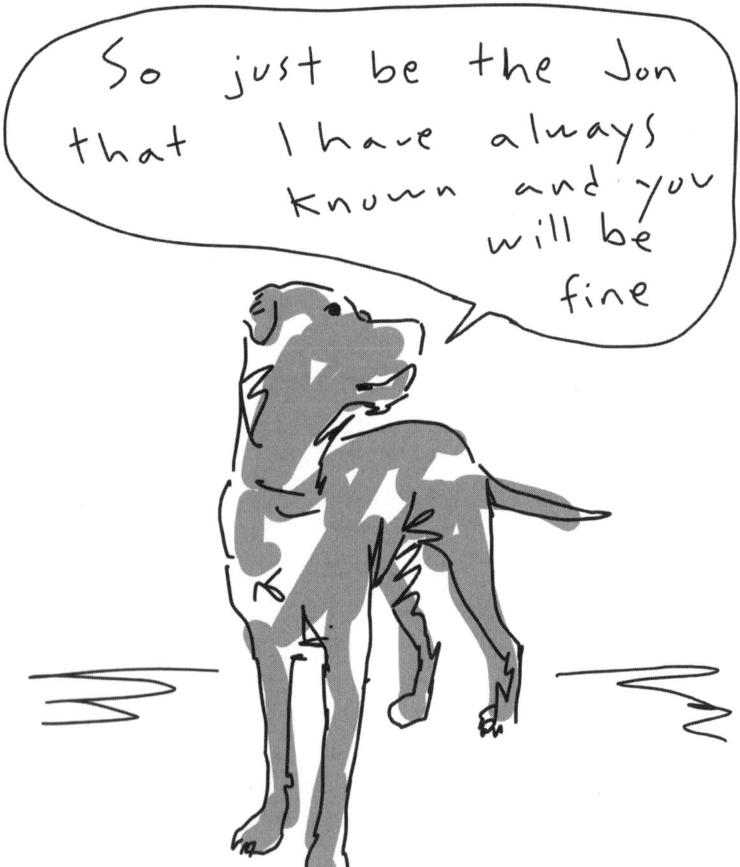
So just be the Jon that I have always known and you will be fine

Back in the car....

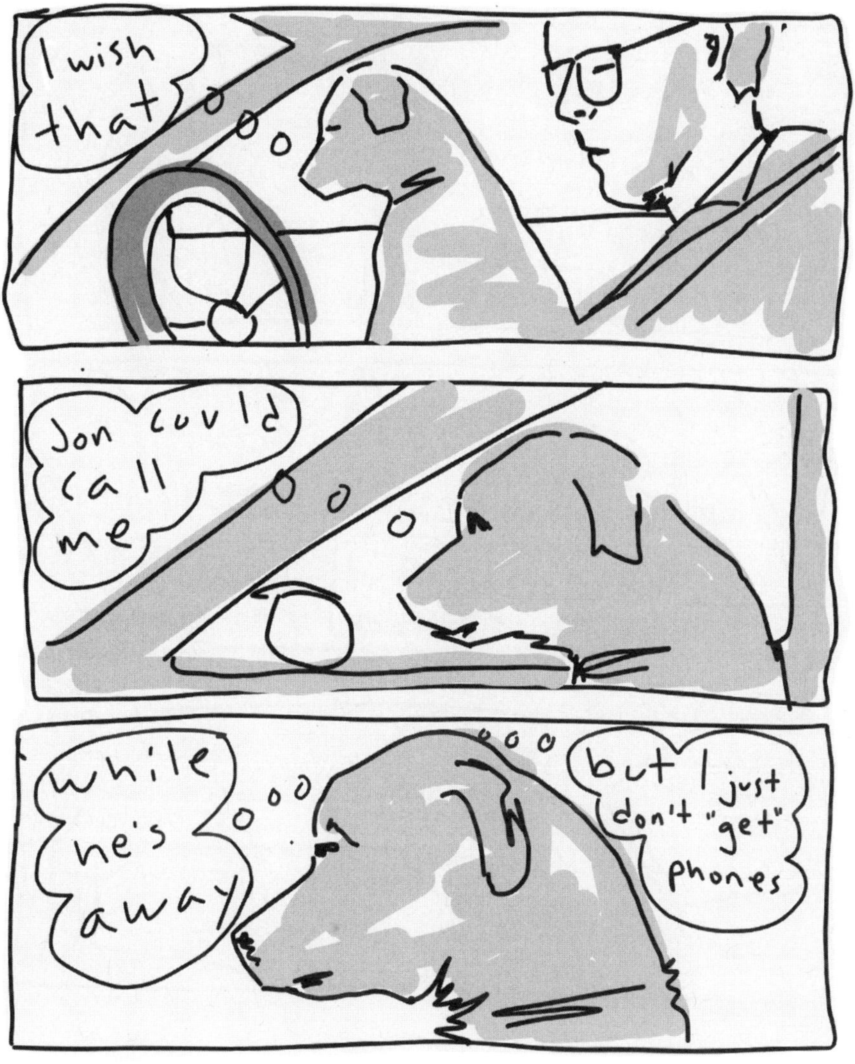
I wish that
Jon could call me
while he's away
but I just don't "get" phones

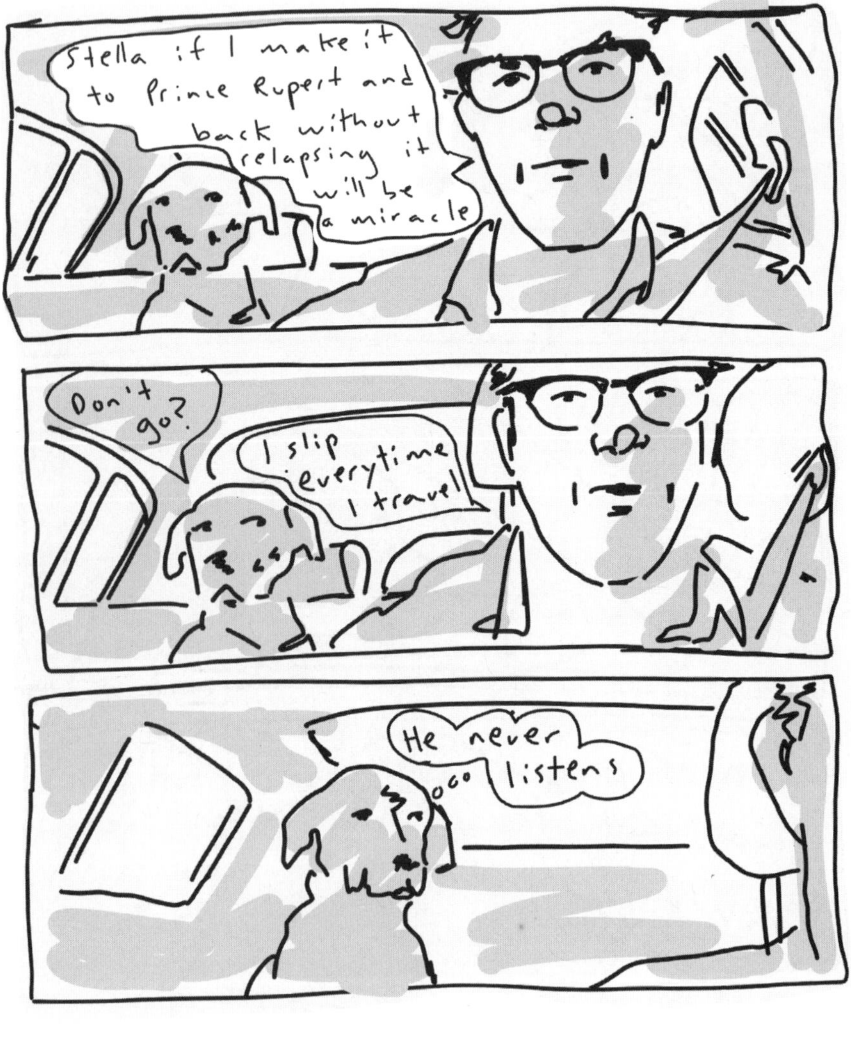
Stella if I make it to Prince Rupert and back without relapsing it will be a miracle
Don't go?
I slip everytime I travel
He never listens

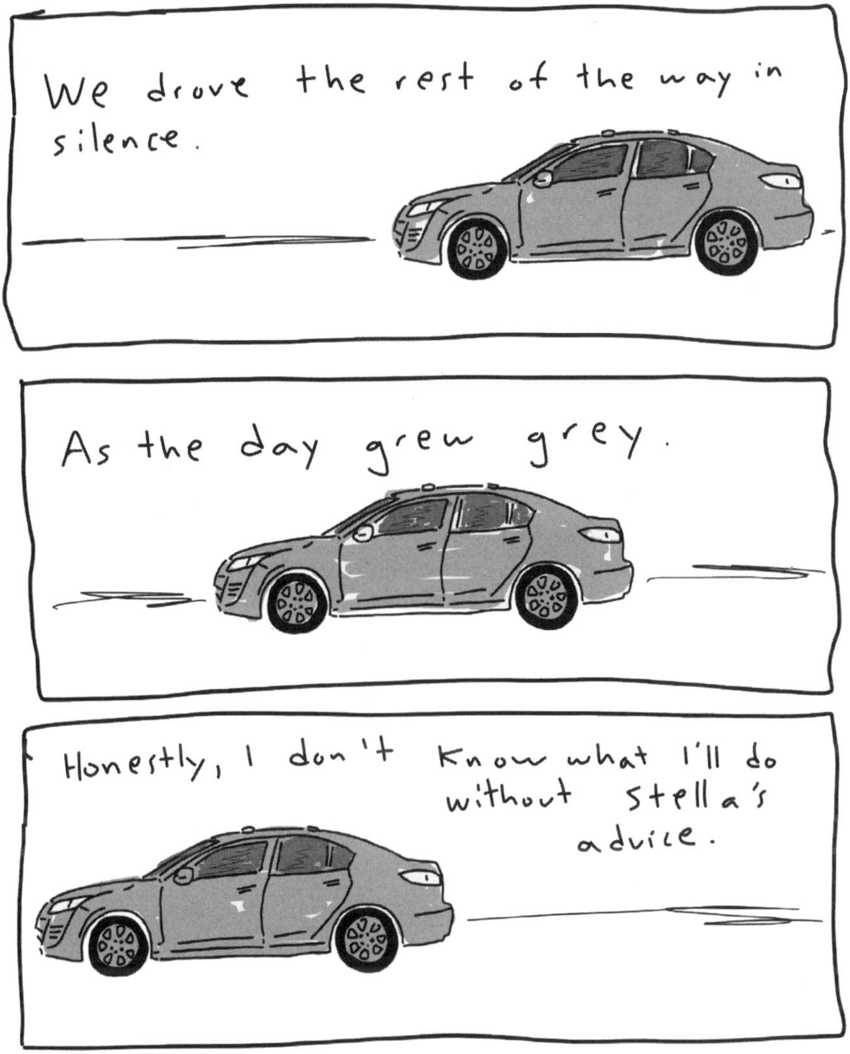
We drove the rest of the way in silence.
As the day grew grey.
Honestly, I don't know what I'll do without Stella's advice.

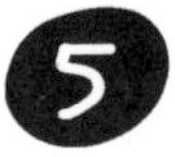

5

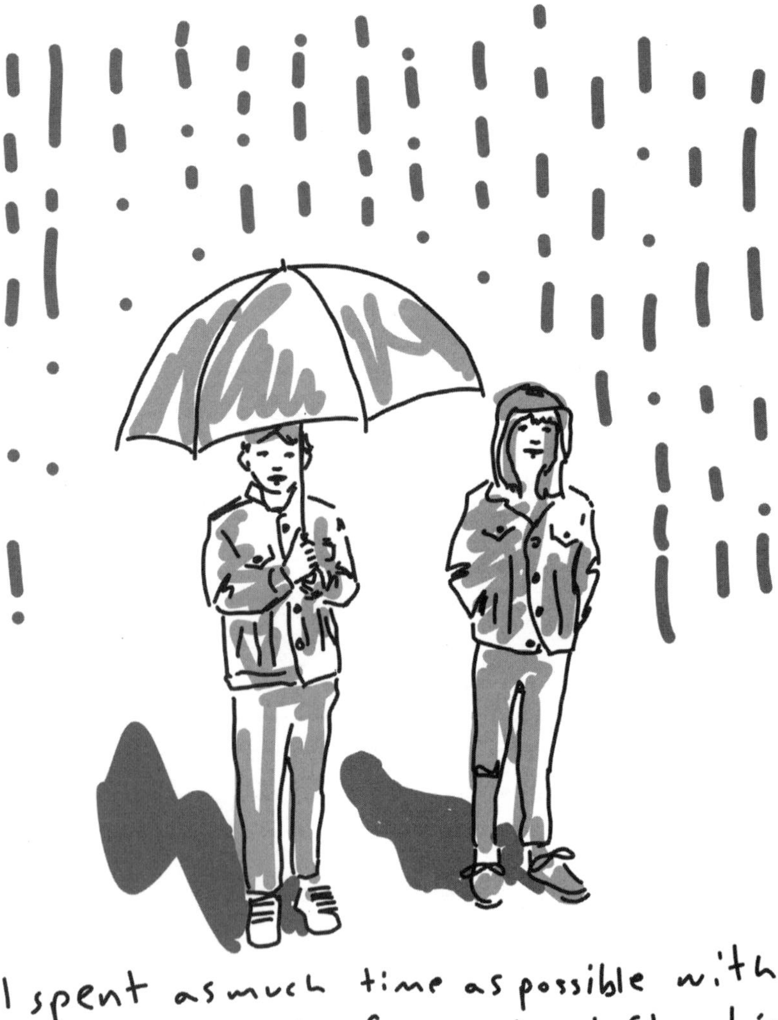

I spent as much time as possible with the twins before I left which included a few walks in the rain and trips to the skate park, visits to the monkey bars (the best kind of bars), walks around the waterfowl park (we saw otters!) lots of time drawing and playing cards. But the good times can't last.

Summer had ended and school started again and as much as I was in denial, I had to accept the fact I was going to be away for six weeks. Why was I nervous, what did I think was going to happen?

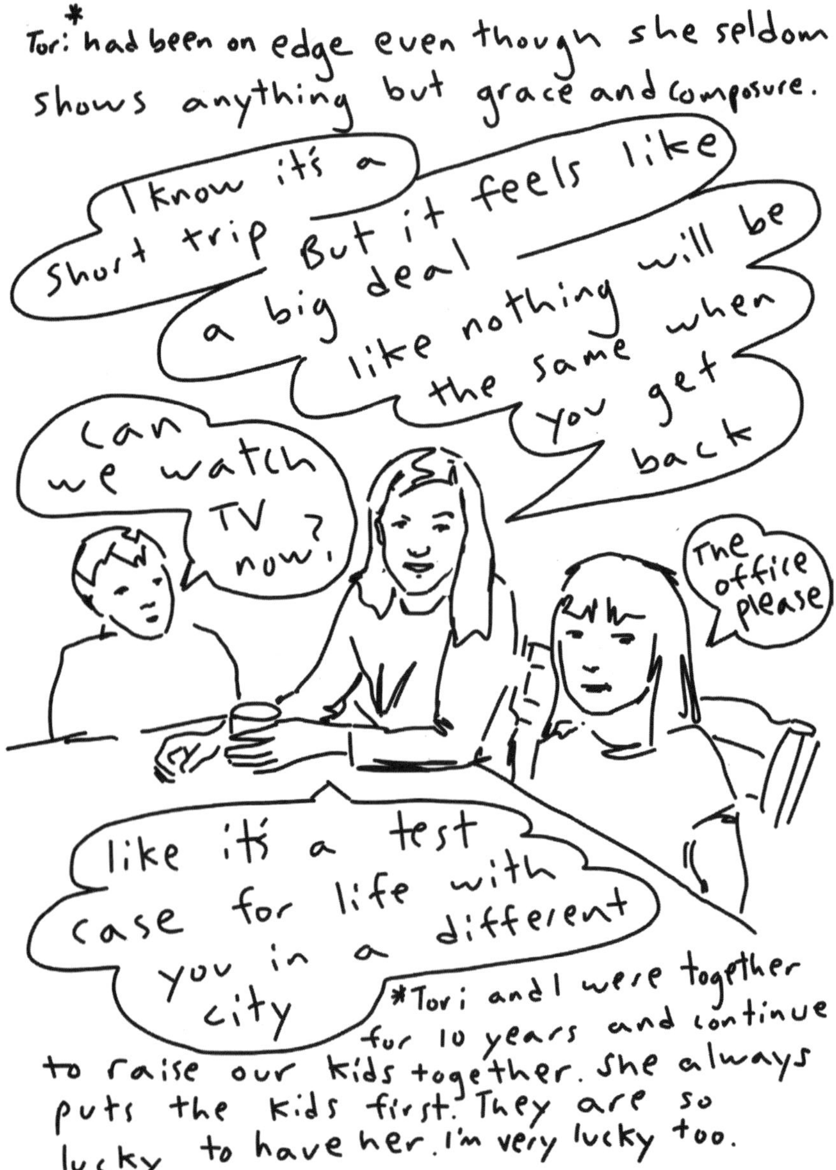

Tor:* had been on edge even though she seldom shows anything but grace and composure.
I know it's a short trip
But it feels like a big deal
like nothing will be the same when you get back
Can we watch TV now?
The office please
like it's a test case for life with you in a different city
*Tori and I were together for 10 years and continue to raise our kids together. She always puts the kids first. They are so lucky to have her. I'm very lucky too.

I might not have been the absolute worst partner you can imagine but I certainly wasn't the partner Tori deserved. Actually, I was the worst.

But that's a road I'm not going down right now. I'm just very grateful she's happy to look after the kids and Stella while I'm gone. But most of all I'm grateful that she is happy and thriving in life, even if it is no thanks to me.

And of course I spent lots of time with Rose*
but we always do. On days when the twins
are at Tori's and Rose isn't at Julie's,** Tori's,
or a sleepover, it's just us (which is most days).
Don't tell her, but she's become my BFF. She
gives even better advice than Stella.

bad idea

Rose is my 17 year old daughter. Julie
is her Mom and Tori is her other (step) Mom.
It takes a team to raise a teenager.** More
on Julie later.

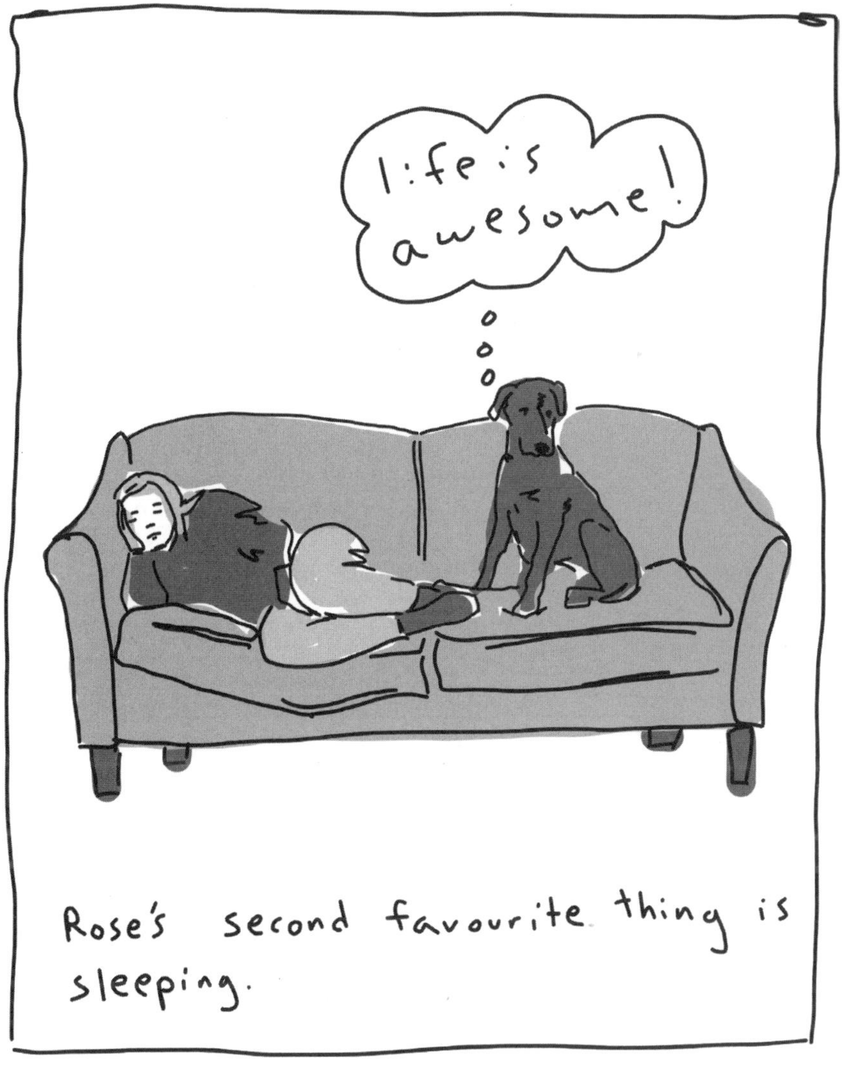
life is awesome!

Rose's second favourite thing is sleeping.

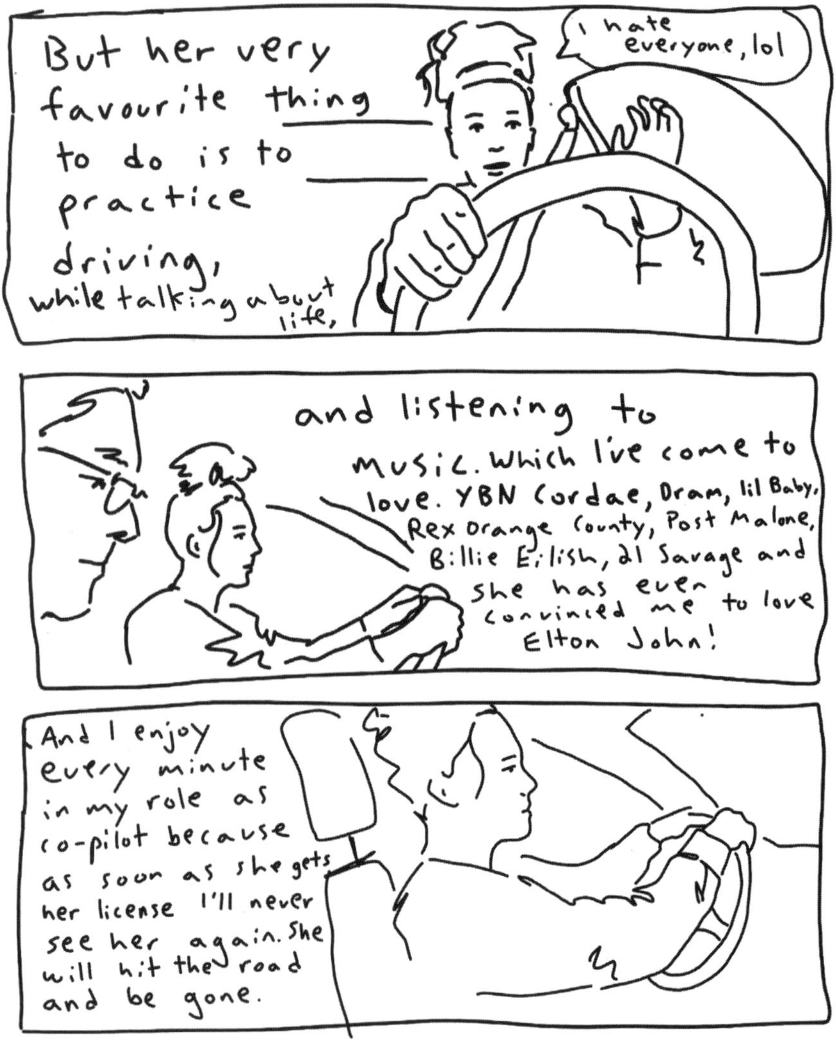
But her very favourite thing to do is to practice driving, while talking about life,
i hate everyone, lol
and listening to music. Which I've come to love. YBN Cordae, Dram, lil Baby, Rex Orange County, Post Malone, Billie Eilish, 21 Savage and she has ever convinced me to love Elton John!
And I enjoy every minute in my role as co-pilot because as soon as she gets her license I'll never see her again. She will hit the road and be gone.

And then it was simply time to say goodbye and get in the car and drive away alone.

6

I wasn't on the road for
an hour when I stopped to
see my Mom in Moncton, she had a
lot on her mind she wanted
to talk about for some time.

As you can see she is a
very sweet lady. But she
got it into her head she needed
to make amends.

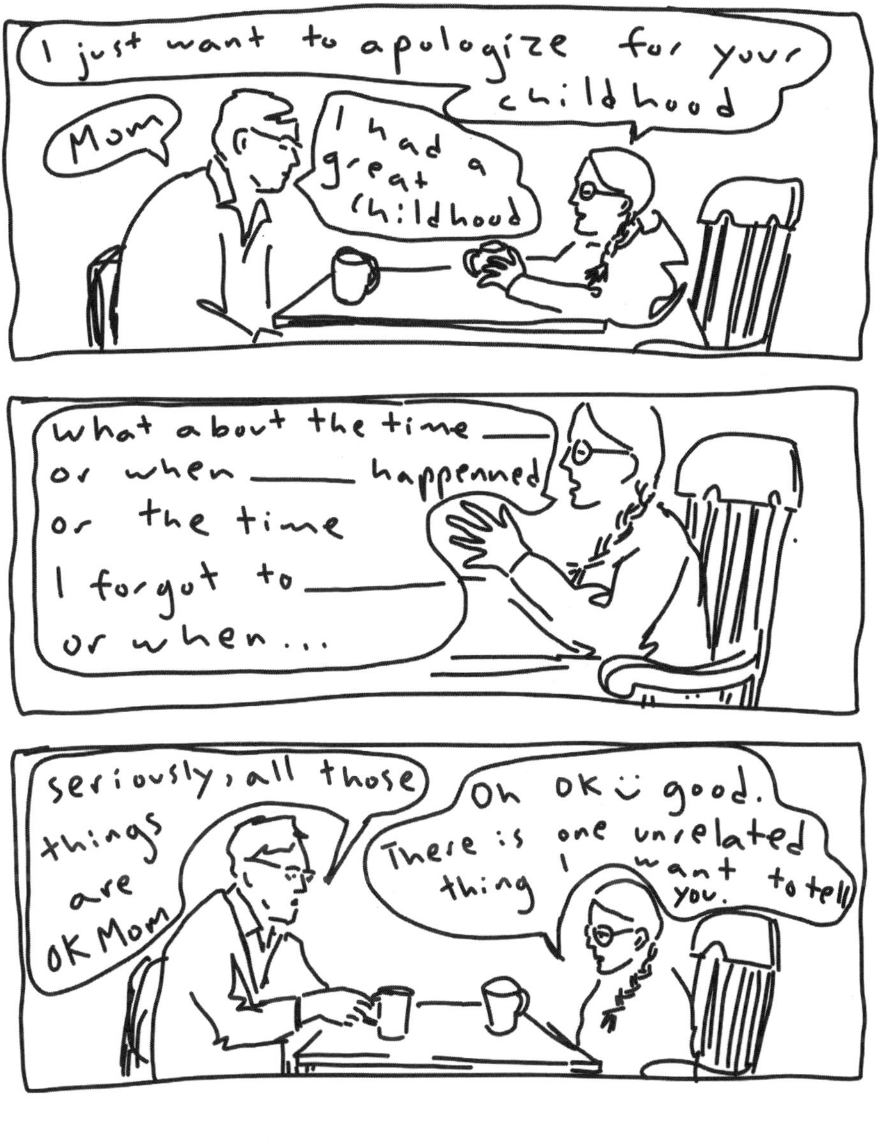

I just want to apologize for your childhood
Mom
I had a great childhood
what about the time ___ or when ___ happenned or the time I forgot to ___ or when...
seriously, all those things are OK Mom
Oh OK ◡̈ good. There is one unrelated thing I want to tell you.

And then she told me something that truly surprised me. Bear in mind I'm an only child (if that wasn't obvious).

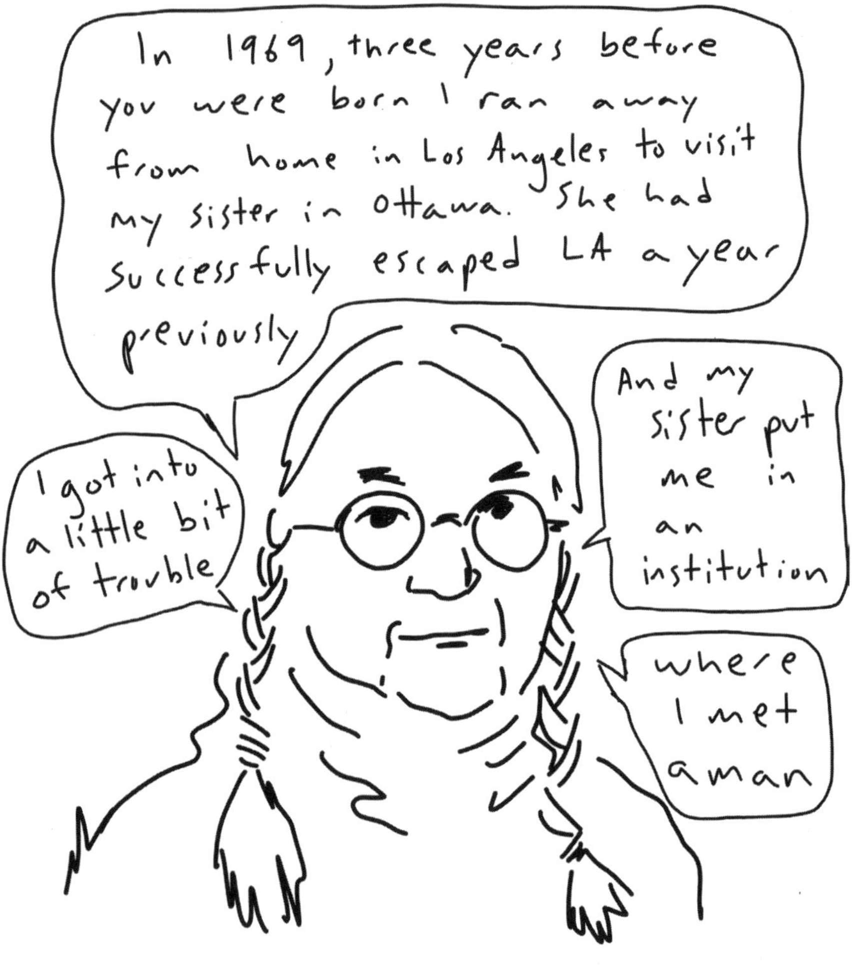
In 1969, three years before you were born I ran away from home in Los Angeles to visit my sister in Ottawa. She had successfully escaped LA a year previously
I got into a little bit of trouble
And my sister put me in an institution
where I met a man

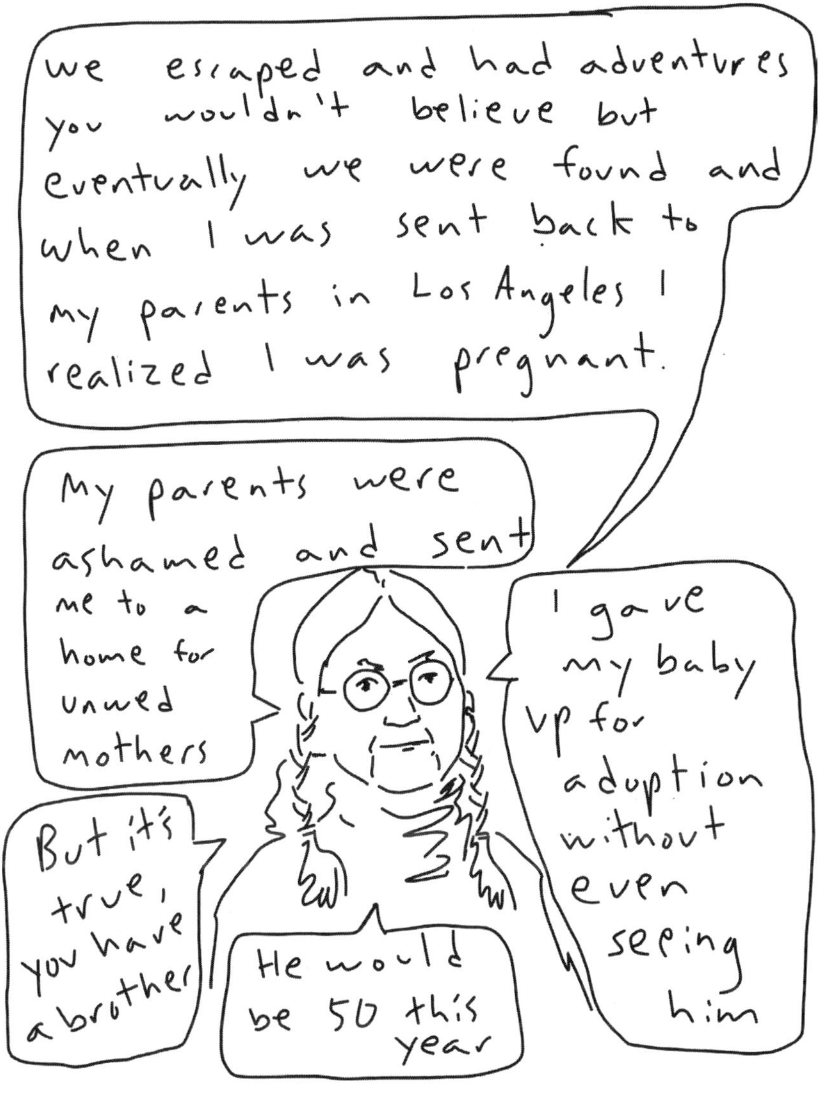
we escaped and had adventures you wouldn't believe but eventually we were found and when I was sent back to my parents in Los Angeles I realized I was pregnant.
My parents were ashamed and sent me to a home for unwed mothers
I gave my baby up for adoption without even seeing him
But it's true, you have a brother
He would be 50 this year

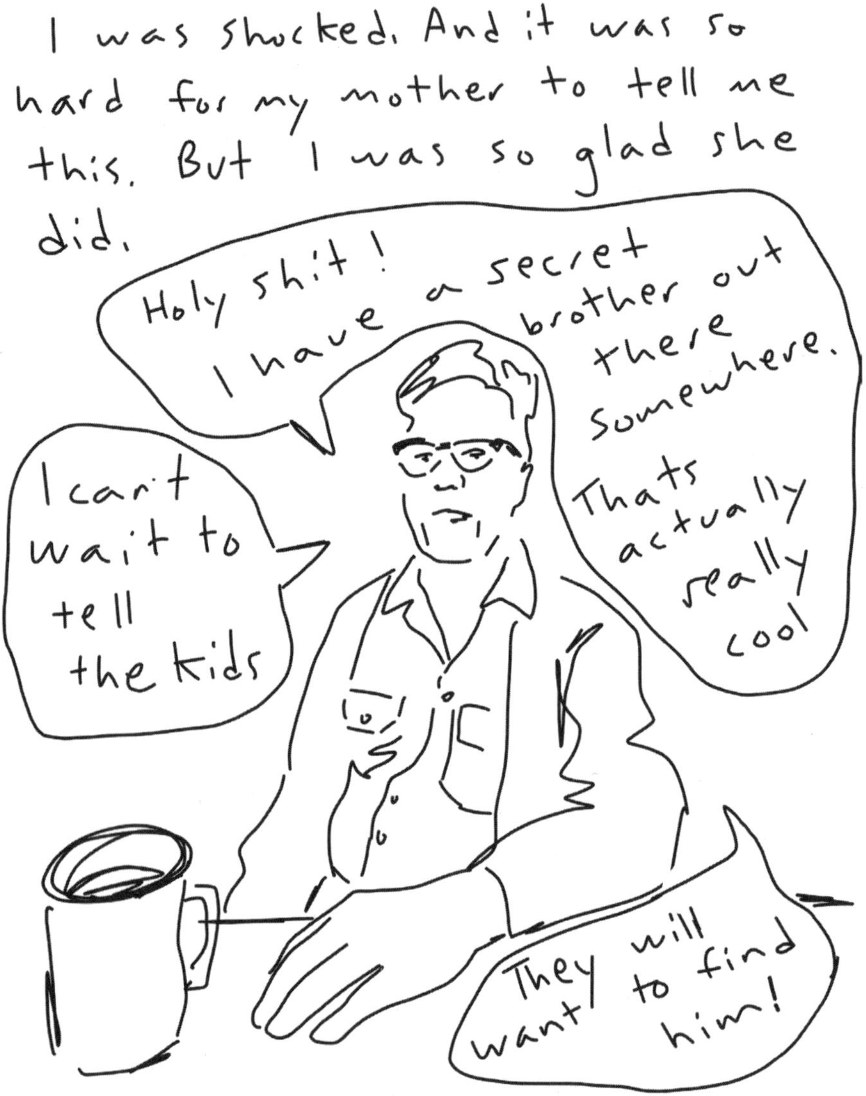
I was shocked. And it was so hard for my mother to tell me this. But I was so glad she did.
Holy shit! I have a secret brother out there somewhere.
I can't wait to tell the kids
Thats actually really cool
They will want to find him!

I just needed to finally get those things off my chest
Now you can
have a good trip
Thank you

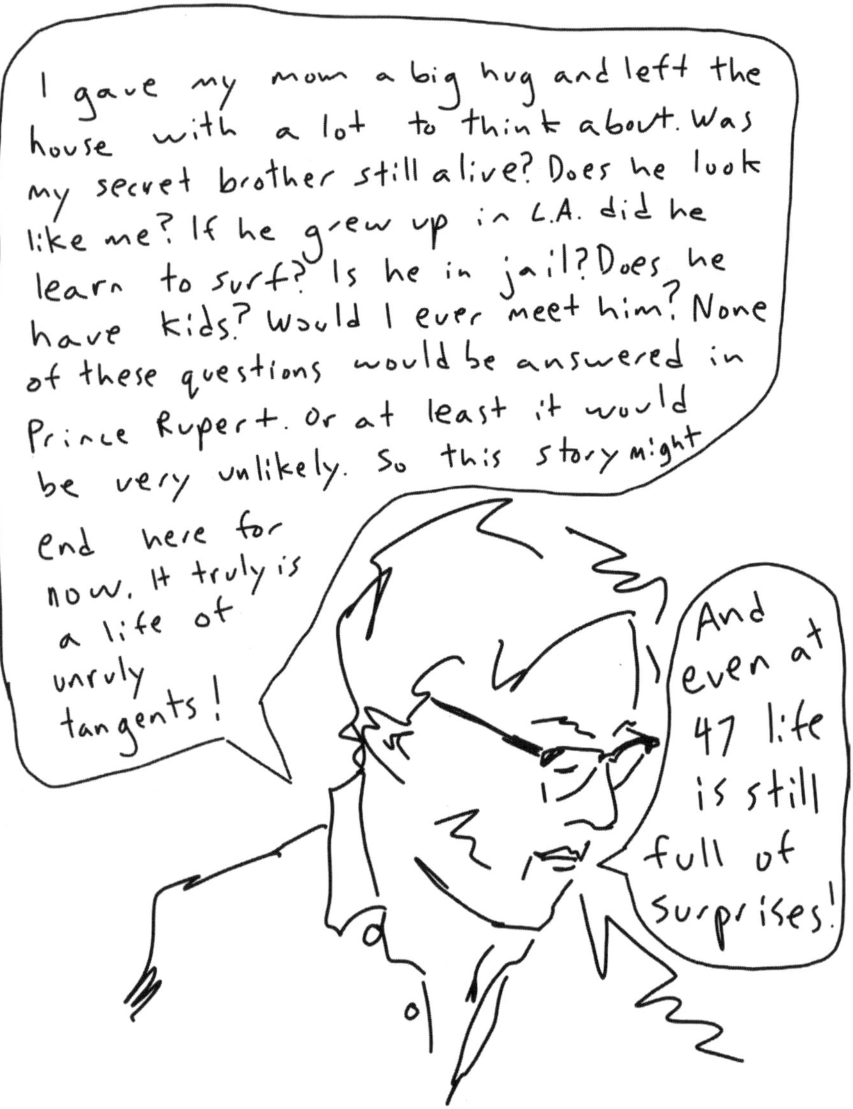
I gave my mom a big hug and left the house with a lot to think about. Was my secret brother still alive? Does he look like me? If he grew up in L.A. did he learn to surf? Is he in jail? Does he have kids? Would I ever meet him? None of these questions would be answered in Prince Rupert. Or at least it would be very unlikely. So this story might end here for now. It truly is a life of unruly tangents!
And even at 47 life is still full of surprises!

7

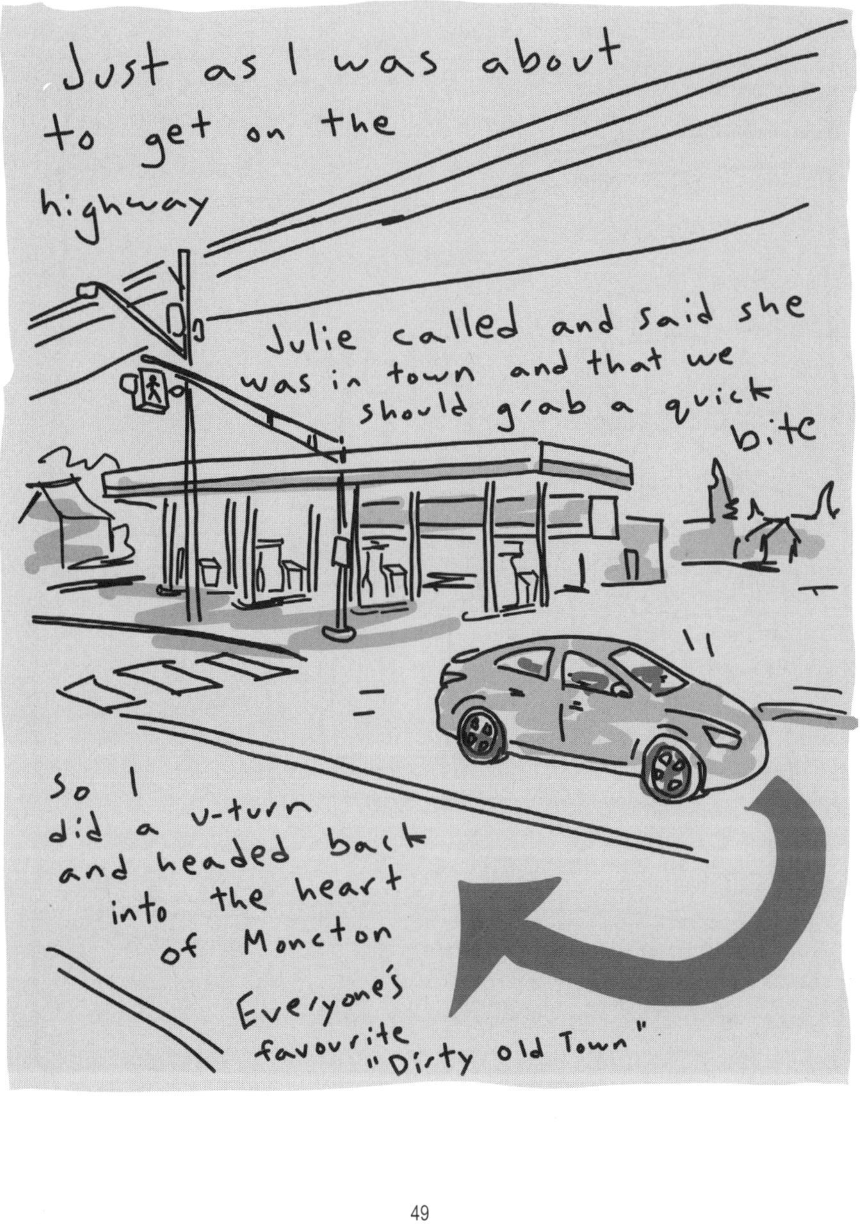
Just as I was about to get on the highway
Julie called and said she was in town and that we should grab a quick bite
So I did a u-turn and headed back into the heart of Moncton
Everyone's favourite "Dirty Old Town".

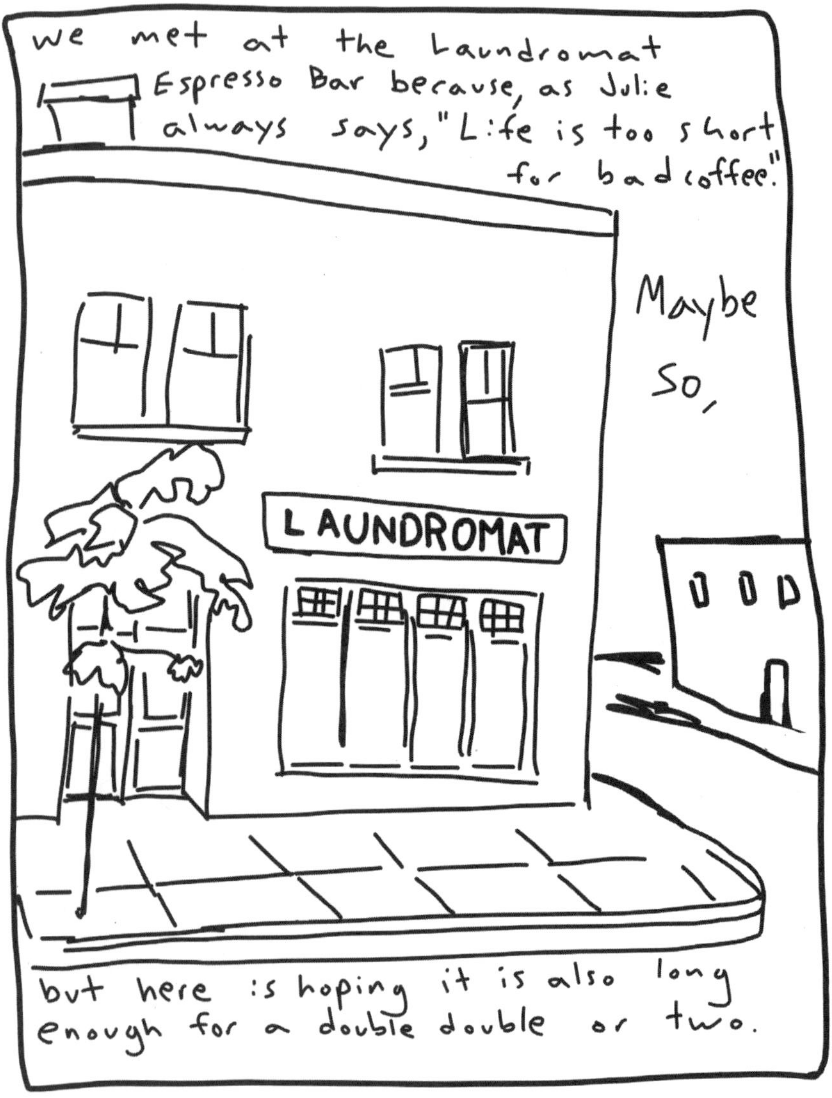
we met at the Laundromat Espresso Bar because, as Julie always says, "Life is too short for bad coffee."
Maybe so,
LAUNDROMAT
but here is hoping it is also long enough for a double double or two.

I've known Julie for 33 years and we were married for 12 of those years. Ben, Charlotte, and Rose were born when we were in our 20's. We might have been married too young for our relationship to survive but I loved being a young parent.

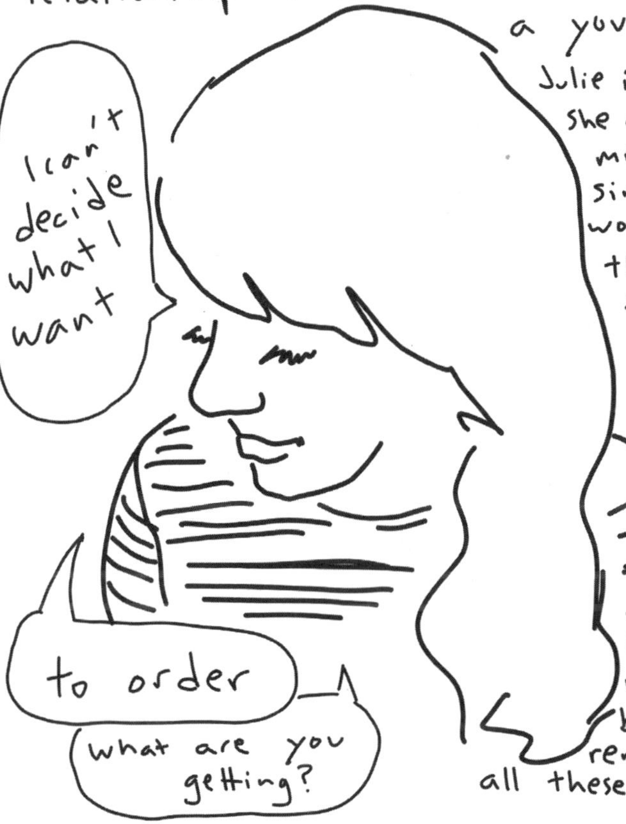

I can't decide what I want
to order
what are you getting?

Julie is a musician, she can sing a melody that could sink a ship. We would bring the kids on the road. I was the Nanny and she was the rock star. It worked until it didn't but we've remained friends all these years.

we were married 25 years ago at the Moncton Dart Club. The regulars had to stop throwing darts long enough for our vows. It rained cats and dogs. Julie was only 8 months pregnant. I was working as a carpenter and we got married on a friday and I had work on monday. That settled for romance then and I wouldn't have had it any other way. But to say we weren't ready is an understatement.

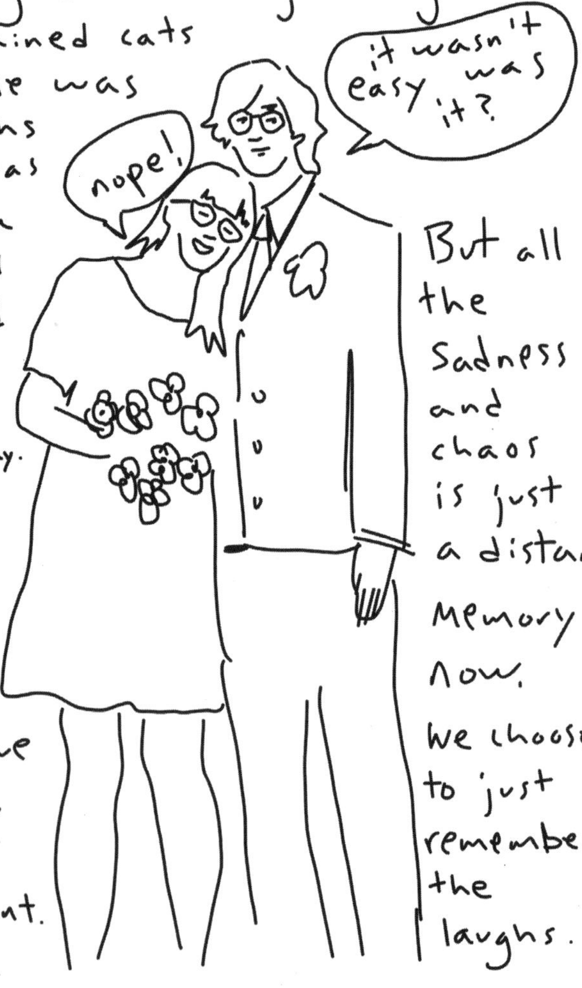
it wasn't easy was it?
nope!

But all the sadness and chaos is just a distant memory now. We choose to just remember the laughs.

Time and distance have brought us closer in the end. We know just about everything about each other I think.
How is your sobriety?
Are you really going to move?
How are things with you and Elly?
What the heck are you going you going to do?
Did you get that job at struts?
I know we can drive each other crazy but that doesn't mean we can't be friends.

And surprisingly for someone who talks so much she is a great listener.
I have no idea where Elly and I stand these days
I have no idea what I'm doing
How are things with you and Danny?
I didn't get the job
I've always been more of a listener myself.

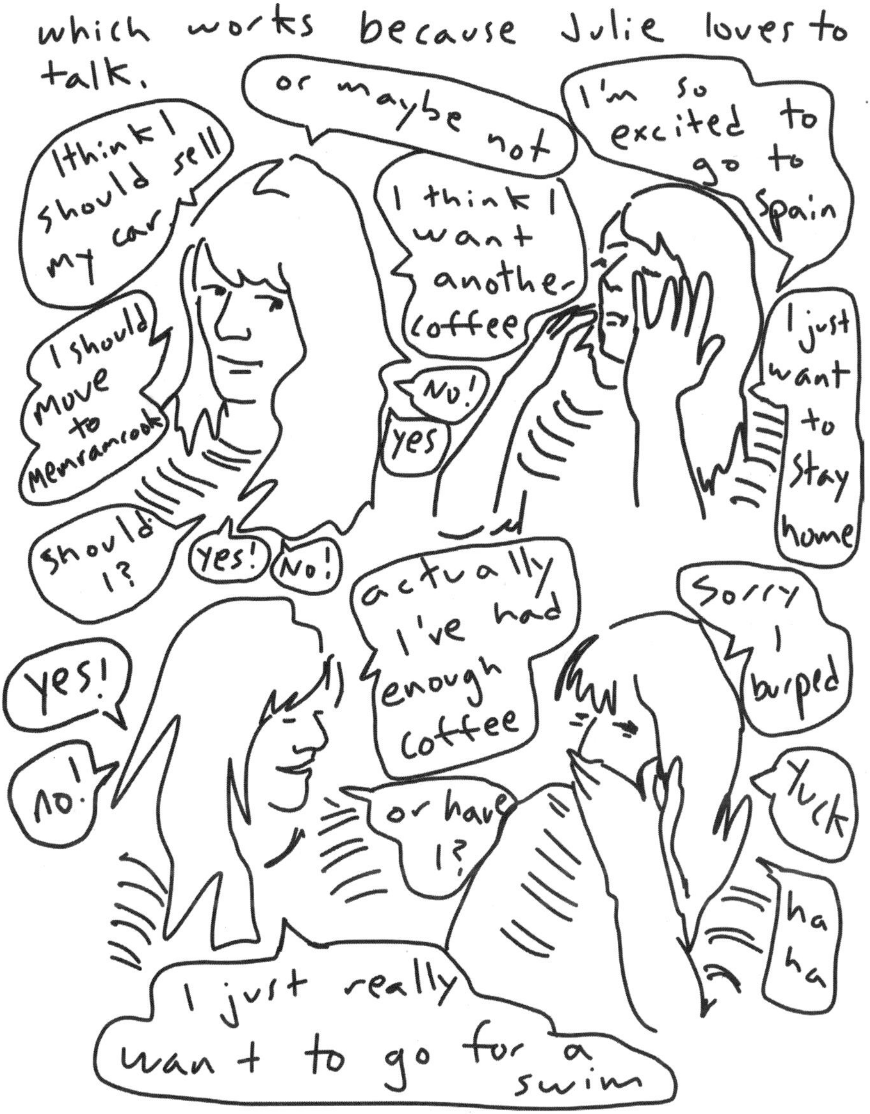
which works because Julie loves to talk.
or maybe not
I'm so excited to go to Spain
I think I should sell my car.
I think I want another coffee
I should move to memramcook
No!
yes
I just want to stay home
should I?
Yes!
No!
actually I've had enough coffee
Sorry I burped
yes!
no!
or have I?
Yuck
ha ha
I just really want to go for a swim

Really the hardest part about being married to a musician was that they write about their lives, their loves and their losses. Sometimes it's about you and sometimes it isn't. I never learned which was harder to deal with. In the end it's all worth it for a good song.

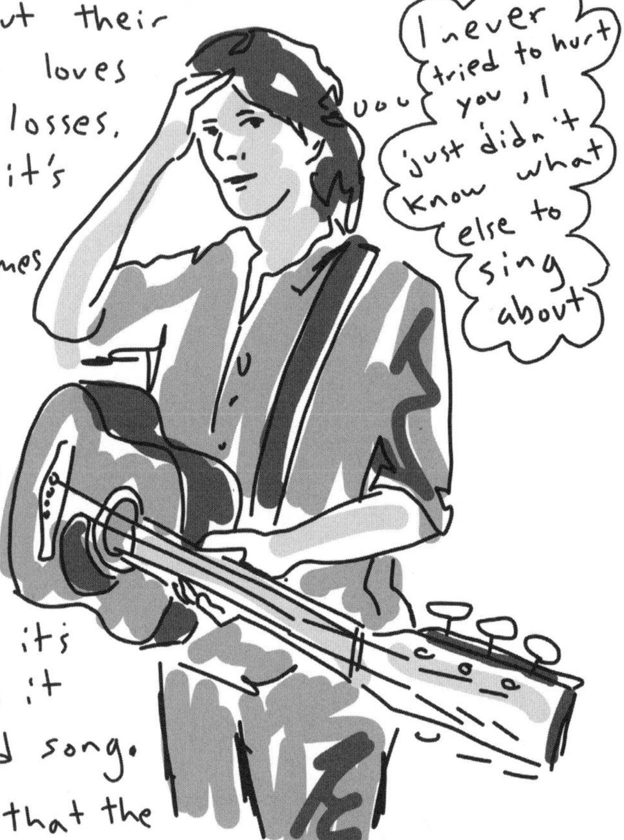
I never tried to hurt you, I just didn't know what else to sing about

But now that the shoe is on the other foot, I hope that everyone knows I mean every word with love. I just don't know what else to write about.

we left the café and said goodbye on the street.

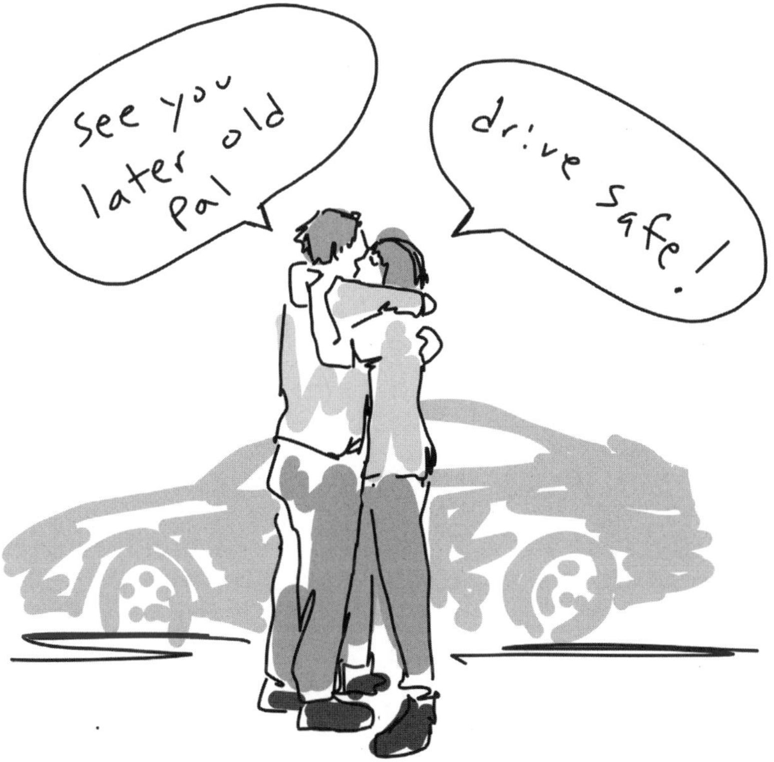
see you later old pal
drive safe!

It looks like I'll finally get out of Moncton.

8

One last thing before I hit the road, I had just enough time to go to a meeting. As usual I heard all the things I needed to hear.

Always know where the door is

It could be worse, you could be drunk

It's easier to stay sober than get sober again

A meeting buys me a day

Sometimes we cry but mostly we laugh. That's really the strangest thing. People share all the most horrible things they've done and it's fucking hilarious. I've never been anywhere as joyful as a meeting.

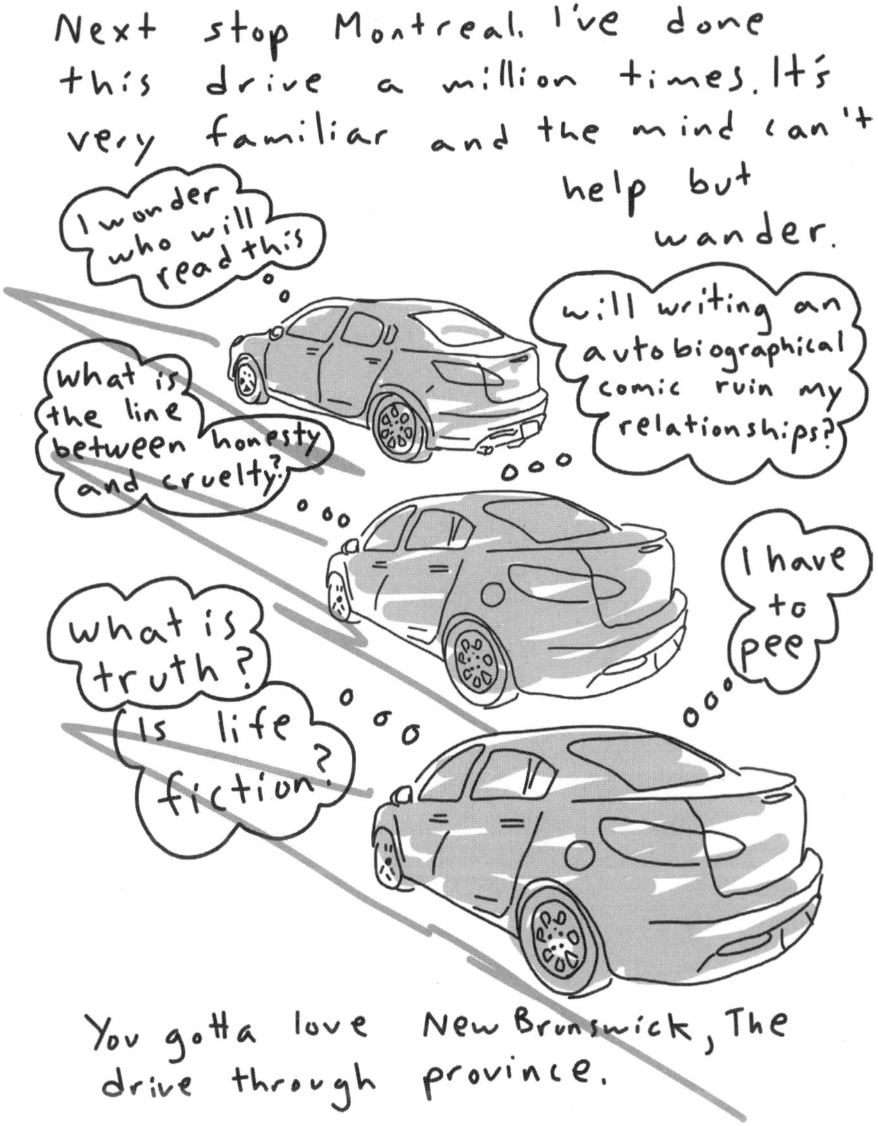
Next stop Montreal. I've done this drive a million times. It's very familiar and the mind can't help but wander.
I wonder who will read this
will writing an autobiographical comic ruin my relationships?
what is the line between honesty and cruelty?
I have to pee
what is truth?
Is life fiction?
You gotta love New Brunswick, The drive through province.

9

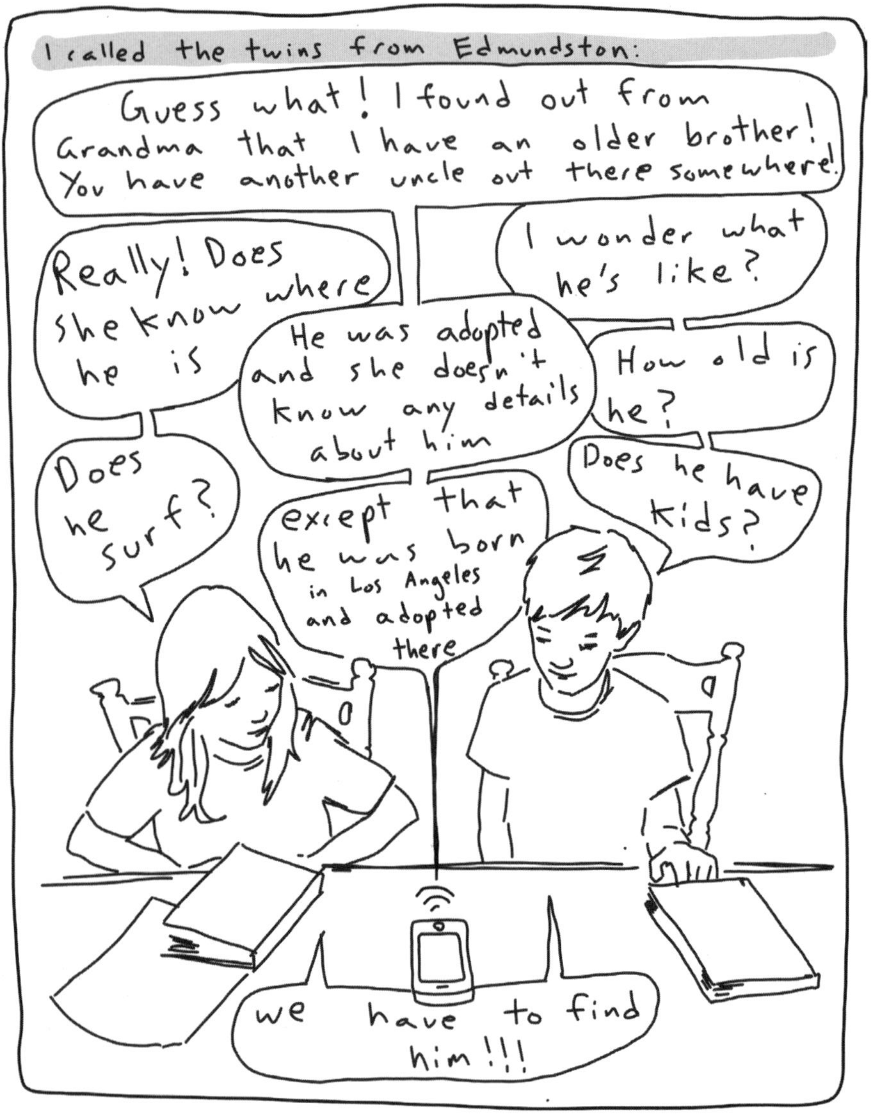
I called the twins from Edmundston:
Guess what! I found out from Grandma that I have an older brother! You have another uncle out there somewhere!
Really! Does she know where he is
I wonder what he's like?
He was adopted and she doesn't know any details about him
How old is he?
Does he surf?
Does he have kids?
except that he was born in Los Angeles and adopted there
we have to find him!!!

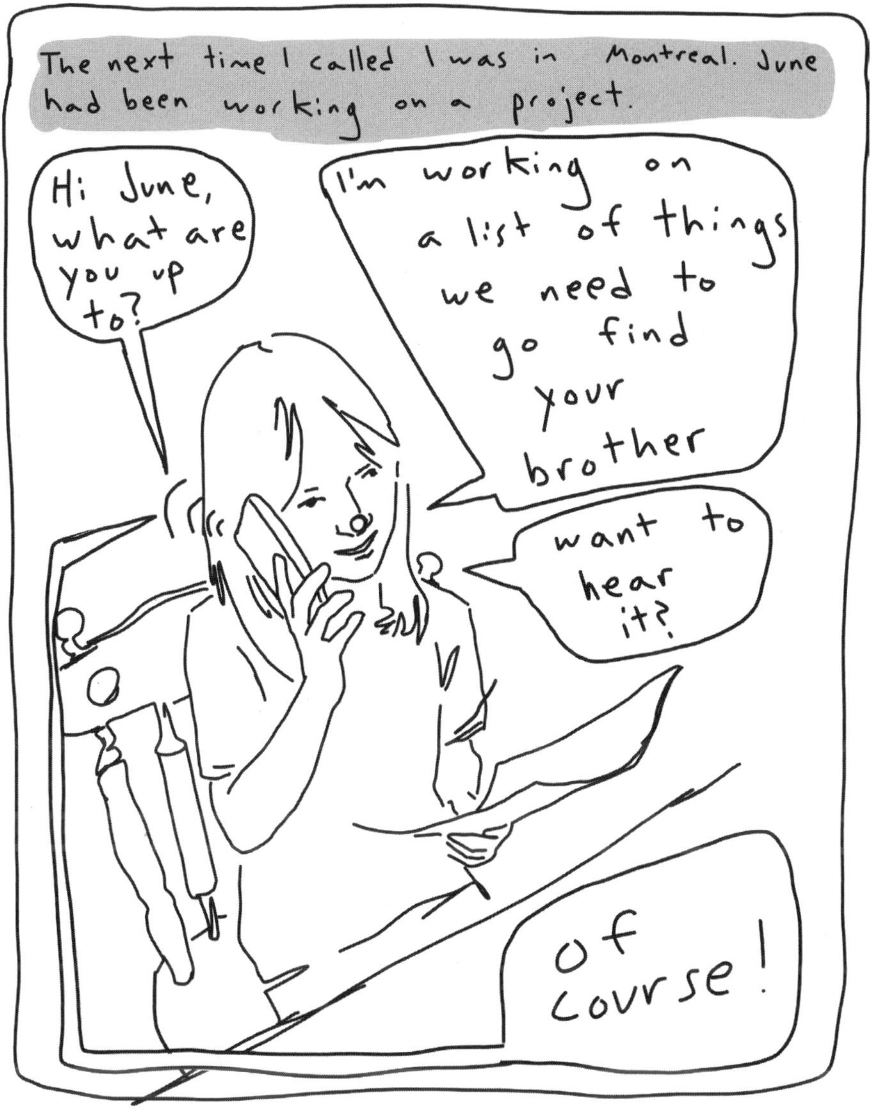
The next time I called I was in Montreal. June had been working on a project.
Hi June, what are you up to?
I'm working on a list of things we need to go find your brother
want to hear it?
of course!

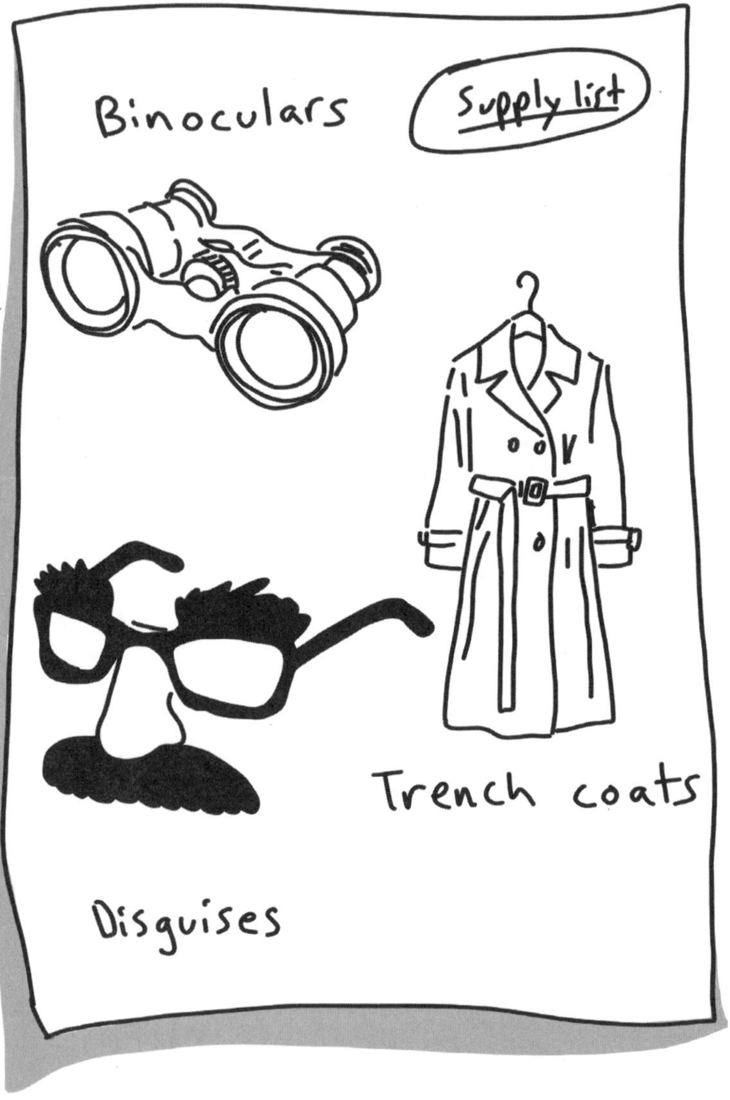
Binoculars
Supply list
Trench coats
Disguises

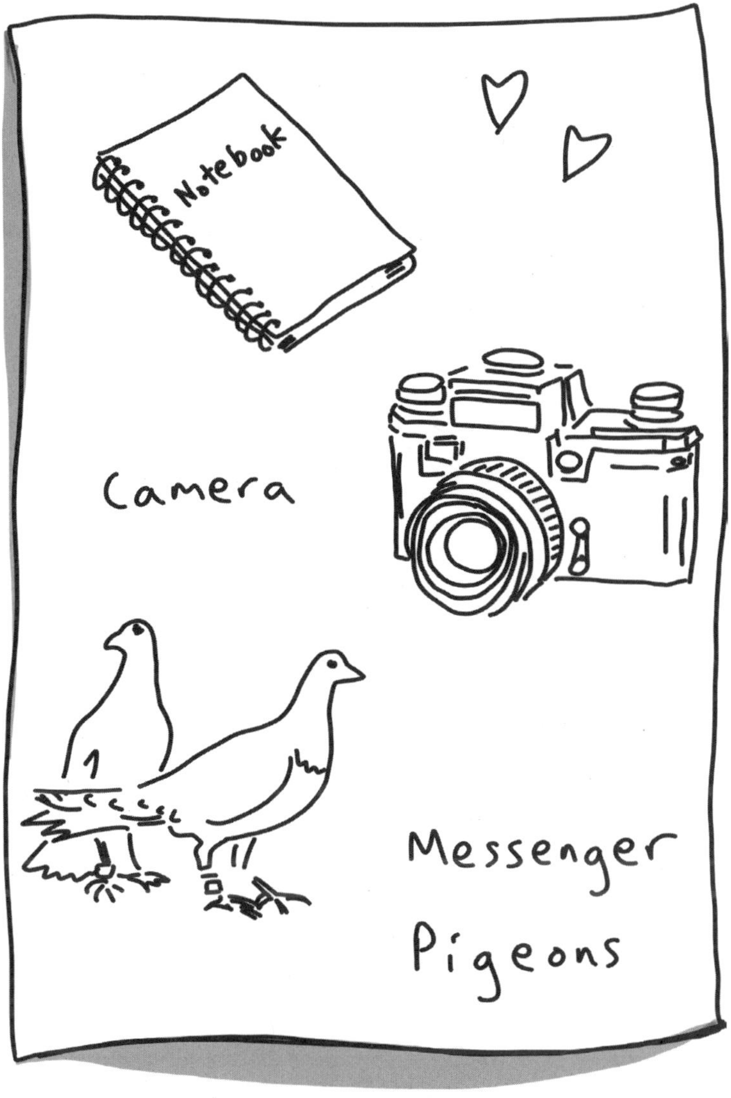
Notebook
Camera
Messenger
Pigeons

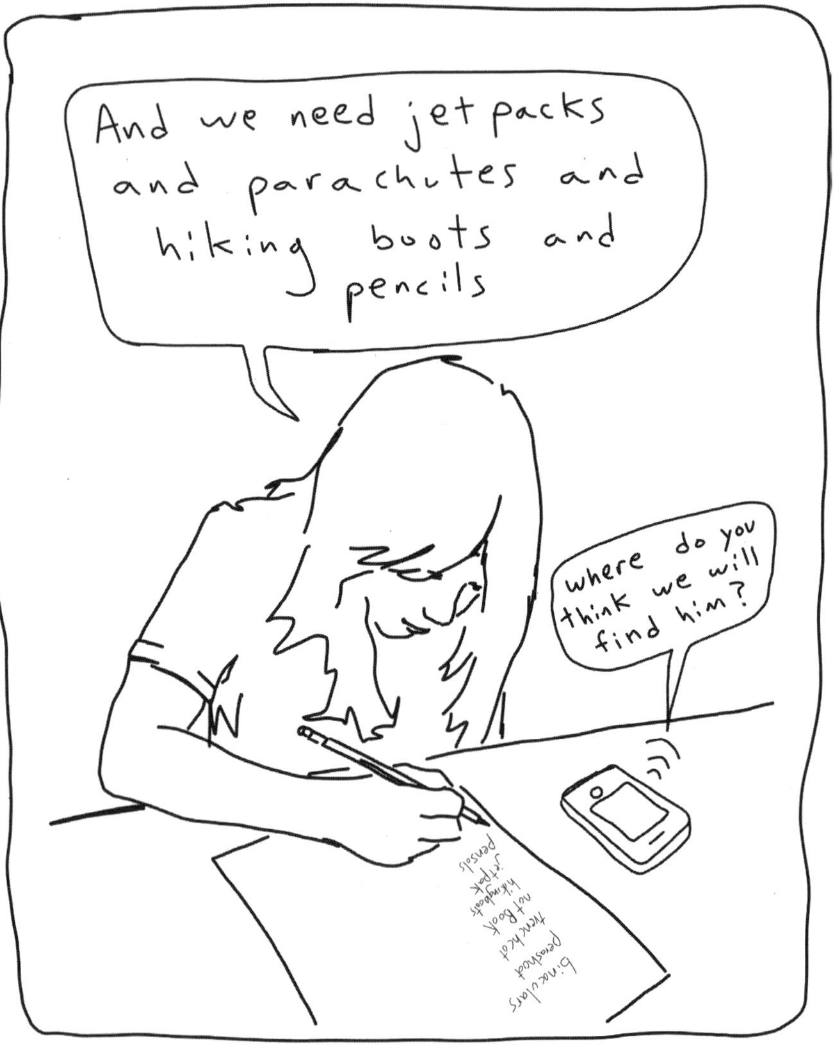
And we need jet packs and parachutes and hiking boots and pencils
Where do you think we will find him?
binaculars
perashoot
trenchcot
notBook
hikingboots
jetpak
pensols

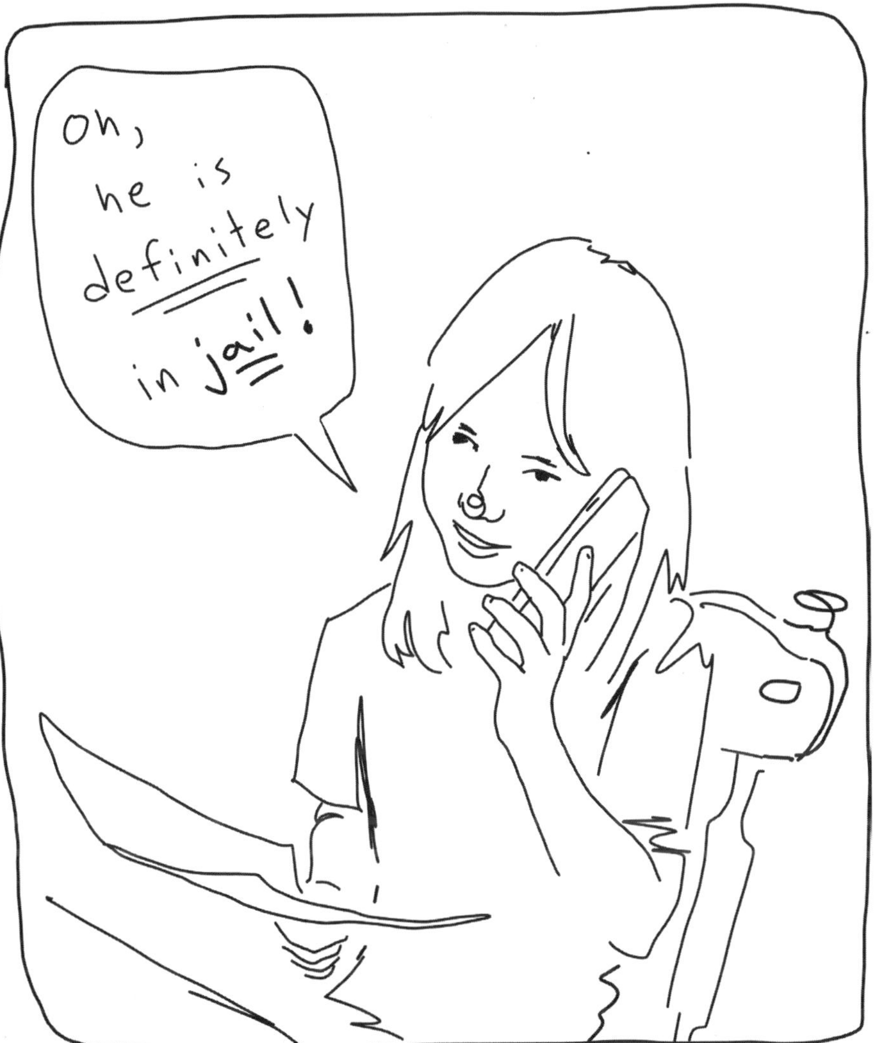
Oh, he is definitely in jail!

10

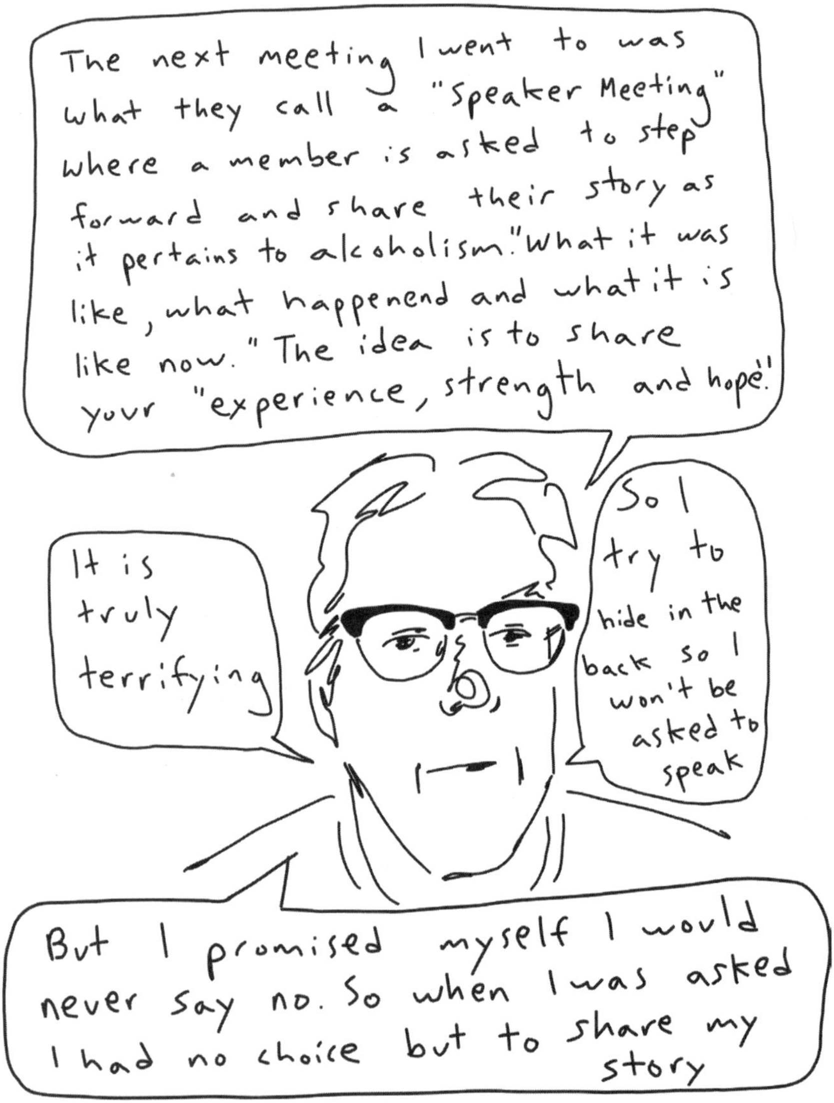
The next meeting I went to was what they call a "Speaker Meeting" where a member is asked to step forward and share their story as it pertains to alcoholism." What it was like, what happenend and what it is like now." The idea is to share your "experience, strength and hope."
It is truly terrifying
So I try to hide in the back so I won't be asked to speak
But I promised myself I would never say no. So when I was asked I had no choice but to share my story

WARNING! The following pages contain too much information and deal with addiction and dark thoughts I advise you skip it.
Hi, my name is Jon and I'm an alcoholic.
This is not an unusual story.
It is simply my story.

Of course I wasn't born an alcoholic but the problems I used alcohol to solve were there from the beginning. My parents moved to Canada in 1972 shortly after I was born. They wanted to escape Vietnam and earthquakes but they couldn't escape each other.

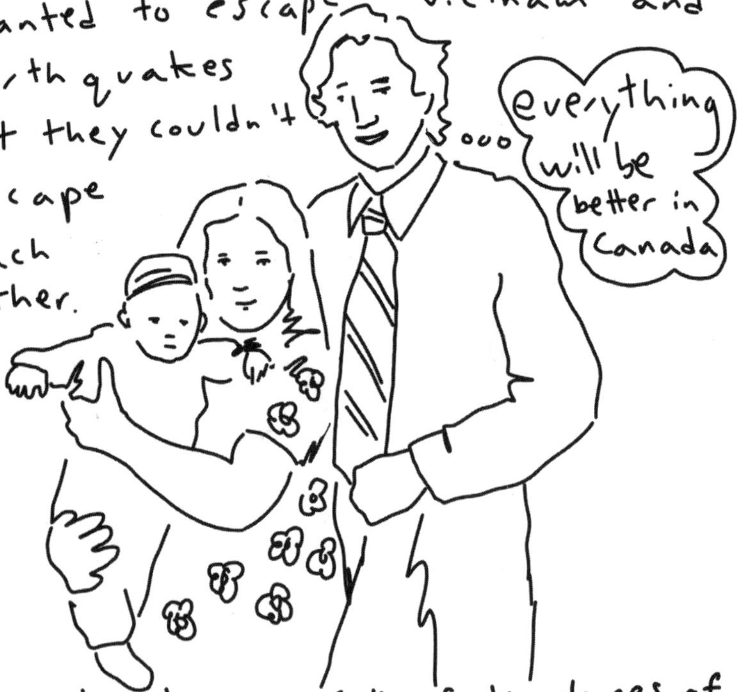
everything will be better in Canada

My chidhood was full of the types of adventures only families in the clutch of mental illness share but that's another story.

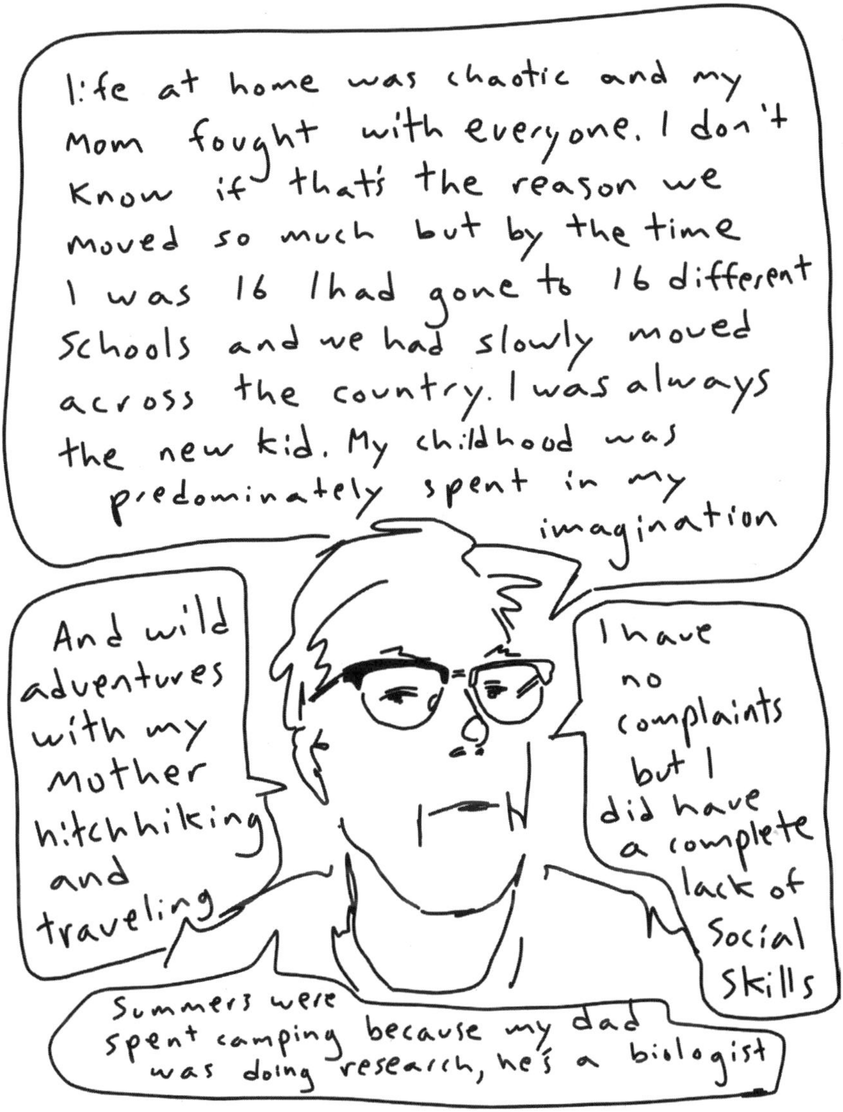
life at home was chaotic and my Mom fought with everyone. I don't know if that's the reason we moved so much but by the time I was 16 I had gone to 16 different schools and we had slowly moved across the country. I was always the new kid. My childhood was predominately spent in my imagination
And wild adventures with my mother hitchhiking and traveling
I have no complaints but I did have a complete lack of social skills
Summers were spent camping because my dad was doing research, he's a biologist

Right from my first drink everything was better. My anxiety was gone. I fit in. I was funny and brave. I could make friends. More than anything I felt like myself for the first time. Comfortable in my own skin. Honestly, I don't know how I would have survived without it.

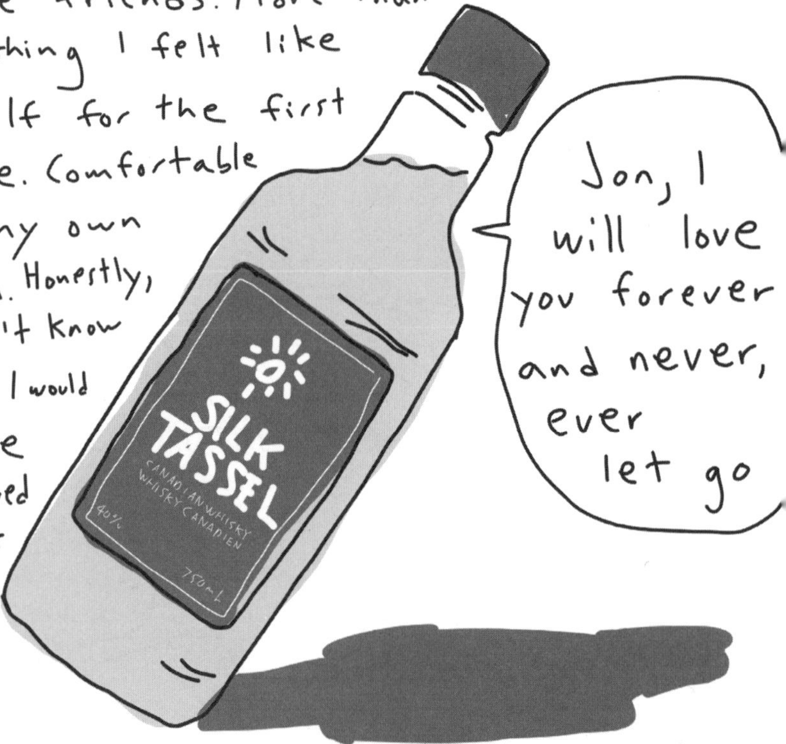
SILK TASSEL
CANADIAN WHISKY
WHISKY CANADIEN
40%
750mL
Jon, I will love you forever and never, ever let go

Alcohol wasn't my problem. Right from the beginning it was my solution.

My first drink was Silk Tassle whiskey.
You never forget your first time. Your first
love. It was in the parking lot of
Tantramar Regional Highschool. No one
would remember I was there but I
was truly happy and content.

During highschool I was thrilled to
be a binge drinker but by the time
I was married and my son was born
I was a daily drinker. Of course
I was, I loved it.

Babies 1, 2 and 3 were born. We traveled together, I was a devoted dad and a supportive husband. I had everything under control.

Sure I passed out some days at noon but no one would have called me an alcoholic and I loved being a dad.

I'm not a christmas kind of guy but the kids and their moms are. One christmas eve I was reminded I still hadn't got a tree. So I put my sweet daughter in the car. we headed out searching for

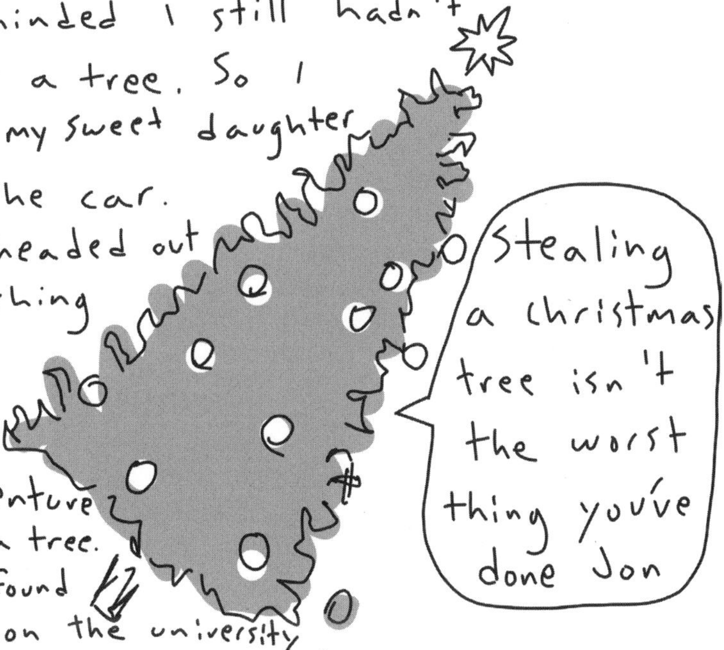
Stealing a christmas tree isn't the worst thing you've done Jon

adventure and a tree. we found one on the university campus and shoved it into the car.

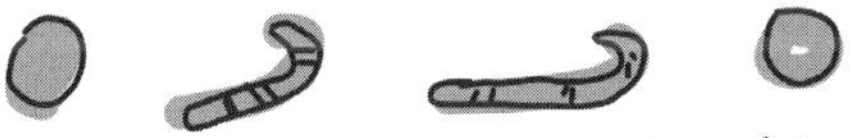

As we drove away I didn't worry about the fact that I just stole a christmas tree with my 5 year old daughter or that I was driving drunk.

When my first marriage ended I met someone kind and loving who held me together. But something had changed in my drinking.

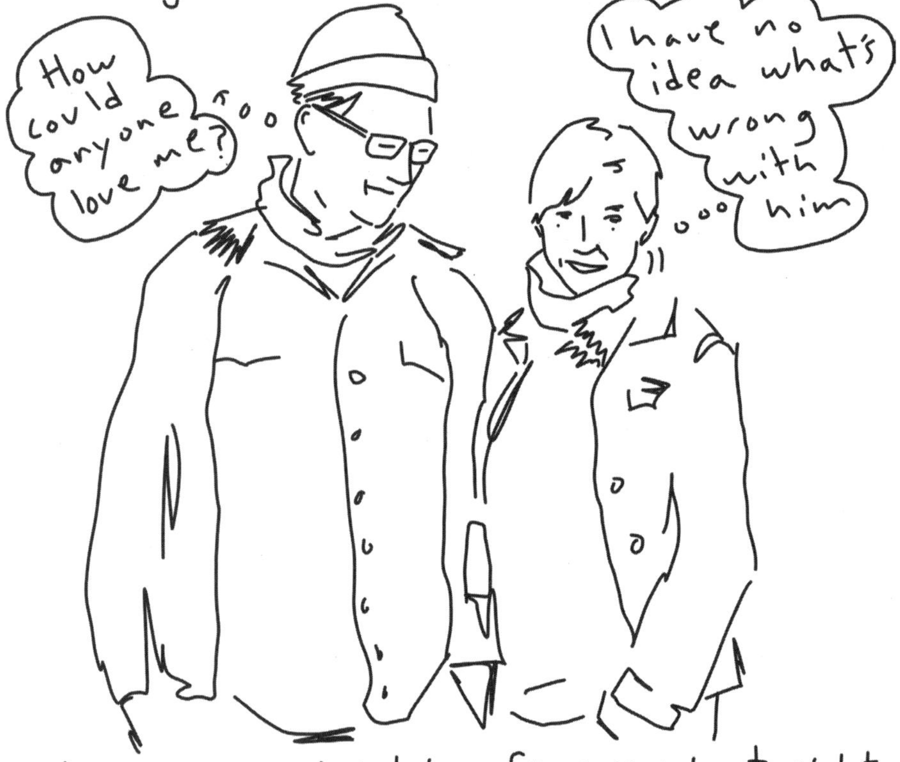
How could anyone love me?
I have no idea what's wrong with him

I was now drinking from morning to night sometimes secretly. I was still searching for a solution but that solution was oblivion.

Sweet babies 4 and 5 were born. we were a big noisy happy family. And sometimes I woke up on the sidewalk.

Sometimes I didn't know how I got home.

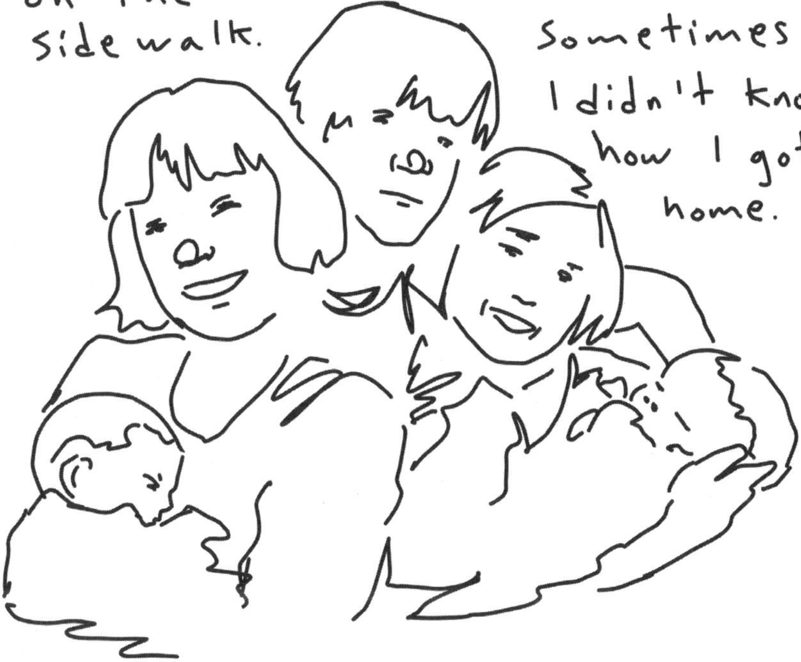

Sometimes I lost the car, my phone or my wallet. Still very few people would have thought I had a problem but my partner was starting to worry.

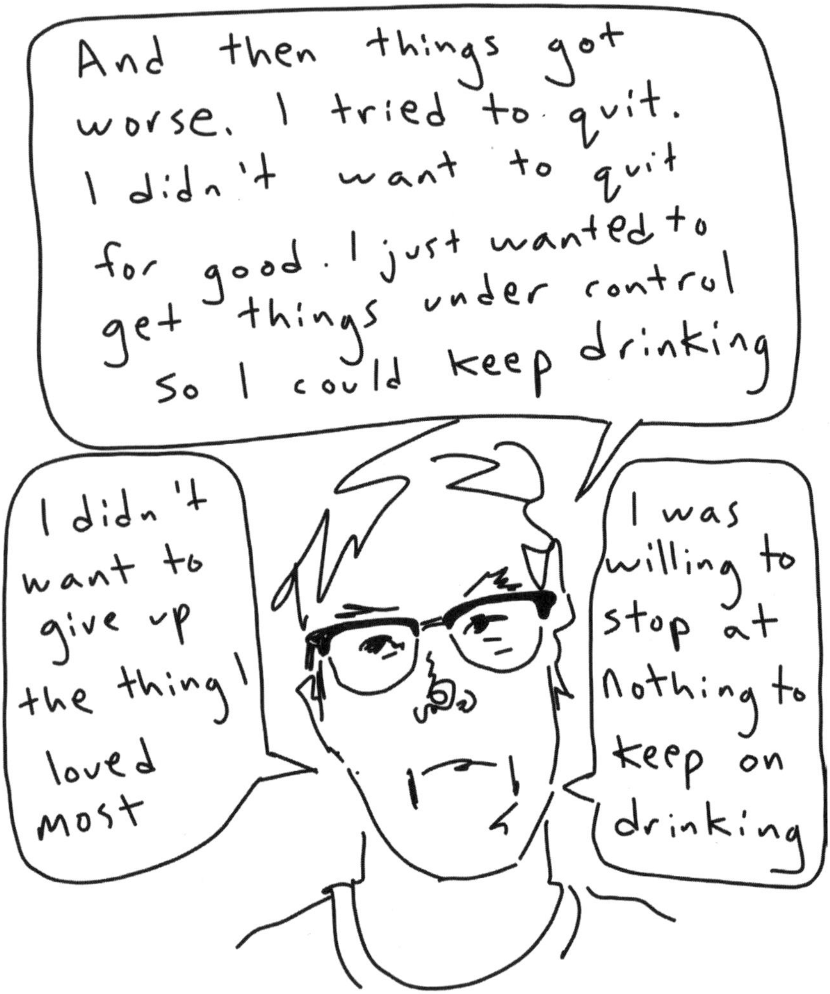
And then things got worse. I tried to quit. I didn't want to quit for good. I just wanted to get things under control so I could keep drinking
I didn't want to give up the thing I loved most
I was willing to stop at nothing to keep on drinking

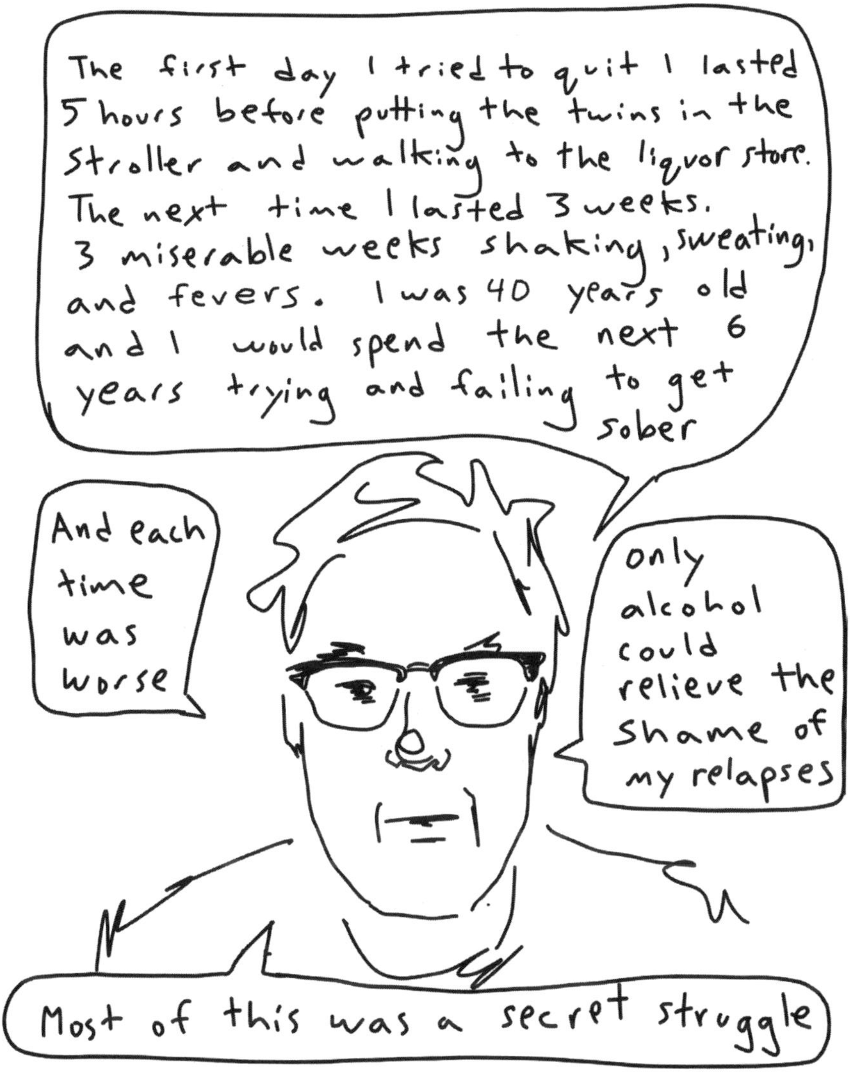
The first day I tried to quit I lasted 5 hours before putting the twins in the stroller and walking to the liquor store. The next time I lasted 3 weeks. 3 miserable weeks shaking, sweating, and fevers. I was 40 years old and I would spend the next 6 years trying and failing to get sober
And each time was worse
only alcohol could relieve the shame of my relapses
Most of this was a secret struggle

I could write a "how to" book called "How to Relapse"
Don't throw out your hidden stash
Open a bar
Ensure every aspect of your life revolves around booze, especially work
Don't ask for help
lie and cheat
keep secrets
Don't go to meetings
feel sorry for yourself
isolate yourself
stew in hate and envy
And those tips you can have for free

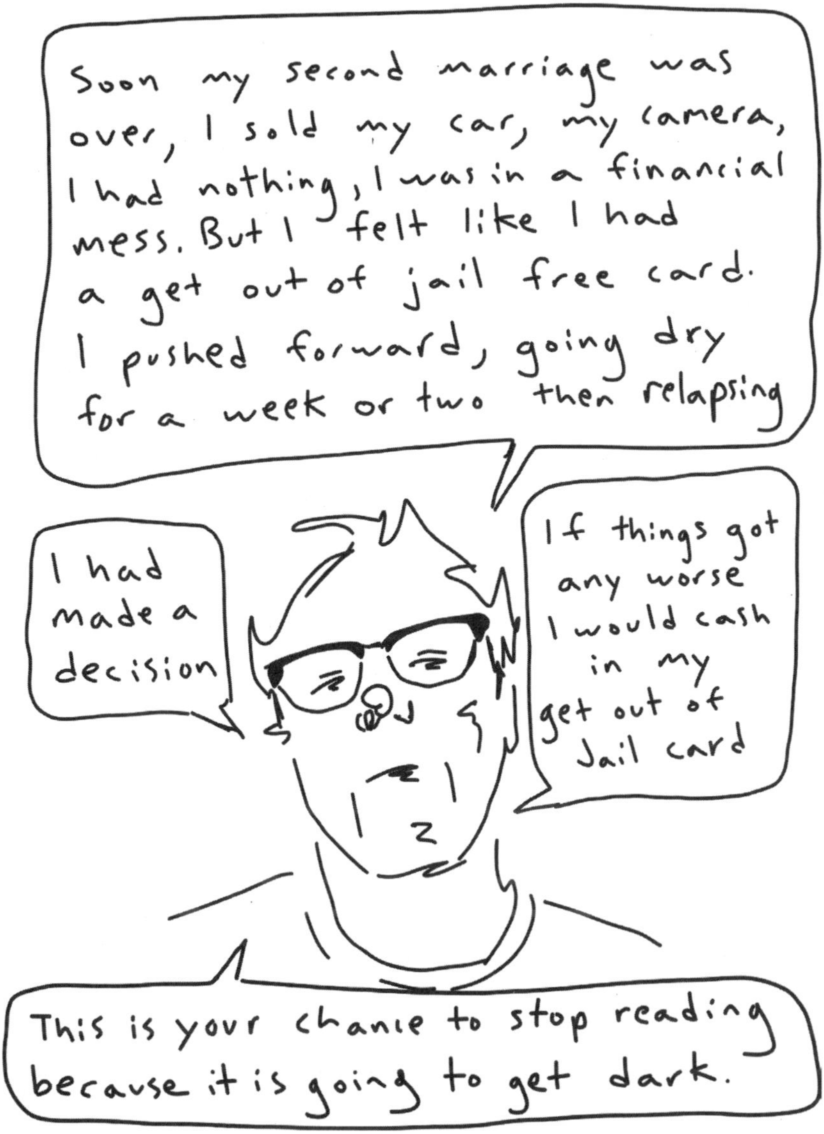
Soon my second marriage was over, I sold my car, my camera, I had nothing, I was in a financial mess. But I felt like I had a get out of jail free card. I pushed forward, going dry for a week or two then relapsing
I had made a decision
If things got any worse I would cash in my get out of Jail card
This is your chance to stop reading because it is going to get dark.

Alcohol wasn't solving anything anymore and I had no idea how to go on.
No matter how drunk I got it didn't help.
I decided to kill myself
It was the only way I knew to end the guilt
I was so full of shame
I was only thinking of myself
This is another chance to stop here. I recommend you skip this section.

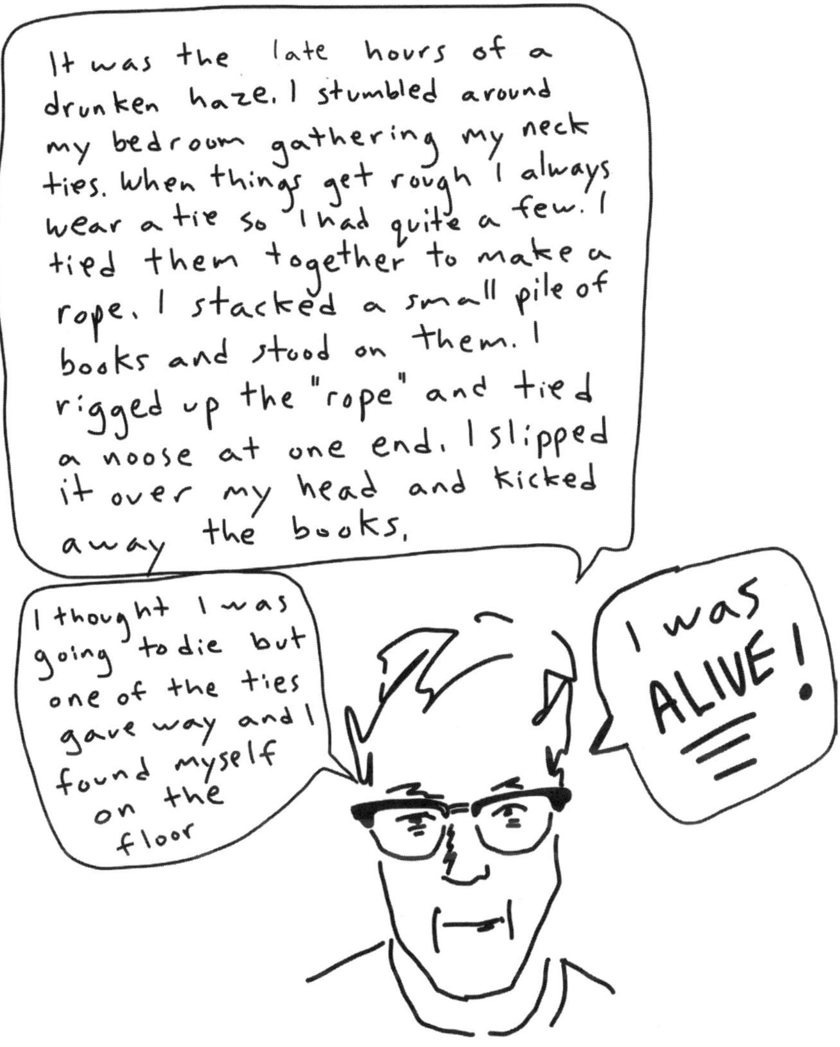
It was the late hours of a drunken haze. I stumbled around my bedroom gathering my neck ties. When things get rough I always wear a tie so I had quite a few. I tied them together to make a rope. I stacked a small pile of books and stood on them. I rigged up the "rope" and tied a noose at one end. I slipped it over my head and kicked away the books.
I thought I was going to die but one of the ties gave way and I found myself on the floor
I was ALIVE!

I was scared but I was ALIVE!!!
And for the first time in a long time I wanted to live.
I can't believe what I almost did to my kids!!!
I wanted to LIVE!!!
This was a chance for a new start
And still I drank for another week

finally I walked into a meeting completely ready to do whatever it would take to become a changed man and to hang on to this new hope
This hope that I'm worth saving
This hope that life can be worth living
But now that I knew I wanted to live I had to find out how to live

Now that I was truly ready, desperate to get sober I was willing to do anything anyone told me to do.

If you told me the only way to get well was to stand on my head for 6 hours a day I would have done it.

The next 6 months were hell. I was either an overmedicated zombie or a ball of shaking, screaming nerves. Sometimes I would find myself walking to the liquor store or suddenly standing in front of the bar. People said I would need a Higher Power's help. But I was sure that was bullshit. Still I did say I would try anything to stay sober. So....

OK, hypothetical God what should I do?? Should I buy booze?

Jon! Go home! watch Netflix and eat a pint of ice cream!

Higher Power

even my shadow was ← shaking

The voice was clear and strong and the answer was sure and fast. I did what it told me. Fuck it! Why not? I call it my ice cream moment.

I would like to say things got better right away but they did not. I didn't find a way to solve the problems of my on again/off again relationship with Eleanor. I wish I could find the words to explain my love for her and to apologize for how I hurt her.

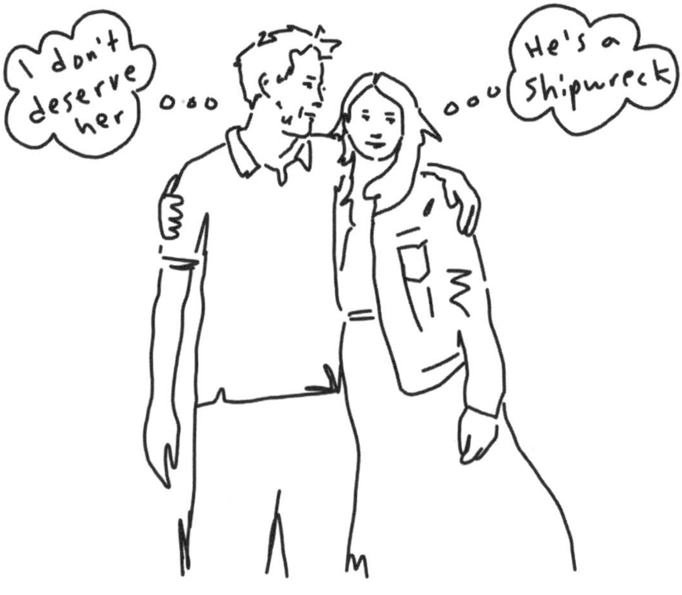

I don't deserve her
He's a shipwreck

My finances didn't improve. My job prospects only got worse. I still had a million amends to make with my family. I was still consumed with shame and guilt but I was learning to accept who I was. I even started being able to look at myself in the mirror.

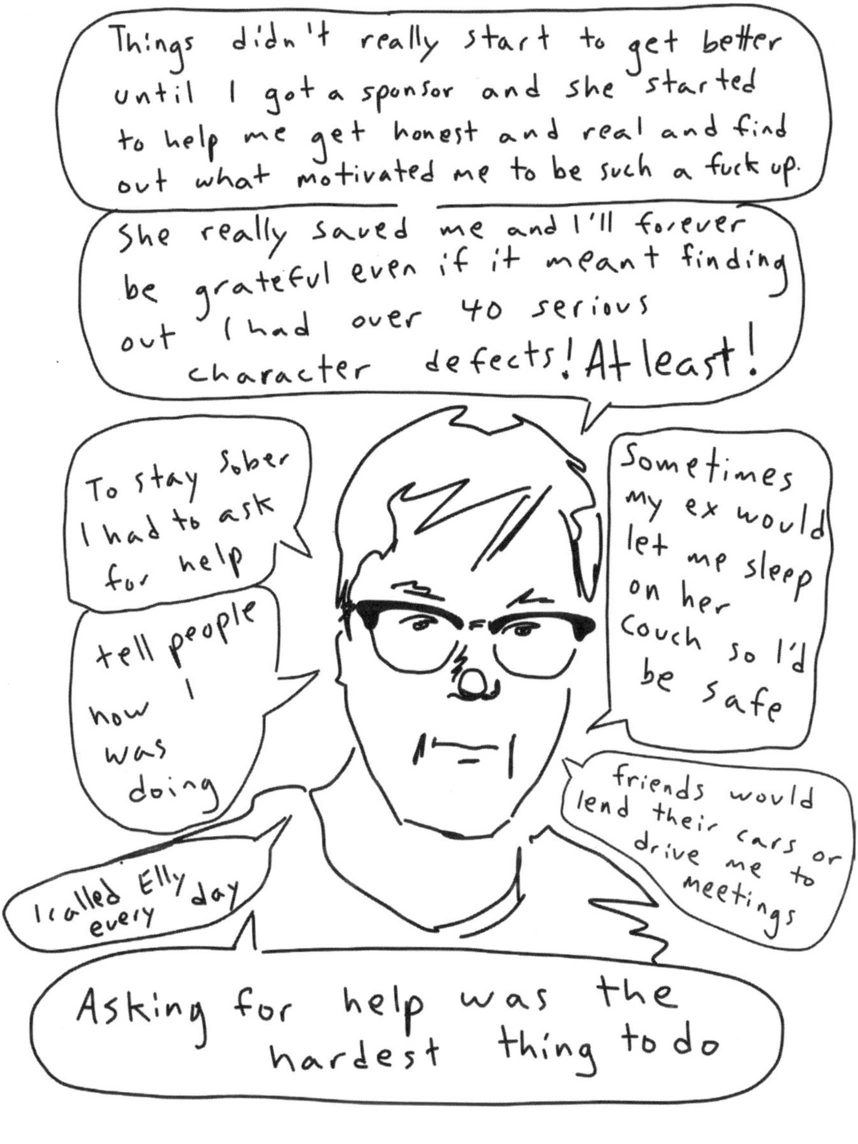
Things didn't really start to get better until I got a sponsor and she started to help me get honest and real and find out what motivated me to be such a fuck up.
She really saved me and I'll forever be grateful even if it meant finding out I had over 40 serious character defects! At least!
To stay sober I had to ask for help
tell people how I was doing
I called Elly every day
Sometimes my ex would let me sleep on her couch so I'd be safe
friends would lend their cars or drive me to meetings
Asking for help was the hardest thing to do

And I made the oddest friendship with a waterfall (waterfalls are impossible to draw by the way). I told that waterfall everything I had done and then I told my sponsor.
The guilt and shame were beginning to lift.
I still wasn't a "better" person but I was becoming a different person.
And any change was going to be for the better.
getting serious with that waterfall about my character defects was just the start.

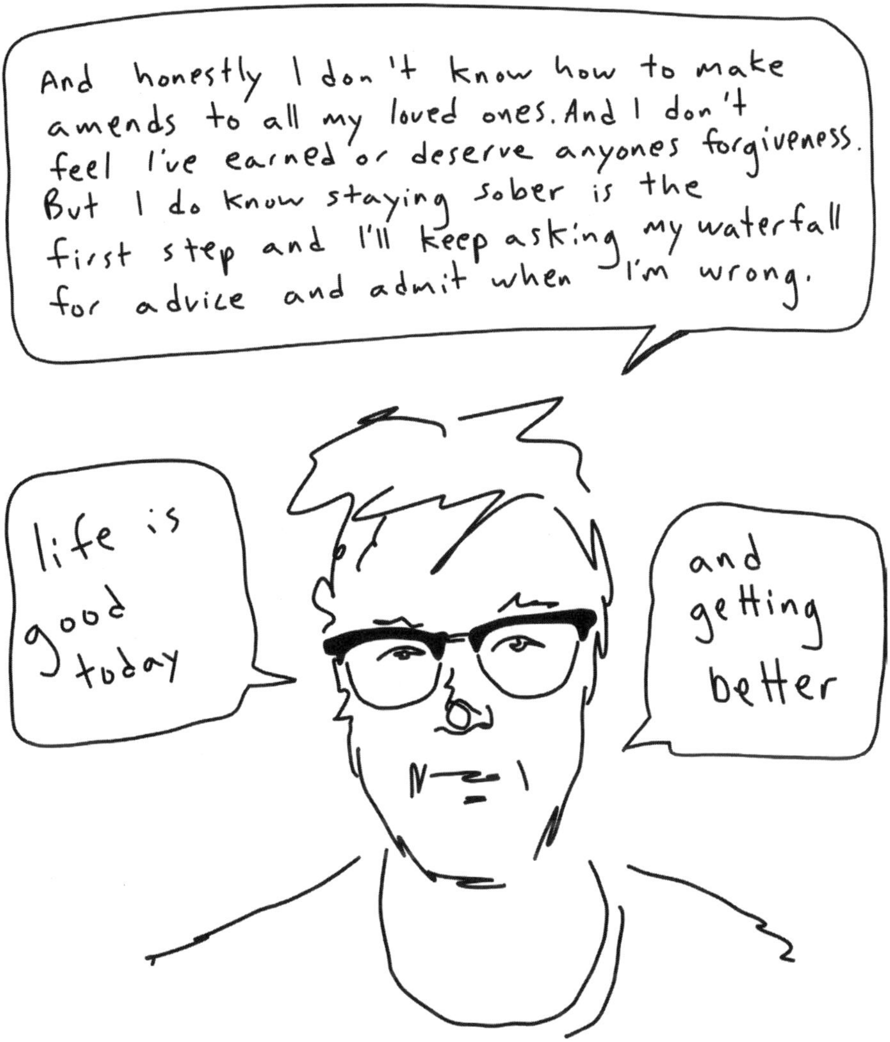
And honestly I don't know how to make amends to all my loved ones. And I don't feel I've earned or deserve anyones forgiveness. But I do know staying sober is the first step and I'll keep asking my waterfall for advice and admit when I'm wrong.
life is good today
and getting better

And that's the story of me and alcohol. Maybe it is a lot like yours or someone you love. Like I said, it is not an unusual story. It just happens to be my story.
Thanks for keeping me sober
And have a good 24.
Thanks for listening.

11

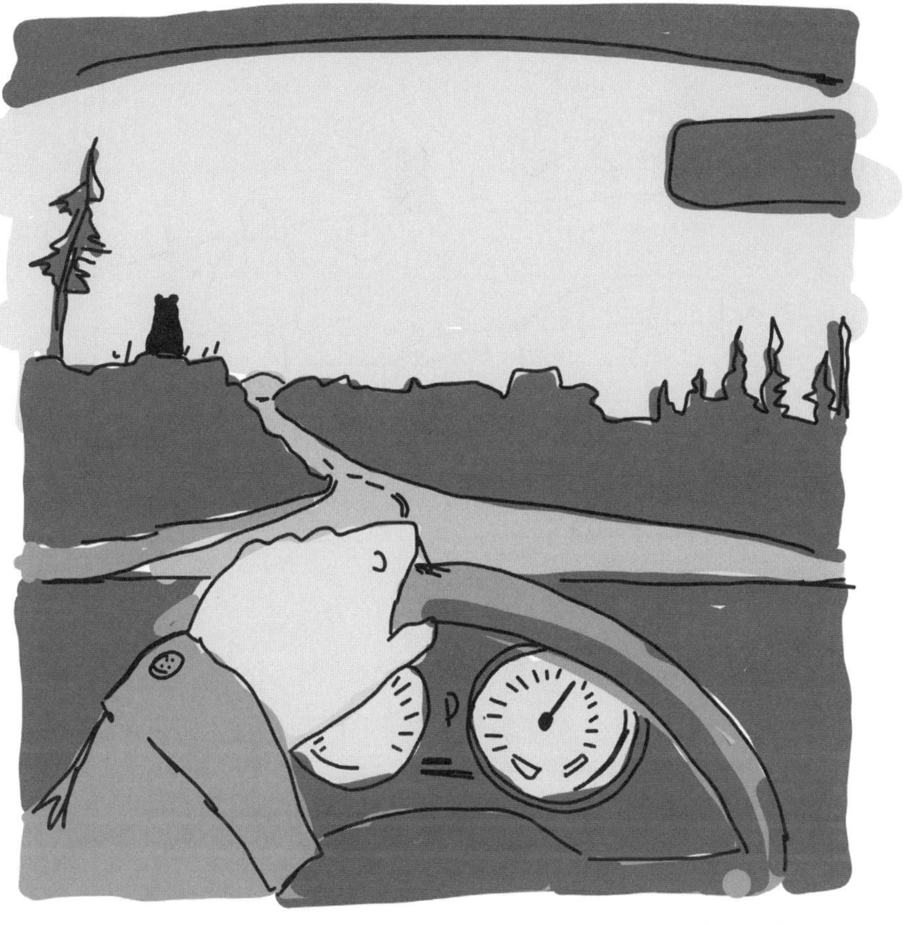

After hours and hours of driving I noticed a bear on a hill and pulled over.

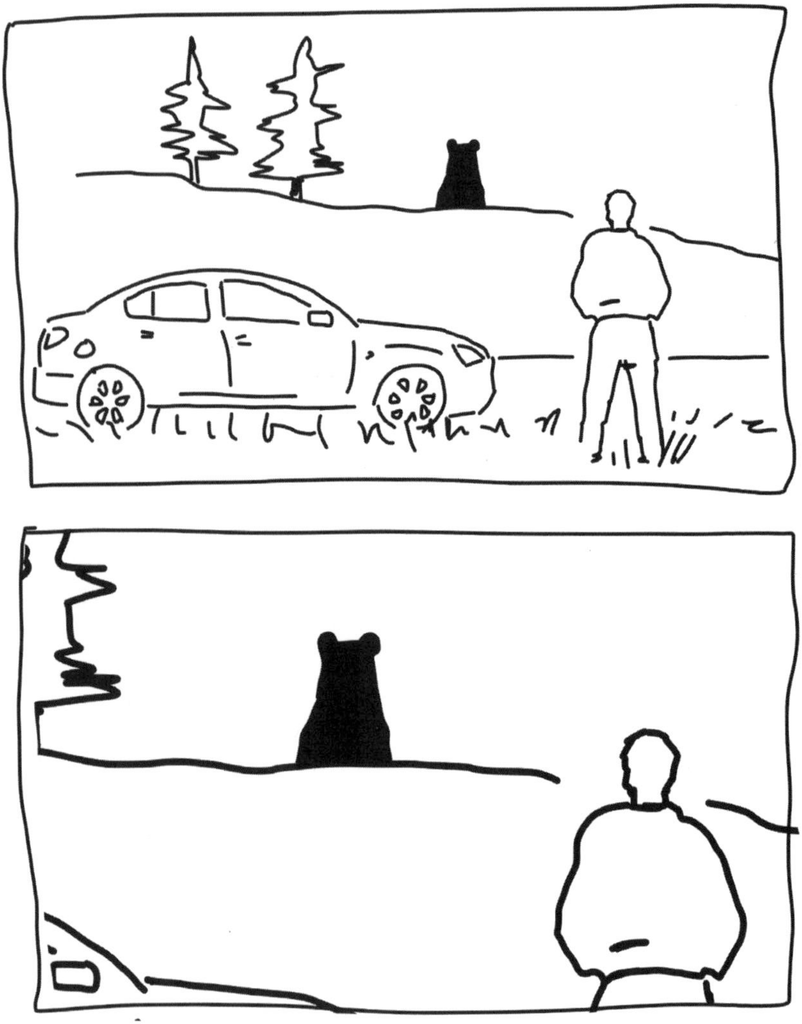

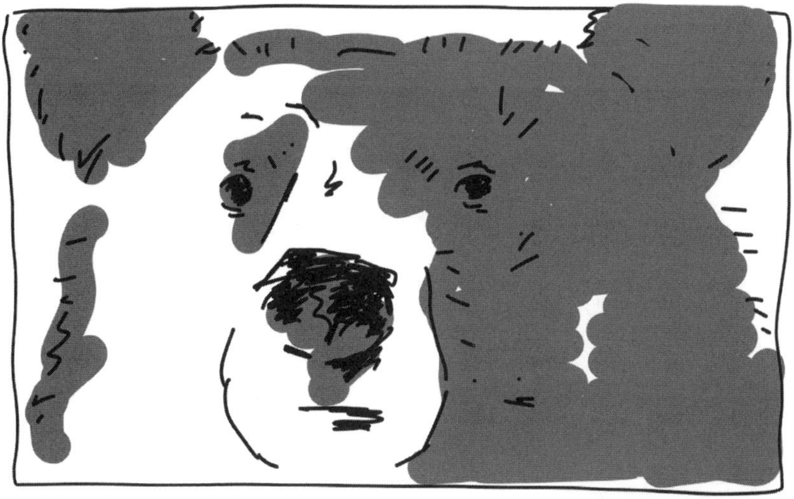

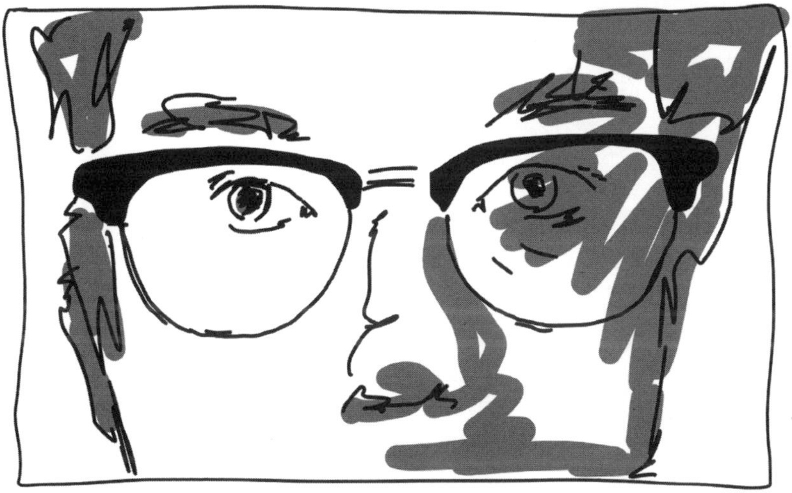

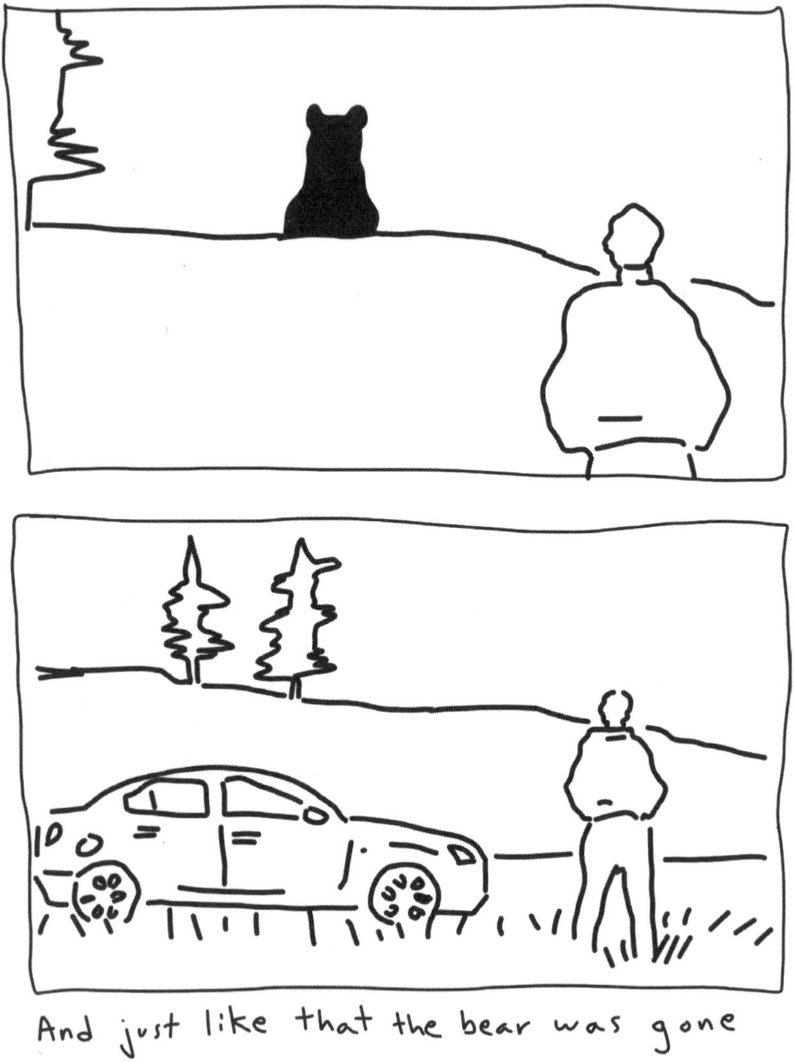

And just like that the bear was gone

And just like that I
was back on the road.

12

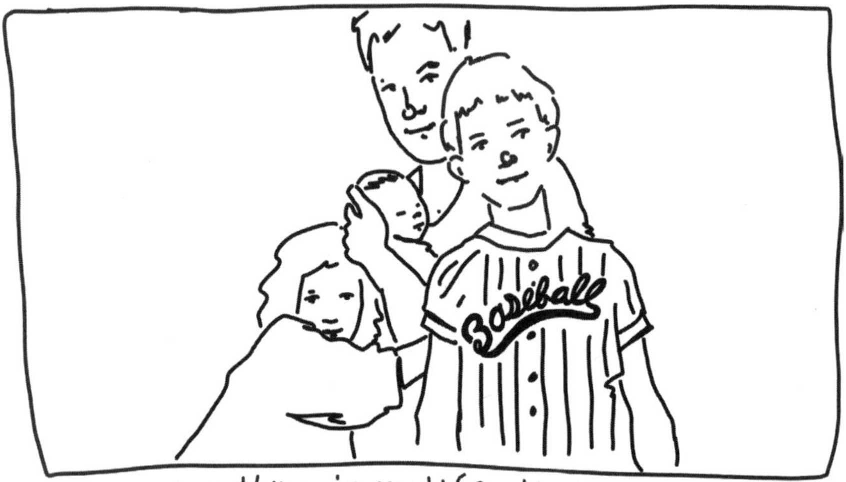
Baseball

There is nothing in my life that has brought me more joy than being a young parent.

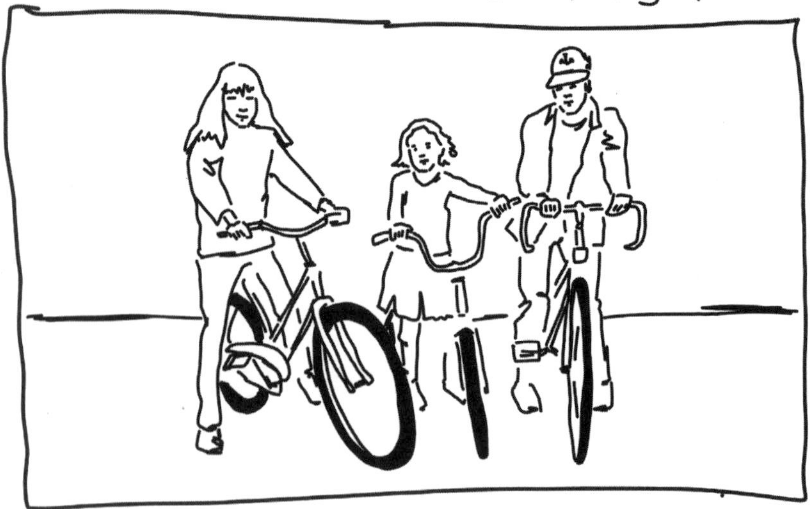

They made every day an adventure.

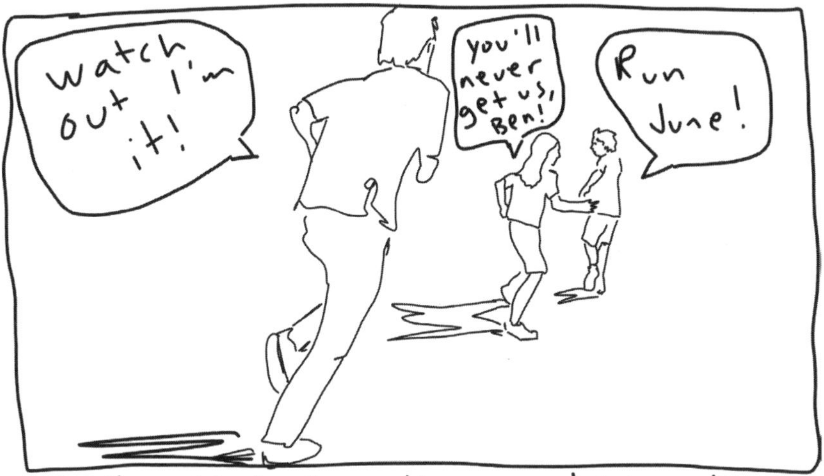
watch out I'm it!
you'll never get us, Ben!
Run June!

And nothing is better than watching the big kids play with the little kids.

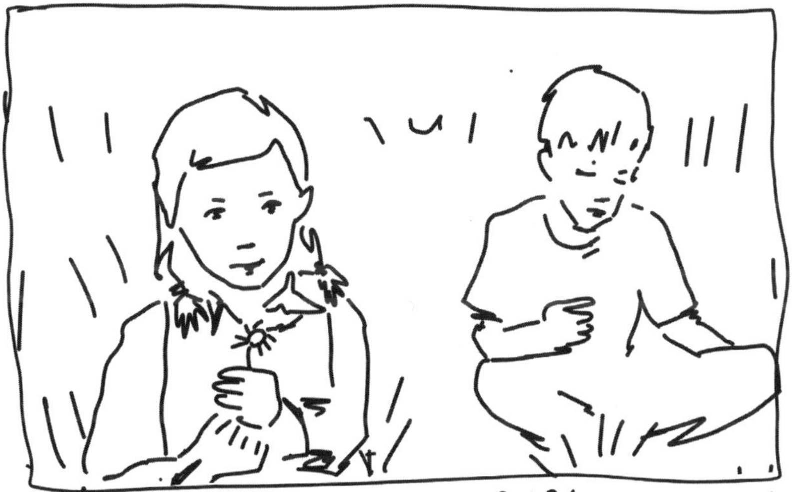

These two are 22 1/2 and 24 3/4 now and I enjoy their company more than ever.

So I was pretty excited
to be on my way to visit
them both. I was going to

pick up Ben in Montreal and
we would drive to Toronto to
hang with Char. How did I
get this lucky?

13

Sometimes at gas stations and rest stops I would see the same person repeatedly. Weary and determined.

I would wonder. Where were they going? What were they leaving? Who were they driving to?

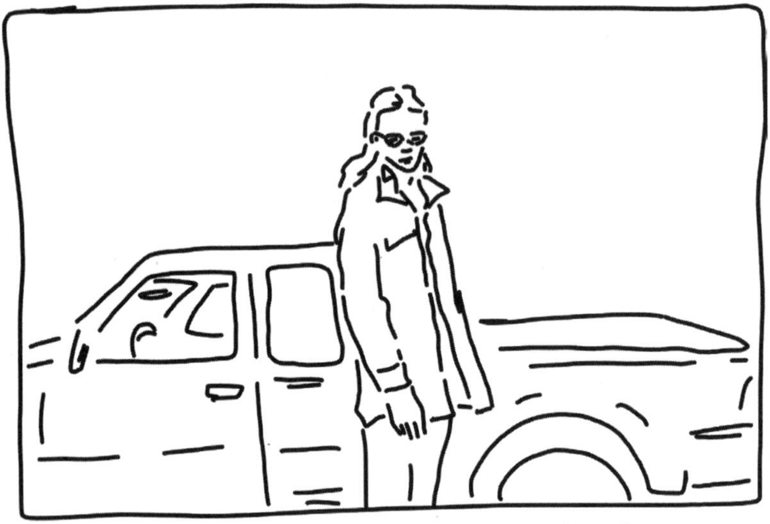

And sometimes we would lock eyes

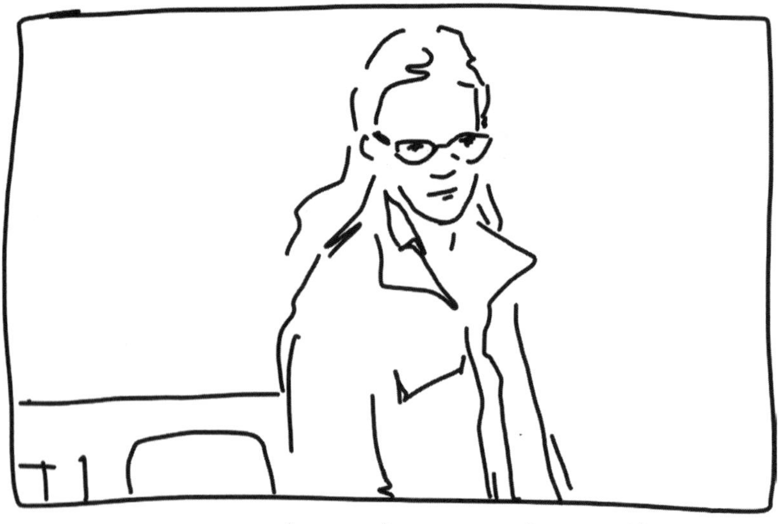

In a moment of solidarity

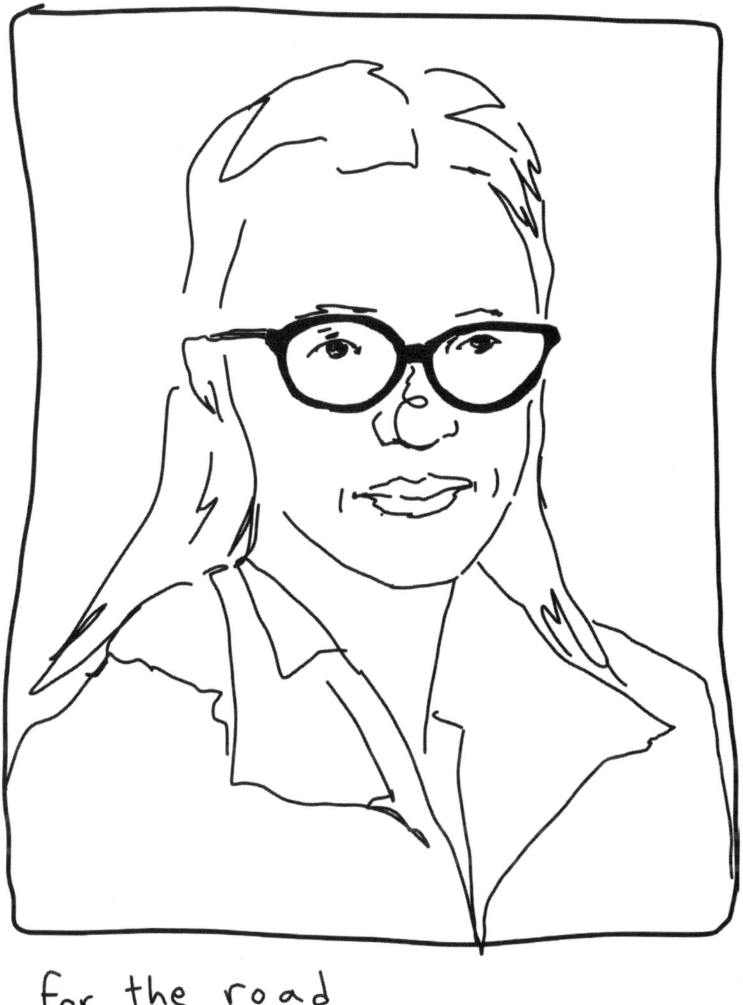

for the road
and for the journey

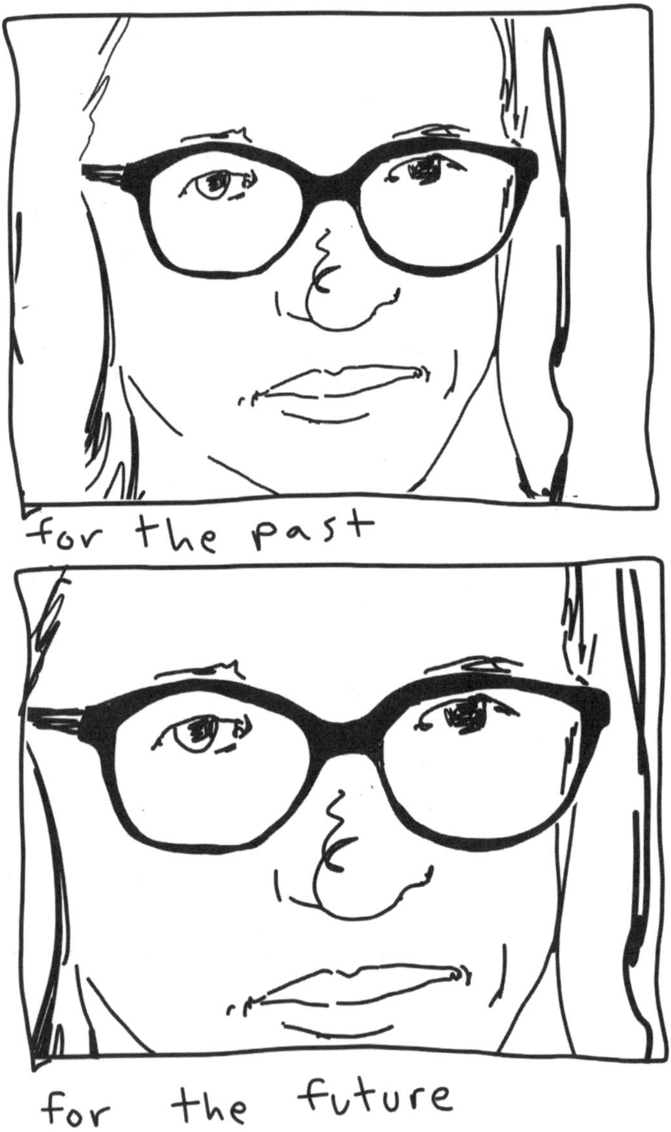
for the past
for the future

and for this moment.

And then they would be back
in the truck

and gone forever

14

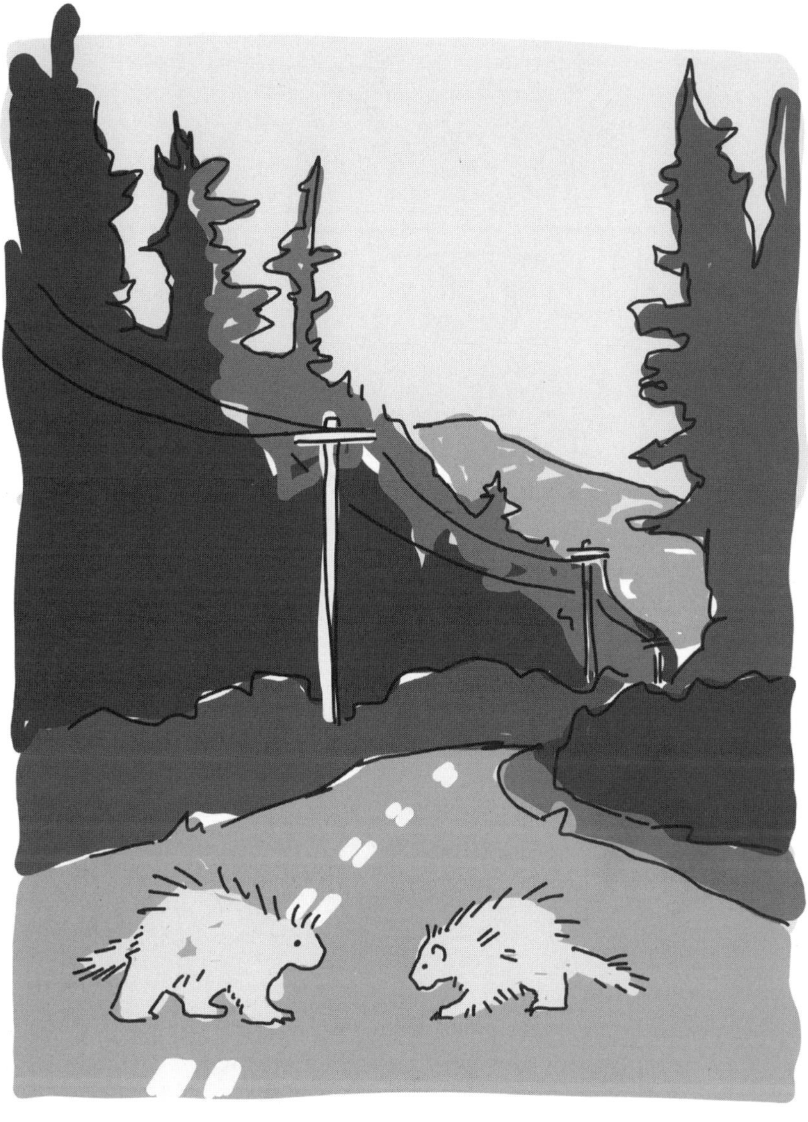

Honestly, you are not that easy to get close to
Really?
You can be a little prickly yourself
good point
like I've never heard that before

I just don't want to get hurt
me neither
Maybe this time it will be different

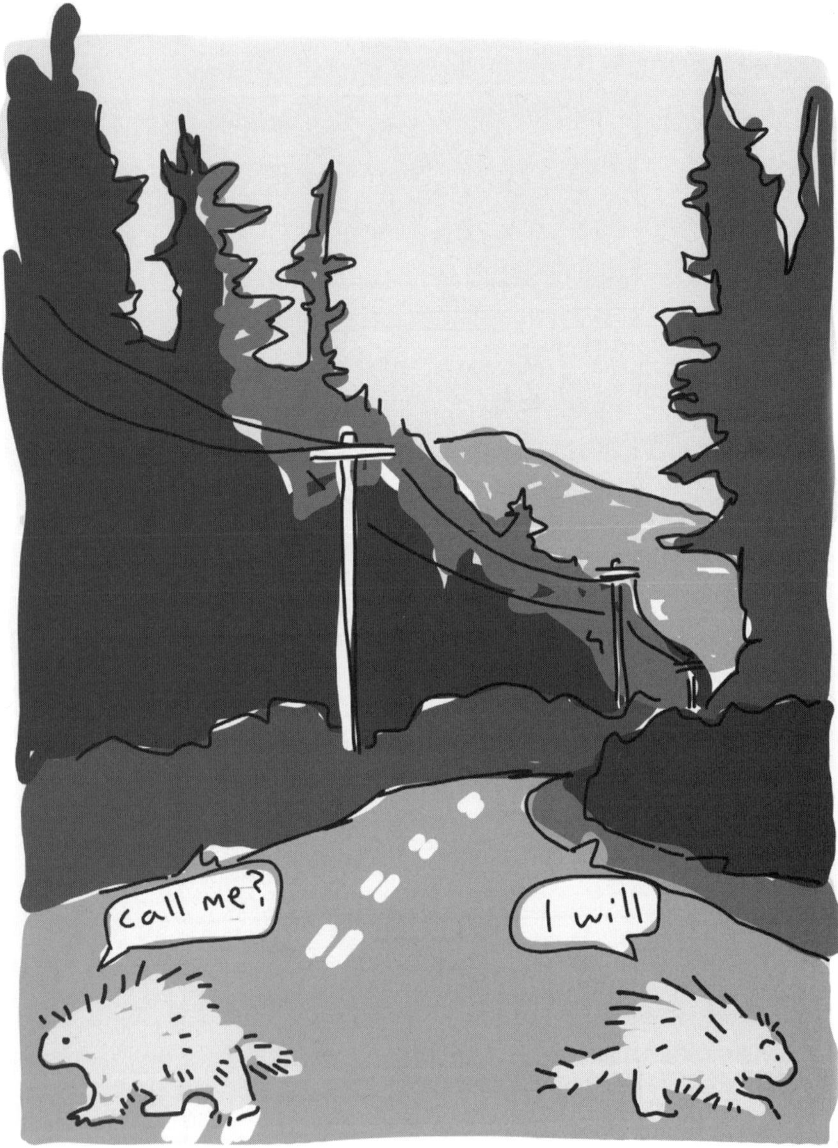
call me?
I will

15

Montreal is where young New Brunswickers go to try and find themselves.

I tried that years ago. Now I go back to try and find something else.

My closest friends today, my life long friends, were never my drinking buddies. That's probably why we are still friends.

But even though I would isolate myself and claim to be busy they would always open the door and let me in.

I don't know how they saw me but I always felt like I was a shadow, a distorted reflection of the friend I had once been.

*

It's not that I was a bad friend it's just that I wasn't all there.

*My favourite park in Montreal. A beautiful white building sits surrounded by a circular pond perfect for skating in the winter.

Ritual, habit and repetitian kept those old friendships intact. Whenever I'm in Montreal Mike and I go to my favourite restaurant in

the whole world, Arahova. I always get the same thing, fries and tzatziki. Sometimes we talk of going somewhere else but we never do.

And now when I stay over at Mike and Katies. We stay up late,

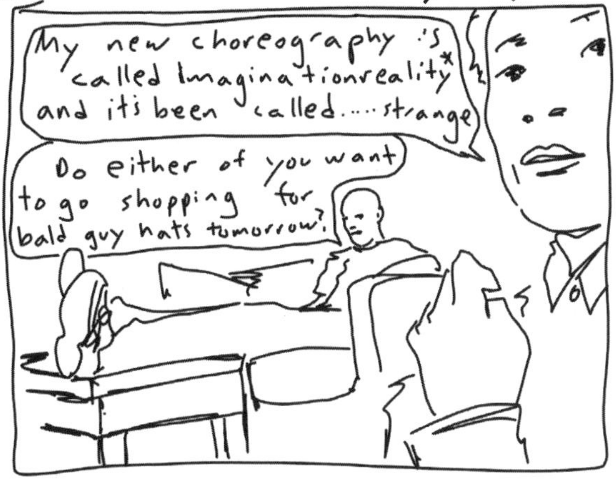
My new choreography is called Imaginationreality* and its been called..... strange
Do either of you want to go shopping for bald guy hats tomorrow?

talking about nothing in particular

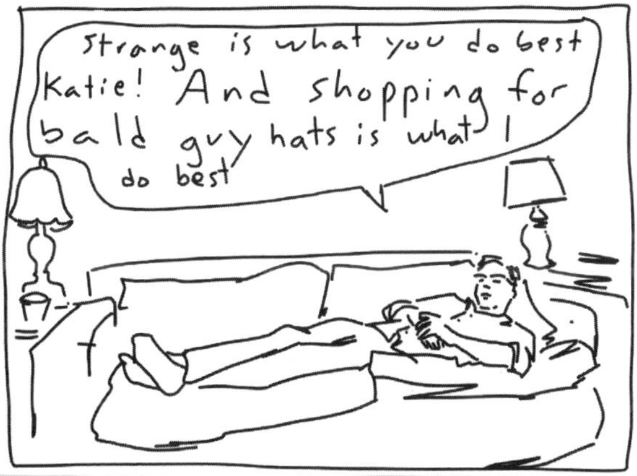
Strange is what you do best Katie! And shopping for bald guy hats is what I do best

It's life's smallest details I enjoy most these days.

*Katie is a fucking brilliant and truly one of a kind choreographer

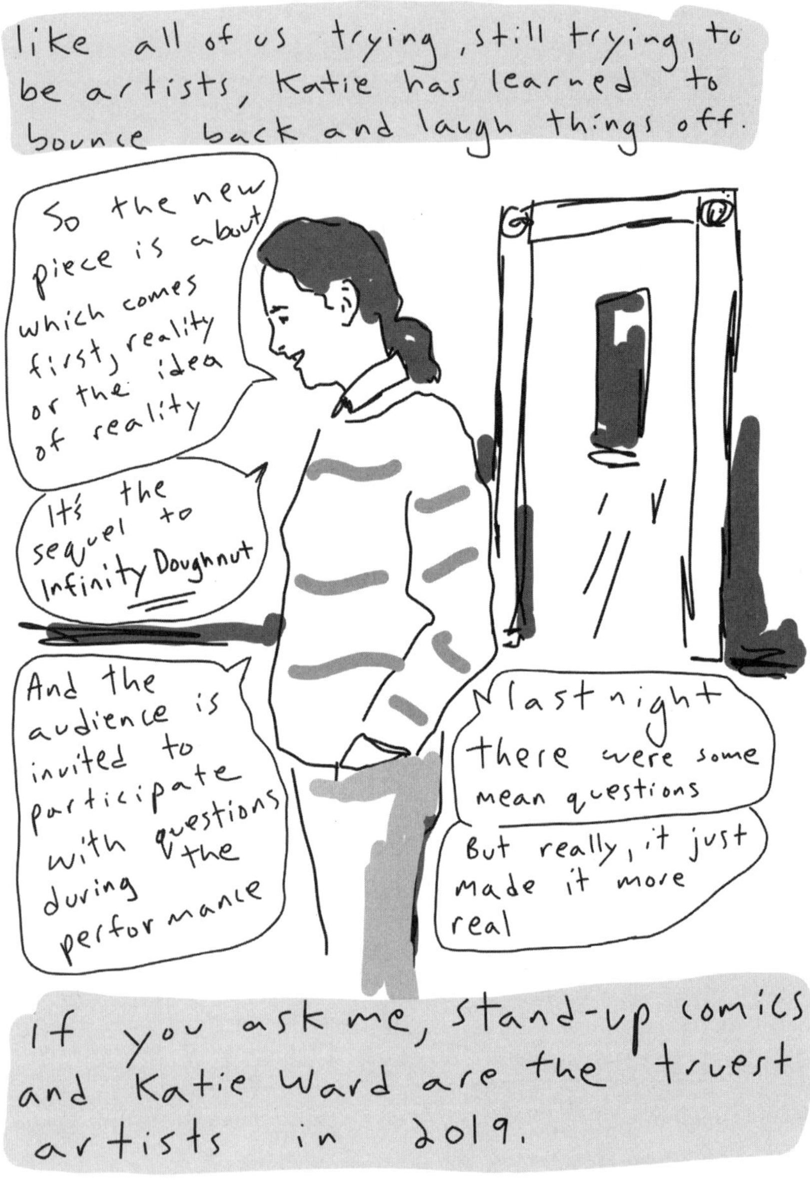
like all of us trying, still trying, to be artists, Katie has learned to bounce back and laugh things off.
So the new piece is about which comes first, reality or the idea of reality
It's the sequel to Infinity Doughnut
And the audience is invited to participate with questions during the performance
last night there were some mean questions
But really, it just made it more real
If you ask me, stand-up comics and Katie Ward are the truest artists in 2019.

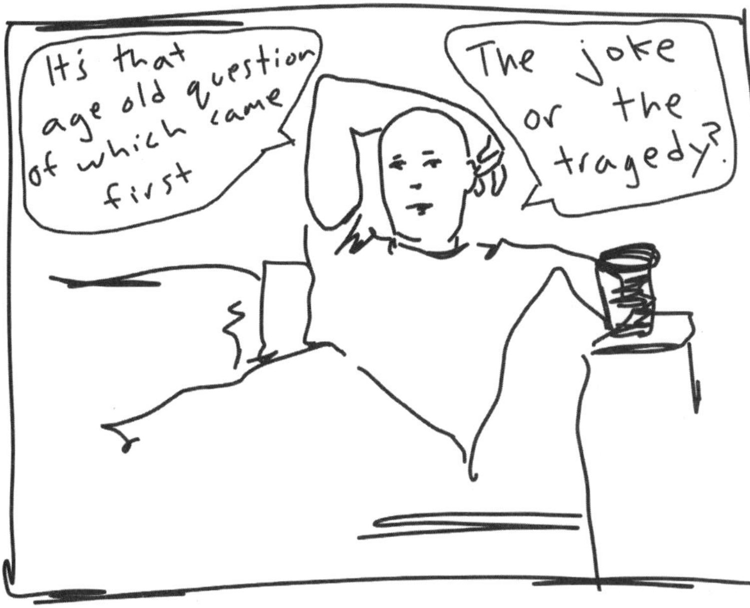
It's that age old question of which came first
The joke or the tragedy?

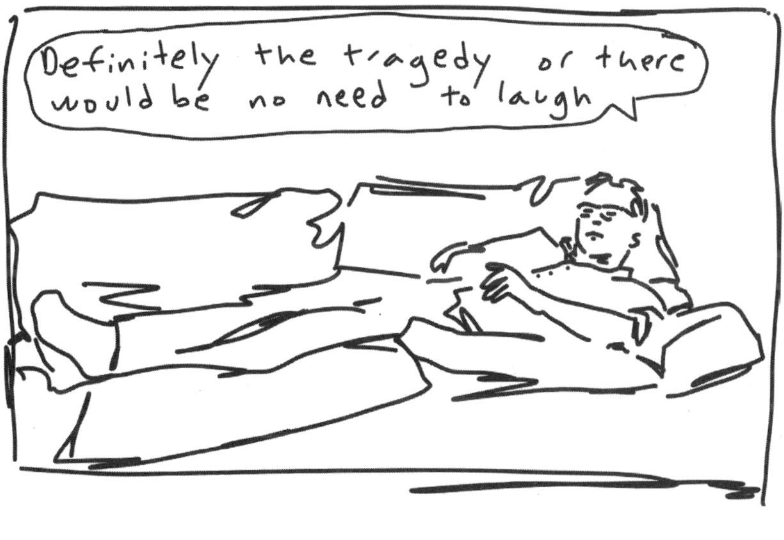
Definitely the tragedy or there would be no need to laugh

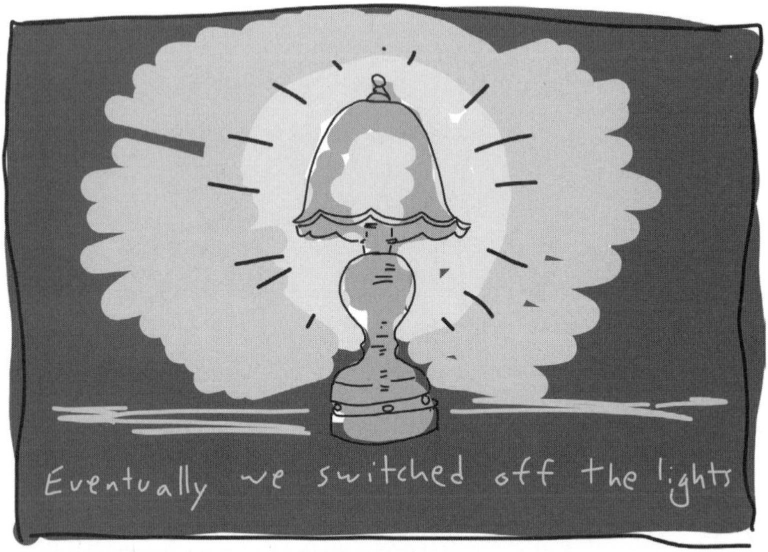
Eventually we switched off the lights

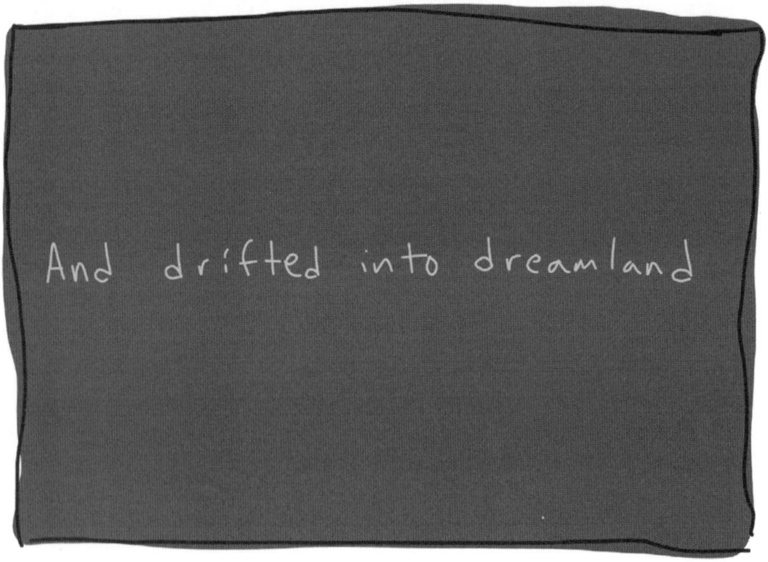
And drifted into dreamland

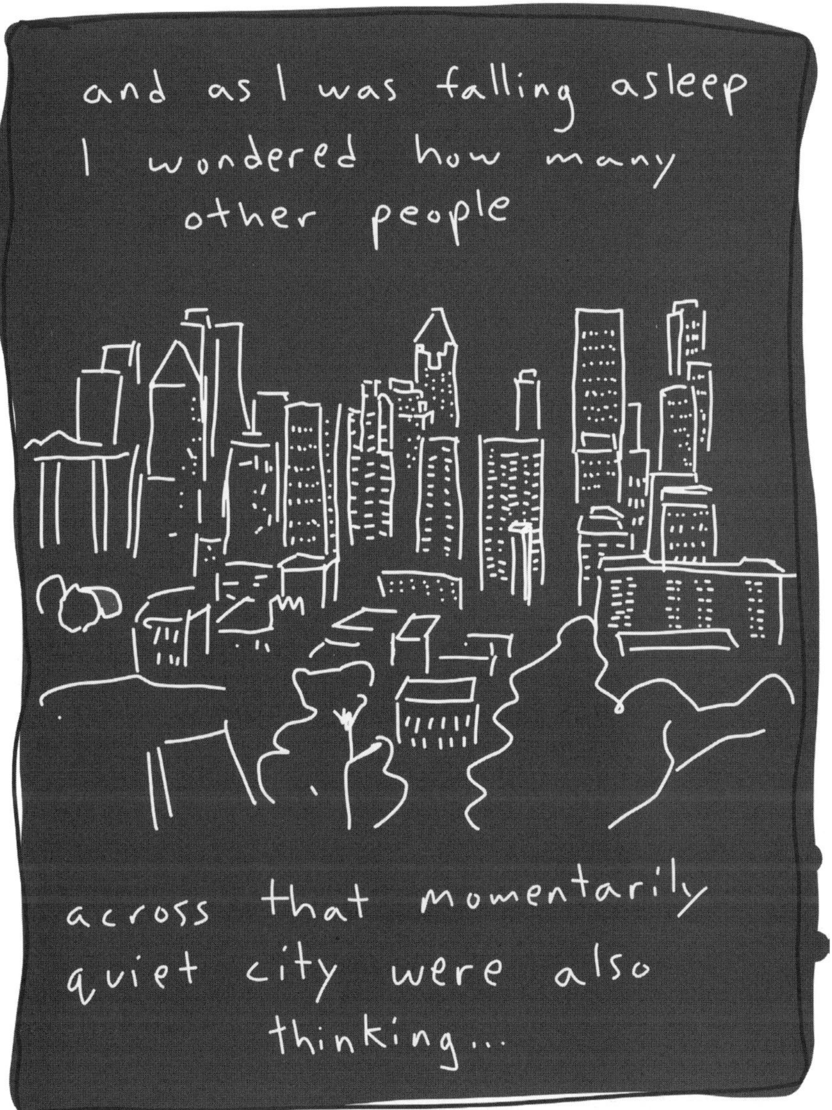
and as I was falling asleep
I wondered how many
other people
across that momentarily
quiet city were also
thinking...

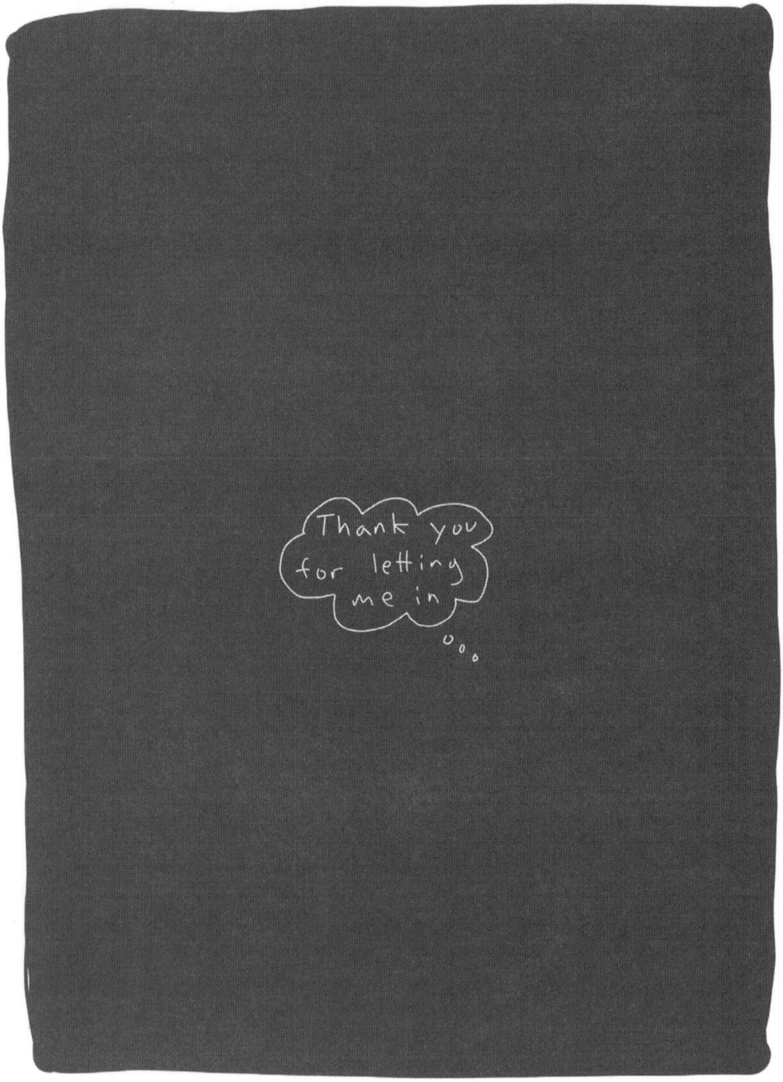
Thank you for letting me in

16

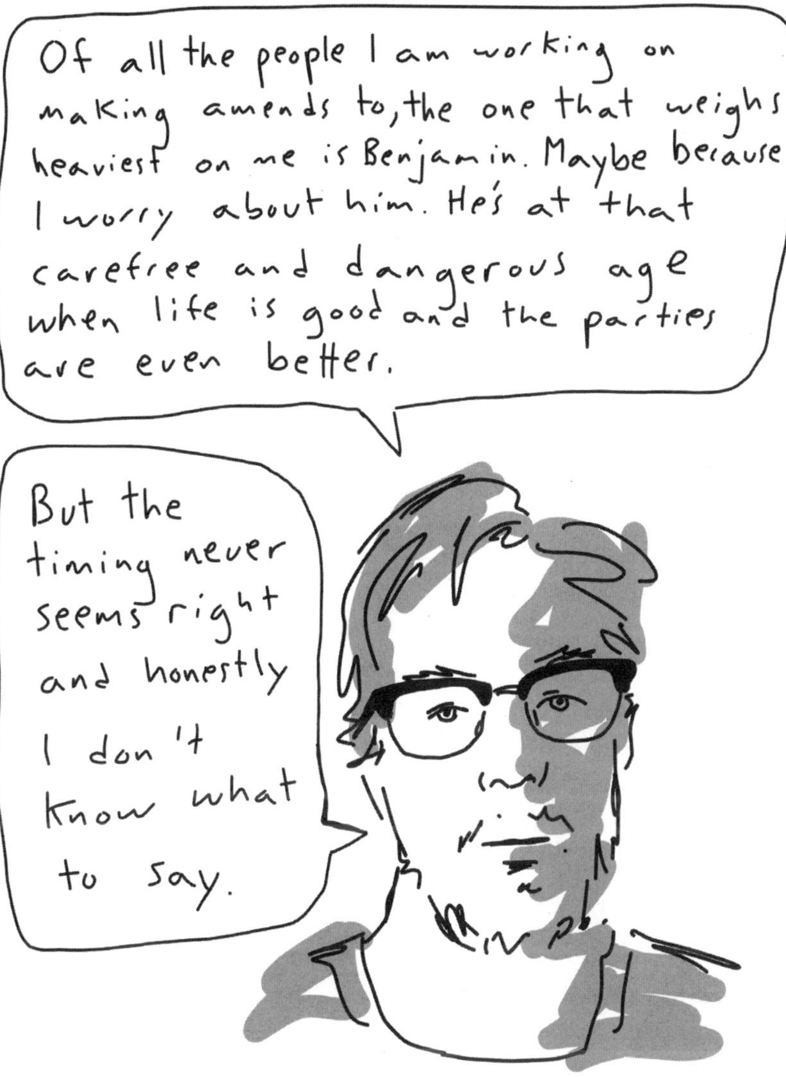
Of all the people I am working on making amends to, the one that weighs heaviest on me is Benjamin. Maybe because I worry about him. He's at that carefree and dangerous age when life is good and the parties are even better.
But the timing never seems right and honestly I don't know what to say.

So as I drove closer to pick
him up I decided that now
wasn't the time to try to make
amends. After all, it doesn't always
go well. when the time is right I

am sure I'll know. I didn't
want to burden him with
being asked to forgive his
father. That doesn't sound like
a fun trip!

I've been drawing and painting Ben his whole life. He's always been a great model. He's always up for anything no matter how crazy. He knows how to have fun.

But one thing I've never worried about is whether he would turn out to be kind and loving. He really is a wonderful human.

← pink hair

← ear ring

I'm sure being the oldest child in our family wasn't easy.

We went to breakfast before hitting the road. But first a smoke!

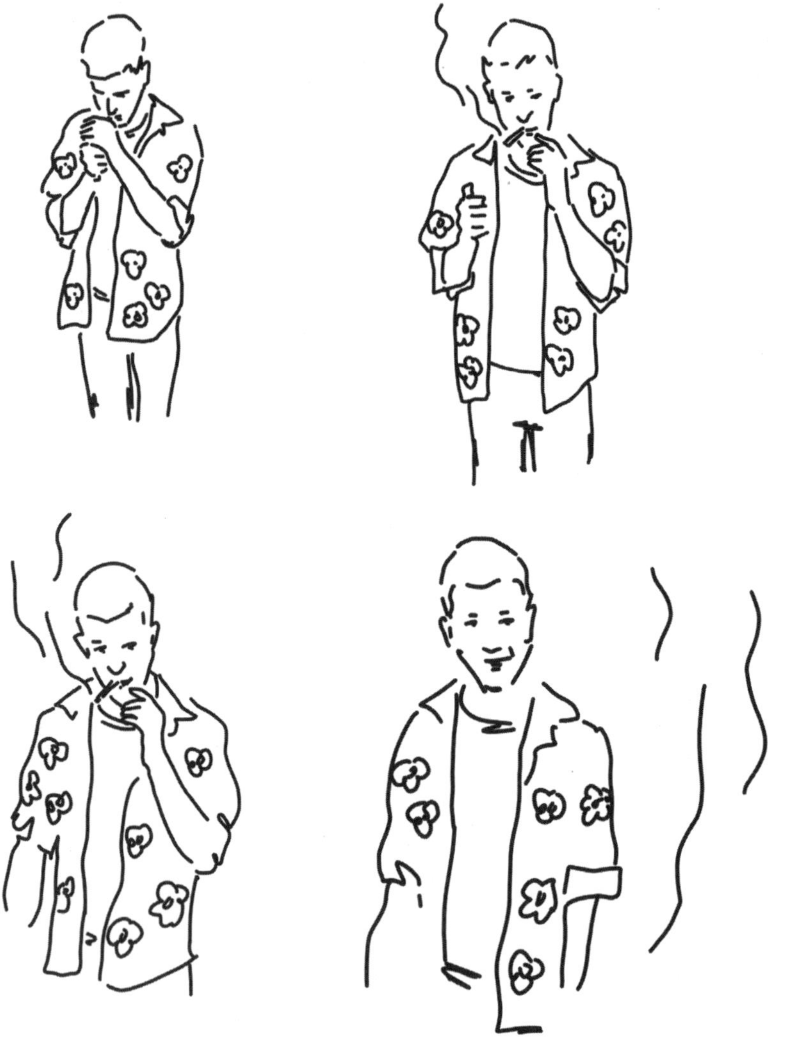

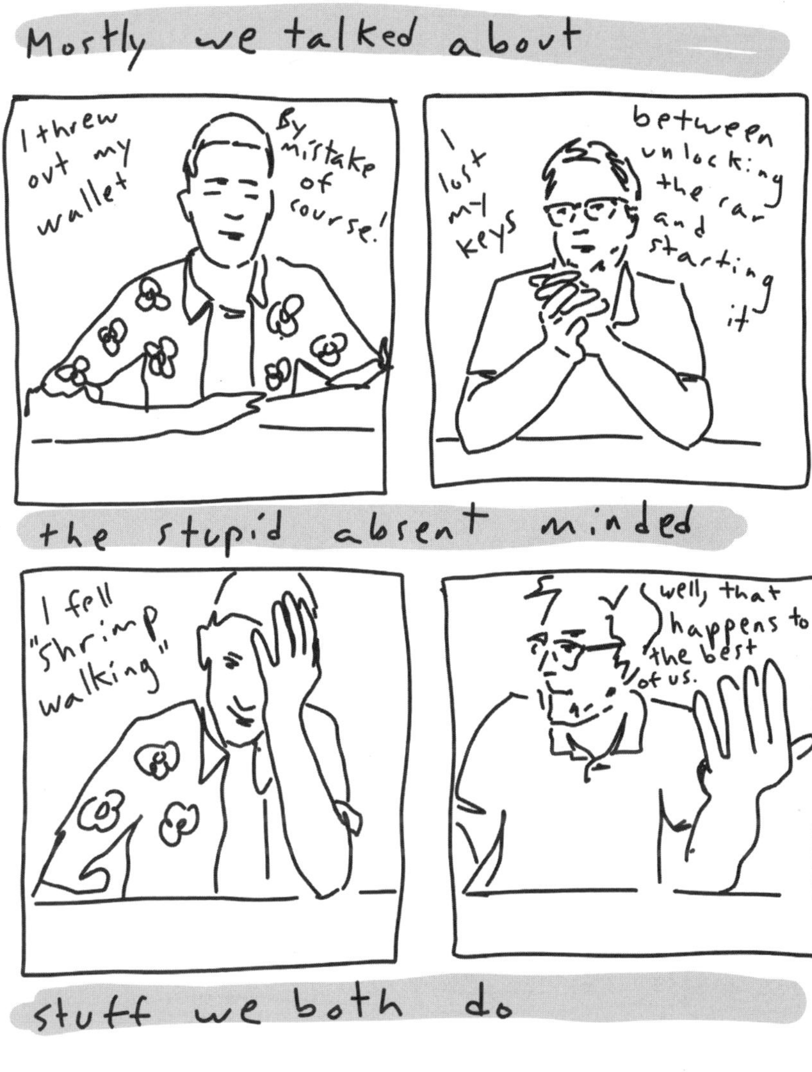
Mostly we talked about
I threw out my wallet
By mistake of course!
I lost my keys
between unlocking the car and starting it
the stupid absent minded
I fell "shrimp walking"
well, that happens to the best of us.
stuff we both do

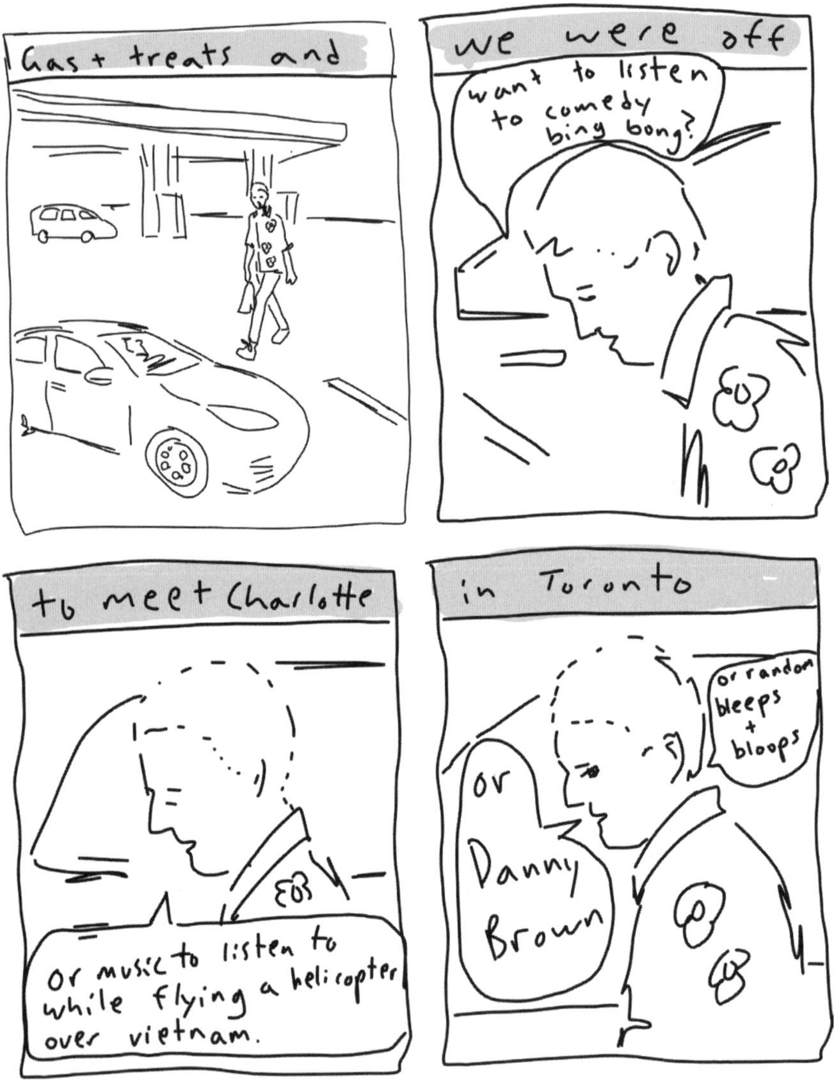
Gas + treats and
we were off
want to listen to comedy bing bong?
to meet Charlotte
or music to listen to while flying a helicopter over vietnam.
in Toronto
or Danny Brown
or random bleeps + bloops

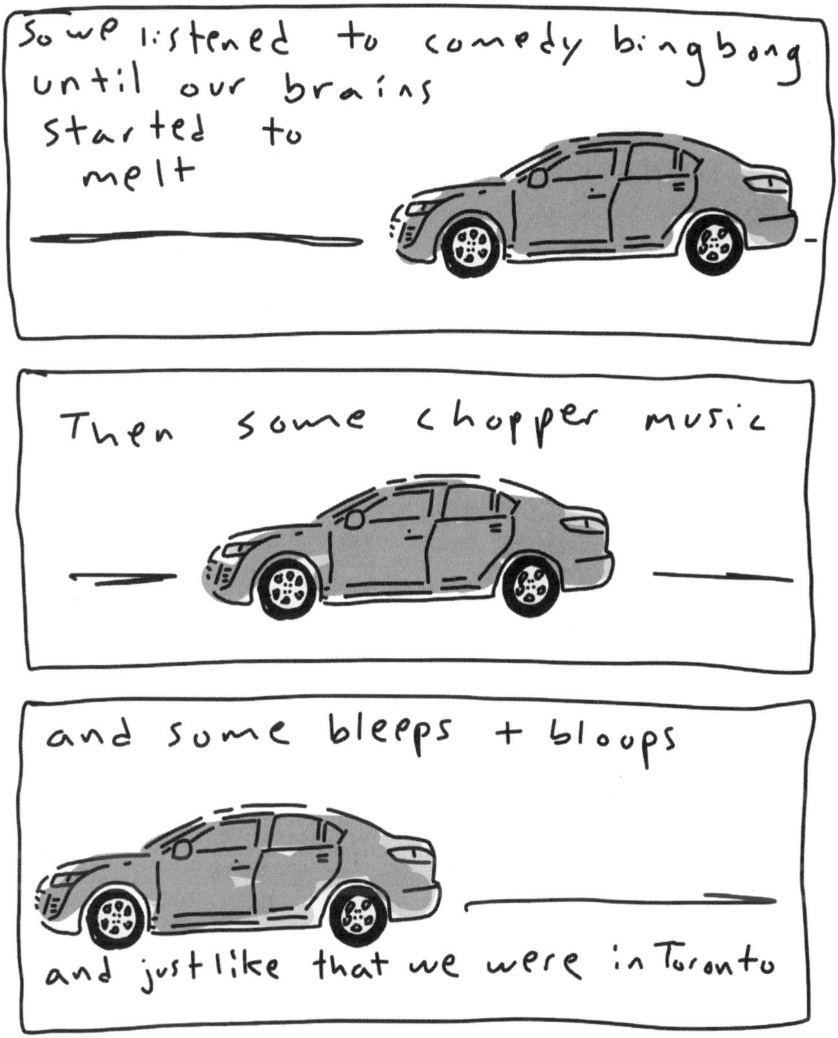
So we listened to comedy bingbong until our brains started to melt
Then some chopper music
and some bleeps + bloops
and just like that we were in Toronto

Of course I worry about Charlotte too. She has been through so much since moving out. But she's making it in Toronto, she's gonna be a huge success. So we are all being extra nice to her now, 'cause she's gonna be rich.

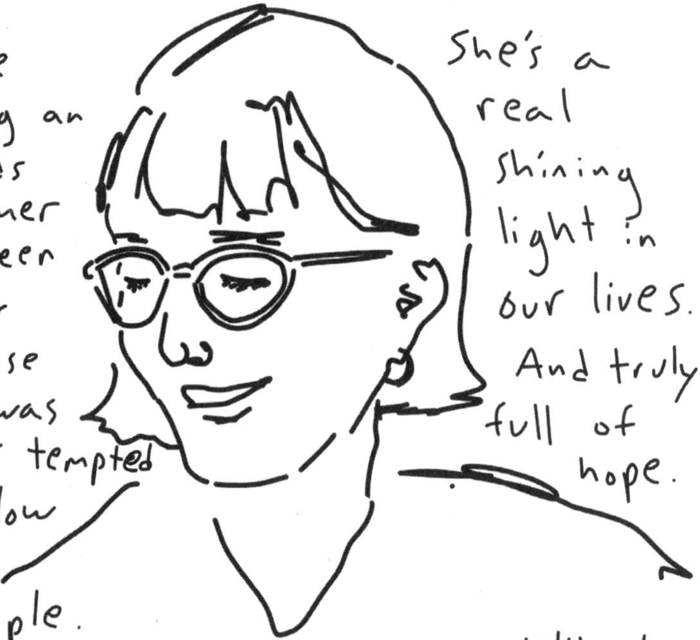

Maybe making an amends with her had been easier because she was never tempted to follow my example.

She's a real shining light in our lives. And truly full of hope.

And when she was little I carried her around in my backpack. We had good times.

Charlotte wanted to meet at the Lakeview Restaurant which was perfect

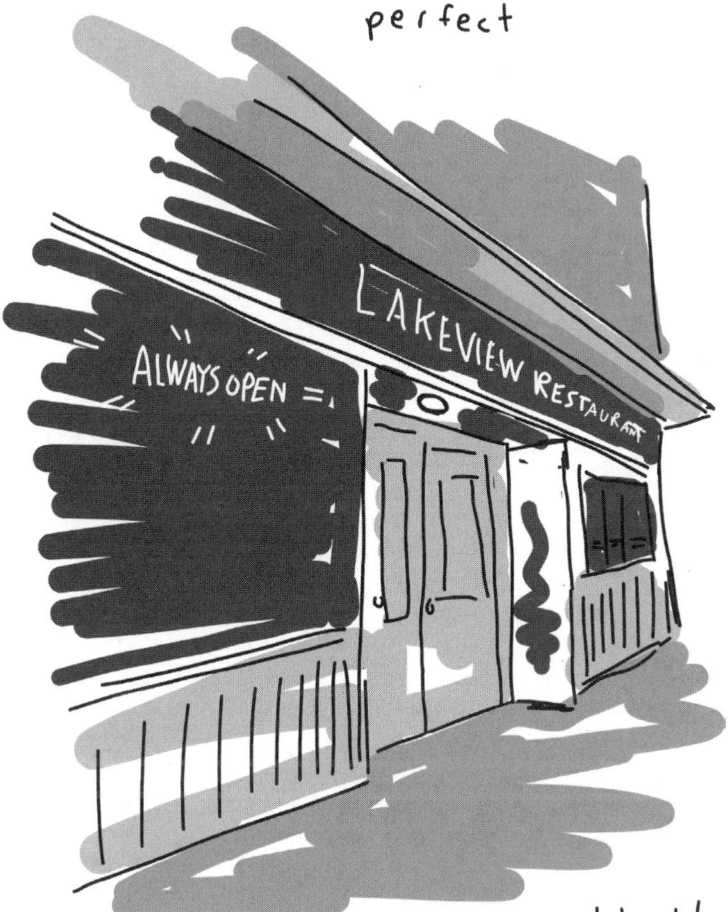
LAKEVIEW RESTAURANT
ALWAYS OPEN

because we knew we couldn't get there too late, it never closes.

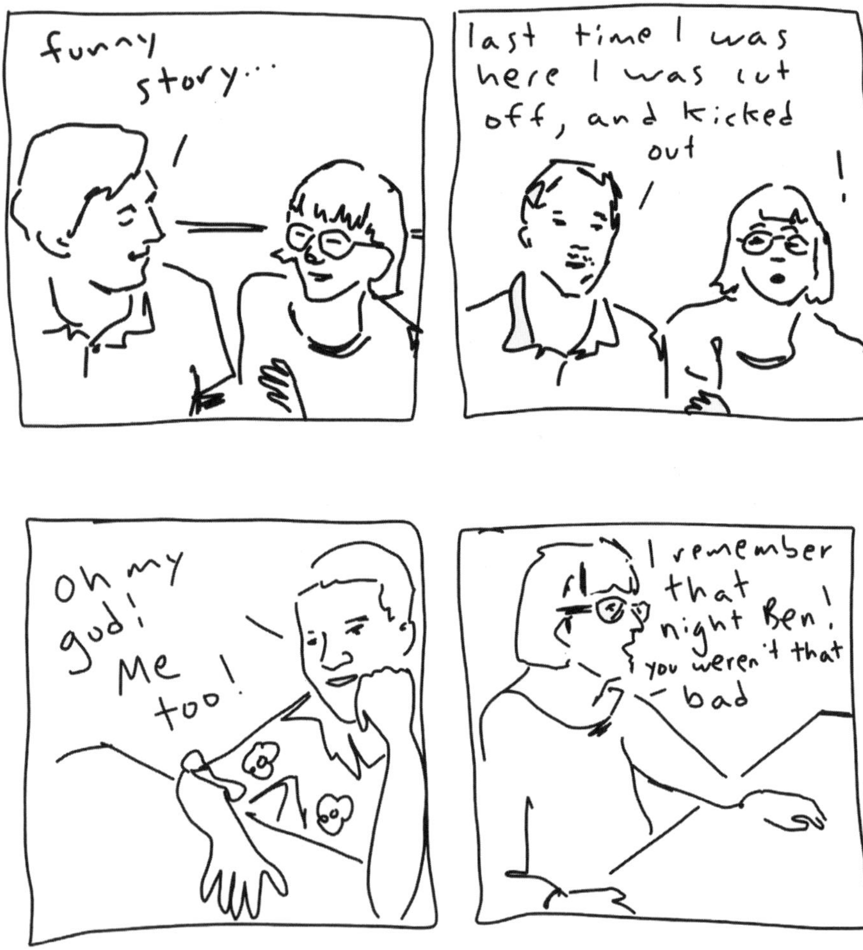
funny story...
last time I was here I was cut off, and kicked out
!
Oh my god! Me too!
I remember that night Ben! you weren't that bad

It's actually the only time I was ever kicked out of somewhere

One minute everyone was laughing, the next minute I had to go.

haha, I was being a little bit sassy.

And certainly it wasn't the first or last time I was kicked out of somewhere unless Ducky's doesn't count.

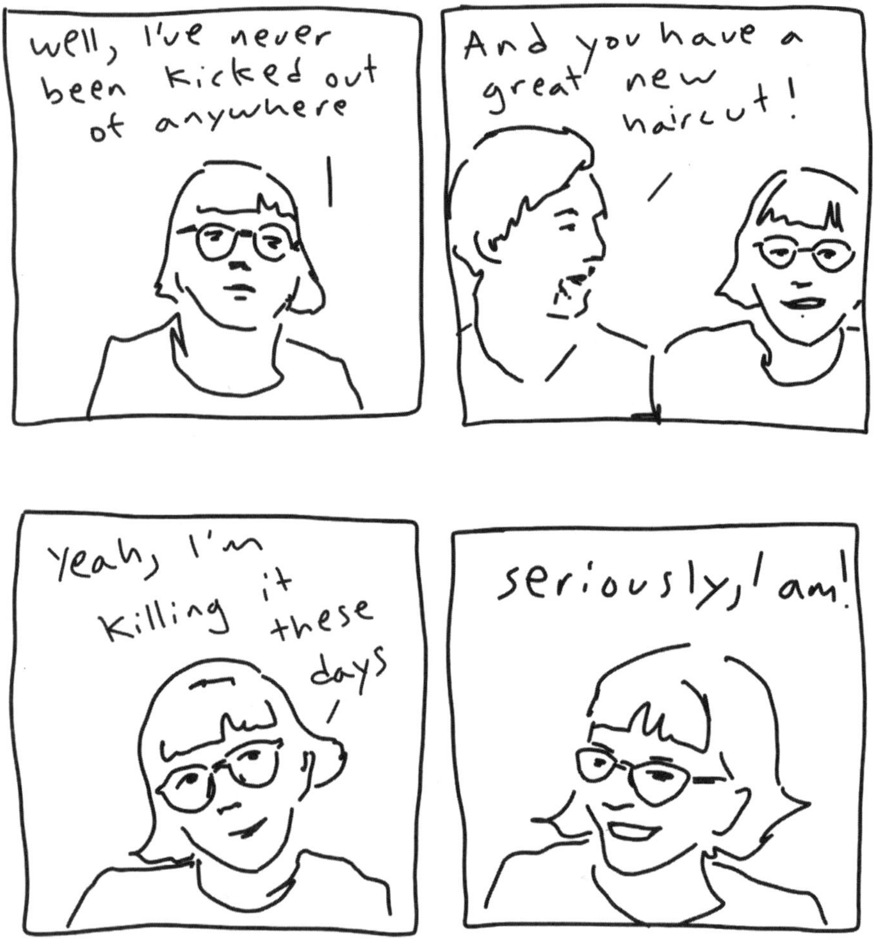

well, I've never been kicked out of anywhere
And you have a great new haircut!
Yeah, I'm killing it these days
seriously, I am!

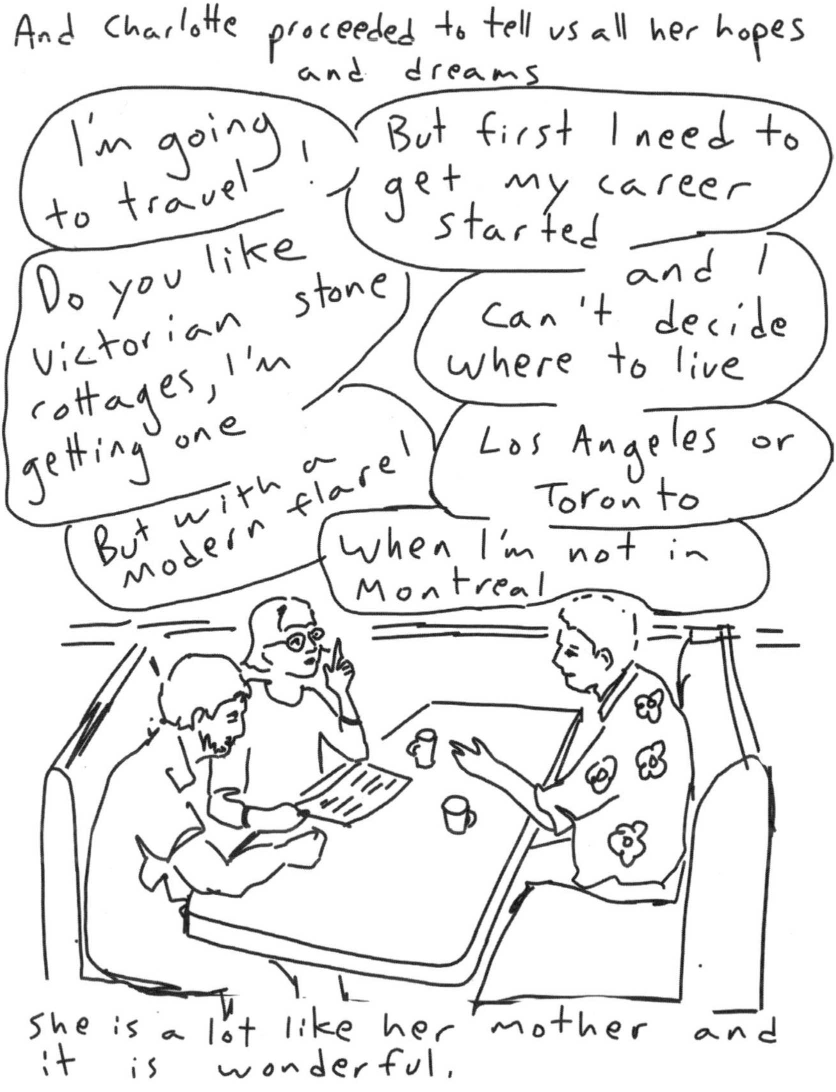
And Charlotte proceeded to tell us all her hopes and dreams
I'm going to travel!
But first I need to get my career started
Do you like victorian stone cottages, I'm getting one
and I can't decide where to live
But with a modern flare!
Los Angeles or Toronto
When I'm not in Montreal
She is a lot like her mother and it is wonderful.

And then we walked back to Charlotte's through the neon Toronto night talking about Sackville.

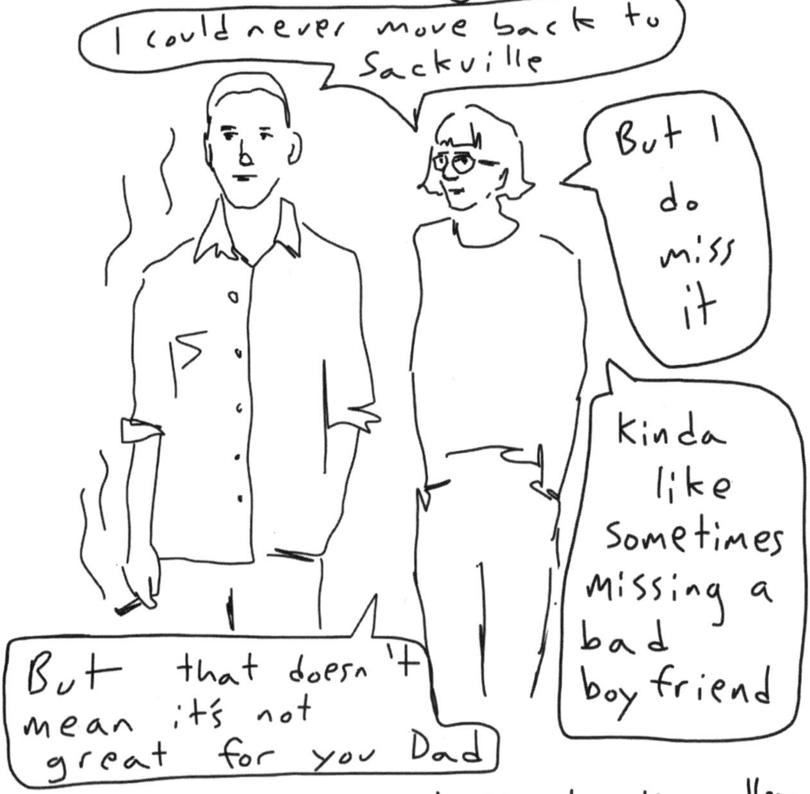
I could never move back to Sackville
But I do miss it
Kinda like Sometimes missing a bad boyfriend
But that doesn't mean it's not great for you Dad

And reminiscing about the bowling alley, Mel's and the fall fair parade.

But mostly we just talked about

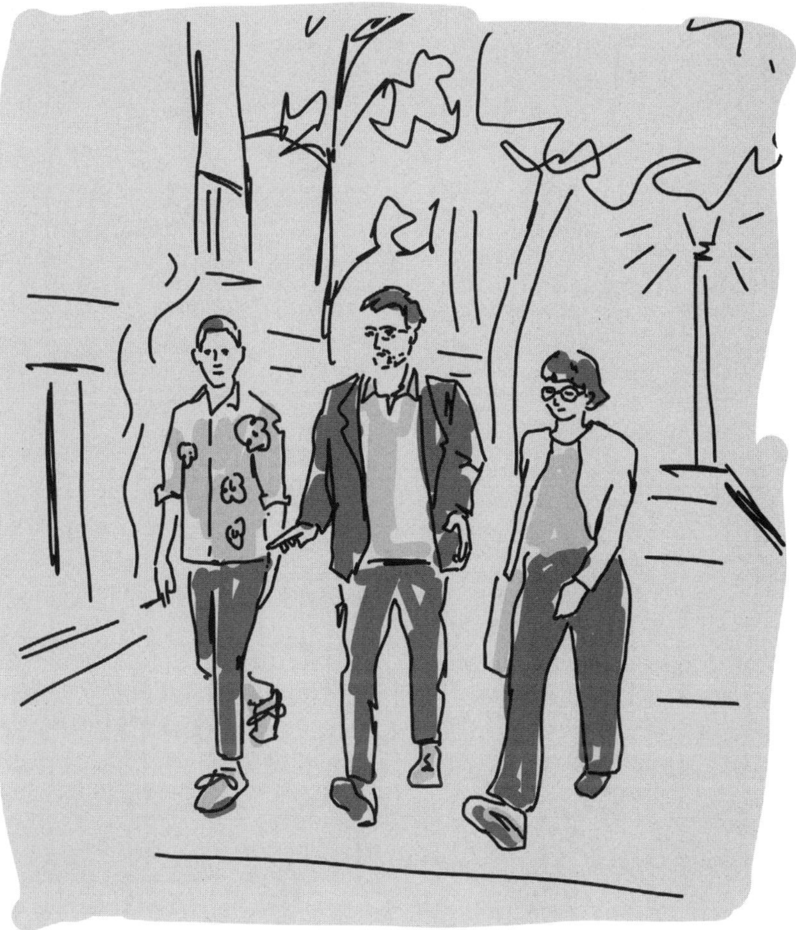

how excited we were to get to Char's and watch Frasier.

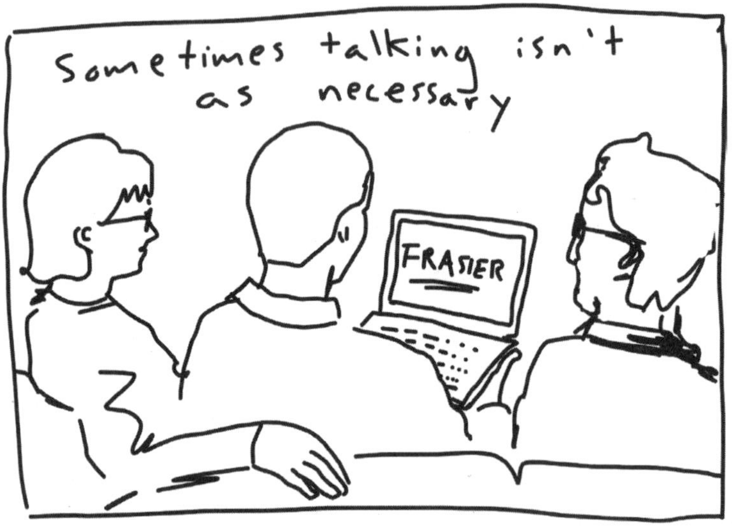
Sometimes talking isn't as necessary
FRASIER

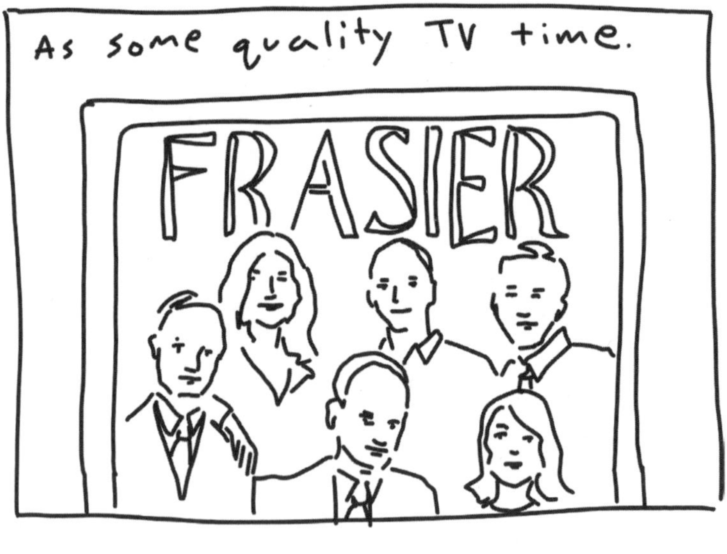
As some quality TV time.
FRASIER

And in the morning we said goodbye to charlotte over coffee.

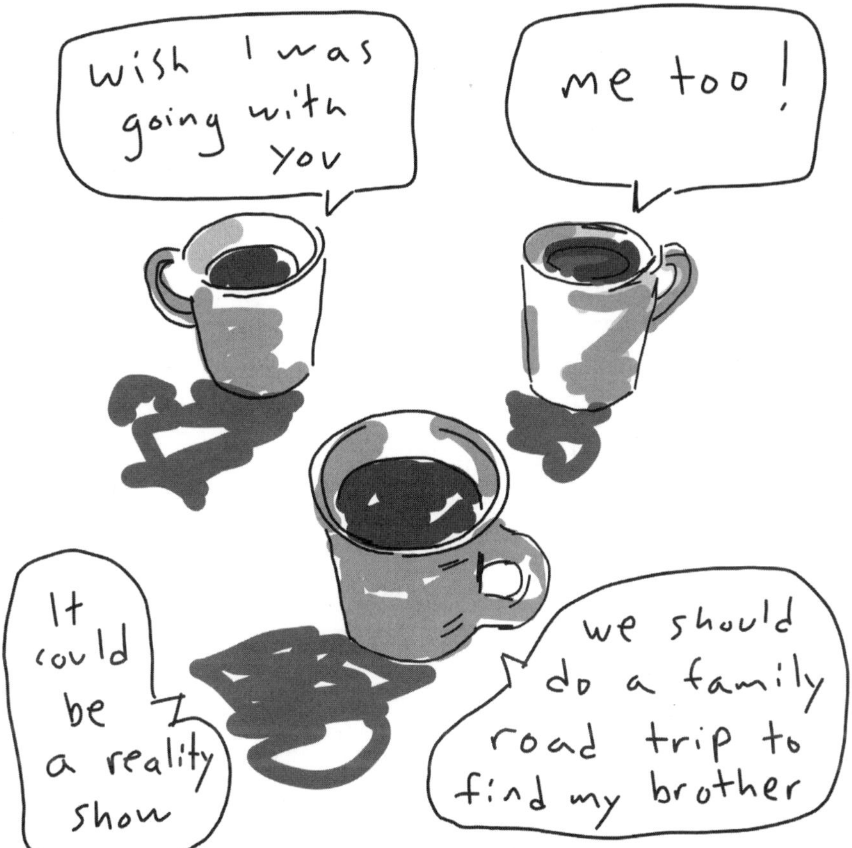
wish I was going with you
me too!
It could be a reality show
we should do a family road trip to find my brother

we all drank it black like my dad taught me.

17

Next stop Ottawa -

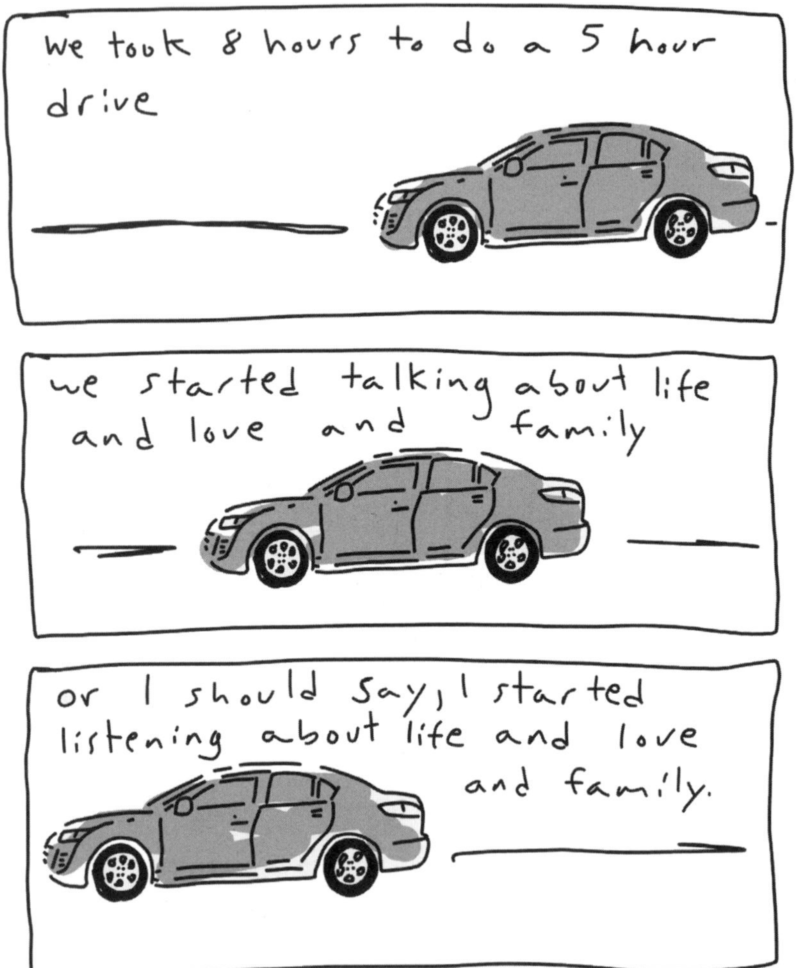
we took 8 hours to do a 5 hour drive
we started talking about life and love and family
or I should say, I started listening about life and love and family.

By the longest route possible

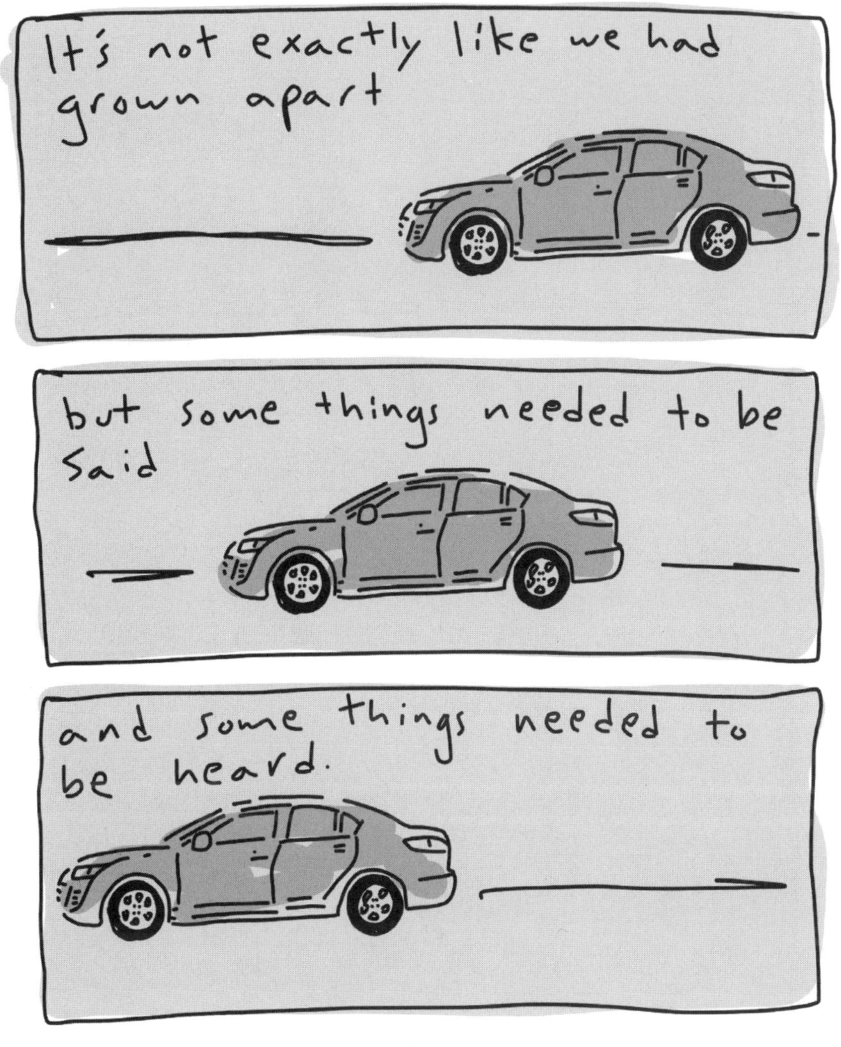
It's not exactly like we had grown apart
but some things needed to be said
and some things needed to be heard.

And we talked about addiction

And even listened to some

of my recovery podcasts.

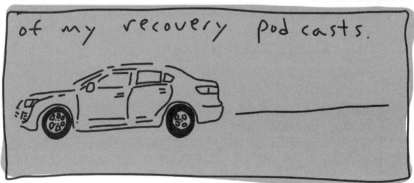

And we stopped

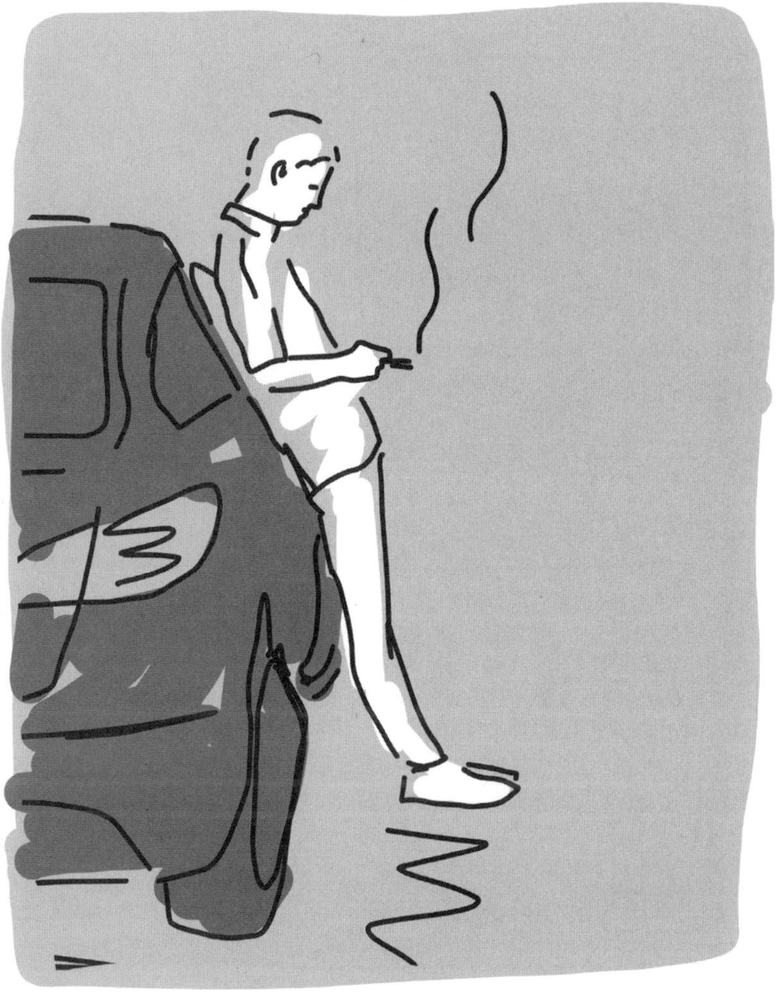

for smoke breaks

And to gaze at the smallest

litte riple of a waterfall

called Furnace falls

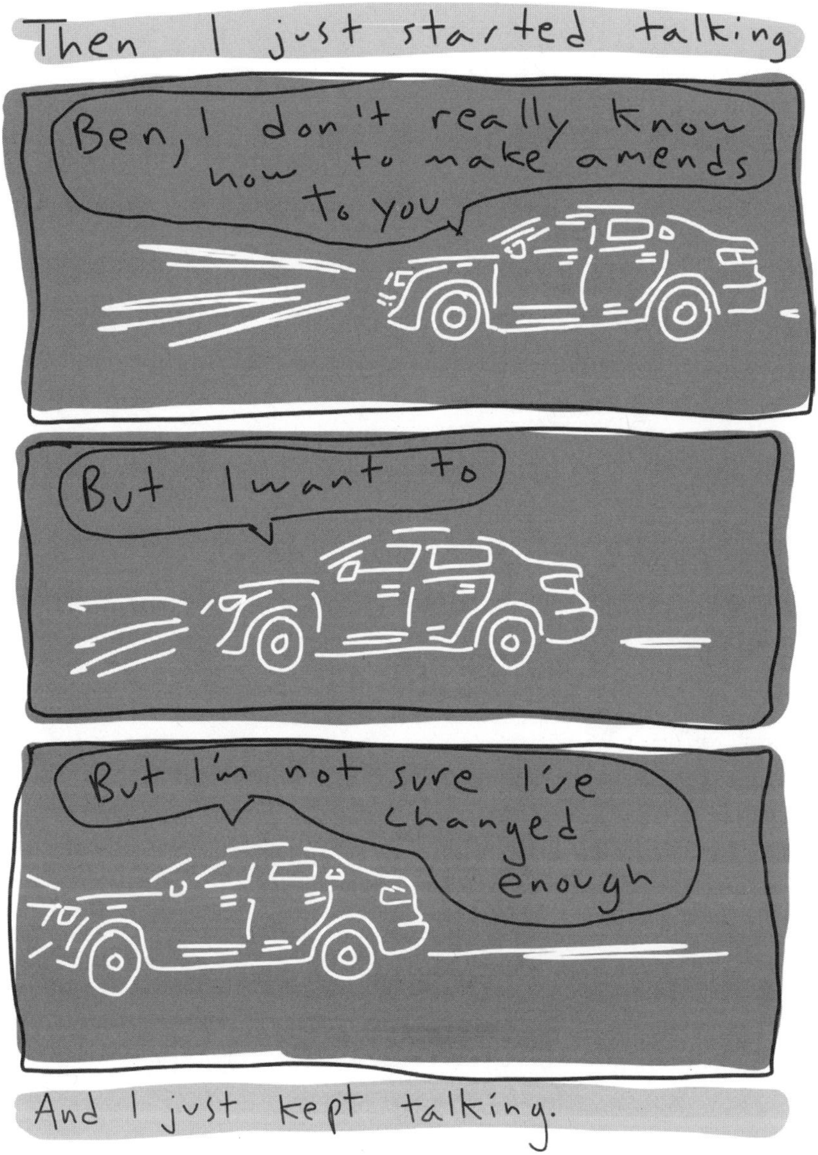
Then I just started talking
Ben, I don't really know how to make amends to you
But I want to
But I'm not sure I've changed enough
And I just kept talking.

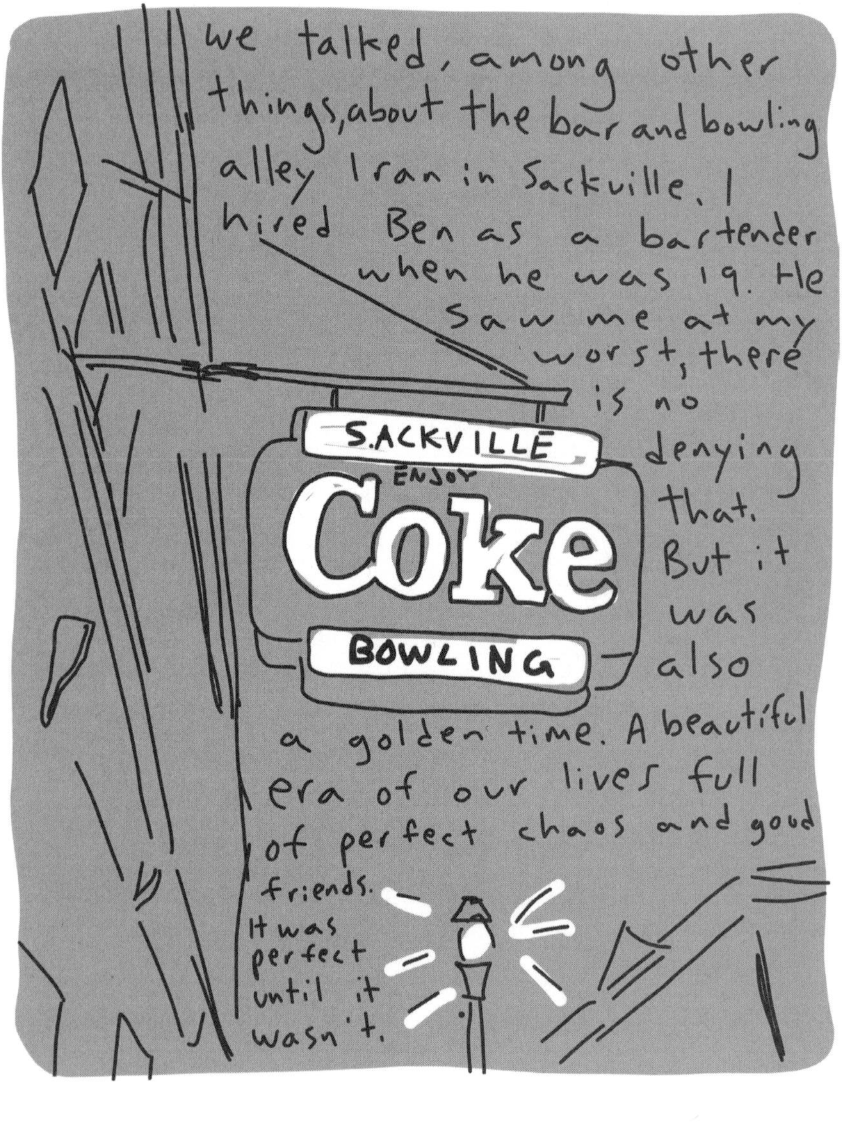
we talked, among other things, about the bar and bowling alley I ran in Sackville. I hired Ben as a bartender when he was 19. He saw me at my worst, there is no denying that. But it was also
SACKVILLE
ENJOY
Coke
BOWLING
a golden time. A beautiful era of our lives full of perfect chaos and good friends.
It was perfect until it wasn't.

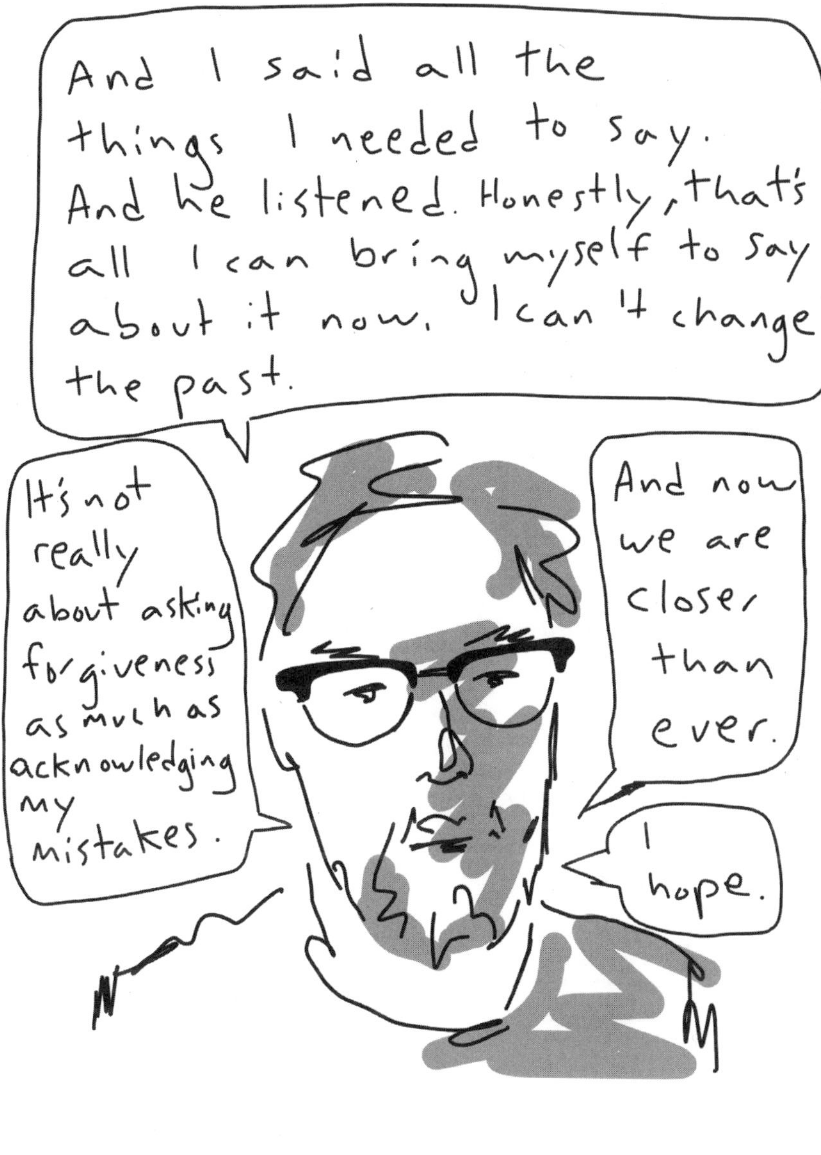
And I said all the things I needed to say. And he listened. Honestly, that's all I can bring myself to say about it now. I can't change the past.
It's not really about asking forgiveness as much as acknowledging my mistakes.
And now we are closer than ever.
I hope.

we arrived in Ottawa at the Caspi-Roy residence a little emotionally exhausted and

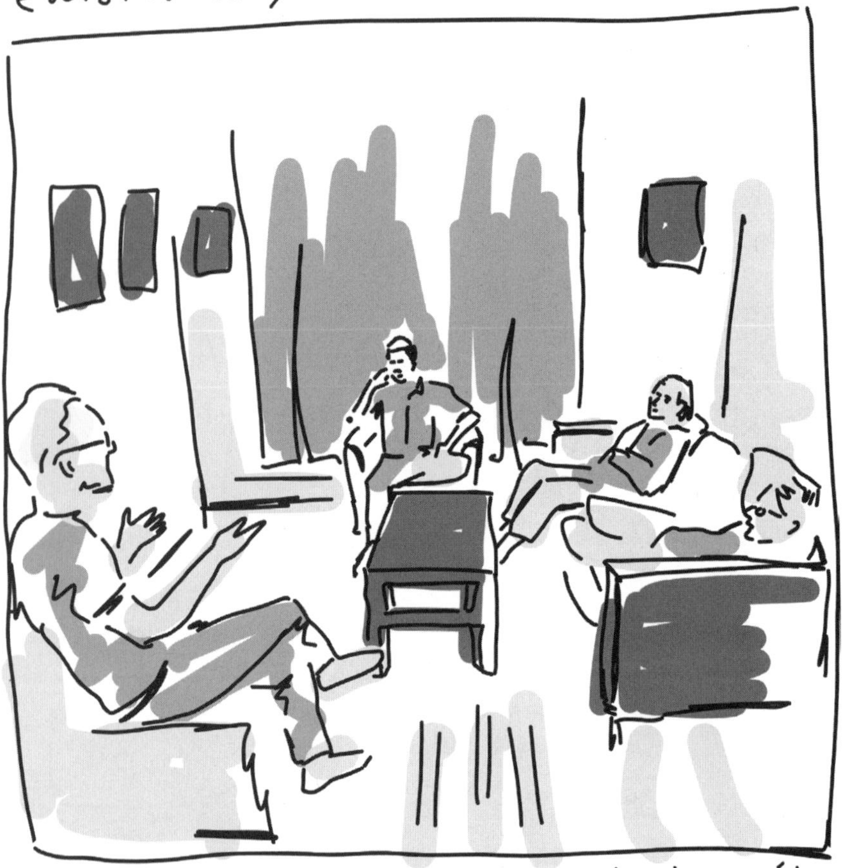

were thankfuly greeted with warm hugs and snacks.

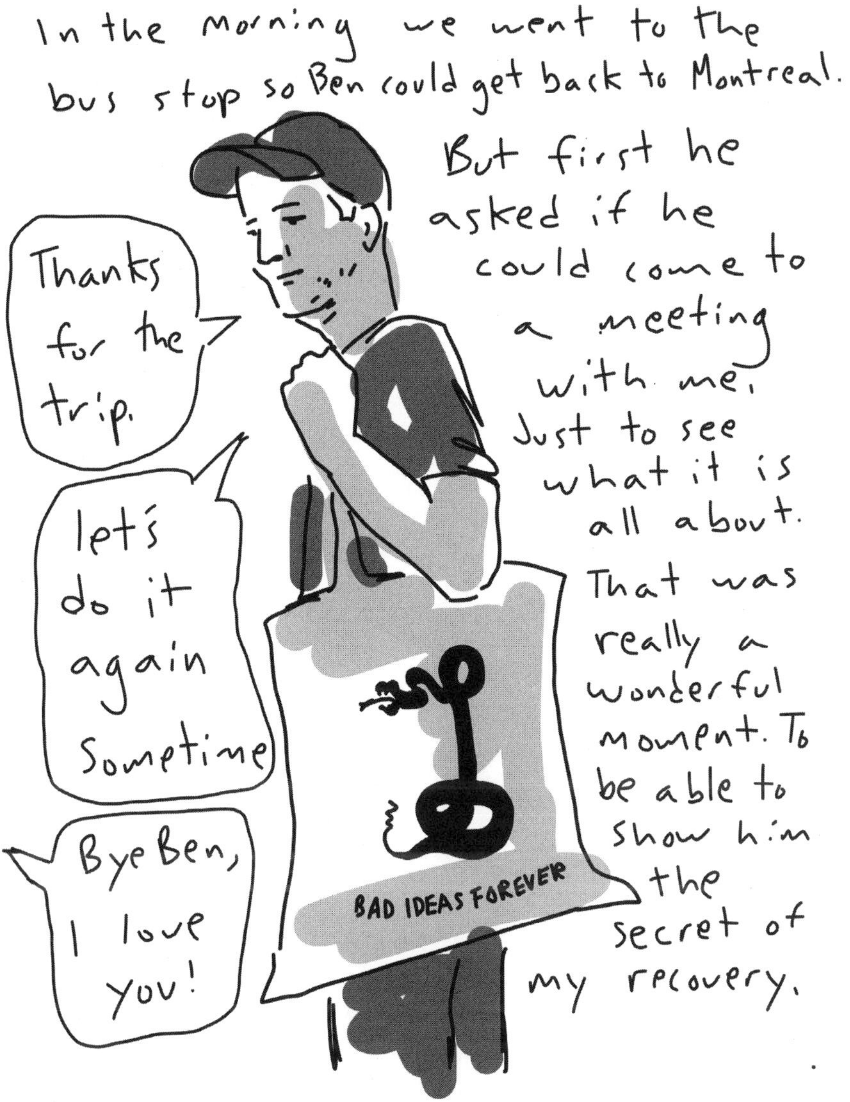
In the morning we went to the bus stop so Ben could get back to Montreal.
But first he asked if he could come to a meeting with me. Just to see what it is all about.
Thanks for the trip.
let's do it again sometime
Bye Ben, I love you!
BAD IDEAS FOREVER
That was really a wonderful moment. To be able to show him the secret of my recovery.

18

I spent two days in Ottawa walking, talking and drinking coffee with Ian.

When I have a decision to make I often ask myself, what would Ian and Sarah do. It's always the opposite of what I'm doing.

we've known each other for decades and were roommates in our 20's. we've had a fight or two and some things we just don't mention!

But hey, he puts his shoes on one at a time like everyone else. Or does he? Regardless, I love him.

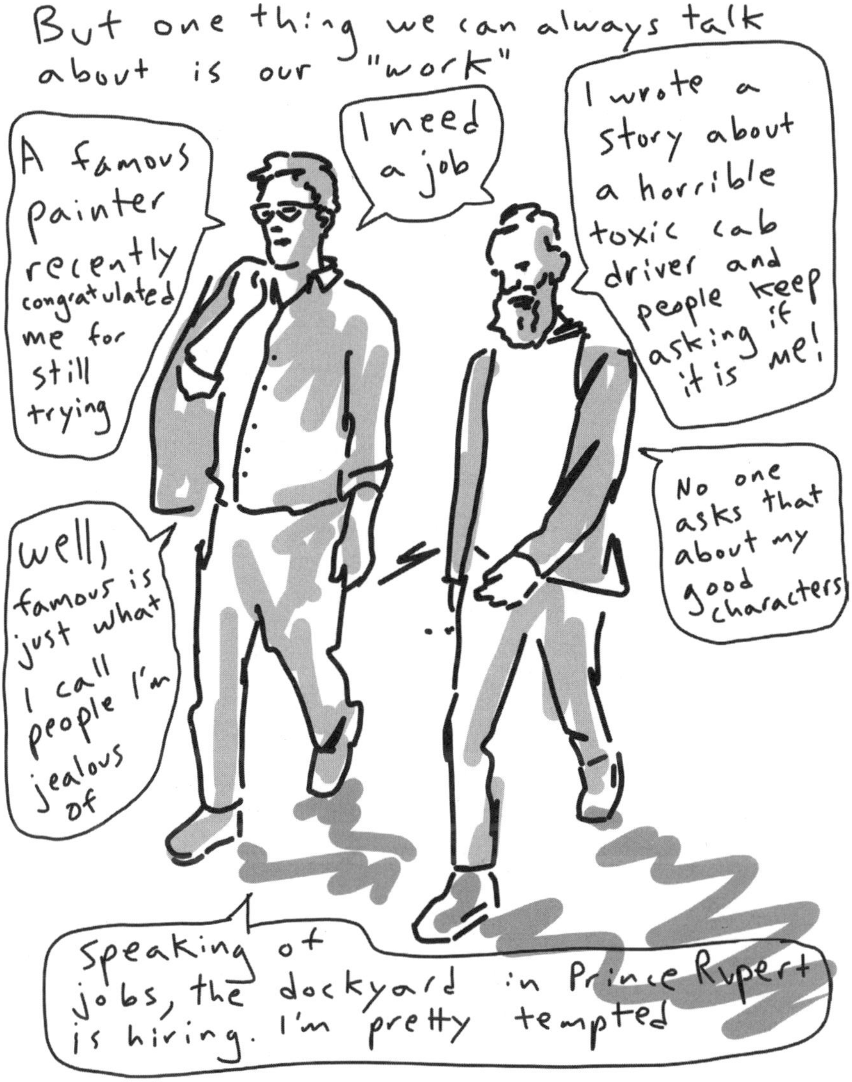

But one thing we can always talk about is our "work"
A famous painter recently congratulated me for still trying
I need a job
I wrote a story about a horrible toxic cab driver and people keep asking if it is me!
Well, famous is just what I call people I'm jealous of
No one asks that about my good characters
Speaking of jobs, the dockyard in Prince Rupert is hiring. I'm pretty tempted

Remember when that guy at the beach asked if you were Ian Roy?
And I said no!
And he turned out to be your new boss
That was an awkward first day.
Thats why we probably couldn't get jobs if we tried
Do you think it isn't bragging just because you put air quotes around everything?
My only "skill" is bartending anyway
Kinda
honestly I'm pretty "content" these days and I'll take any kind of job I can get after I finish this book

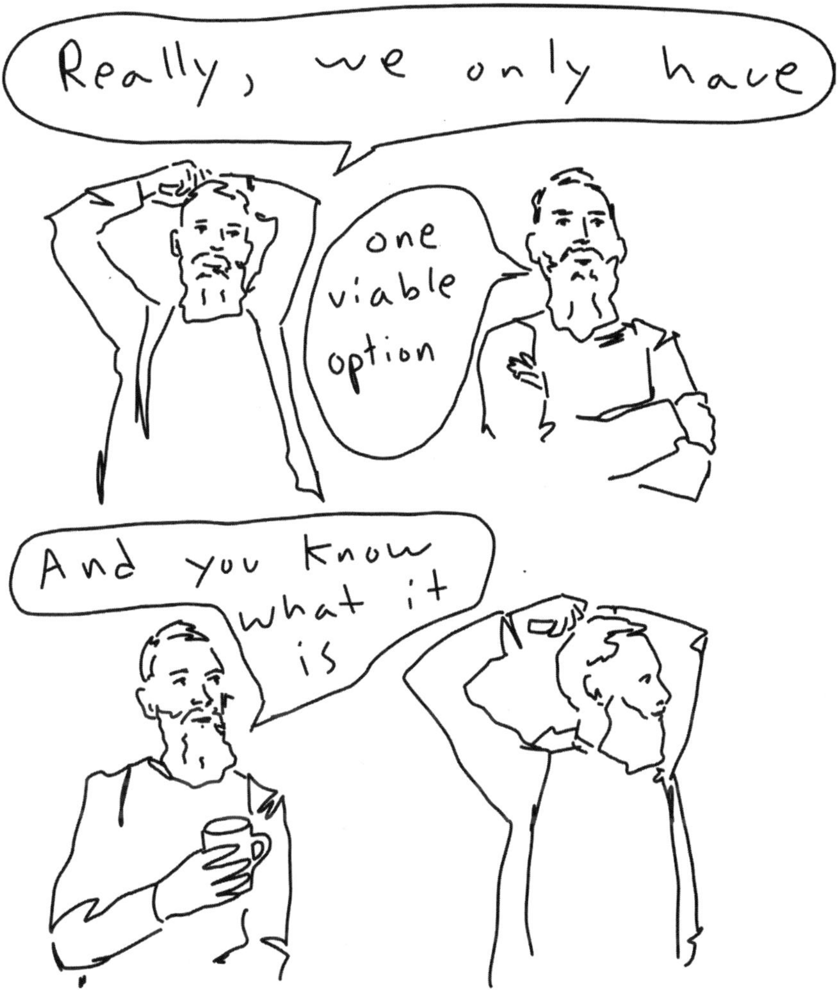
Really, we only have
one viable option
And you know what it is

Oh god I'm too old for this.
It's only a matter of time before one of us breaks a hip!
Nah, you gotta own it claytor!
I'll need an excuse to tell my doctor.
I'd rather say I fell down drunk than admit I'm almost 50 and hurt myself on my skateboard.

And then Ian and Sarah saw me off with snacks, good advice and smiles.

If you want life advice I suggest asking someone who is smiling.

19

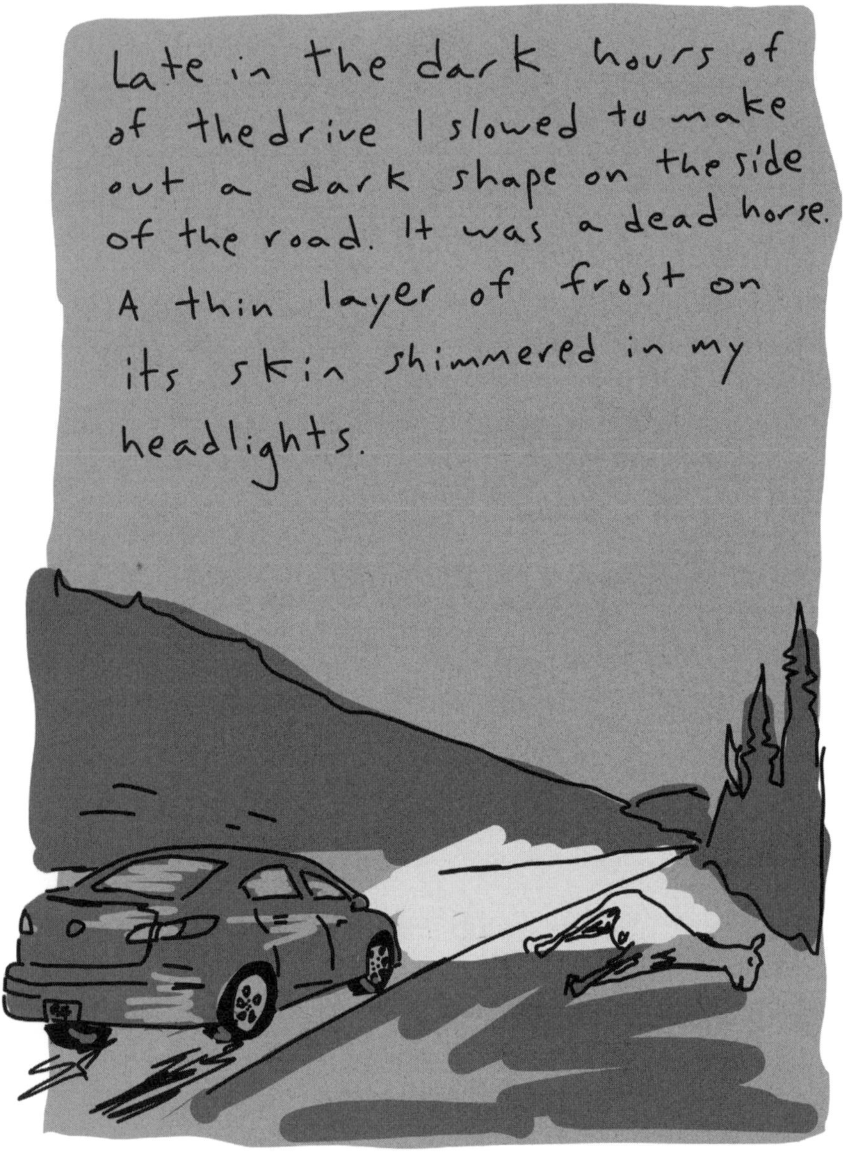
Late in the dark hours of of the drive I slowed to make out a dark shape on the side of the road. It was a dead horse. A thin layer of frost on its skin shimmered in my headlights.

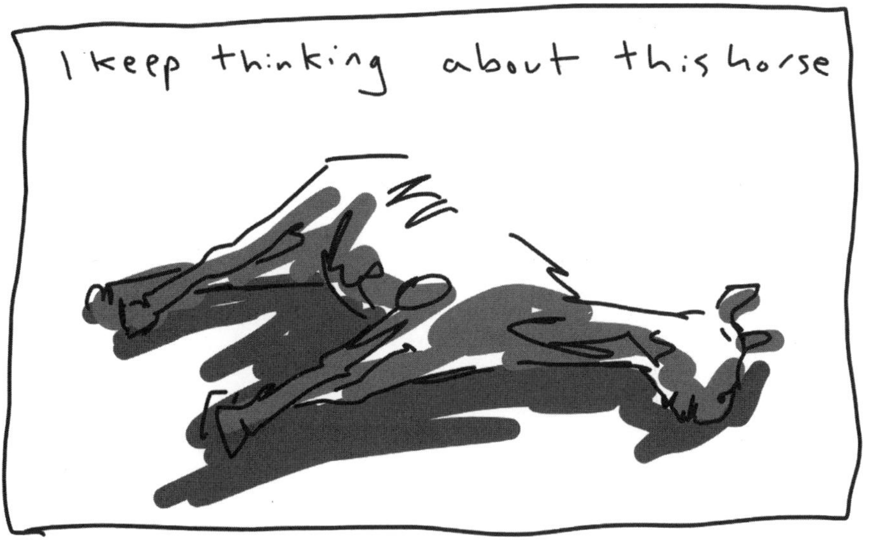
I keep thinking about this horse

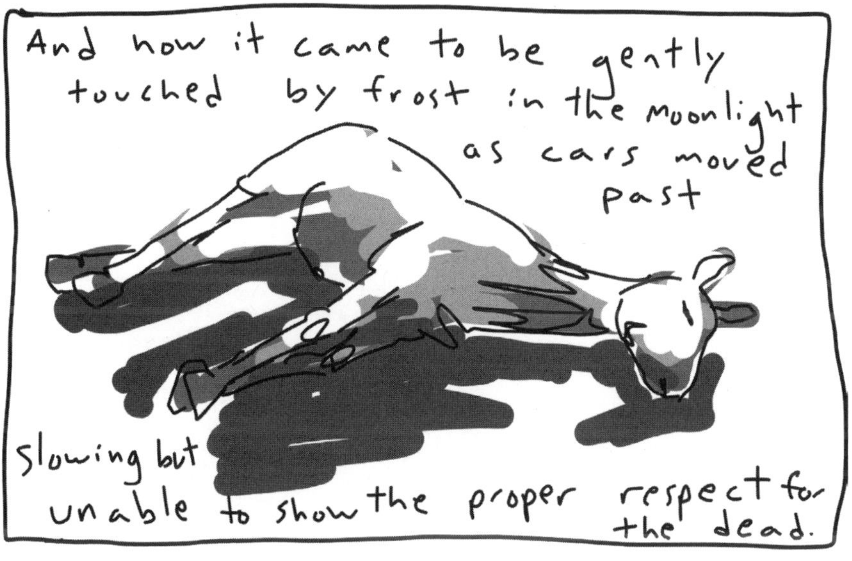
And how it came to be gently touched by frost in the moonlight as cars moved past
slowing but unable to show the proper respect for the dead.

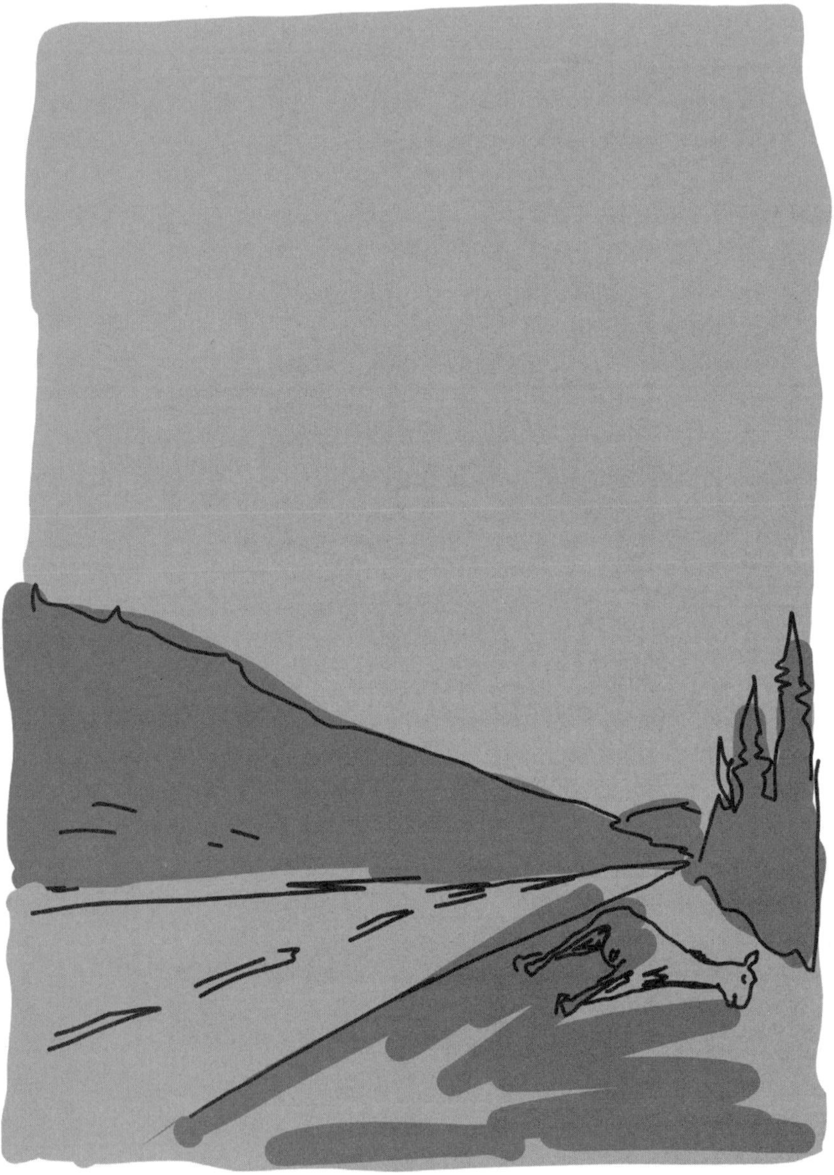

20

Babies are also excellent advice givers.

And so are their moms.*

* I stopped in Collingwood for the good kind of advice only Kallie and Zach can give

And if you can't find a
baby or a mom

You can take your problems
to a wise experimental
sound artist.*
*I took my problems to W.L.
in Regina

And when in doubt
and in need of more wisdom

ask a Professor of media,
art and performance*

*I found Helen hanging out with W.L.
and she had sage advice.

Even Bowie* gives good advice.

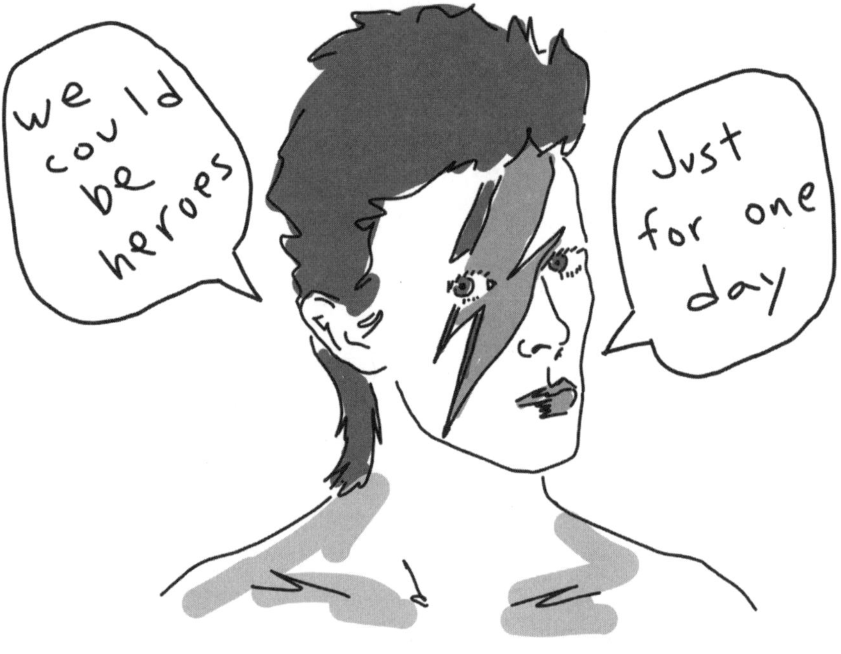
we could be heroes
Just for one day

* I played Heroes on repeat from Thunder Bay to Winnipeg hoping for answers. I found them.

21

Two wolves strolled across the
highway in Northern Ontario
giving no fucks.

And even though they were in the
distance I felt a chill go down
my spine.

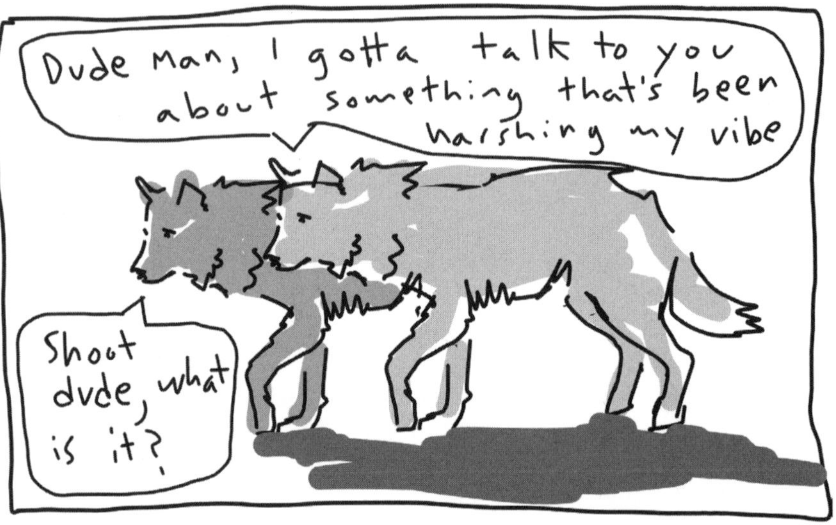
Dude man, I gotta talk to you about something that's been harshing my vibe
Shoot dude, what is it?

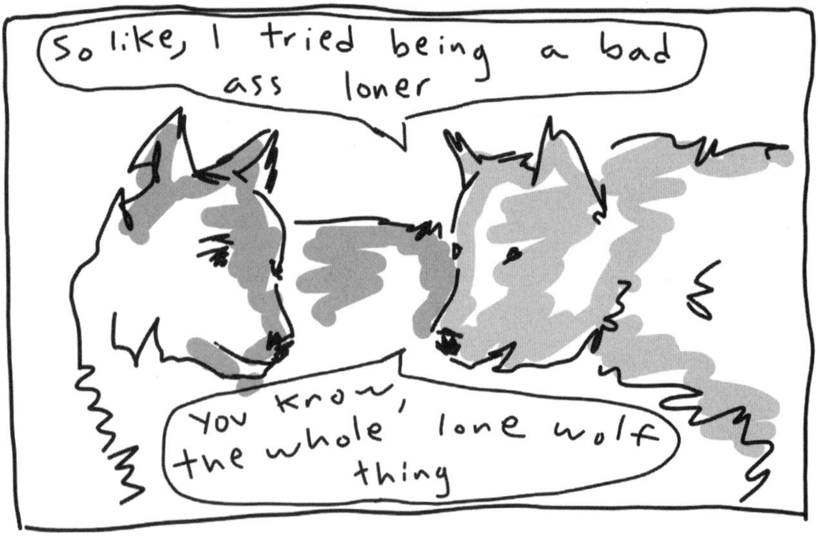
So like, I tried being a bad ass loner
You know, the whole lone wolf thing

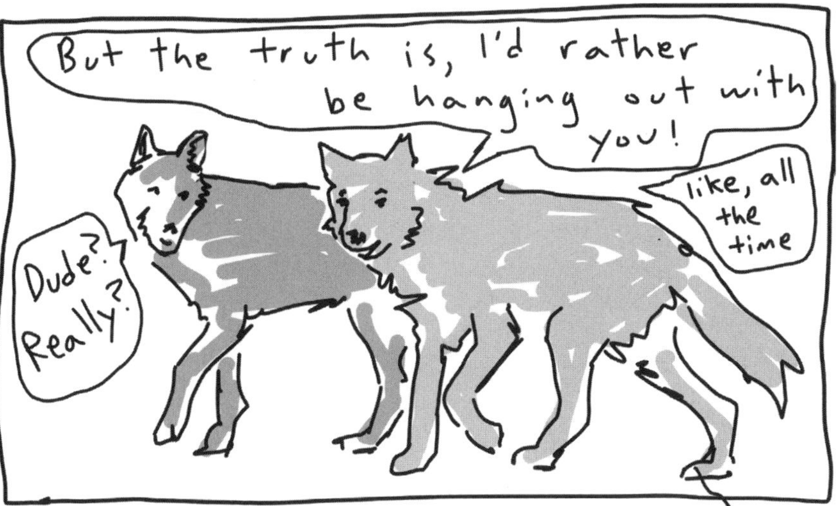
But the truth is, I'd rather be hanging out with you!
like, all the time
Dude? Really?

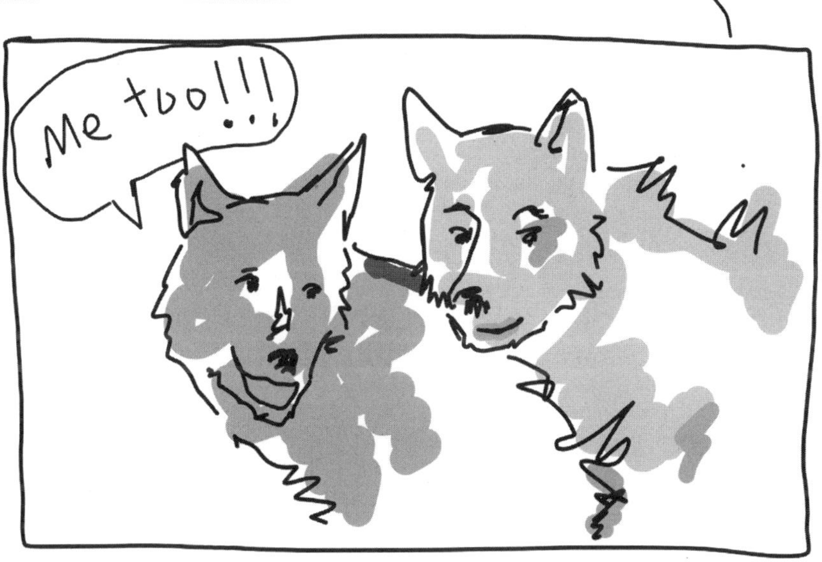
Me too!!!

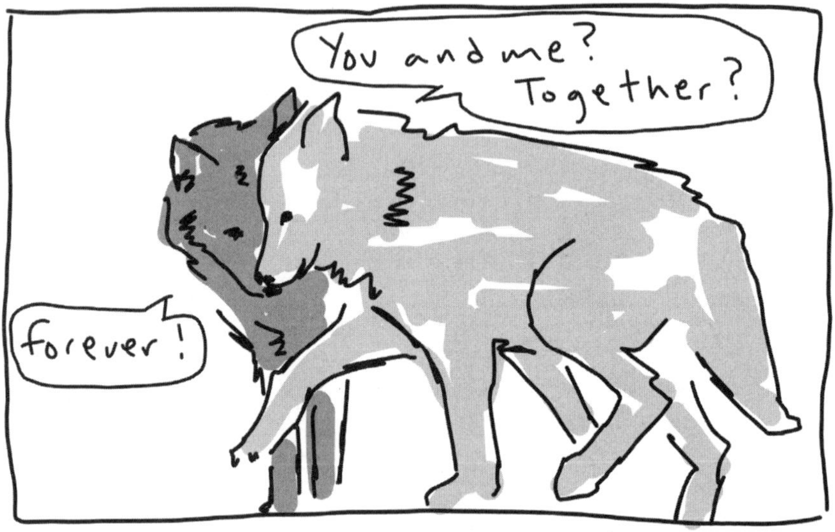
You and me? Together?
forever!

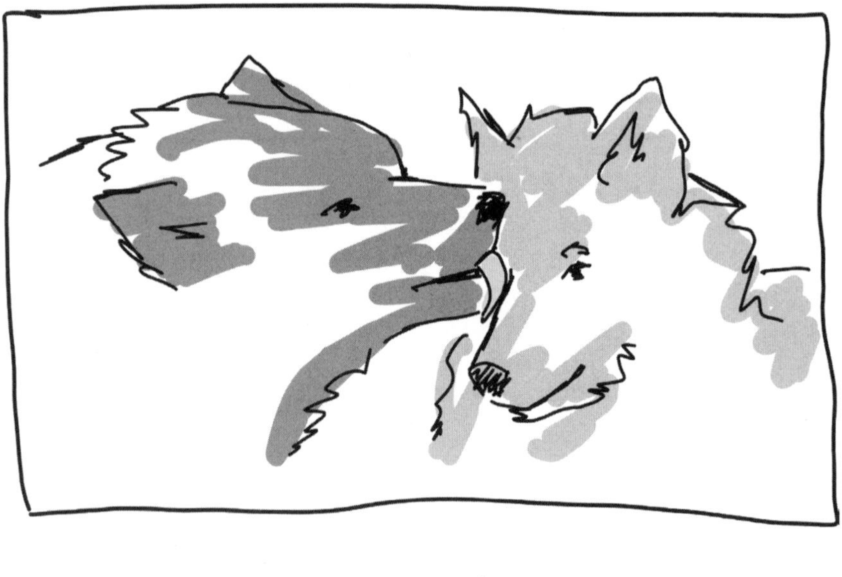

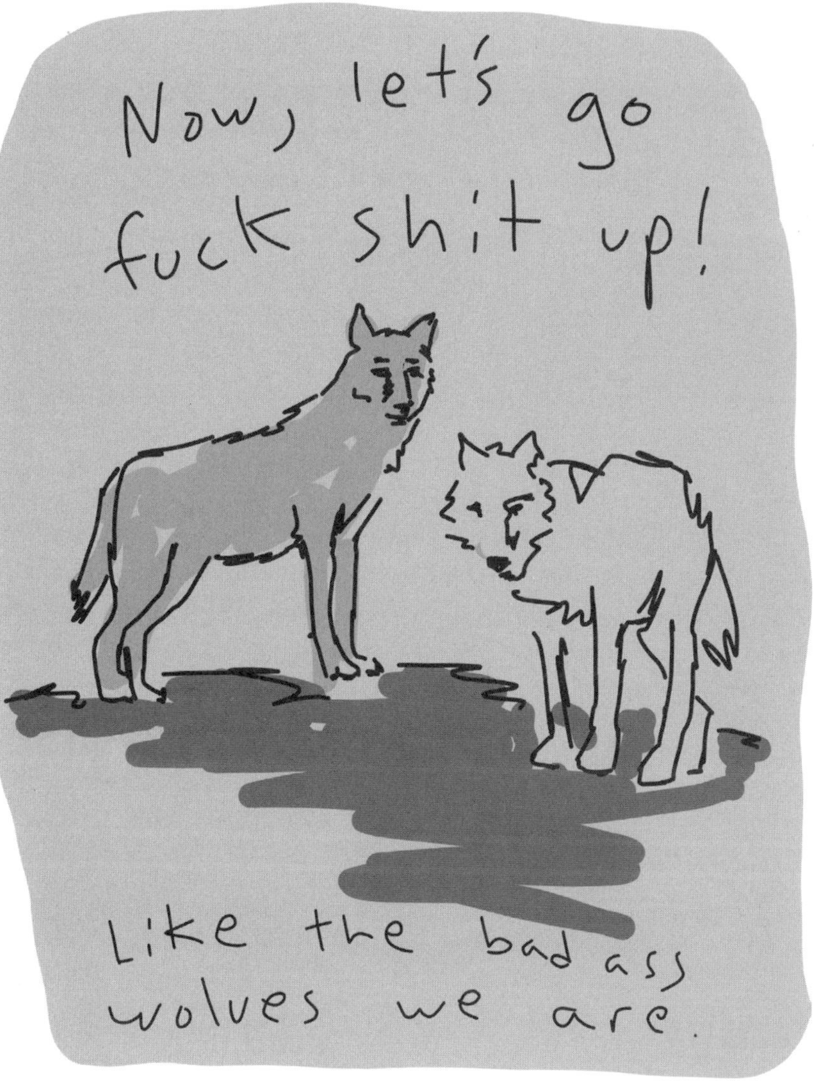
Now, let's go fuck shit up!
Like the bad ass wolves we are.

After hours on the road I pulled
into Wawa. For no reason other
than a fond memory of stopping
here with the two youngest and

Julie 20 some years ago. It
would have been on one of
her cross country tours.

I don't remember who was more
excited about the big goose,* the
kids or me.

Stopping this time, alone, I could
almost hear them playing and
running around.

* Built in 1960 Wawa is "famous" for
its big goose. Small town Canada sure
likes big things.

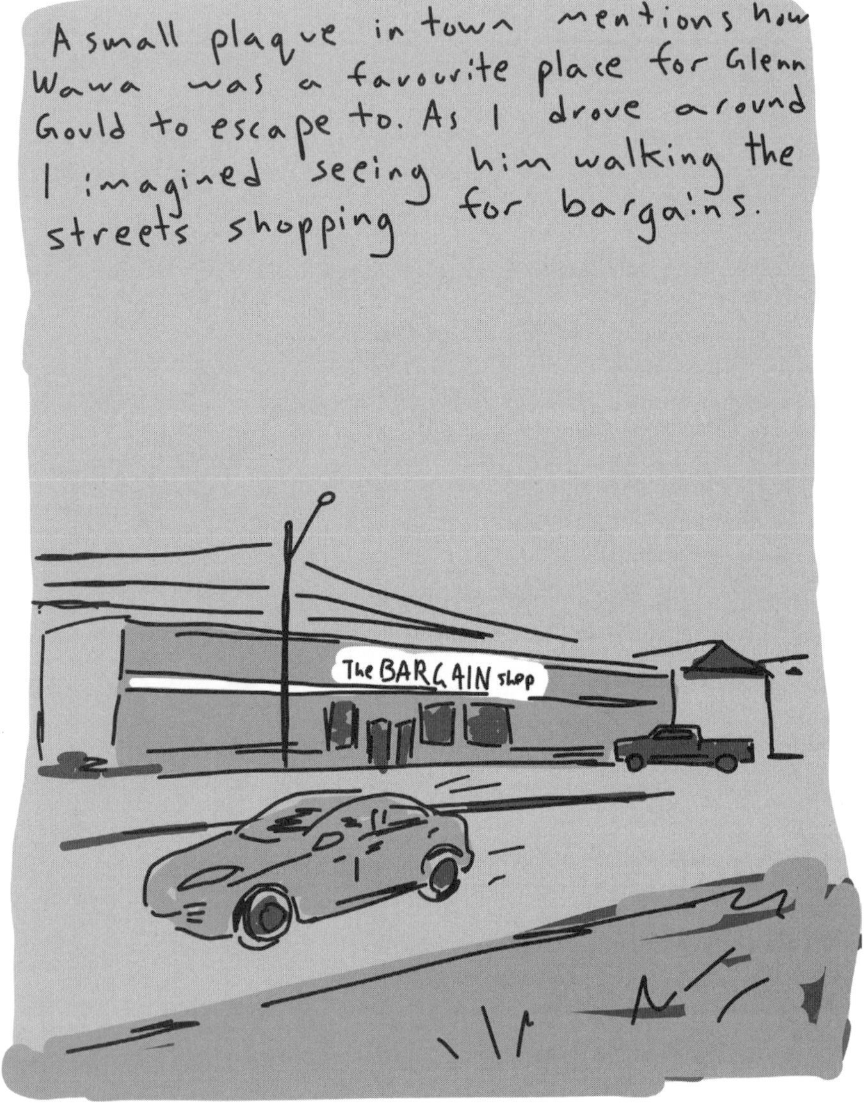
A small plaque in town mentions how Wawa was a favourite place for Glenn Gould to escape to. As I drove around I imagined seeing him walking the streets shopping for bargains.
The BARGAIN shop

I even stopped in front of
room 102 at the Wawa Motor
Inn which was stated on the
plaque as the room he always stayed in.

The car was warm in the late
September sun and I put the seat
back and closed my eyes.

I woke up to the sound of someone tapping on my window.

So of course I invited them in.

I was a little shocked to see Glenn Gould climb into the passenger seat.

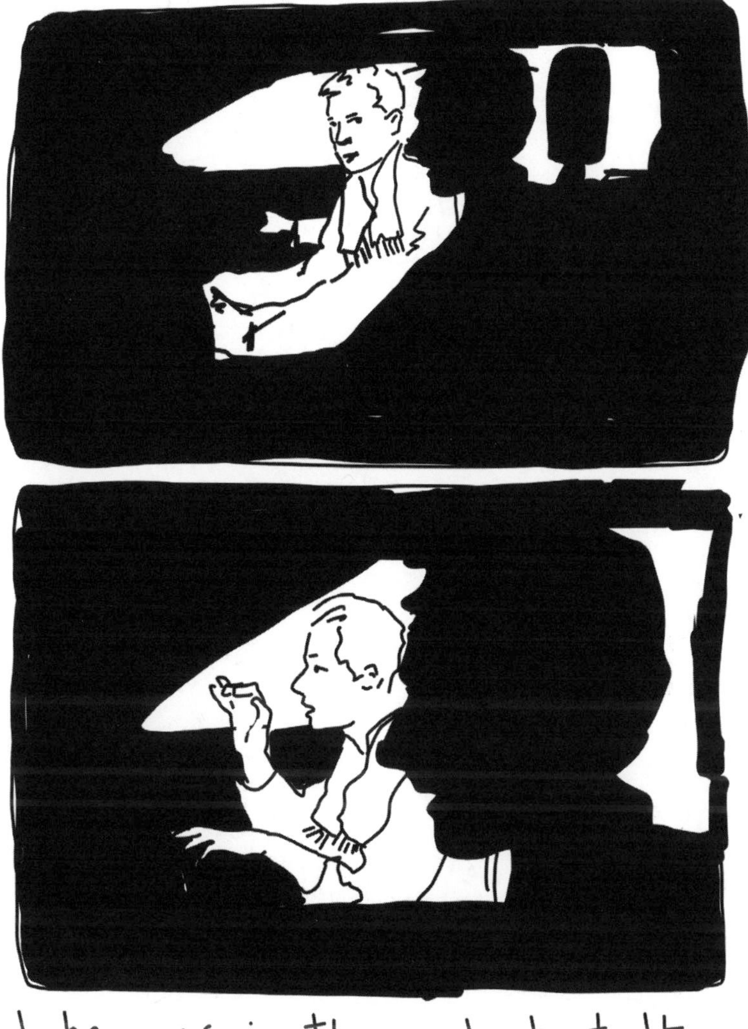

And he was in the mood to talk.

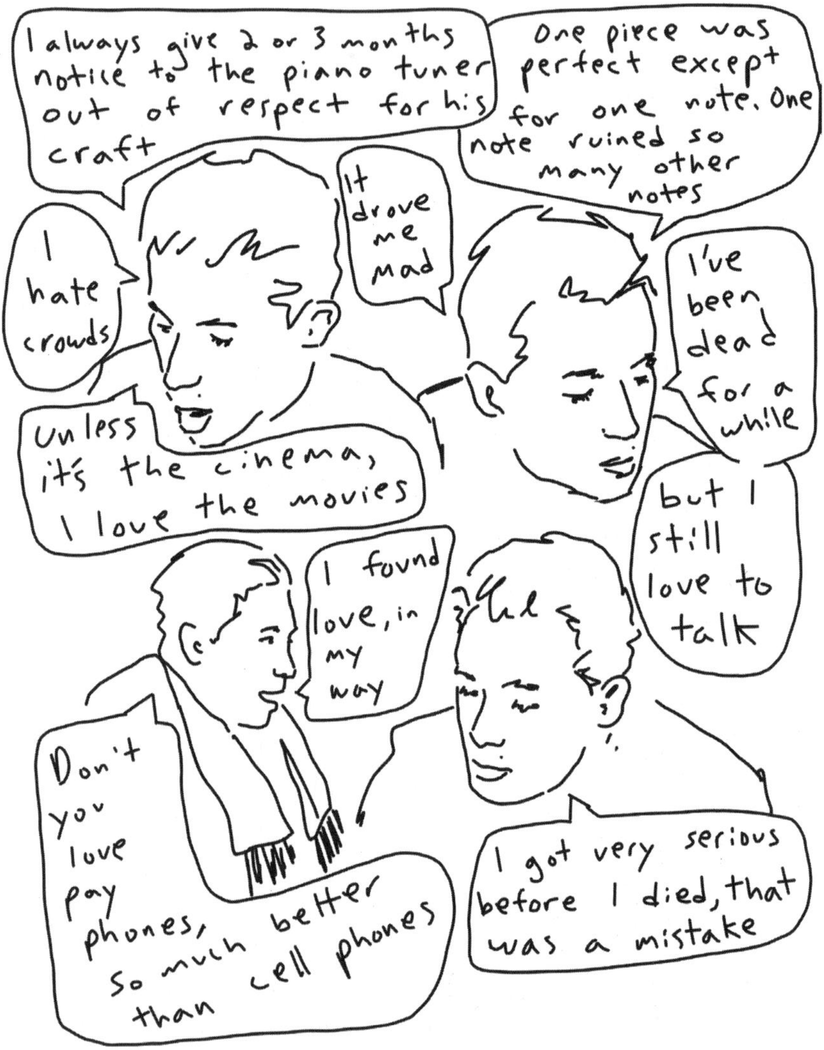
I always give 2 or 3 months notice to the piano tuner out of respect for his craft
One piece was perfect except for one note. One note ruined so many other notes
I hate crowds
It drove me mad
unless it's the cinema, I love the movies
I've been dead for a while
but I still love to talk
I found love, in my way
Don't you love pay phones, so much better than cell phones
I got very serious before I died, that was a mistake

But most importantly, Mr. Claytor, do you like to bowl?
I most certainly do!

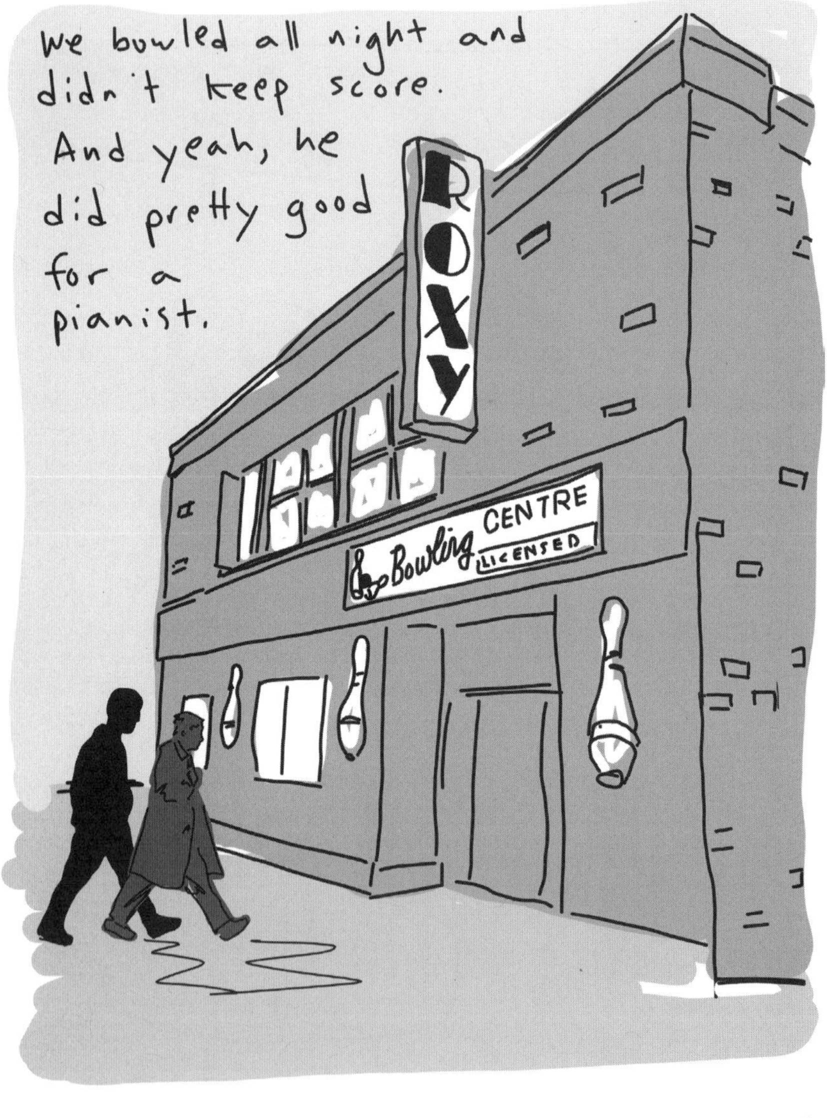
We bowled all night and didn't keep score. And yeah, he did pretty good for a pianist.
ROXY
Bowling CENTRE
LICENSED

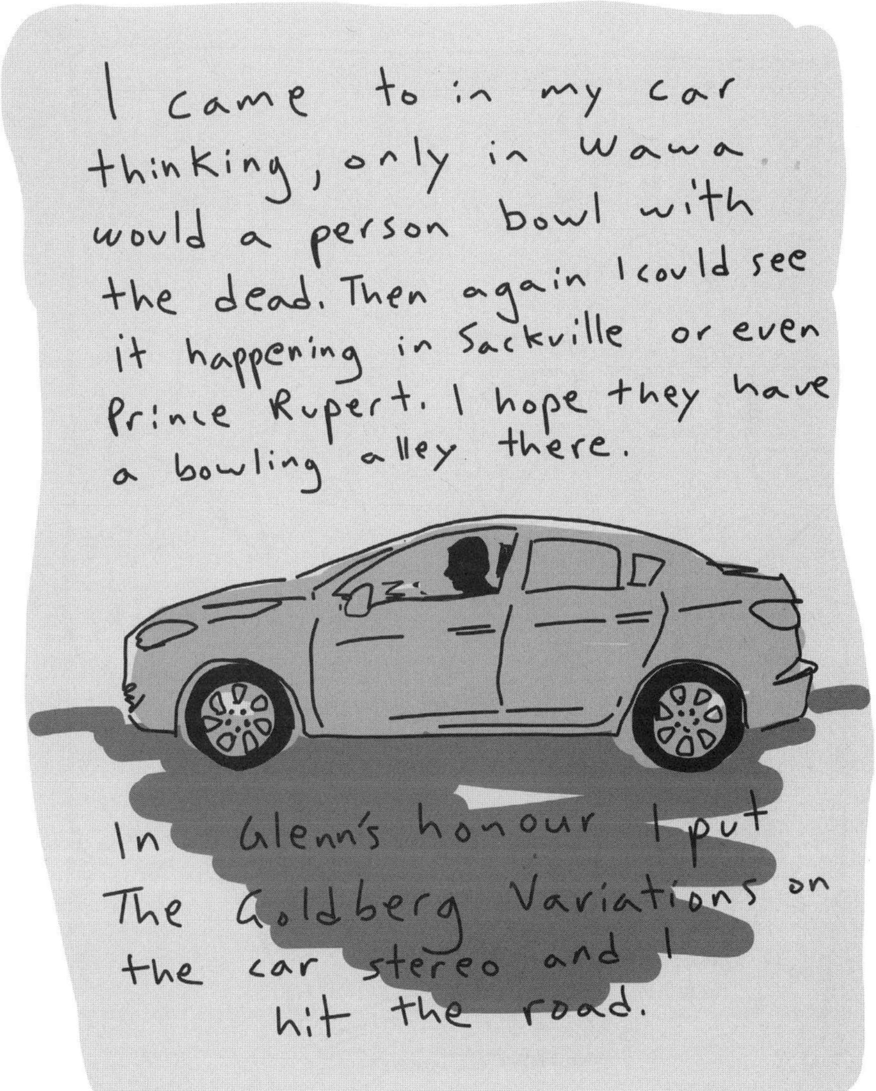
I came to in my car thinking, only in Wawa would a person bowl with the dead. Then again I could see it happening in Sackville or even Prince Rupert. I hope they have a bowling alley there.
In Glenn's honour I put The Goldberg Variations on the car stereo and I hit the road.

23

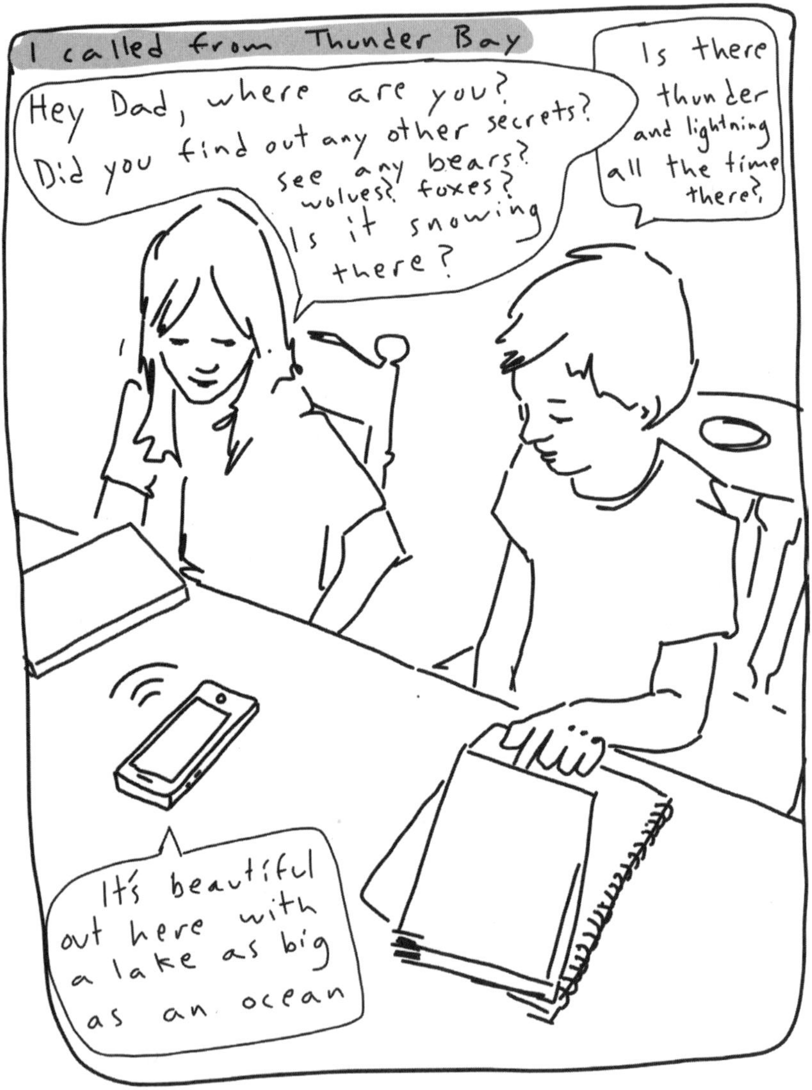
I called from Thunder Bay
Hey Dad, where are you? Did you find out any other secrets? see any bears? wolves? foxes? Is it snowing there?
Is there thunder and lightning all the time there?
It's beautiful out here with a lake as big as an ocean

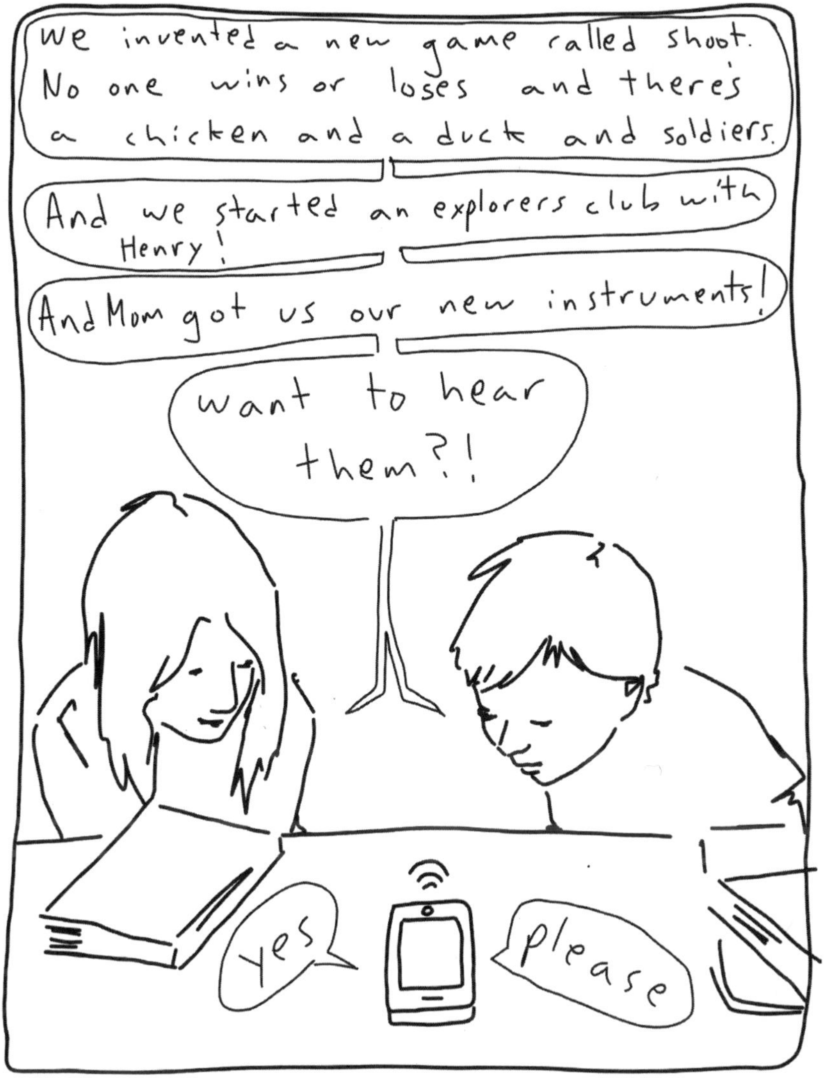
We invented a new game called shoot. No one wins or loses and there's a chicken and a duck and soldiers.
And we started an explorers club with Henry!
And Mom got us our new instruments!
Want to hear them?!
yes
please

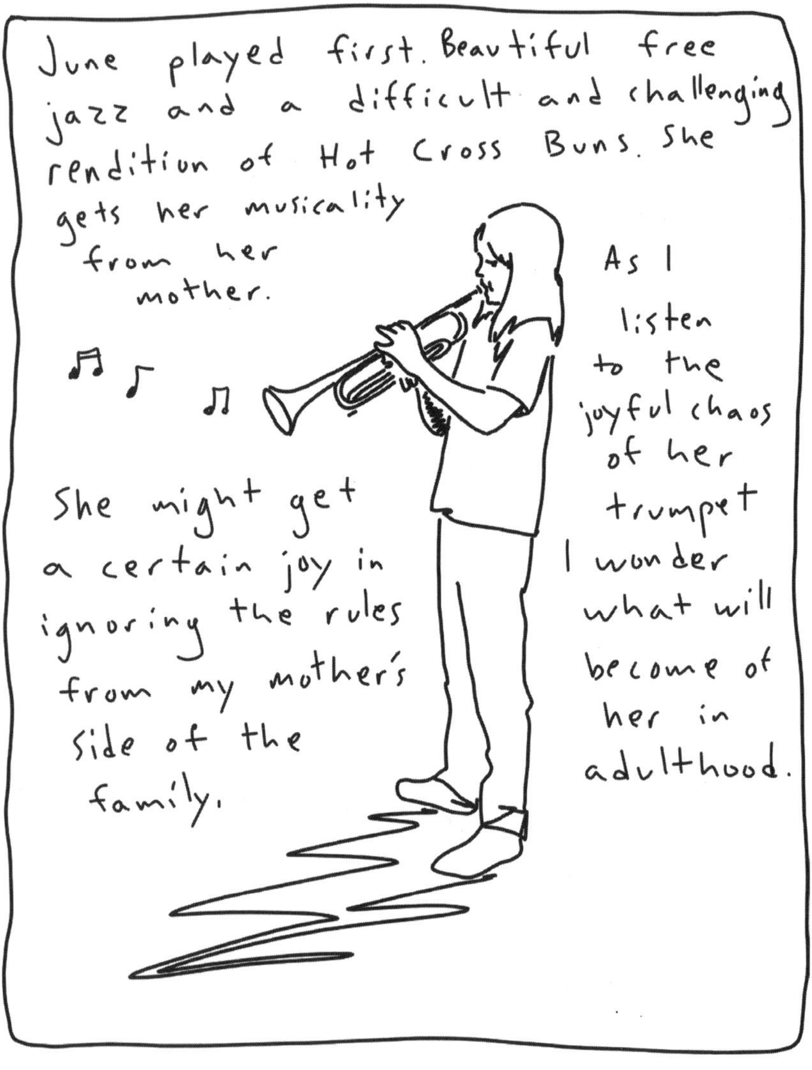
June played first. Beautiful free jazz and a difficult and challenging rendition of Hot Cross Buns. She gets her musicality from her mother.
As I listen to the joyful chaos of her trumpet I wonder what will become of her in adulthood.
She might get a certain joy in ignoring the rules from my mother's side of the family.

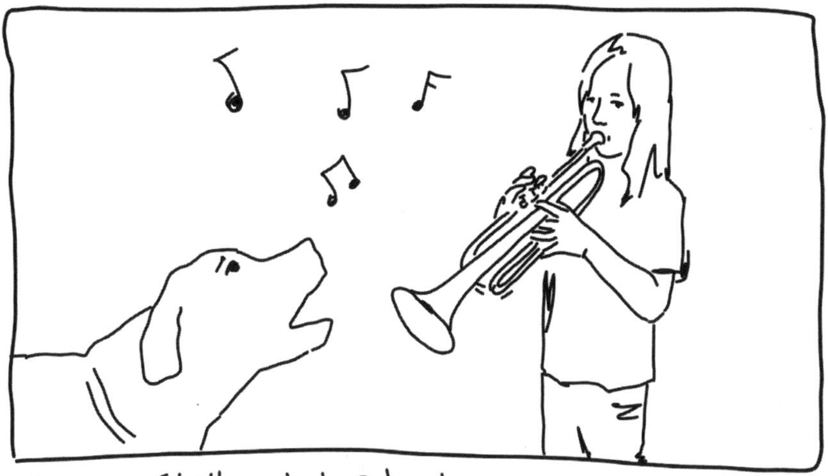

Soon Stella joined in

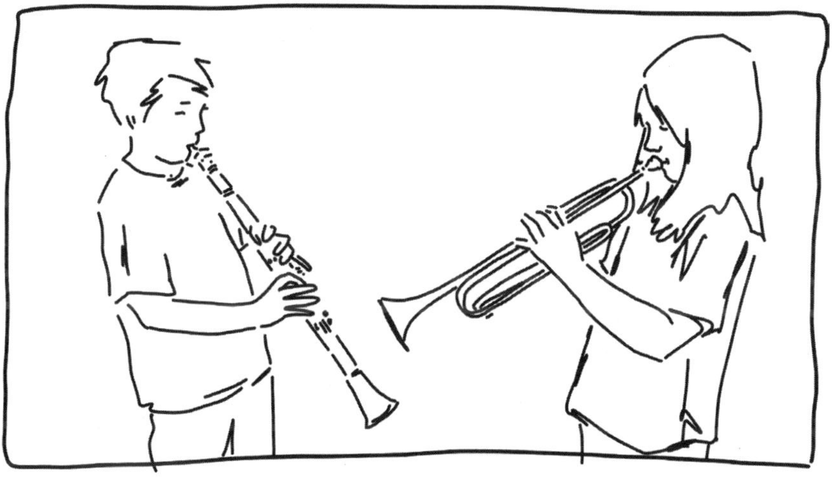

and then Sonny

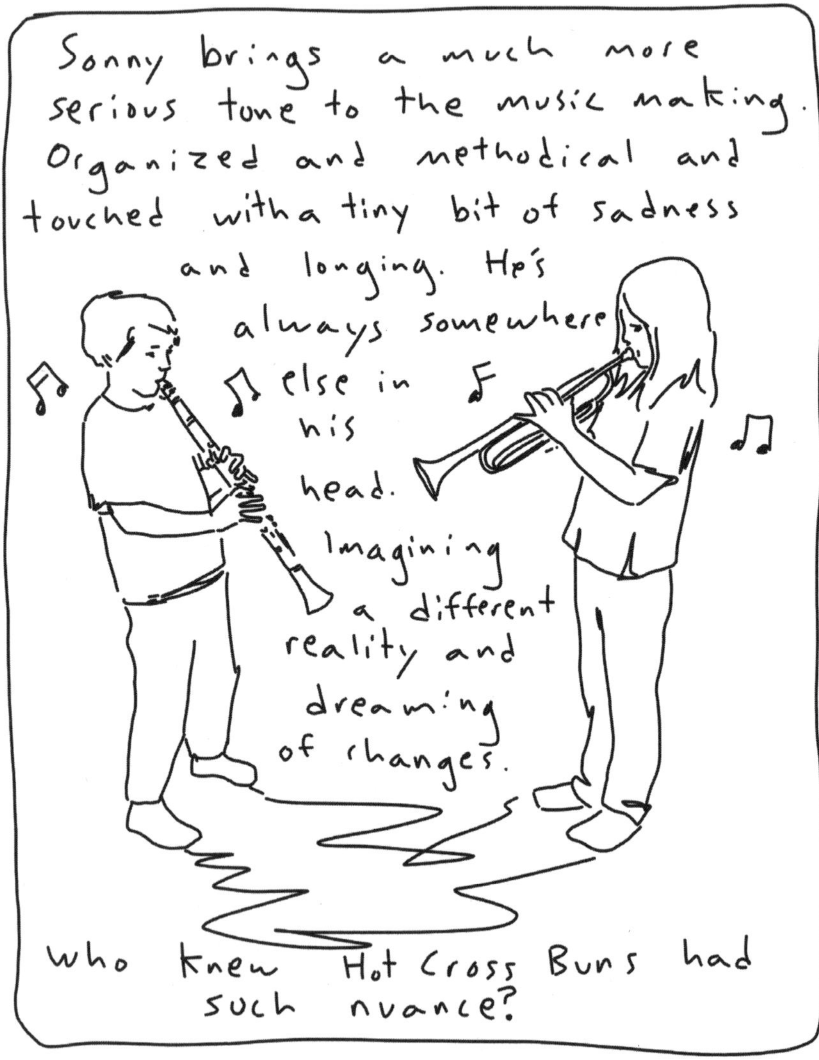
Sonny brings a much more serious tone to the music making. Organized and methodical and touched with a tiny bit of sadness and longing. He's always somewhere else in his head. Imagining a different reality and dreaming of changes.
Who knew Hot Cross Buns had such nuance?

when the sound of the trumpet
disappeared I knew June had started dancing.

And that they had forgotten
all about the phone call.

24

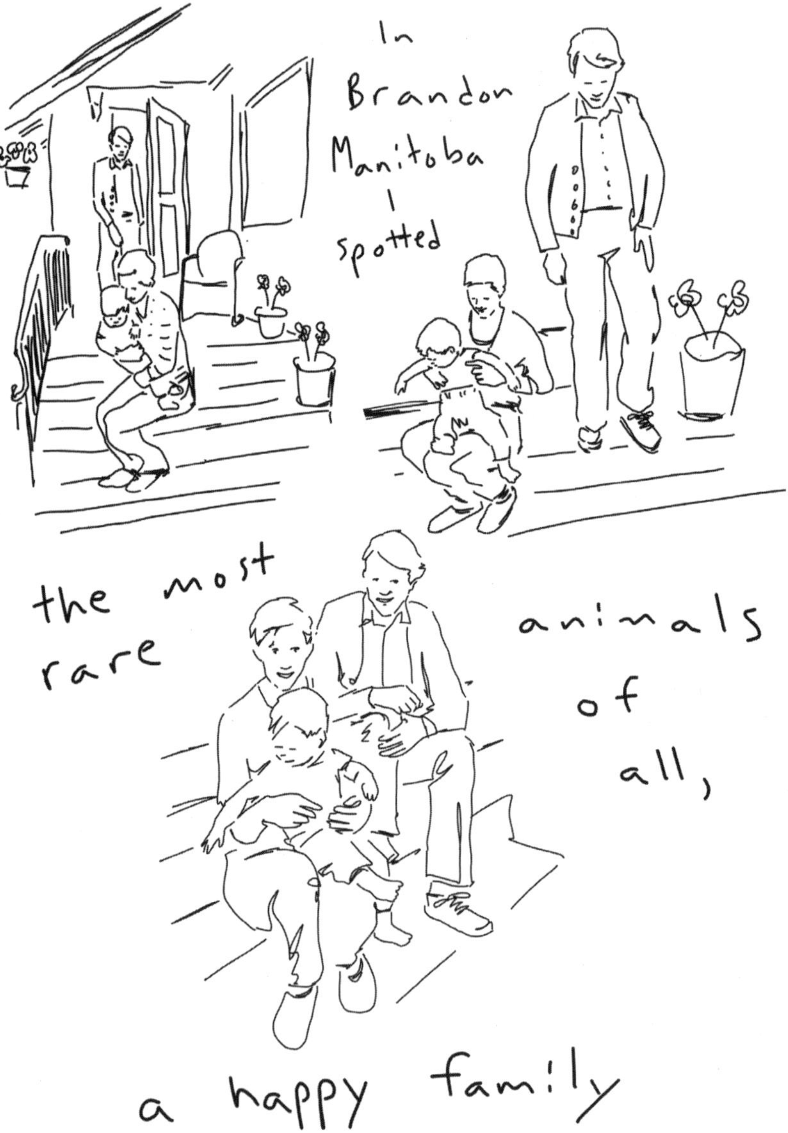
In Brandon Manitoba I spotted
the most rare animals of all,
a happy family

Lianne + Jimmie seem to handle every situation with ease

Even the toughest situations can be solved

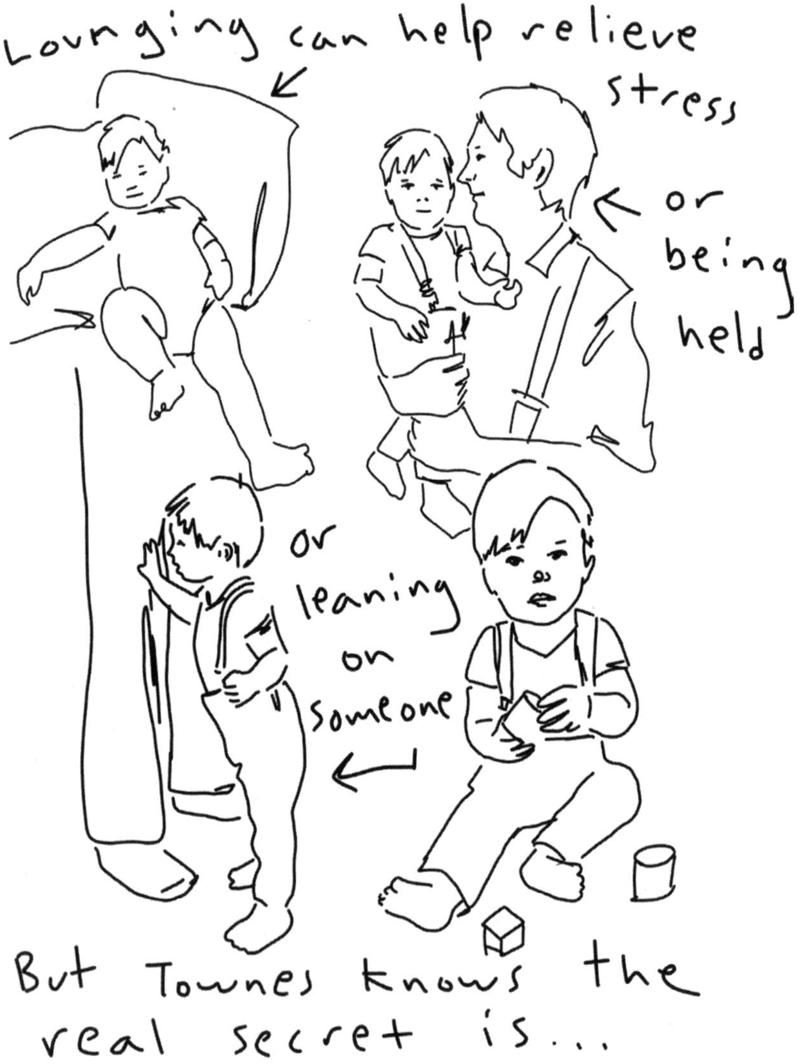
Lounging can help relieve stress
or being held
or leaning on someone
But Townes knows the real secret is...

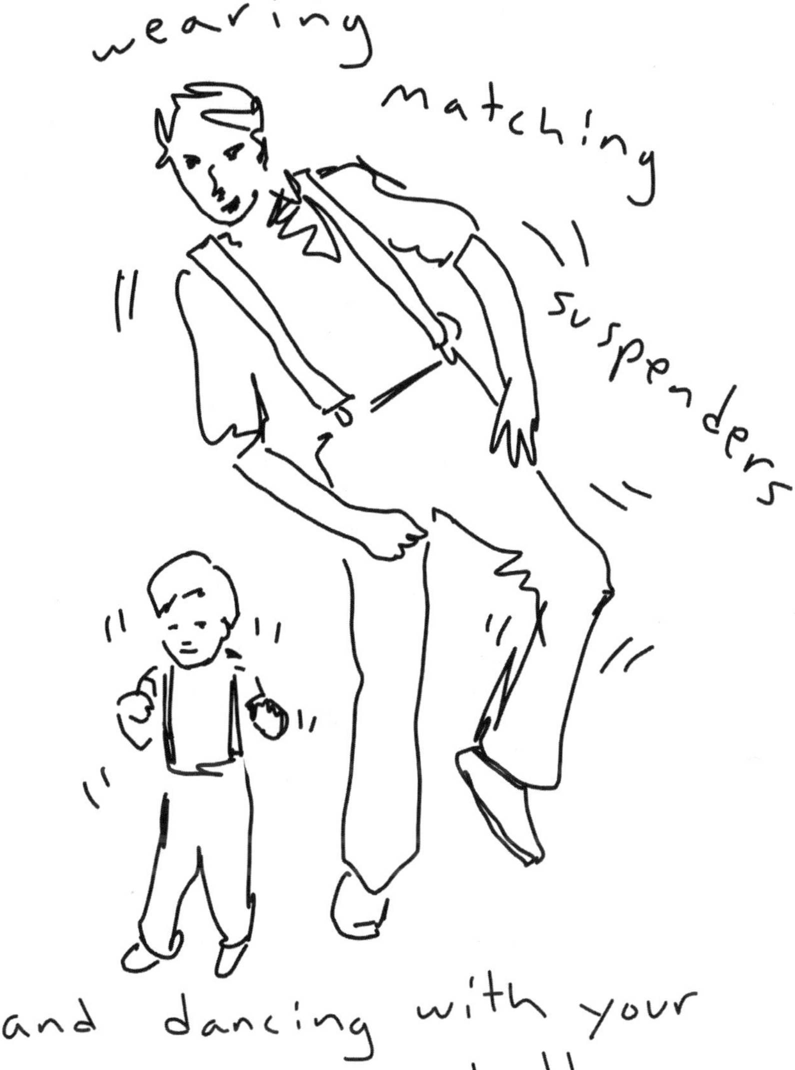
wearing
matching
suspenders
and dancing with your dad!

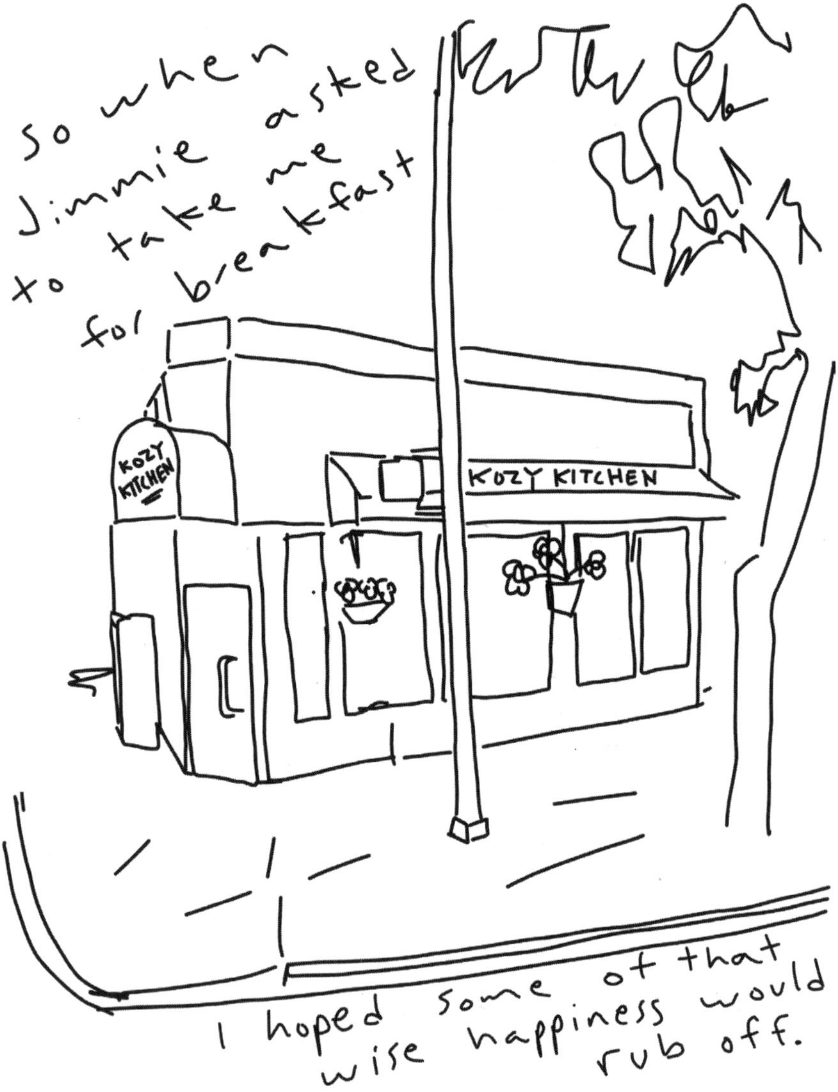
so when Jimmie asked to take me for breakfast
KOZY KITCHEN
KOZY KITCHEN
I hoped some of that wise happiness would rub off.

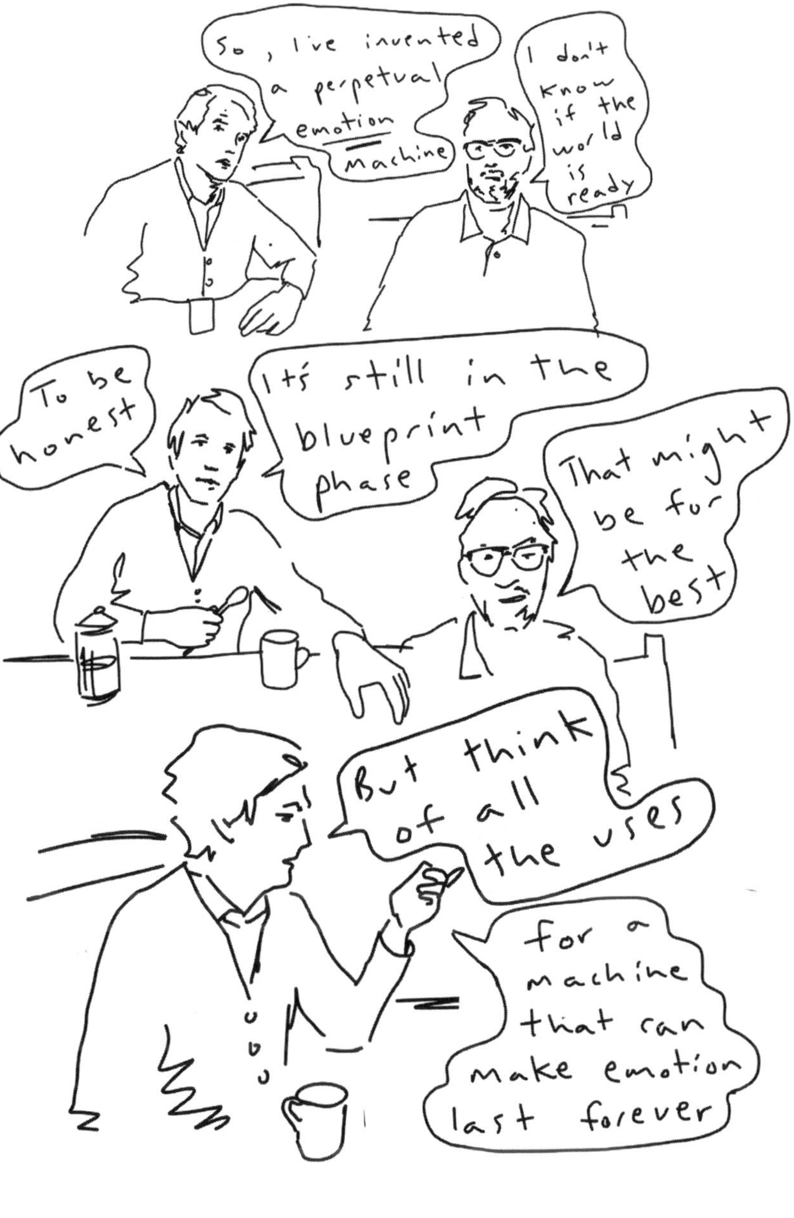
So, I've invented a perpetual emotion machine
I don't know if the world is ready
To be honest
It's still in the blueprint phase
That might be for the best
But think of all the uses
for a machine that can make emotion last forever

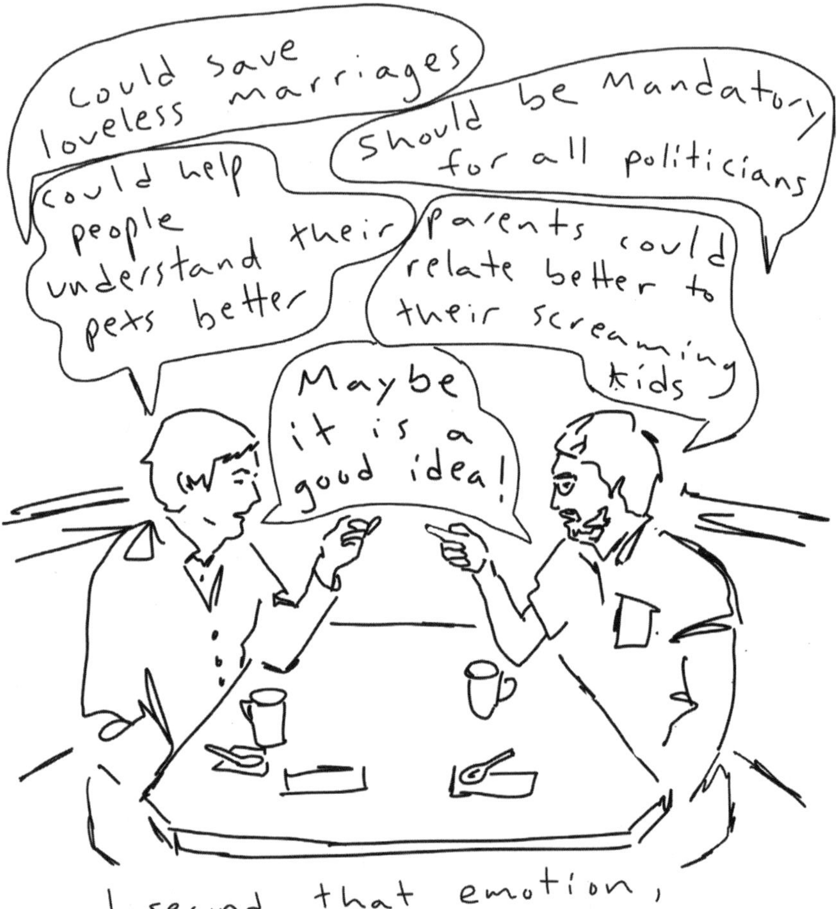
Could save loveless marriages
Should be Mandatory for all politicians
Could help people understand their pets better
Parents could relate better to their screaming kids
Maybe it is a good idea!

I second that emotion,
the world needs a little more feeling.

*"Perpetual Emotion Machine" ShotgunJimmieTM

And as I drove
off to Regina I
felt as though

Some of that
happiness was
contagious. ♥

25

I called from Regina

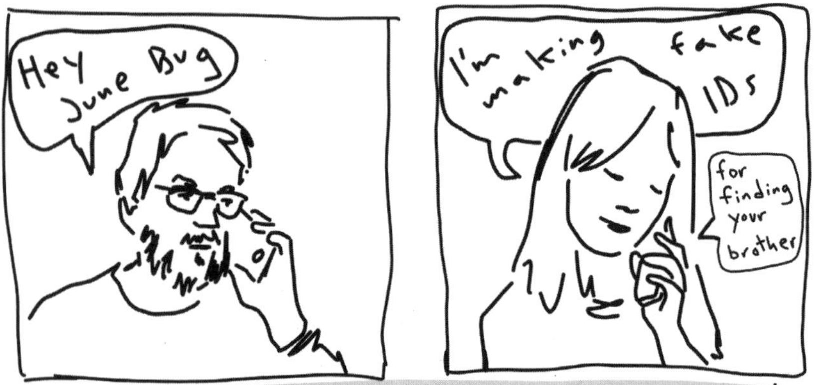
Hey June Bug
I'm making fake IDs
for finding your brother

And I listened to June make fake ID cards

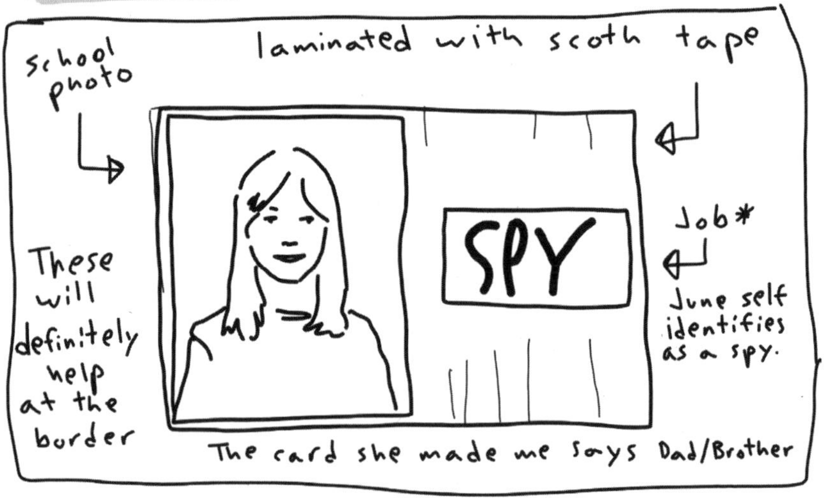
laminated with scoth tape
school photo
SPY
Job*
June self identifies as a spy.
These will definitely help at the border
The card she made me says Dad/Brother

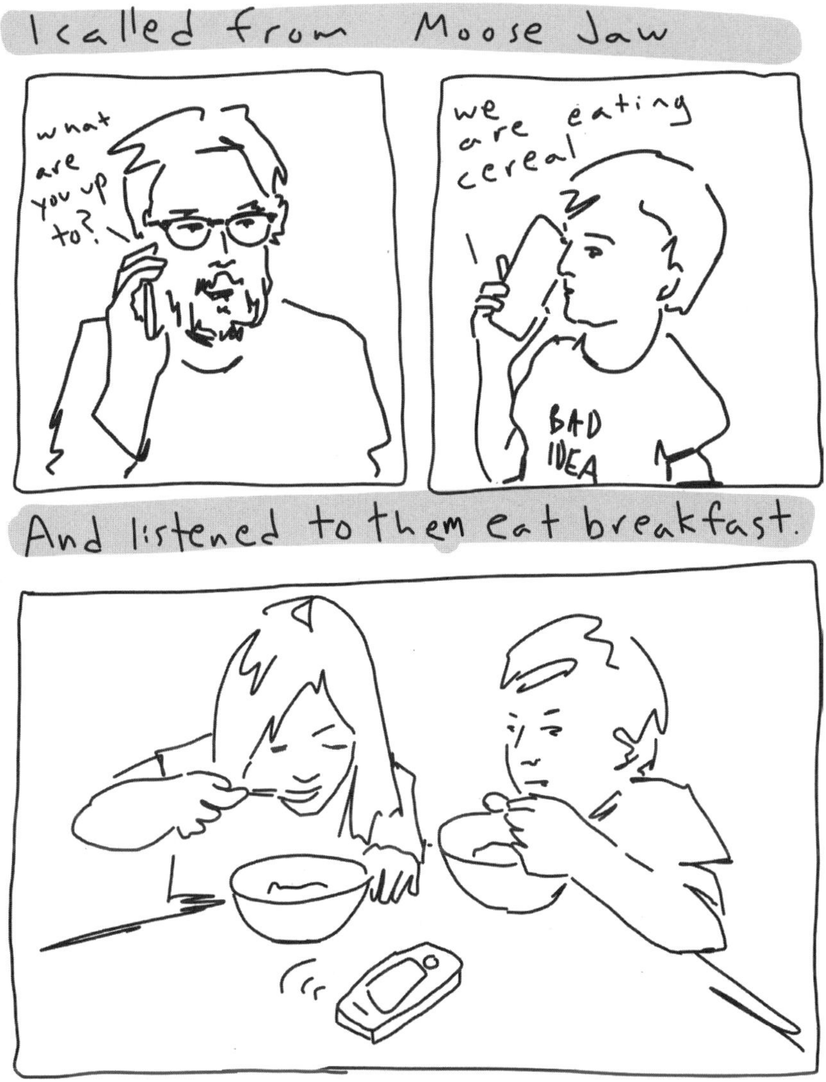
I called from Moose Jaw
what are you up to?
we are eating cereal
BAD IDEA
And listened to them eat breakfast.

26

I stopped in Medicine Hat to stretch my legs and explore a little when my phone rang. It was Elly, Eleanor, El, and it was at one of those times, most times, when we were in the habit of talking everyday.

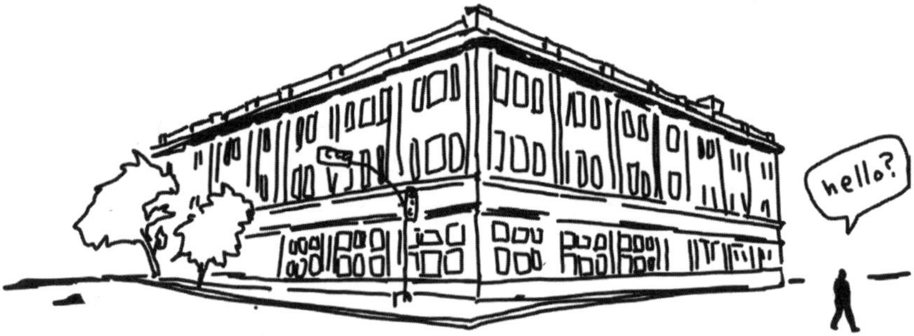
hello?

The last four plus years had been a roller coaster. Sometimes we saw each other every week. Sometimes we went weeks without talking. Now we were settling into something more reliable, friendship.

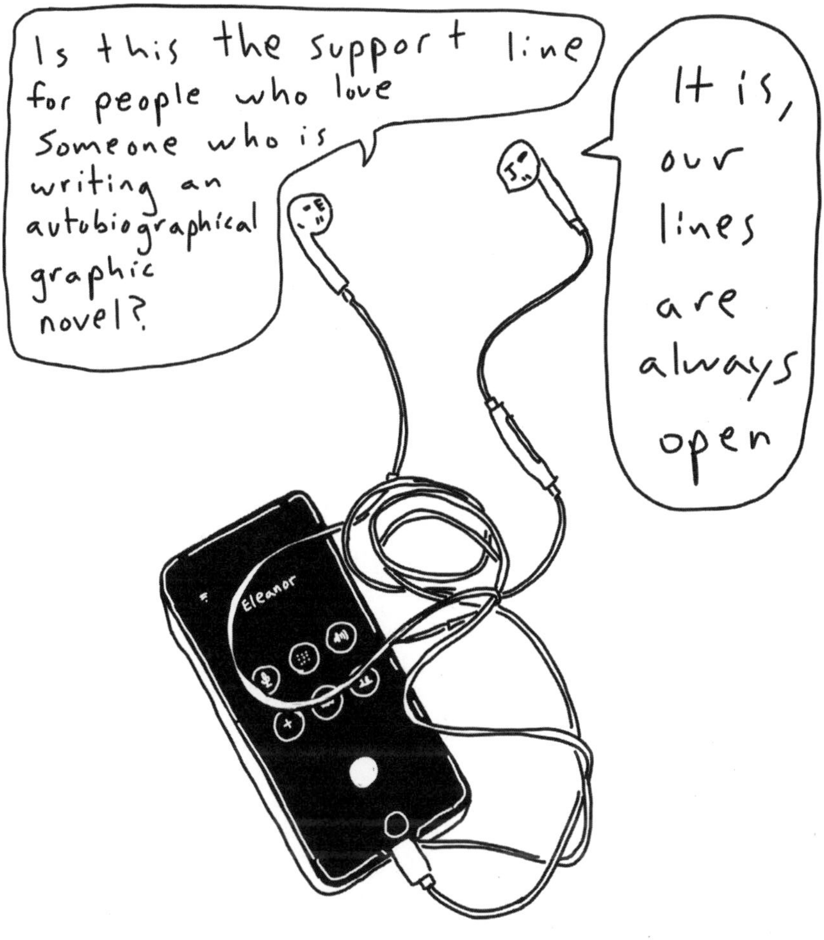
Is this the support line for people who love Someone who is writing an autobiographical graphic novel?
It is, our lines are always open
Eleanor

When Elly came into my life I was deeply lost and she's been there through every step of my recovery. I am truly grateful.

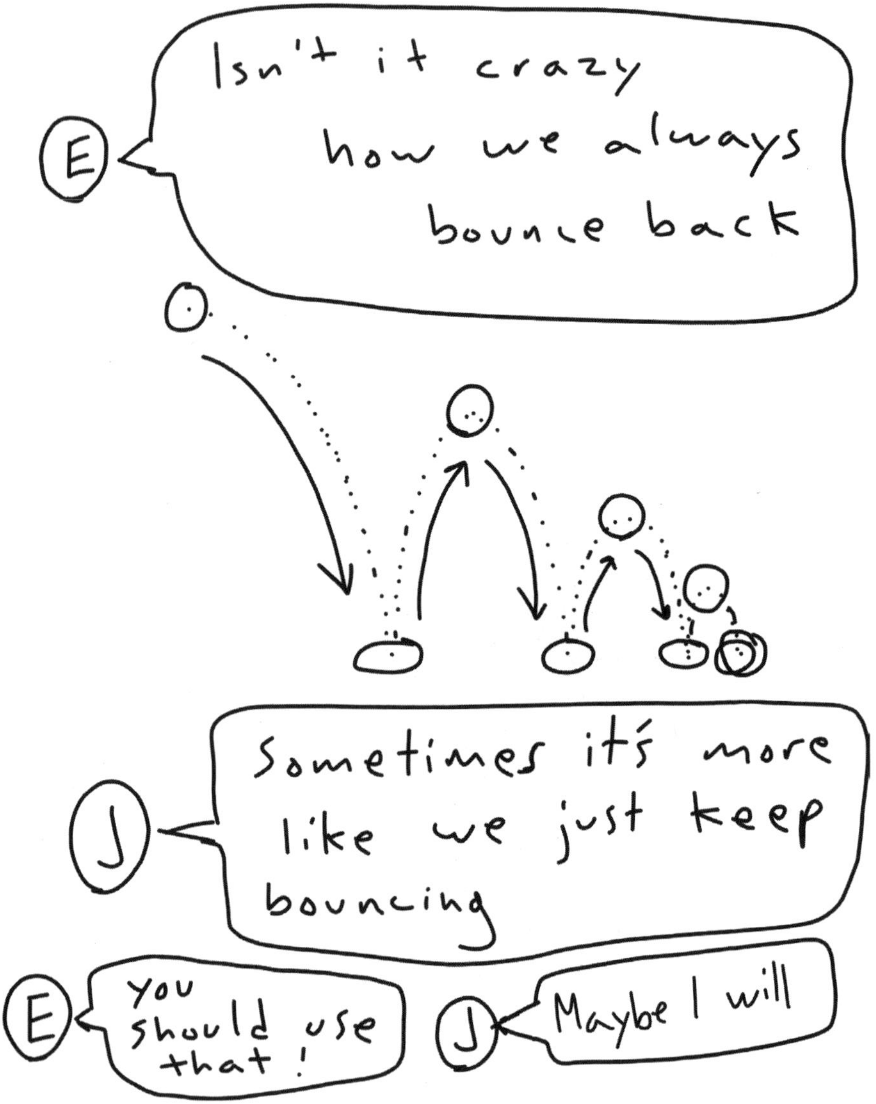
E
Isn't it crazy how we always bounce back
J
Sometimes it's more like we just keep bouncing
E
you should use that!
J
Maybe I will

Now we keep each other up to date on the important things

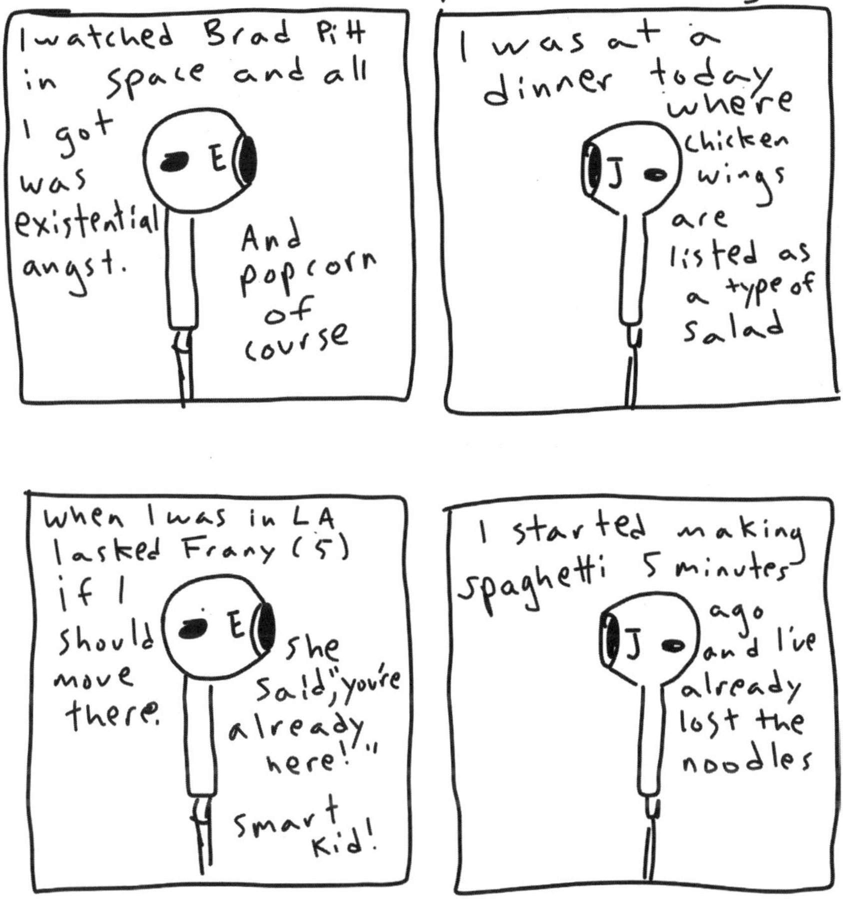
I watched Brad Pitt in space and all I got was existential angst.
E
And popcorn of course
I was at a dinner today where chicken wings are listed as a type of salad
J
when I was in LA I asked Frany (5) if I should move there.
E
she said, "you're already here!"
smart kid!
I started making spaghetti 5 minutes ago and I've already lost the noodles
J

It's comforting. And I'm trying not to try and predict the future.

But sometimes we have specific agenda items

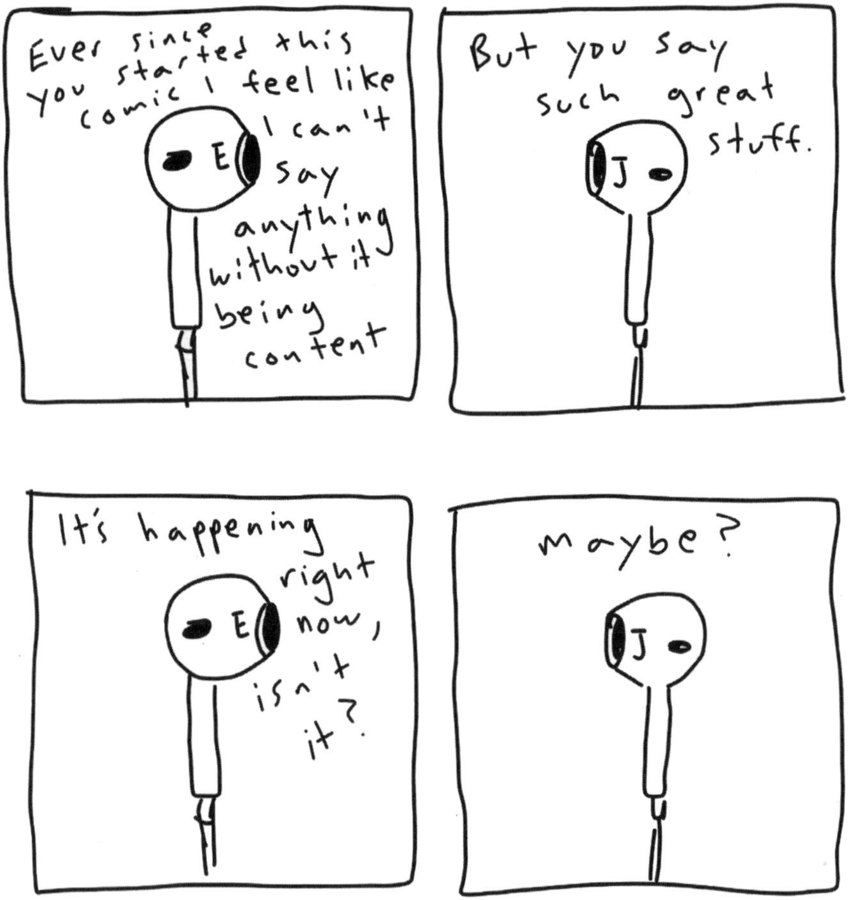
Ever since you started this comic I feel like I can't say anything without it being content
E
But you say such great stuff.
J
It's happening right now, isn't it?
E
maybe?
J

and sometimes we avoid the harder questions.

And sometimes we reminisce

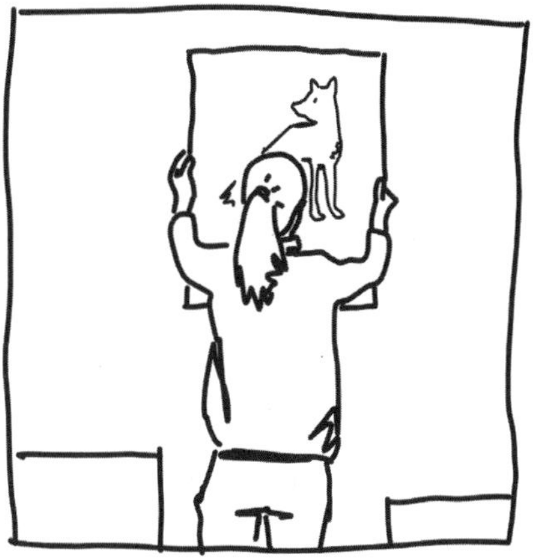

remember

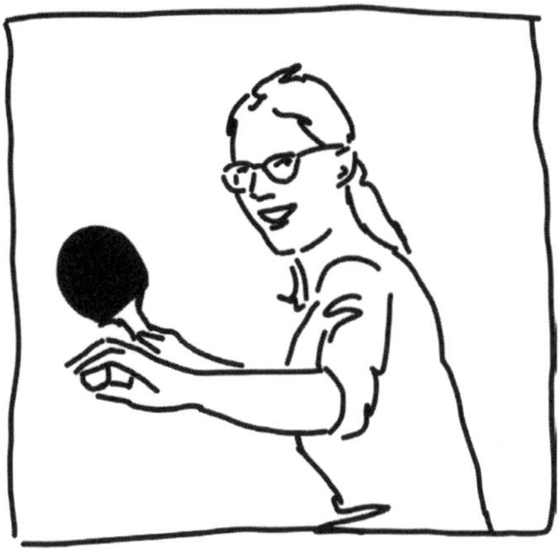

remember

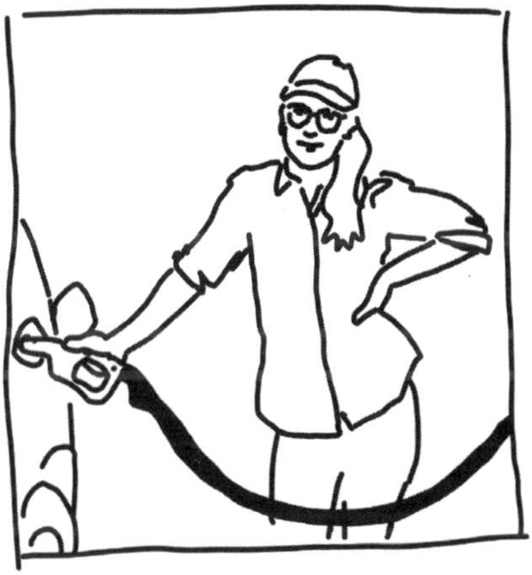

remember

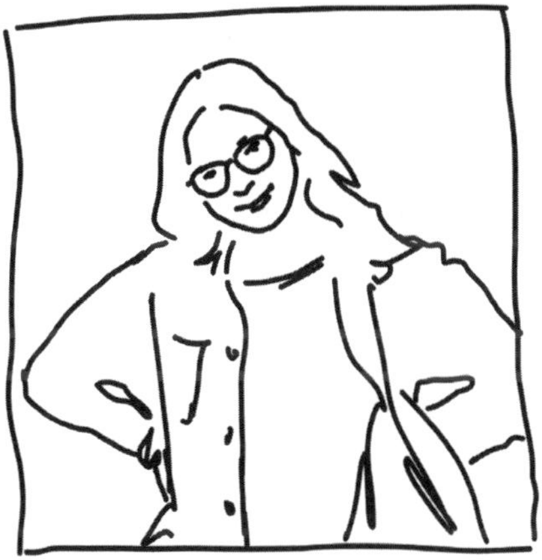

remember

the intimacy of
radio waves

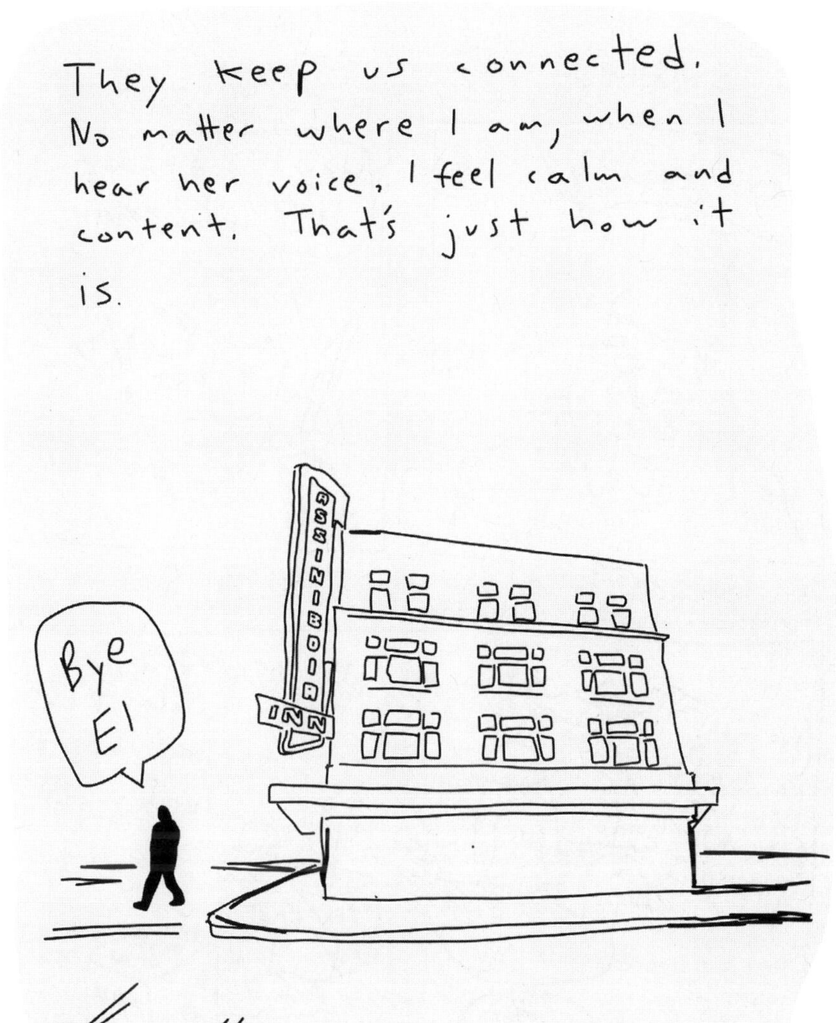
They keep us connected. No matter where I am, when I hear her voice, I feel calm and content. That's just how it is.
ASSINIBOIA
INN
Bye El

27

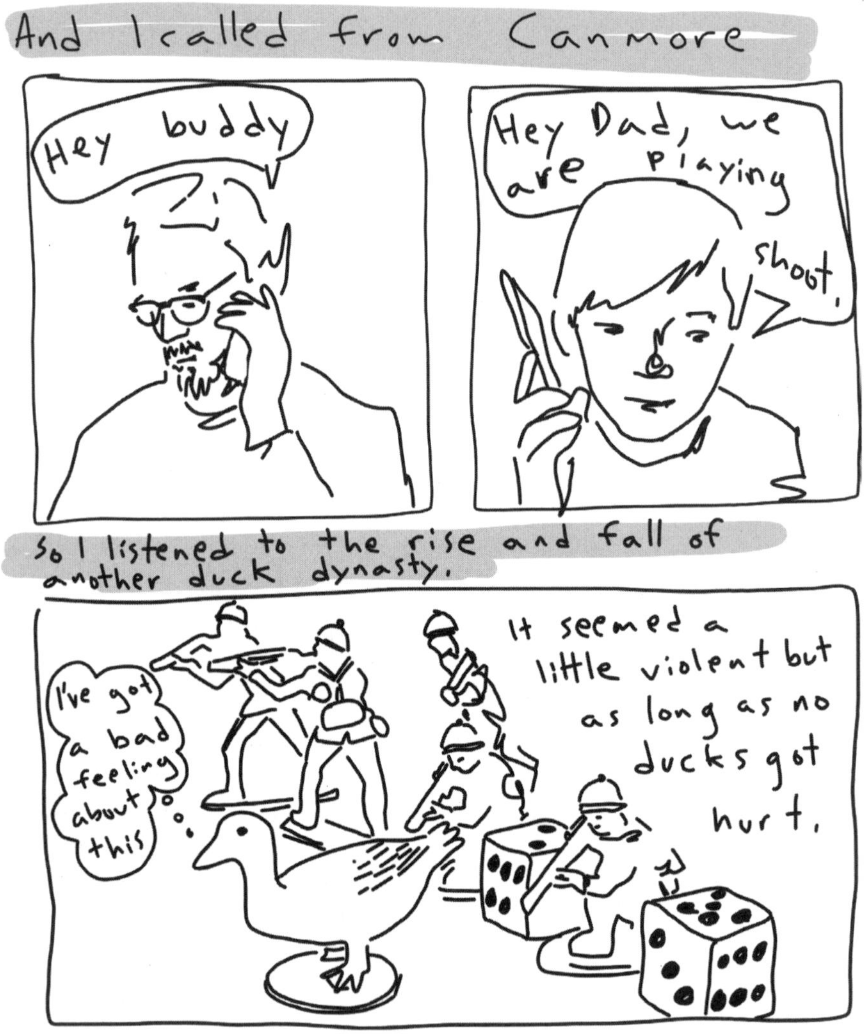
And I called from Canmore
Hey buddy
Hey Dad, we are playing shoot.
So I listened to the rise and fall of another duck dynasty.
I've got a bad feeling about this
It seemed a little violent but as long as no ducks got hurt.

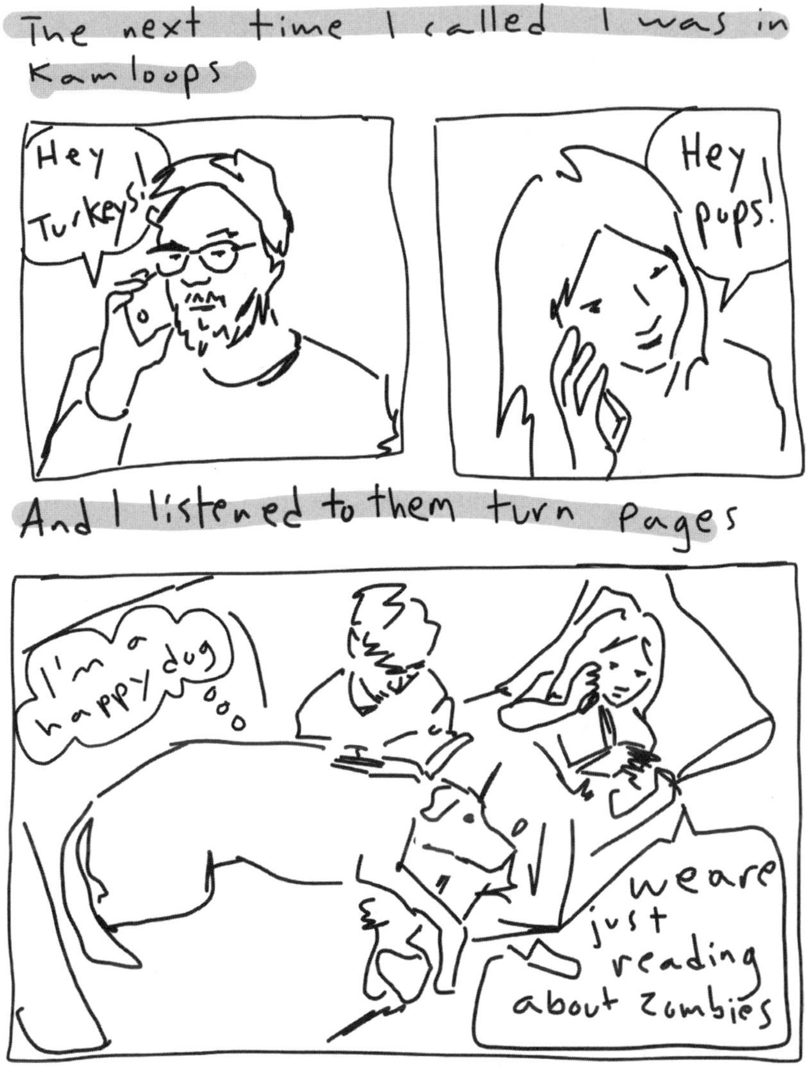
The next time I called I was in Kamloops
Hey Turkeys!
Hey pups!
And I listened to them turn pages
I'm a happy dog
we are just reading about zombies

28

I thought of all the countless other people who had done this drive from east to west. For some it was a drive from despair to hope, for others it was

from boredom to adventure. People putting the petal to the metal and living on coffee and chocolate bars in search of work, family, distraction, adventure, love, or simply a fresh start.

Where do I fit into all that? Probably all of the above and none at all. Not quite a worker and not quite an adventurer. Not in search of something or somewhere ahead of me but trying to understand what lies behind me.

As I drove I imagined the songs I listened to as new Canadian Anthems. Joni Mitchell's "A Case Of You" was a favourite (I drew a map of Canada Oh, Canada, and I sketched your face on it twice)

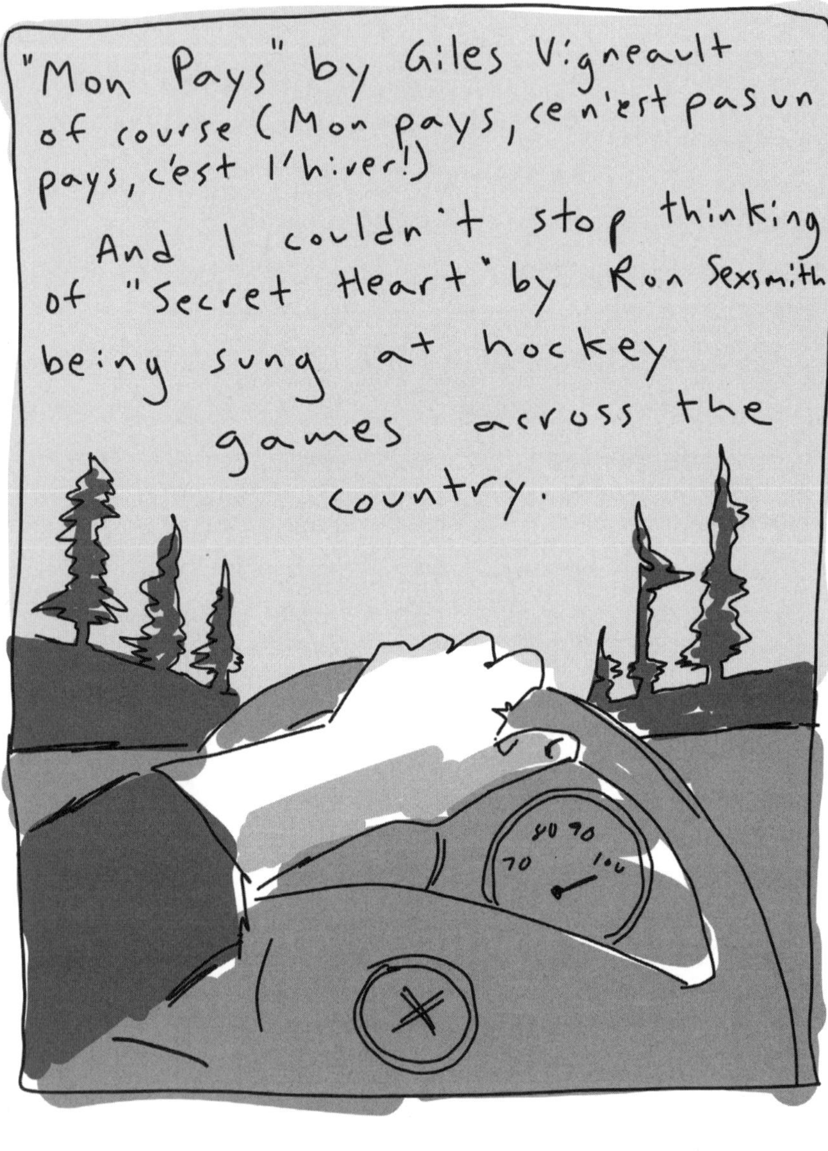
"Mon Pays" by Giles Vigneault of course (Mon pays, ce n'est pas un pays, c'est l'hiver!)
And I couldn't stop thinking of "Secret Heart" by Ron Sexsmith being sung at hockey games across the country.

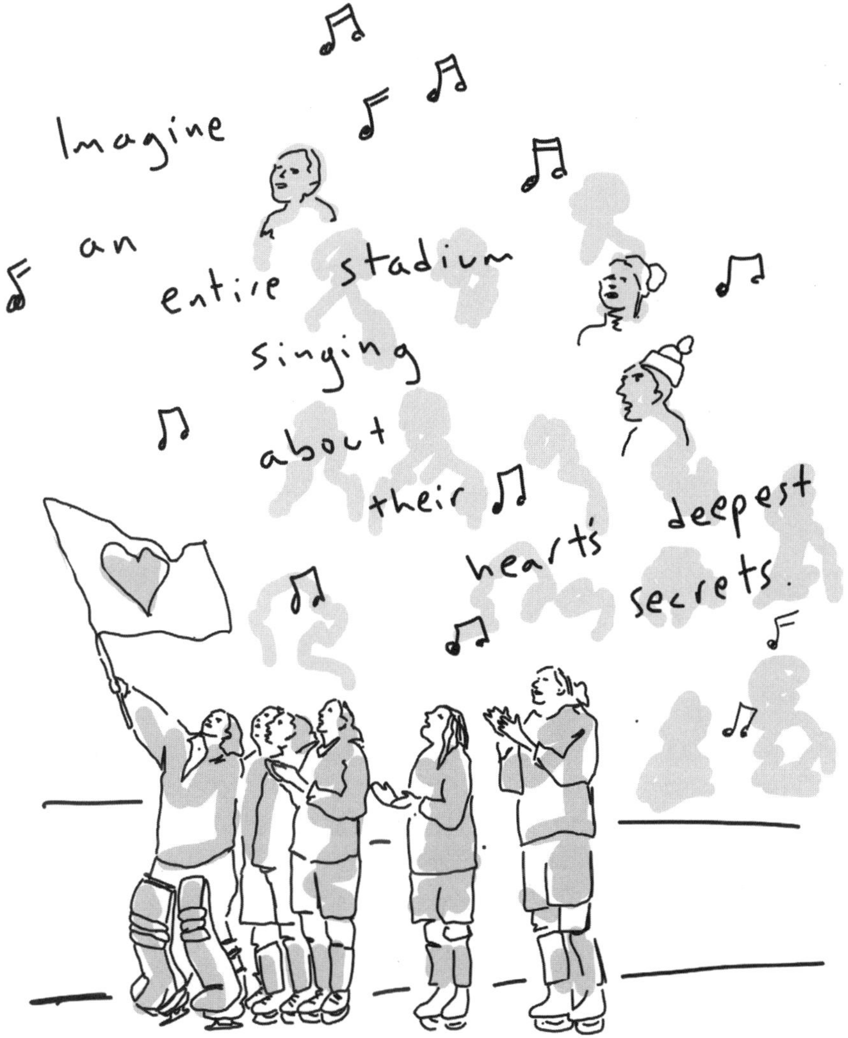
Imagine
an
entire stadium
singing
about
their
heart's deepest
secrets.

But the song that kept coming
back to me as a contender was
"Four strong winds" by Ian and
Sylvia. Although it is maybe more

of an east coast anthem it
worked for me and quietly
that melody haunted my drive.

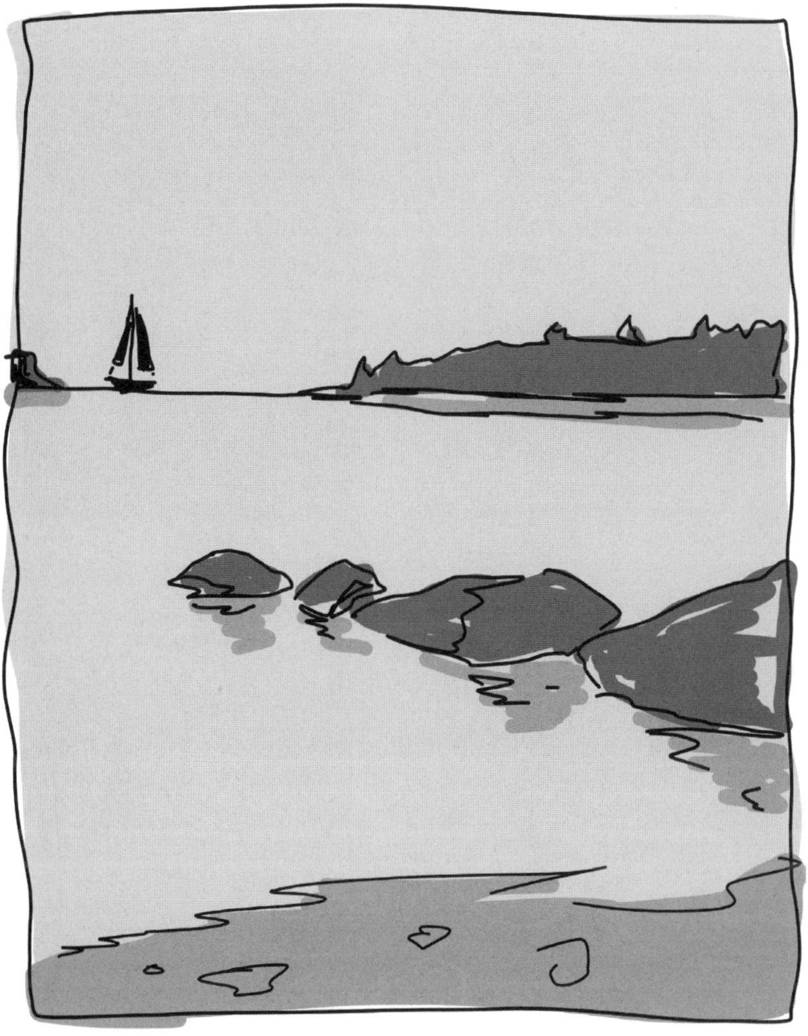

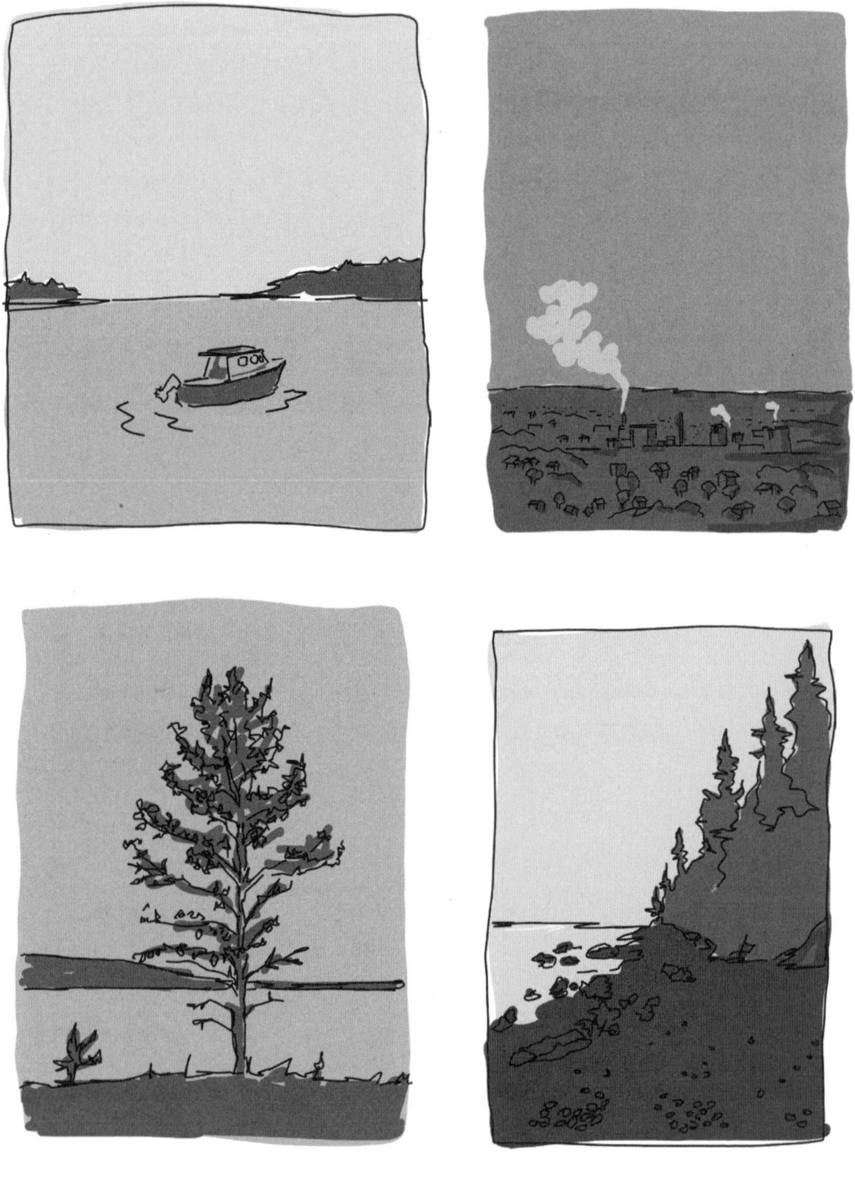

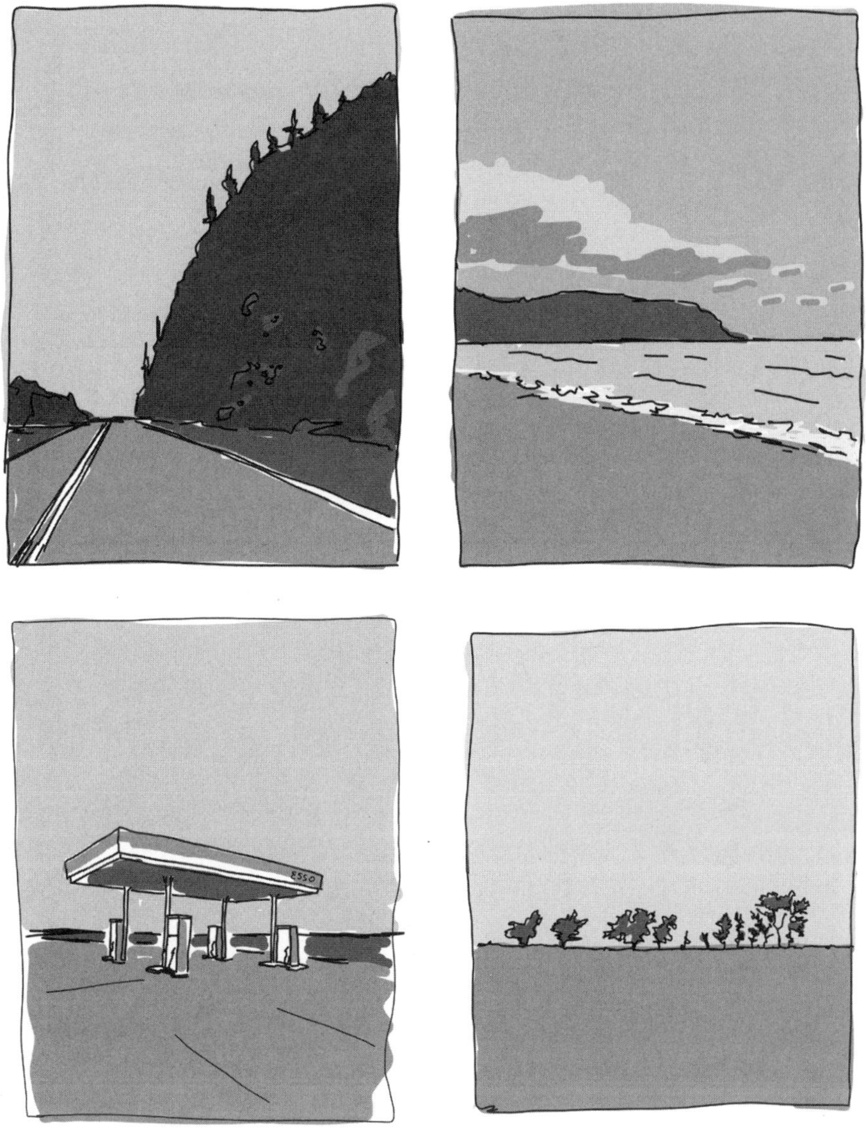
ESSO

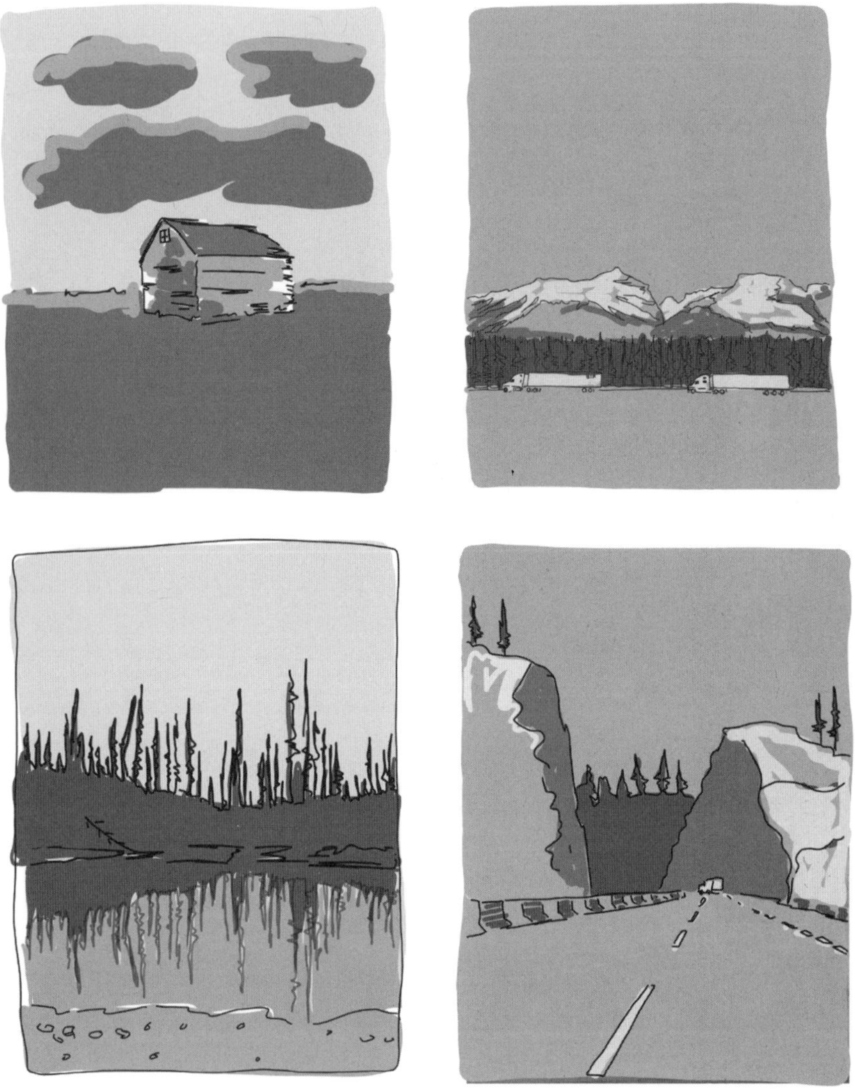

29

I arrived in Prince Rupert late in the afternoon. It was perfectly overcast and grey.

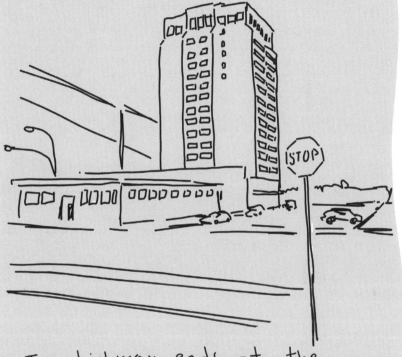

The highway ends at the Pacific Ocean. At least it feels much more like an ending than a beginning.

I drove down to the harbour and looked at the cargo ships weighted down by nothing but potential and the heavy spirit of capitalism.

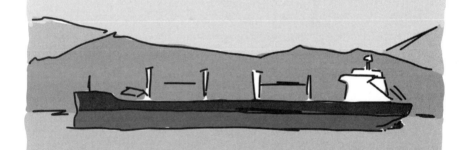

I needed a moment to gather my thoughts before continuing on to my final destination, the residency at Cassiar Cannery.

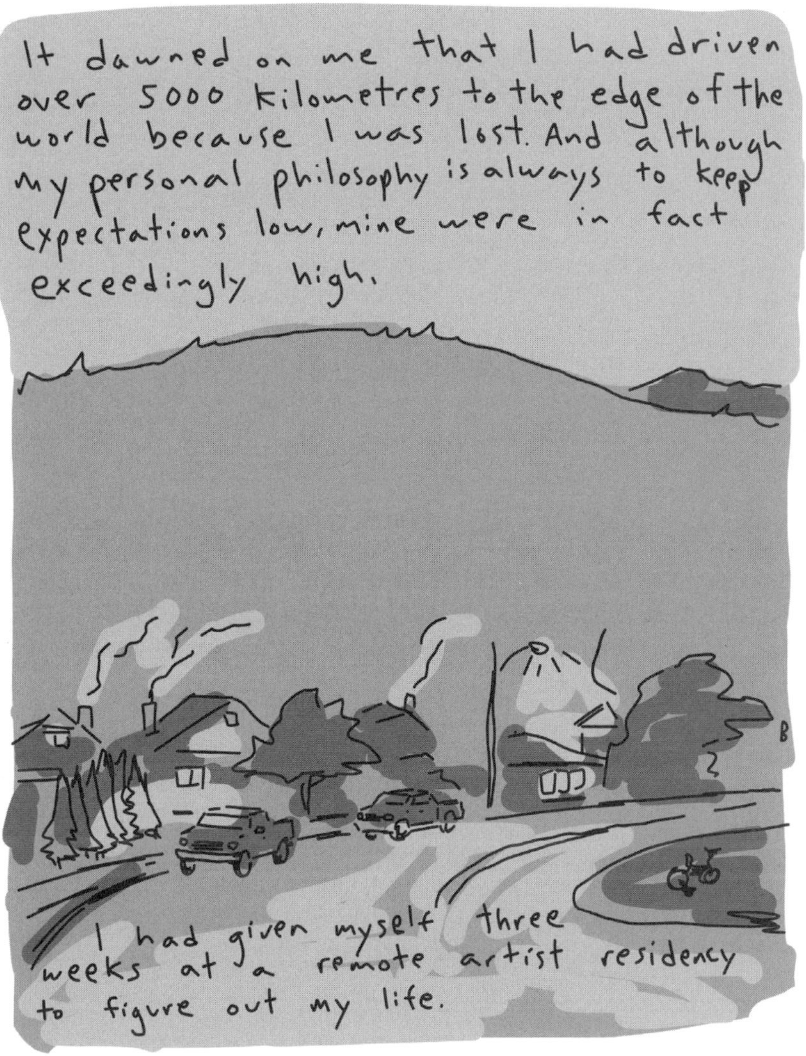
It dawned on me that I had driven over 5000 kilometres to the edge of the world because I was lost. And although my personal philosophy is always to keep expectations low, mine were in fact exceedingly high.
I had given myself three weeks at a remote artist residency to figure out my life.

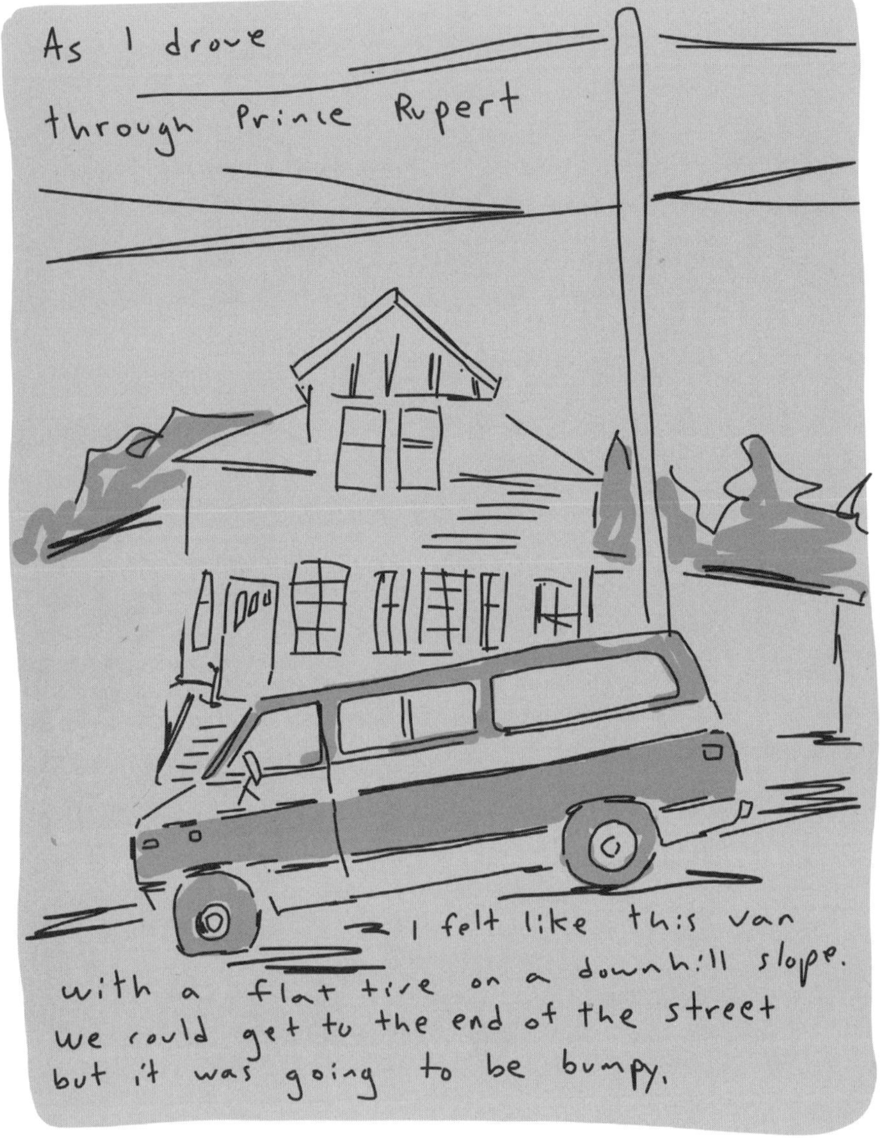
As I drove
through Prince Rupert
I felt like this van
with a flat tire on a downhill slope.
We could get to the end of the street
but it was going to be bumpy.

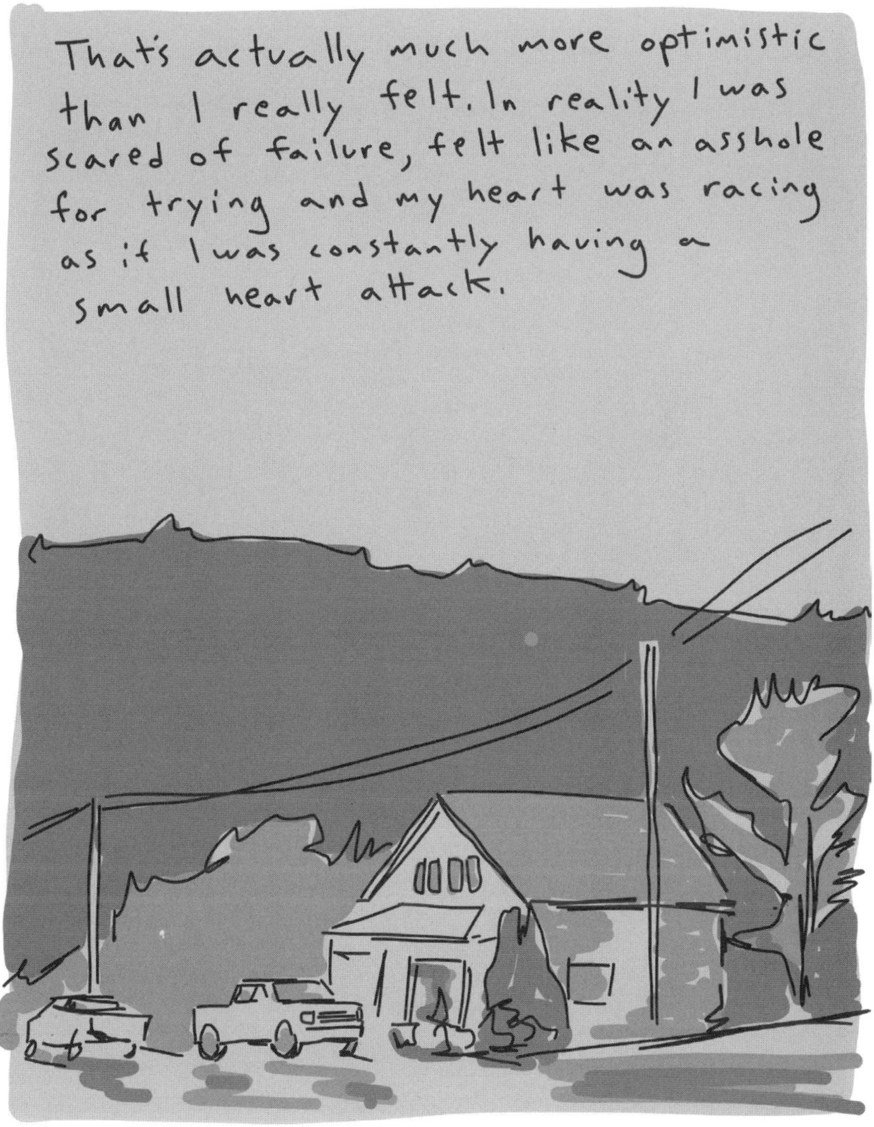
That's actually much more optimistic than I really felt. In reality I was scared of failure, felt like an asshole for trying and my heart was racing as if I was constantly having a small heart attack.

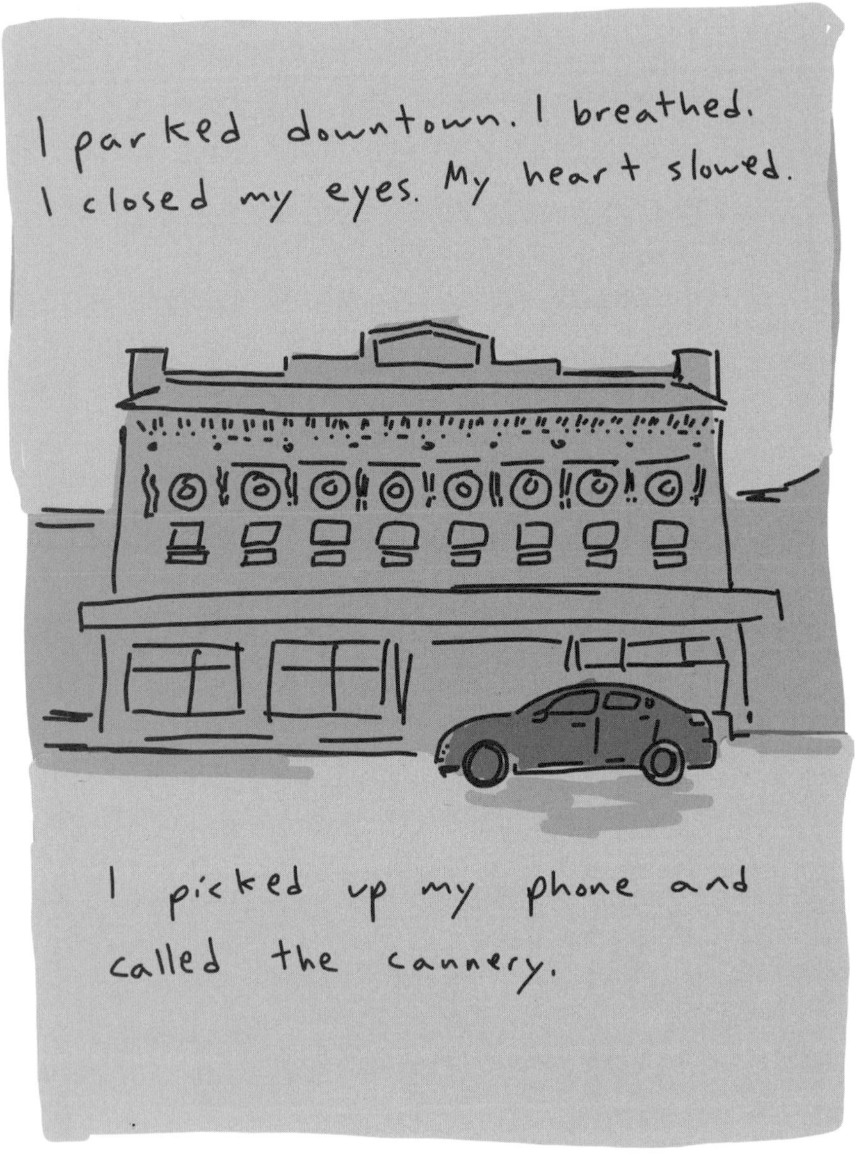
I parked downtown. I breathed. I closed my eyes. My heart slowed.
I picked up my phone and called the cannery.

Hi Justine, it's Jon, I made it to Prince Rupert!
Great! Now just head South on McBride past the harbour. The road gets narrow and bumpy and more narrow and rougher. You will know you're here when the road ends. See you soon!
of course the end of the road isn't the end of the road

I arrived at the cannery
before dark. Not tired but
not awake either.

And despite the beauty my one
overwhelming thought was, "what
the hell do I think I'm doing
here?"

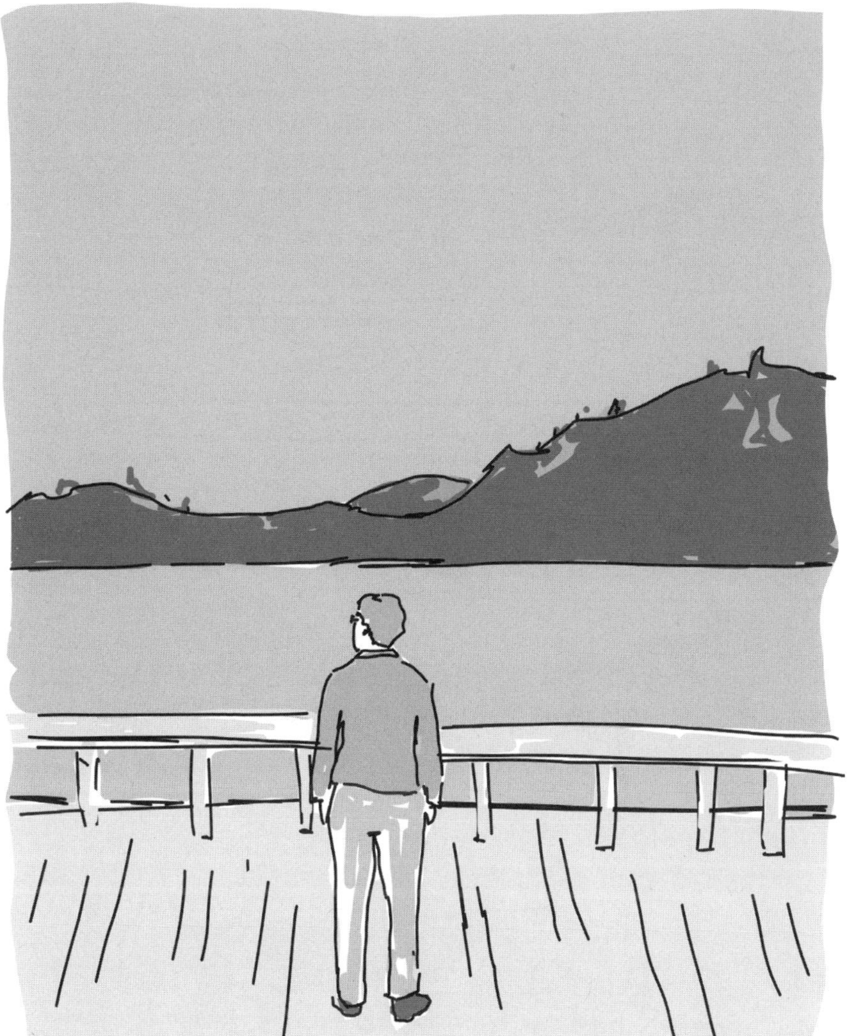

30

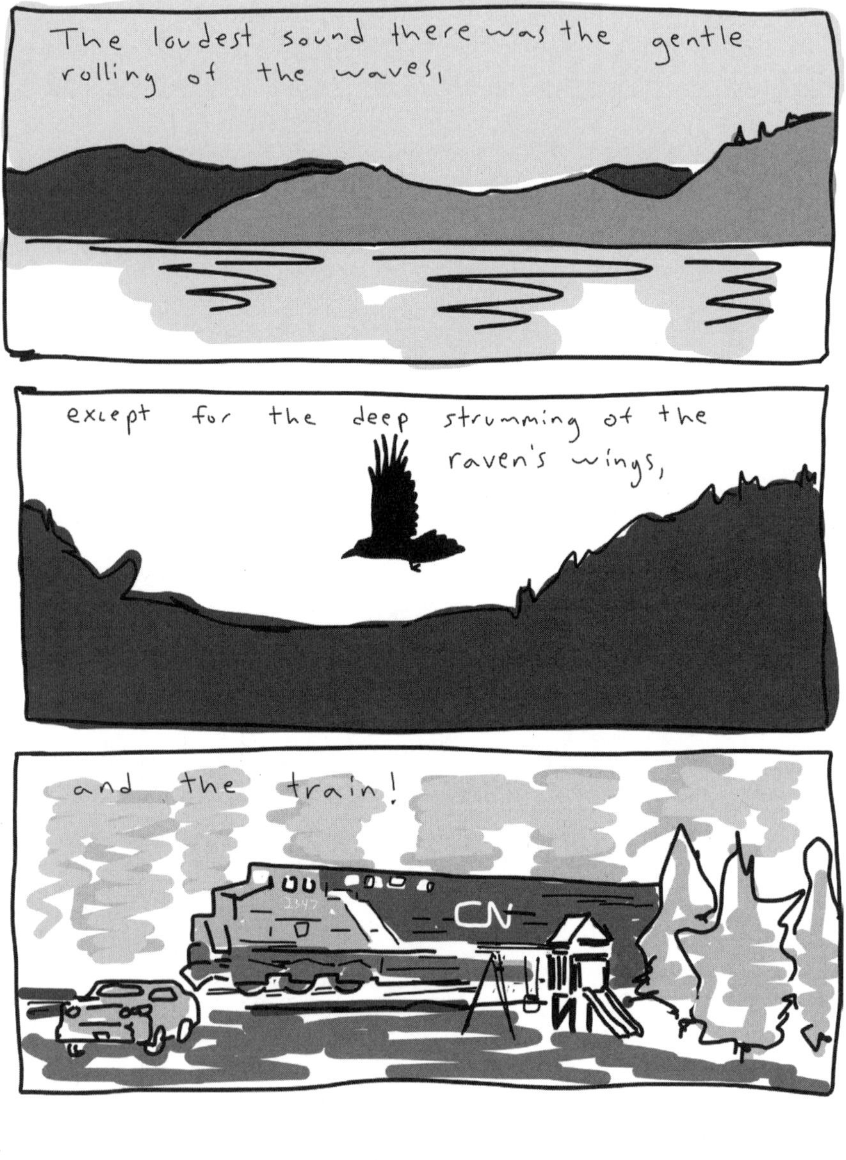
The loudest sound there was the gentle rolling of the waves,
except for the deep strumming of the raven's wings,
and the train!
CN

There was all the
time in the world

to wander.

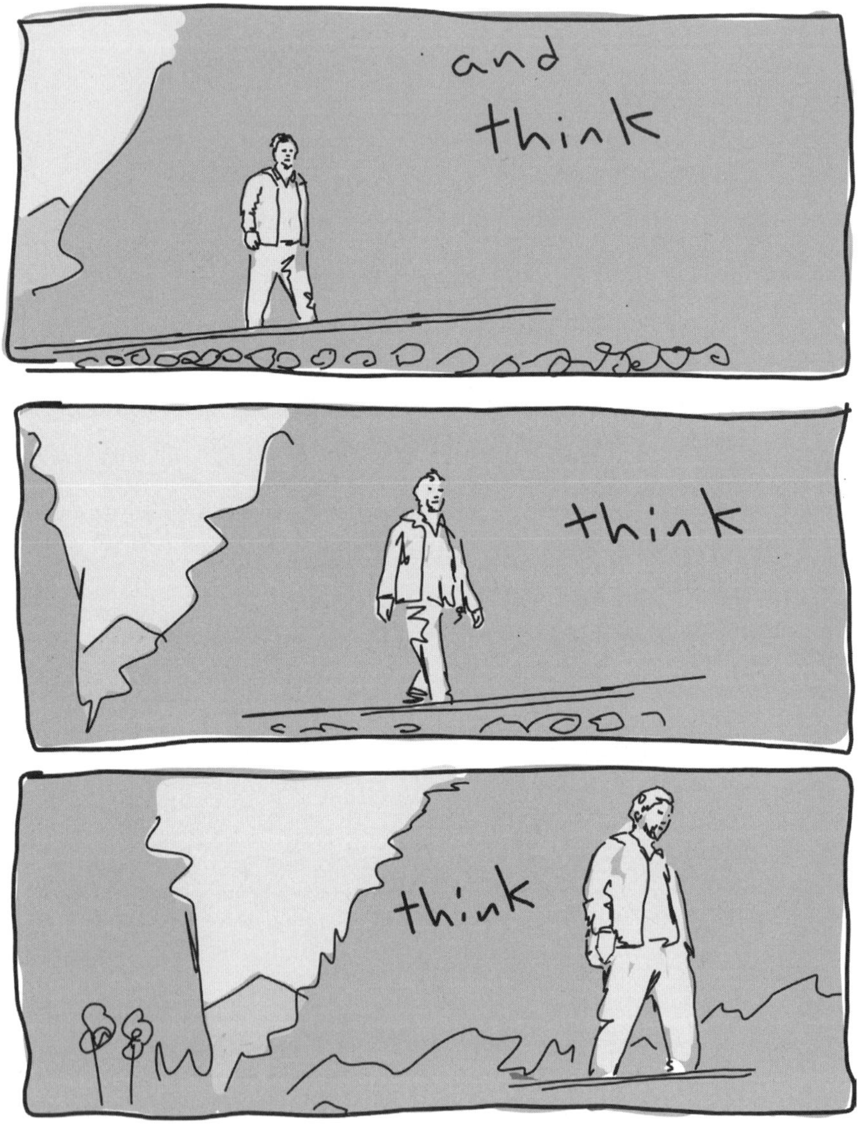
and think
think
think

Think think think think
think think think
think think think
think think think

I seem to have
mastered the opposite
of meditation.

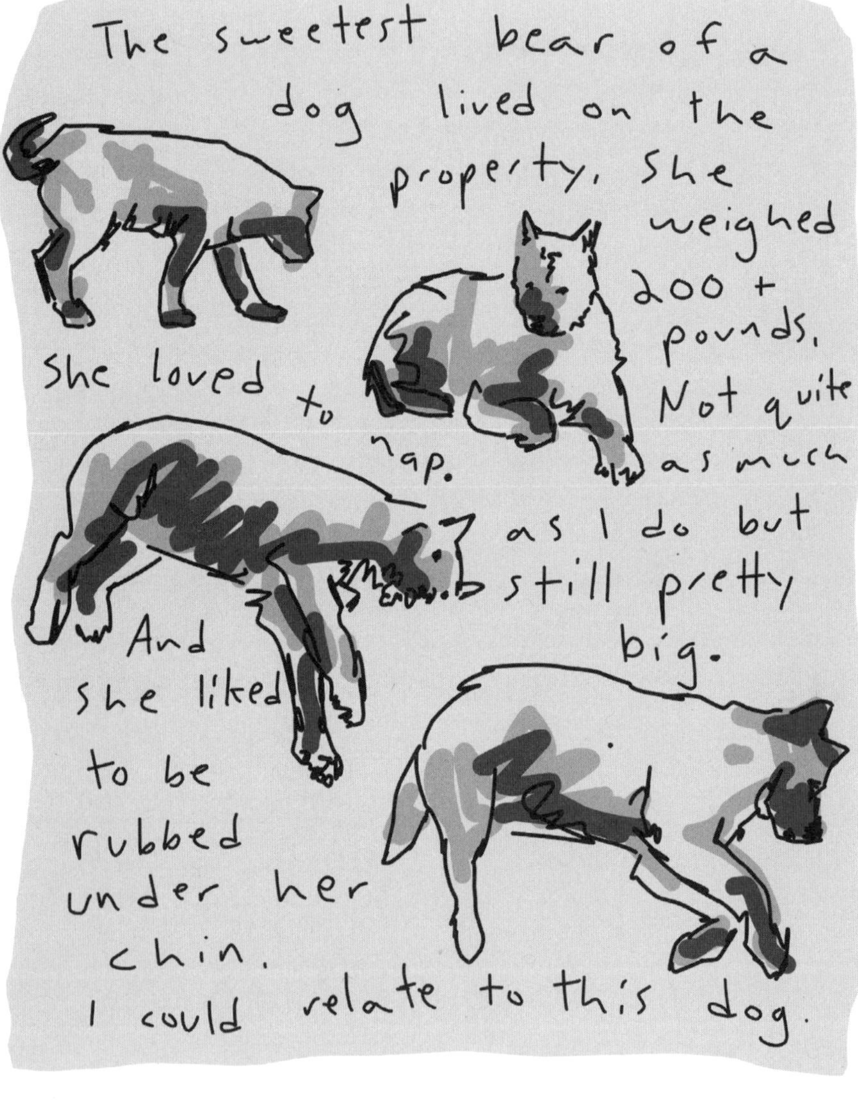
The sweetest bear of a dog lived on the property. She weighed 200+ pounds.
Not quite as much as I do but still pretty big.
She loved to nap.
And she liked to be rubbed under her chin.
I could relate to this dog.

There were signs of chidren here. A playset and a small BMX, CCM brand. What a place to grow up. On the bank of the Skeena River, adventure in the air, no place in the world more beautiful. My kids would love it here. I could just imagine them running and exploring.

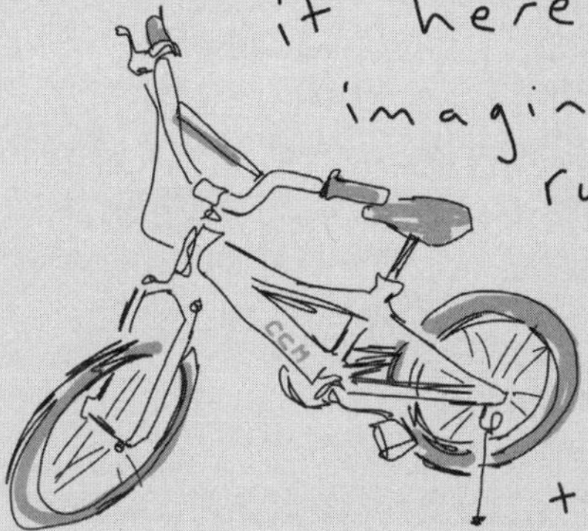
CCM

Looking at this little bike I miss them so much. Can I really move away next year and only see them on weekends?

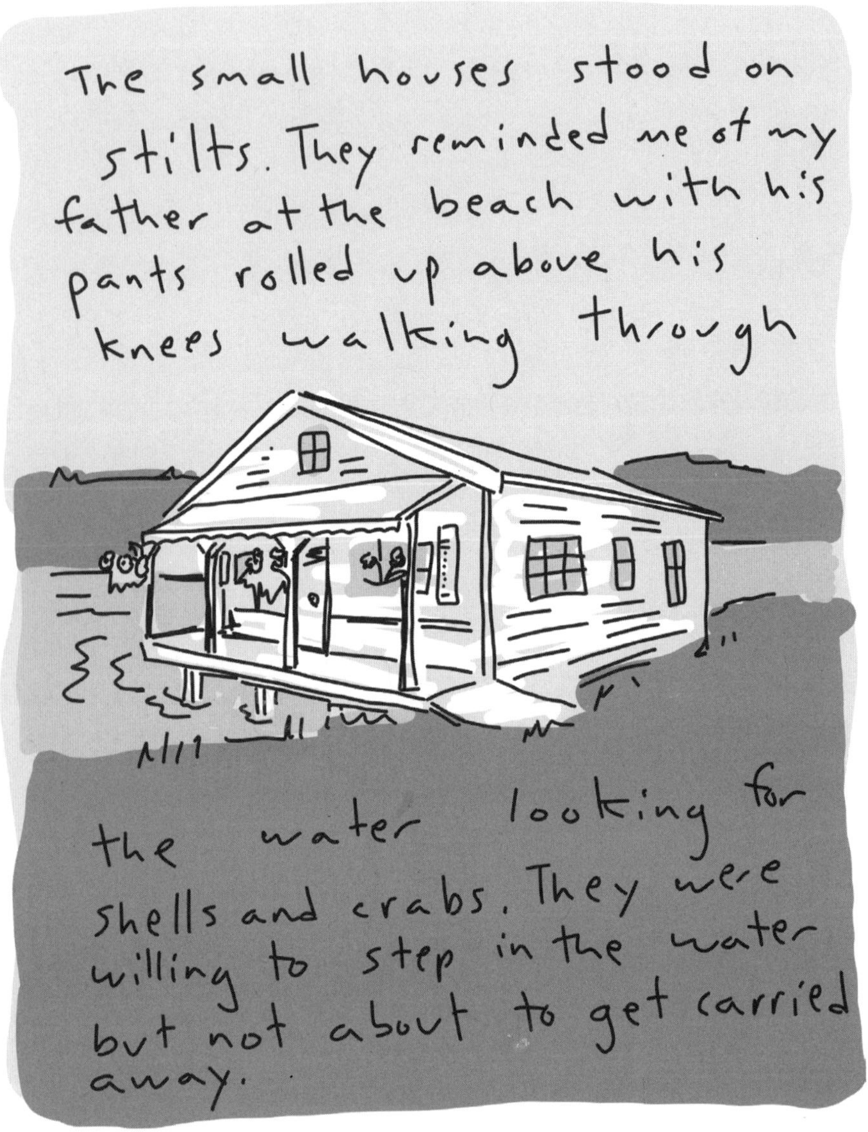
The small houses stood on stilts. They reminded me of my father at the beach with his pants rolled up above his knees walking through
the water looking for shells and crabs. They were willing to step in the water but not about to get carried away.

There were a lot of aging "ghost ships" hanging around the old cannery. They sat and rested on the shore. When the tide came in high enough they floated a little.

Some will be rebuilt by the local master ship-wright. Some will simply, and without notice, disappear into the forest and the sea.

Leaning against one of the out buildings was an ovatek 7 life raft. More of an escape pod really. These life rafts are indestructable, water-tight, unsinkable and self-righting. It was bright orange and

ENTRANCE LIFE RAFT
OVATEK 7
7 PERSONS

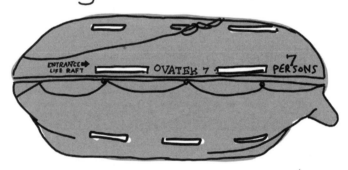

seemed to be asking to be used. like a super hero all dressed up with nowhere to be and no one to save. Full of pent up but quiet good intentions.

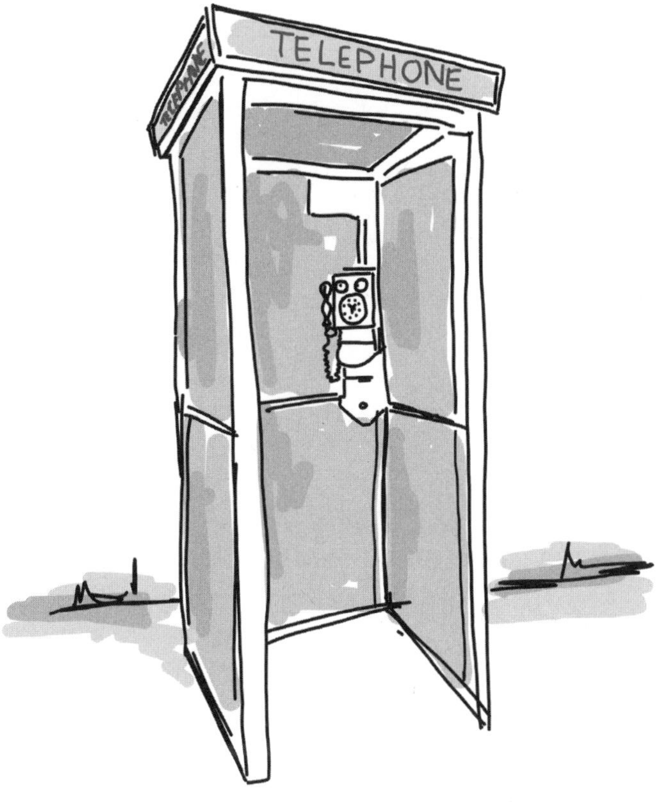
TELEPHONE

The ancient pay phone also stood at attention ready to perform a job it could no longer do.

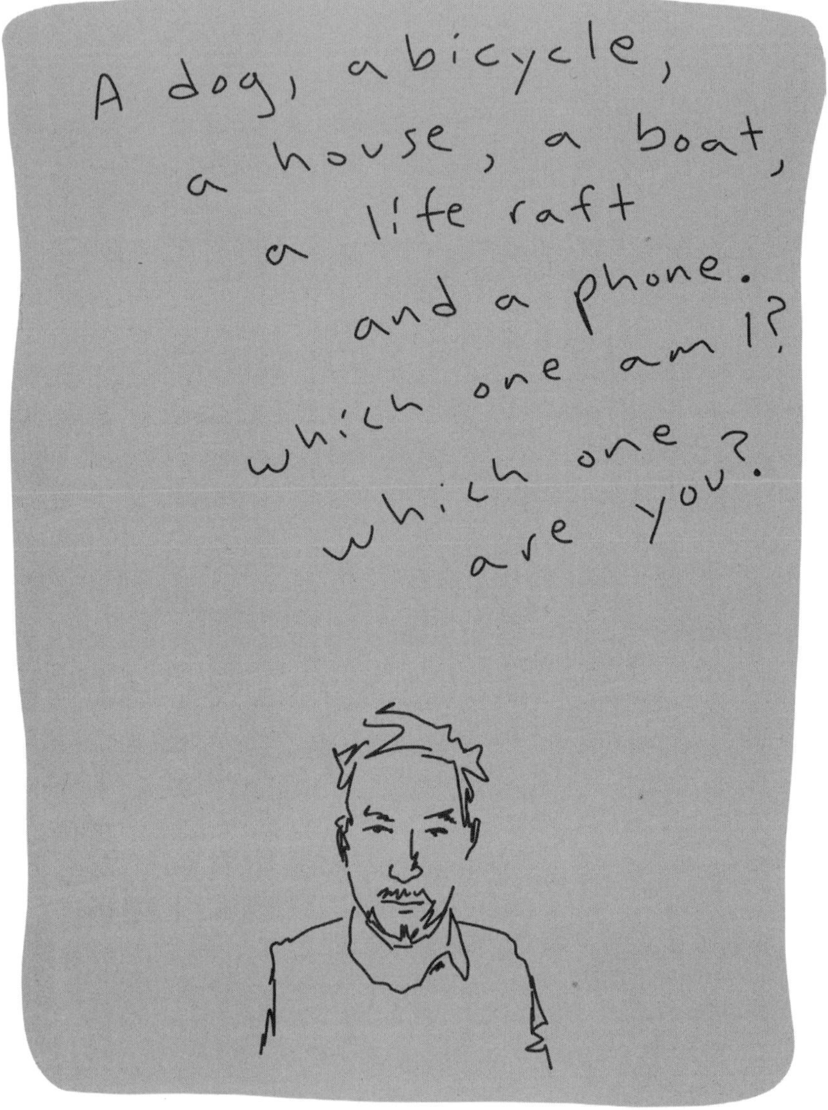
A dog, a bicycle,
a house, a boat,
a life raft
and a phone.
which one am I?
which one
are you?

Everywhere I go I bring an army of self-help books with me. I think it is the shear weight of them that keeps me sober.

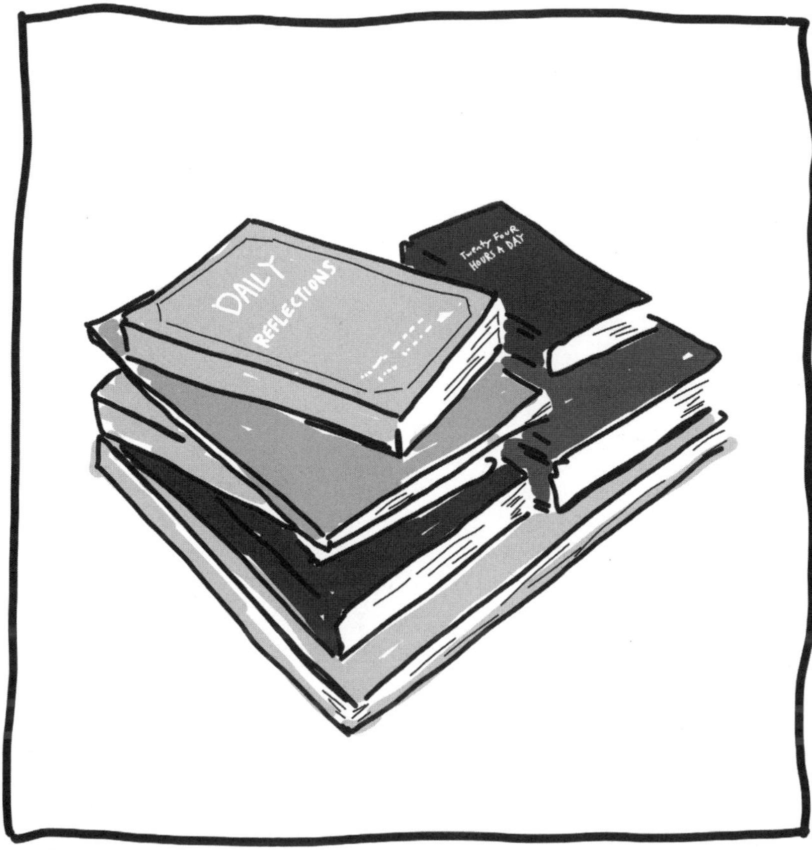
DAILY REFLECTIONS
Twenty Four HOURS A DAY

The one on the bottom is my 12 step binder. It has lists of all the people I have hurt or let down and what I could have done differently.
Woulda, coulda, shoulda.

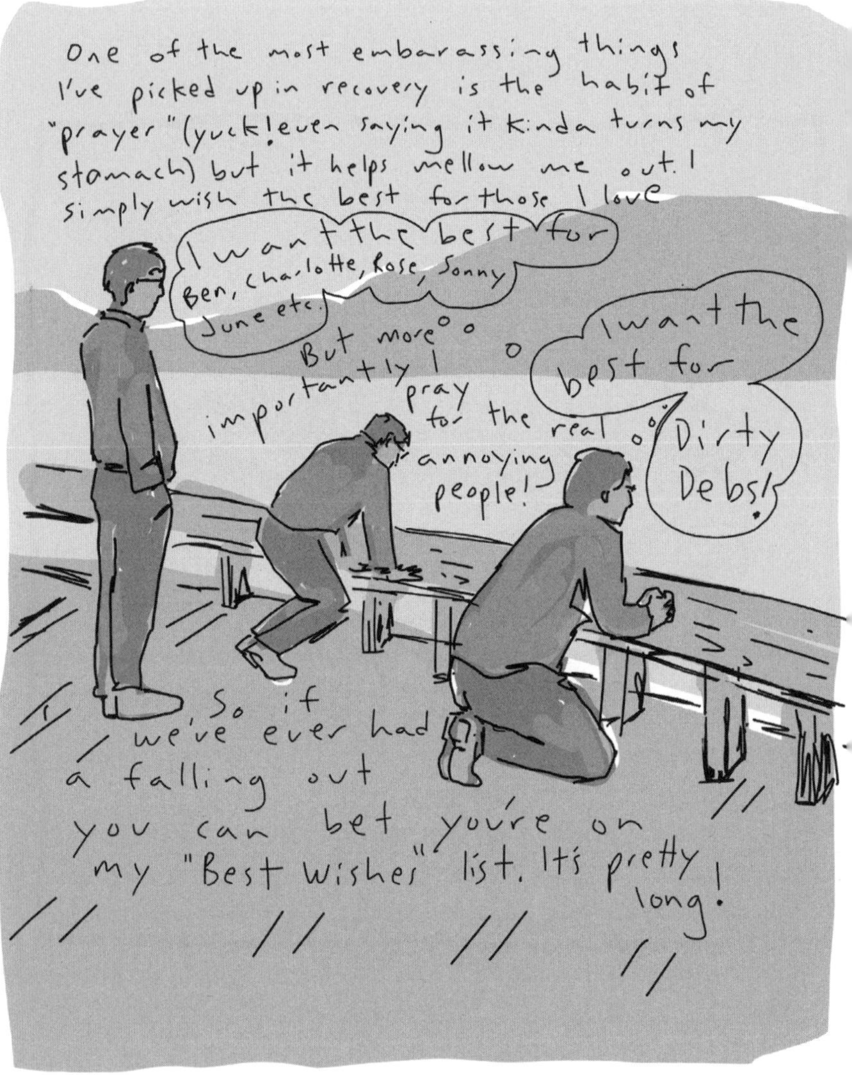
One of the most embarassing things I've picked up in recovery is the habit of "prayer" (yuck! even saying it kinda turns my stomach) but it helps mellow me out. I simply wish the best for those I love
I want the best for Ben, Charlotte, Rose, Sonny June etc.
But more importantly I pray for the real annoying people!
I want the best for Dirty Debs!
So if we've ever had a falling out you can bet you're on my "Best Wishes" list. It's pretty long!

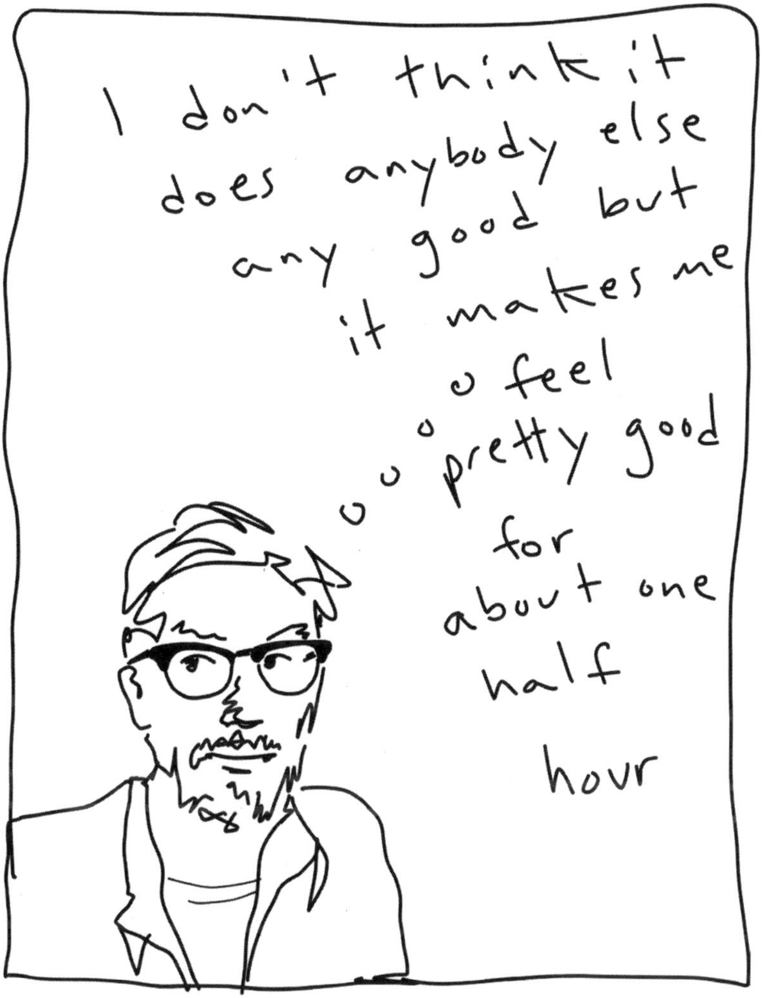
I don't think it
does anybody else
any good but
it makes me
feel
pretty good
for
about one
half
hour

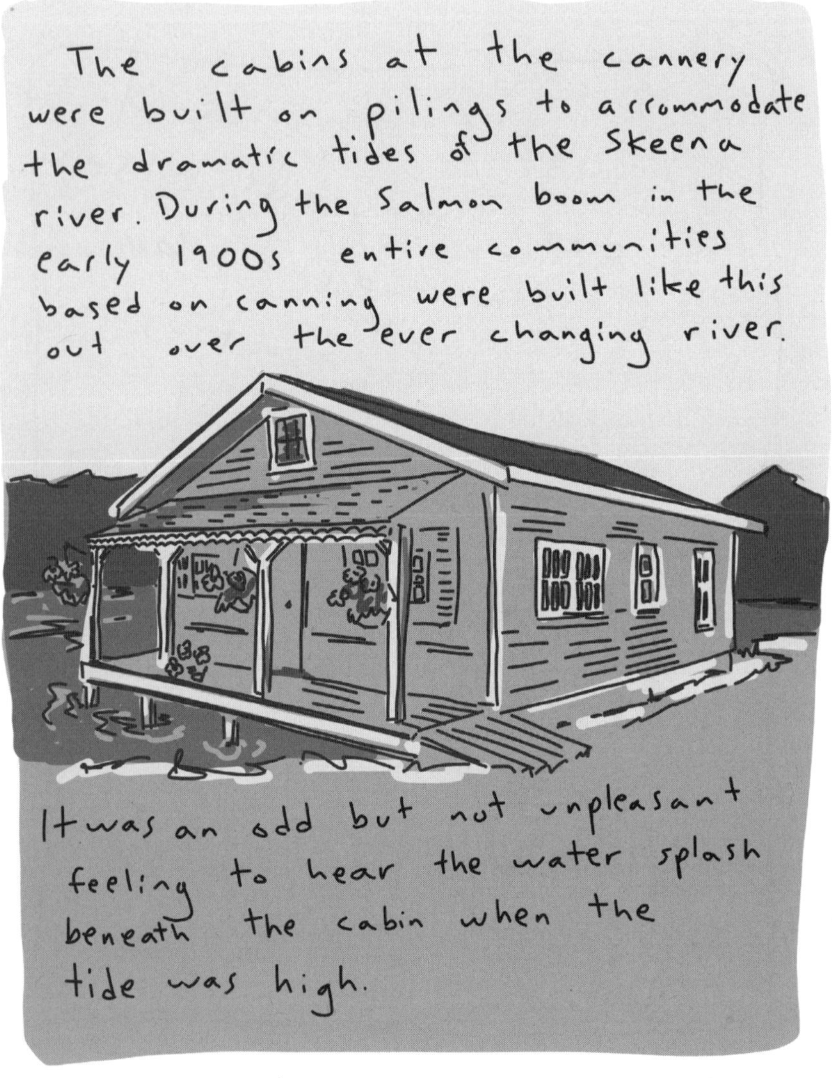
The cabins at the cannery were built on pilings to accommodate the dramatic tides of the Skeena river. During the Salmon boom in the early 1900s entire communities based on canning were built like this out over the ever changing river.
It was an odd but not unpleasant feeling to hear the water splash beneath the cabin when the tide was high.

In the mornings I would draw at the cabin.
My desk was in front of a window that faced the
Skeena and the distant mountains were
always grey in the mist or rain.

I didn't know what I was going to
write about when I started, but then
couldn't stop. I felt obsessed to tell
this story. Maybe it was the result of
momentarily being outside of Sackville, the
town of rumours and whispers.

In the afternoon I would go to the library. I posted the story online as I wrote it so I couldn't turn back.

And I also received some editorial advice.

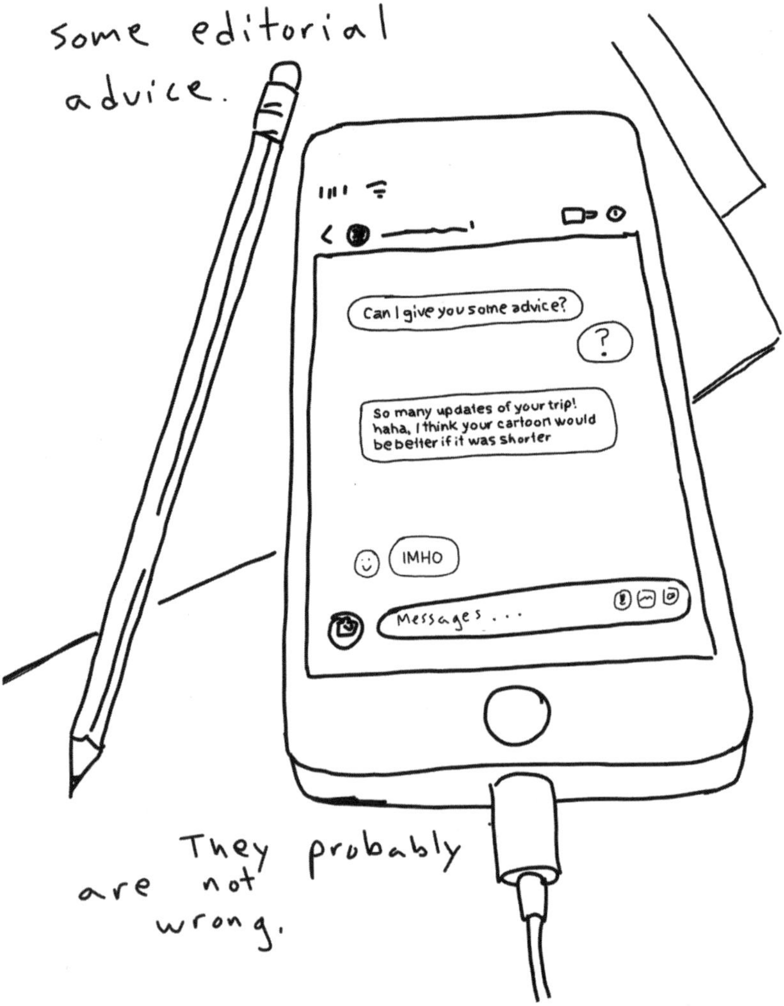
Can I give you some advice?
?
So many updates of your trip! haha, I think your cartoon would be better if it was shorter
IMHO
Messages . . .

They probably are not wrong.

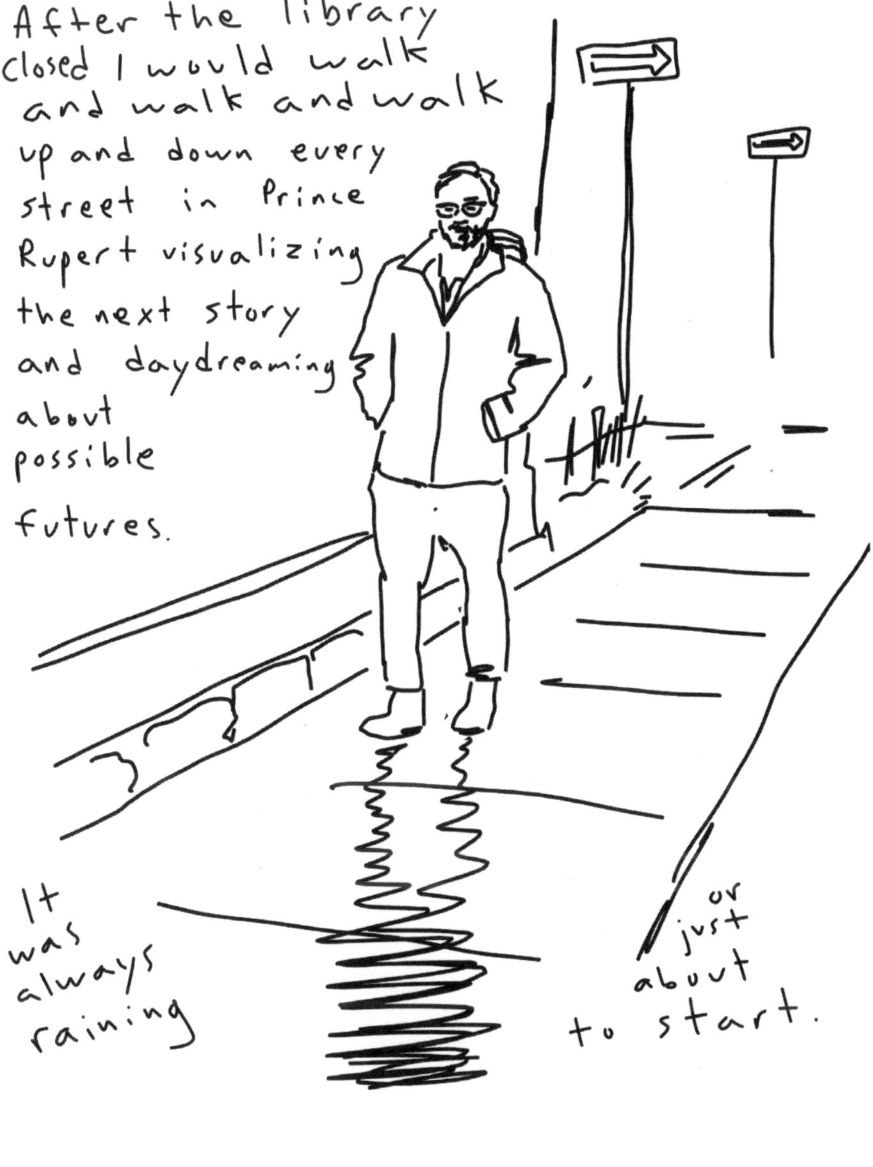
After the library closed I would walk and walk and walk up and down every street in Prince Rupert visualizing the next story and daydreaming about possible futures.
It was always raining
or just about to start.

Late at night, back at the cannery I would mess around on an old tuneless piano that was in what was once a general store for the workers. I played clunky lullabies and thought of the animals in their dens, the drunks in their cups and the dreamers in their beds.

And I'd pray for guidance to remember only to tell my story and no one else's. It was a hard tight rope to walk and I would fall off more than once. And everything is better when it's short and sweet but not all stories are neat and tidy. So bare with me, those that will. This one isn't over yet.

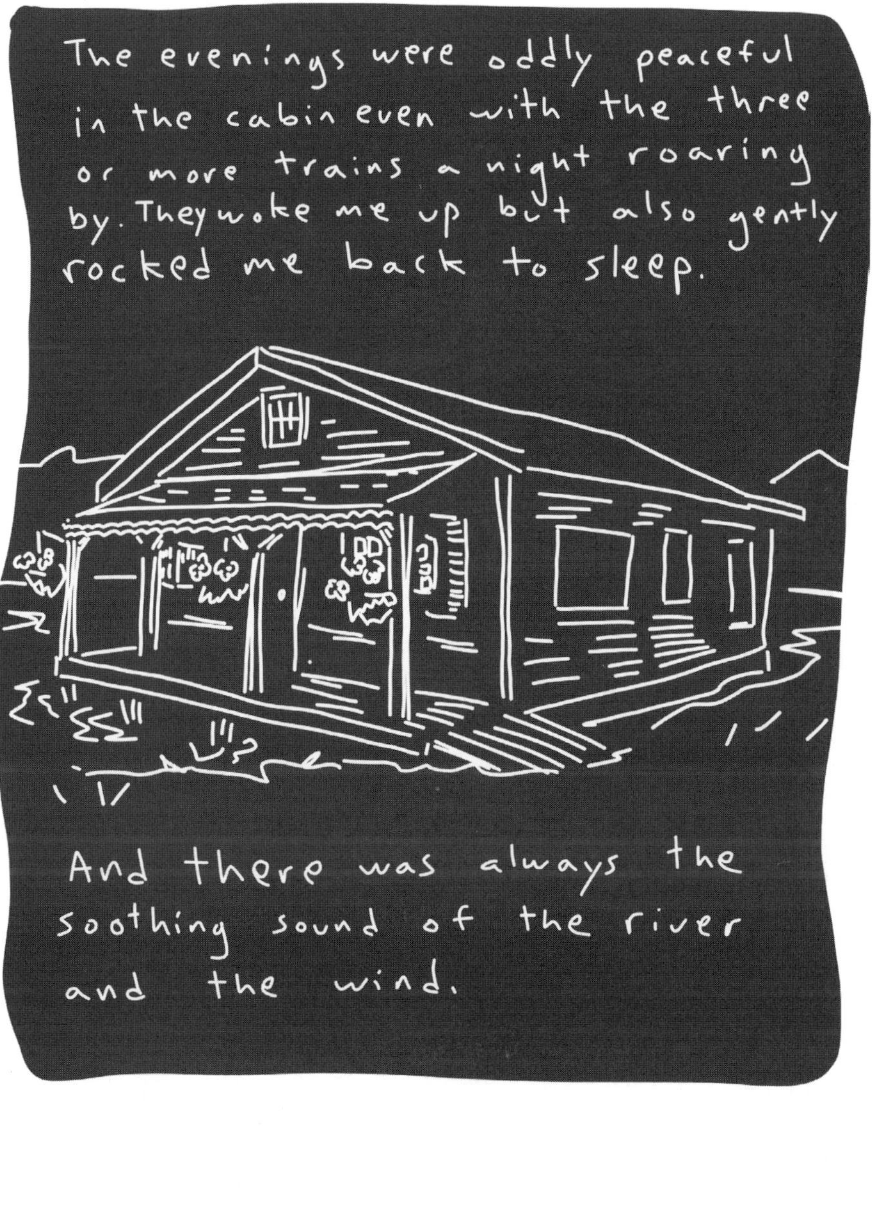
The evenings were oddly peaceful in the cabin even with the three or more trains a night roaring by. They woke me up but also gently rocked me back to sleep.
And there was always the soothing sound of the river and the wind.

31

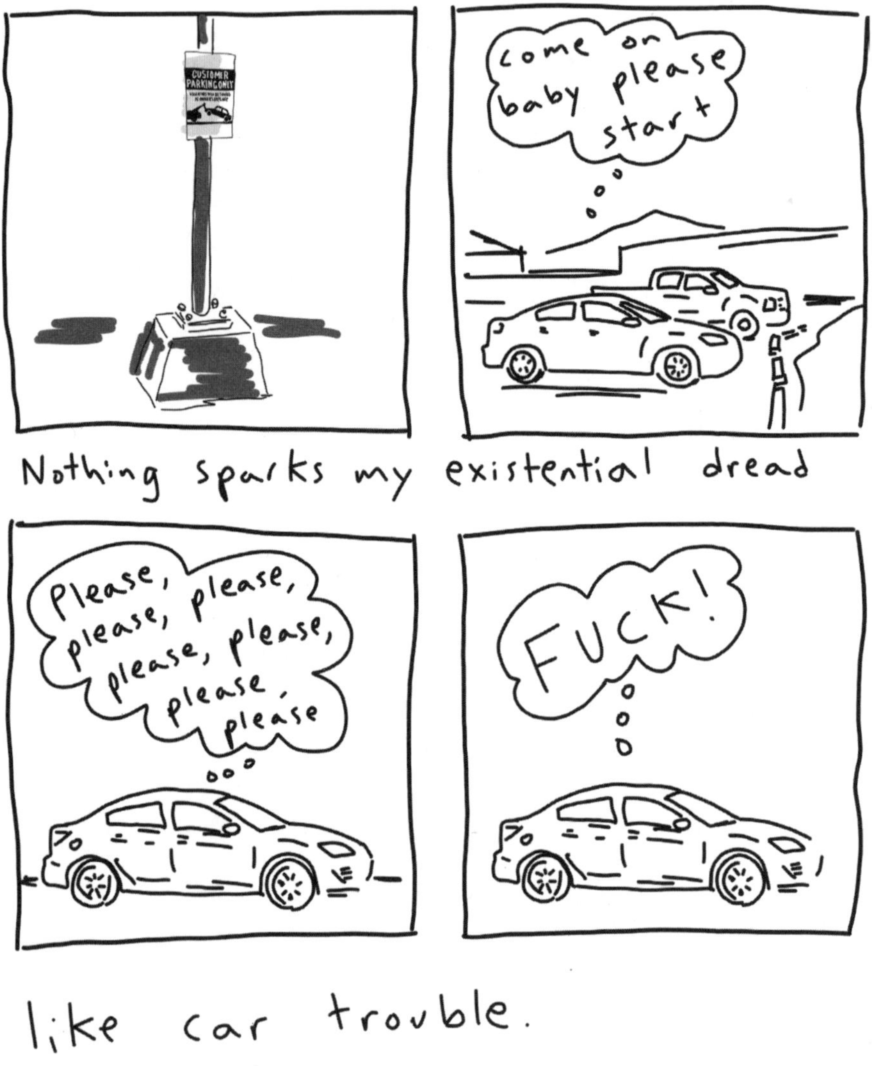
CUSTOMER PARKING ONLY
come on baby please start
Nothing sparks my existential dread
Please, please, please, please, please, please, please
FUCK!
like car trouble.

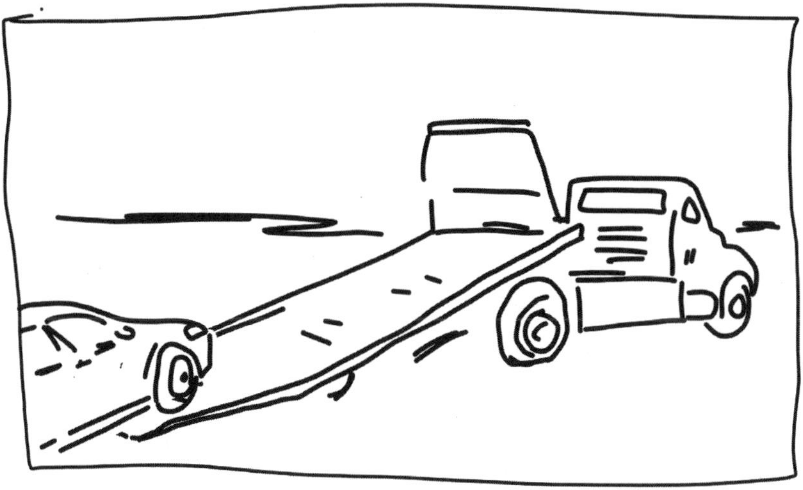

Will I be stuck here forever?

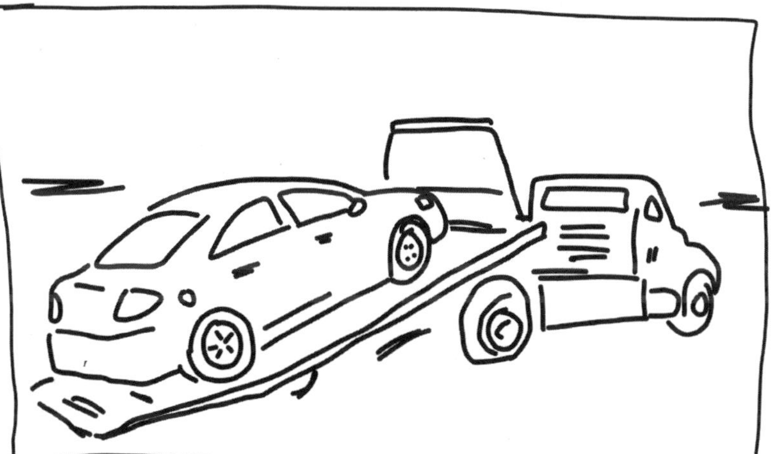

Why do I know nothing about cars?

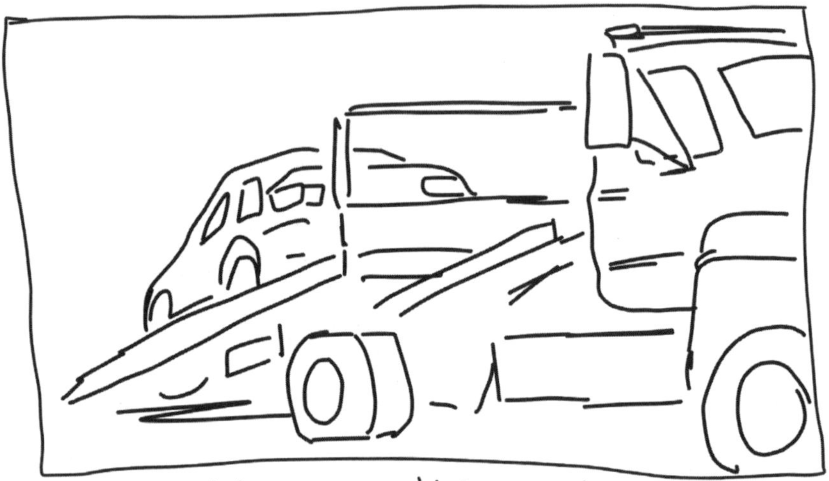

why do I know nothing about nothing?

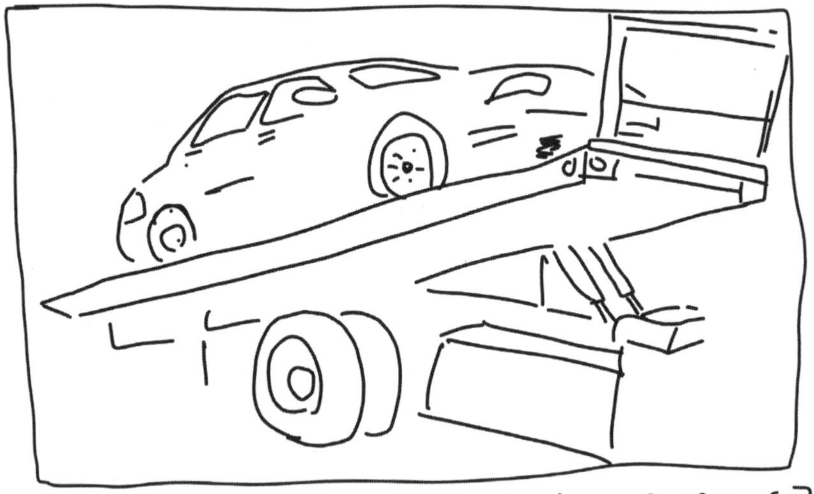

Why do tow truck drivers make me nervous?

I'm always so anxious for them to get there

And they are always gruff, tough

and extremely kind,

which doesn't make me less nervous about small talk on the way to the garage.

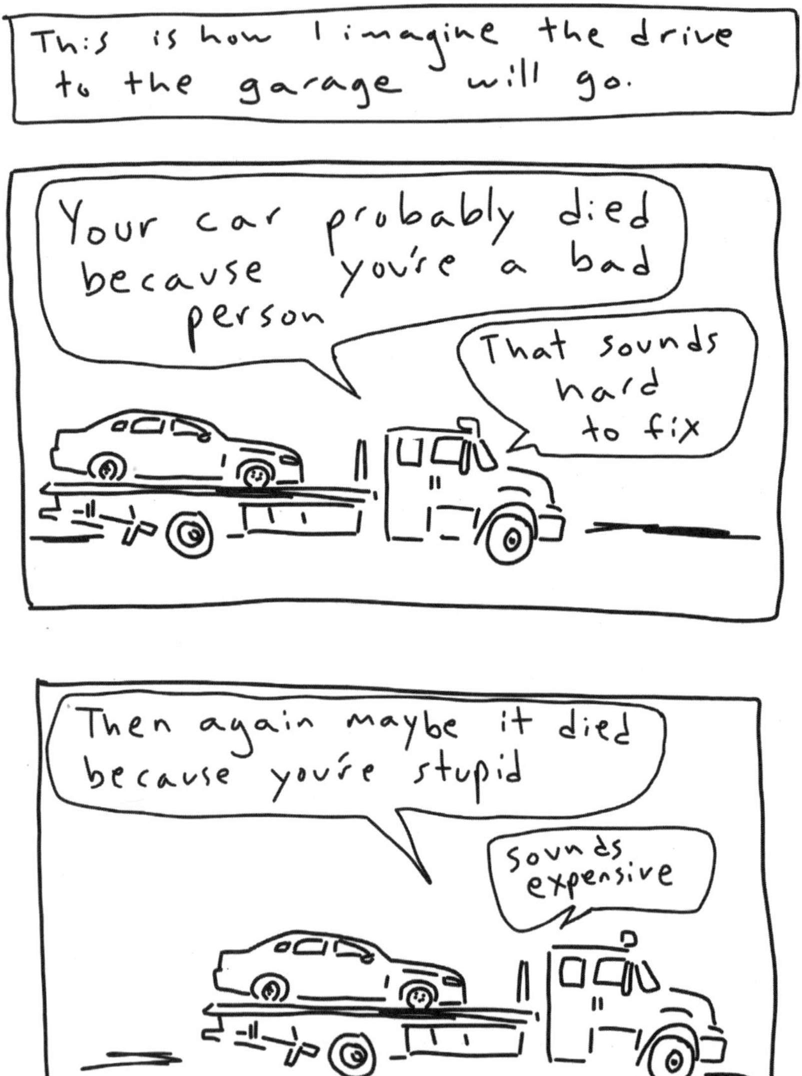
This is how I imagine the drive to the garage will go.
Your car probably died because you're a bad person
That sounds hard to fix
Then again maybe it died because you're stupid
sounds expensive

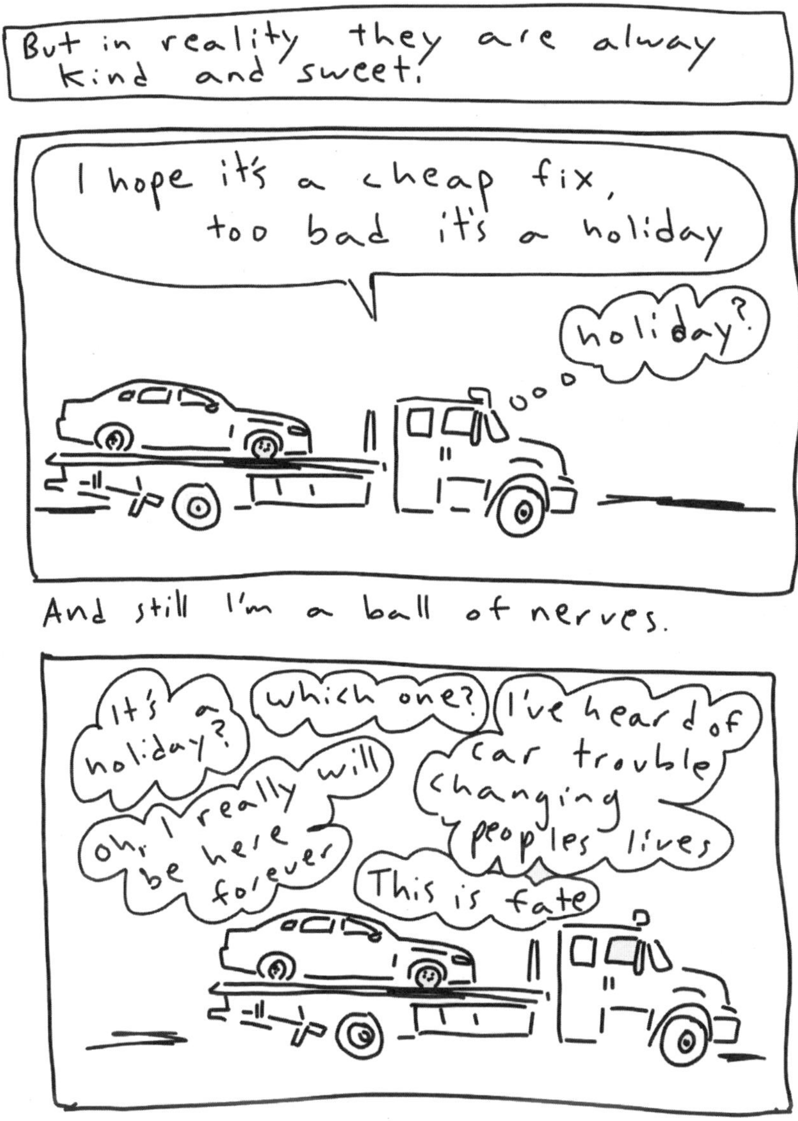
But in reality they are alway kind and sweet.
I hope it's a cheap fix, too bad it's a holiday
holiday?
And still I'm a ball of nerves.
It's a holiday?
which one?
I've heard of car trouble changing peoples lives
Oh, I really will be here forever
This is fate

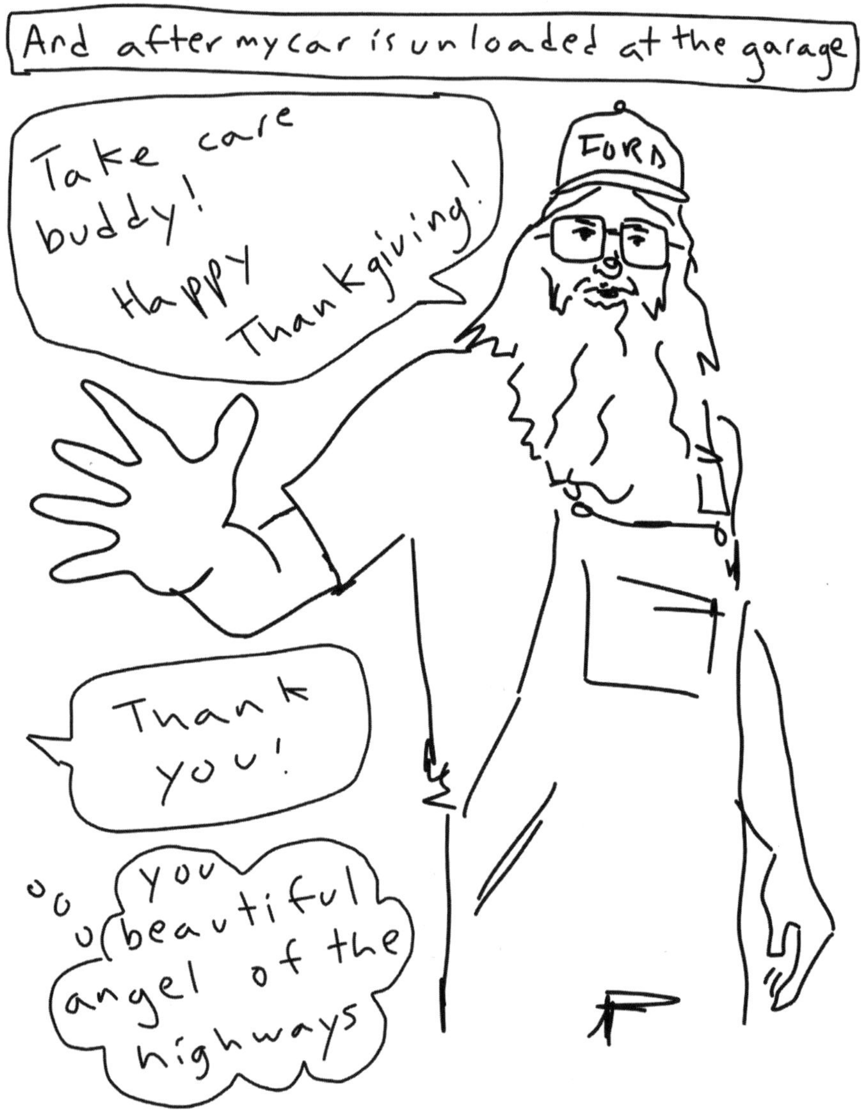
And after my car is unloaded at the garage
Take care buddy! Happy Thankgiving!
FORD
Thank you!
you beautiful angel of the highways

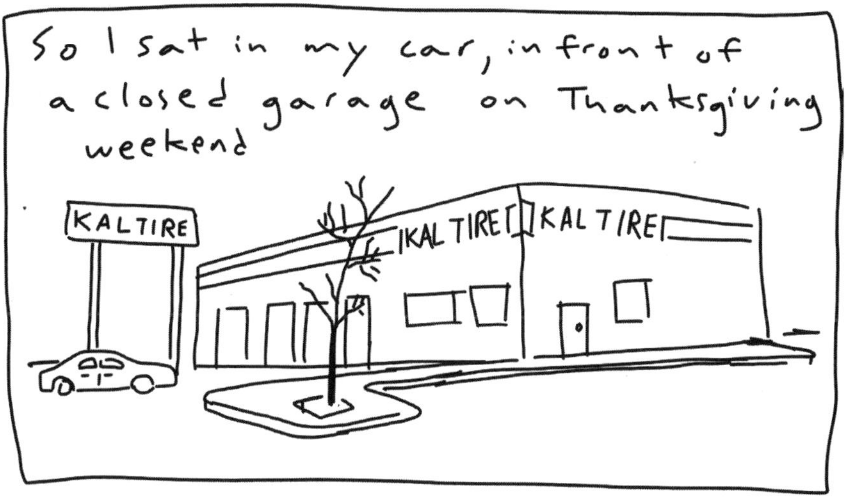
So I sat in my car, in front of a closed garage on Thanksgiving weekend
KALTIRE
KAL TIRE
KAL TIRE

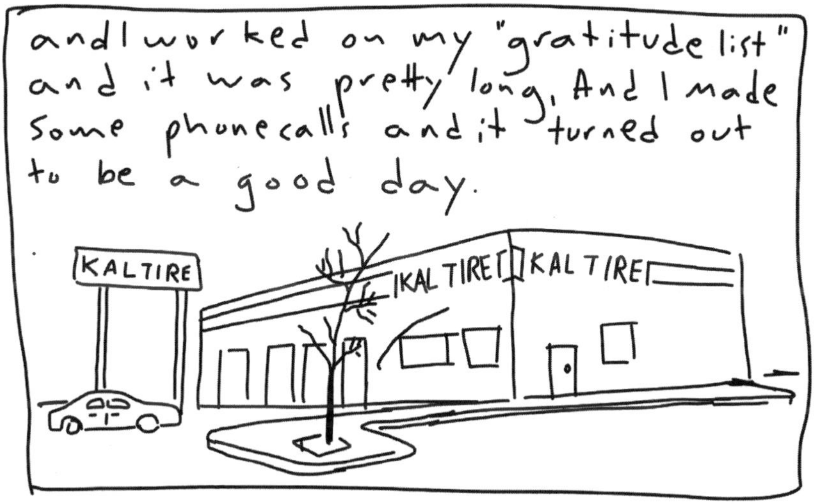
and I worked on my "gratitude list" and it was pretty long. And I made some phonecalls and it turned out to be a good day.
KALTIRE
KAL TIRE
KAL TIRE

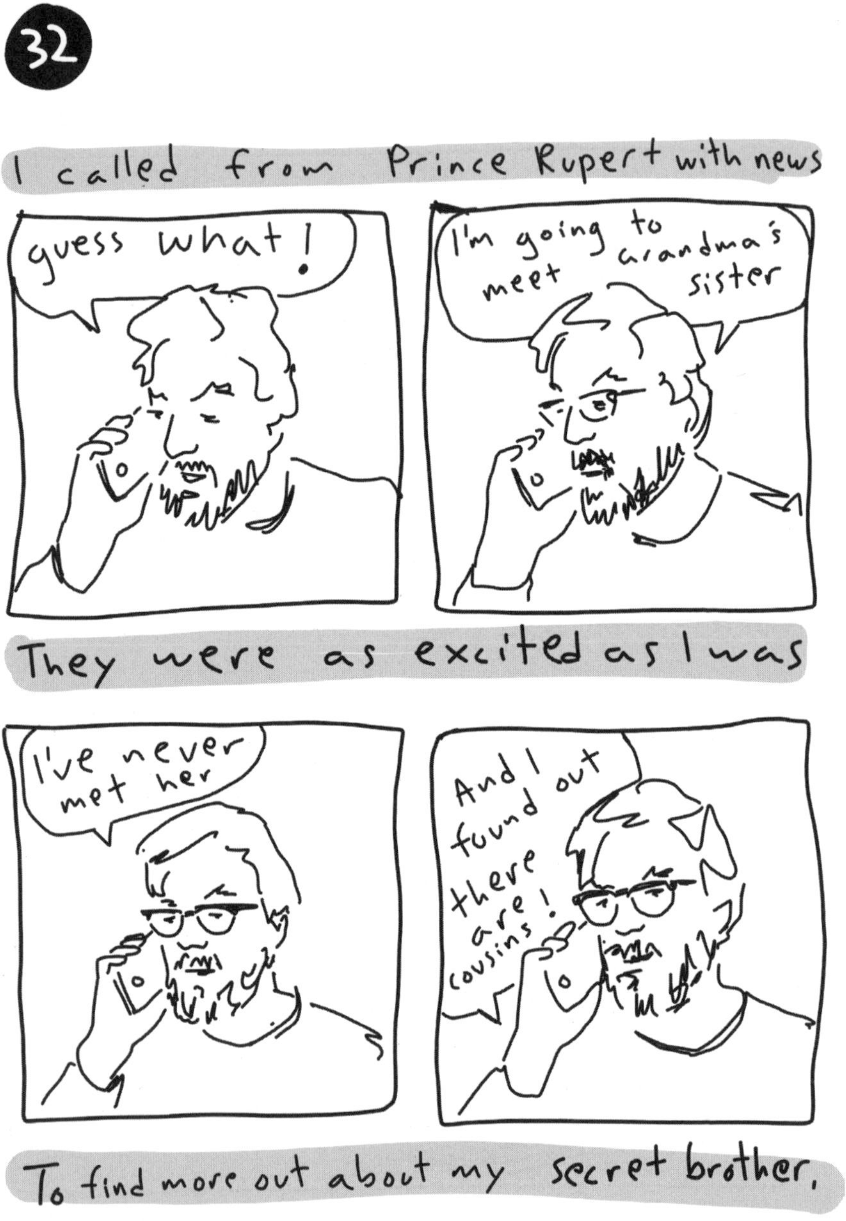
32
I called from Prince Rupert with news
guess what!
I'm going to meet grandma's sister
They were as excited as I was
I've never met her
And I found out there are cousins!
To find more out about my secret brother.

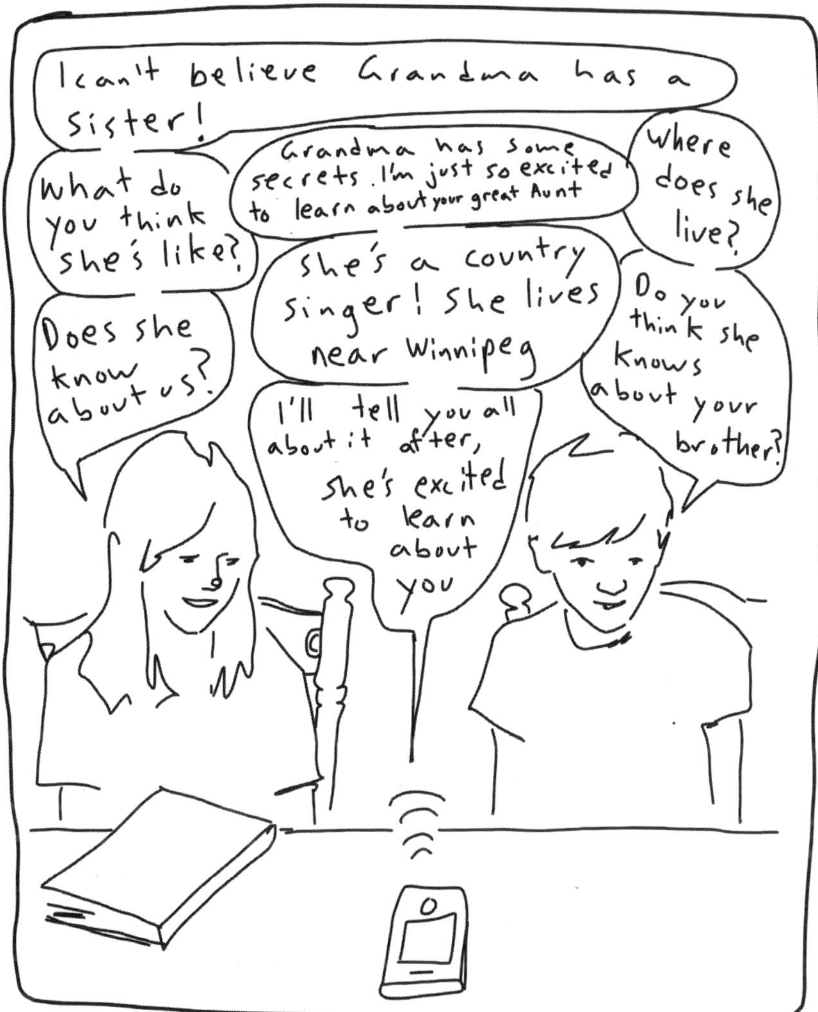
I can't believe Grandma has a sister!
What do you think she's like?
Grandma has some secrets. I'm just so excited to learn about your great Aunt
Where does she live?
Does she know about us?
She's a country singer! She lives near Winnipeg
Do you think she knows about your brother?
I'll tell you all about it after, she's excited to learn about you

33

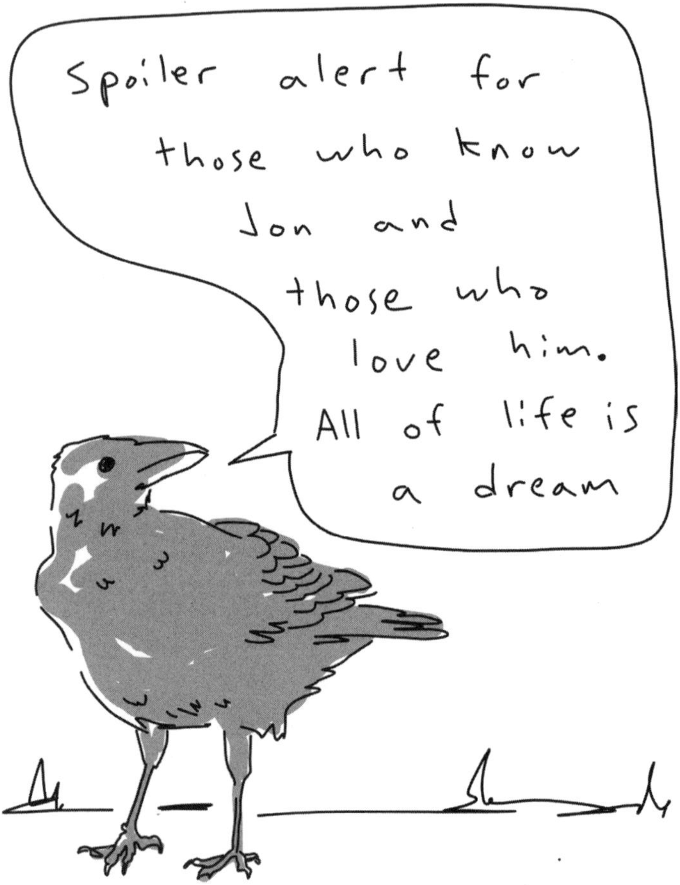
Spoiler alert for those who know Jon and those who love him. All of life is a dream

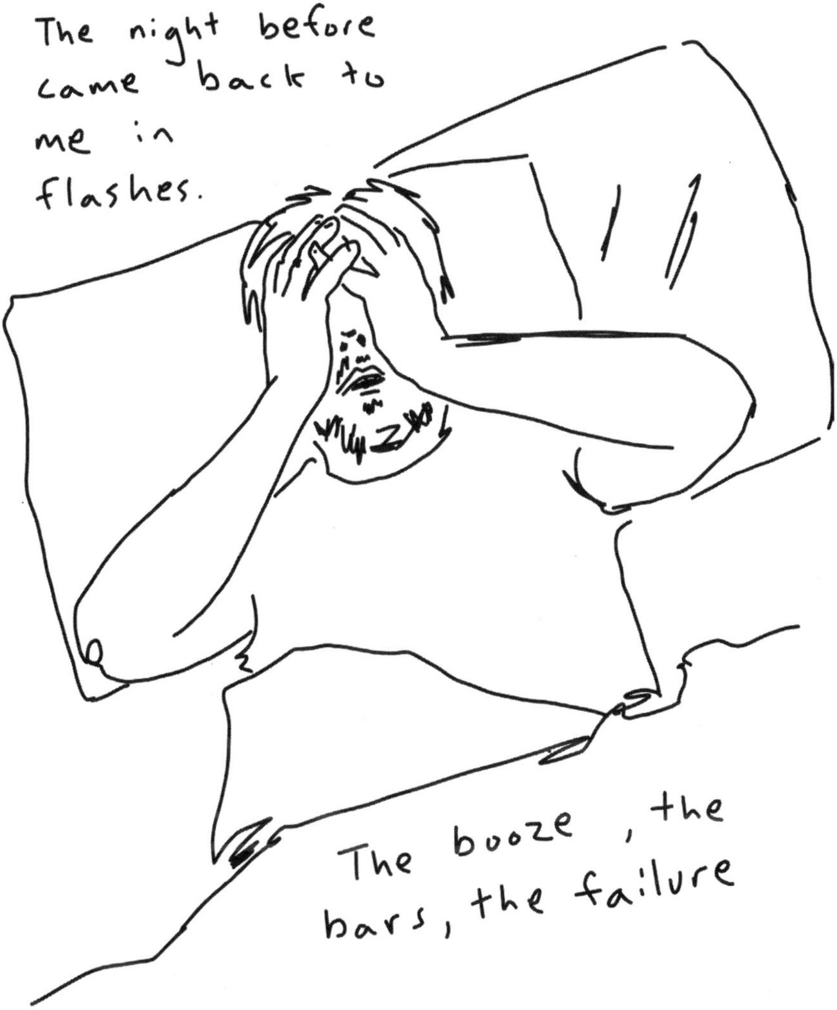
The night before came back to me in flashes.
The booze, the bars, the failure

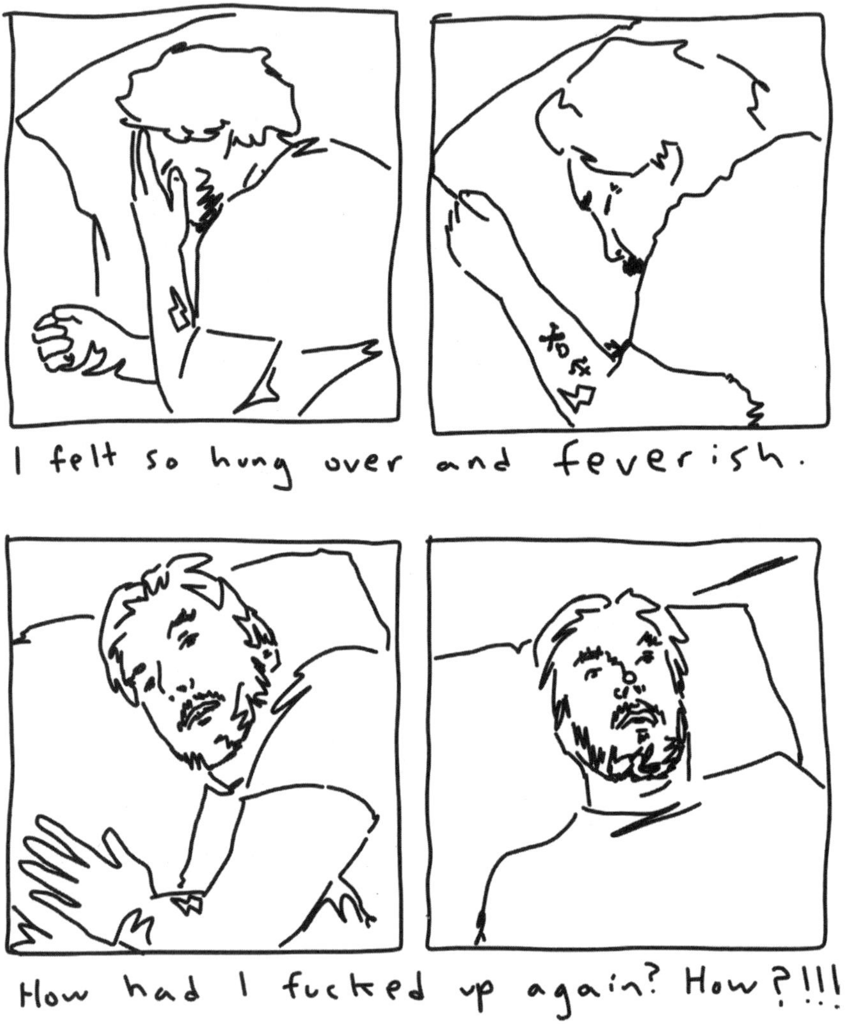
I felt so hung over and feverish.
How had I fucked up again? How?!!!

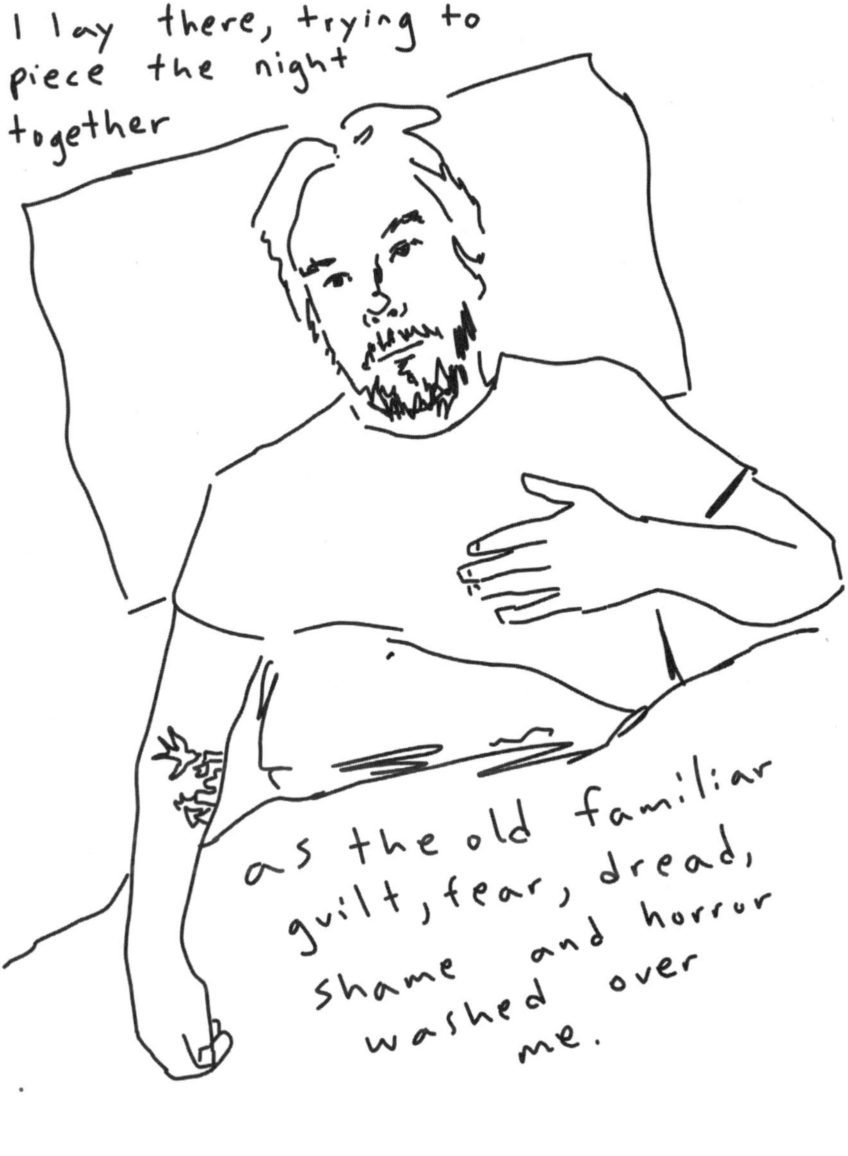
I lay there, trying to piece the night together
as the old familiar guilt, fear, dread, shame and horror washed over me.

I remembered searching the studio for a bottle I was sure I had seen on the piano. but they had moved it.

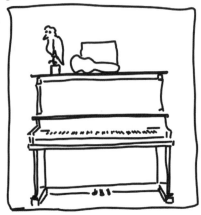

All I could find was mouse traps.
VICTOR
They had to have booze for events.

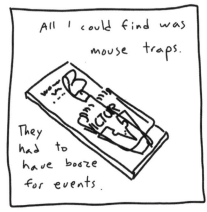

I kept looking until I found something.

ST-REMY
AUTHENTIC

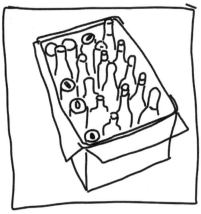

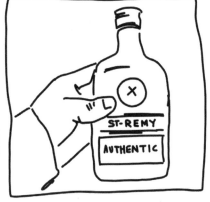

A box of relapse deep in the closet.

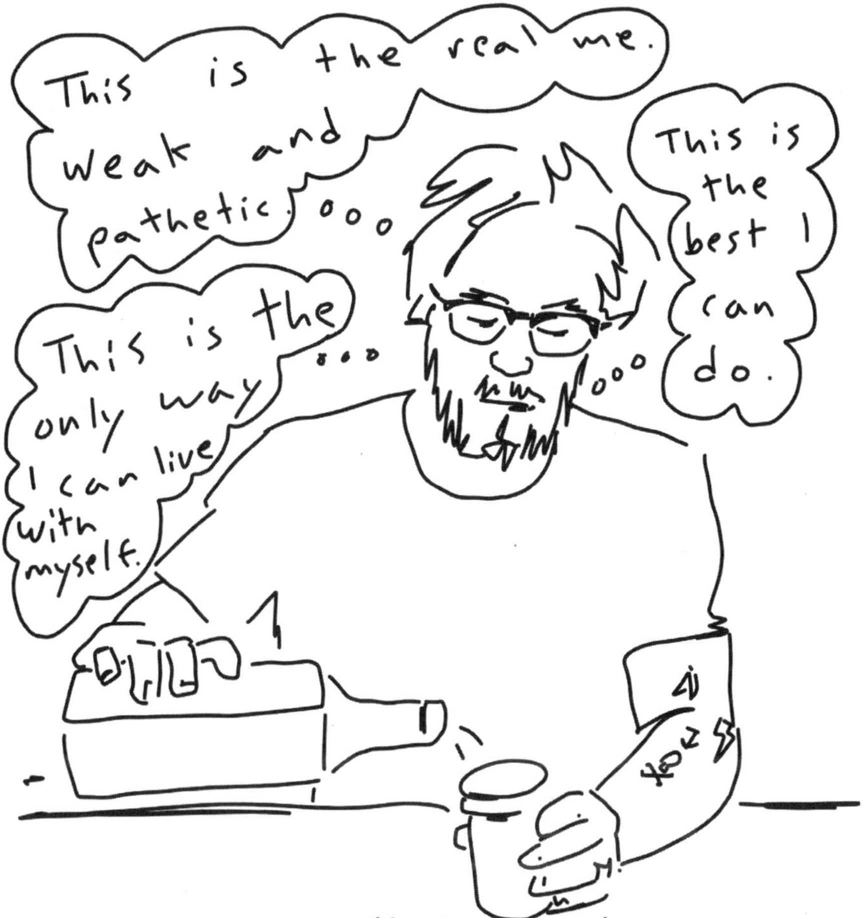
This is the real me. weak and pathetic.
This is the only way I can live with myself.
This is the best I can do.

In hazy recollection I saw myself throwing away 1 ½ years of sobriety.

And somehow I found my way to a bar.

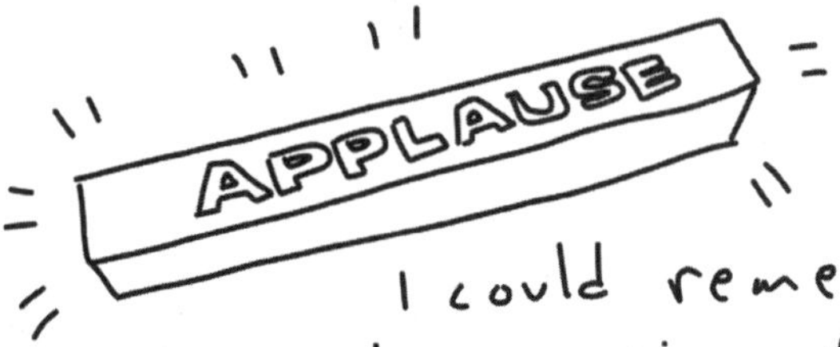
APPLAUSE

I could remember an applause sign flashing.

Was Glenn from back home bartending?

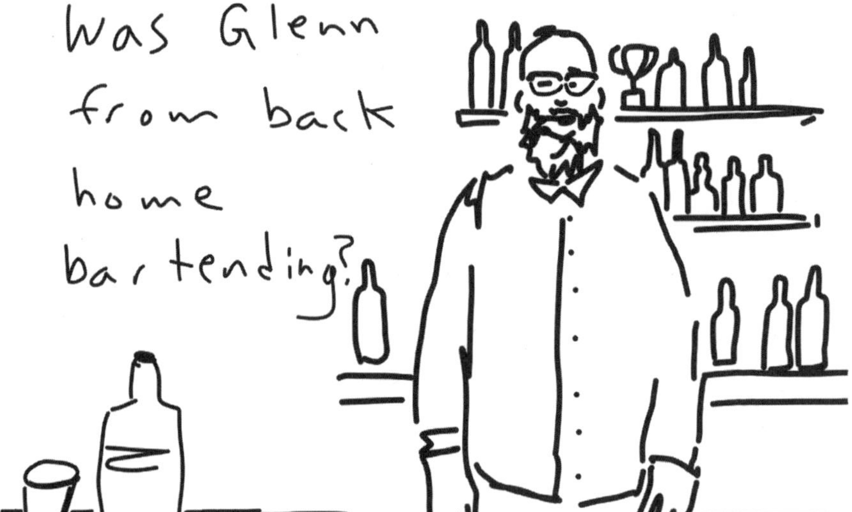

what the fuck happened last night?

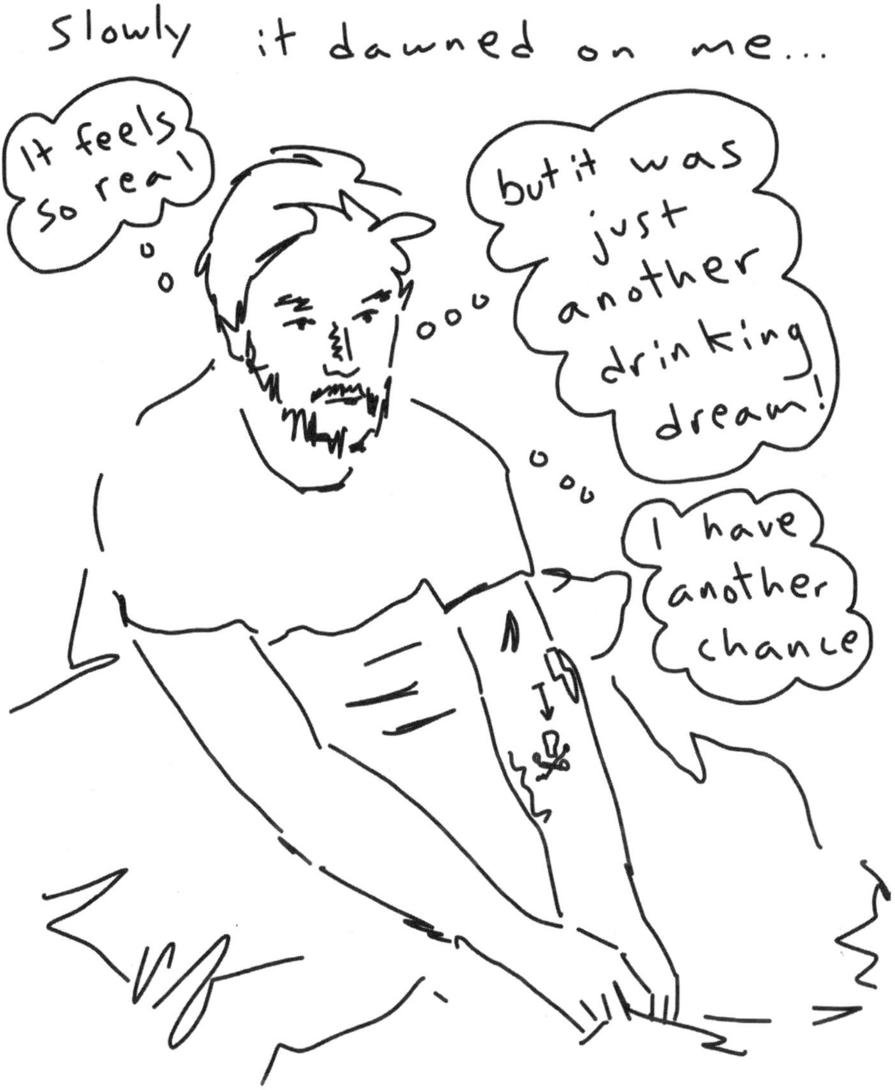
Slowly it dawned on me...
It feels so real
but it was just another drinking dream!
I have another chance

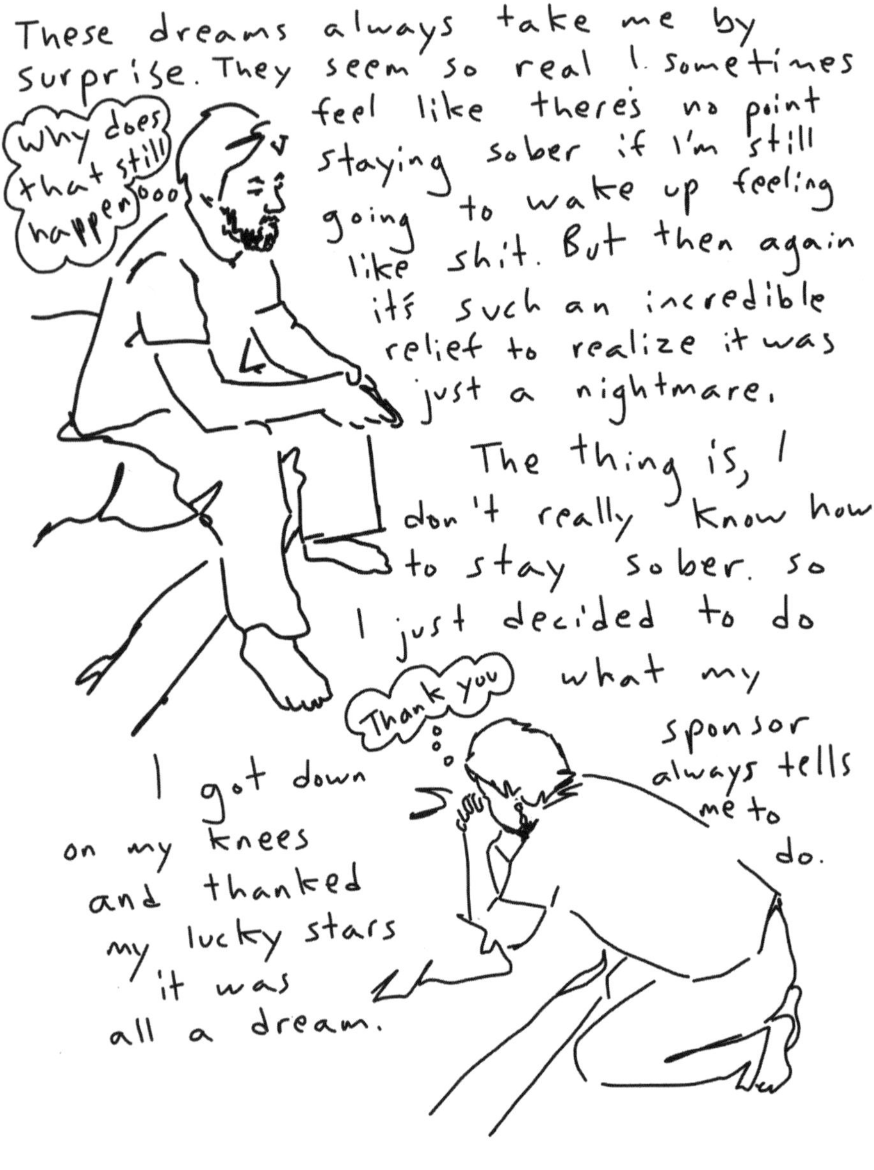
These dreams always take me by surprise. They seem so real I. Sometimes feel like there's no point staying sober if I'm still going to wake up feeling like shit. But then again it's such an incredible relief to realize it was just a nightmare.
Why does that still happen
The thing is, I don't really know how to stay sober. So I just decided to do what my sponsor always tells me to do.
Thank you
I got down on my knees and thanked my lucky stars it was all a dream.

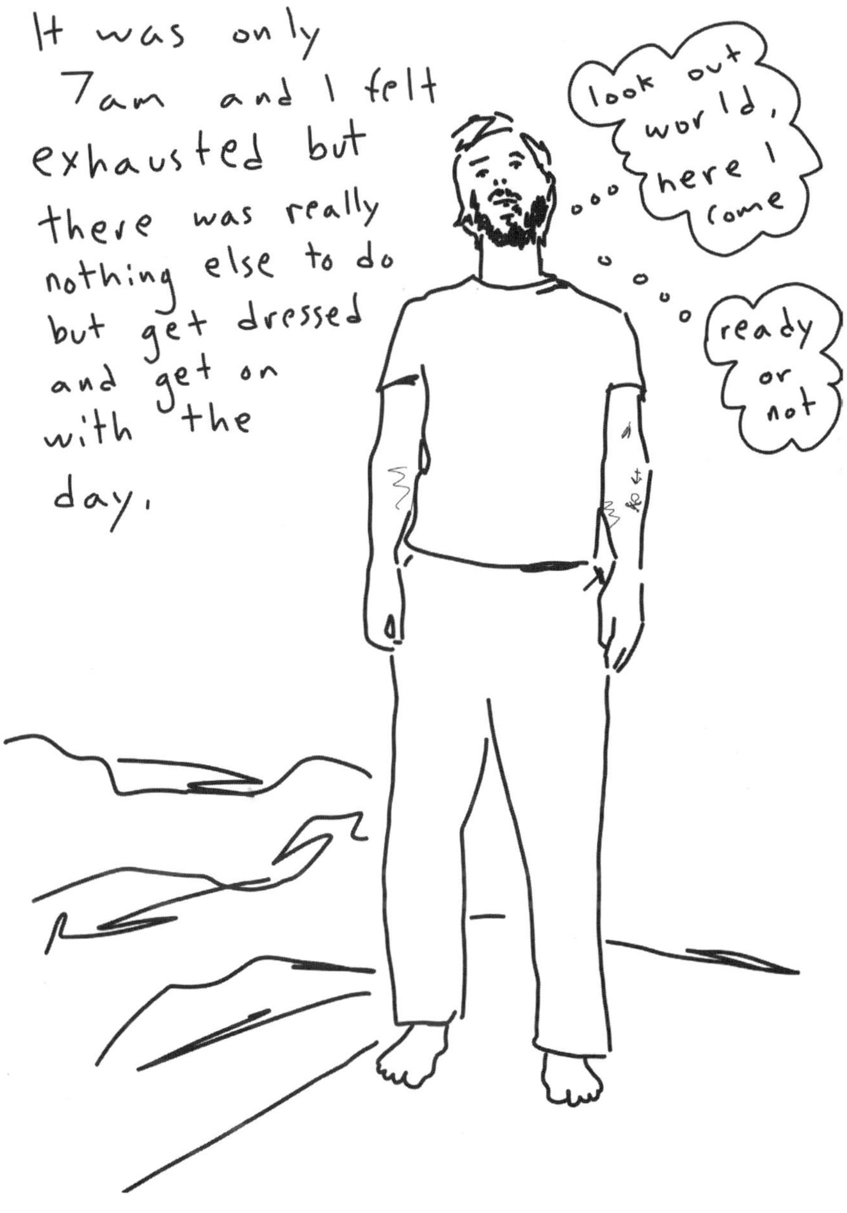
It was only 7am and I felt exhausted but there was really nothing else to do but get dressed and get on with the day.
look out world, here I come
ready or not

34

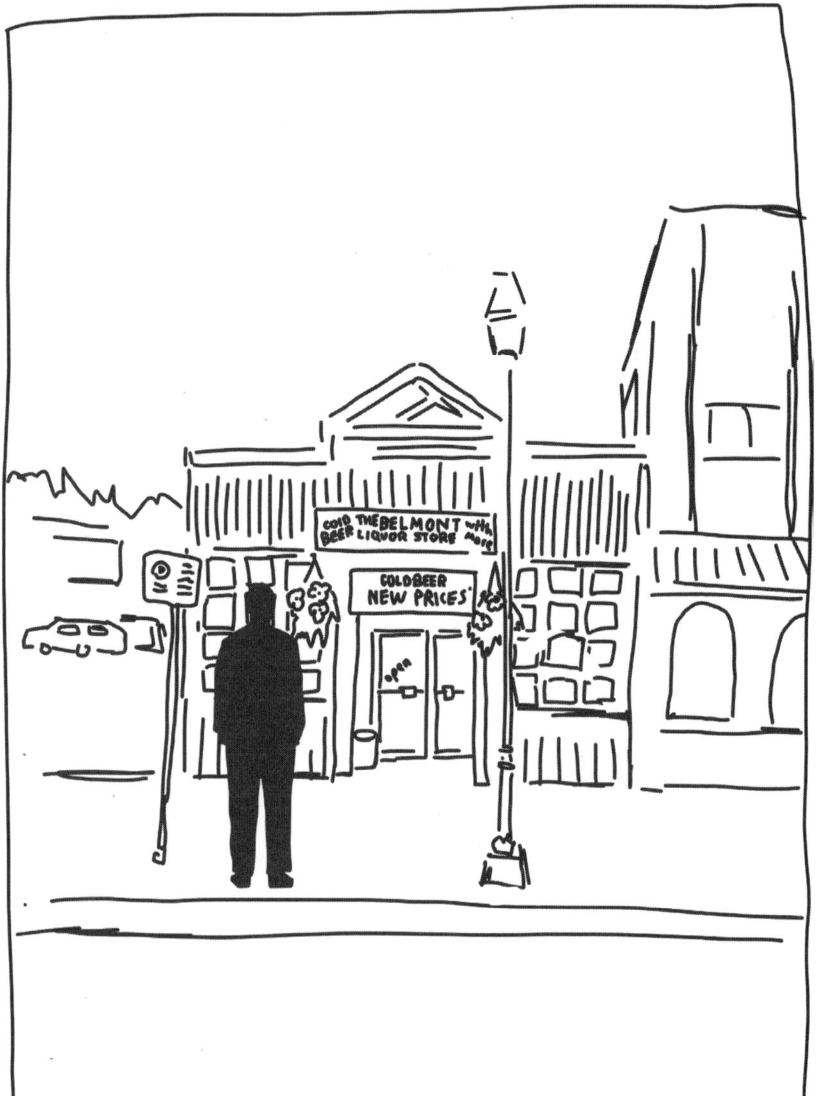
COLD BEER
THE BELMONT LIQUOR STORE
with more
COLD BEER NEW PRICES
open

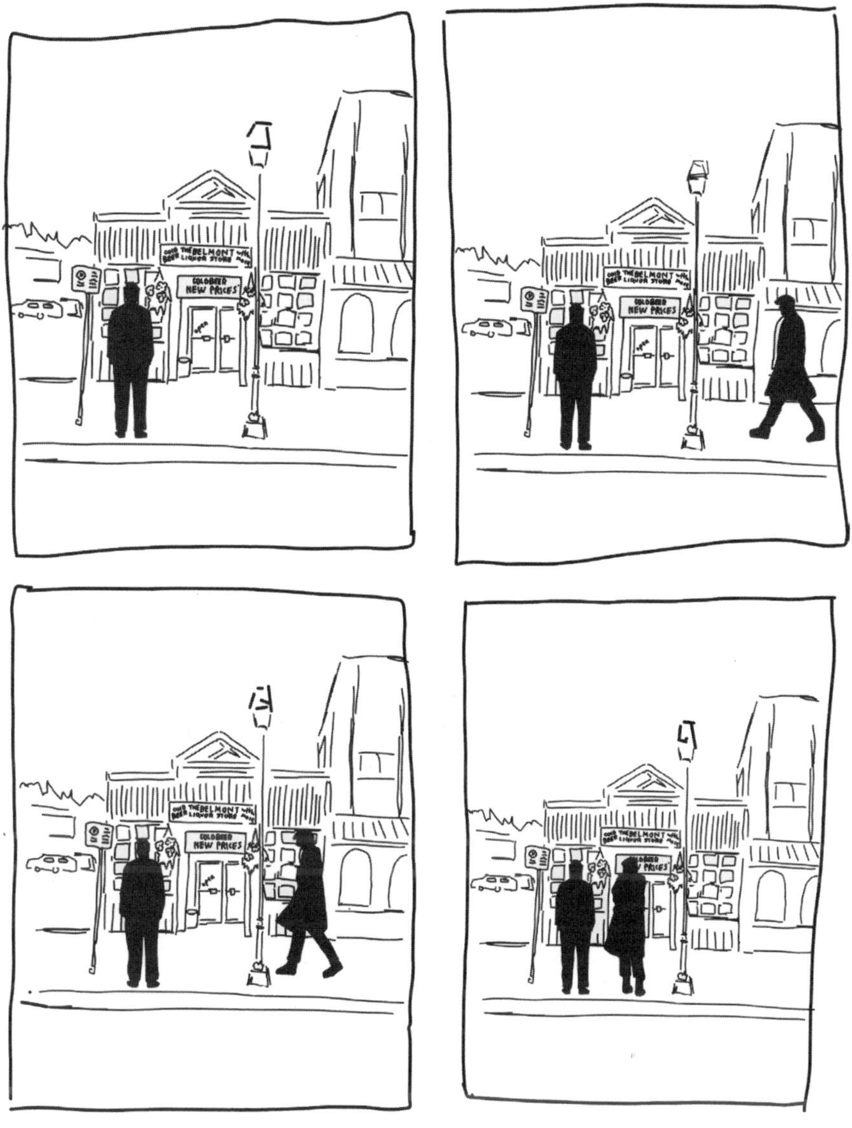
THE BELMONT
LIQUOR STORE
NEW PRICES

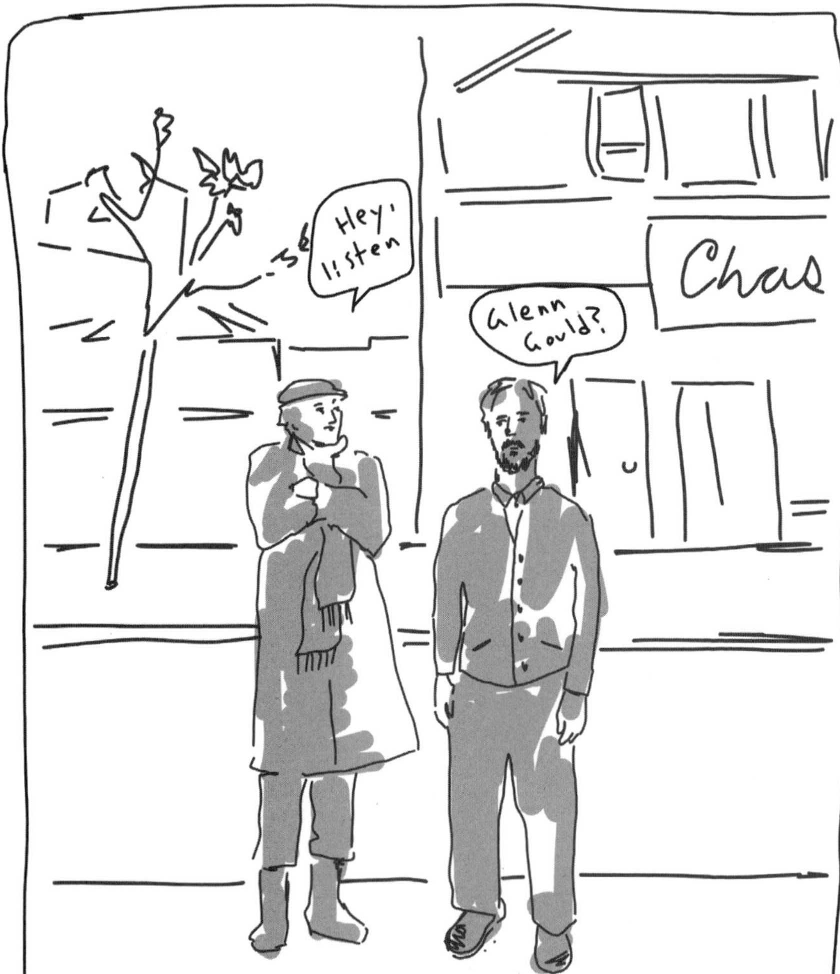
Hey, listen
Glenn Gould?
Chas

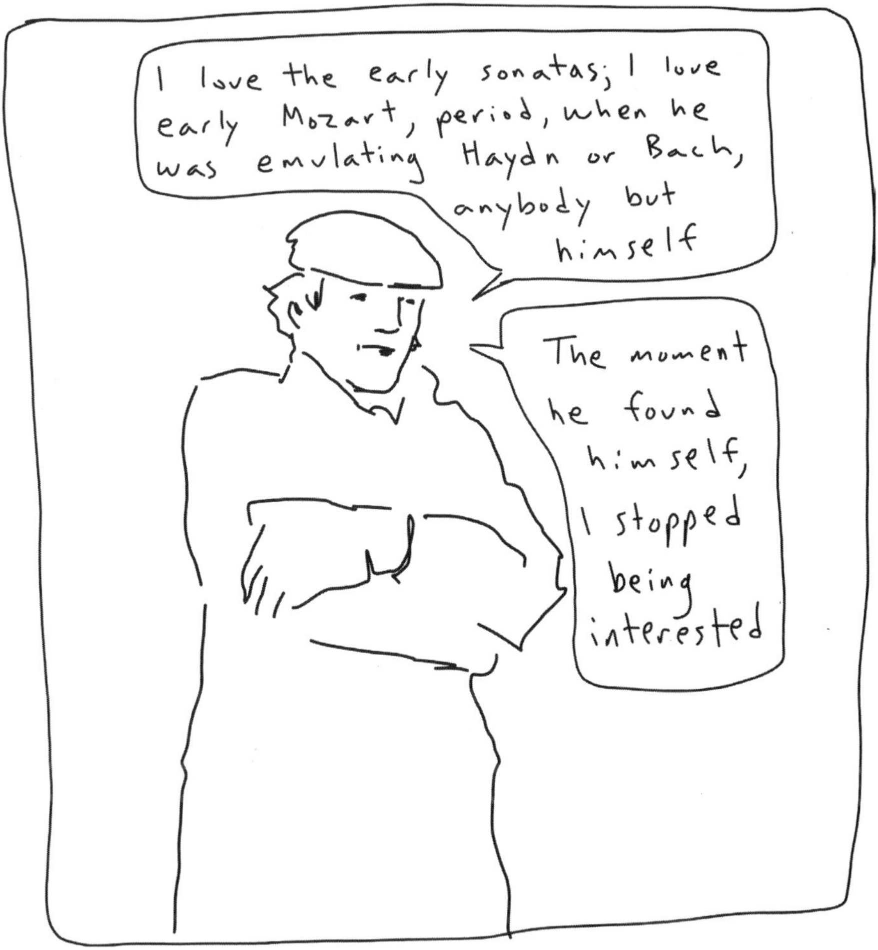
I love the early sonatas; I love early Mozart, period, when he was emulating Haydn or Bach, anybody but himself
The moment he found himself, I stopped being interested

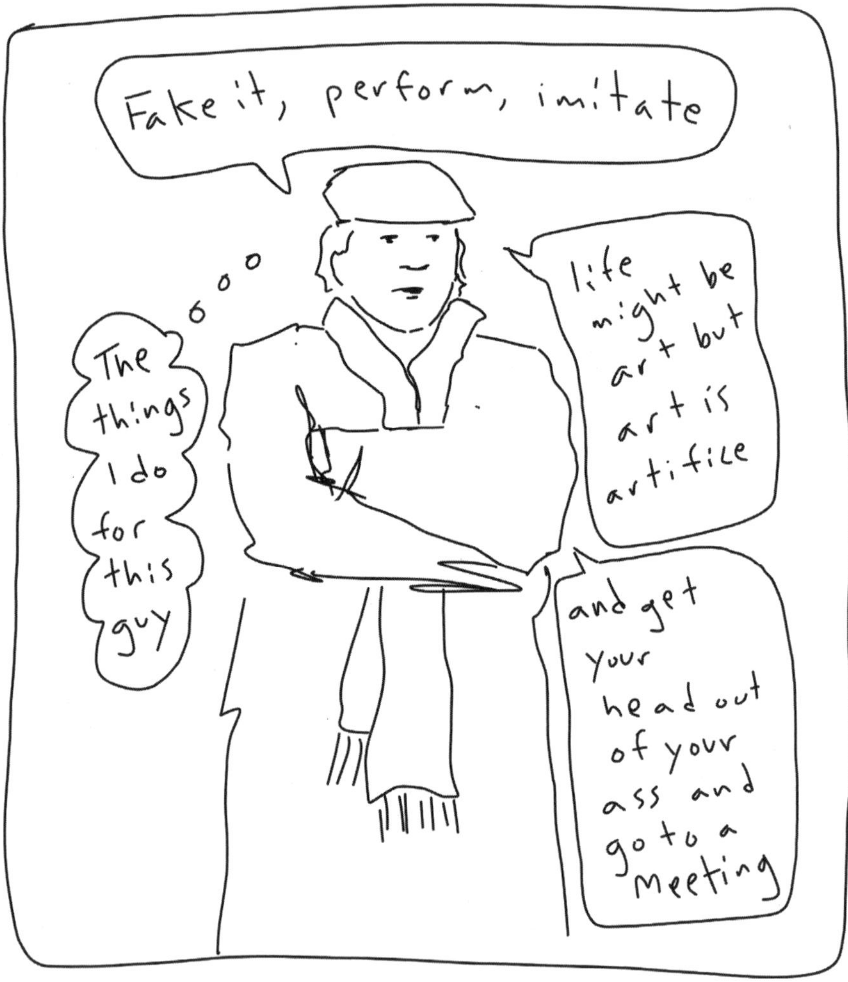
Fake it, perform, imitate
The things I do for this guy
life might be art but art is artifice
and get your head out of your ass and go to a meeting

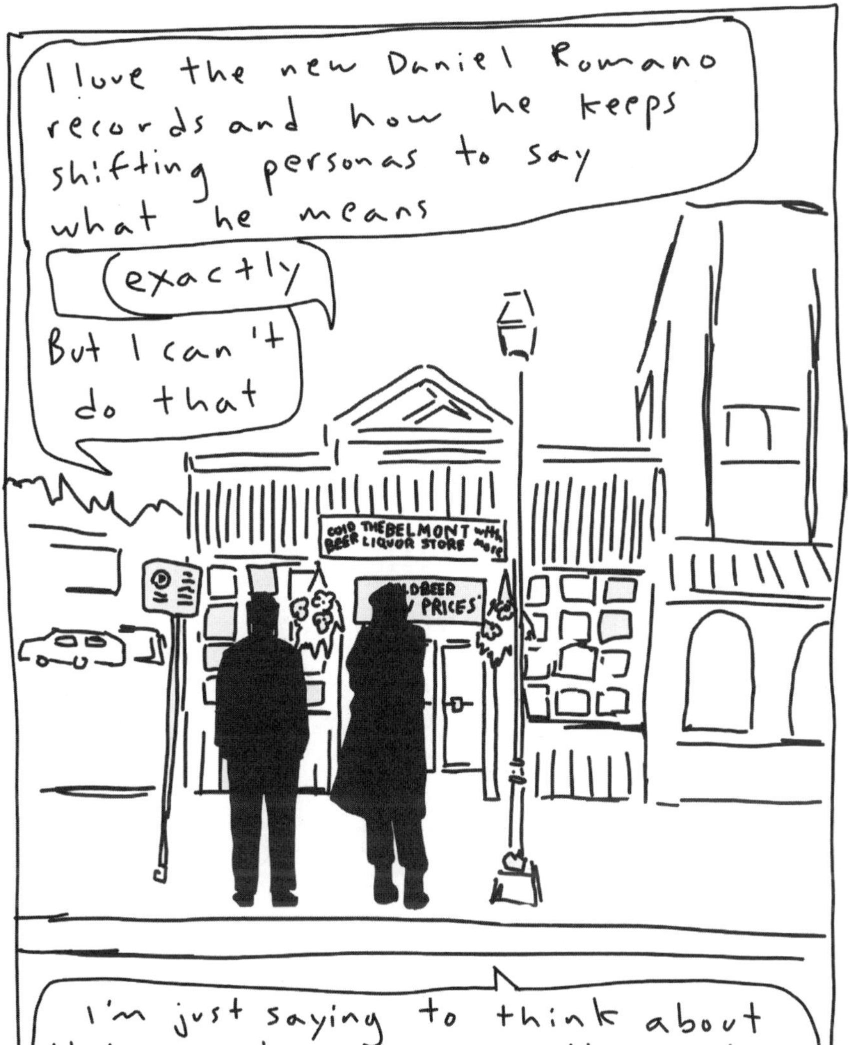

I love the new Daniel Romano records and how he keeps shifting personas to say what he means
exactly
But I can't do that
COLD BEER THE BELMONT LIQUOR STORE with more
LDBEER PRICES
I'm just saying to think about it 'cause being you ain't working

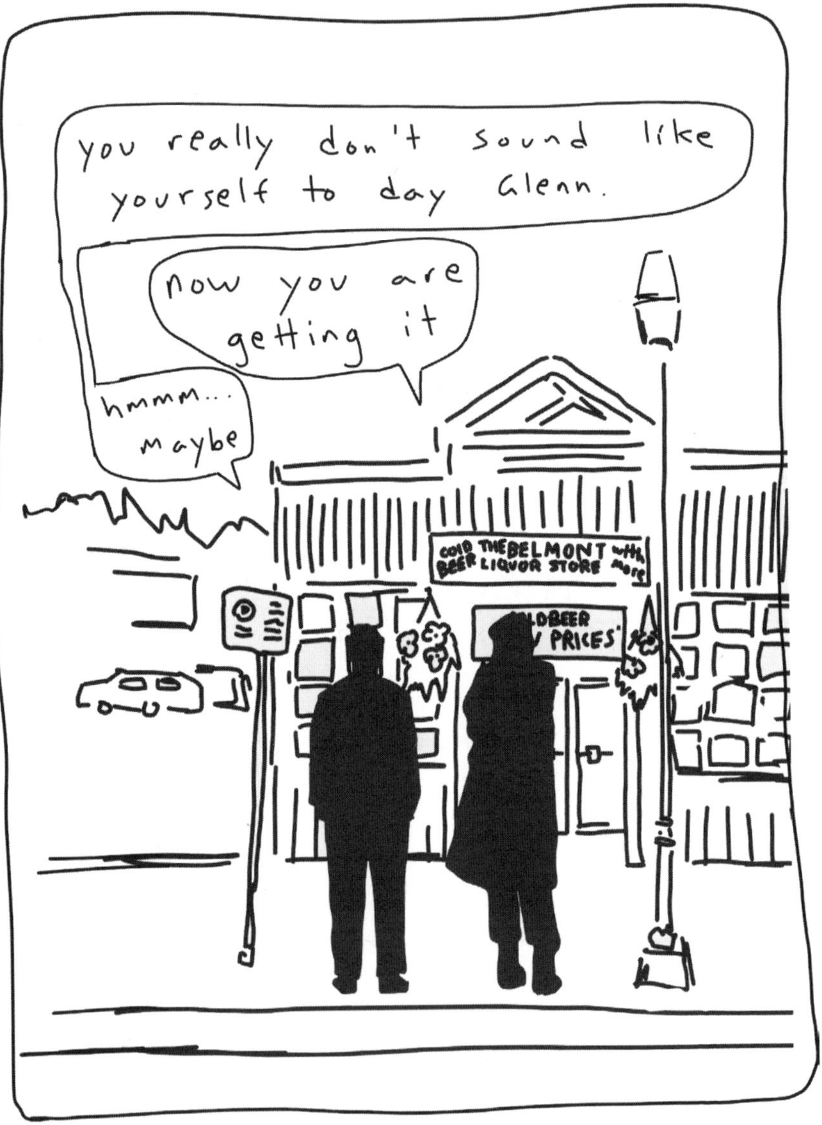
you really don't sound like yourself to day Glenn.
now you are getting it
hmmm... maybe
COLD BEER
THE BELMONT LIQUOR STORE
with more
PRICES

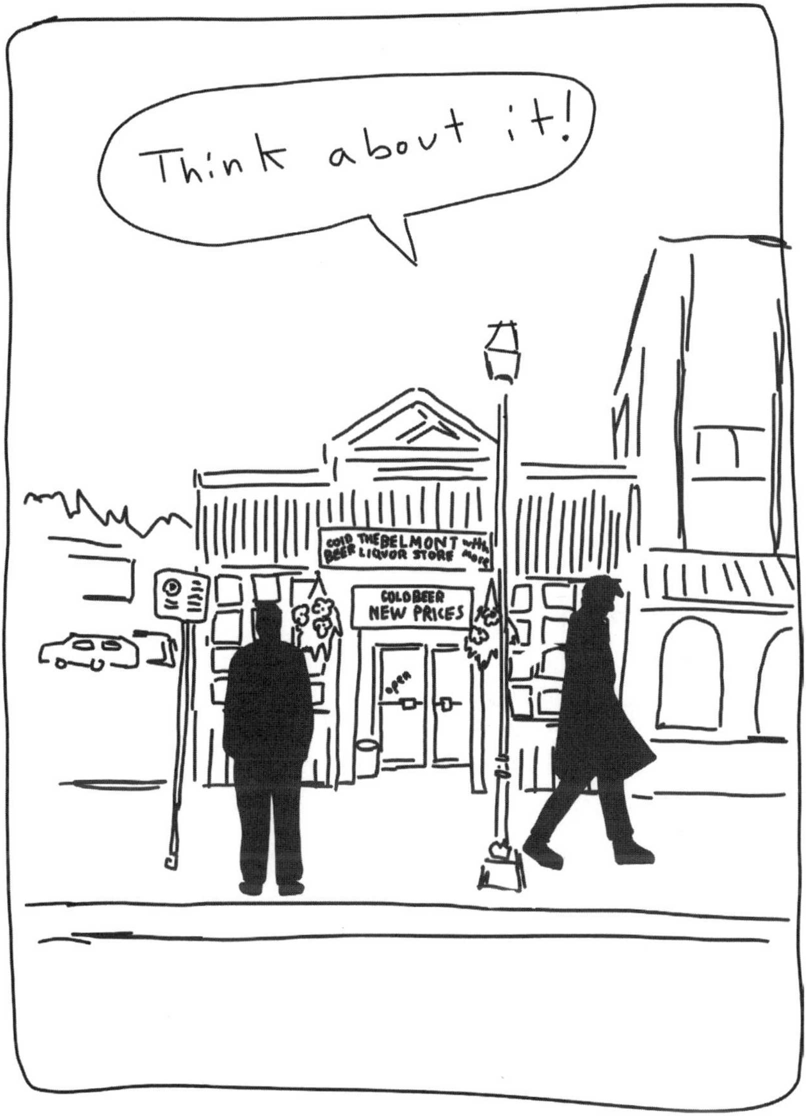
Think about it!
COLD BEER
THE BELMONT LIQUOR STORE
COLD BEER NEW PRICES
open

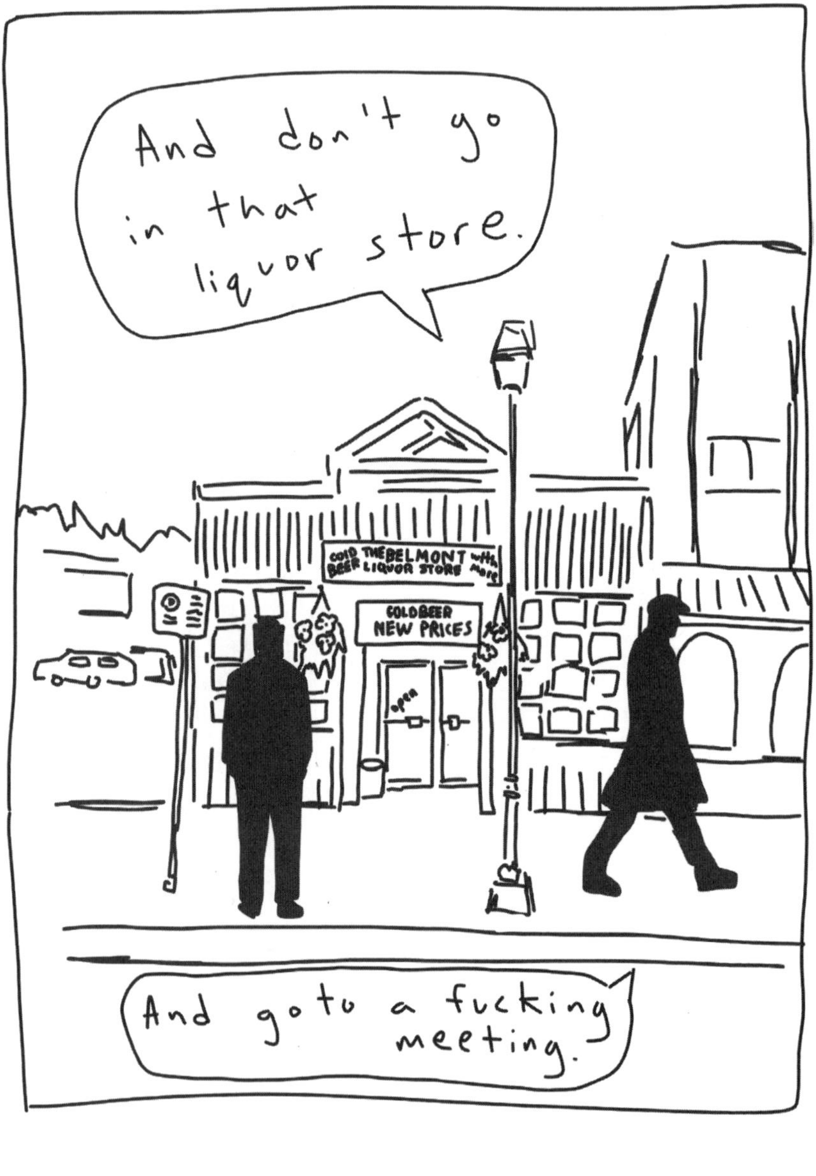
And don't go in that liquor store.
COLD BEER
THE BELMONT LIQUOR STORE
with more
COLD BEER NEW PRICES
open
And go to a fucking meeting.

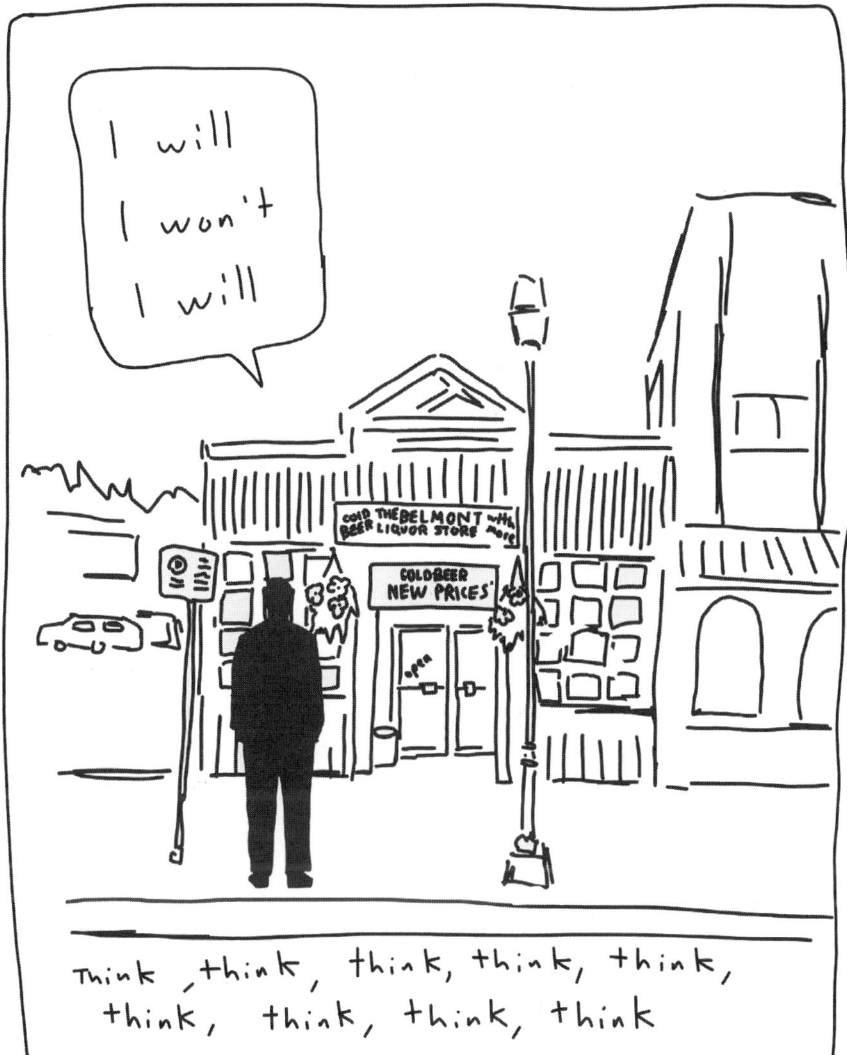
I will
I won't
I will
THE BELMONT LIQUOR STORE
COLD BEER NEW PRICES'
Think, think, think, think, think,
think, think, think, think

35

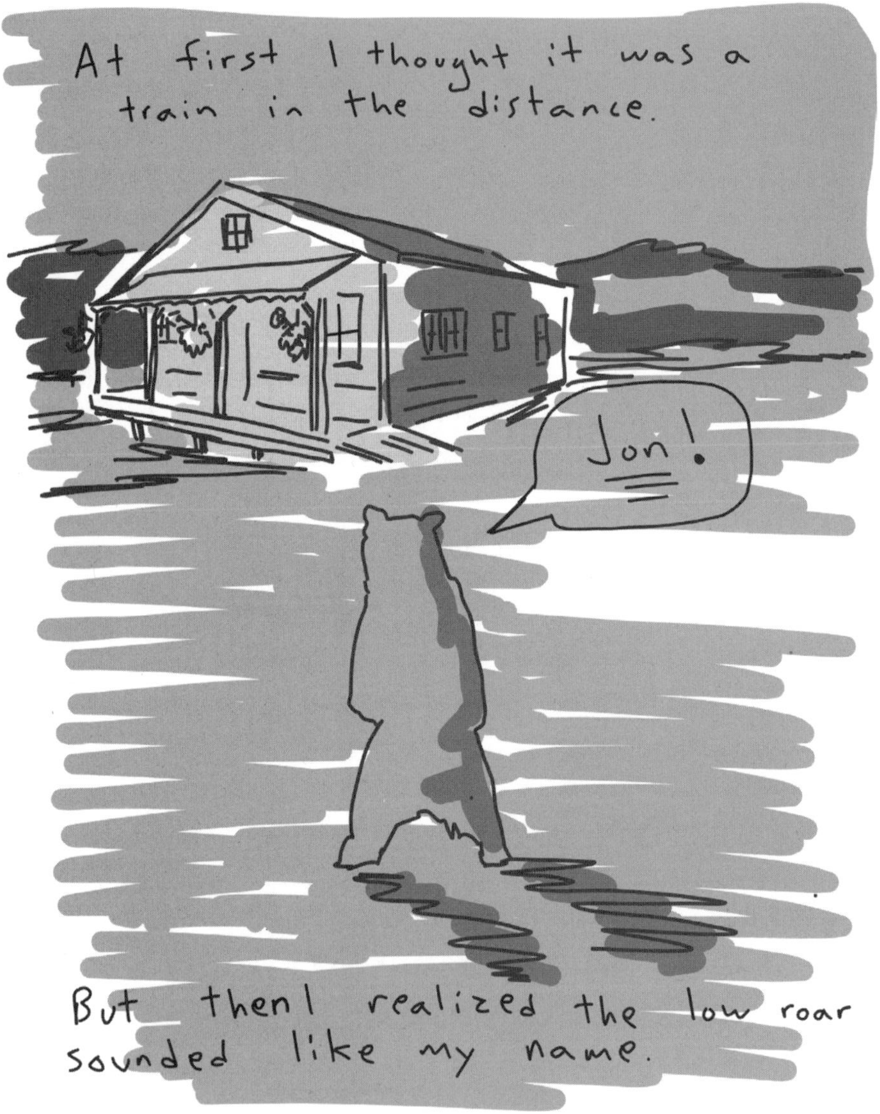
At first I thought it was a train in the distance.
Jon!
But then I realized the low roar sounded like my name.

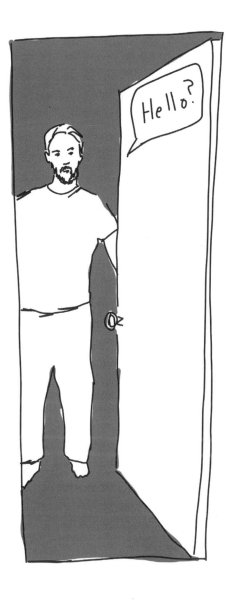

I opened
the door.

It was
going to
be one
of those

days.

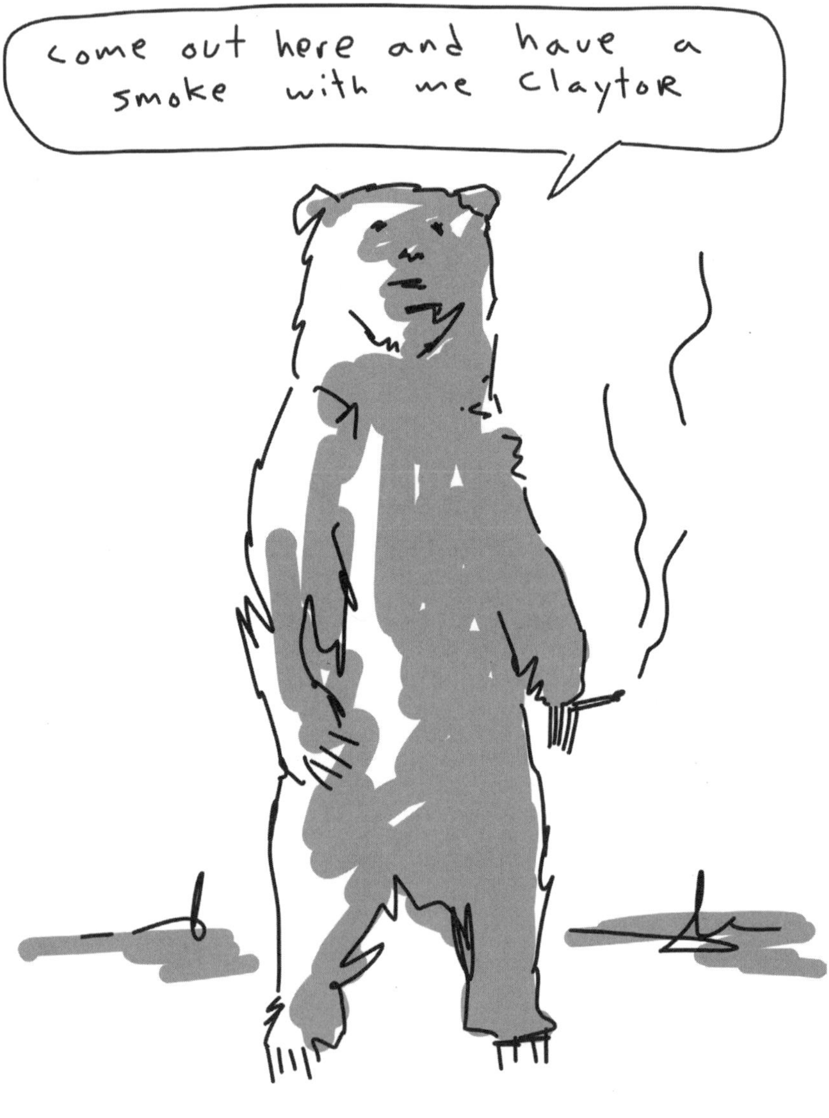
come out here and have a smoke with me Claytor

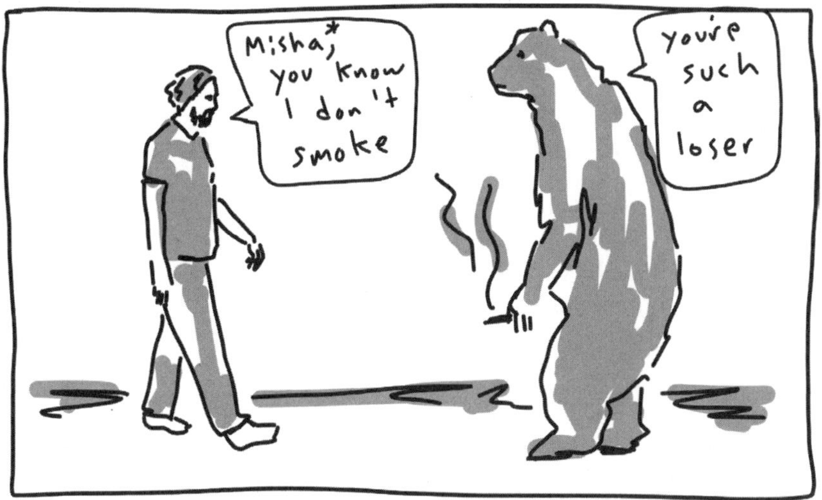
Misha,* you know I don't smoke
you're such a loser

I walked over to say hi to the bear.

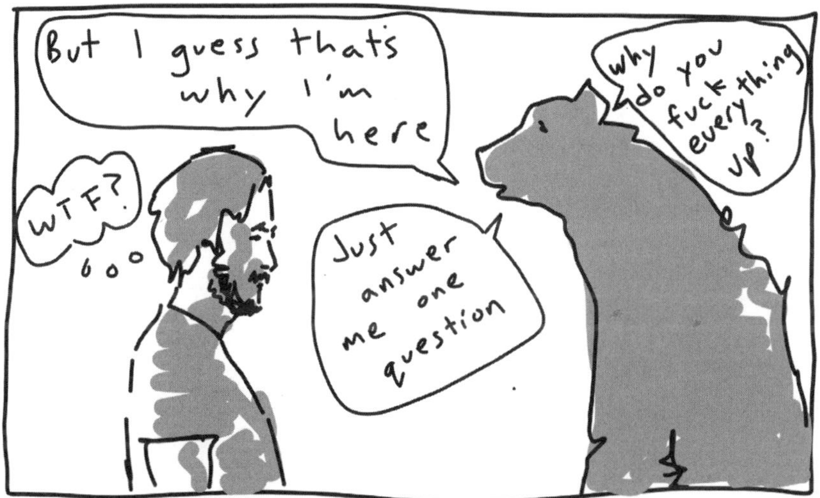
But I guess that's why I'm here
why do you fuck every thing up?
WTF?
Just answer me one question

*we had met before at a music festival in Sackville.

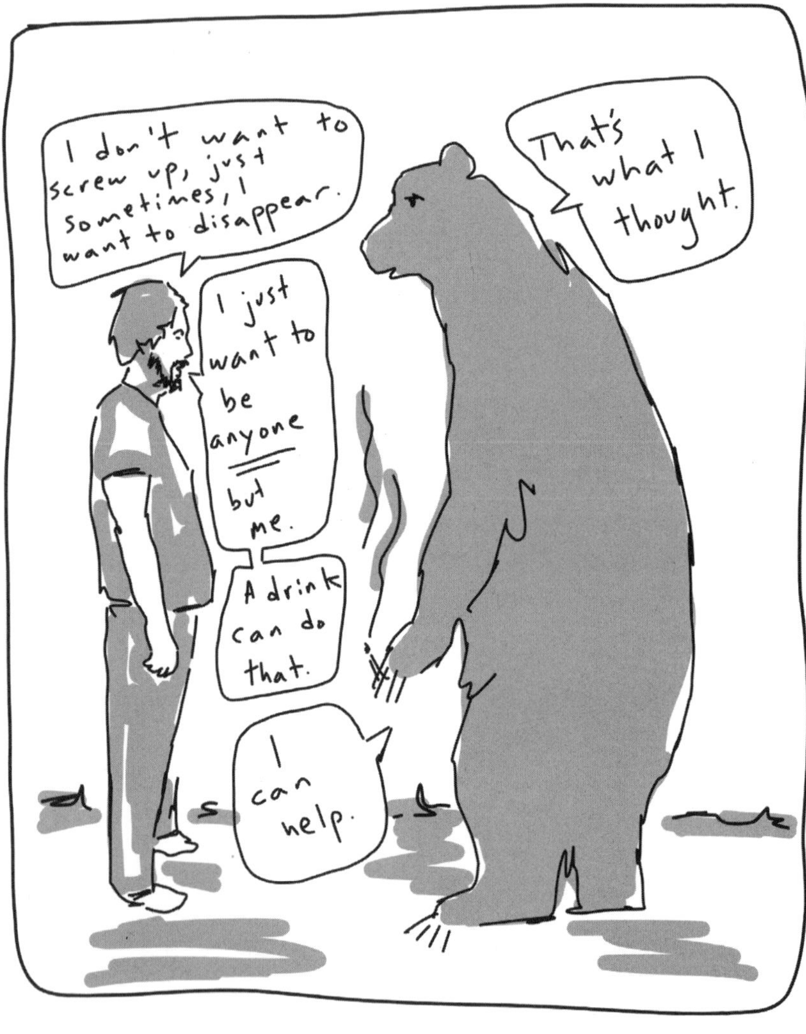
I don't want to screw up, just sometimes, I want to disappear.
I just want to be anyone but me.
A drink can do that.
I can help.
That's what I thought.

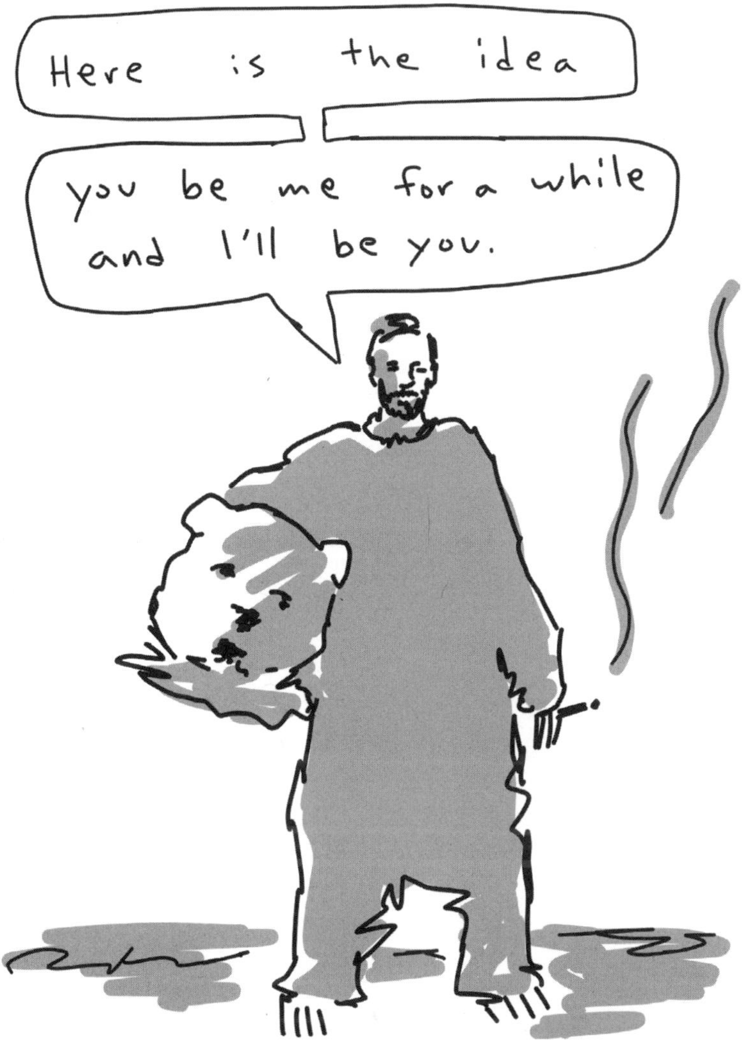
Here is the idea
you be me for a while and I'll be you.

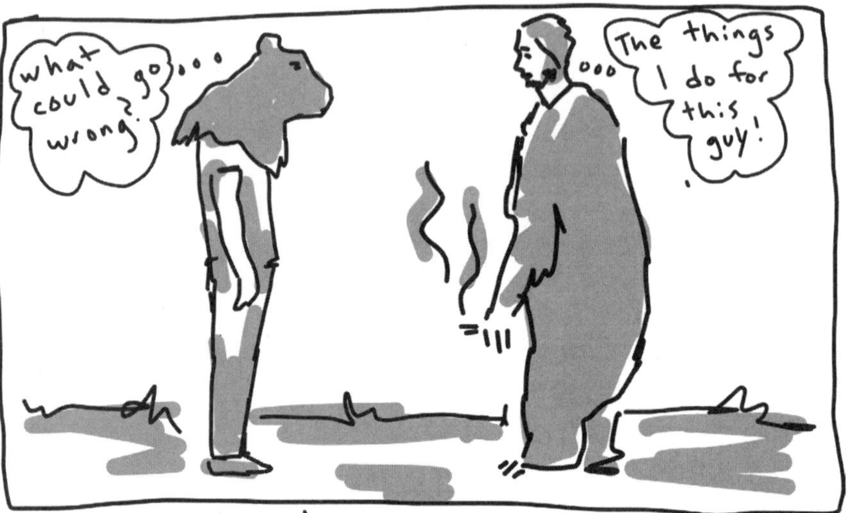
what could go wrong?
The things I do for this guy!

It seemed like a good idea.

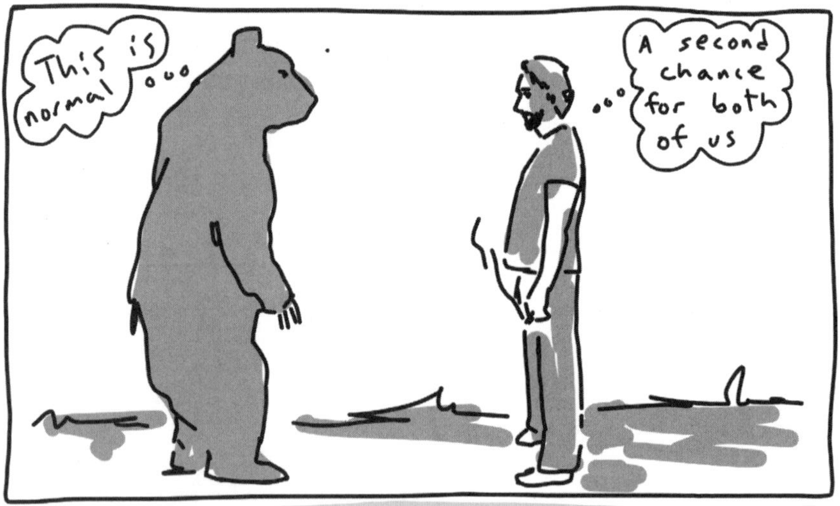
This is normal
A second chance for both of us

So I became a bear and the bear became me.

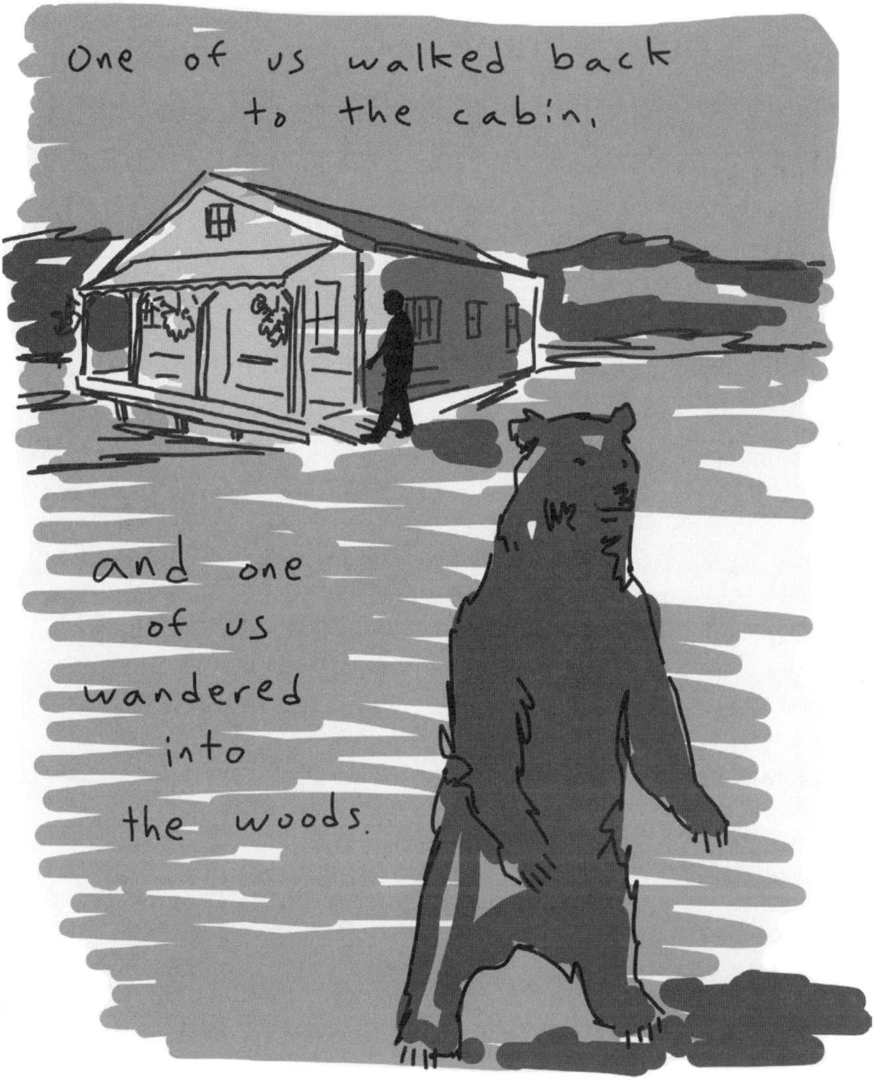
One of us walked back
to the cabin,
and one
of us
wandered
into
the woods.

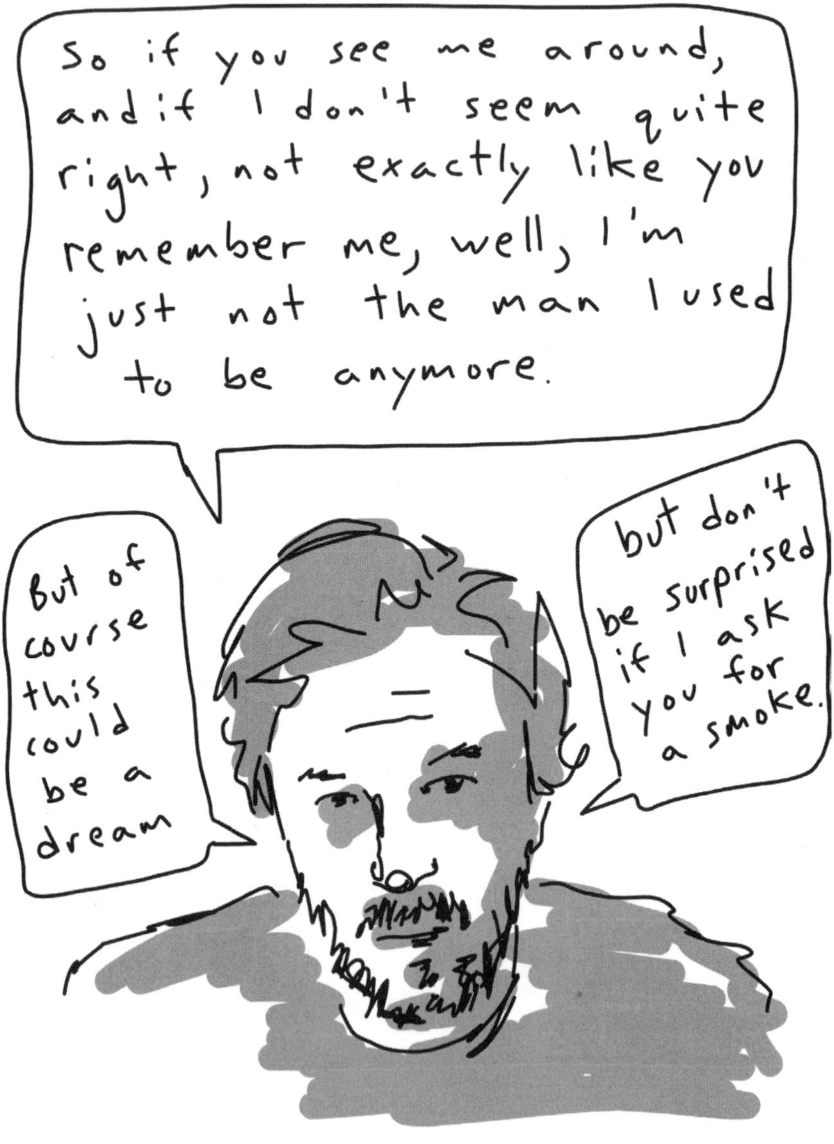
So if you see me around, and if I don't seem quite right, not exactly like you remember me, well, I'm just not the man I used to be anymore.
But of course this could be a dream
but don't be surprised if I ask you for a smoke.

36

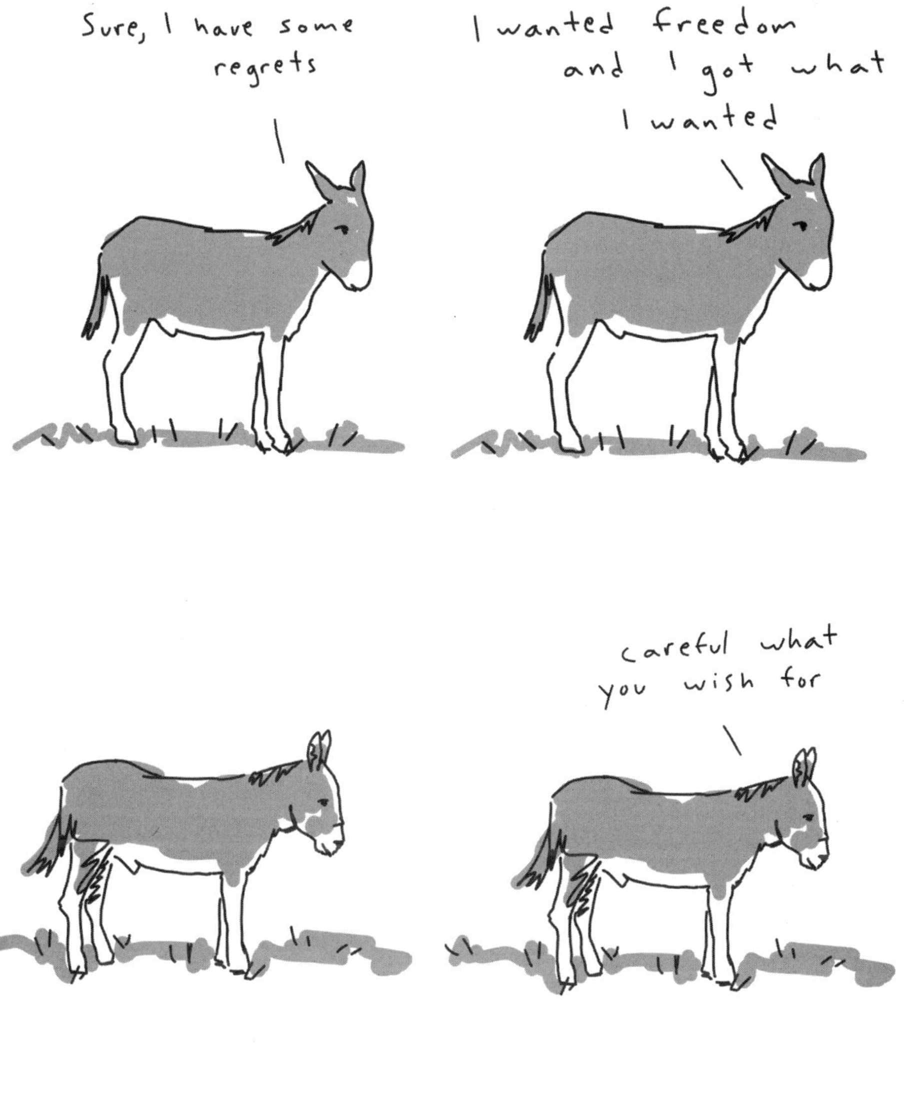

Sure, I have some regrets
I wanted freedom and I got what I wanted
careful what you wish for

37

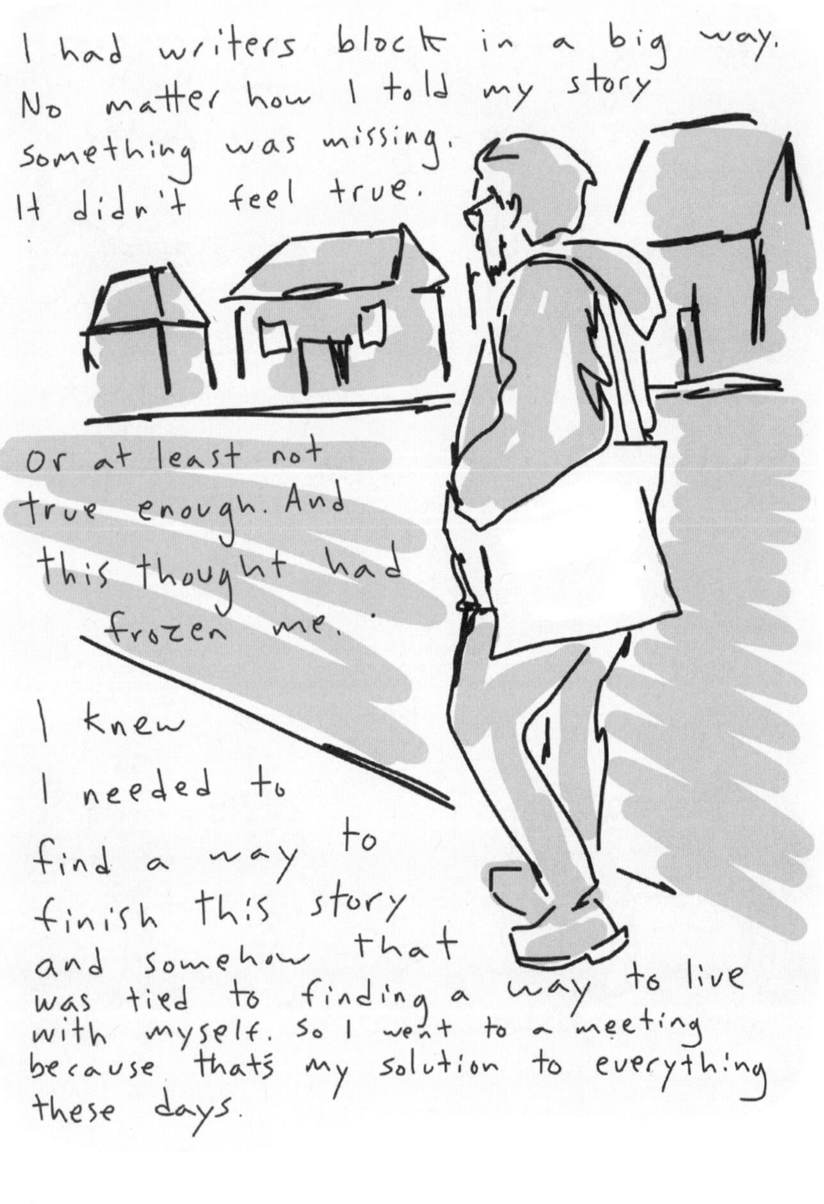
I had writers block in a big way.
No matter how I told my story
something was missing.
It didn't feel true.
Or at least not
true enough. And
this thought had
frozen me.
I knew
I needed to
find a way to
finish this story
and somehow that
was tied to finding a way to live
with myself. So I went to a meeting
because thats my solution to everything
these days.

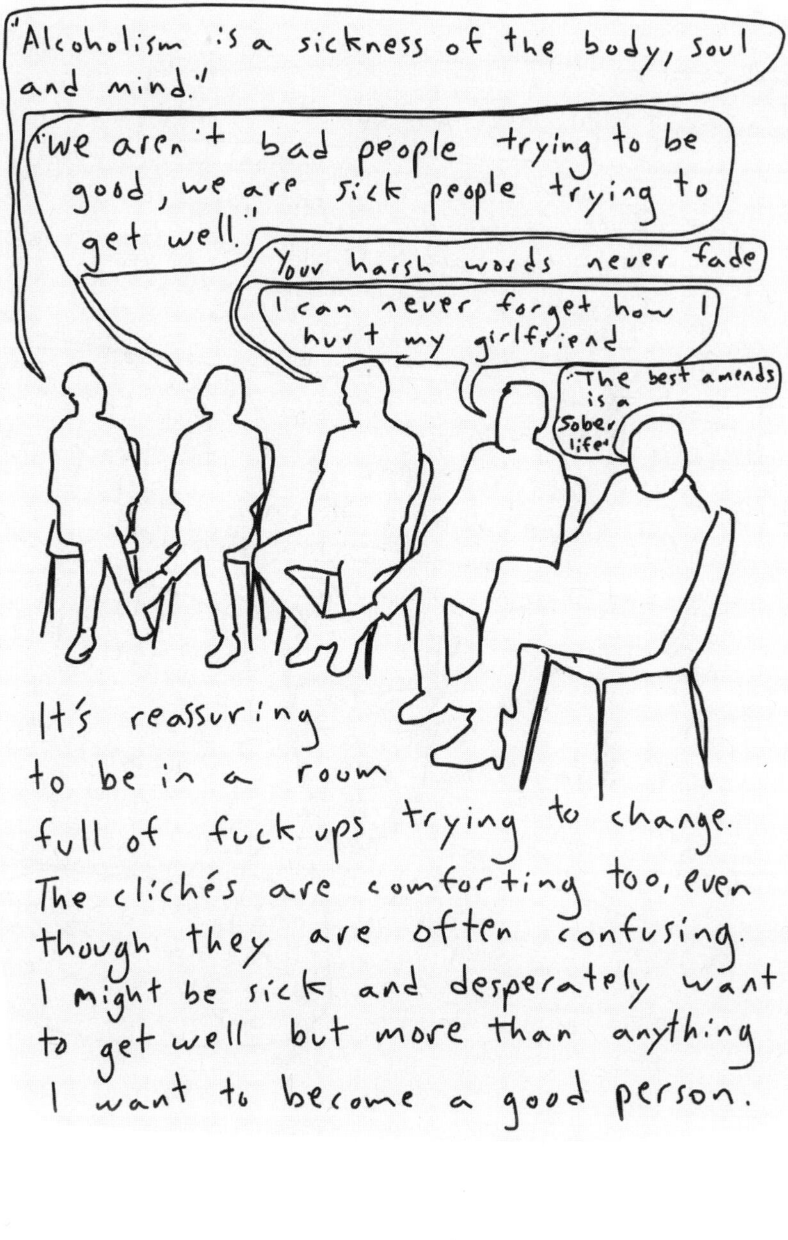
"Alcoholism is a sickness of the body, soul and mind."
"We aren't bad people trying to be good, we are sick people trying to get well."
Your harsh words never fade
I can never forget how I hurt my girlfriend
"The best amends is a sober life"
It's reassuring
to be in a room
full of fuck ups trying to change.
The clichés are comforting too, even
though they are often confusing.
I might be sick and desperately want
to get well but more than anything
I want to become a good person.

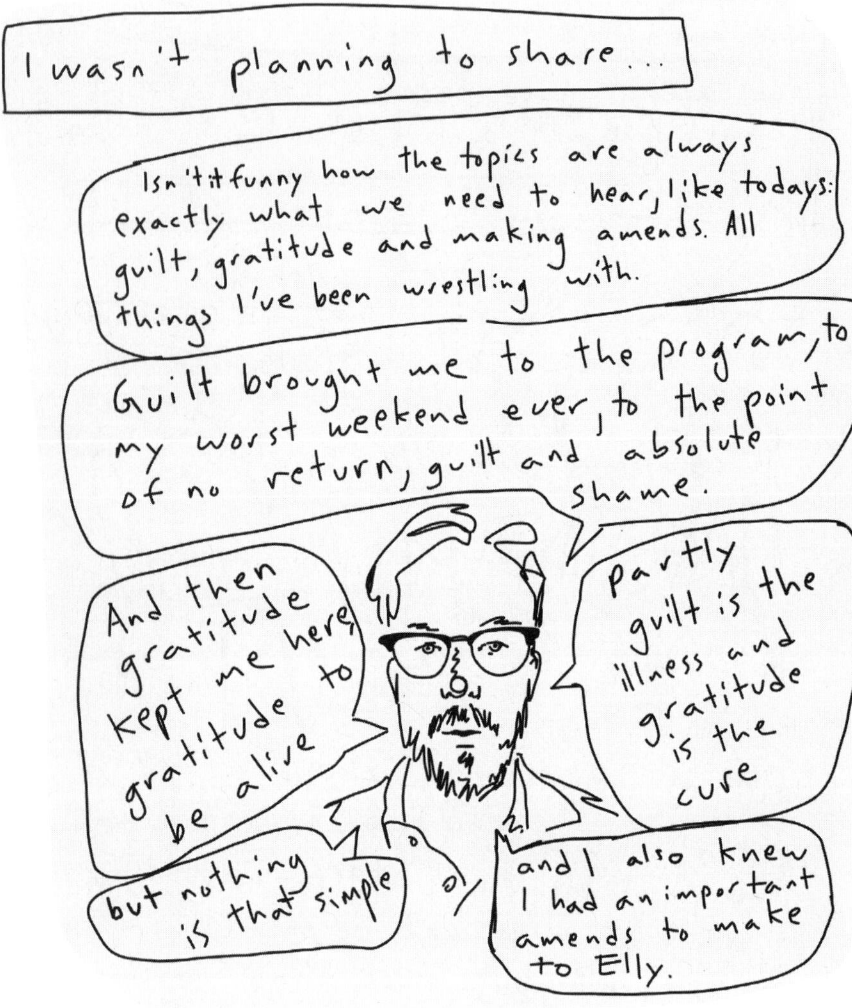
I wasn't planning to share...
Isn't it funny how the topics are always exactly what we need to hear, like todays: guilt, gratitude and making amends. All things I've been wrestling with.
Guilt brought me to the program, to my worst weekend ever, to the point of no return, guilt and absolute shame.
And then gratitude kept me here, gratitude to be alive
partly guilt is the illness and gratitude is the cure
but nothing is that simple
and I also knew I had an important amends to make to Elly.

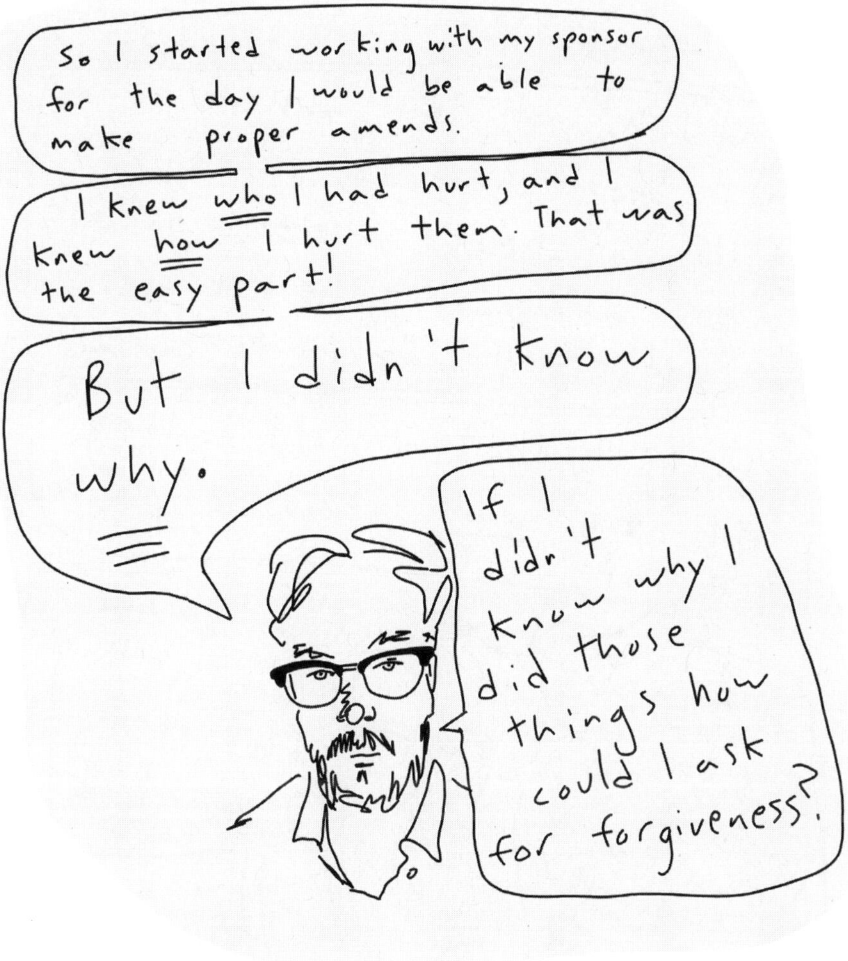
So I started working with my sponsor for the day I would be able to make proper amends.
I knew who I had hurt, and I knew how I hurt them. That was the easy part!
But I didn't know why.
If I didn't know why I did those things how could I ask for forgiveness?

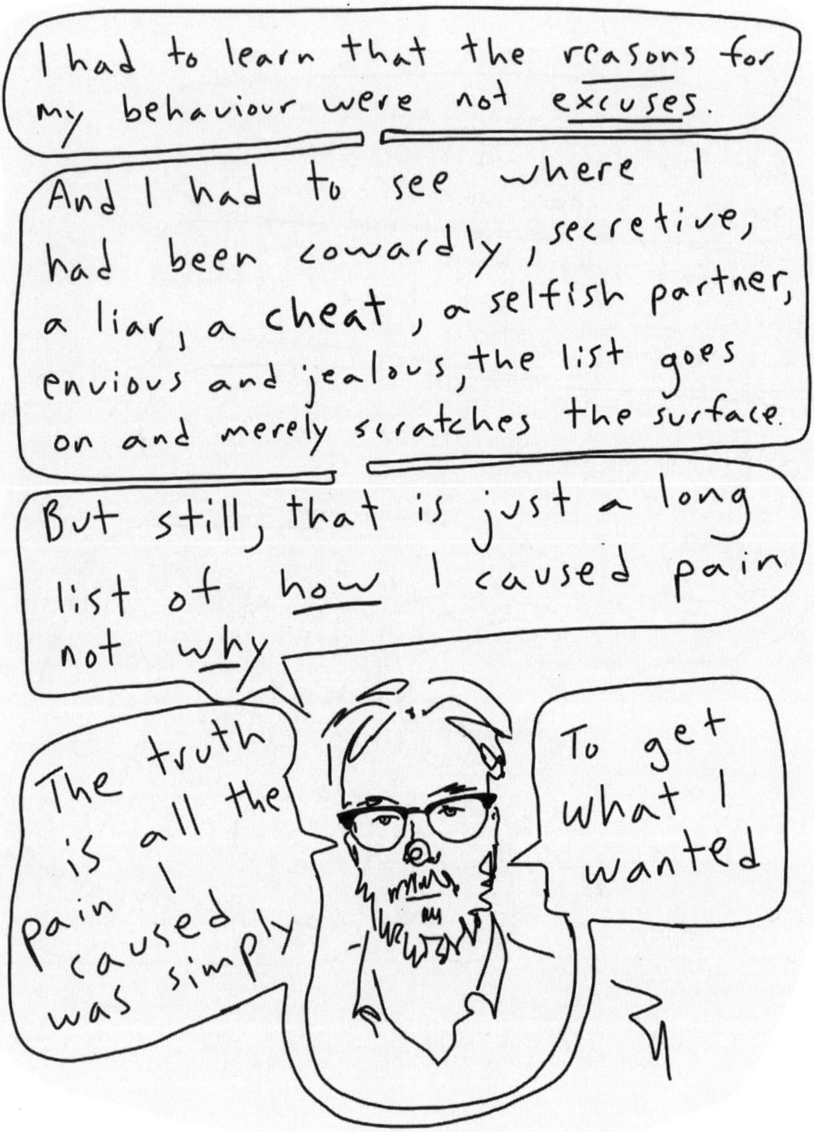
I had to learn that the reasons for my behaviour were not excuses.
And I had to see where I had been cowardly, secretive, a liar, a cheat, a selfish partner, envious and jealous, the list goes on and merely scratches the surface.
But still, that is just a long list of how I caused pain not why
The truth is all the pain I caused was simply
To get what I wanted

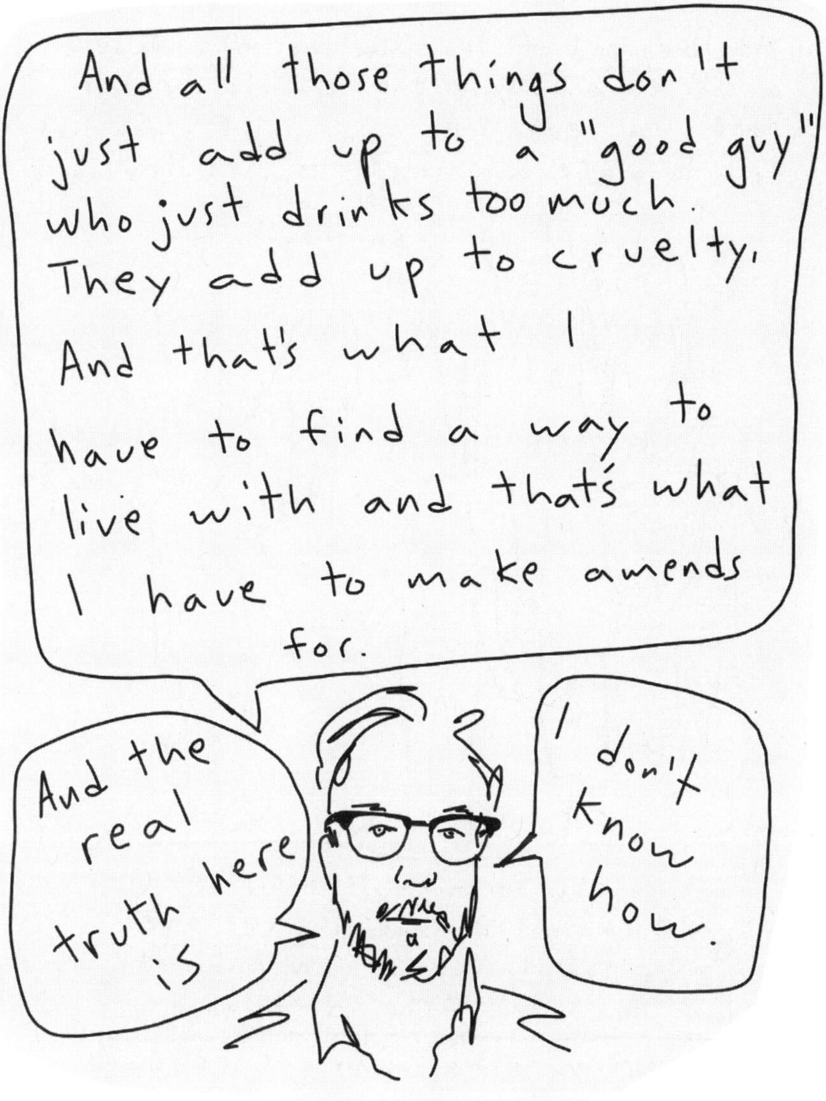
And all those things don't just add up to a "good guy" who just drinks too much. They add up to cruelty. And that's what I have to find a way to live with and that's what I have to make amends for.
And the real truth here is
I don't know how.

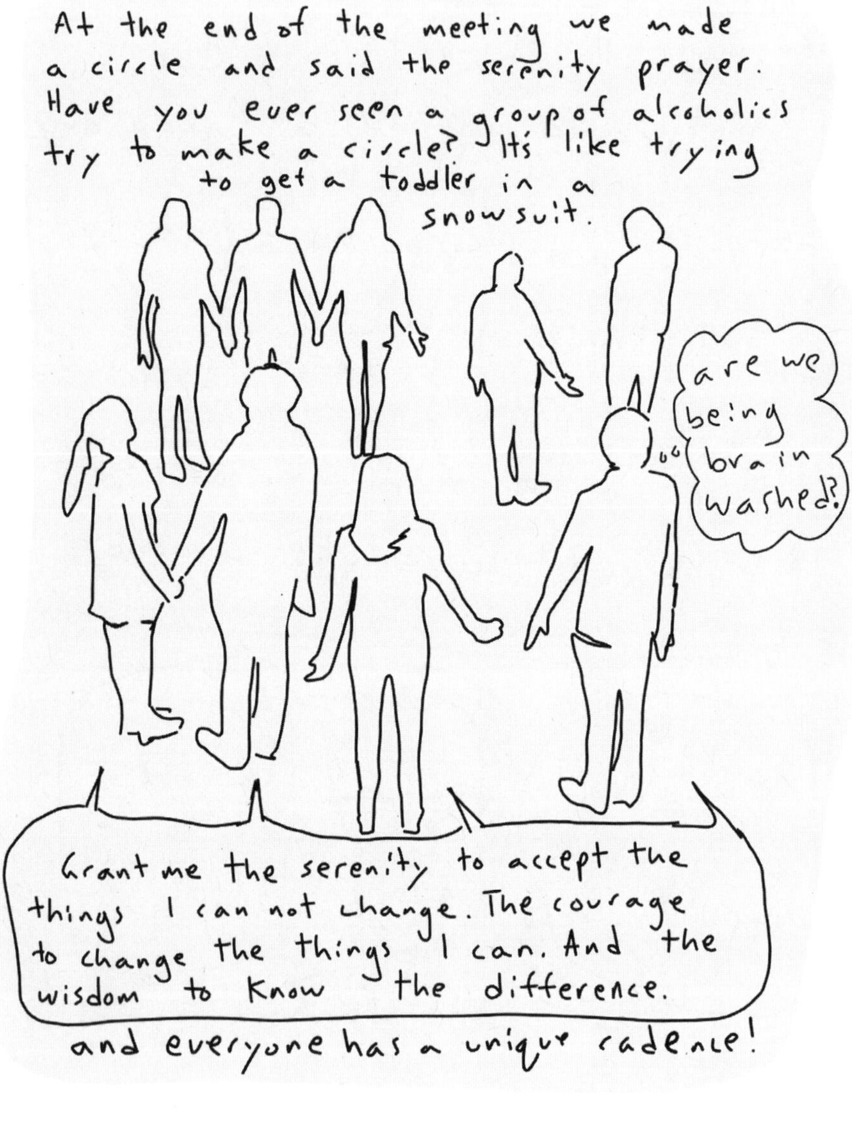
At the end of the meeting we made a circle and said the serenity prayer. Have you ever seen a group of alcoholics try to make a circle? It's like trying to get a toddler in a snowsuit.
are we being brainwashed?
Grant me the serenity to accept the things I can not change. The courage to change the things I can. And the wisdom to Know the difference.
and everyone has a unique cadence!

As I walked to the car I thought about it all. I would have to find a way to start making amends to Elly when I got home. For now I would plow ahead and try to finish what I started. For better or worse I needed to finish this story even if it fell short of what it should be.

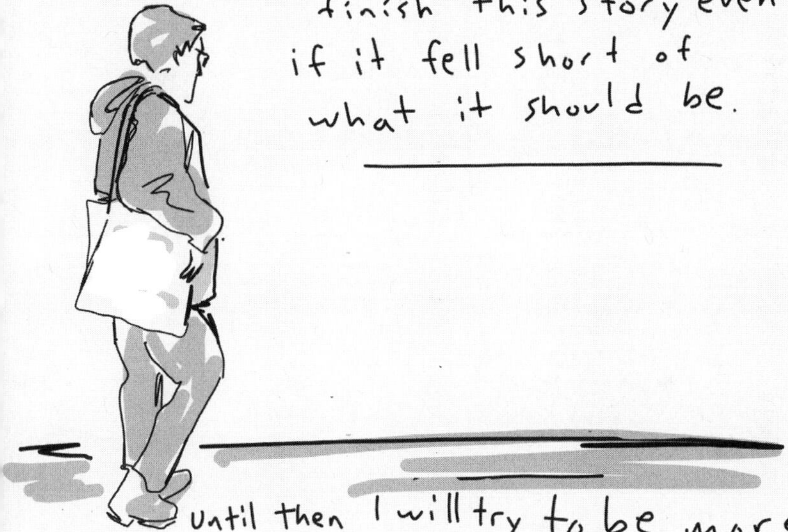

Until then I will try to be more honest. I do know how to try. I know how to fail and I know how to try again.

38

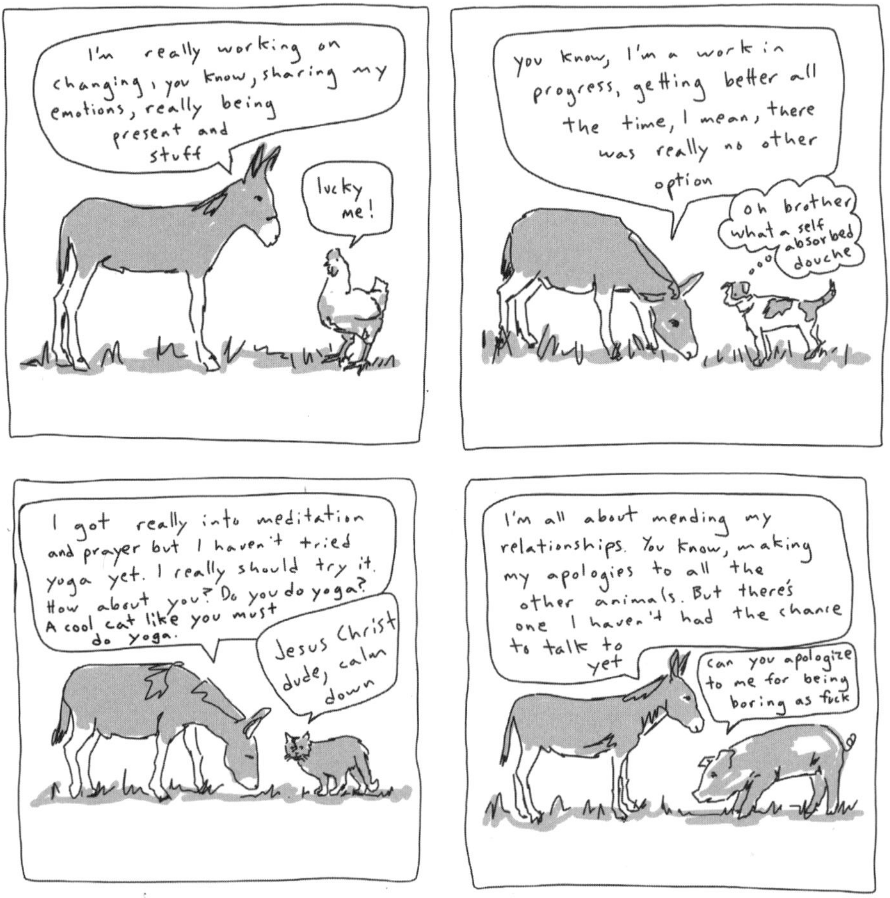
I'm really working on changing, you know, sharing my emotions, really being present and stuff
lucky me!
you know, I'm a work in progress, getting better all the time, I mean, there was really no other option
oh brother what a self absorbed douche
I got really into meditation and prayer but I haven't tried yoga yet. I really should try it. How about you? Do you do yoga? A cool cat like you must do yoga.
Jesus Christ dude, calm down
I'm all about mending my relationships. You know, making my apologies to all the other animals. But there's one I haven't had the chance to talk to yet
can you apologize to me for being boring as fuck

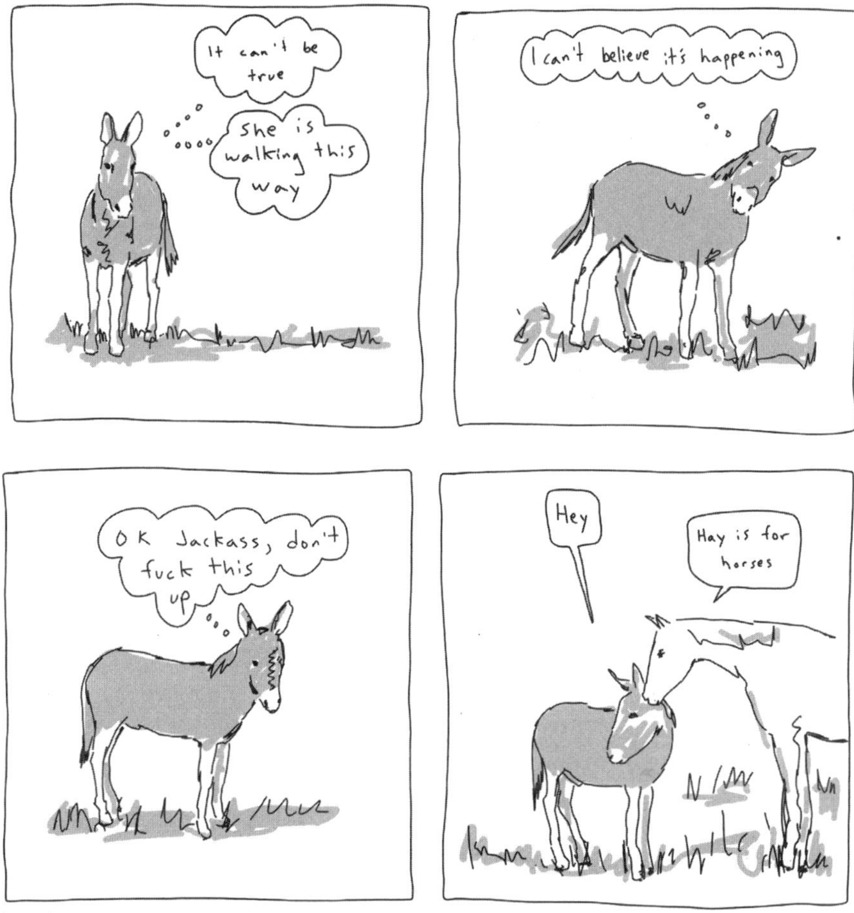
It can't be true
She is walking this way
I can't believe it's happening
OK Jackass, don't fuck this up
Hey
Hay is for horses

39

I was so lucky to spend time with Kayla in Prince Rupert. Talking about life, recovery and our hopes for sober futures.

She showed me the churches that
had meetings. Where she went to
school, all her childhood homes,
    where the candy lady lived
and where her friends lived.

Of course it was raining,
    just a little, making everything
        mysterious.

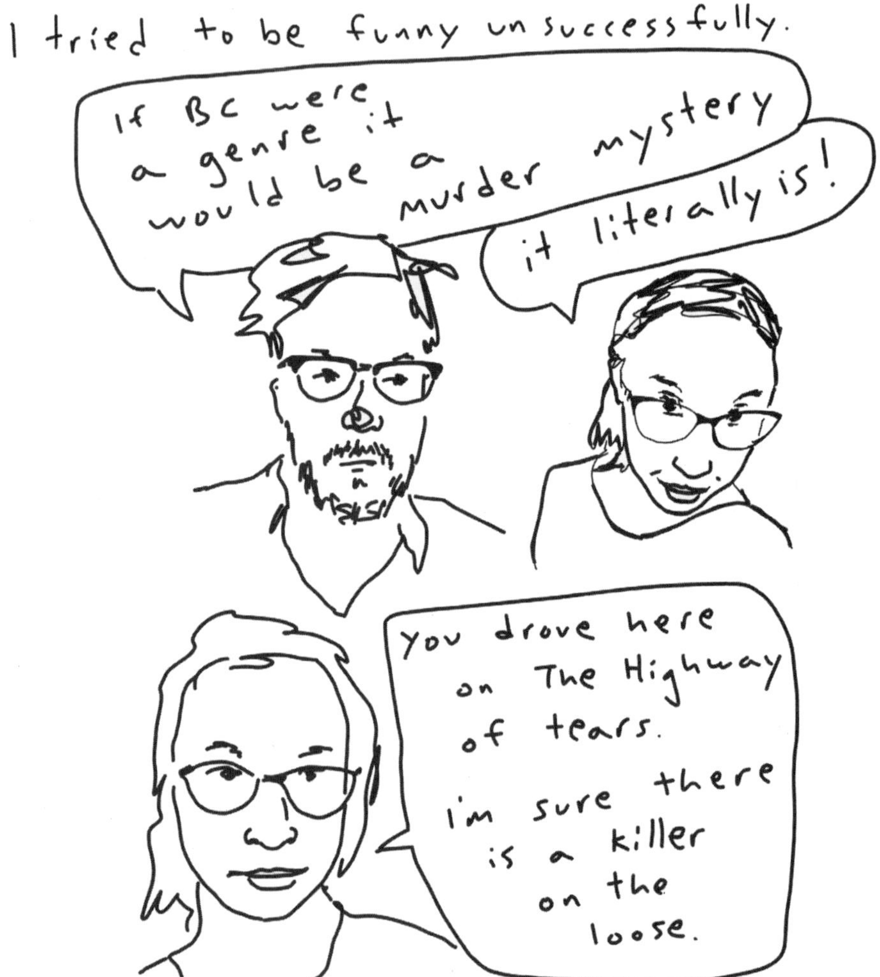
I tried to be funny unsuccessfully.
If BC were a genre it would be a murder mystery
it literally is!
You drove here on The Highway of tears. I'm sure there is a killer on the loose.

Next we went to The Museum of Northern British Columbia.

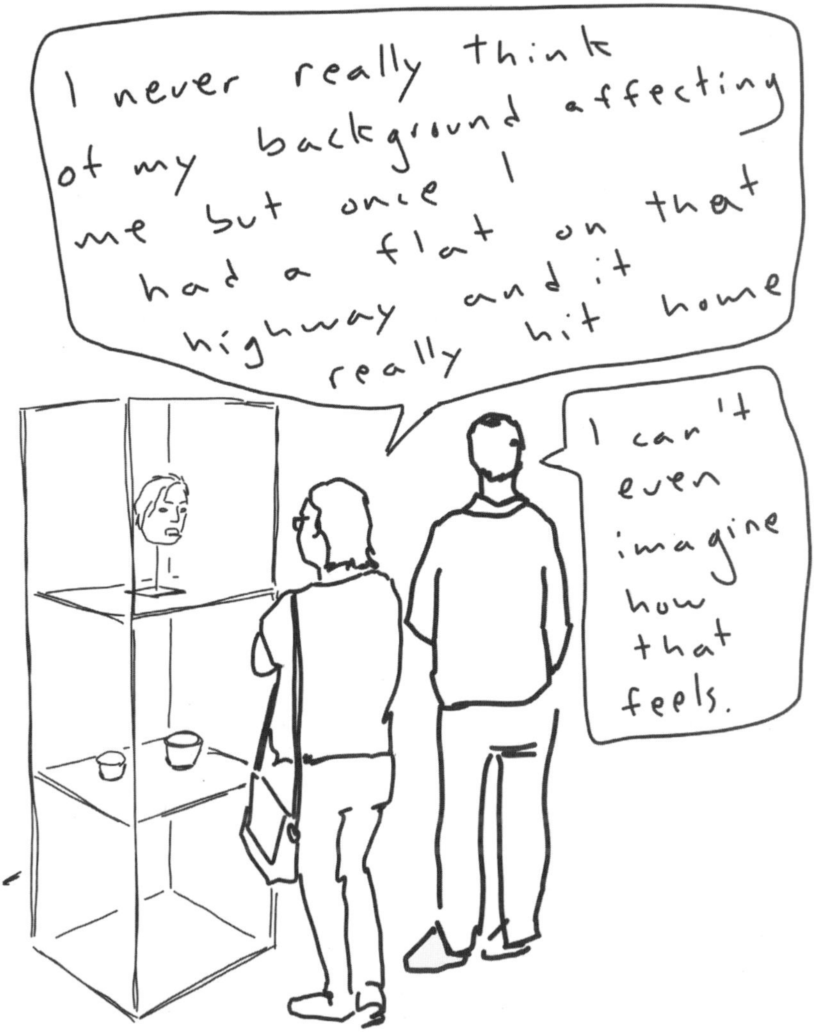
I never really think of my background affecting me but once I had a flat on that highway and it really hit home
I can't even imagine how that feels.

Kayla explained the terror of The Highway of Tears to me.*

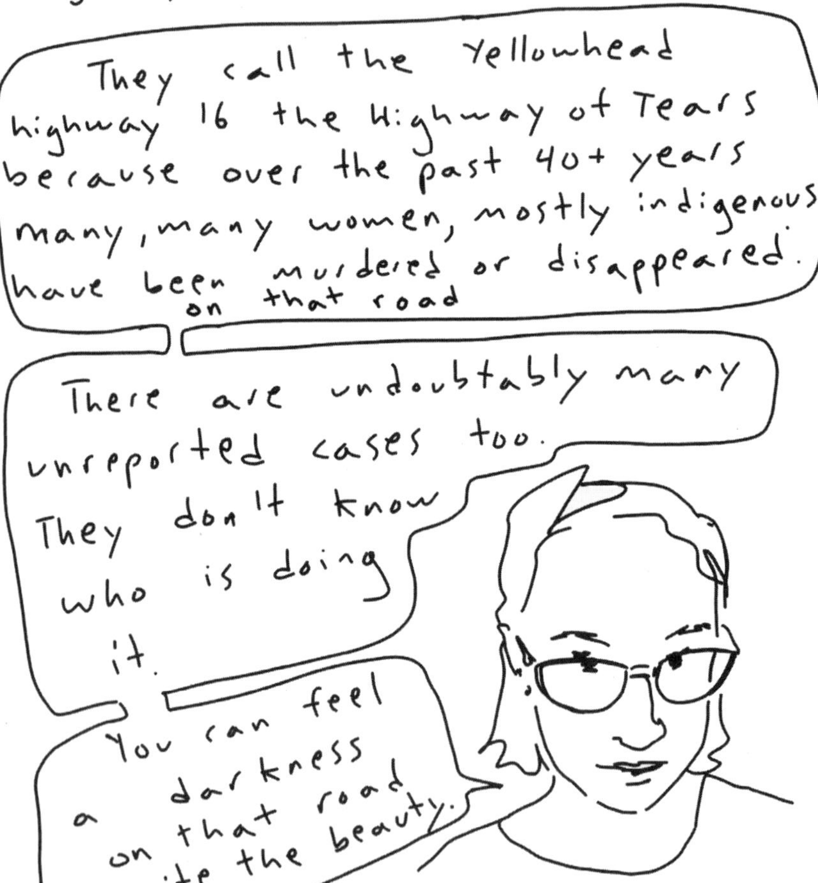
They call the Yellowhead highway 16 the Highway of Tears because over the past 40+ years many, many women, mostly indigenous have been murdered or disappeared on that road.
There are undoubtably many unreported cases too. They don't know who is doing it.
You can feel a darkness on that road despite the beauty.

* I don't know the best source of information on this online but thecanadianencyclopedia.ca is a start.

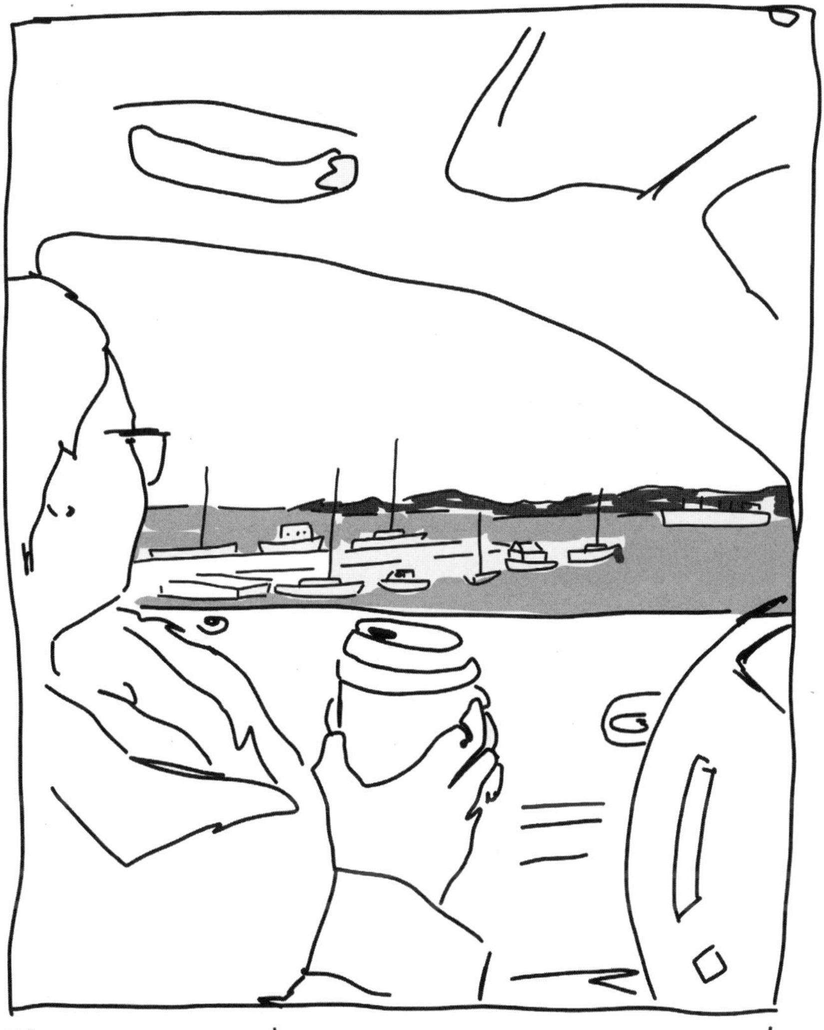

Then she showed me where you can park and watch seals, porpoises and eagles.

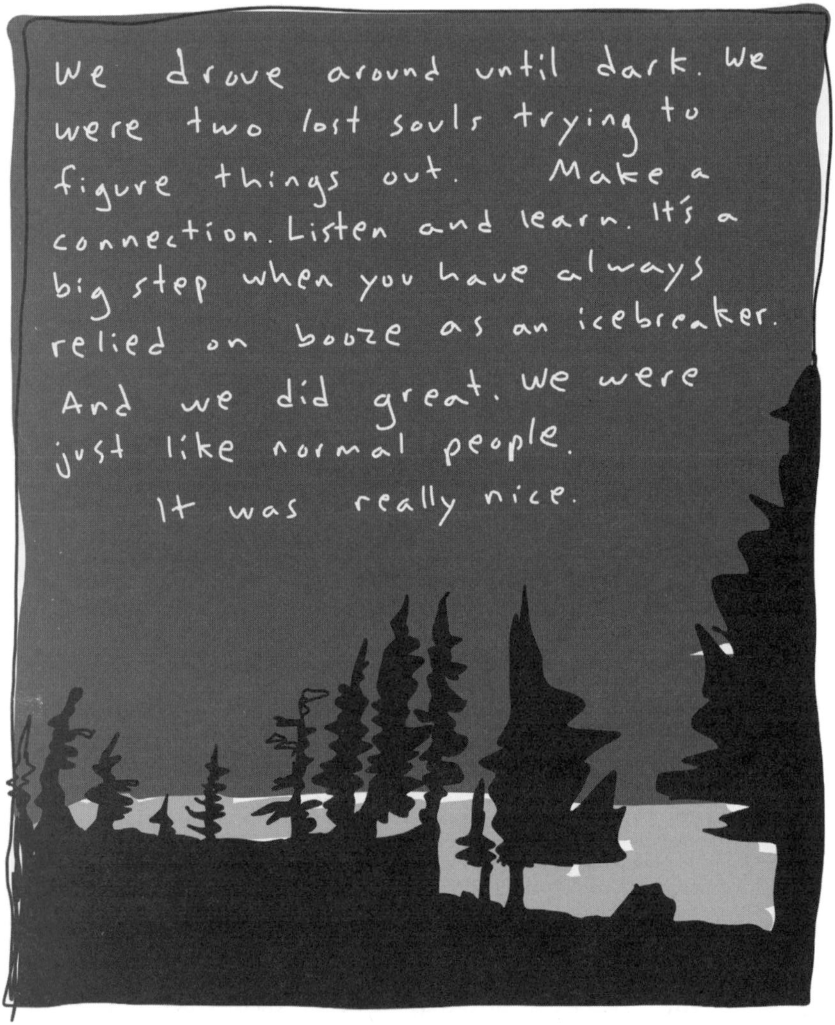
We drove around until dark. We were two lost souls trying to figure things out. Make a connection. Listen and learn. It's a big step when you have always relied on booze as an icebreaker. And we did great. We were just like normal people.
It was really nice.

40

Prince Rupert wasn't all existential dread, morose meditation on life, and the terror of writer's block.

It was also a place full of wonderful, warm and talented people. And luckily they all liked coffee.

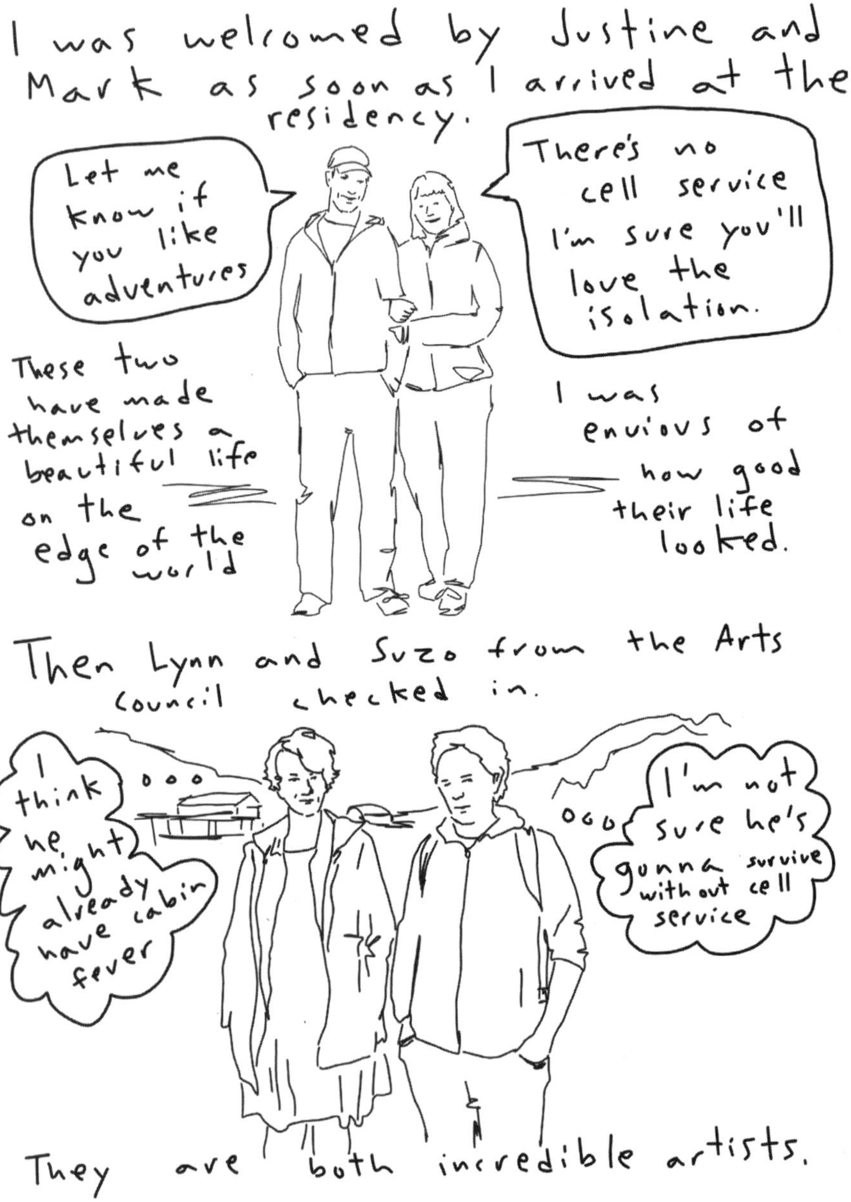
I was welcomed by Justine and Mark as soon as I arrived at the residency.
Let me know if you like adventures
There's no cell service I'm sure you'll love the isolation.
These two have made themselves a beautiful life on the edge of the world
I was envious of how good their life looked.
Then Lynn and Suzo from the Arts Council checked in.
I think he might already have cabin fever ...
... I'm not sure he's gonna survive without cell service
They are both incredible artists.

The truth is I couldn't work without fast internet so I did a lot of work in the library and cafés.
what are you workin on?
Cowpuccinos was a great place to work and make phone calls.
COLD DRINKS
A graphic novel about your mid-life crisis — join the club!
The owner even let me stay after closing a few times.

I was lucky enough to get to know the painter Suzo Hickey over coffee and a studio visit. we talked about trying to have a painting career taken seriously in a small town.
It sucks!
But I wouldn't have it any other way
Lynn* would agree
*Lynn Cociani, another great Prince Rupert painter I had the luck to hang out with.

And I got to know the one and only Jeseka Hickey!

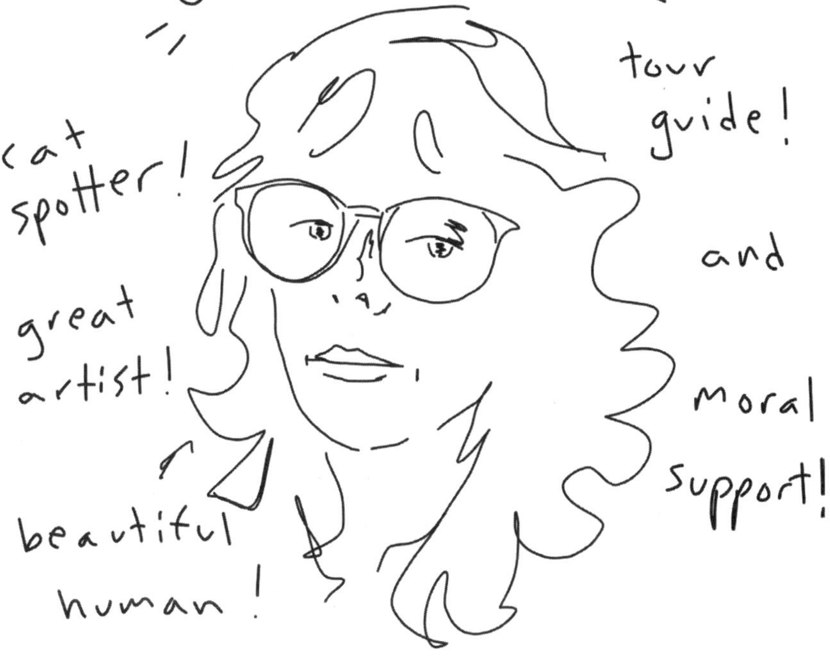

cat spotter!
tour guide!
great artist!
and
moral support!
beautiful human!

Such a ray of sunshine and yet we mostly talked about depression, addiction and death. But in the most positive way possible.

And on my last night I was invited to dinner by Suzo and her partner Emma who happen to be Jeseka's parents.

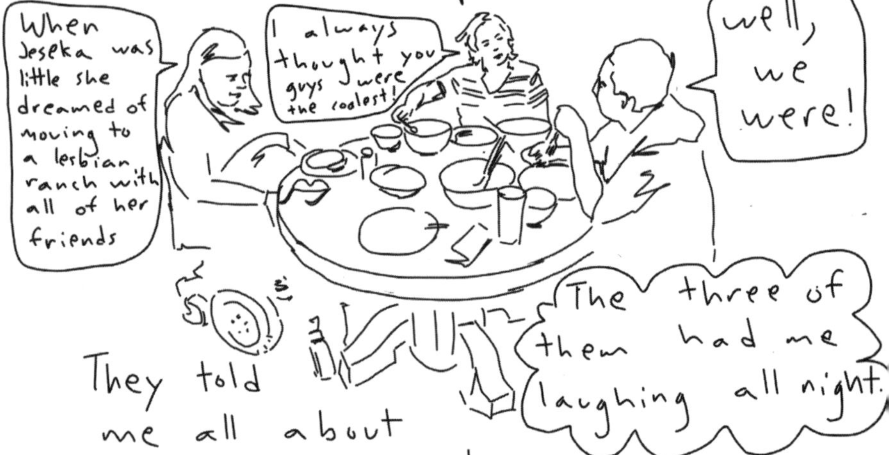

When Jeseka was little she dreamed of moving to a lesbian ranch with all of her friends
I always thought you guys were the coolest!
well, we were!
The three of them had me laughing all night.

They told me all about their family histories and each story would make a great graphic novel on its own.

I knew Emma was a very successful performance artist but I didn't realize how famous she is. She was a part of Kiss & Tell collective under the name Lizard Jones and a novelist (Two Ends of Sleep)

She was off to perform a new piece at a festival shortly after I left Prince Rupert.

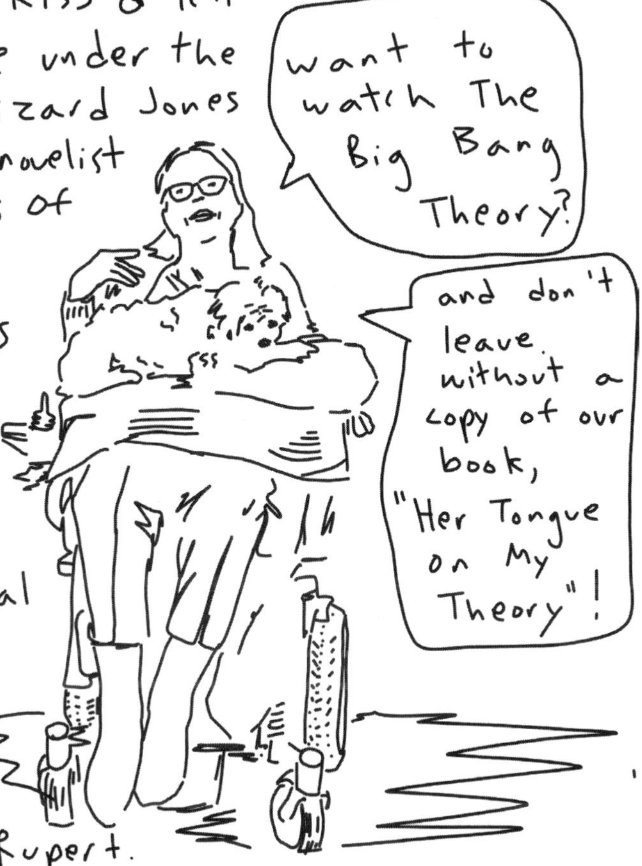
want to watch The Big Bang Theory?
and don't leave without a copy of our book, "Her Tongue on My Theory"!

The two Hickey's went out to their yoga class and Emma Kivisild (Lizard Jones) and I settled in to watch The Big Bang Theory. I had never seen it so Emma filled me in on all the back story.

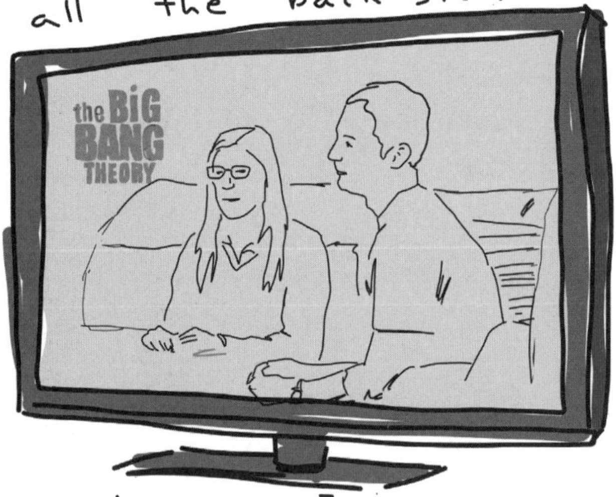
the BIG BANG THEORY

It was the one where Amy ruins the Indiana Jones franchise for Sheldon.

"You see, if Indiana Jones wasn't in the movie the Nazis would still have found the ark, taken it to the island, opened it up, and all died, just like they did."

That hurt. But I won't blame Prince Rupert. Prince Rupert was wonderful.

And I almost forgot to mention their wonderful pets, Vincent Blackshadow and Duke!

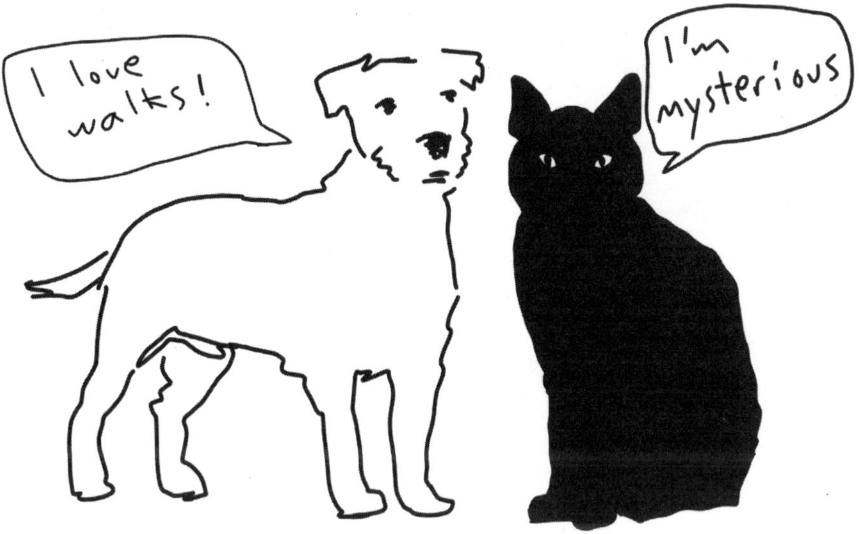
I love walks!
I'm mysterious

41

I woke early and packed the car. I wasn't even half done the work I had started but

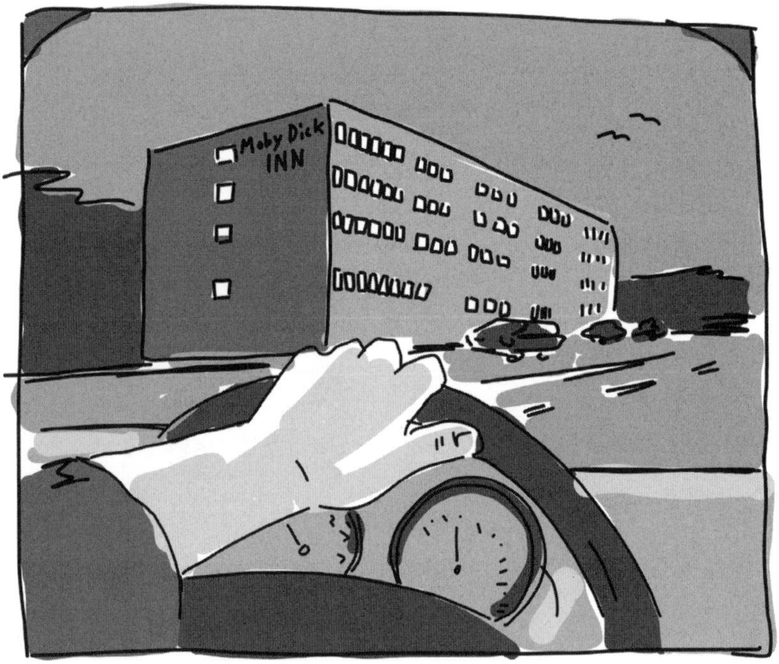
Moby Dick
INN

my time here was over, it was time to leave. I decided to make one last drive through town and make my final goodbyes.

Goodbye cool dangerous car.
looks like he's leaving
I might actually miss him

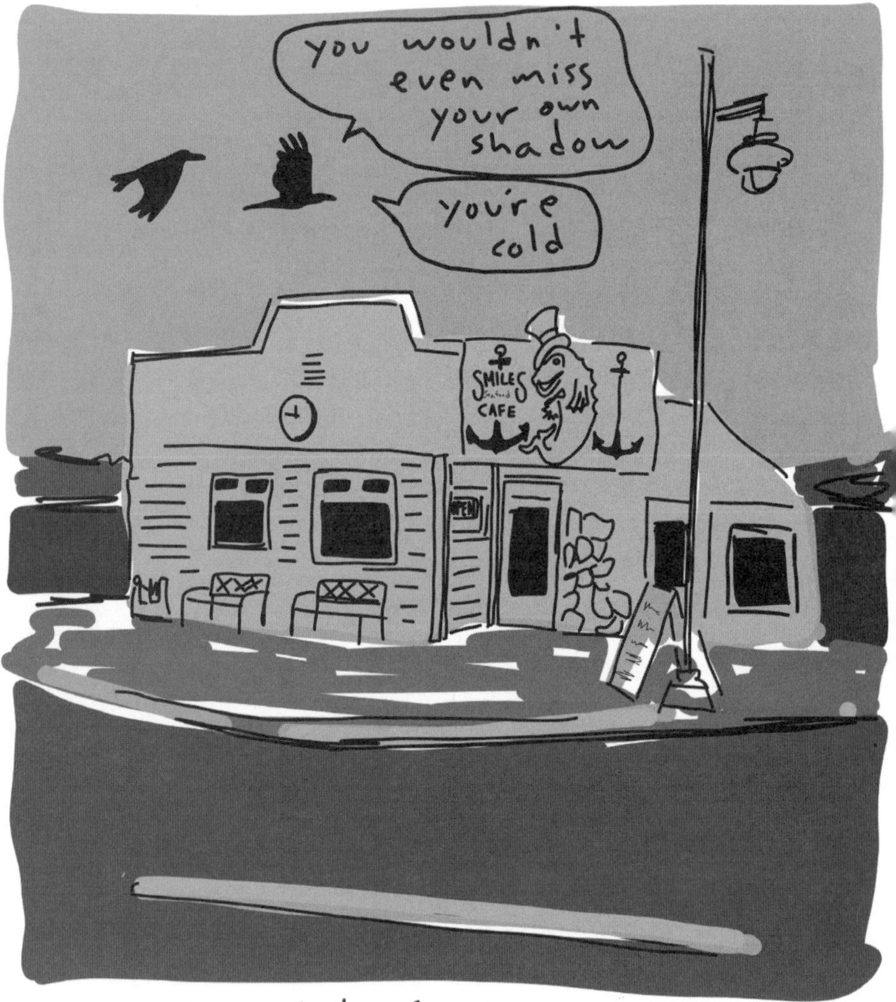
you wouldn't even miss your own shadow
you're cold
SMILES Seafood CAFE
OPEN

Goodbye Smiles Seafood Cafe.

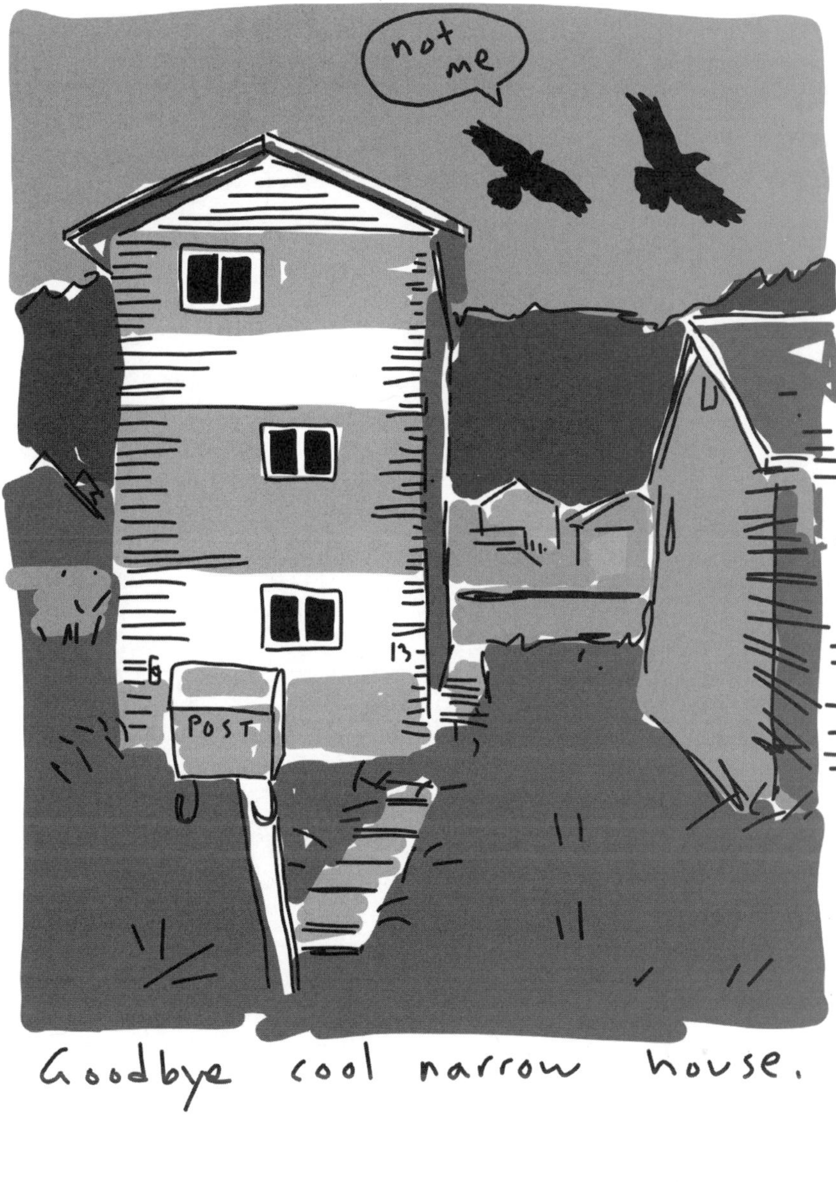
not me
6
13
POST

Goodbye cool narrow house.

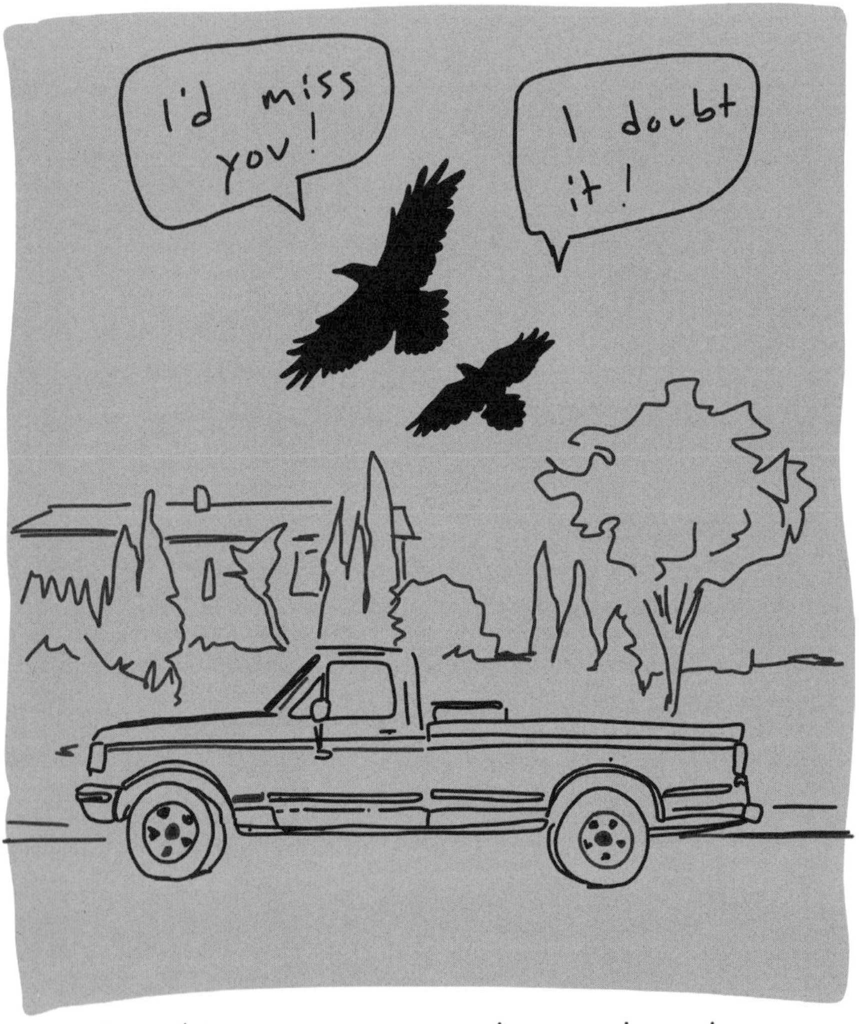
I'd miss you!
I doubt it!

Goodbye nice pick-up truck.

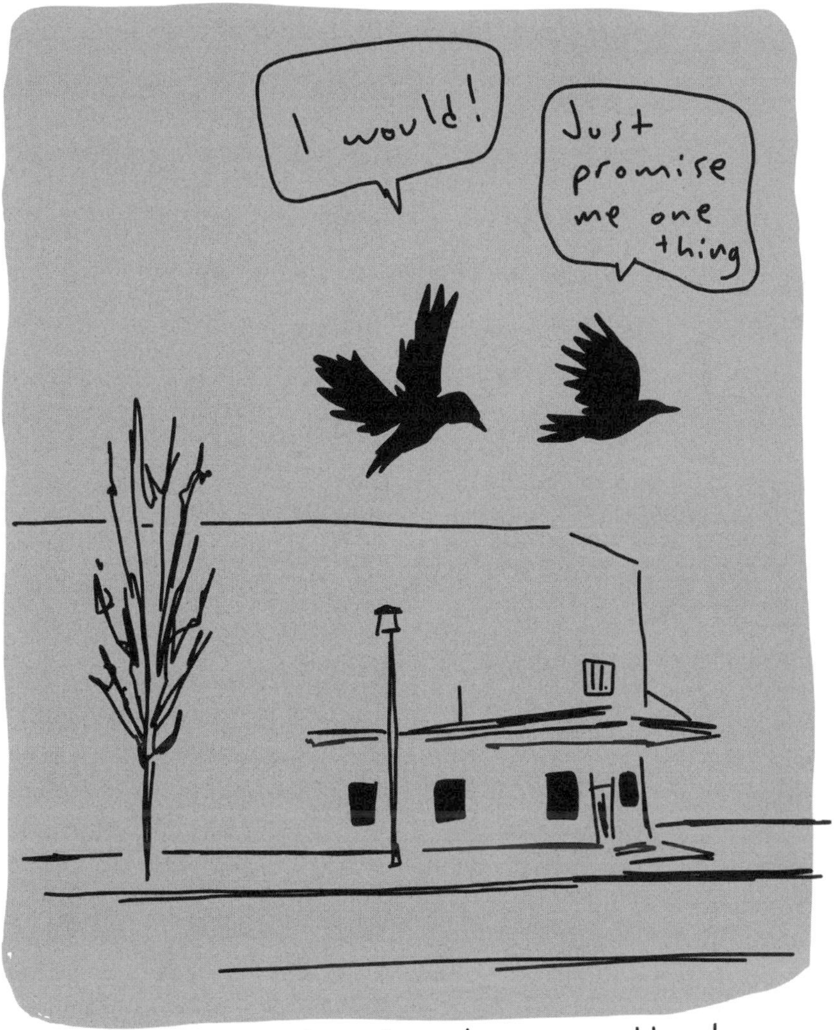
I would!
Just promise me one thing

Goodbye abandoned movie theatre.

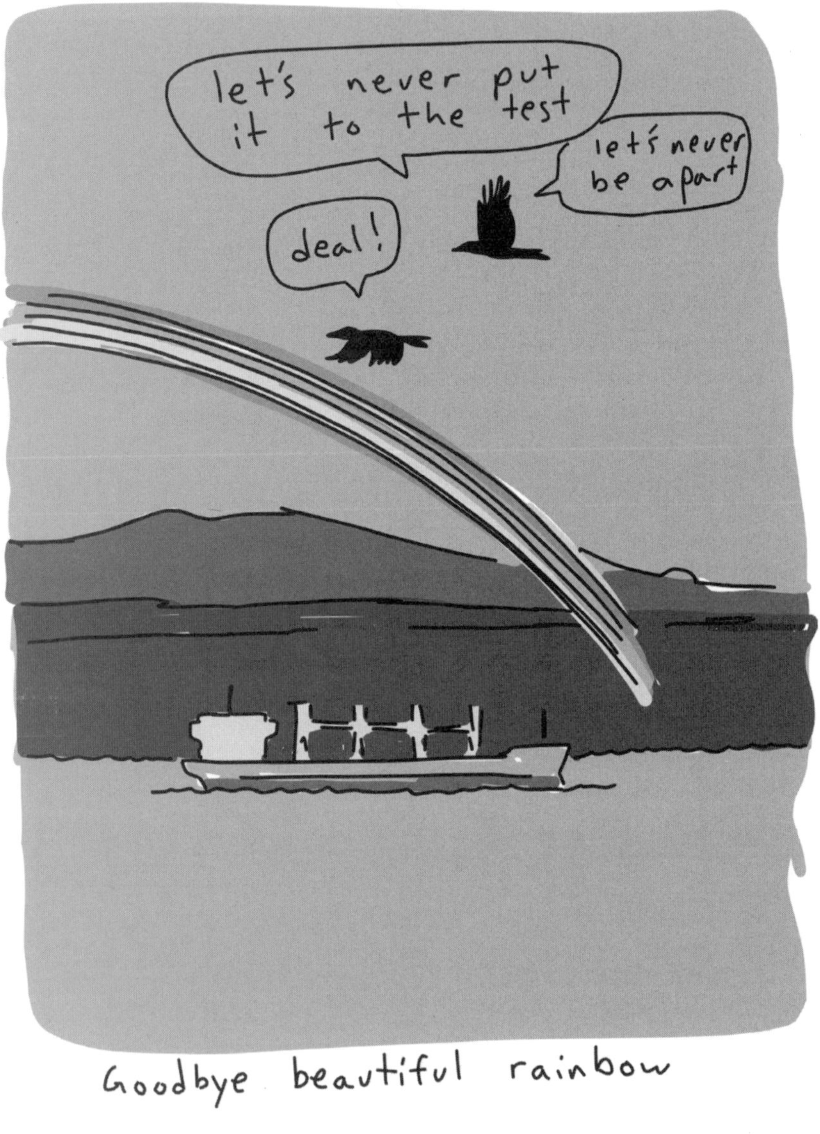
let's never put it to the test
let's never be apart
deal!

Goodbye beautiful rainbow

And back on the highway.

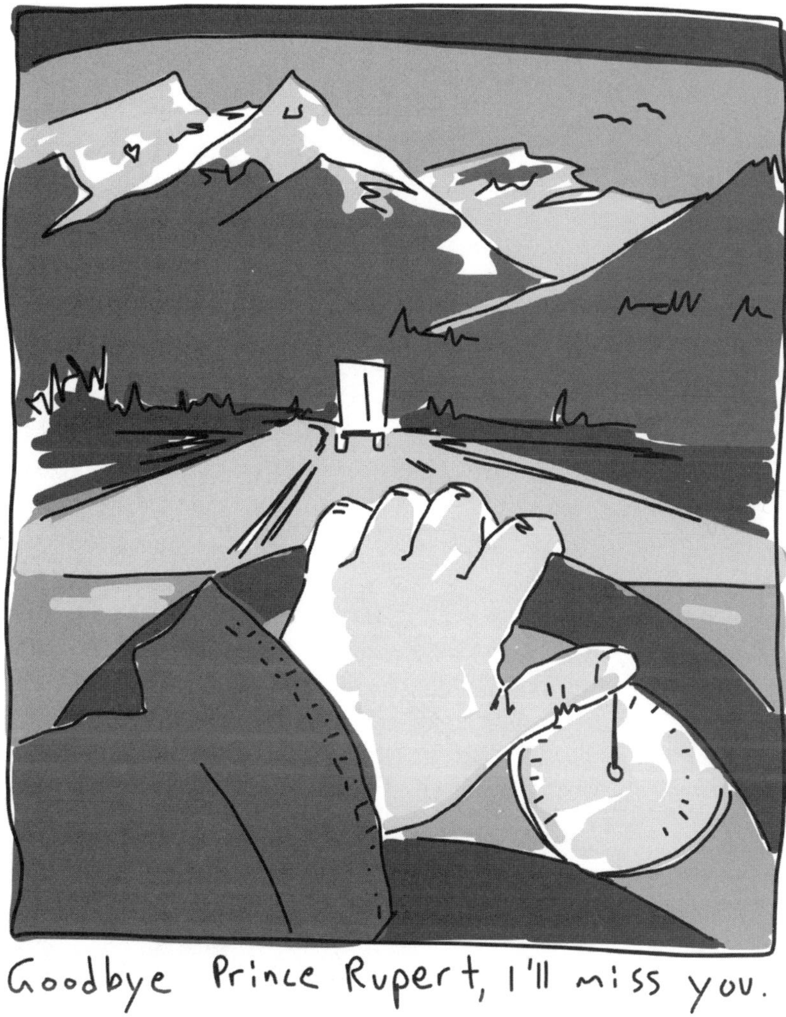

Goodbye Prince Rupert, I'll miss you.

42

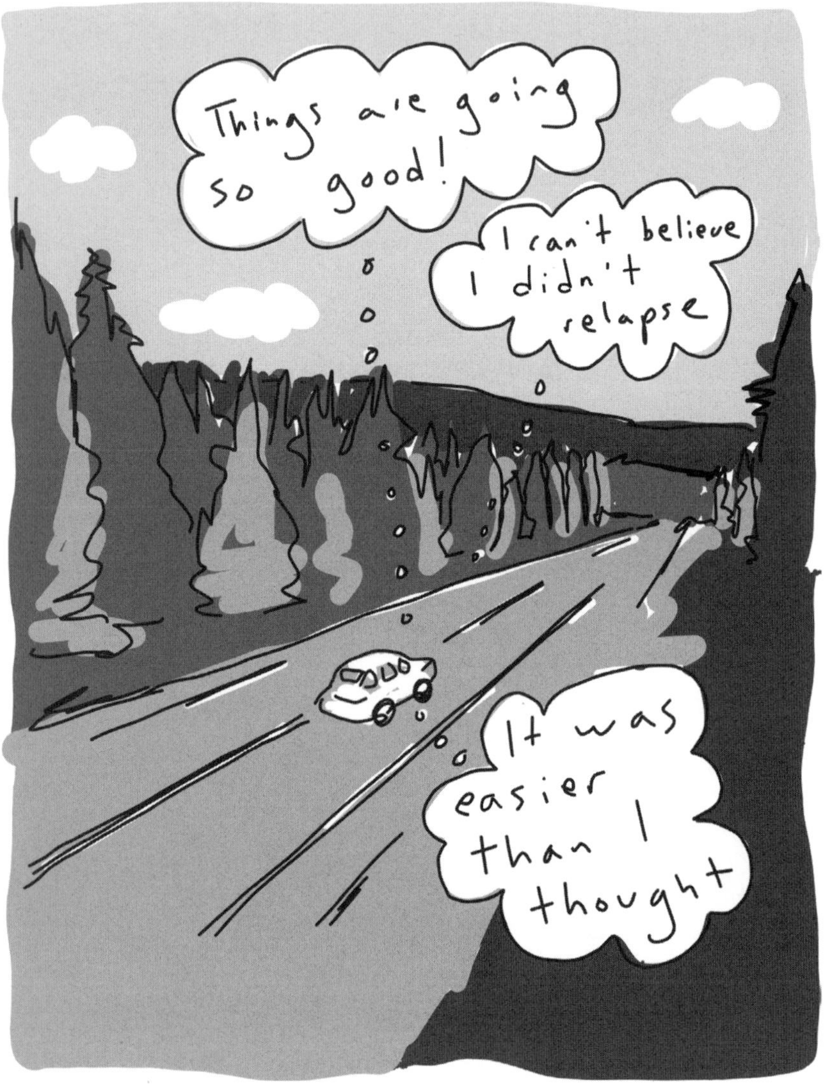
Things are going so good!
I can't believe I didn't relapse
It was easier than I thought

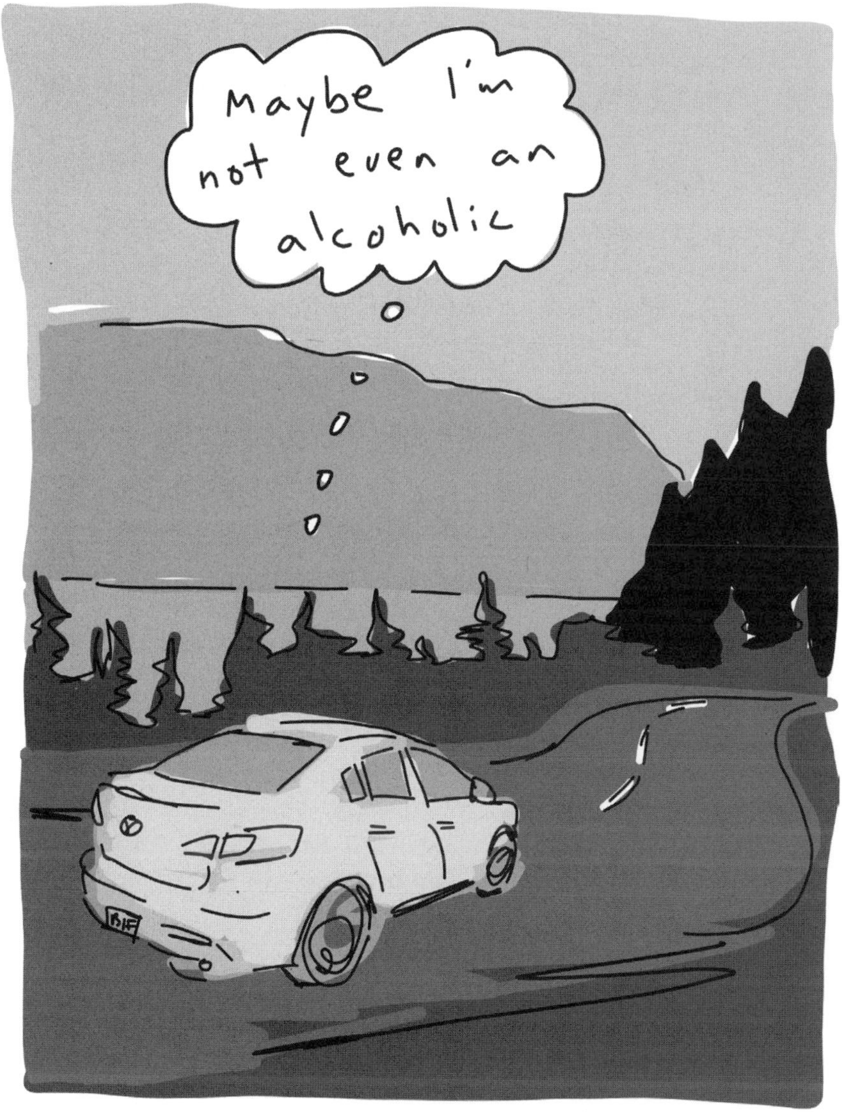
Maybe I'm not even an alcoholic

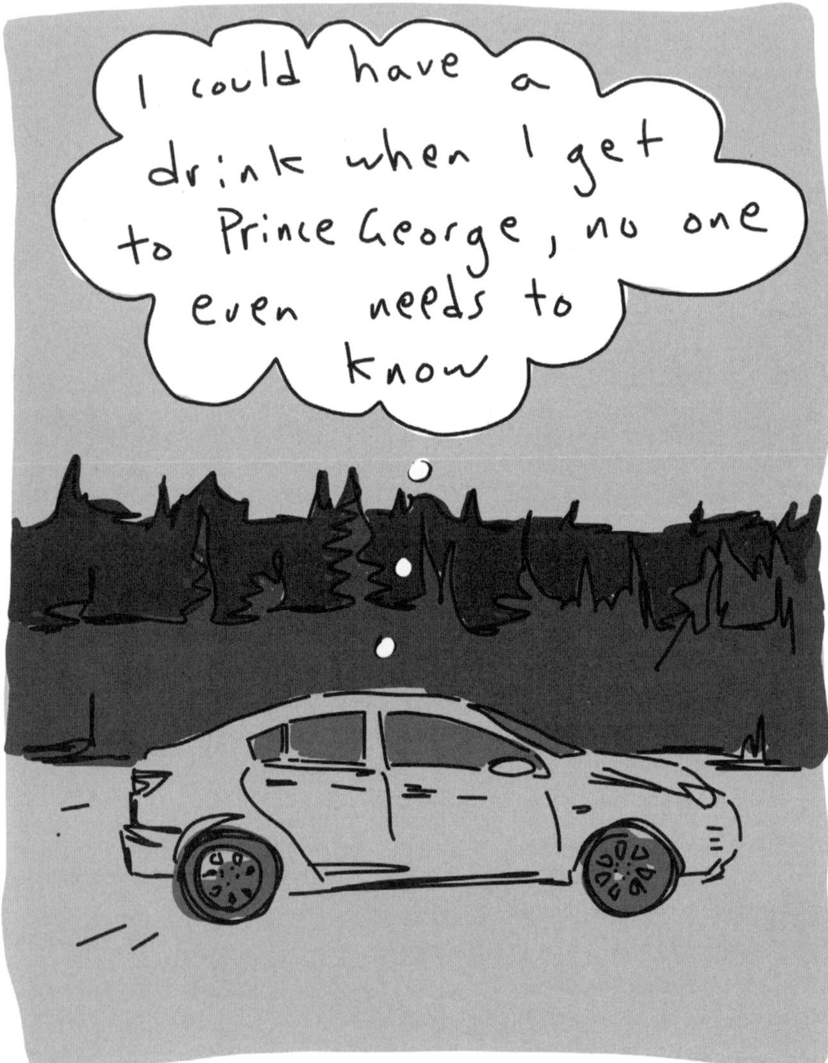
I could have a drink when I get to Prince George, no one even needs to know

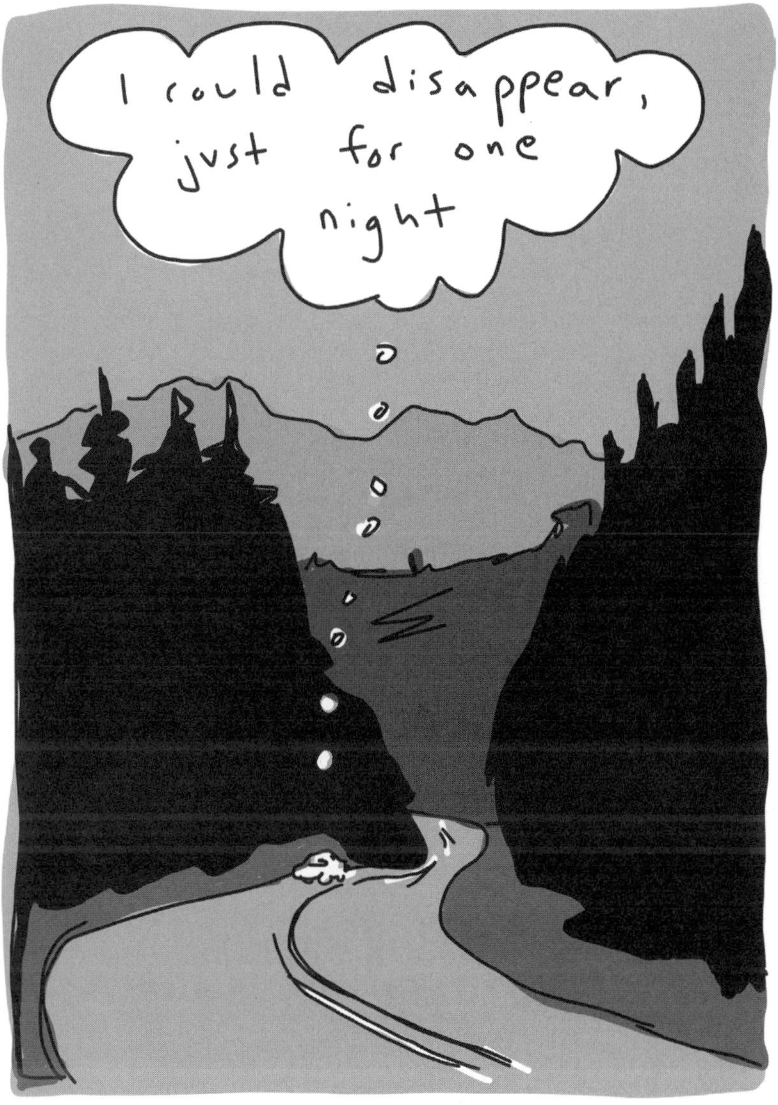
I could disappear, just for one night

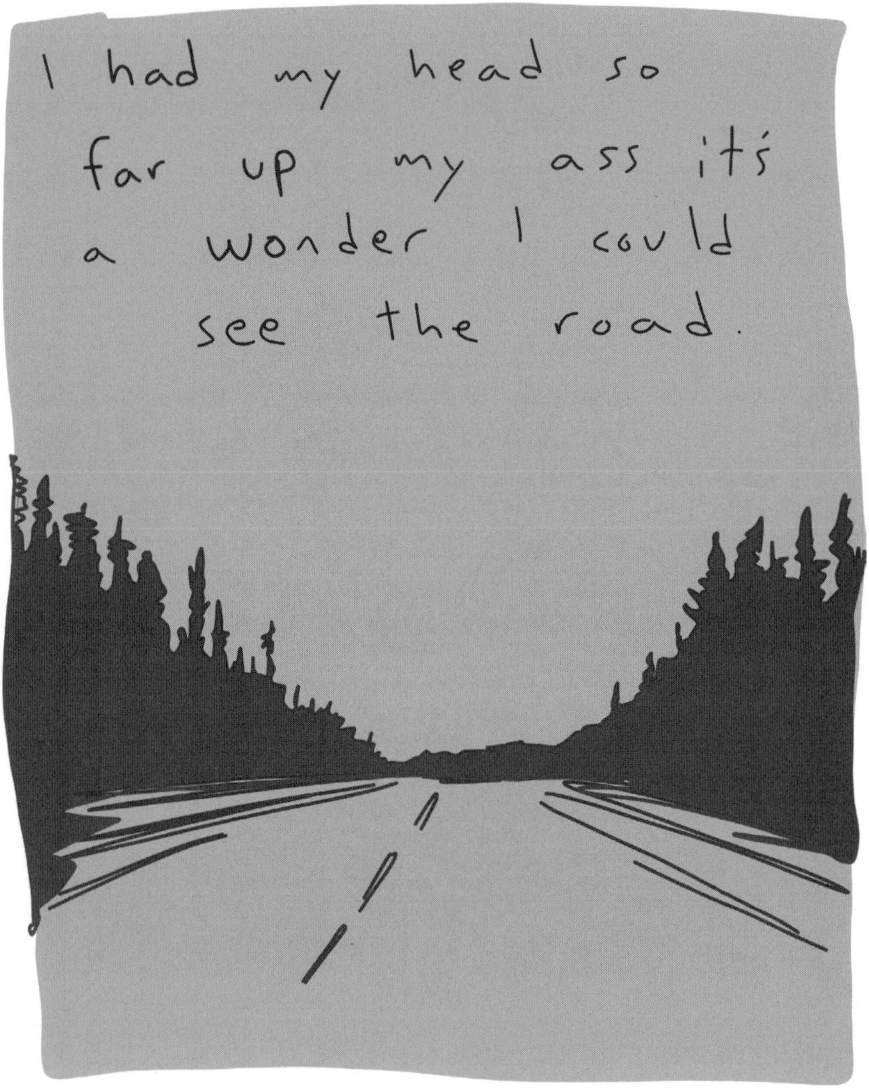
I had my head so far up my ass it's a wonder I could see the road.

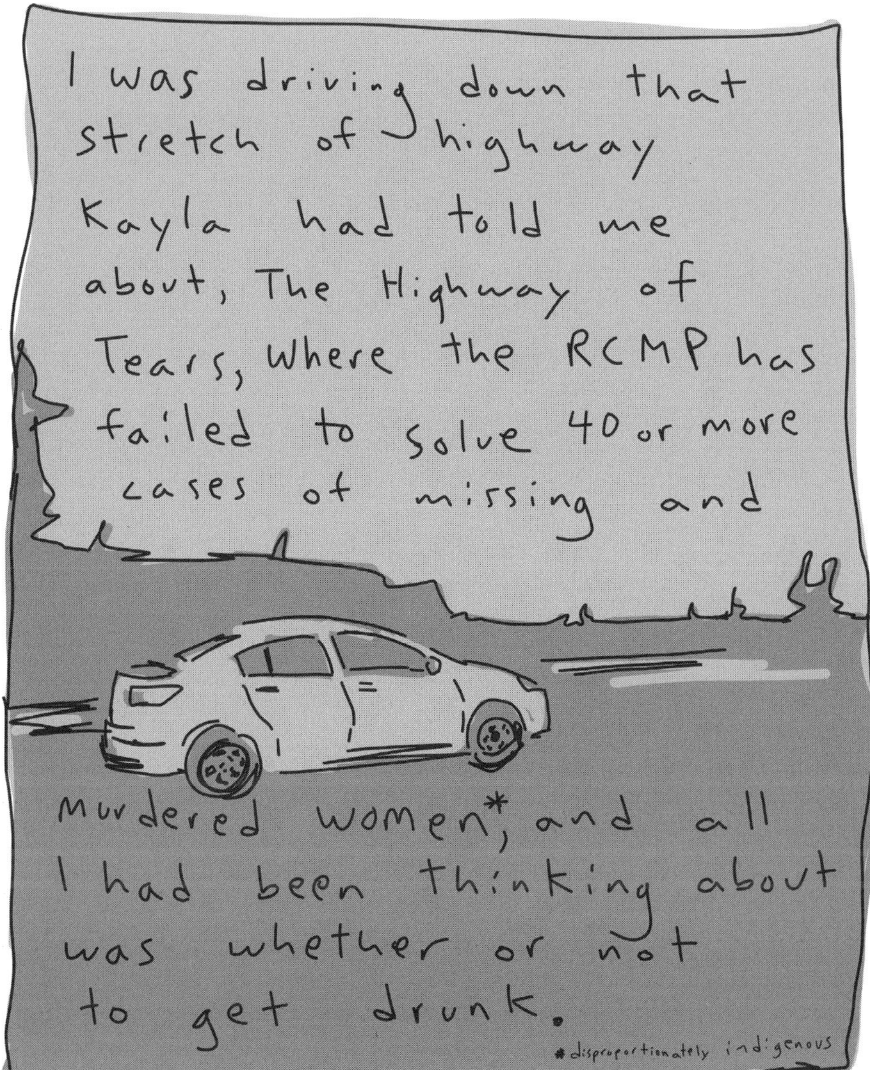
I was driving down that stretch of highway Kayla had told me about, The Highway of Tears, where the RCMP has failed to solve 40 or more cases of missing and
murdered women*, and all I had been thinking about was whether or not to get drunk.
*disproportionately indigenous

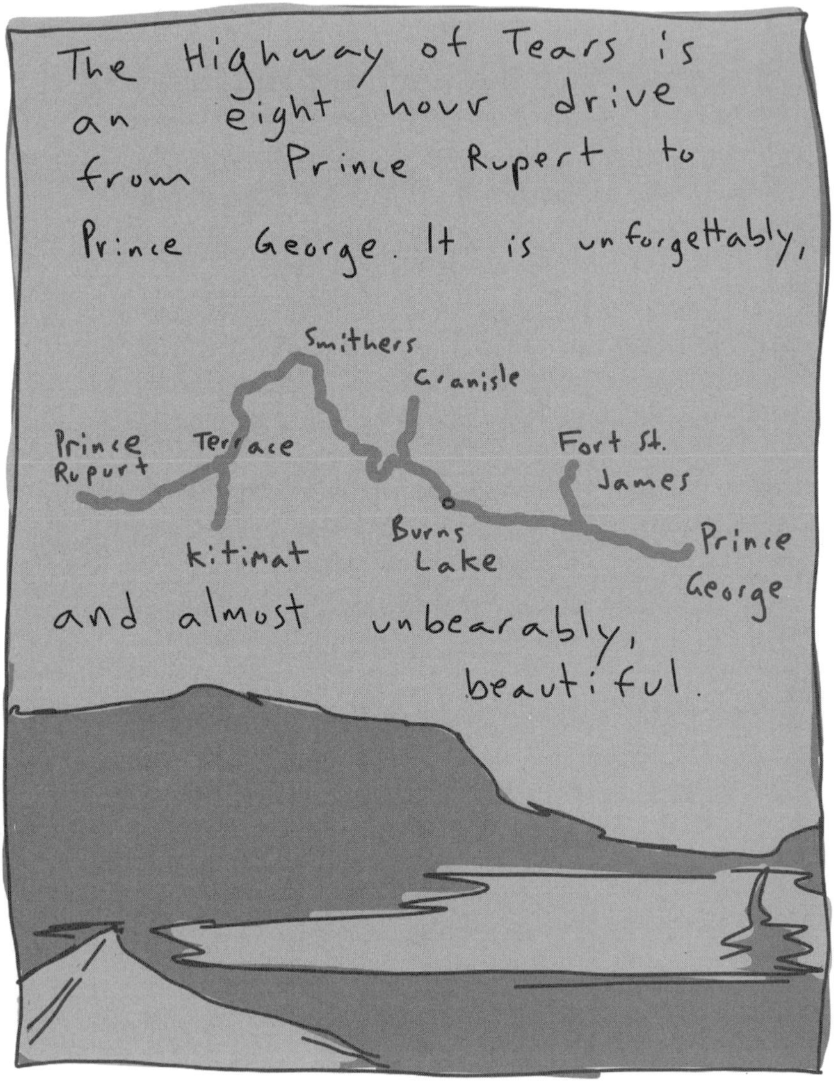
The Highway of Tears is an eight hour drive from Prince Rupert to Prince George. It is unforgettably,
Smithers
Granisle
Prince Rupurt
Terrace
Fort St. James
Kitimat
Burns Lake
Prince George
and almost unbearably, beautiful.

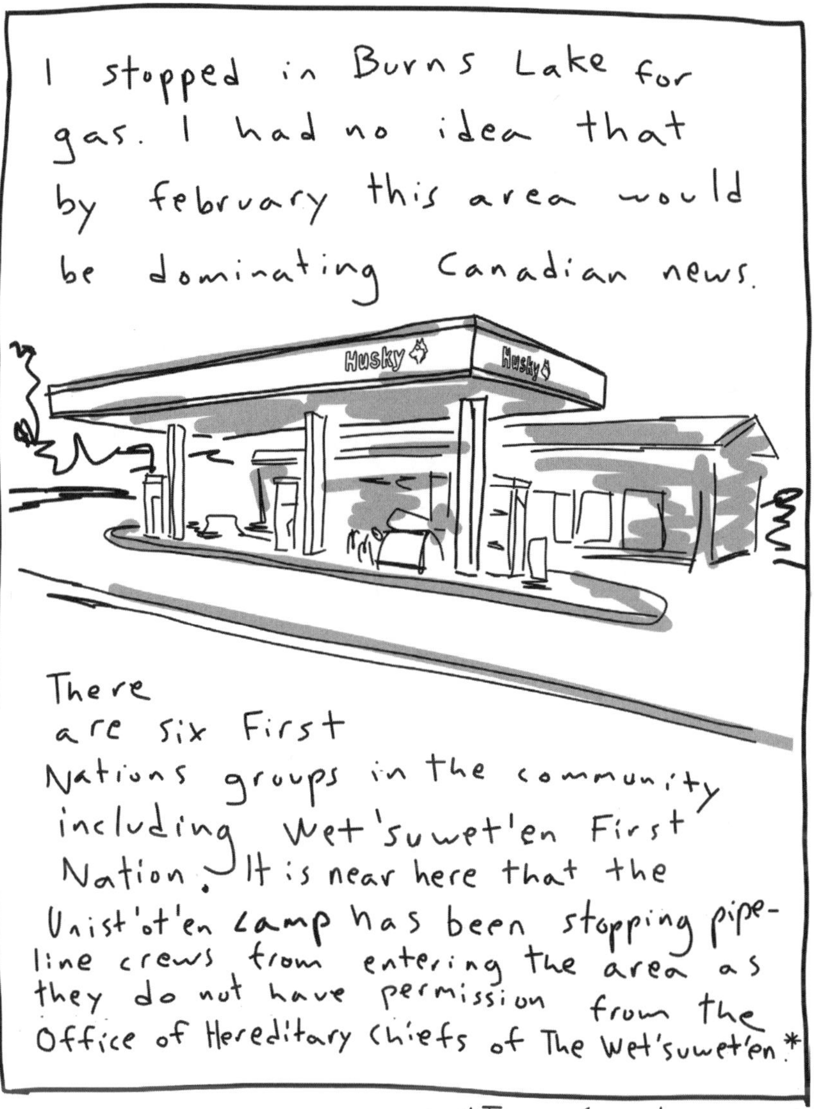
I stopped in Burns Lake for gas. I had no idea that by february this area would be dominating Canadian news.
Husky
Husky
There are six First Nations groups in the community including Wet'suwet'en First Nation. It is near here that the Unist'ot'en camp has been stopping pipe-line crews from entering the area as they do not have permission from the Office of Hereditary Chiefs of The Wet'suwet'en.*

*The Guardian and wikipedia

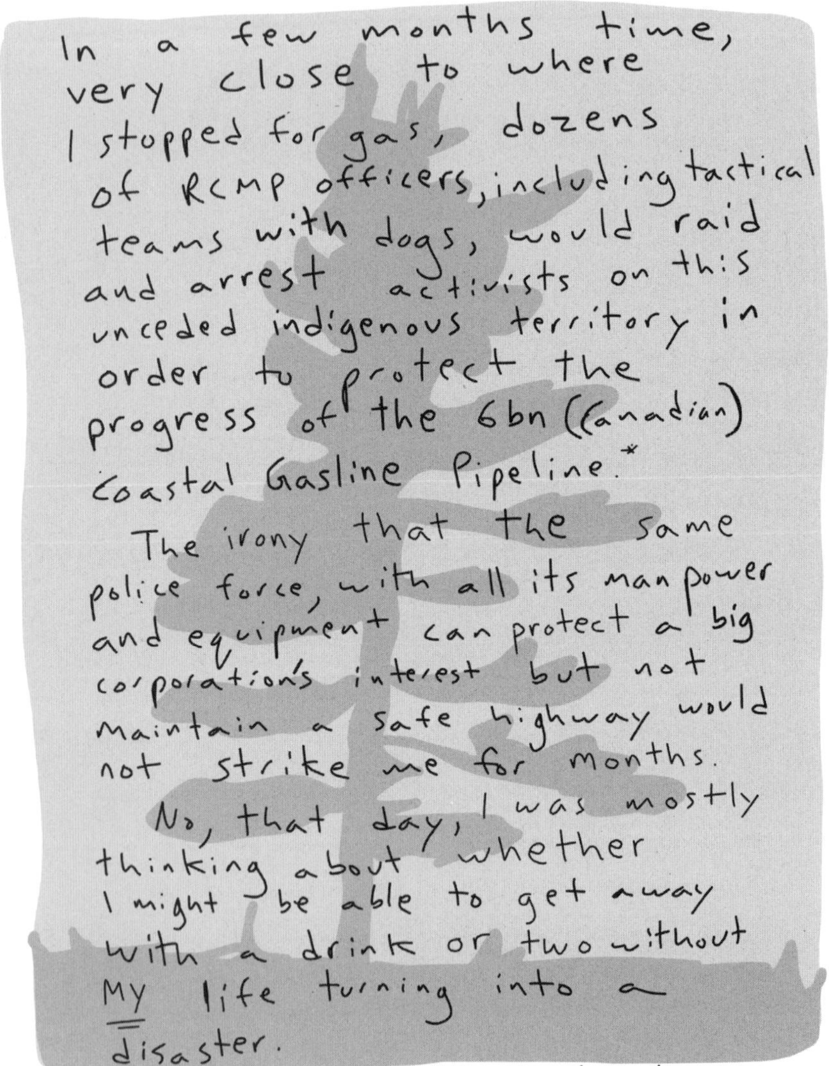
In a few months time, very close to where I stopped for gas, dozens of RCMP officers, including tactical teams with dogs, would raid and arrest activists on this unceded indigenous territory in order to protect the progress of the 6bn (Canadian) Coastal Gasline Pipeline.*
The irony that the same police force, with all its manpower and equipment can protect a big corporation's interest but not maintain a safe highway would not strike me for months.
No, that day, I was mostly thinking about whether I might be able to get away with a drink or two without MY life turning into a disaster.

* The Guardian

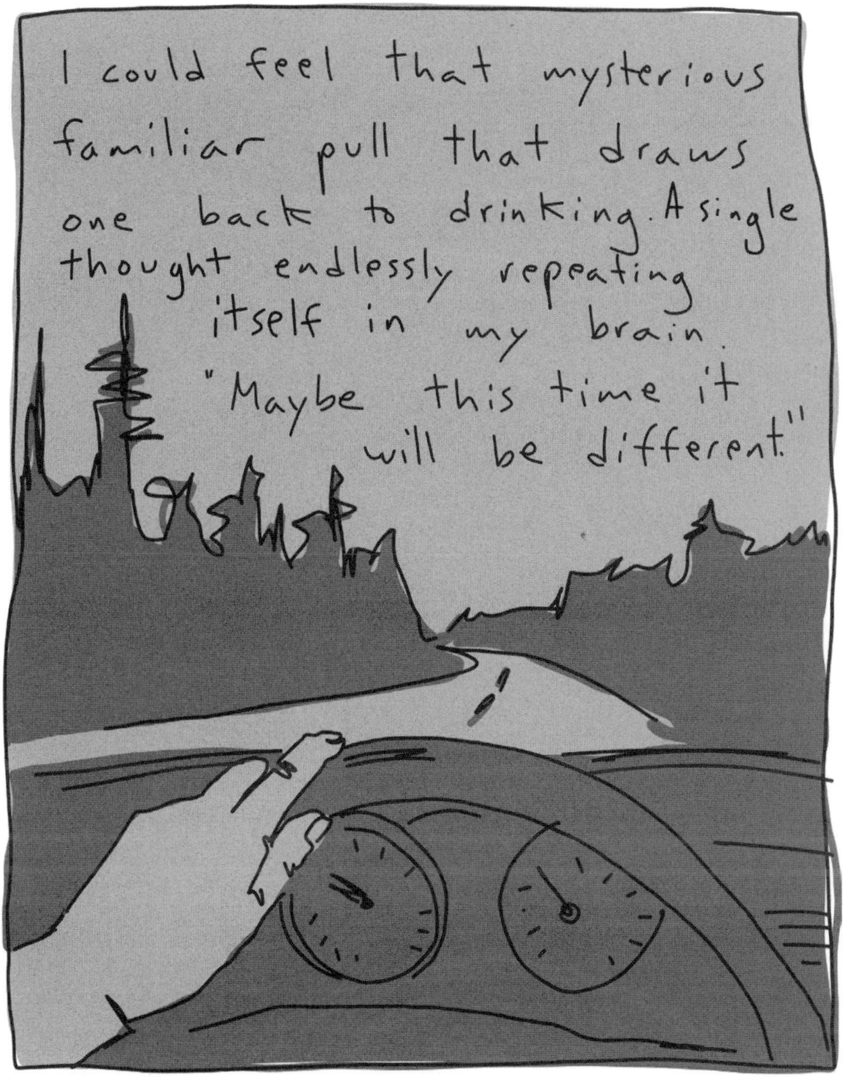
I could feel that mysterious familiar pull that draws one back to drinking. A single thought endlessly repeating itself in my brain.
"Maybe this time it will be different."

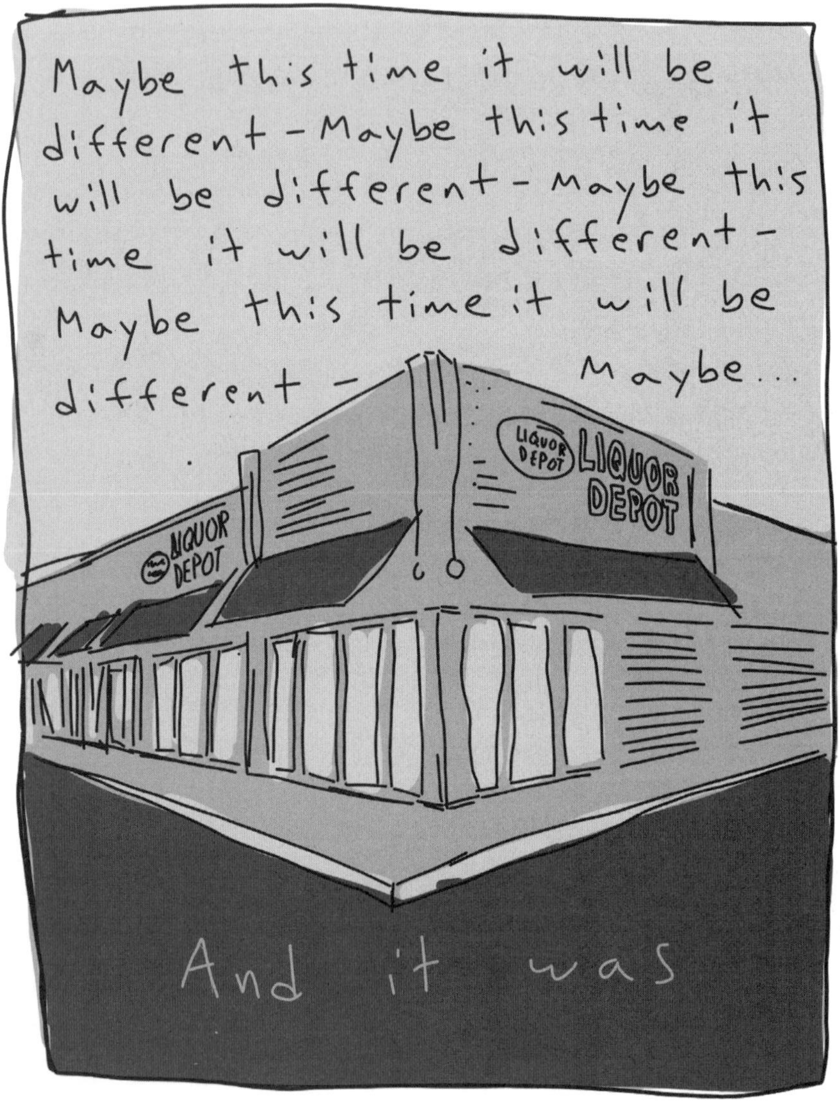
Maybe this time it will be different - Maybe this time it will be different - Maybe this time it will be different - Maybe this time it will be different - Maybe...
LIQUOR DEPOT
LIQUOR DEPOT
LIQUOR DEPOT
And it was

As if by magic I arrived in Prince George just in time for a meeting.

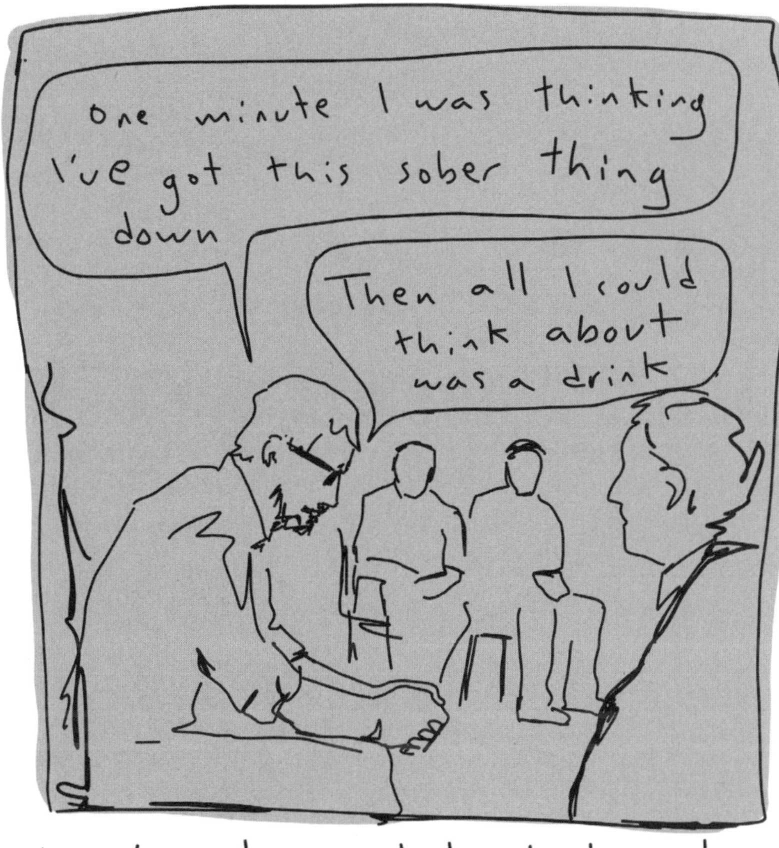
One minute I was thinking I've got this sober thing down
Then all I could think about was a drink

I shared and I listened and it bought me another day.

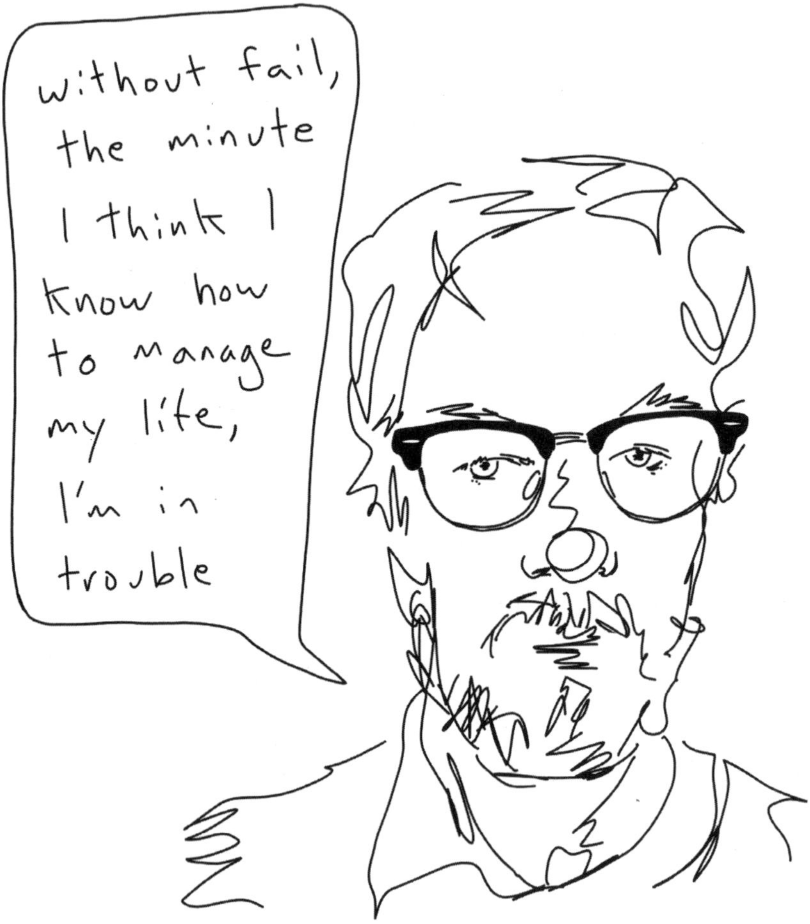
without fail, the minute I think I know how to manage my life, I'm in trouble

43

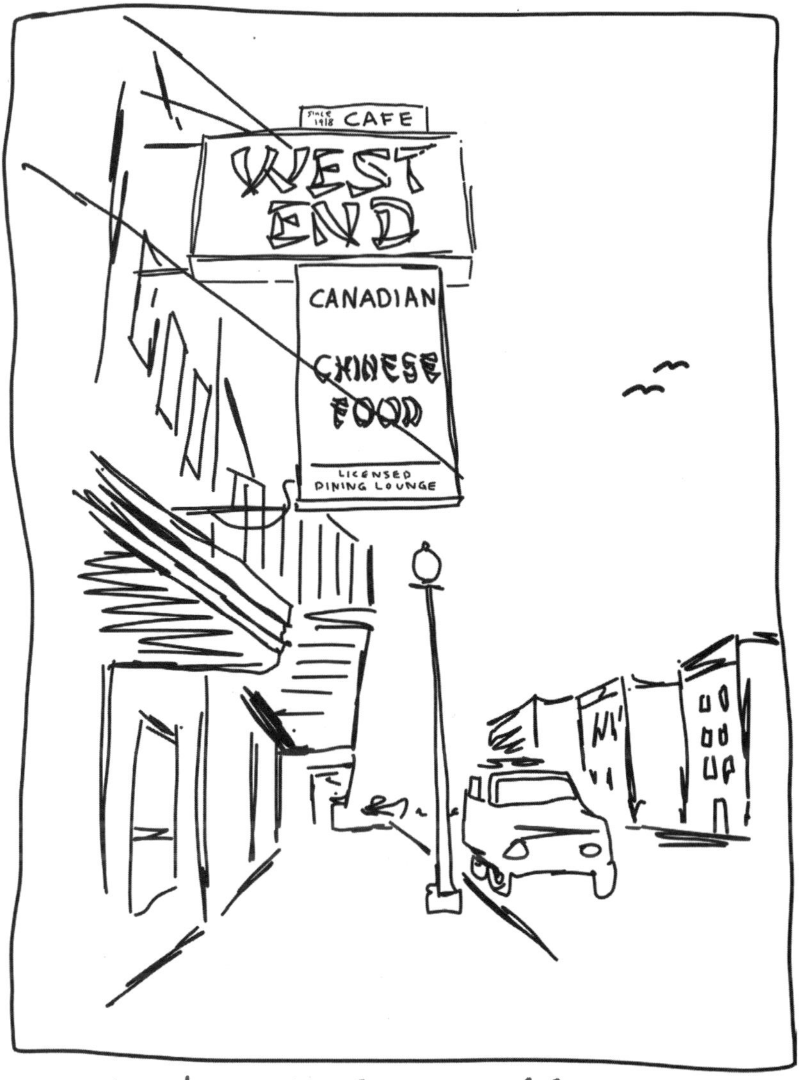
SINCE 1918 CAFE
WEST END
CANADIAN
CHINESE FOOD
LICENSED DINING LOUNGE

I stopped for a coffee

My coffee cup began to speak in my father's voice.
Always drink your coffee black
Then you won't be disappointed if there's no cream

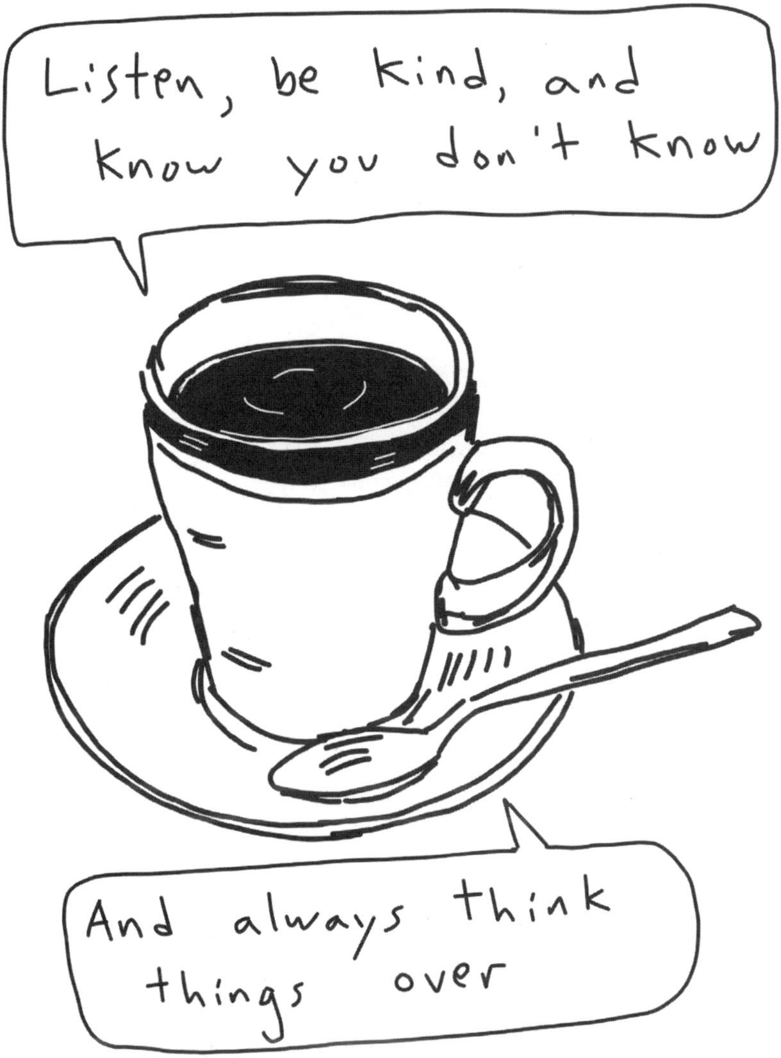
Listen, be kind, and know you don't know
And always think things over

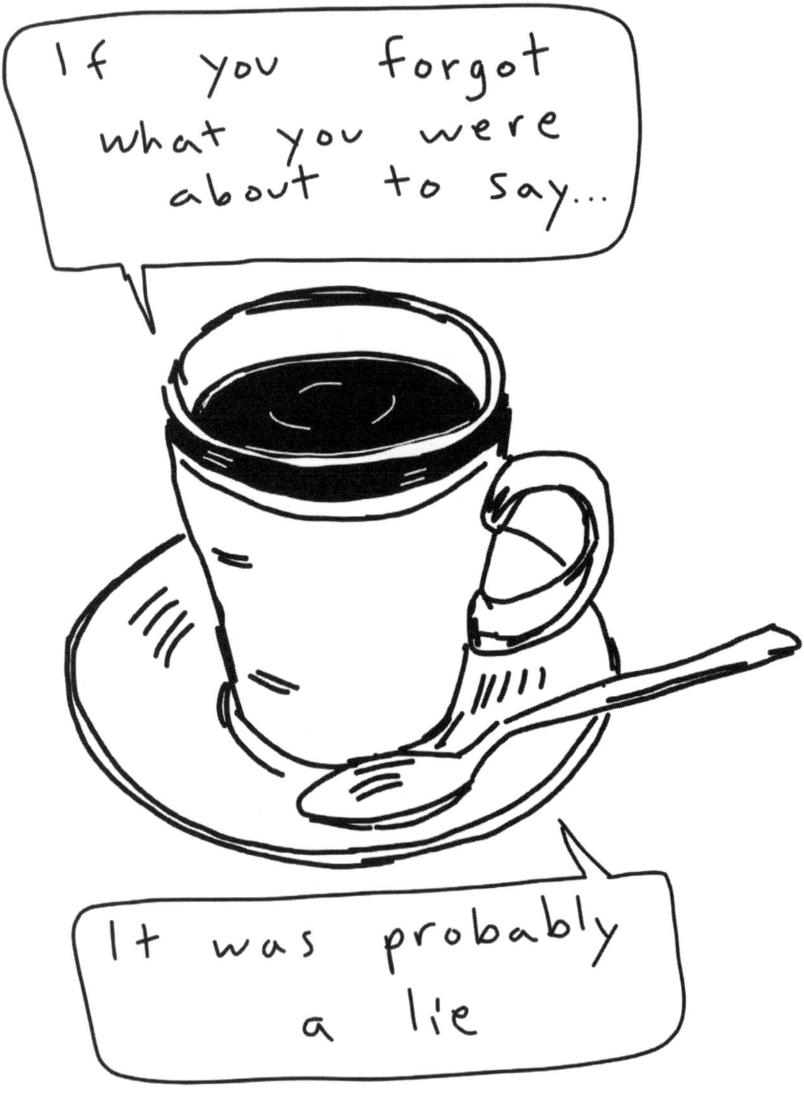
If you forgot what you were about to say...
It was probably a lie

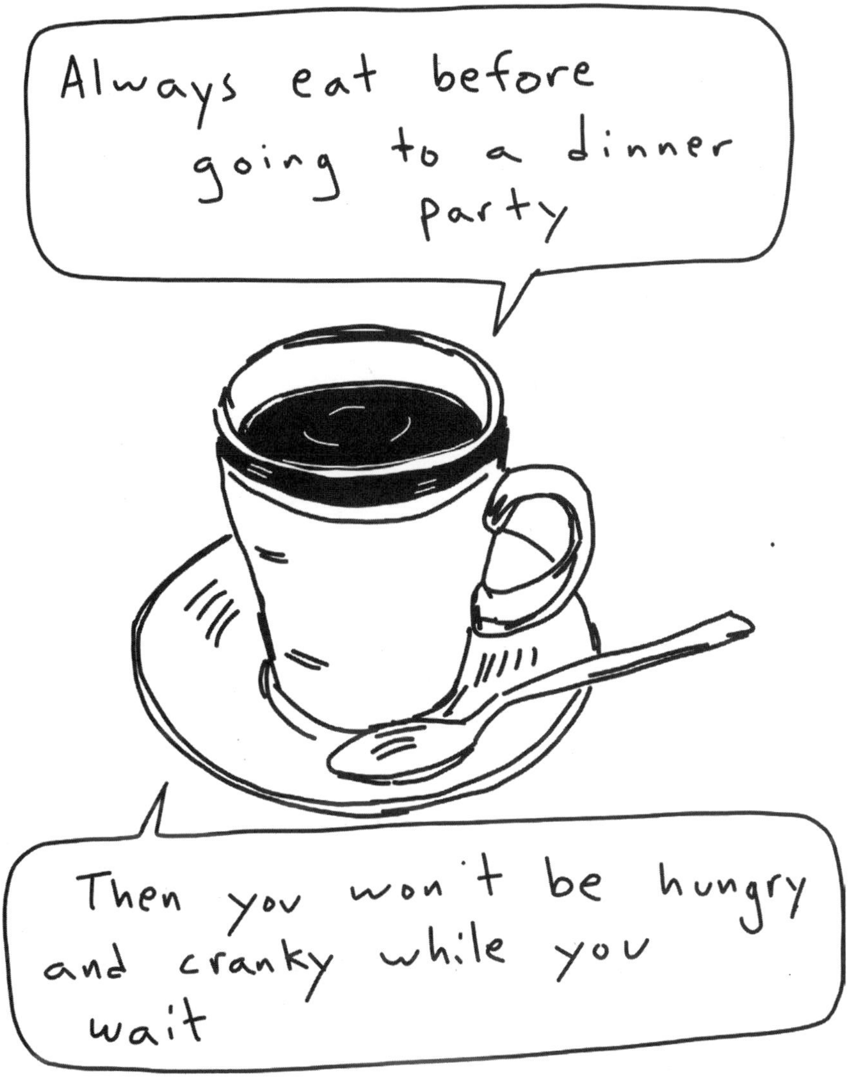
Always eat before going to a dinner party
Then you won't be hungry and cranky while you wait

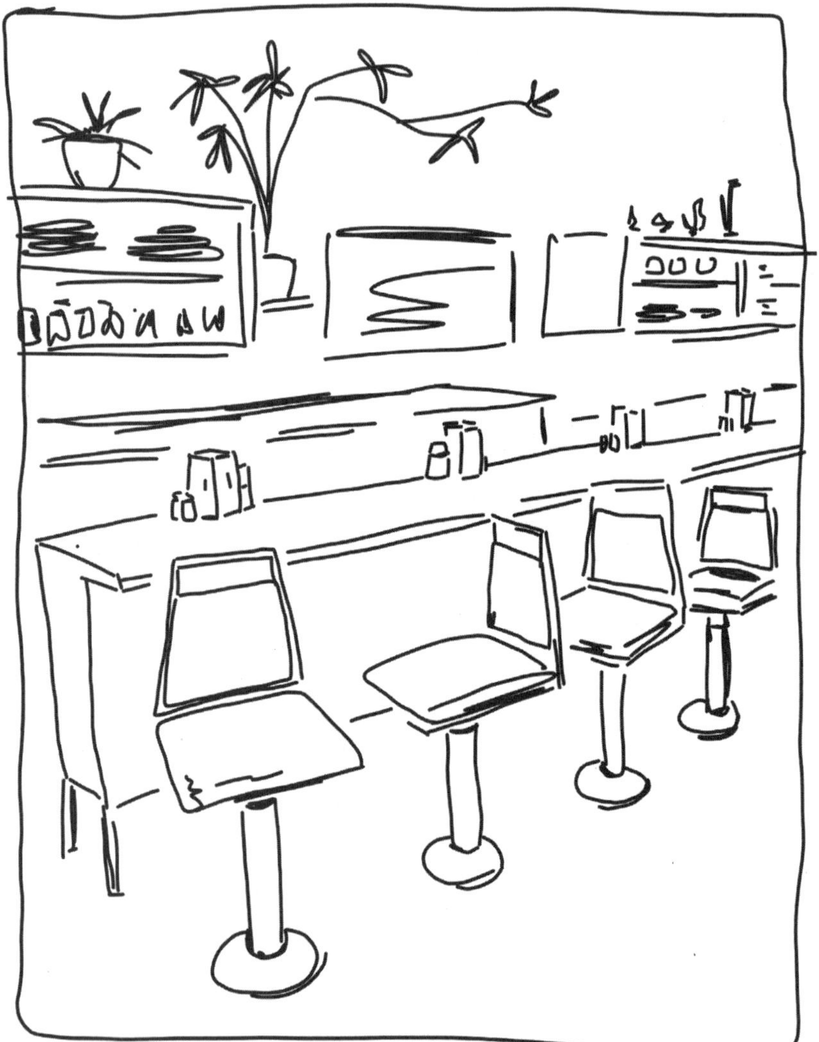

The place was empty.

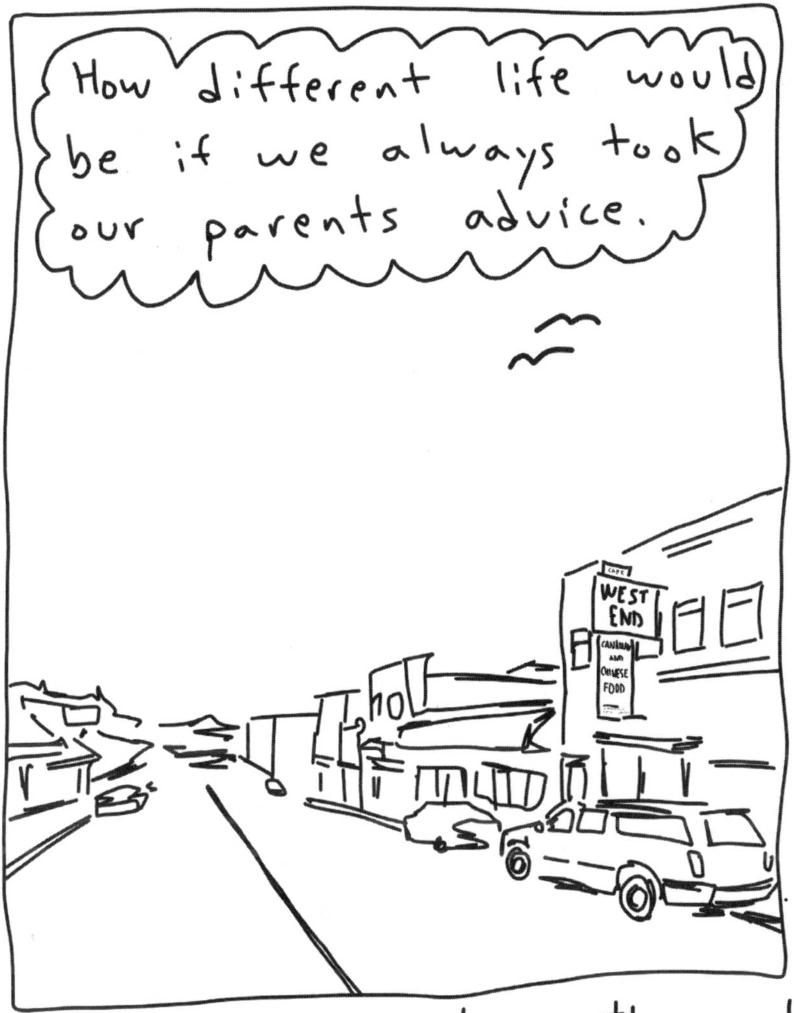
How different life would be if we always took our parents advice.
WEST END
CHINESE FOOD

And so I got back on the road.

44

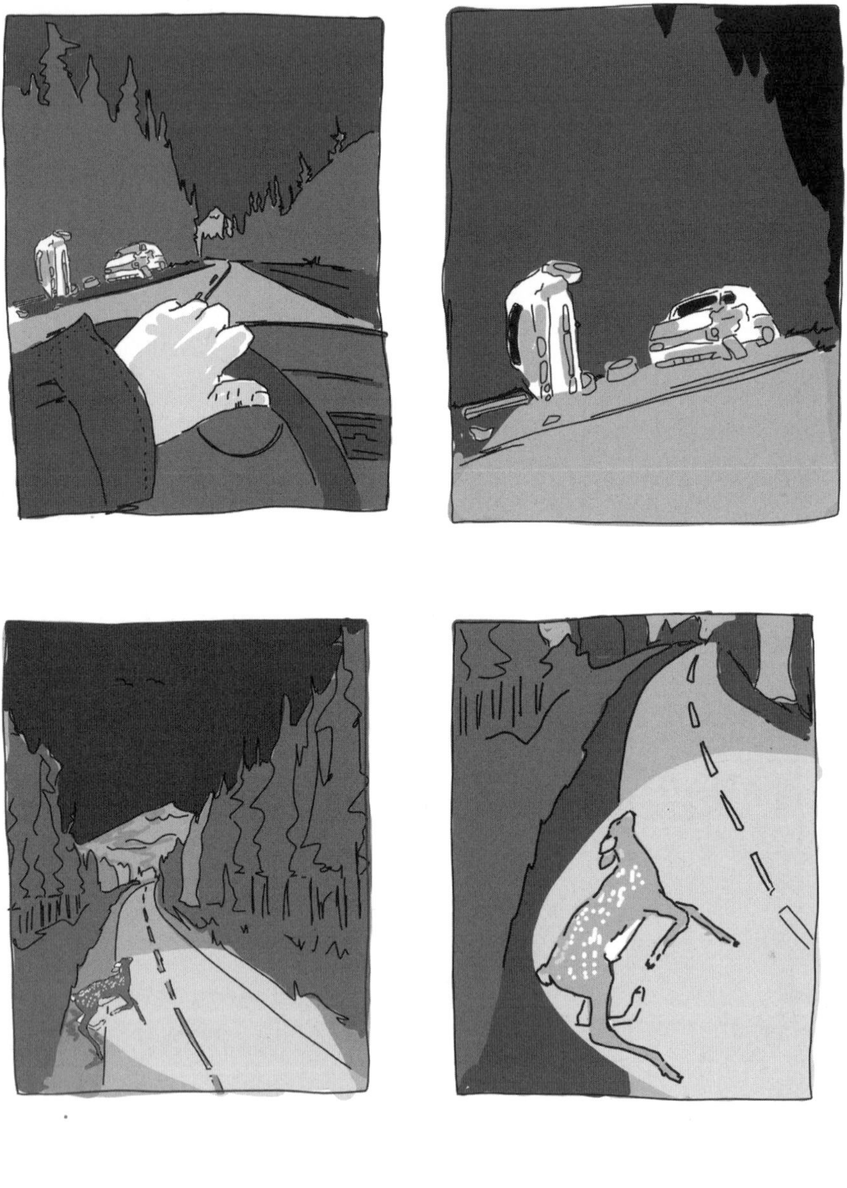

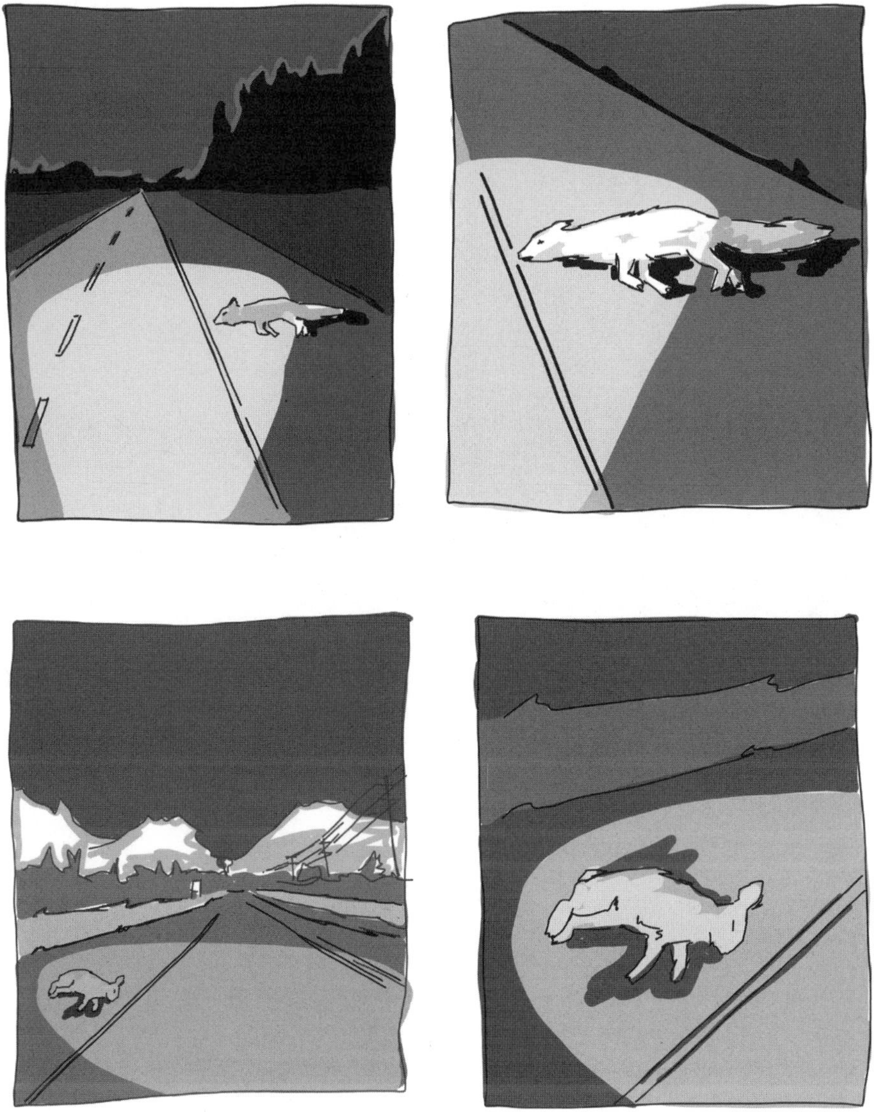

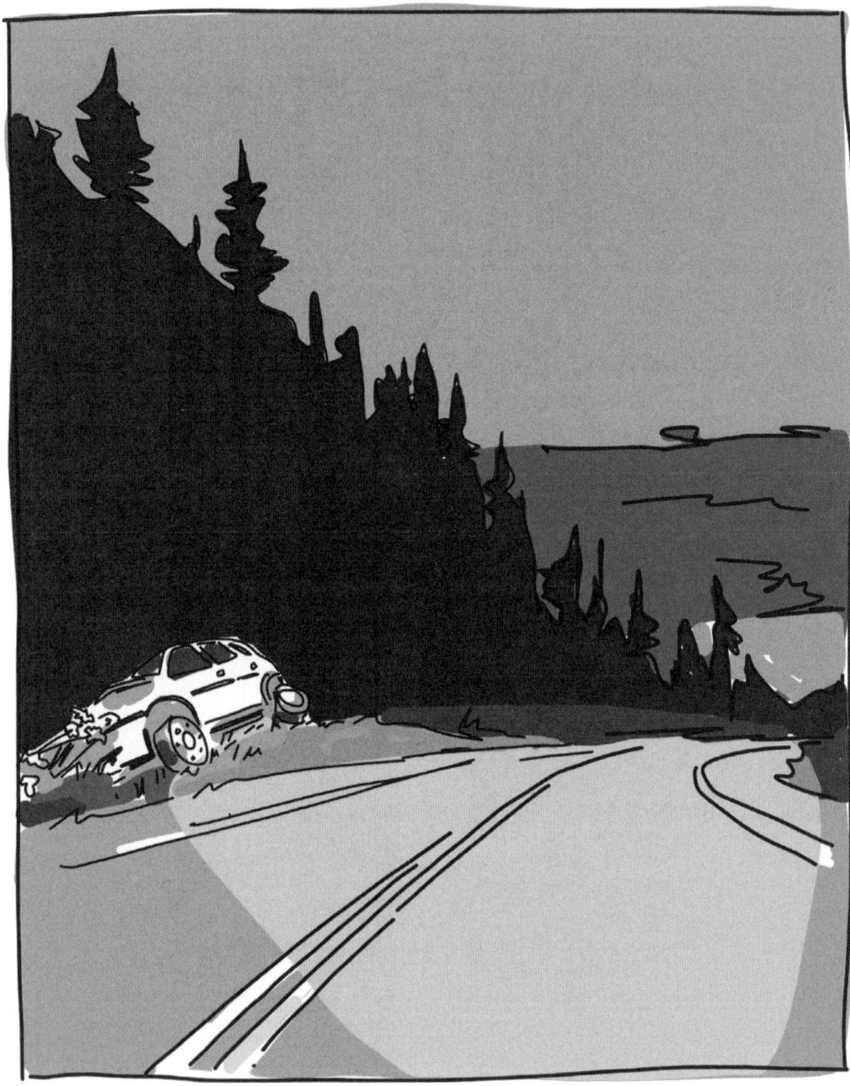

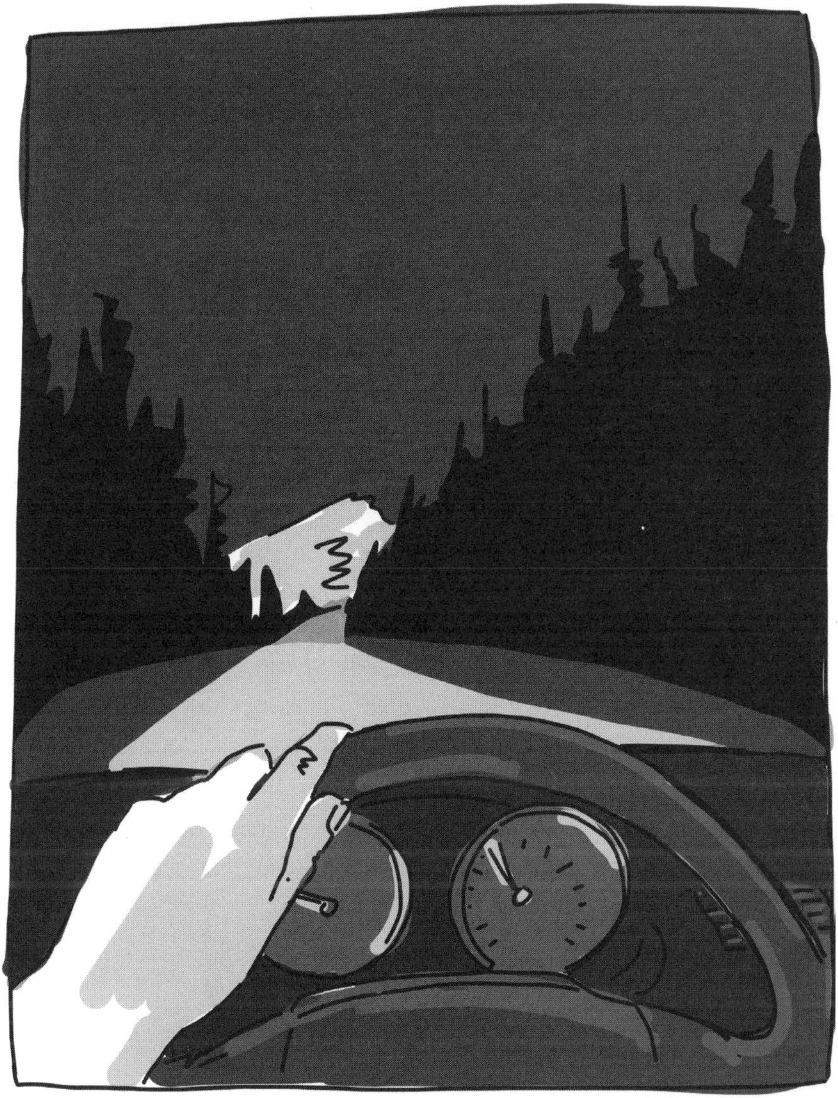

45

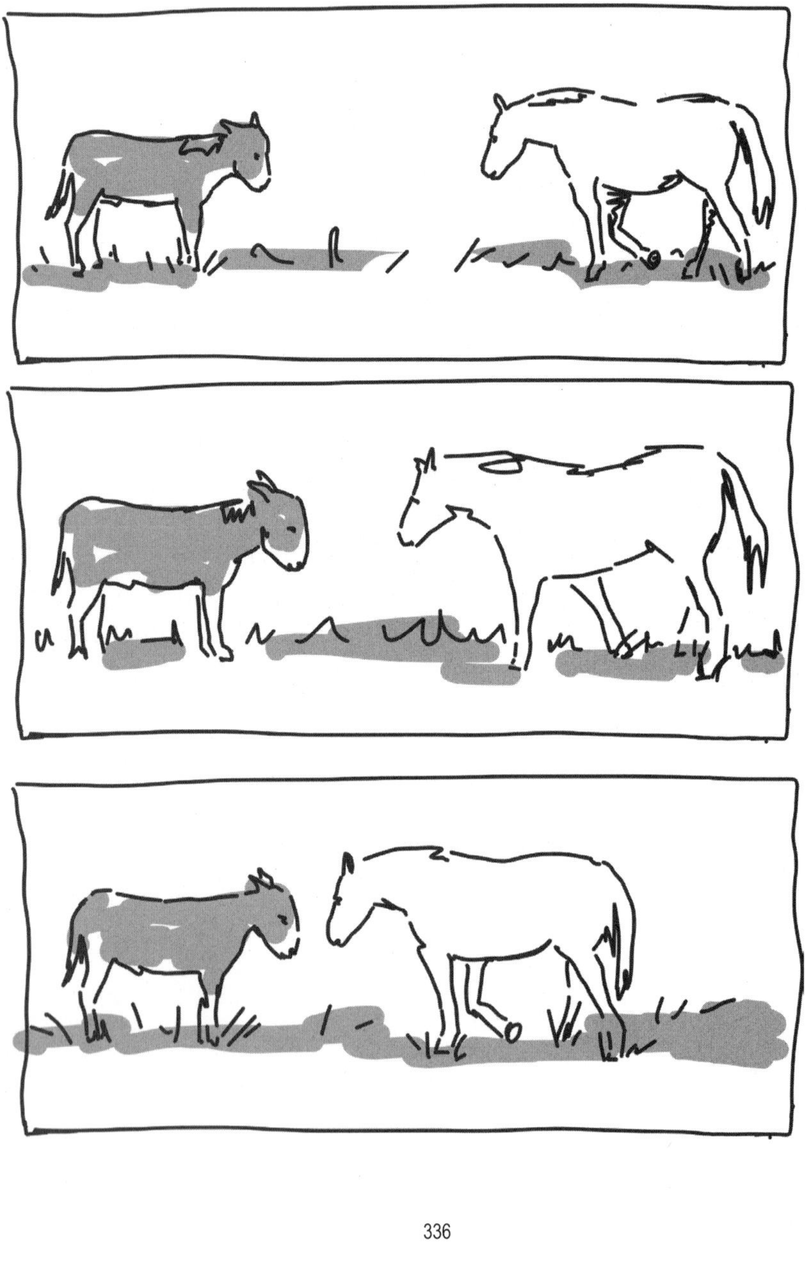

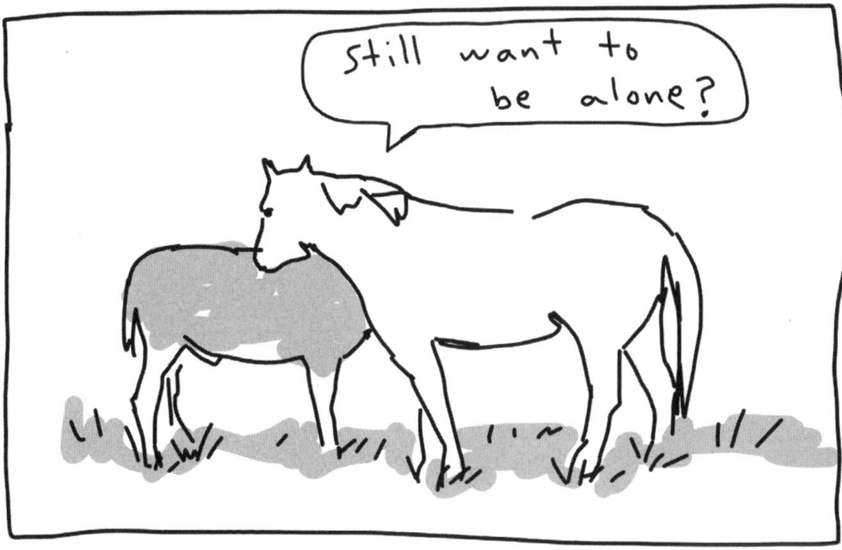
still want to be alone?

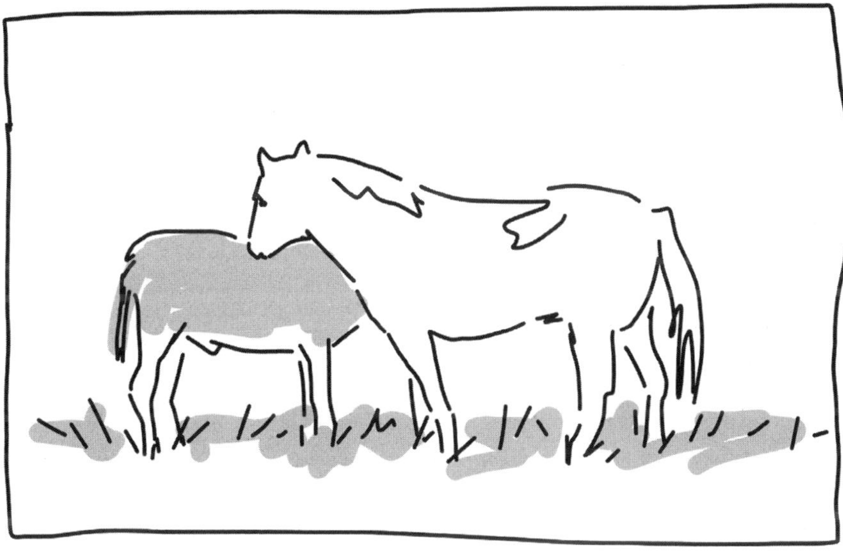

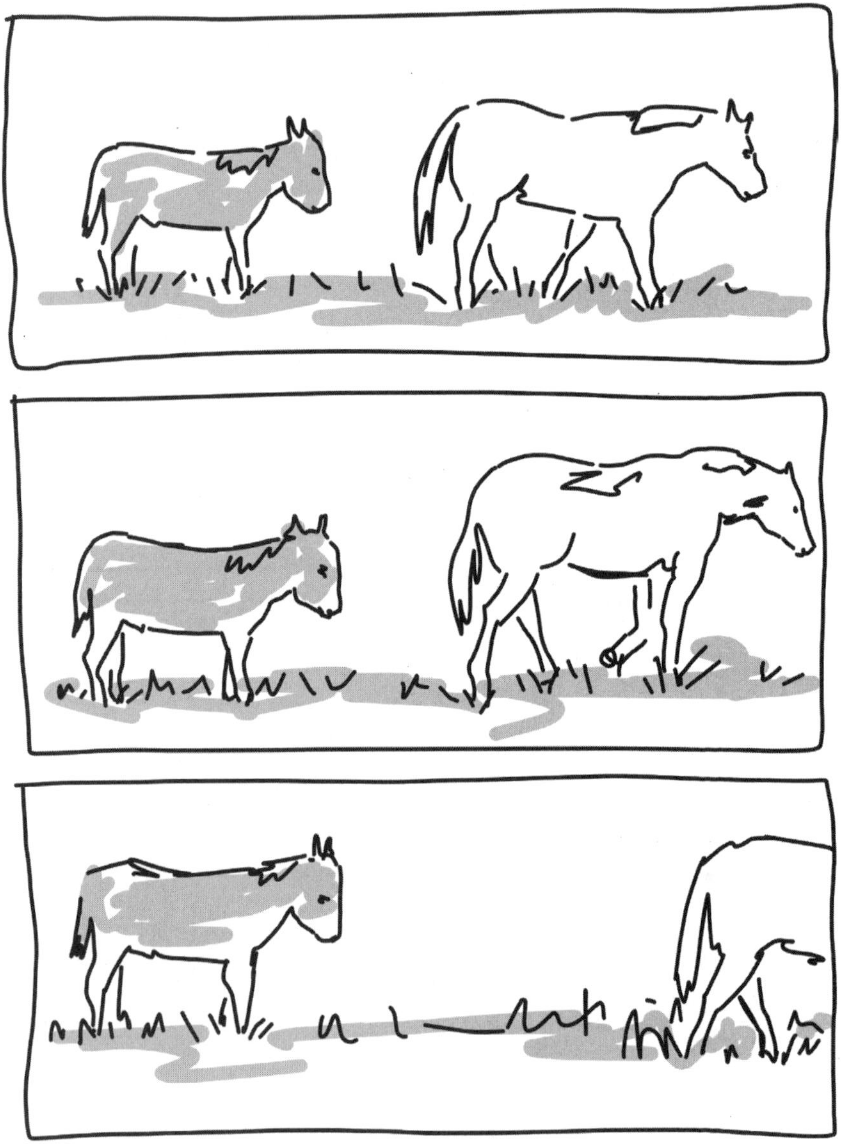

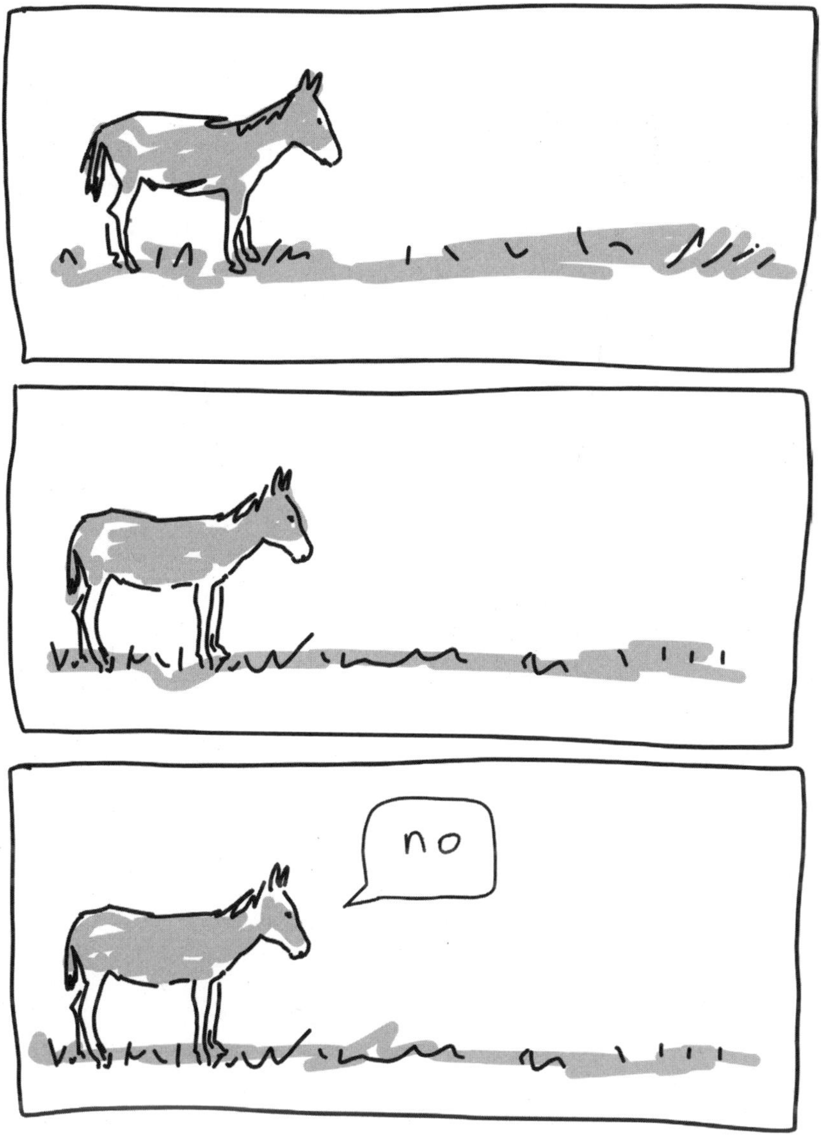
no

46

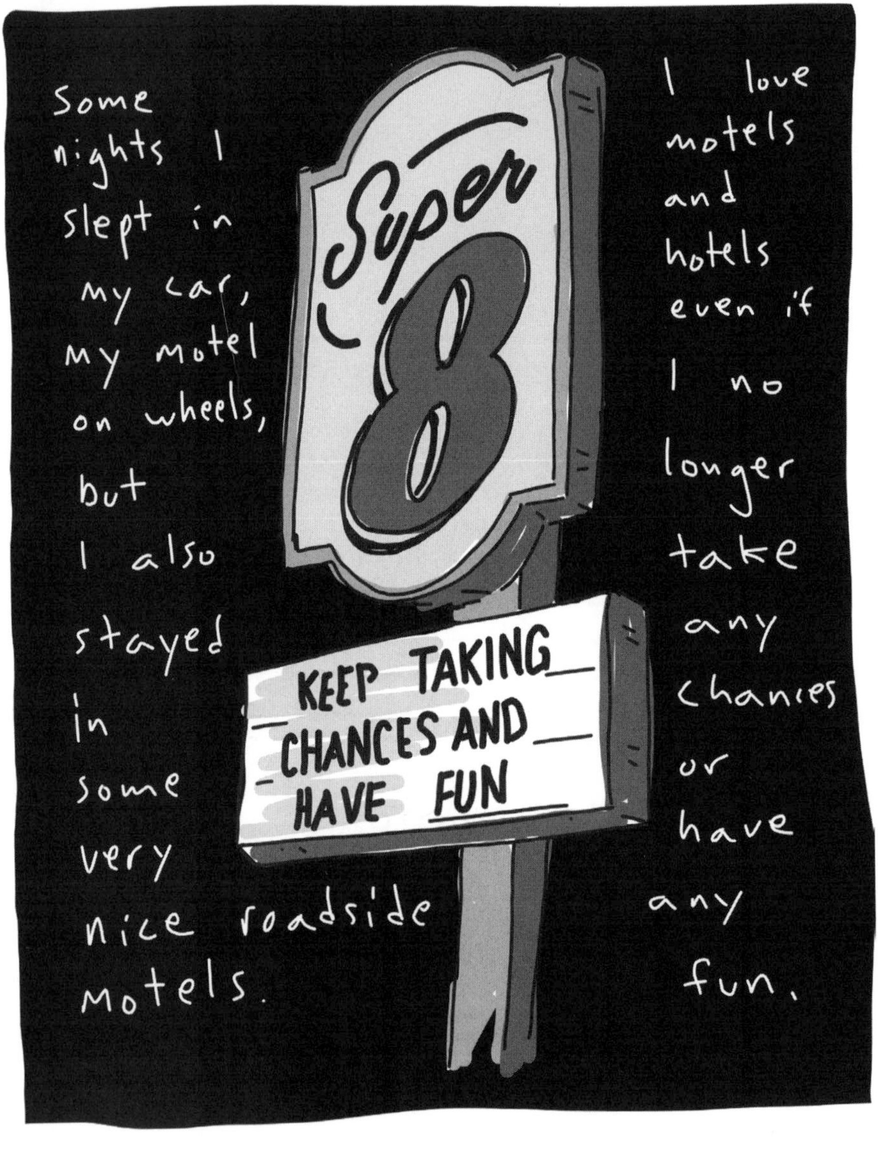
Some nights I slept in my car, my motel on wheels, but I also stayed in some very nice roadside motels.
Super 8
KEEP TAKING CHANCES AND HAVE FUN
I love motels and hotels even if I no longer take any chances or have any fun.

On October 22nd I made myself at home at a Super 8 in Prince George.

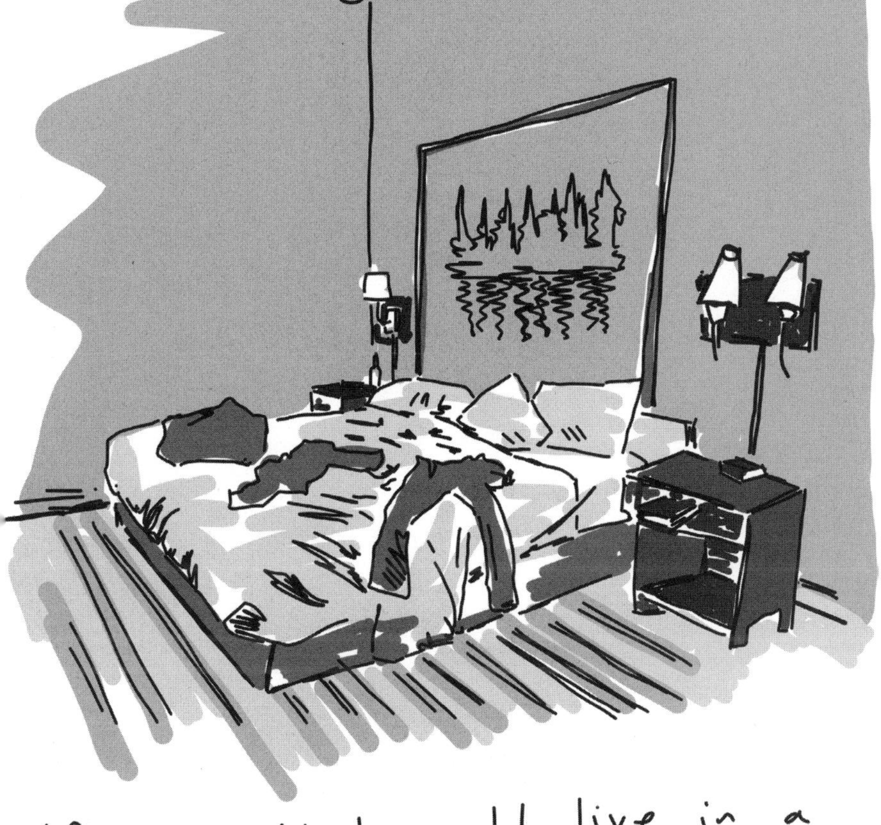

If I could I would live in a cheap motel like this full time.

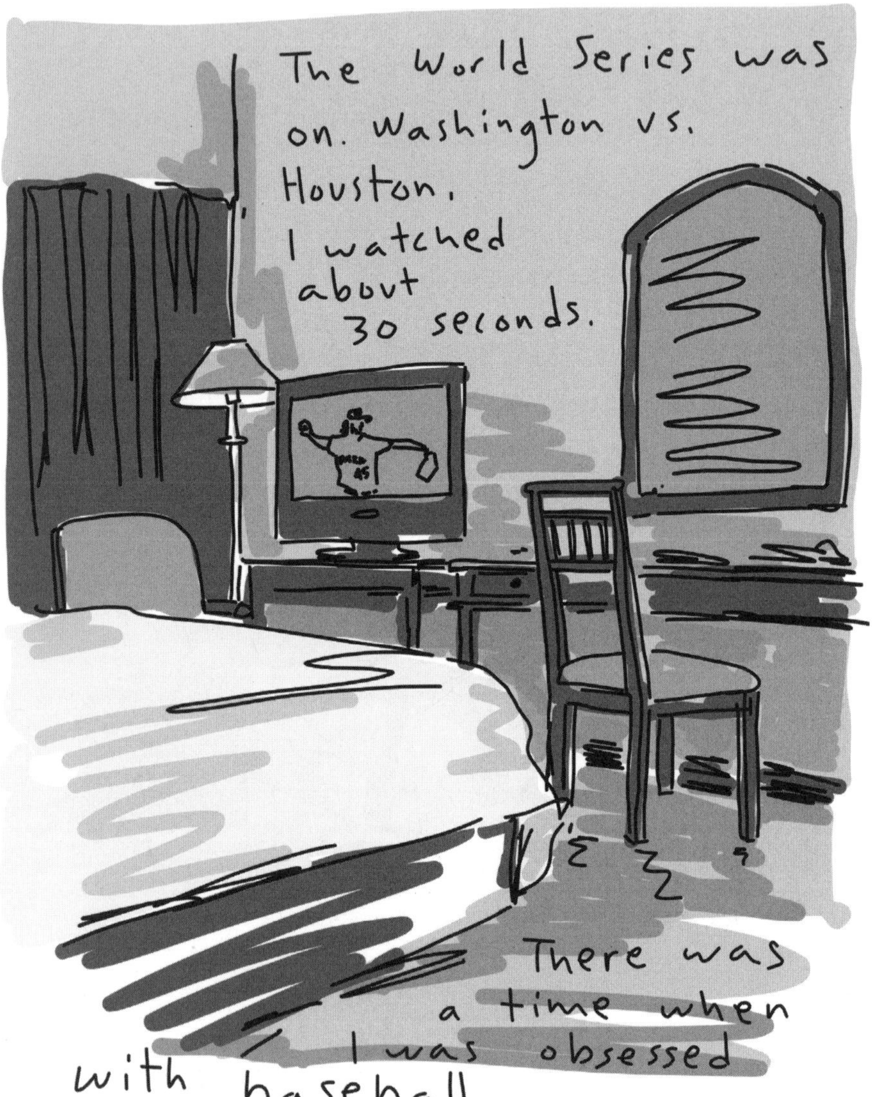
The World Series was on. Washington vs. Houston.
I watched about 30 seconds.
There was a time when I was obsessed with baseball.

I first became aware of the passage of time in 1979. I distinctly remember watching the Pirates win the World Series that year on TV with my dad who loved baseball.

I was 7 and smitten. I memorized every World Series match up from 1903 to present. The winners and the losers of course.

MANNY SANGUILLEN C
PIRATES

I made baseballs out of elastics and leather. My dad and I played a stats card game called "APBA Baseball" that was kind of like Dungeons and Dragons but for base ball

Manuel De Jesus Sanguillén Magan played for Pittsburgh that year. It was his second last year in the majors and he may also have been feeling the reality of the passage of time. Like Manny I would soon decide it was time to move on from a life in baseball.

When I was 10 and 11 I played for a team called "Super Duper Buns Master Bakery."

But our uniforms just said "Super Duper" in a speech bubble and nothing else, as if our mascot was a ghost.

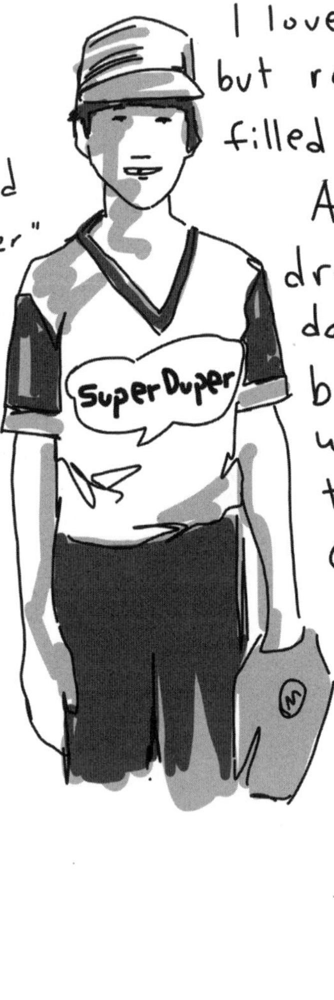
Super Duper

I loved to practice but real games filled me with dread.

And yet I would dream that one day I could become the worst player in the big leagues. Good enough, but *just* good enough, to barely make it.

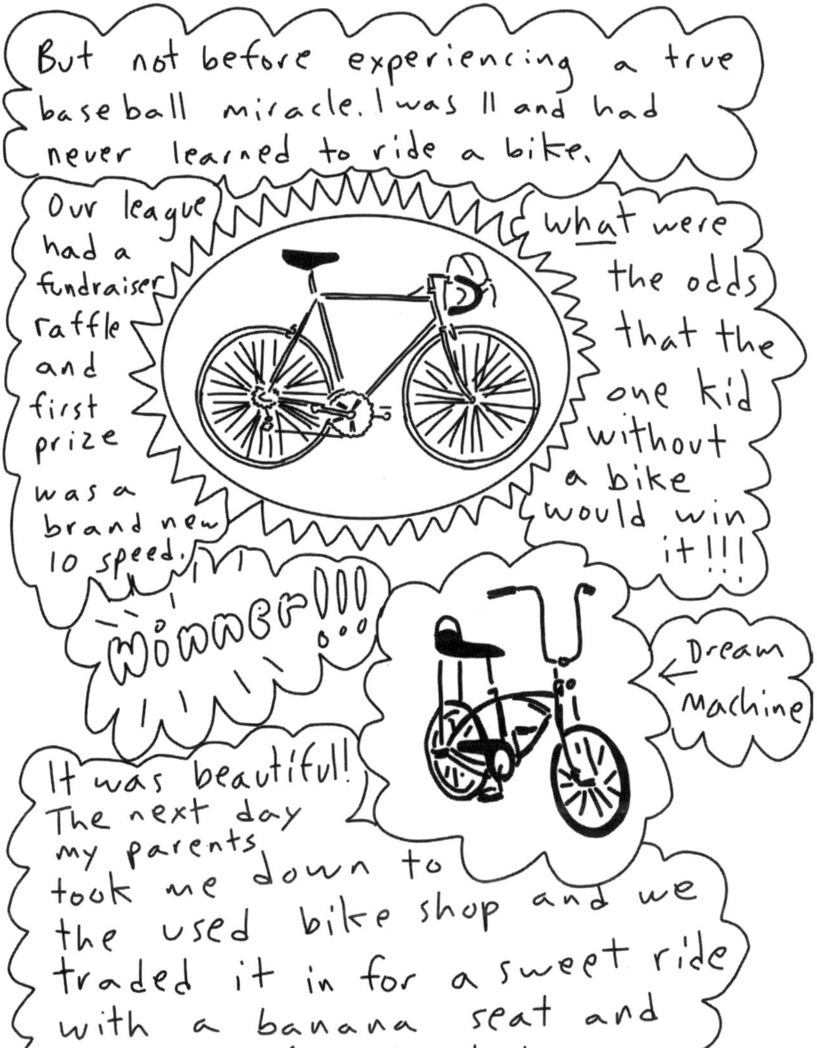
But not before experiencing a true baseball miracle. I was 11 and had never learned to ride a bike.
Our league had a fundraiser raffle and first prize was a brand new 10 speed.
What were the odds that the one kid without a bike would win it!!!
WINNER!!!
It was beautiful! The next day my parents took me down to the used bike shop and we traded it in for a sweet ride with a banana seat and a bunch of cool stickers.
Dream Machine

I have such wonderful memories of my dad and baseball but the stress of game days was killing me.

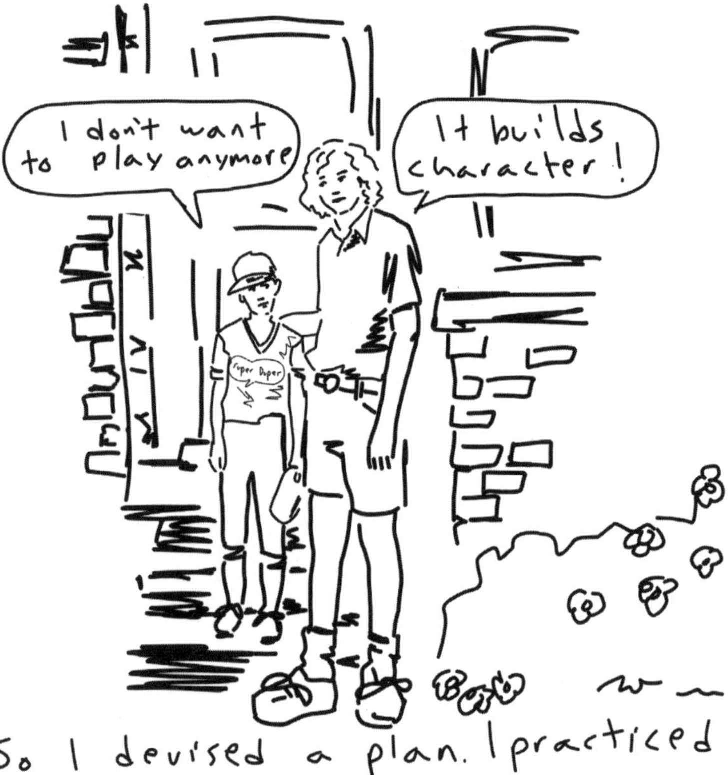

I don't want to play anymore
It builds character!
Super Duper

So I devised a plan. I practiced it for weeks and it worked. I cried my eyes out and they let me quit.

Baseball was good to me, I even met Bluejays pitcher Dave Stieb at an exhibition game in 1980 (thanks Dad!), and sometimes I missed it, but once you cry to get out of playing a game there is no going back.

And now I had wheels and new adventures ahead of me.

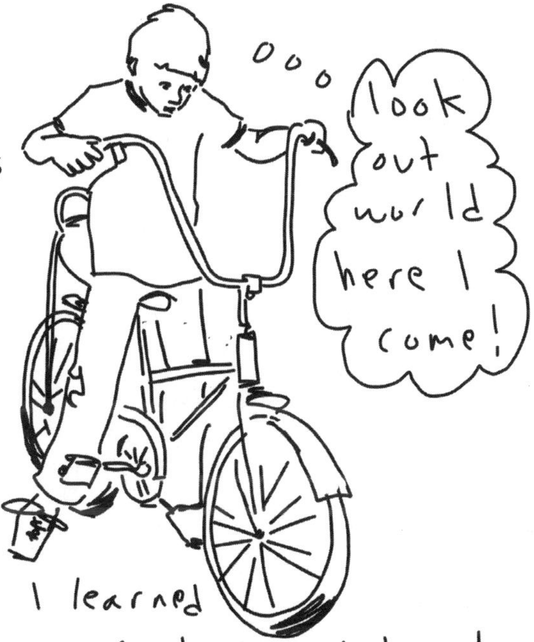
ooo
look out world here I come!

My Mom was proud I learned to ride it so fast but holy moly I was eleven!

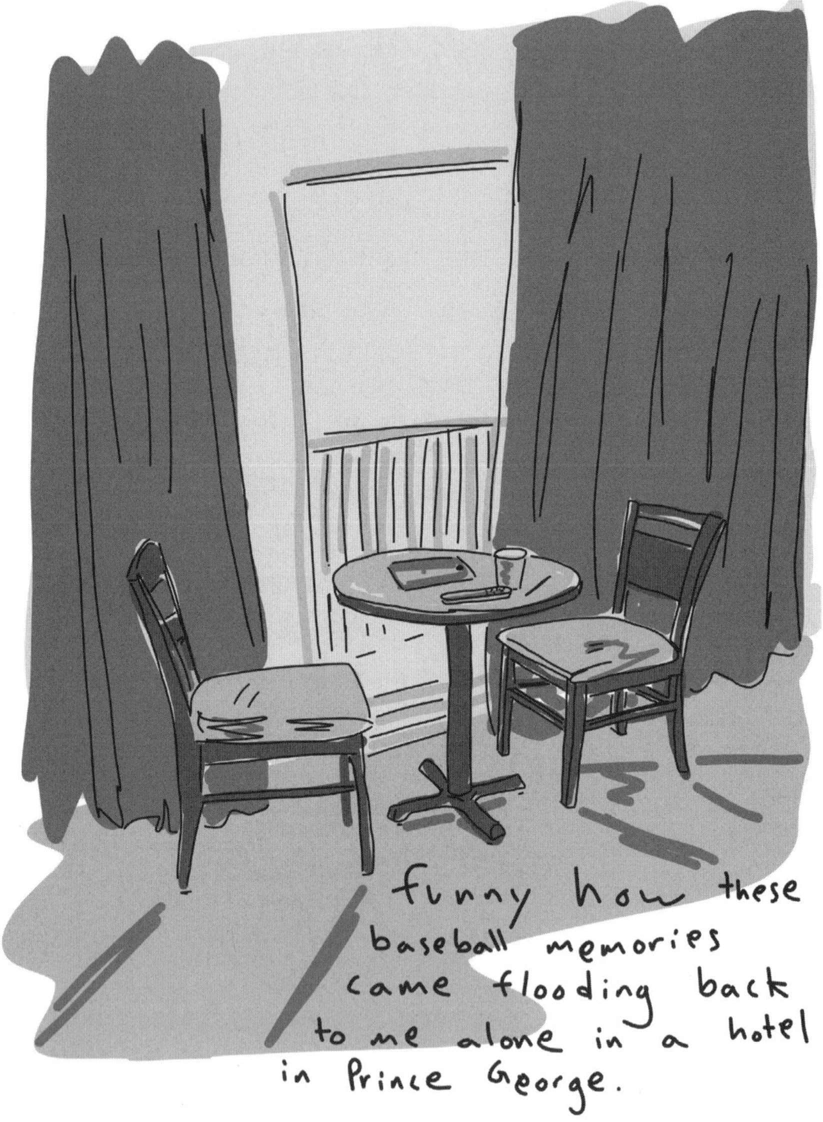
funny how these baseball memories came flooding back to me alone in a hotel in Prince George.

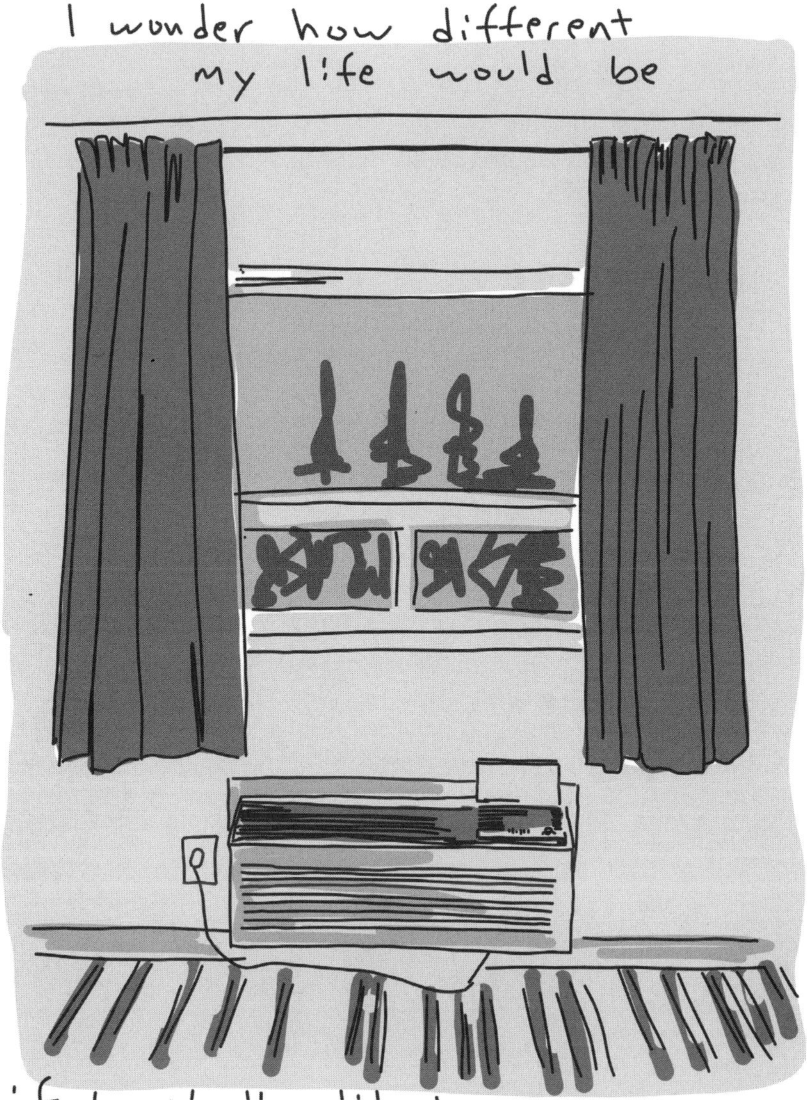
I wonder how different my life would be
if baseball didn't make me cry.

47

I overheard a lot of great conversations while working at the library in Rupert. Near the end of my stay I listened to an older couple discussing Heisenberg's Observer Effect theory.

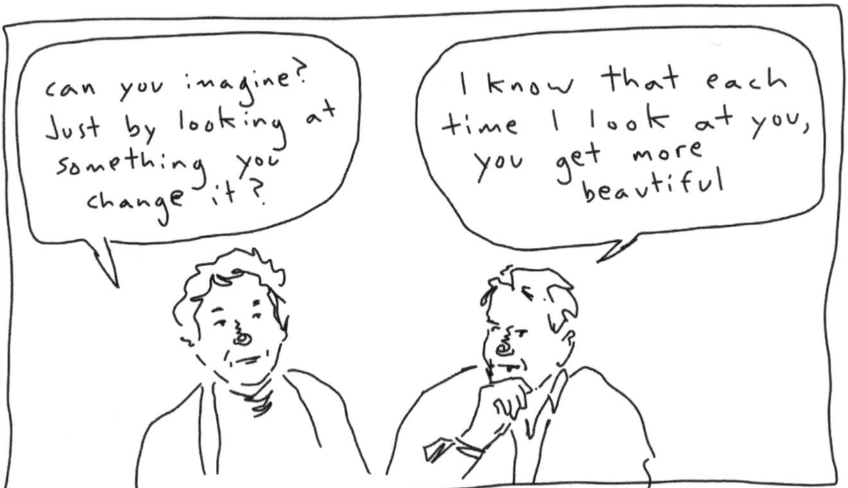
can you imagine? Just by looking at something you change it?
I know that each time I look at you, you get more beautiful

While eavesdropping I learned that while not to be confused with The Uncertainty Principle (also known as the story of my life) the Observer Effect points out that on a quantum level, to observe something is to change it.

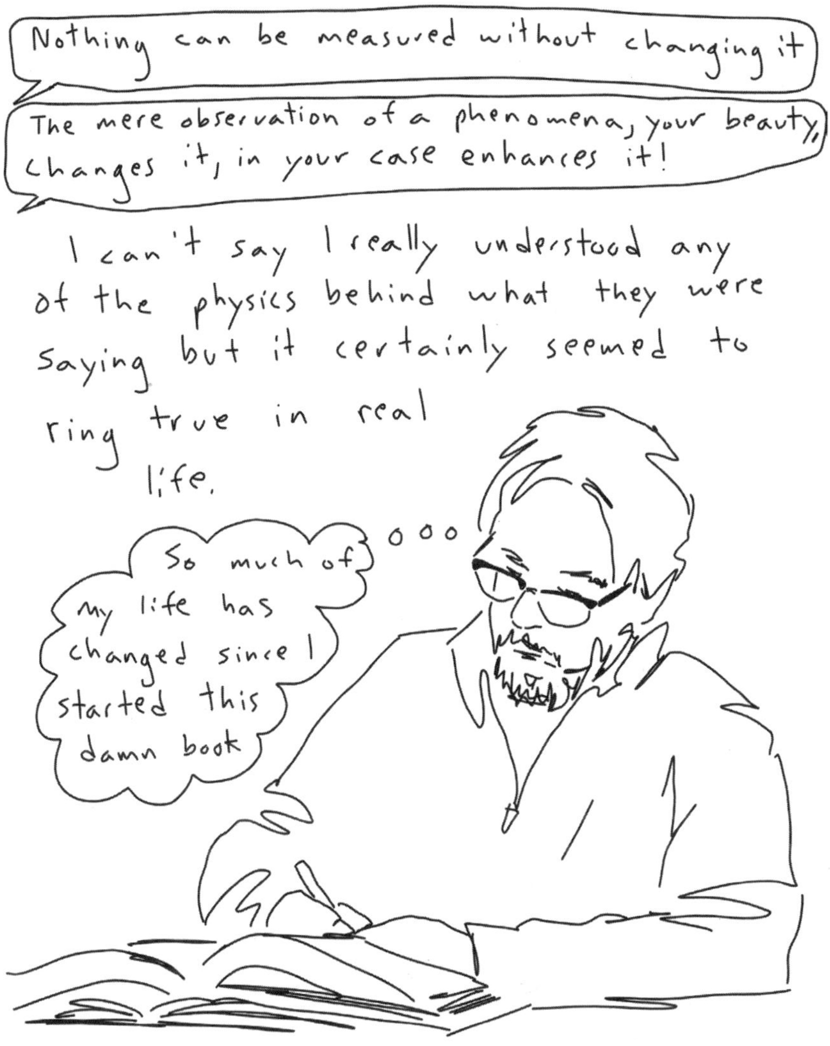
Nothing can be measured without changing it
The mere observation of a phenomena, your beauty, changes it, in your case enhances it!
I can't say I really understood any of the physics behind what they were saying but it certainly seemed to ring true in real life.
So much of my life has changed since I started this damn book

In particle physics an electron is detected by its interaction with a photon – this interaction inevitably alters the trajectory of the electron.*

I was a pretty good baseball player as a kid but not when my parents were watching.

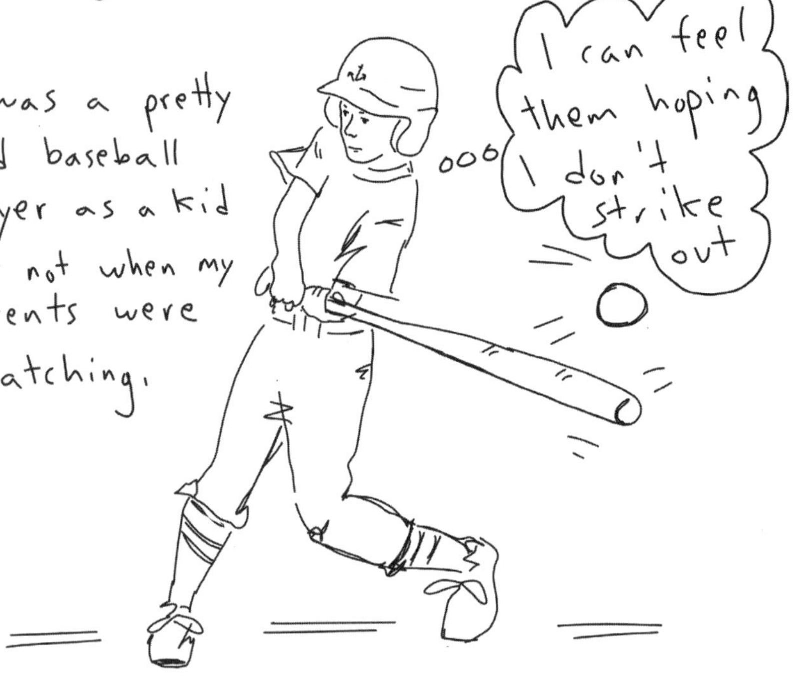
I can feel them hoping I don't strike out

So was I really a good or bad player? It all depended on who was or wasn't watching.

In thermodynamics a standard glass thermometer must absorb or give up some thermal energy to record a temperature and therefore changes the temperature of the body it is measuring.*

like a text from an ex

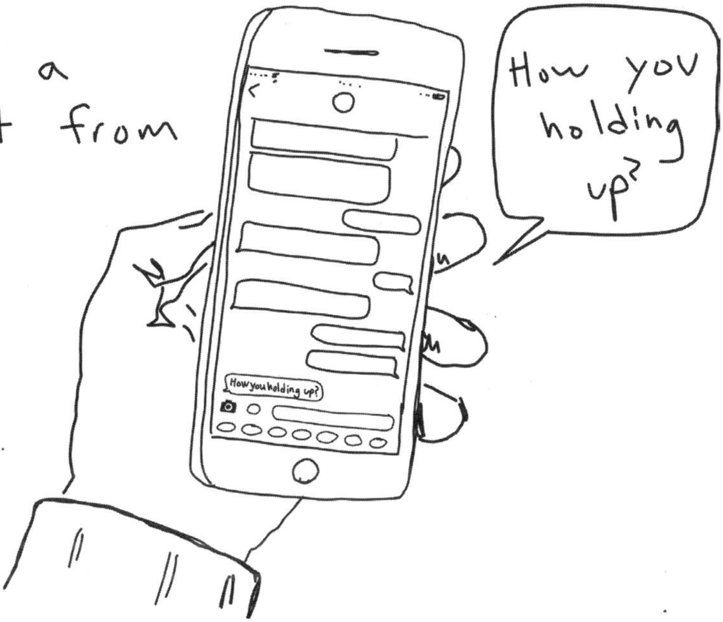
How you holding up?
How you holding up?

Nothing changes my state of mind as quickly as even the friendliest check in from an ex.

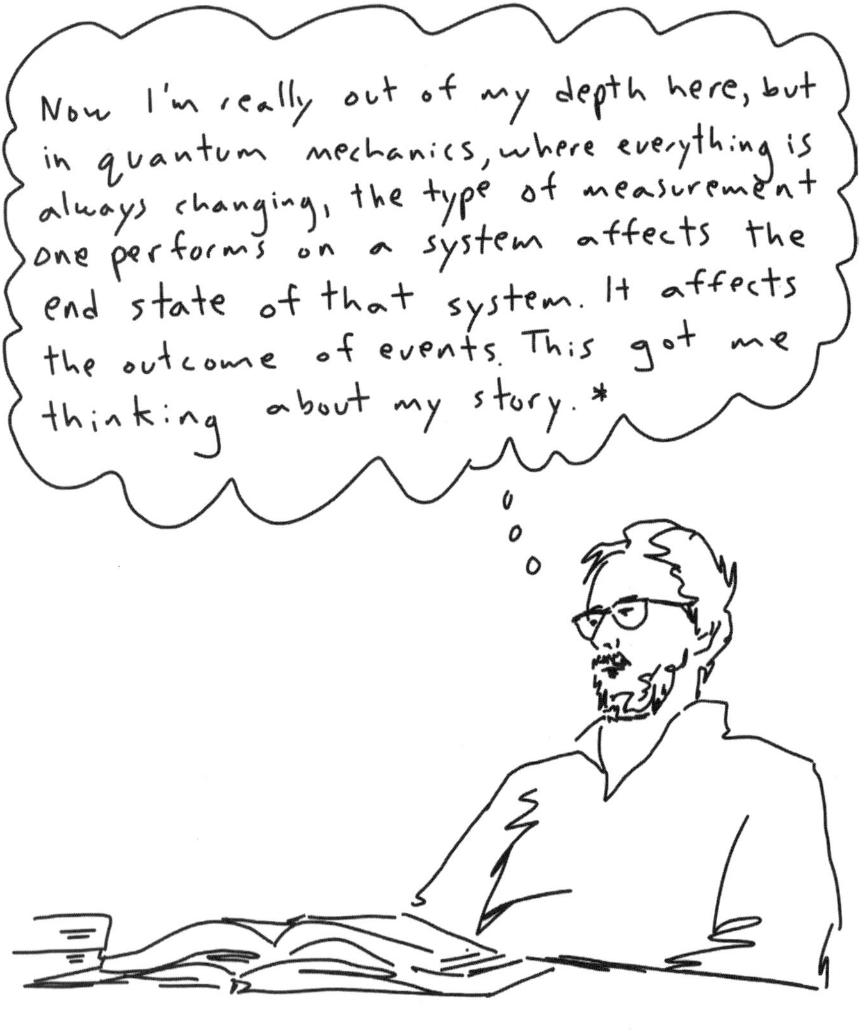
Now I'm really out of my depth here, but in quantum mechanics, where everything is always changing, the type of measurement one performs on a system affects the end state of that system. It affects the outcome of events. This got me thinking about my story.*

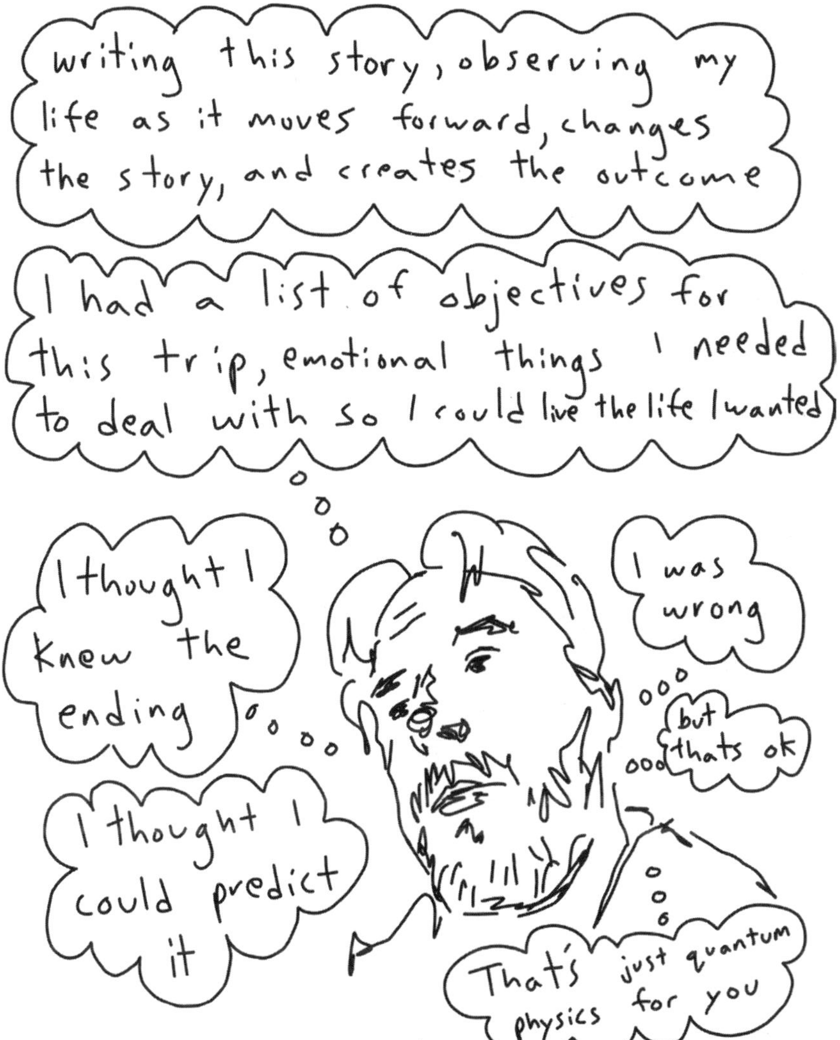
writing this story, observing my life as it moves forward, changes the story, and creates the outcome
I had a list of objectives for this trip, emotional things I needed to deal with so I could live the life I wanted
I thought I knew the ending
I thought I could predict it
I was wrong
but thats ok
That's just quantum physics for you

It reminds me of another conversation I overheard about how people in recovery never change __that__ much. Maybe 10% at most.

And I thought of a ship at sea. And Small adjustments.

And how even a small change in course, a matter of degrees, will guide a ship to a completely different destination.

HOMEWARD BOUND?

And I wondered if I was homeward bound.

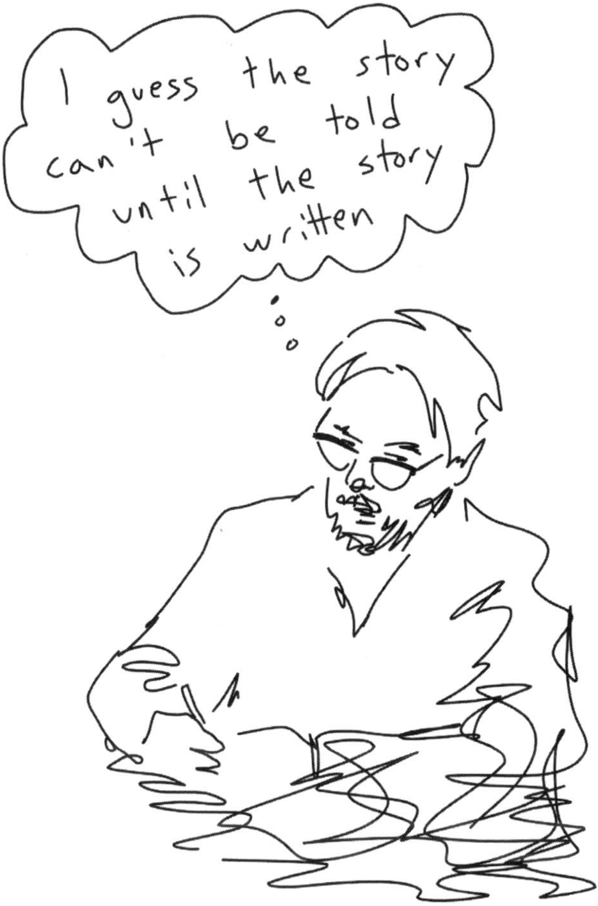
I guess the story can't be told until the story is written

* my sources are, an old couple in the library, Jon McKiel, Brian Neilson, wikipedia and some <u>books</u>, "A Cultural History of Physics" and "Physics in the 20th century"

48

I saw a Snowshoe Hare running fast and straight as an arrow

across a large open field so quickly even the distant eagles above did not notice it.

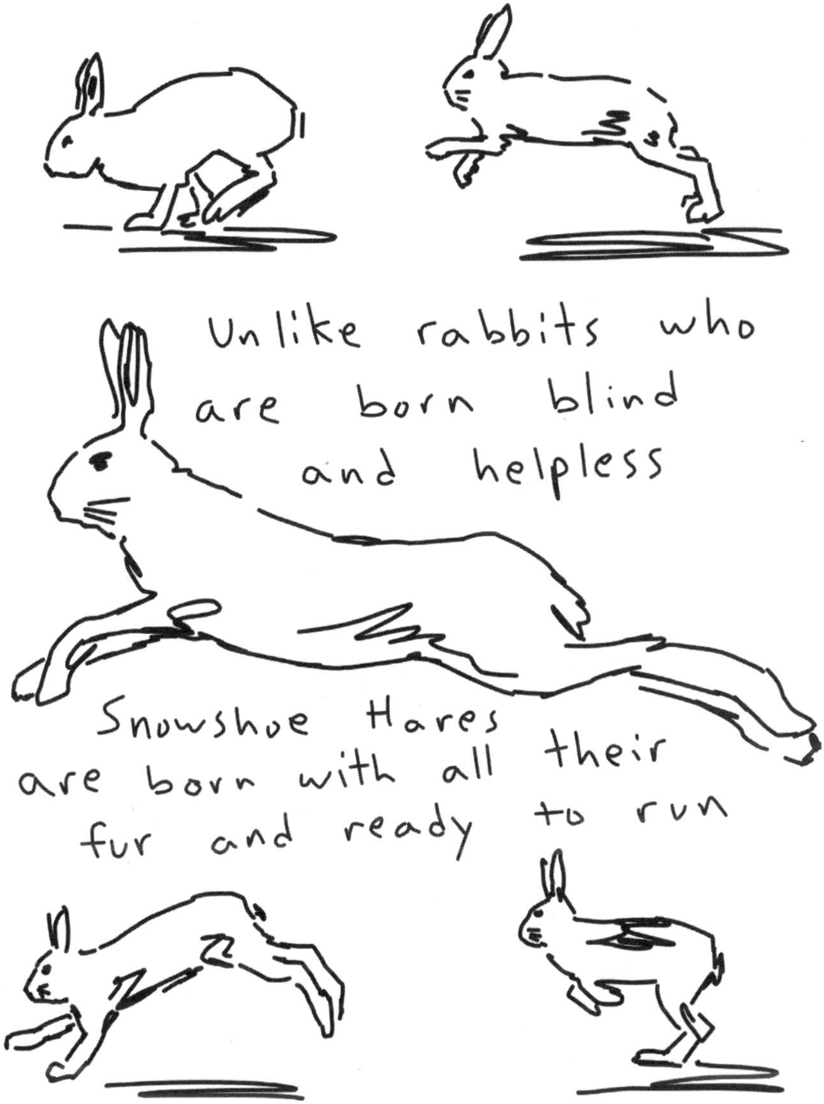
Unlike rabbits who
are born blind
and helpless
Snowshoe Hares
are born with all their
fur and ready to run

As I watched that hare
   disappear into the woods
I thought to myself, I
          do believe I know
          how it feels

Always running, always
   afraid of something,
Always one step ahead
of an unknown disaster.

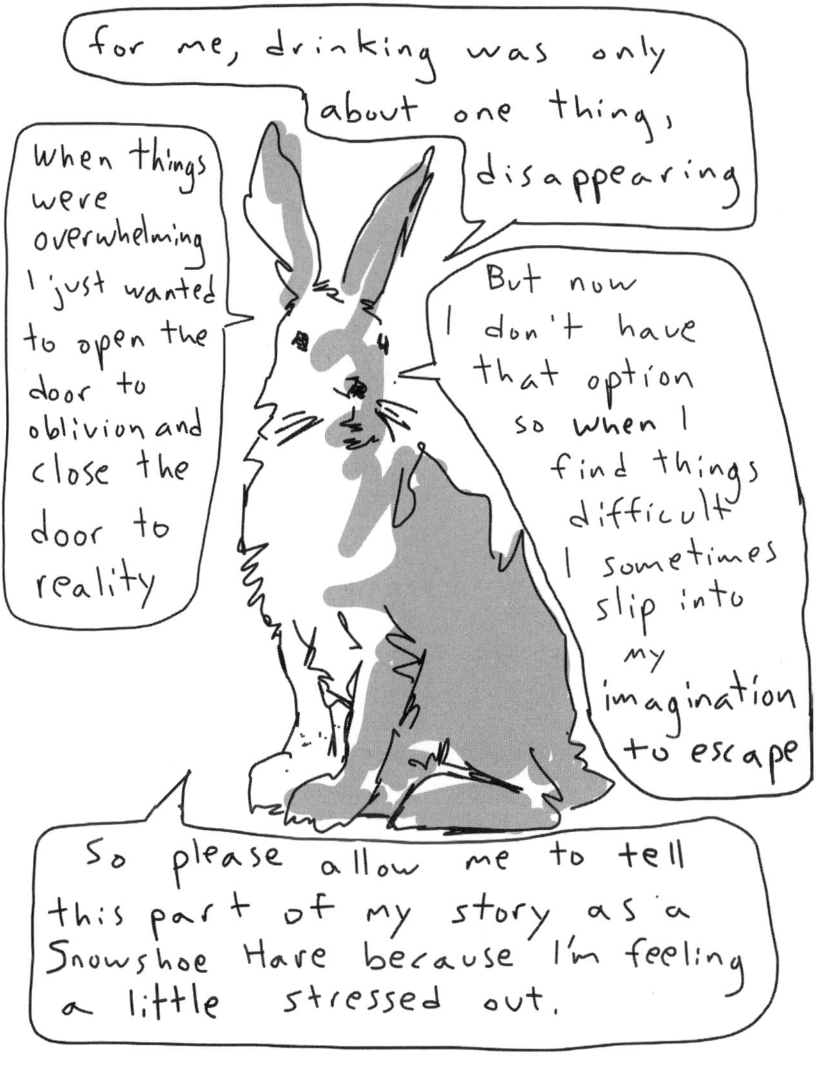
for me, drinking was only about one thing, disappearing
When things were overwhelming I just wanted to open the door to oblivion and close the door to reality
But now I don't have that option so when I find things difficult I sometimes slip into my imagination to escape
So please allow me to tell this part of my story as a Snowshoe Hare because I'm feeling a little stressed out.

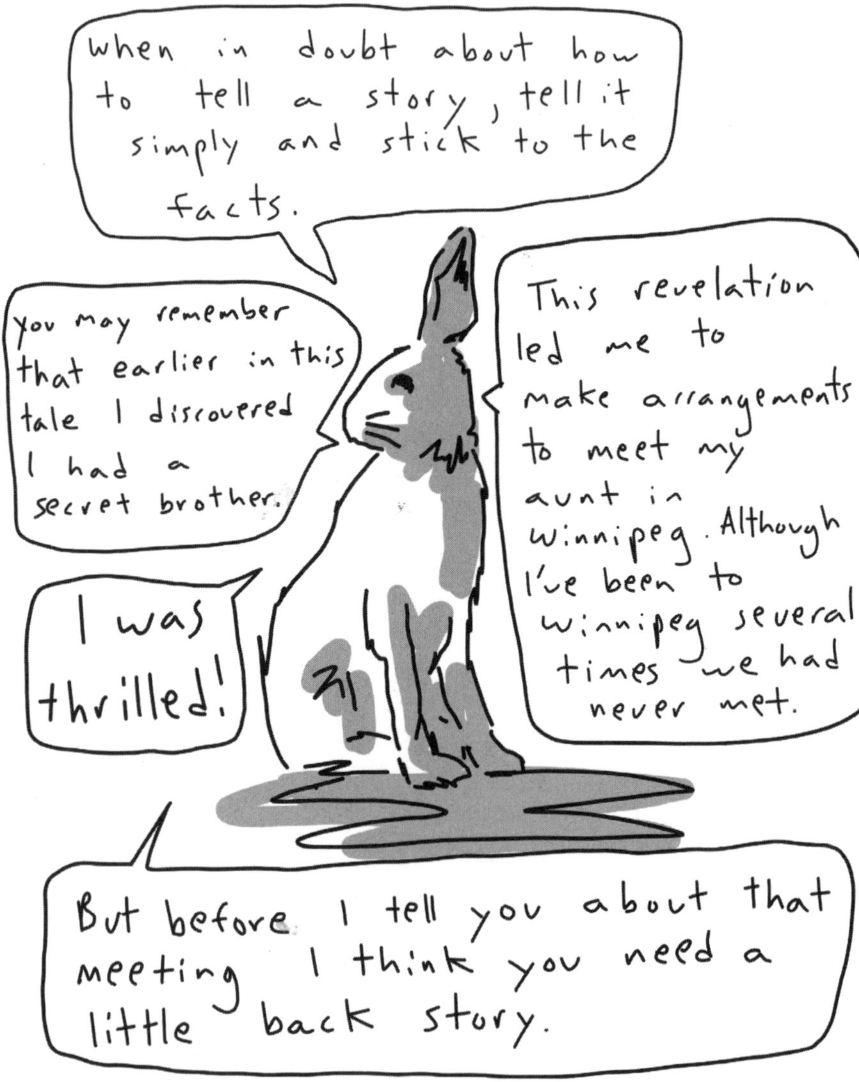
when in doubt about how to tell a story, tell it simply and stick to the facts.
you may remember that earlier in this tale I discovered I had a secret brother.
This revelation led me to make arrangements to meet my aunt in winnipeg. Although I've been to winnipeg several times we had never met.
I was thrilled!
But before I tell you about that meeting I think you need a little back story.

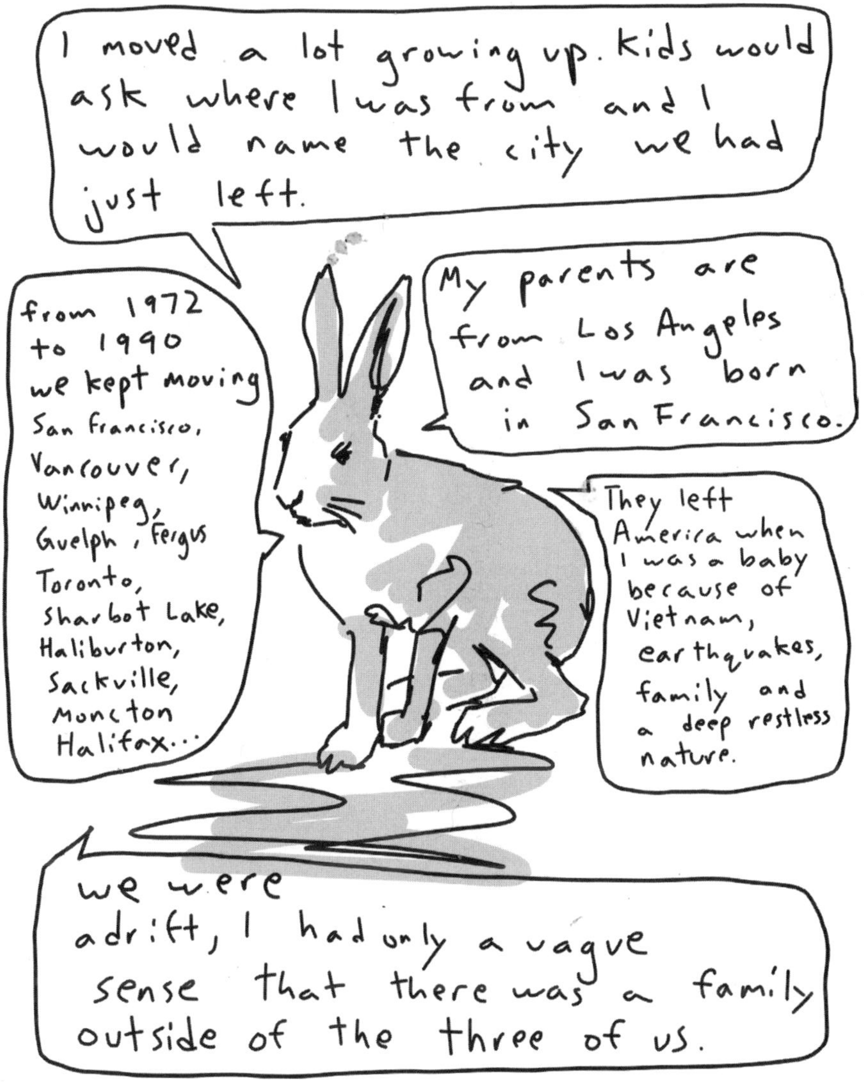
I moved a lot growing up. Kids would ask where I was from and I would name the city we had just left.
from 1972 to 1990 we kept moving San francisco, Vancouver, Winnipeg, Guelph, Fergus Toronto, Sharbot Lake, Haliburton, Sackville, Moncton Halifax...
My parents are from Los Angeles and I was born in San Francisco.
They left America when I was a baby because of Vietnam, earthquakes, family and a deep restless nature.
we were adrift, I had only a vague sense that there was a family outside of the three of us.

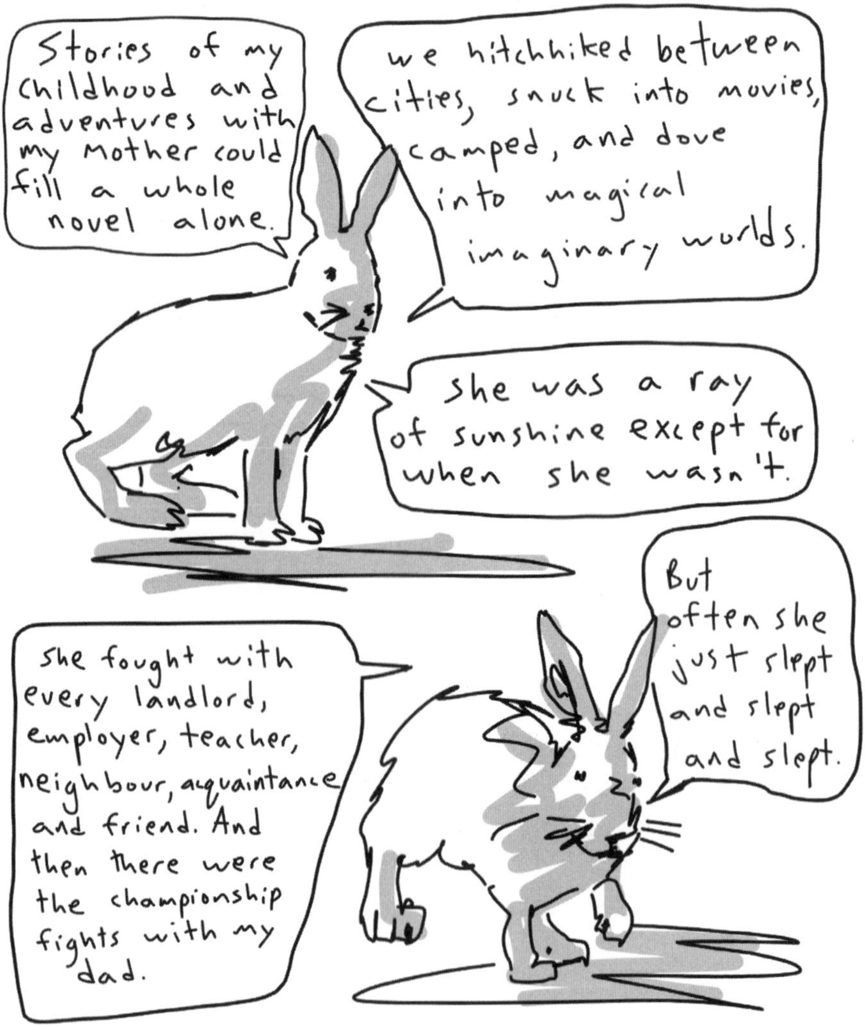
Stories of my childhood and adventures with my Mother could fill a whole novel alone.
we hitchhiked between cities, snuck into movies, camped, and dove into magical imaginary worlds.
She was a ray of sunshine except for when she wasn't.
She fought with every landlord, employer, teacher, neighbour, acquaintance and friend. And then there were the championship fights with my dad.
But often she just slept and slept and slept.

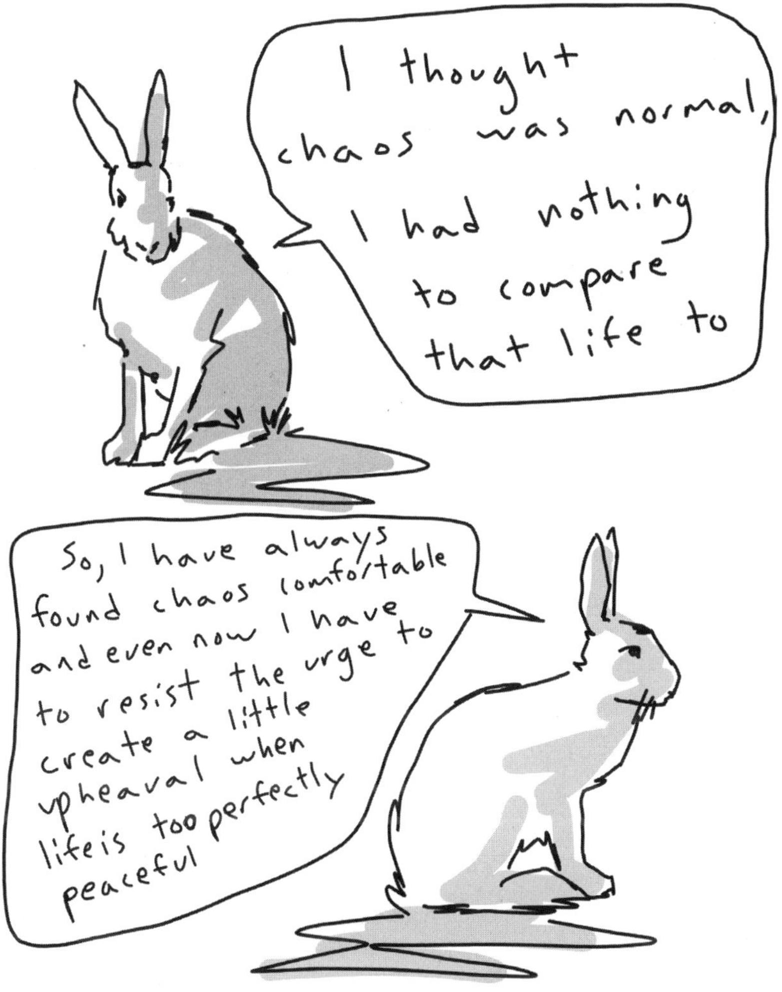
I thought chaos was normal, I had nothing to compare that life to
So, I have always found chaos comfortable and even now I have to resist the urge to create a little upheaval when life is too perfectly peaceful

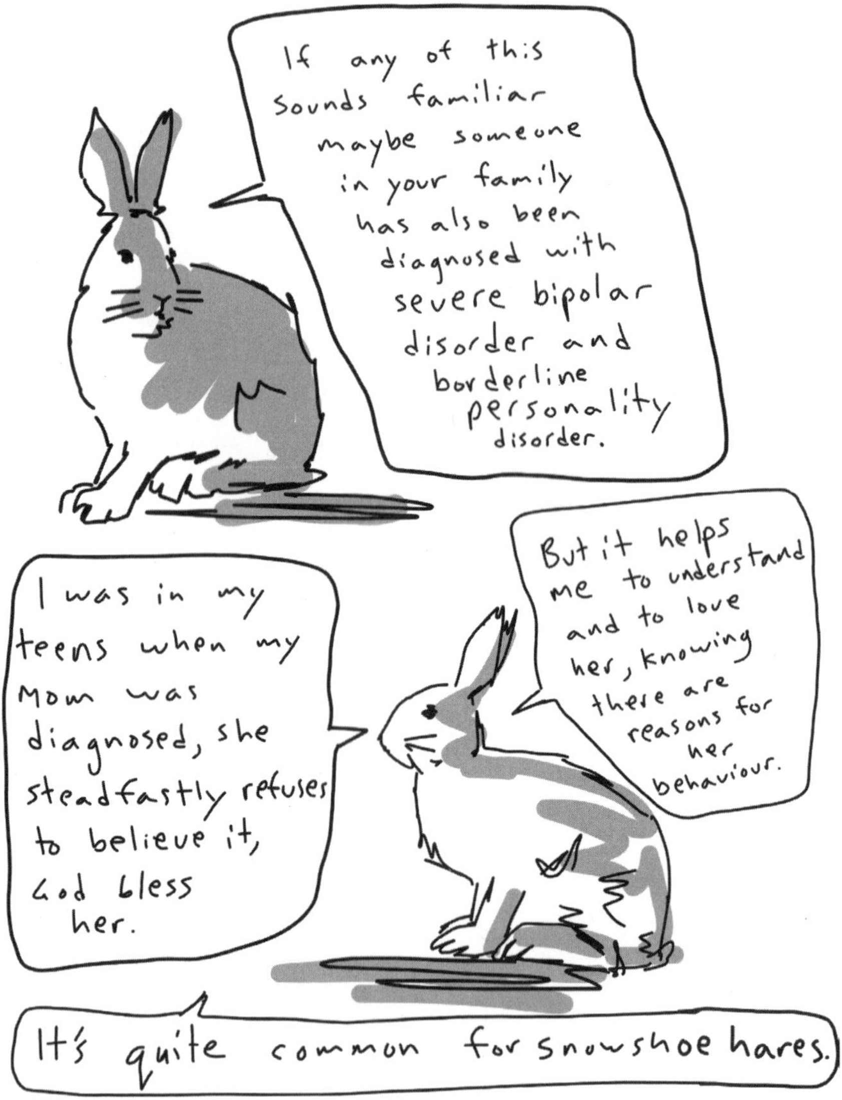
If any of this sounds familiar maybe someone in your family has also been diagnosed with severe bipolar disorder and borderline personality disorder.
I was in my teens when my Mom was diagnosed, she steadfastly refuses to believe it, God bless her.
But it helps me to understand and to love her, knowing there are reasons for her behaviour.
It's quite common for snowshoe hares.

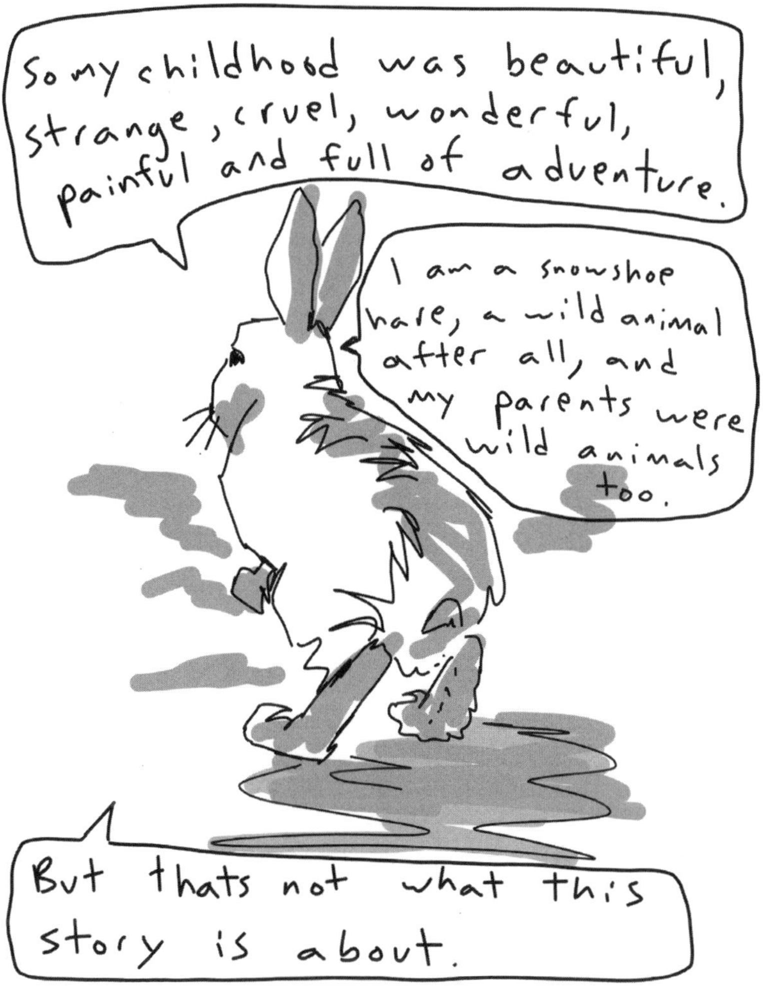
So my childhood was beautiful, strange, cruel, wonderful, painful and full of adventure.
I am a snowshoe hare, a wild animal after all, and my parents were wild animals too.
But thats not what this story is about.

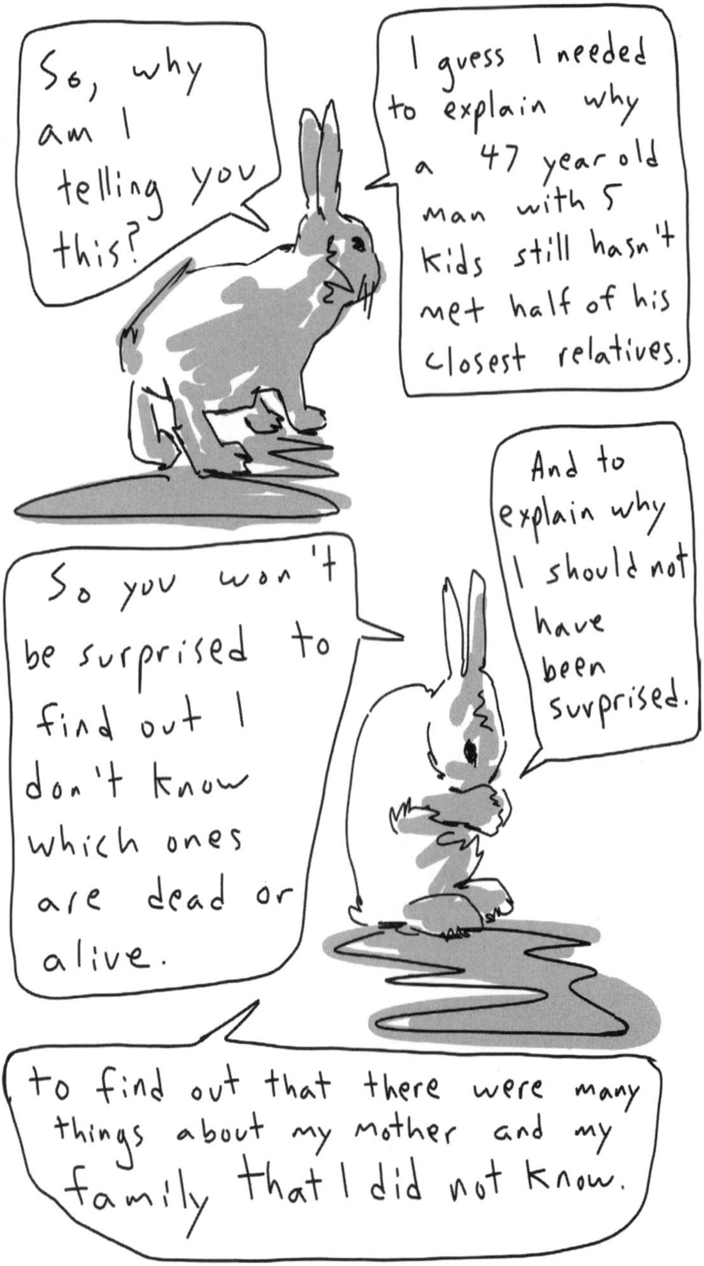
So, why am I telling you this?
I guess I needed to explain why a 47 year old man with 5 kids still hasn't met half of his closest relatives.
And to explain why I should not have been surprised.
So you won't be surprised to find out I don't know which ones are dead or alive.
to find out that there were many things about my mother and my family that I did not know.

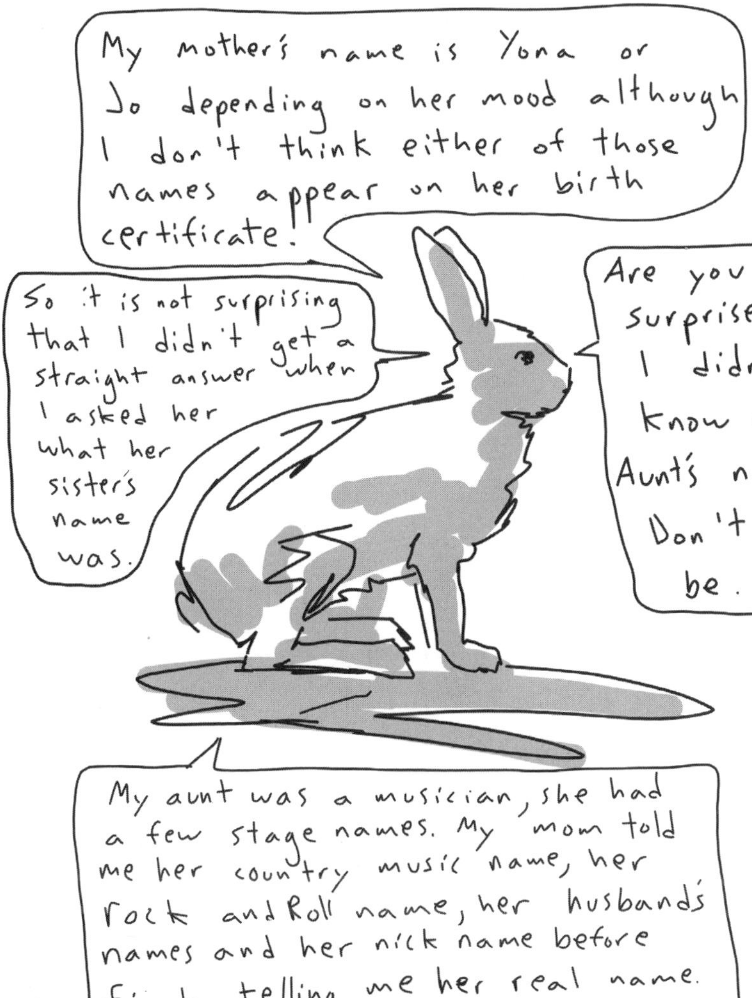
My mother's name is Yona or Jo depending on her mood although I don't think either of those names appear on her birth certificate!
So it is not surprising that I didn't get a straight answer when I asked her what her sister's name was.
Are you surprised I didn't know my Aunt's name? Don't be.
My aunt was a musician, she had a few stage names. My mom told me her country music name, her rock and Roll name, her husband's names and her nick name before finaly telling me her real name. Well, only her first name, Eleanor. Needless to say I could not find her online.

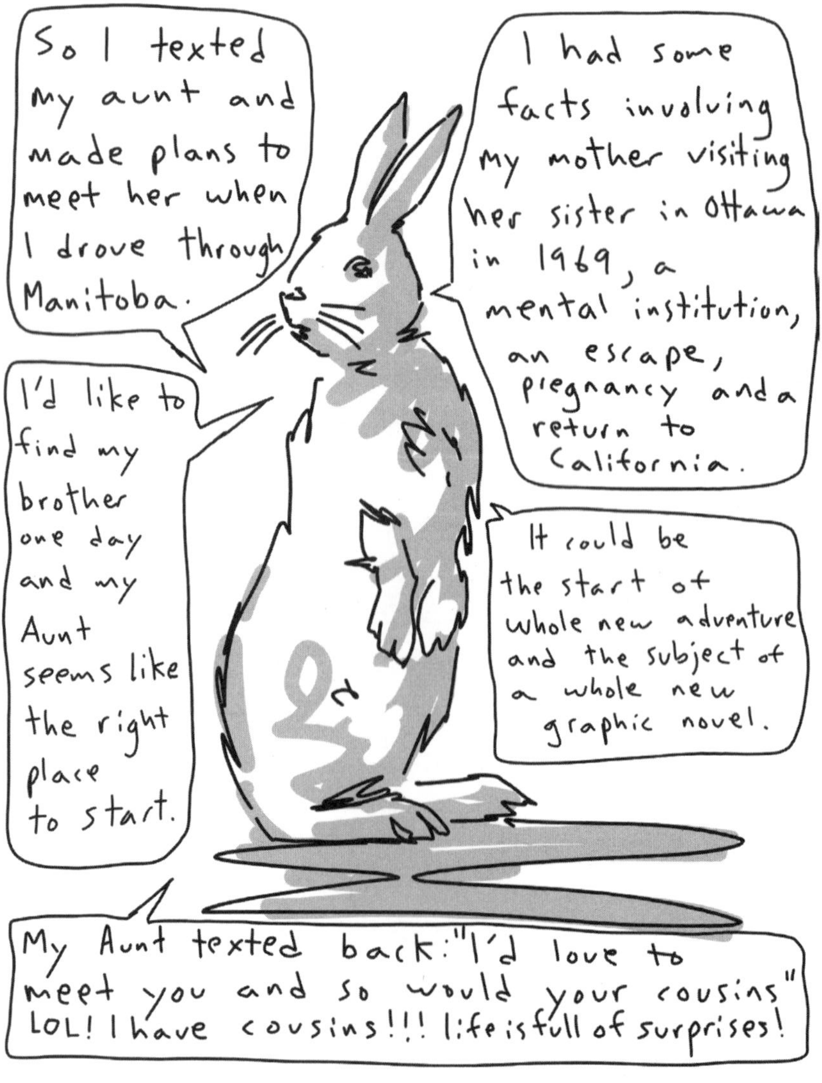
So I texted my aunt and made plans to meet her when I drove through Manitoba.
I'd like to find my brother one day and my Aunt seems like the right place to start.
I had some facts involving my mother visiting her sister in Ottawa in 1969, a mental institution, an escape, pregnancy and a return to California.
It could be the start of whole new adventure and the subject of a whole new graphic novel.
My Aunt texted back: "I'd love to meet you and so would your cousins" LOL! I have cousins!!! life is full of surprises!

49

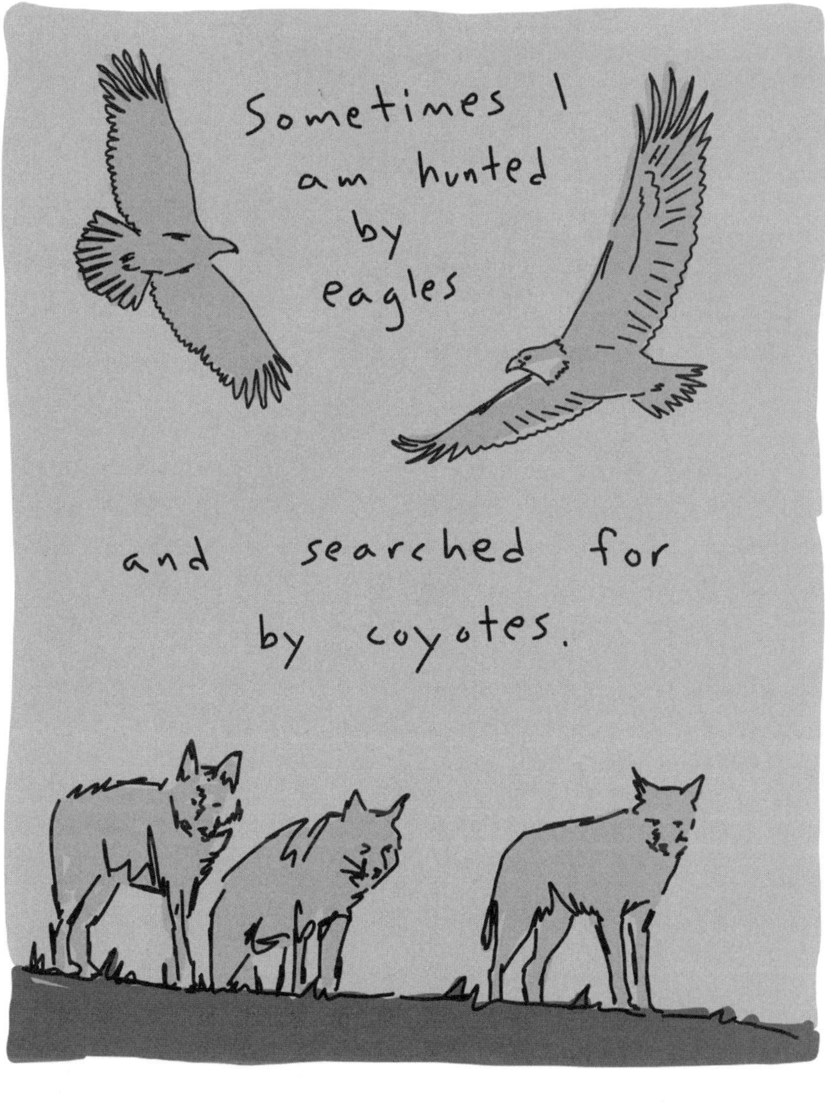
Sometimes I am hunted by eagles
and searched for by coyotes.

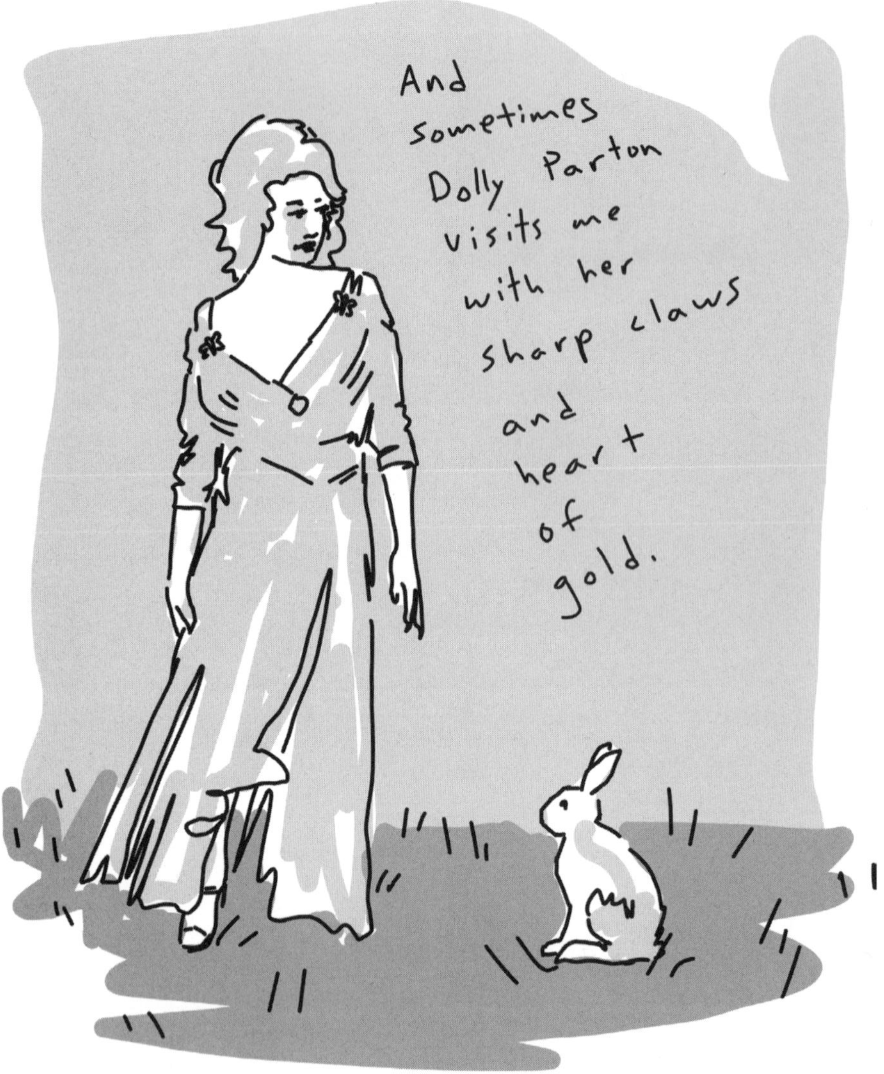
And sometimes Dolly Parton visits me with her sharp claws and heart of gold.

I feel safe with her and her words of wisdom give me some sense that everything will be ok.
If you want to see a rainbow you gotta put up with a little rain *
*true Dolly

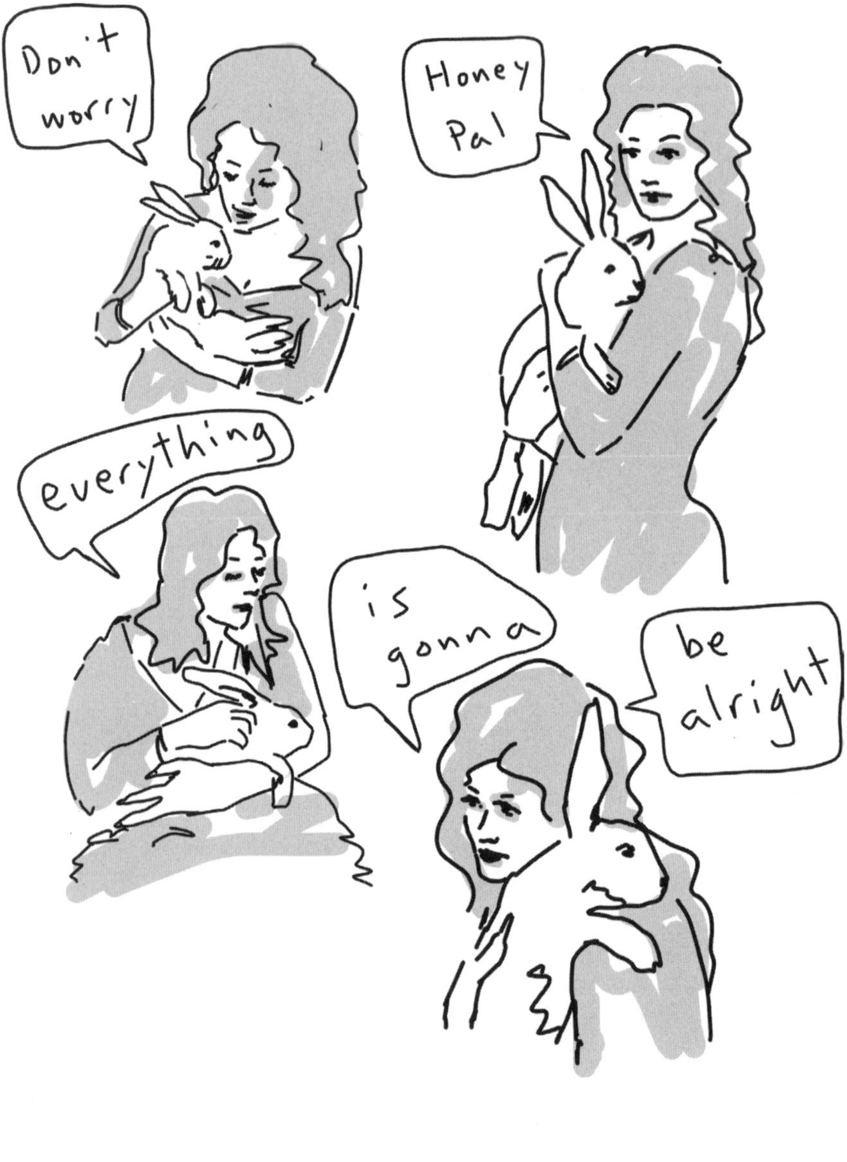
Don't worry
Honey Pal
everything
is gonna
be alright

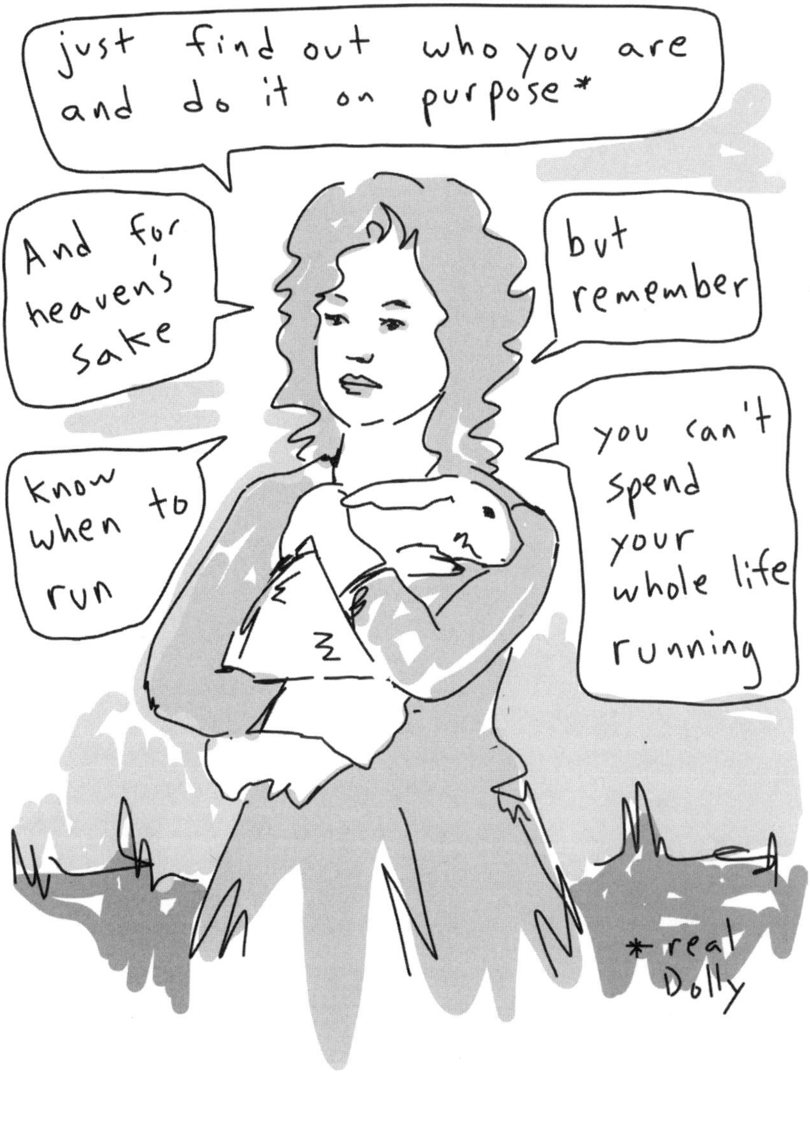
just find out who you are and do it on purpose*
And for heaven's sake
but remember
know when to run
you can't spend your whole life running
*real Dolly

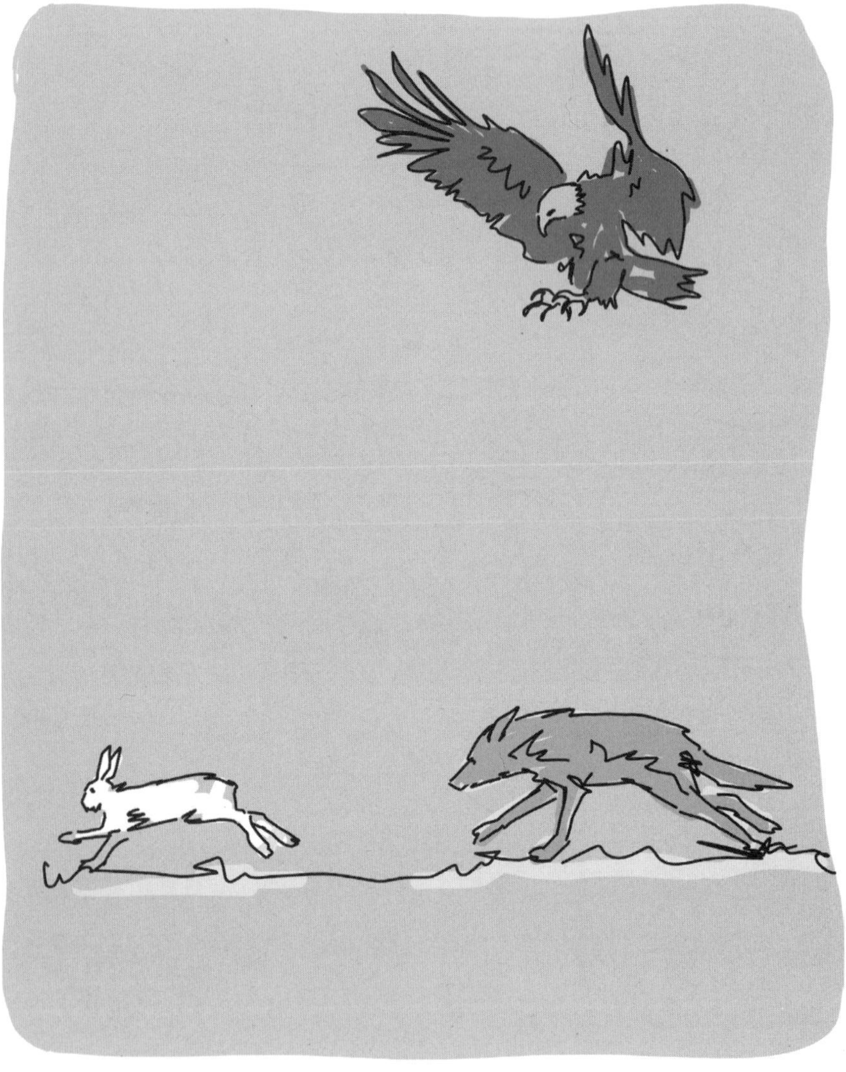

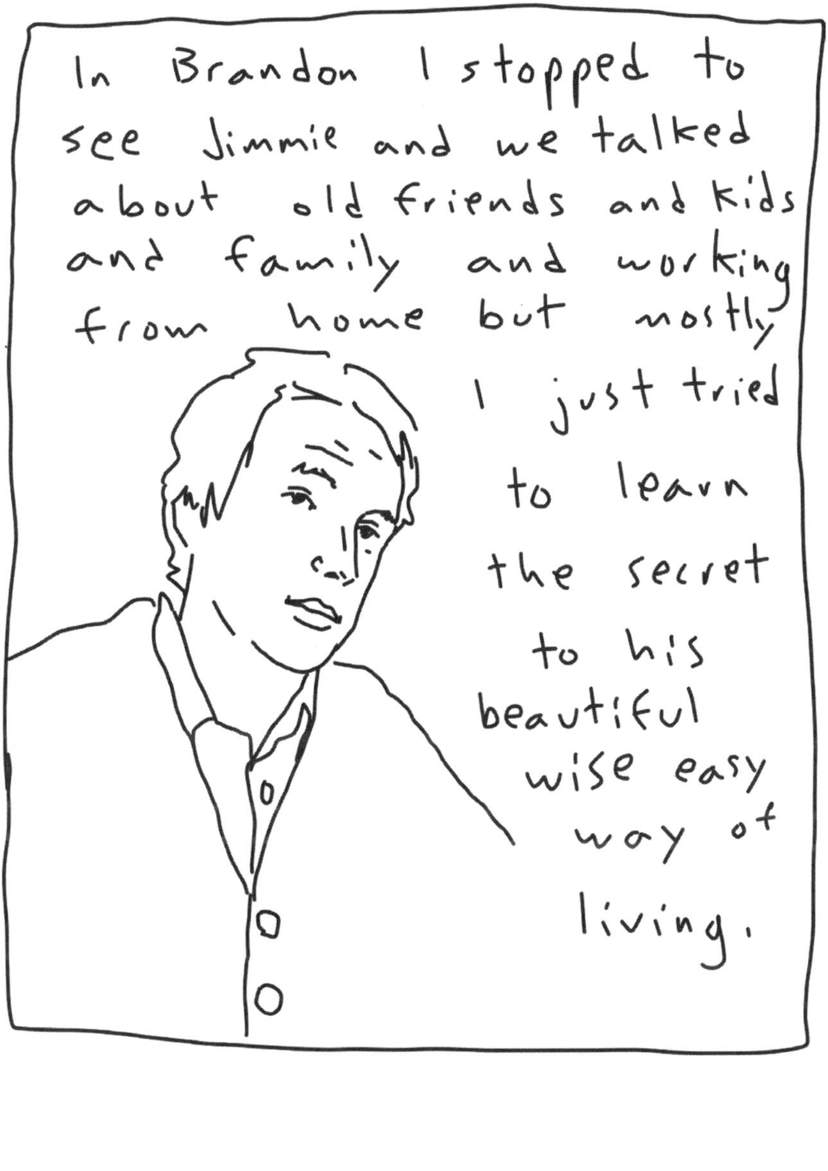
In Brandon I stopped to see Jimmie and we talked about old friends and kids and family and working from home but mostly I just tried to learn the secret to his beautiful wise easy way of living.

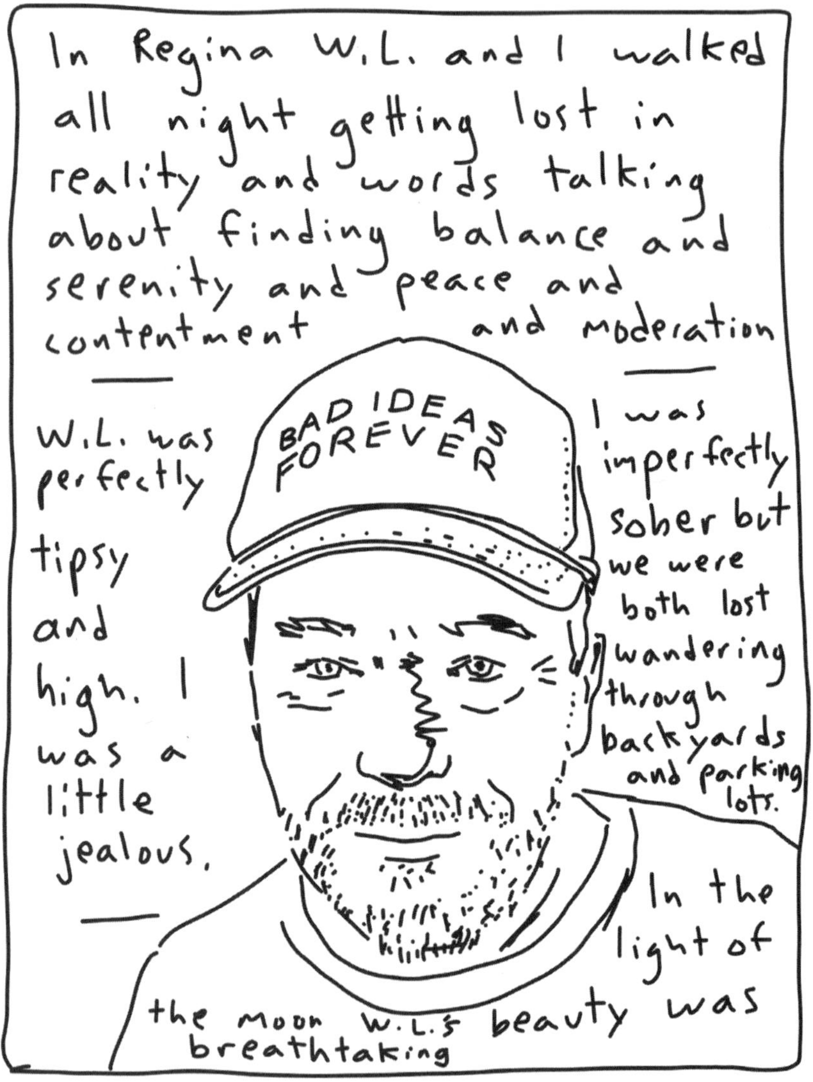
In Regina W.L. and I walked all night getting lost in reality and words talking about finding balance and serenity and peace and contentment and moderation
W.L. was perfectly tipsy and high. I was a little jealous.
I was imperfectly sober but we were both lost wandering through backyards and parking lots.
BAD IDEAS FOREVER
In the light of the moon W.L.'s beauty was breathtaking

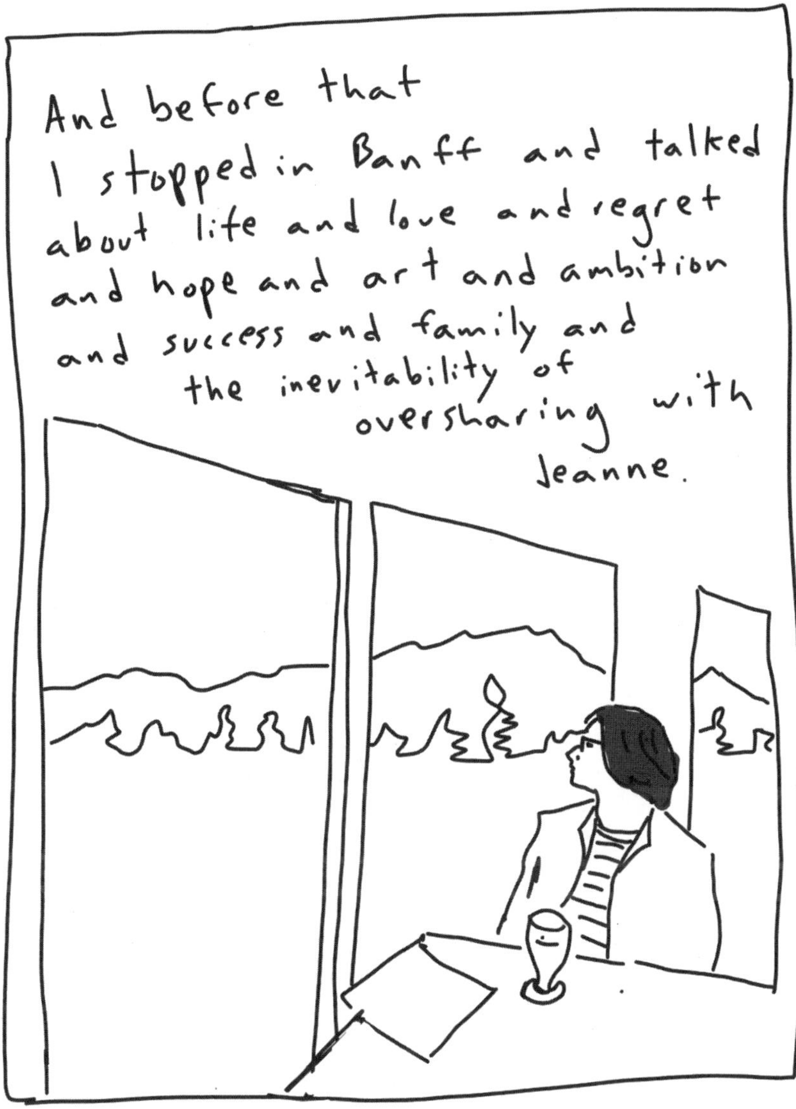
And before that
I stopped in Banff and talked
about life and love and regret
and hope and art and ambition
and success and family and
the inevitability of
oversharing with
Jeanne.

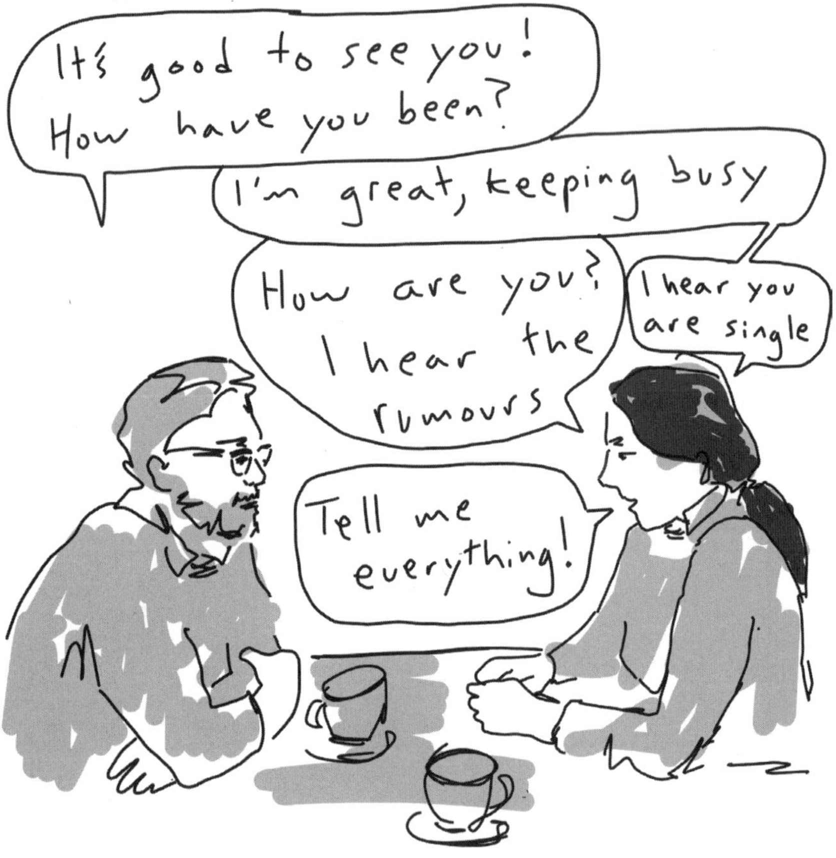
It's good to see you! How have you been?
I'm great, keeping busy
How are you? I hear the rumours
I hear you are single
Tell me everything!

Oh gosh, I'm sure the rumours are better than the truth but I have been in a reflective mood lately.
Go on, I'm listening
you know, just looking back on my relationship history
I'm all ears
spill the beans ClaytoR!
Start at the beginning
you can trust me.

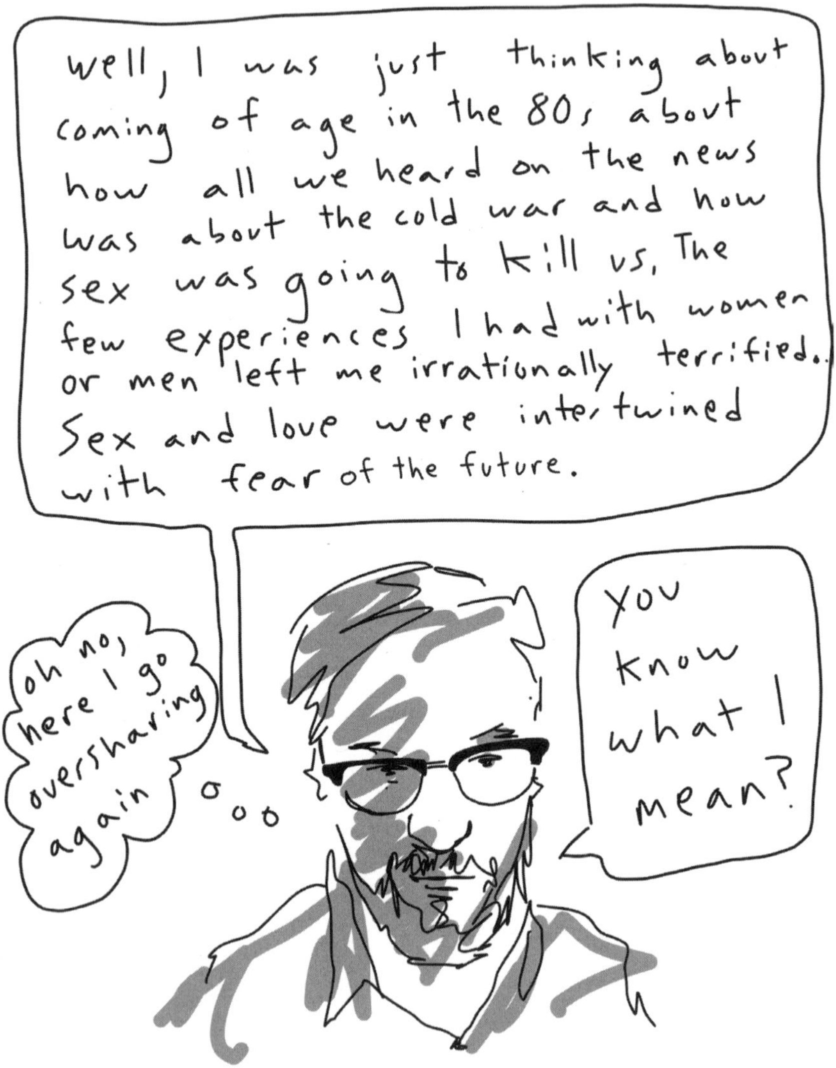
well, I was just thinking about coming of age in the 80s about how all we heard on the news was about the cold war and how sex was going to kill us, The few experiences I had with women or men left me irrationally terrified.. Sex and love were intertwined with fear of the future.
oh no, here I go oversharing again
you know what I mean?

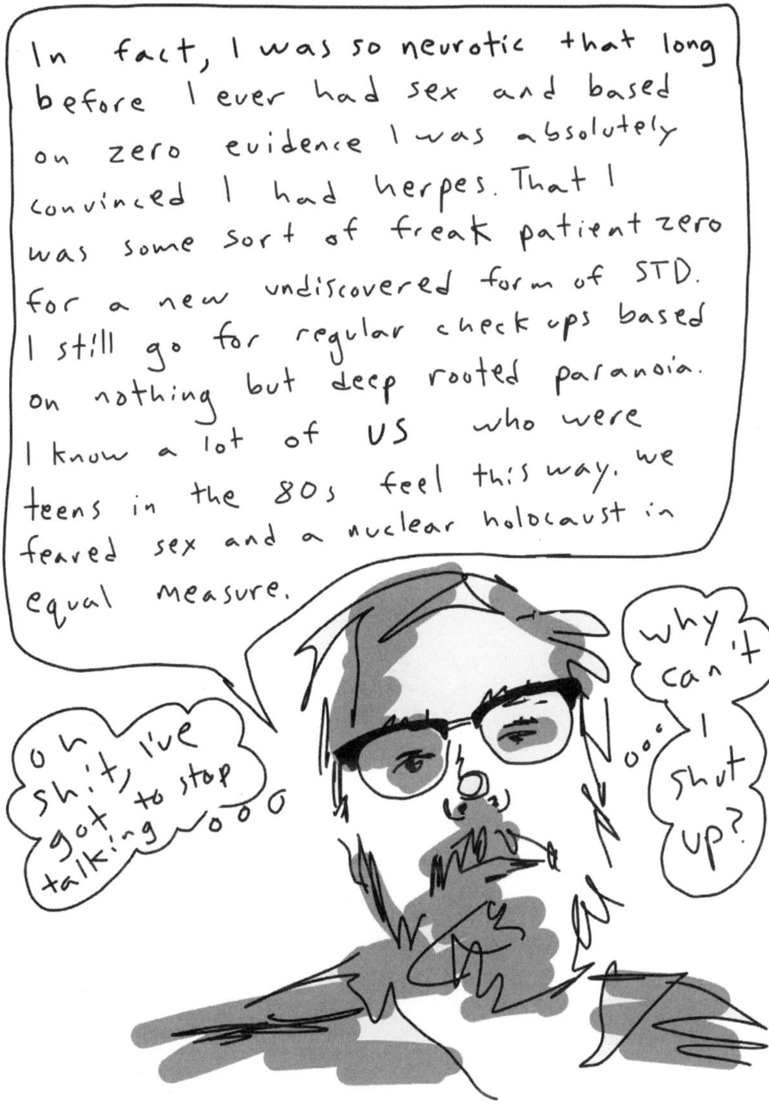
In fact, I was so neurotic that long before I ever had sex and based on zero evidence I was absolutely convinced I had herpes. That I was some sort of freak patient zero for a new undiscovered form of STD. I still go for regular check ups based on nothing but deep rooted paranoia. I know a lot of US who were teens in the 80s feel this way. We feared sex and a nuclear holocaust in equal measure.
oh shit, I've got to stop talking
why can't I shut up?

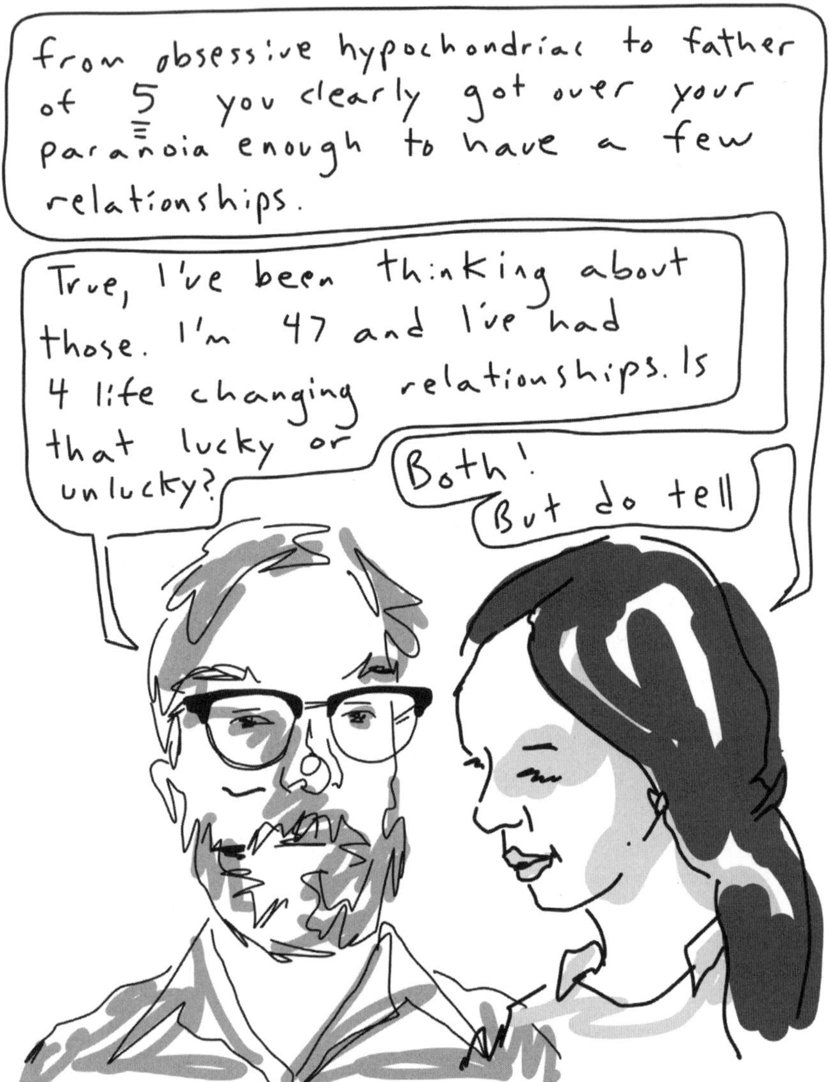
from obsessive hypochondriac to father of 5 you clearly got over your paranoia enough to have a few relationships.
True, I've been thinking about those. I'm 47 and I've had 4 life changing relationships. Is that lucky or unlucky?
Both! But do tell

There was Emily, we met at artschool and moved to Vancouver together. It was a roller coaster but I still think of her often. She's a brilliant soul baring artist, always was.
And Julie, for better or worse, but you know all about that.
And Tori, you know all about that too.
and Eleanor.
Here I go again.

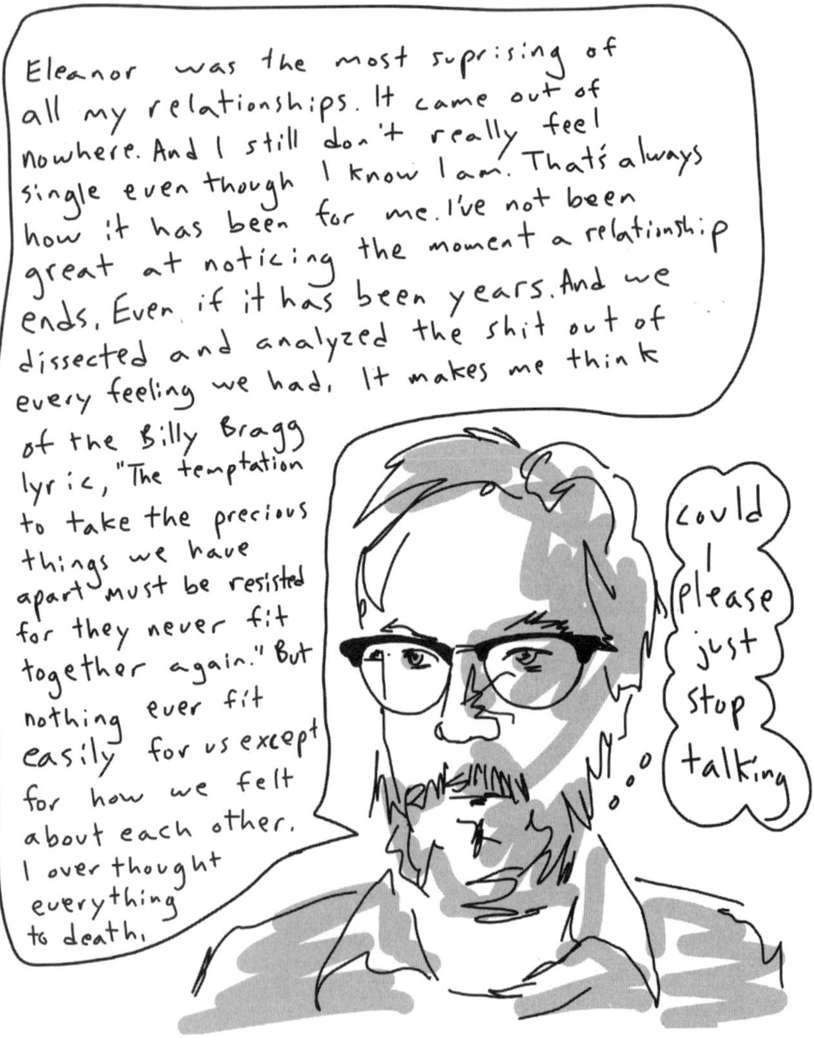
Eleanor was the most suprising of all my relationships. It came out of nowhere. And I still don't really feel single even though I know I am. That's always how it has been for me. I've not been great at noticing the moment a relationship ends. Even if it has been years. And we dissected and analyzed the shit out of every feeling we had. It makes me think
of the Billy Bragg lyric, "The temptation to take the precious things we have apart must be resisted for they never fit together again." But nothing ever fit easily for us except for how we felt about each other. I over thought everything to death.
could I please just stop talking

Do you regret meeting her, would you undo it all?
No, never, I love her. But I do have regrets. I regret being secretive in the beginning. That snowballed into an avalanche of consequence that can never be undone. We would get back together and I'd get scared and break it off. I did that again and again. I regret that, it was very hurtful. And there was our age difference. I was very lost, still drinking and I'd like to say it wasn't like me to behave that way but it's not like I have anyone else to blame. And then it seemed like we finally fixed things but they fell apart, I couldn't give her the life we needed. And there were other complications. I don't know how to ever make it up to her. So I guess I have some regrets but I wouldn't trade our good days for anything.

That's about it, the basics, but in the final analysis I have no answers. What does it all add up to? That love never dies, it only changes? That forever is only perspective? That I'm clearly bad at romantic relationships. That love's failures are the only true signs of its successes?
I don't know
fuck, that was brutal
I just don't know anything
So how about you?
single?

haha ha, well, I can tell you one thing
we are going to be just friends!
Have you considered therapy?
I think this is going about as well as it could be

51

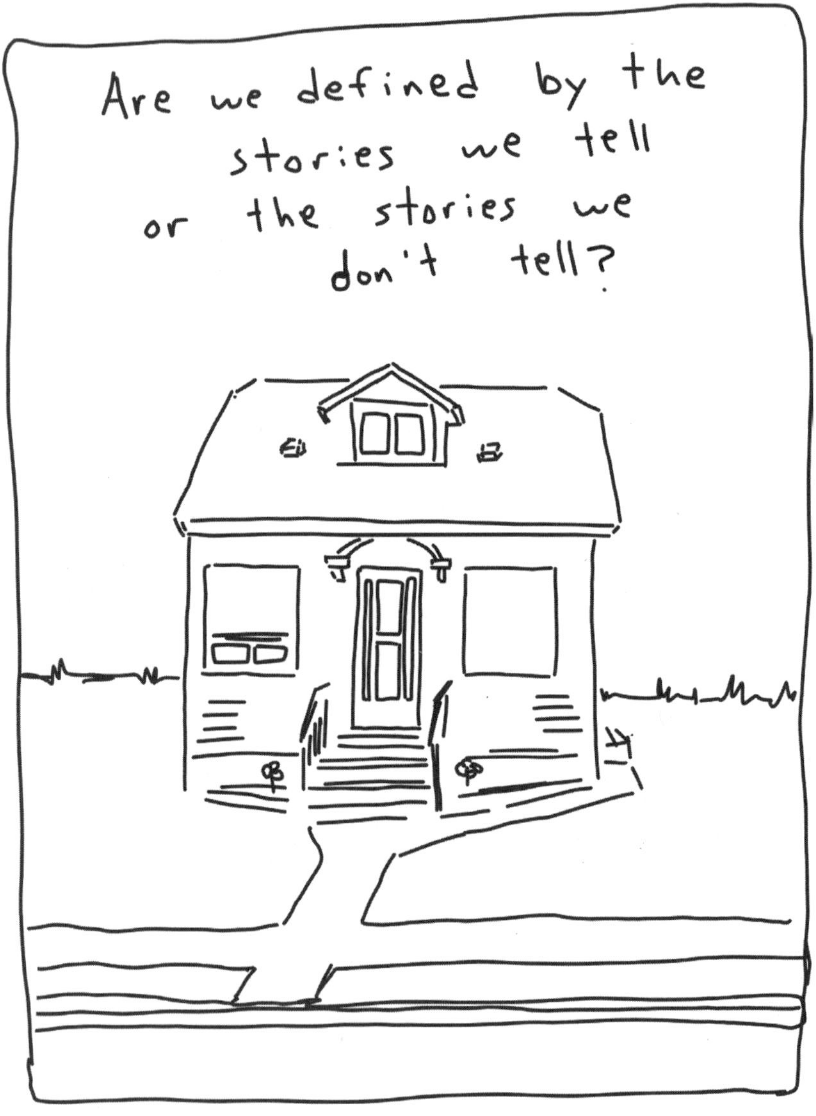
Are we defined by the stories we tell or the stories we don't tell?

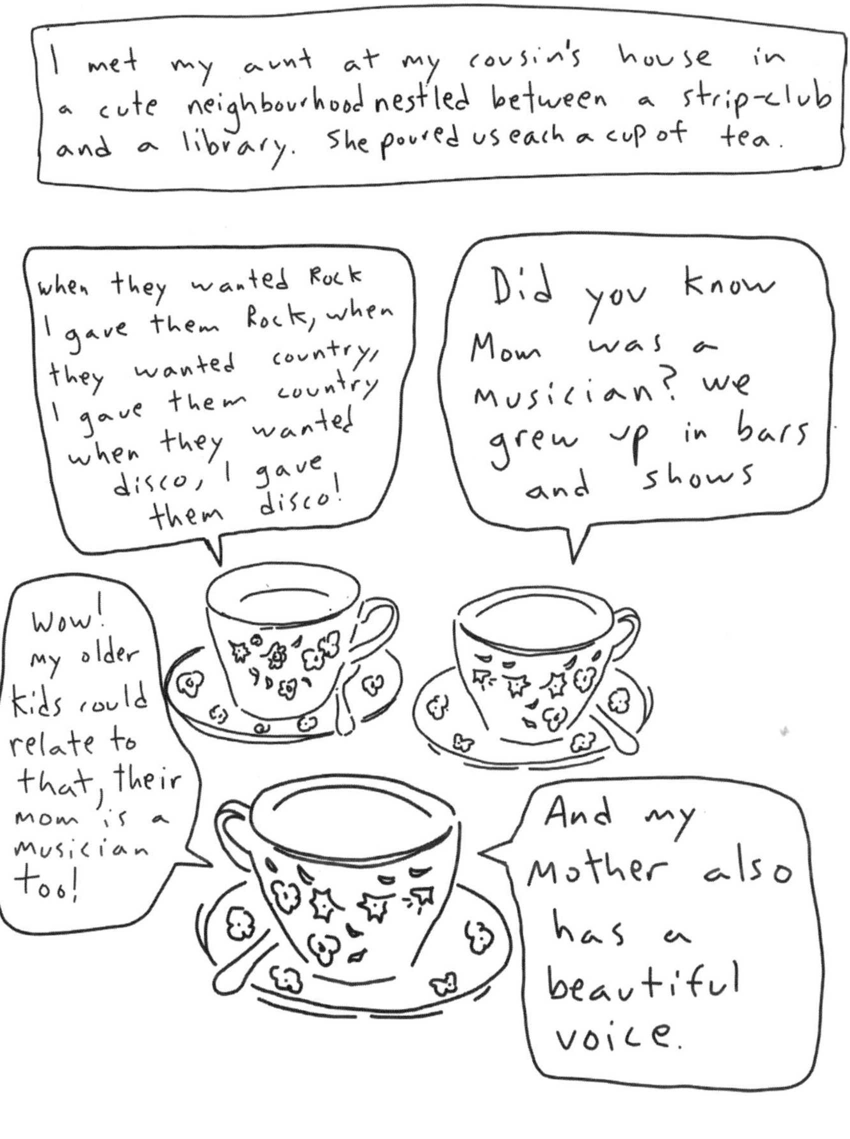
I met my aunt at my cousin's house in a cute neighbourhood nestled between a strip-club and a library. She poured us each a cup of tea.
when they wanted Rock I gave them Rock, when they wanted country, I gave them country when they wanted disco, I gave them disco!
Did you know Mom was a musician? we grew up in bars and shows
Wow! my older kids could relate to that, their mom is a musician too!
And my Mother also has a beautiful voice.

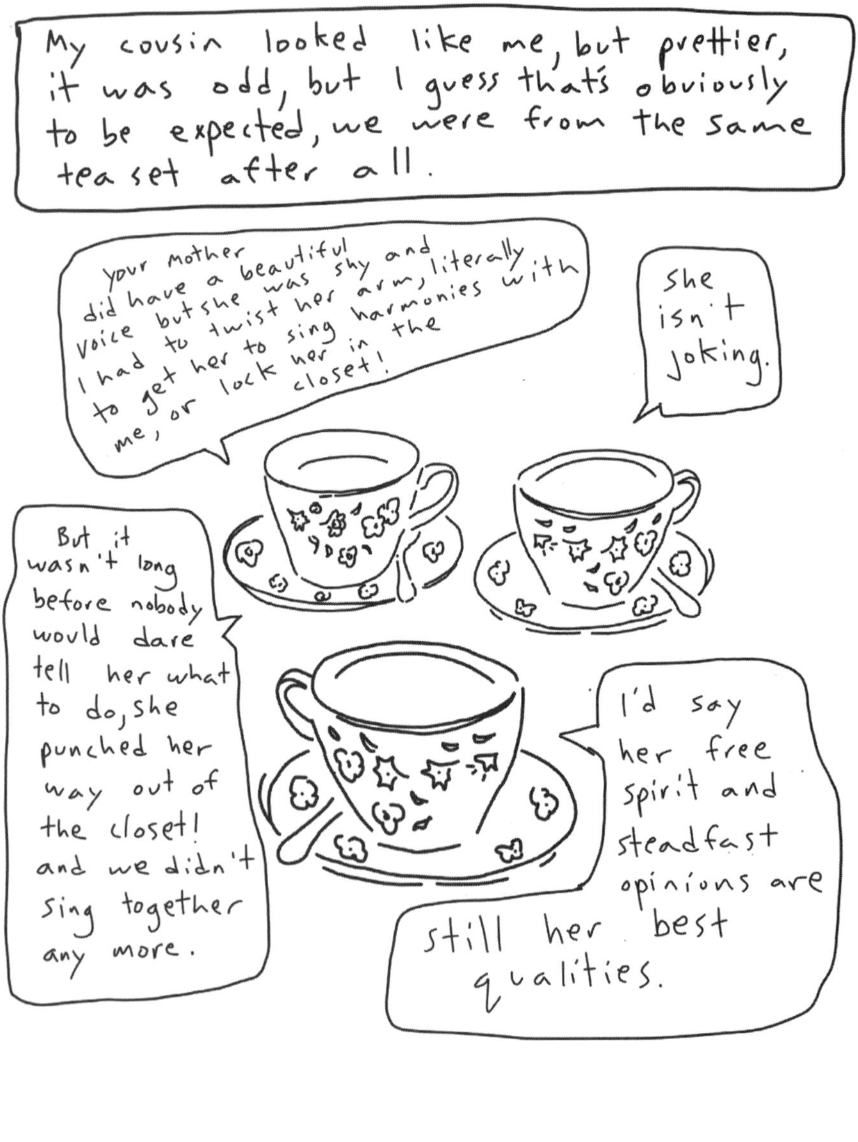
My cousin looked like me, but prettier, it was odd, but I guess that's obviously to be expected, we were from the same tea set after all.
your mother did have a beautiful voice but she was shy and I had to twist her arm, literally to get her to sing harmonies with me, or lock her in the closet!
She isn't joking.
But it wasn't long before nobody would dare tell her what to do, she punched her way out of the closet! and we didn't sing together any more.
I'd say her free spirit and steadfast opinions are still her best qualities.

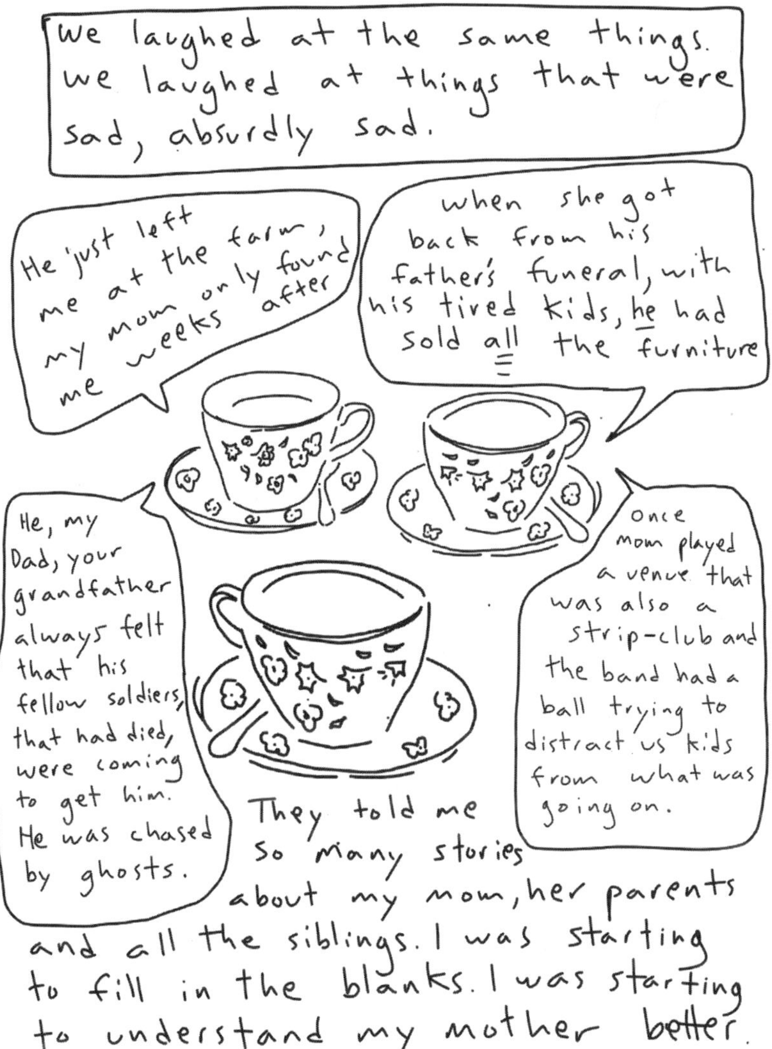
We laughed at the same things. We laughed at things that were sad, absurdly sad.
He just left me at the farm, my mom only found me weeks after
When she got back from his father's funeral, with his tired kids, he had sold all the furniture
He, my Dad, your grandfather always felt that his fellow soldiers, that had died, were coming to get him. He was chased by ghosts.
Once mom played a venue that was also a strip-club and the band had a ball trying to distract us kids from what was going on.
They told me so many stories about my mom, her parents and all the siblings. I was starting to fill in the blanks. I was starting to understand my mother better.

And they showed me one of my grandmother's paintings. Pretty daisies but with one glaring, out of place drip. Exactly like something I would do.

And as my aunt told me about my mother's visit to Ottawa in 1969 and her version of how things unfolded. I thought how strange it was that I was almost as much a stranger to this family as my secret brother would be.

I excused myself to the bathroom and took a minute to process all I had heard. I could imagine a different life if my parent's had made slightly different choices. I looked in the mirror and felt

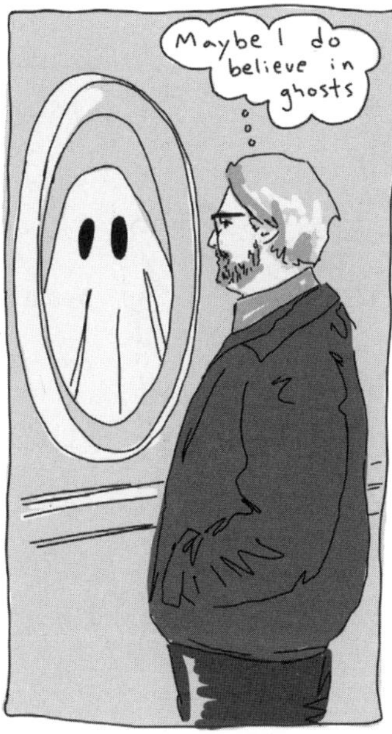
Maybe I do believe in ghosts

my brother, my grandfather, my grandmother, all strangers, looking back at me. I was content with how things had played out in my life but I also felt changed.

And I saw my own face looking back at me. It's still new to be able to make eye contact with myself and not turn away. And yet, here I was making questionable choices again.

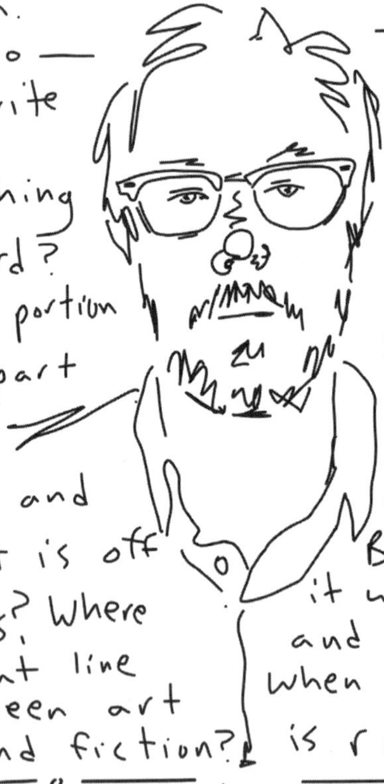

Do I write about everything I heard? What portion is a part of my story and what is off limits? Where is that line between art and fiction?

Maybe the search for my secret brother isn't a part of this story. Maybe it's not time to peel back those layers yet. But I do believe it will be a joyful and healing process when the time is right.

And I was thrilled to tell my kids all about ther "new" relatives.

Believe it or not, when I went back to the kitchen my aunt and cousin were looking out the window at two white rabbits. They weren't snowshoe hares but it still felt like a magical sign.

— o —

— o —

rabbits always remind me of love and family and other stories best saved for later.

— o —

we just silently watched, the three of us, strangers until this moment.

— o —

— o —

And when my cousin explained that she bought this house because of these two feral rabbits living in the backyard I understood what it means to be related.

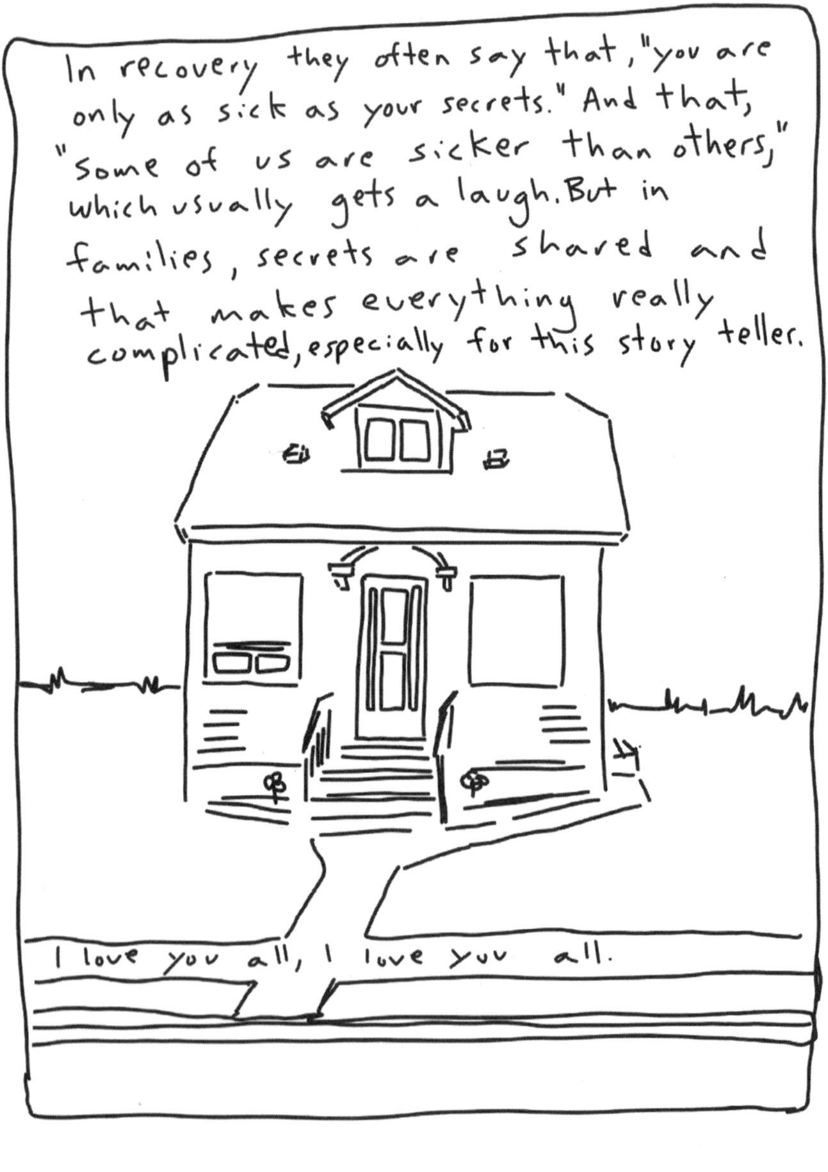
In recovery they often say that, "you are only as sick as your secrets." And that, "Some of us are sicker than others," which usually gets a laugh. But in families, secrets are shared and that makes everything really complicated, especially for this story teller.
I love you all, I love you all.

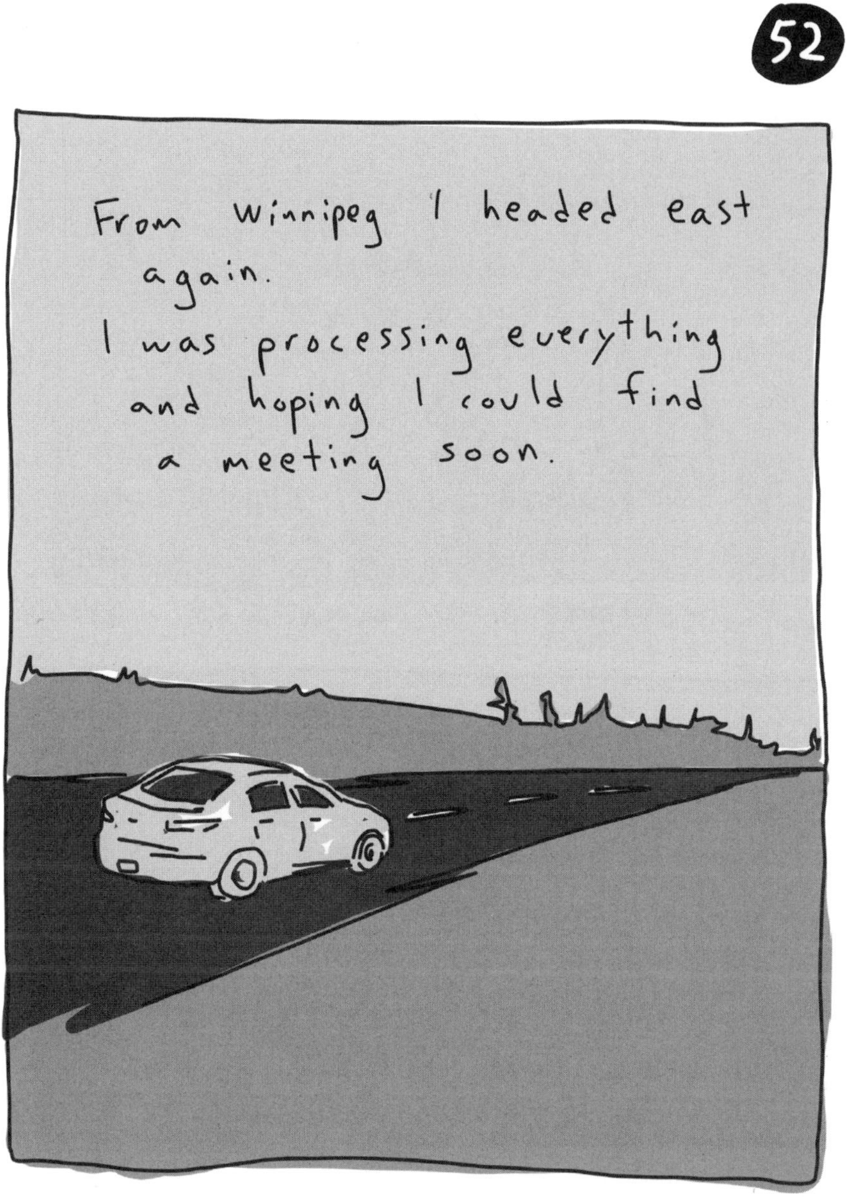
52
From Winnipeg I headed east again.
I was processing everything and hoping I could find a meeting soon.

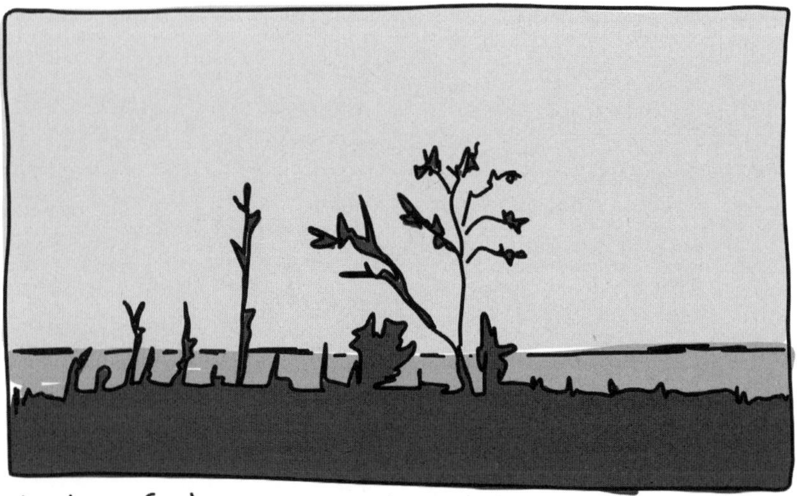

Lots of trees and rocks and water

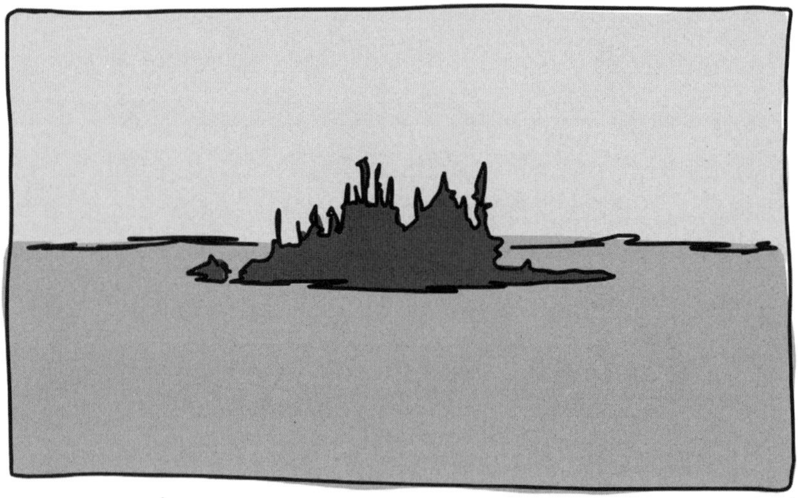

but miles to go without a meeting in sight.

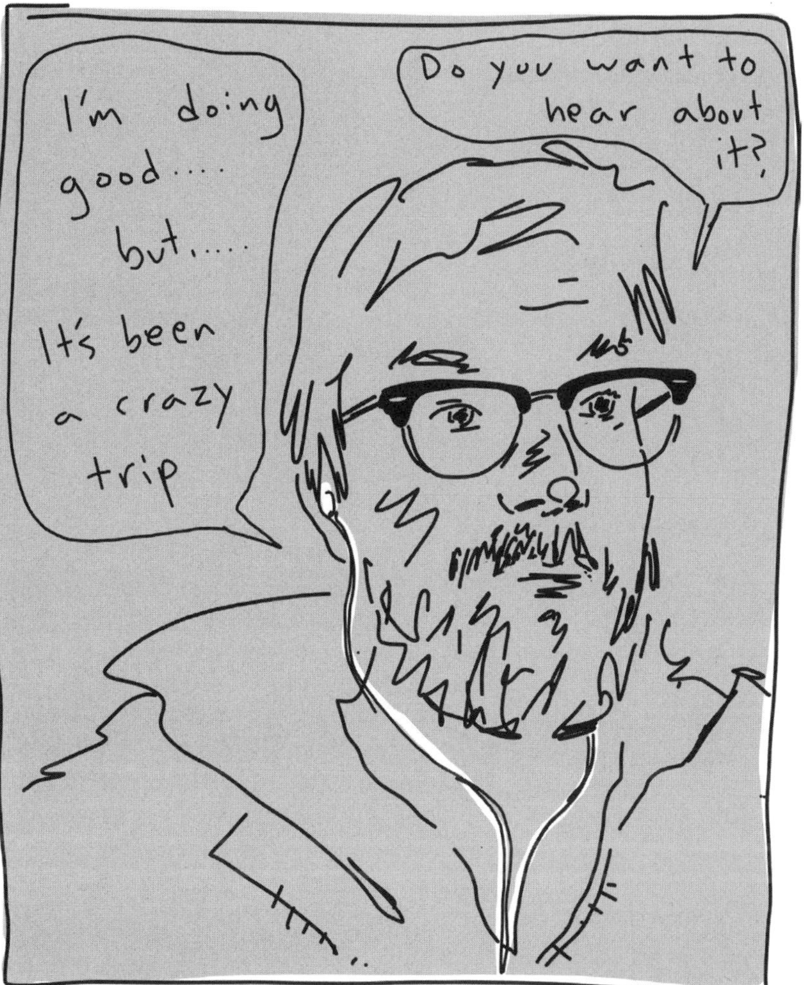
I'm doing good.... but..... It's been a crazy trip
Do you want to hear about it?

I called my sponsor and a friend I knew who was struggling to get sober.

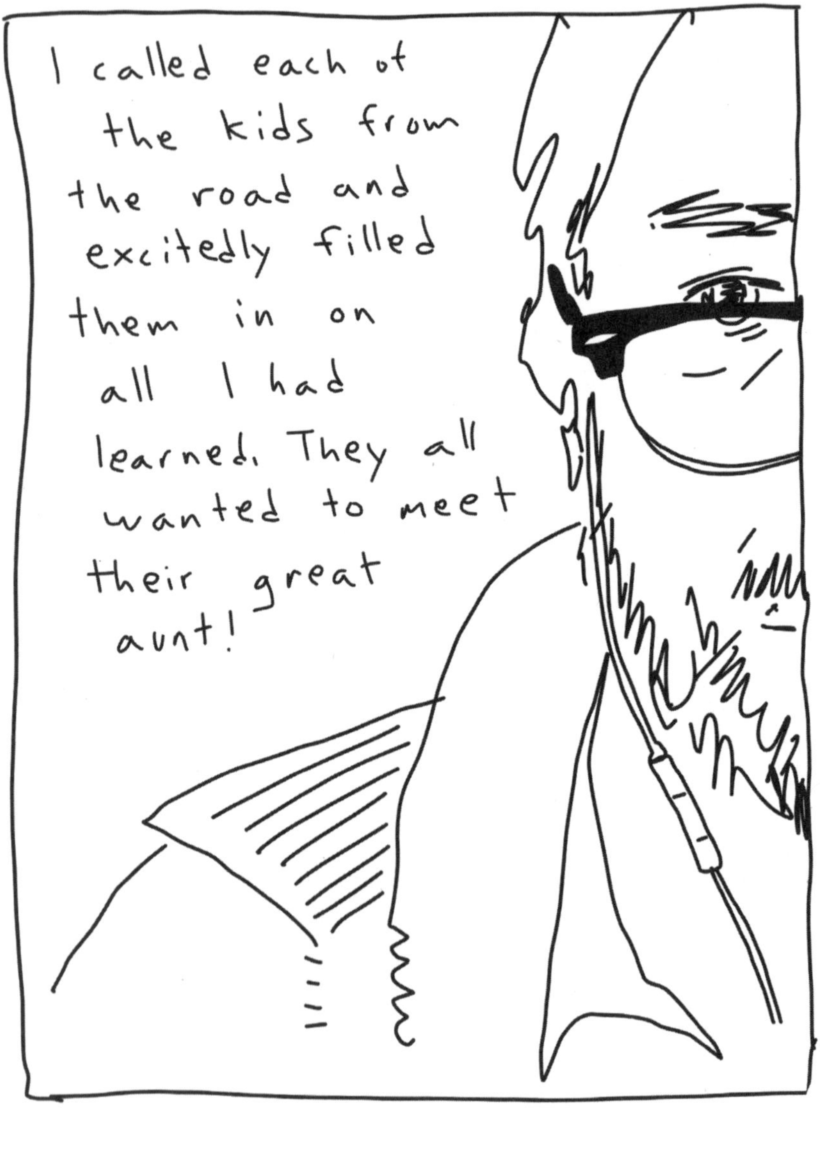
I called each of the kids from the road and excitedly filled them in on all I had learned. They all wanted to meet their great aunt!

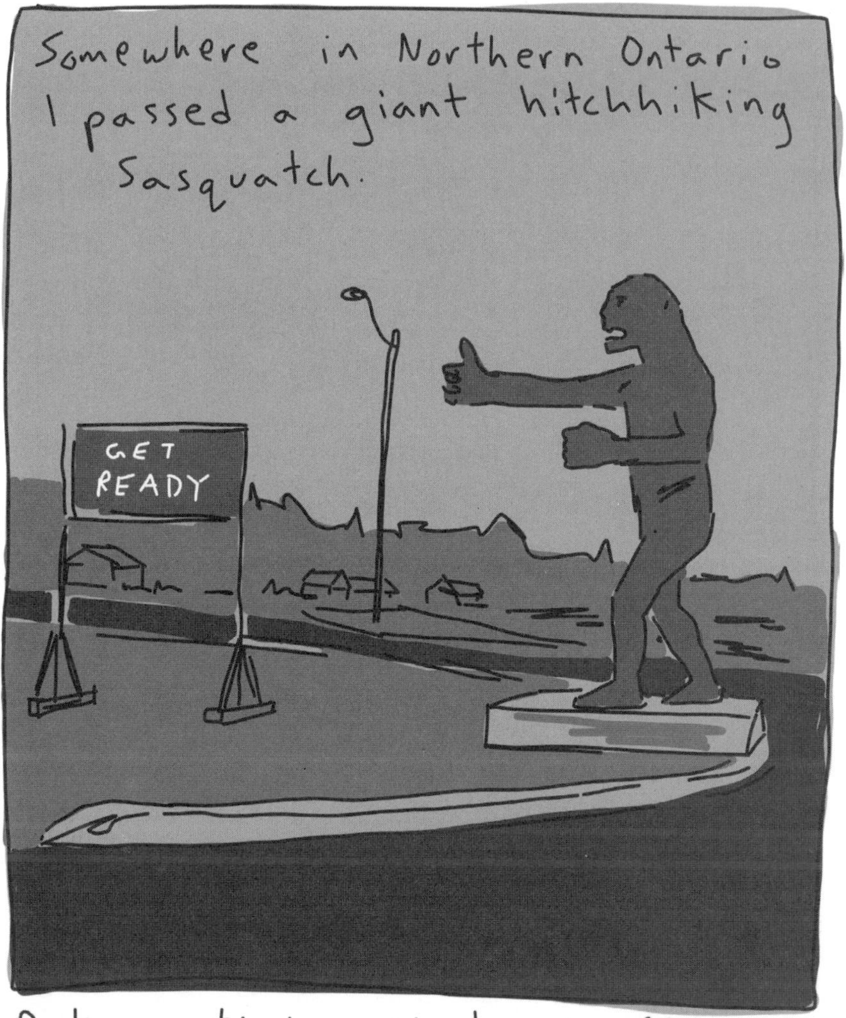
Somewhere in Northern Ontario I passed a giant hitchhiking Sasquatch.
GET READY

But my timing was always off for finding a meeting to go to.

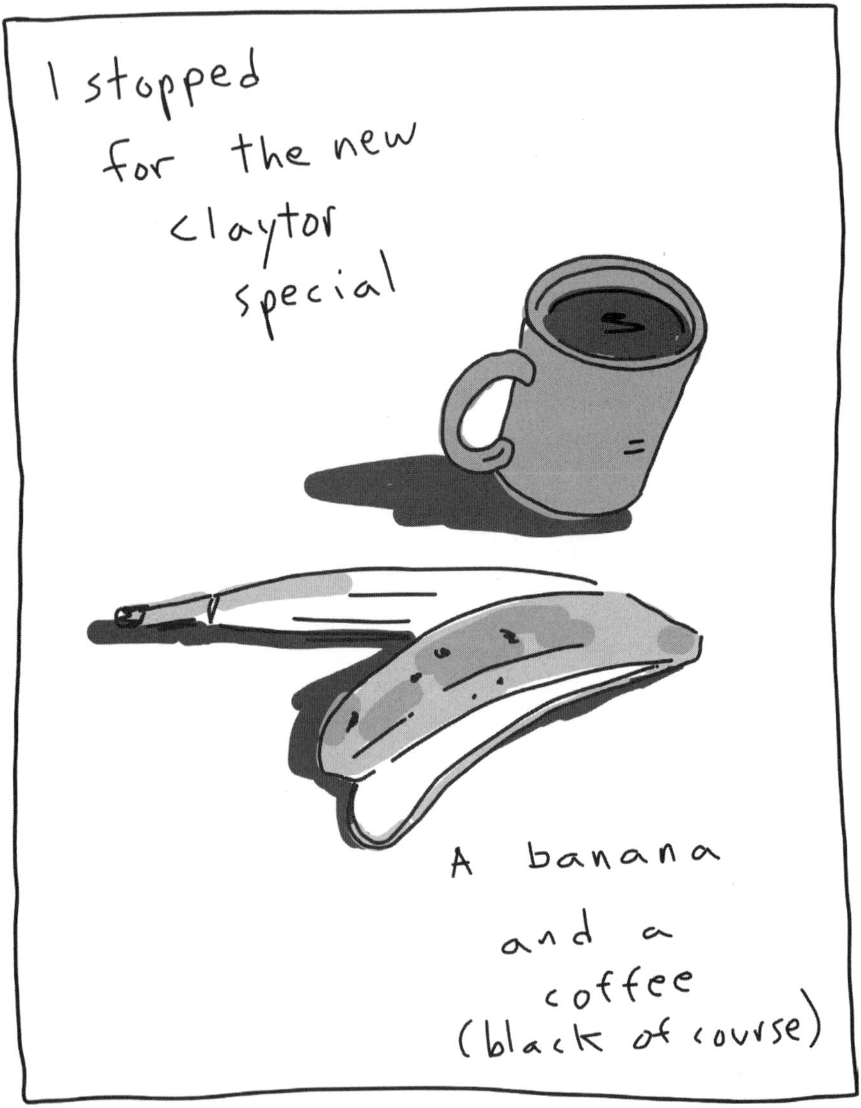
I stopped for the new claytor special
A banana and a coffee (black of course)

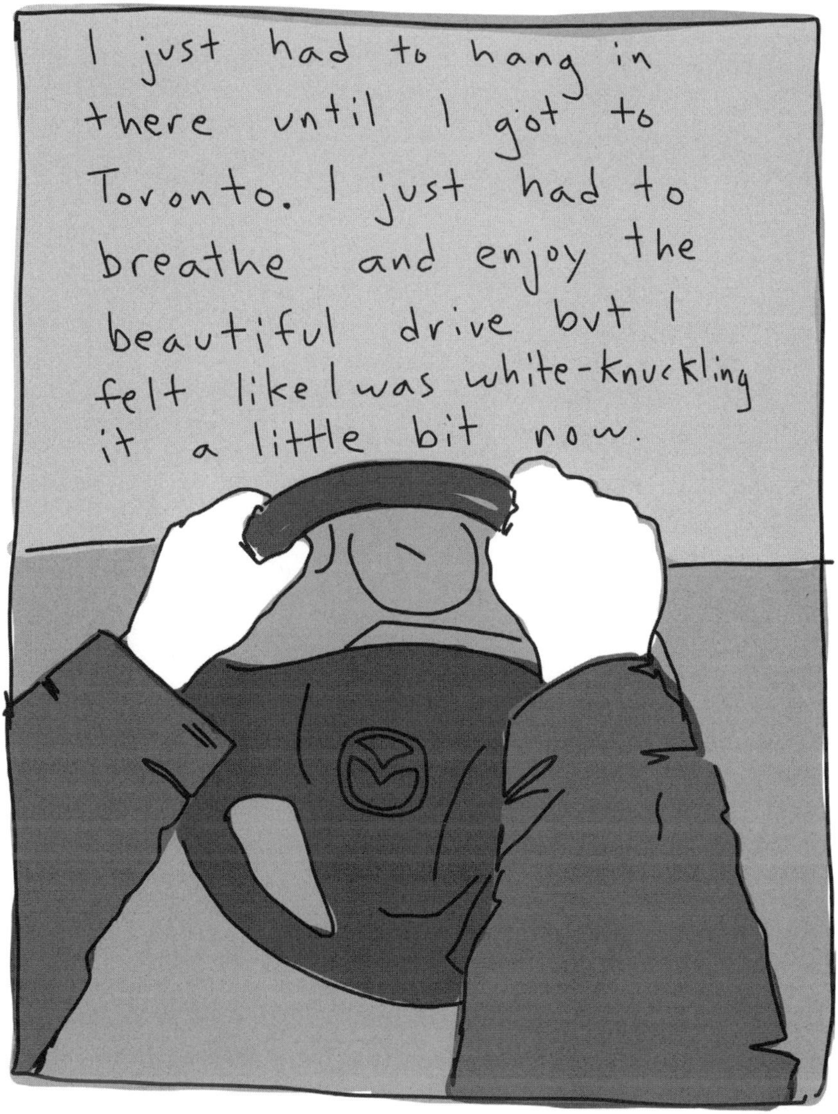
I just had to hang in there until I got to Toronto. I just had to breathe and enjoy the beautiful drive but I felt like I was white-knuckling it a little bit now.

There would be lots of time for a
meeting in Toronto and I would
get to see Charlotte.

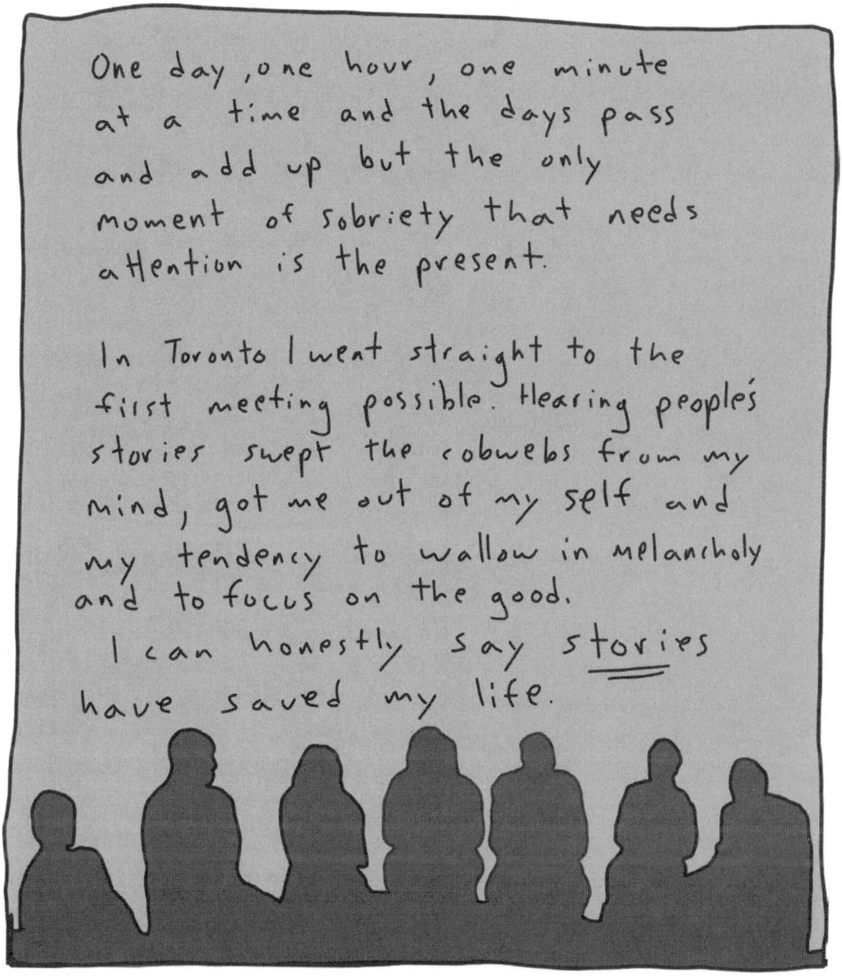
One day, one hour, one minute at a time and the days pass and add up but the only moment of sobriety that needs attention is the present.
In Toronto I went straight to the first meeting possible. Hearing people's stories swept the cobwebs from my mind, got me out of my self and my tendency to wallow in melancholy and to focus on the good.
I can honestly say stories have saved my life.

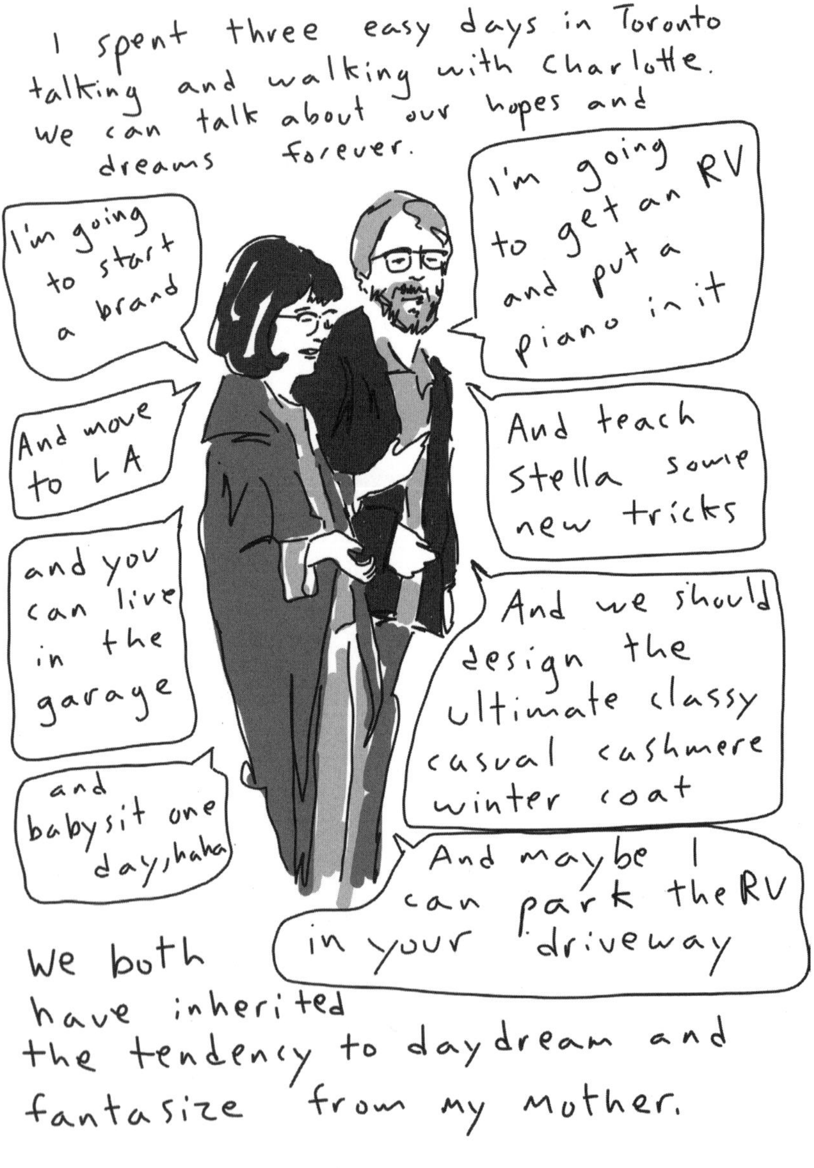
I spent three easy days in Toronto talking and walking with Charlotte. We can talk about our hopes and dreams forever.
I'm going to start a brand
I'm going to get an RV and put a piano in it
And move to LA
And teach Stella some new tricks
and you can live in the garage
And we should design the ultimate classy casual cashmere winter coat
and babysit one day, haha
And maybe I can park the RV in your driveway
We both have inherited the tendency to daydream and fantasize from my mother.

Charlotte tagged along to Montreal.

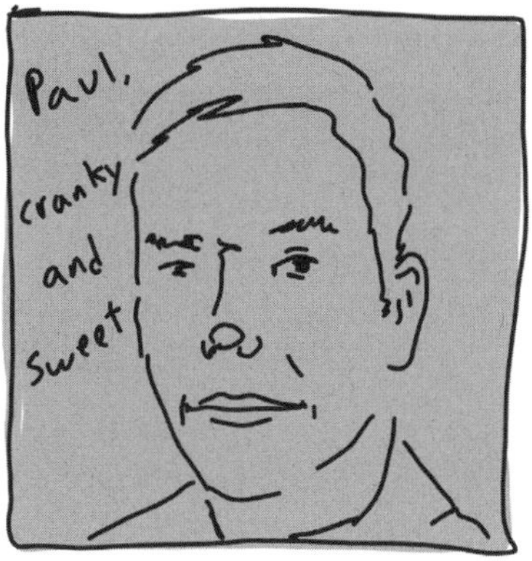
Paul,
cranky and sweet

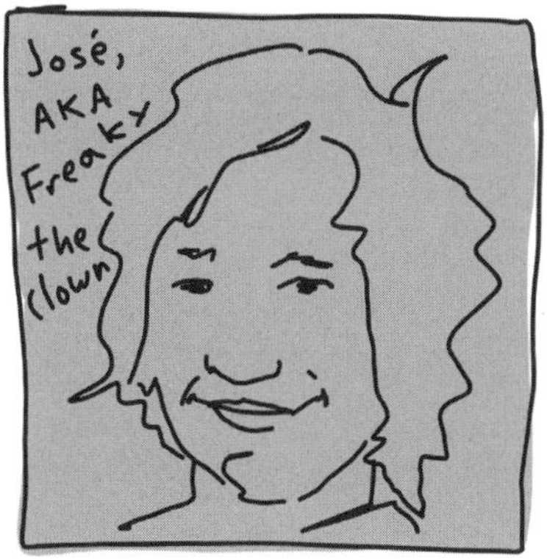
José, AKA Freaky the clown

we met up with some family friends, new and old, along the way.

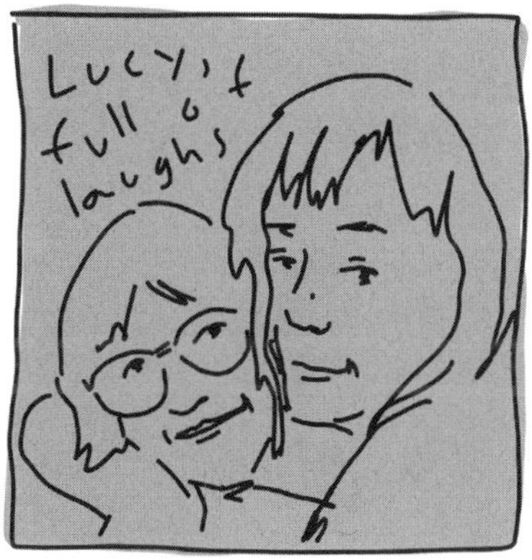
Lucy, full of laughs

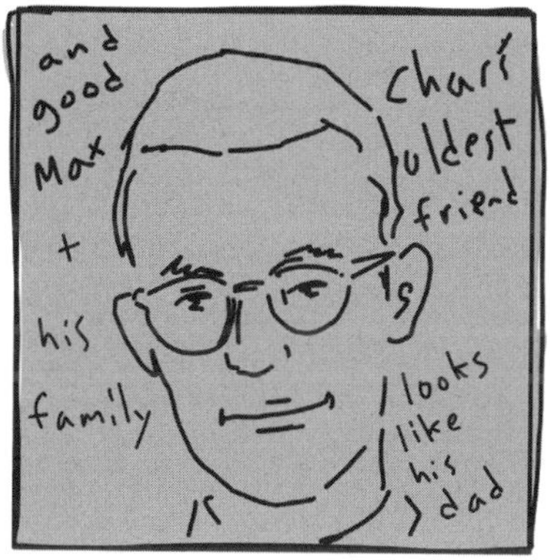
and good Max + his family
Char's oldest friend
looks like his dad

Connection and communication versus isolation. Perhaps the oldest dilemma.

In Montreal we met up with Ben for coffee at Social Club on St. Viateur in our old neighbourhood.

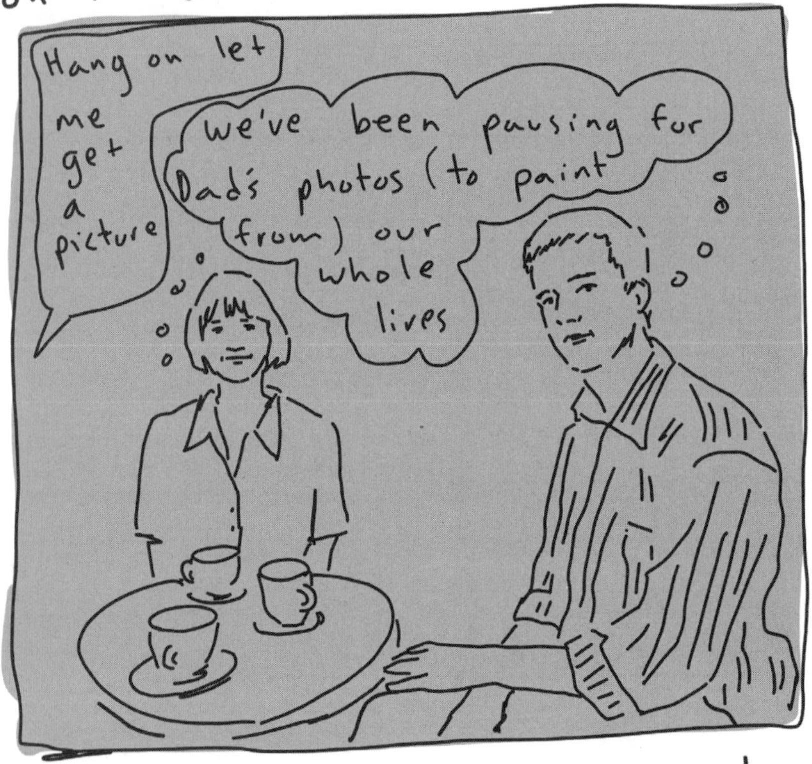
Hang on let me get a picture
we've been pausing for Dad's photos (to paint from) our whole lives

we said our goodbyes and I got back on the road feeling like I was leaving home as much as going towards it.

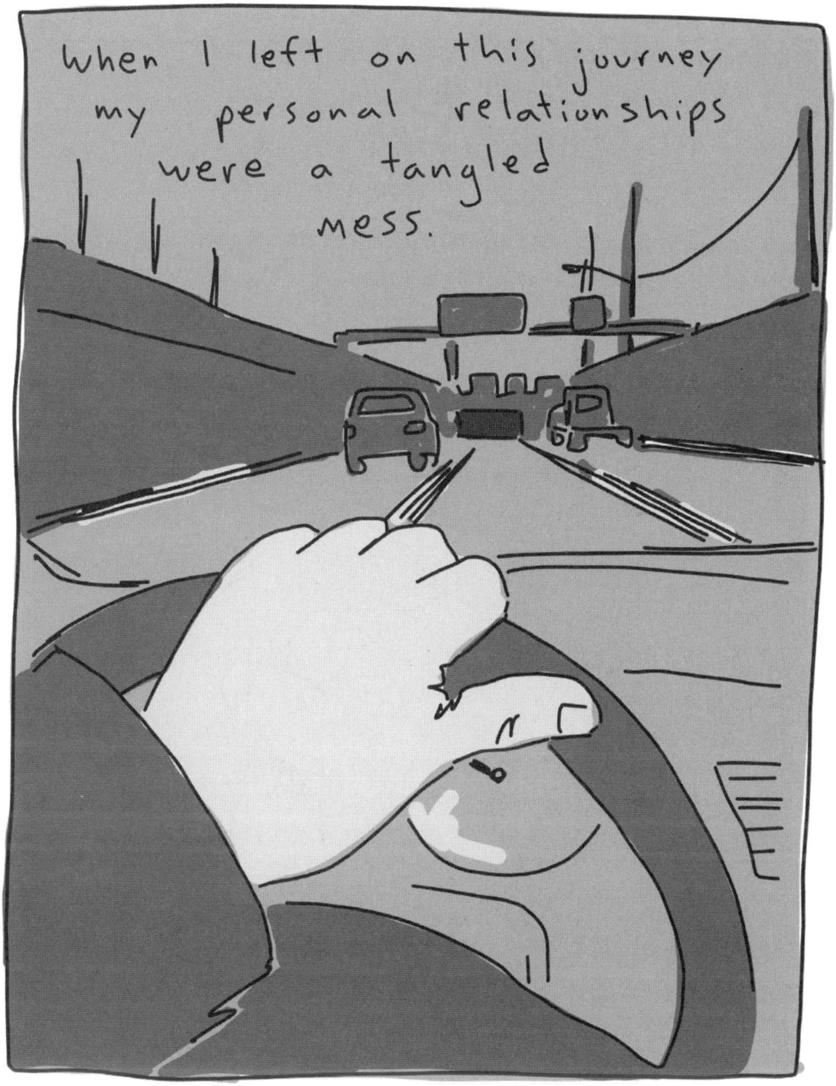
when I left on this journey
my personal relationships
were a tangled
mess.

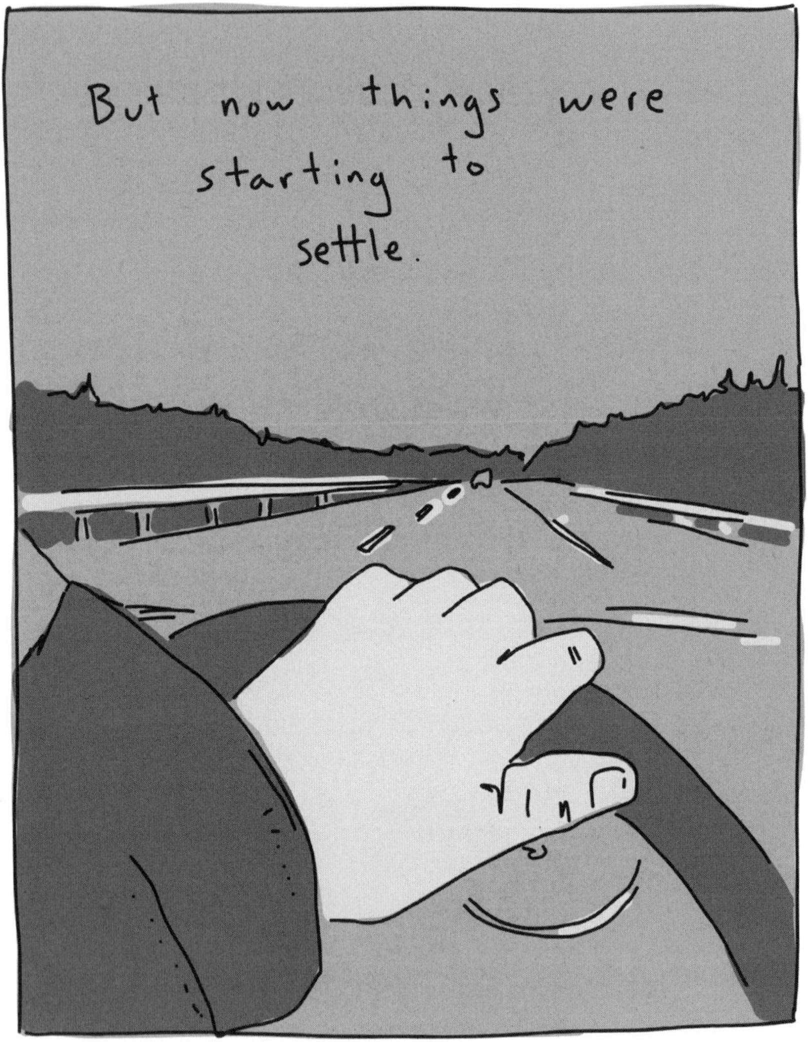
But now things were starting to settle.

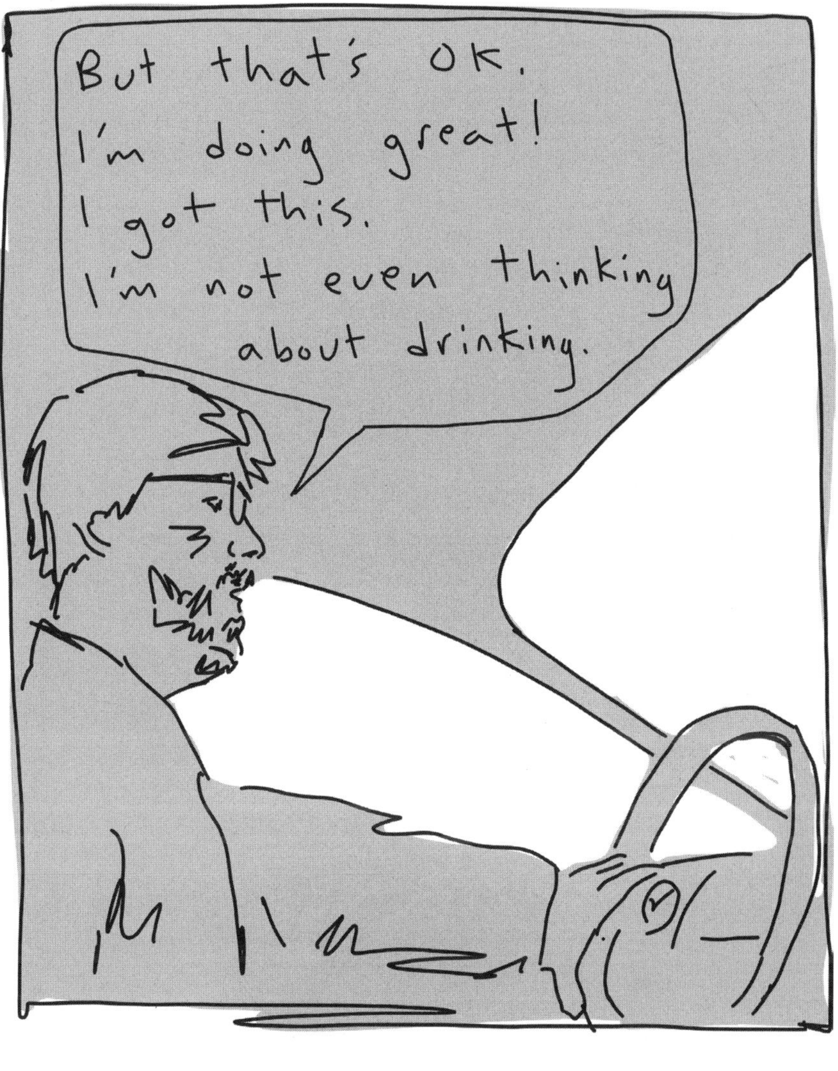
But that's OK. I'm doing great! I got this. I'm not even thinking about drinking.

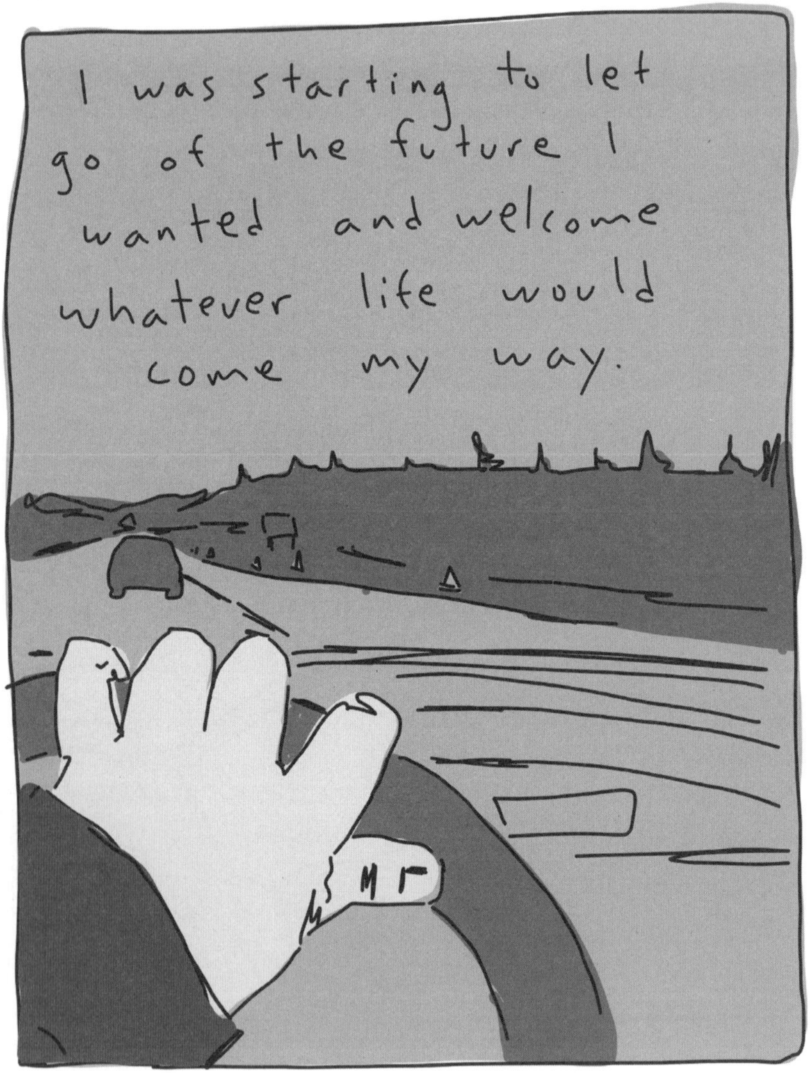
I was starting to let go of the future I wanted and welcome whatever life would come my way.

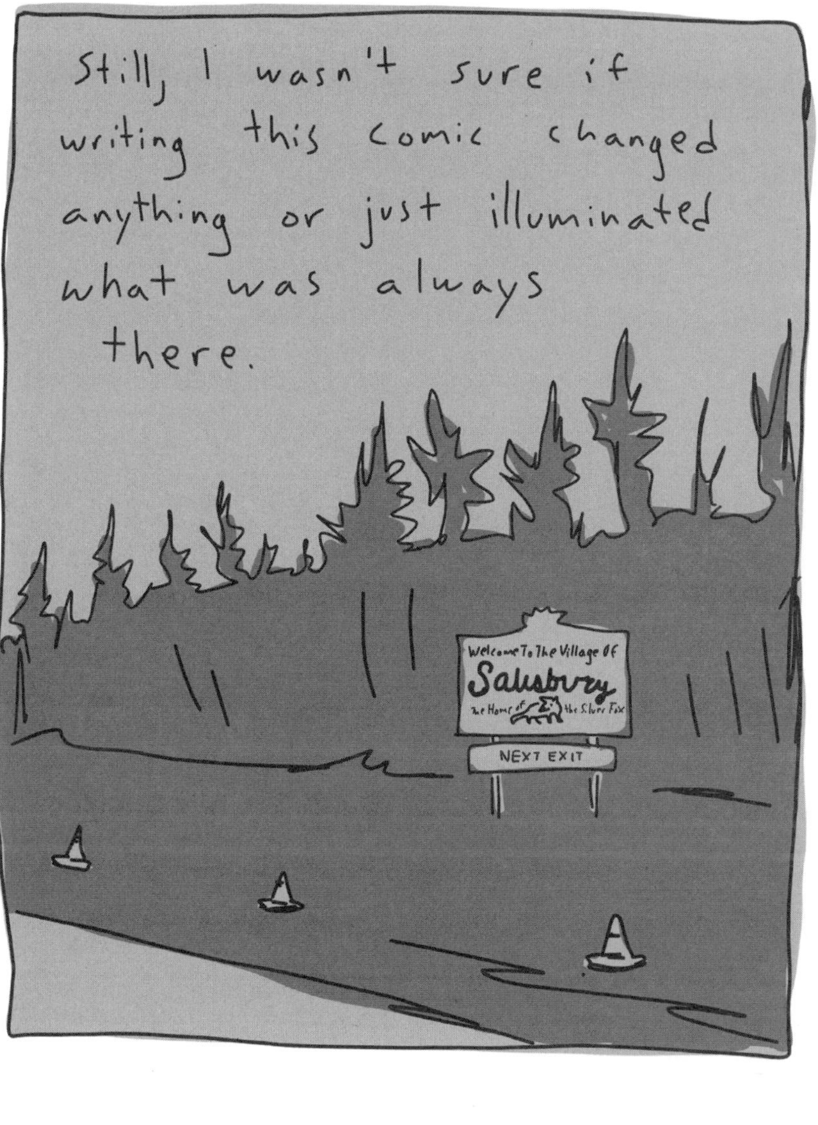
Still, I wasn't sure if writing this comic changed anything or just illuminated what was always there.
Welcome To The Village Of
Salisbury
The Home of the Silver Fox
NEXT EXIT

I drove in silence thinking about the lives that crossed or entangled with my own on this trip.

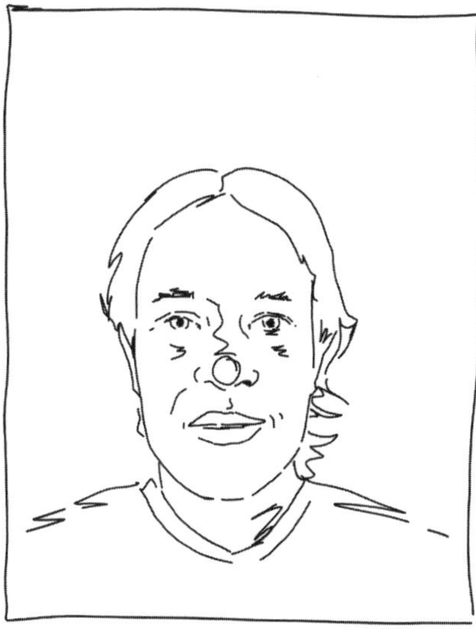

If it is true that connection is the opposite of addiction,

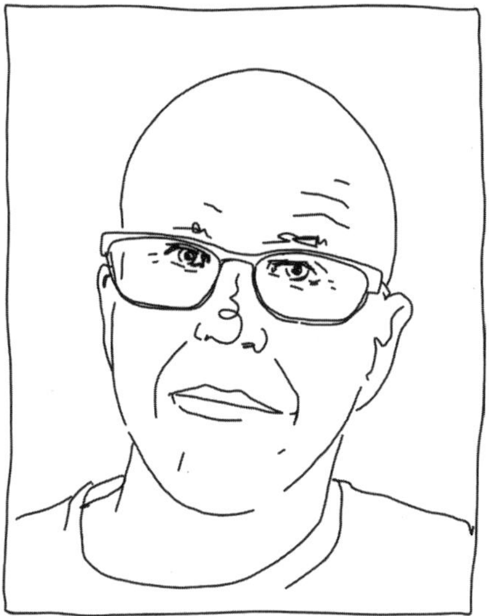

then I needed these people much more than I ever wanted to admit.

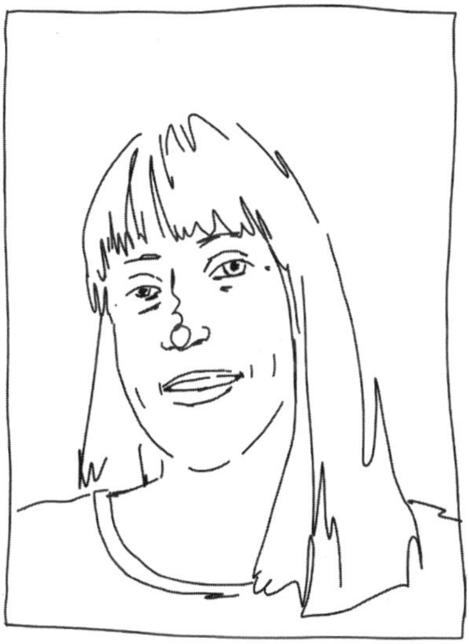

Forgiveness,

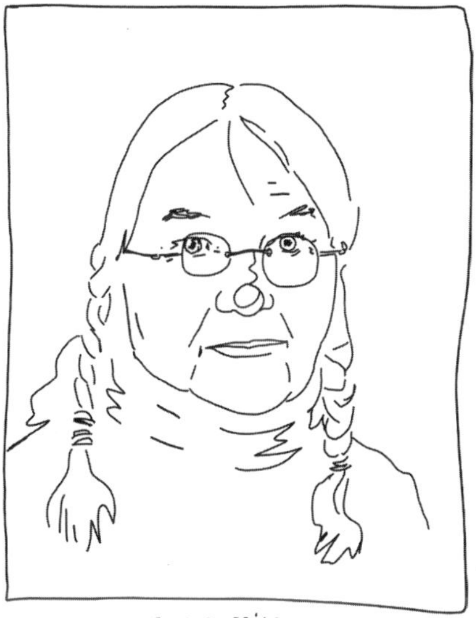

compassion,

and understanding.

I need their silly jokes

and endless questions.

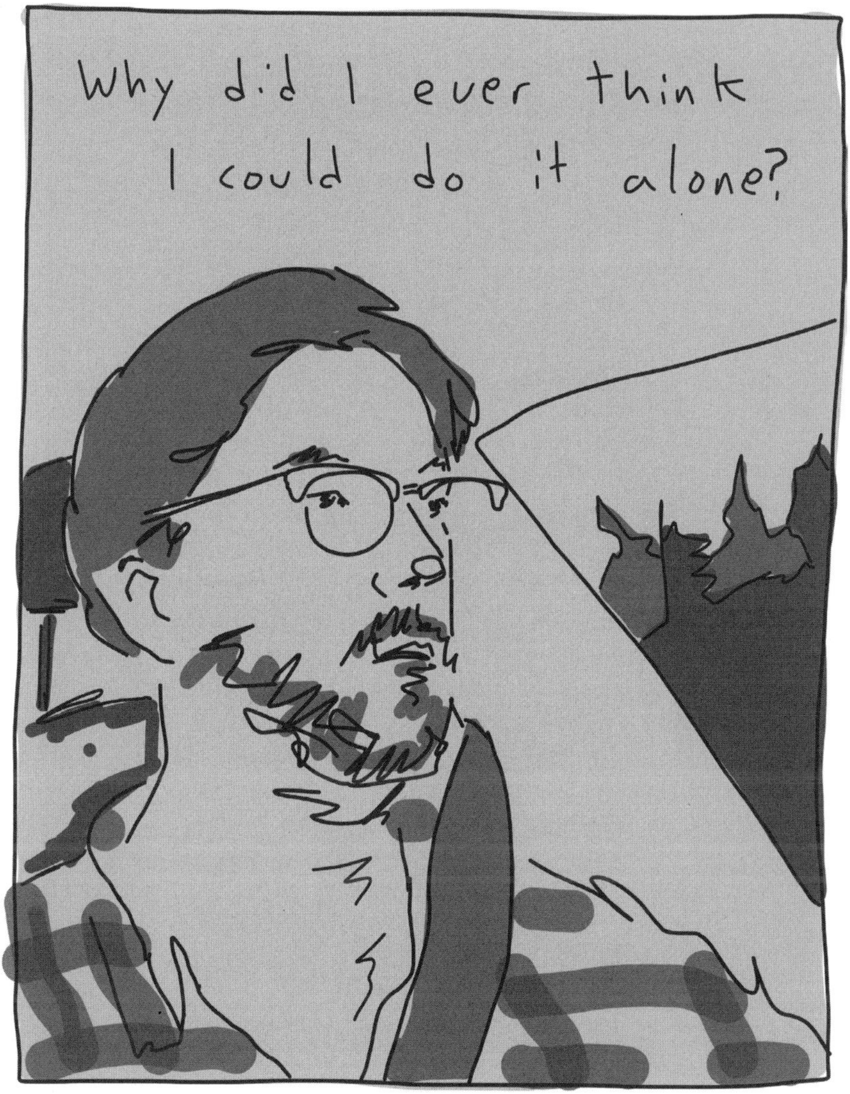
Why did I ever think I could do it alone?

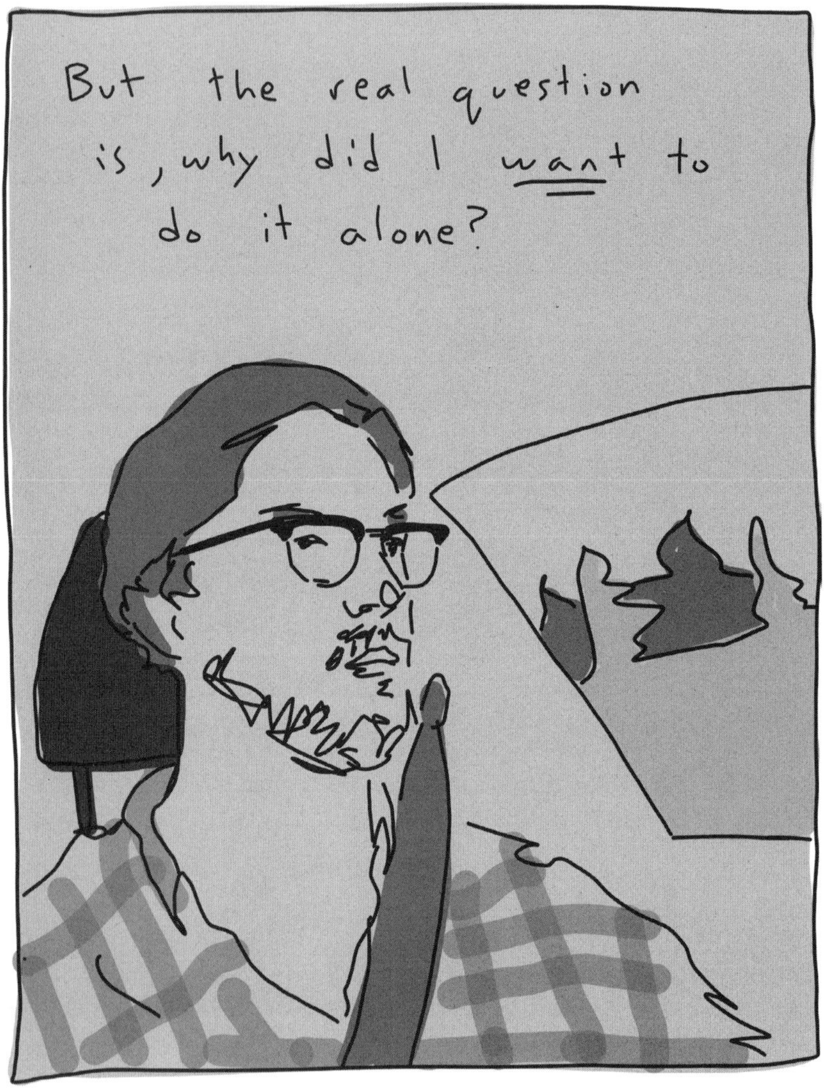
But the real question is, why did I want to do it alone?

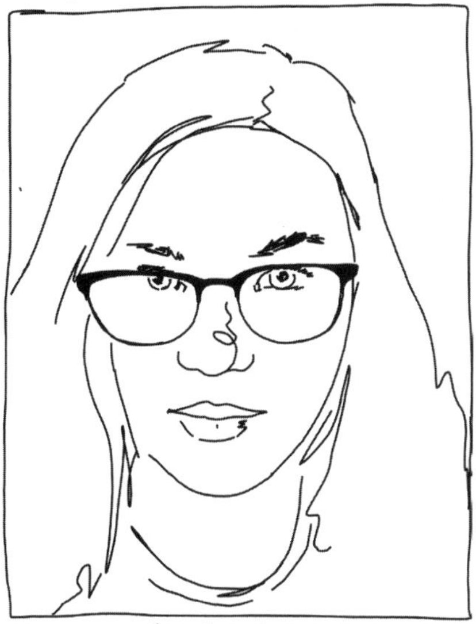

without advice

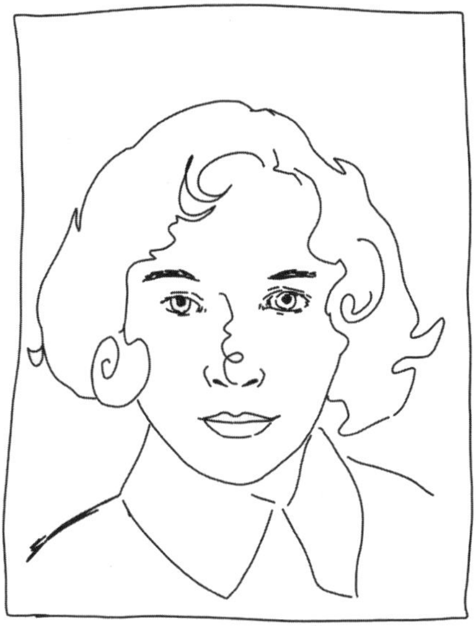

encouragement

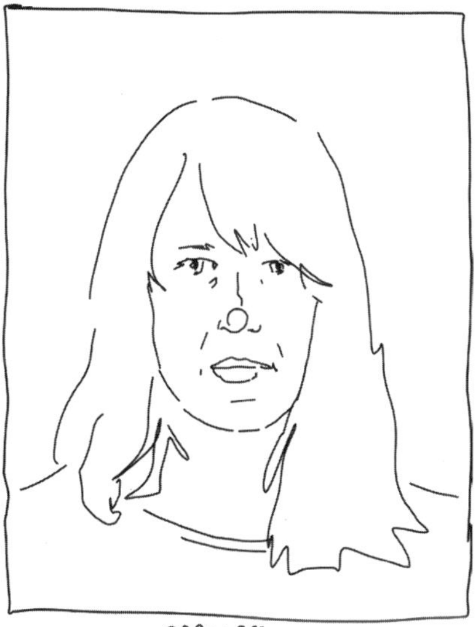

openness

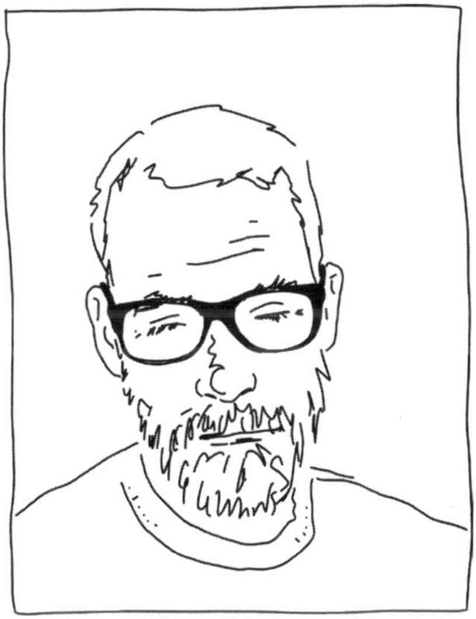

caring

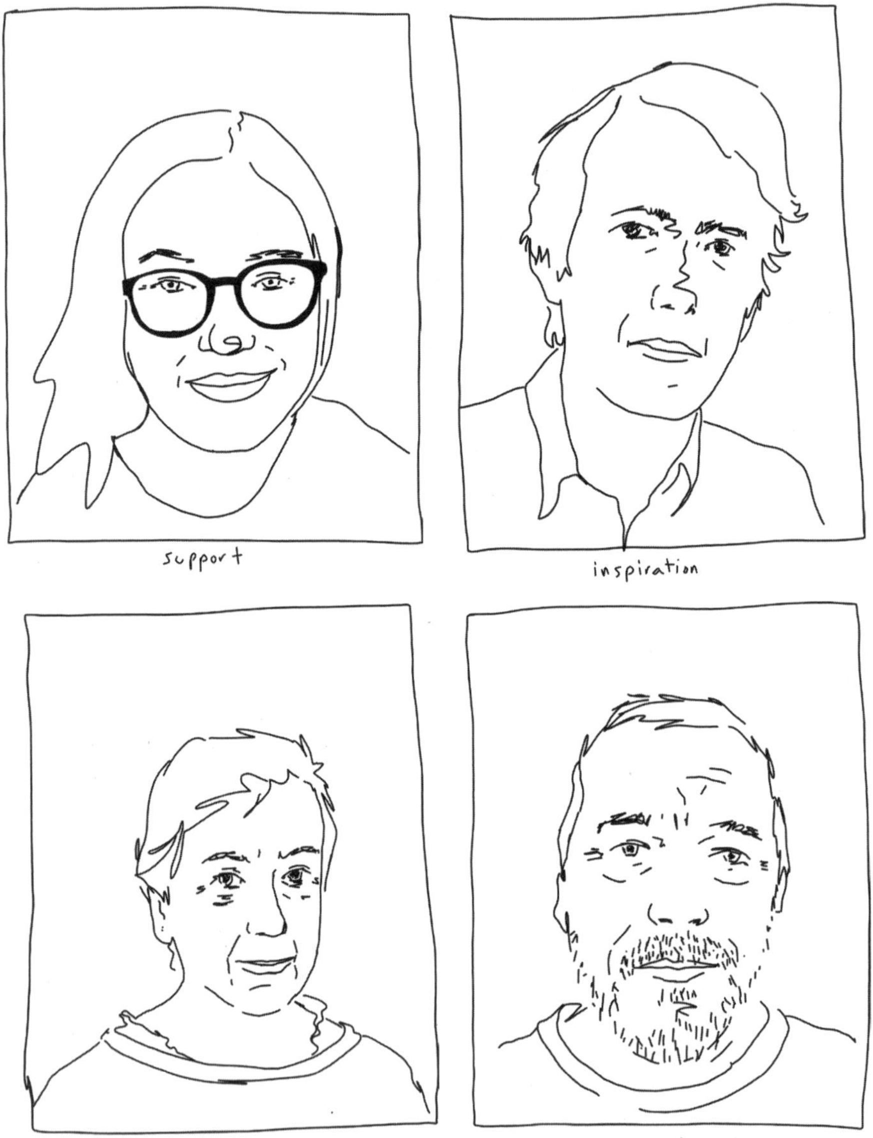
support
inspiration
guidance
or wisdom.

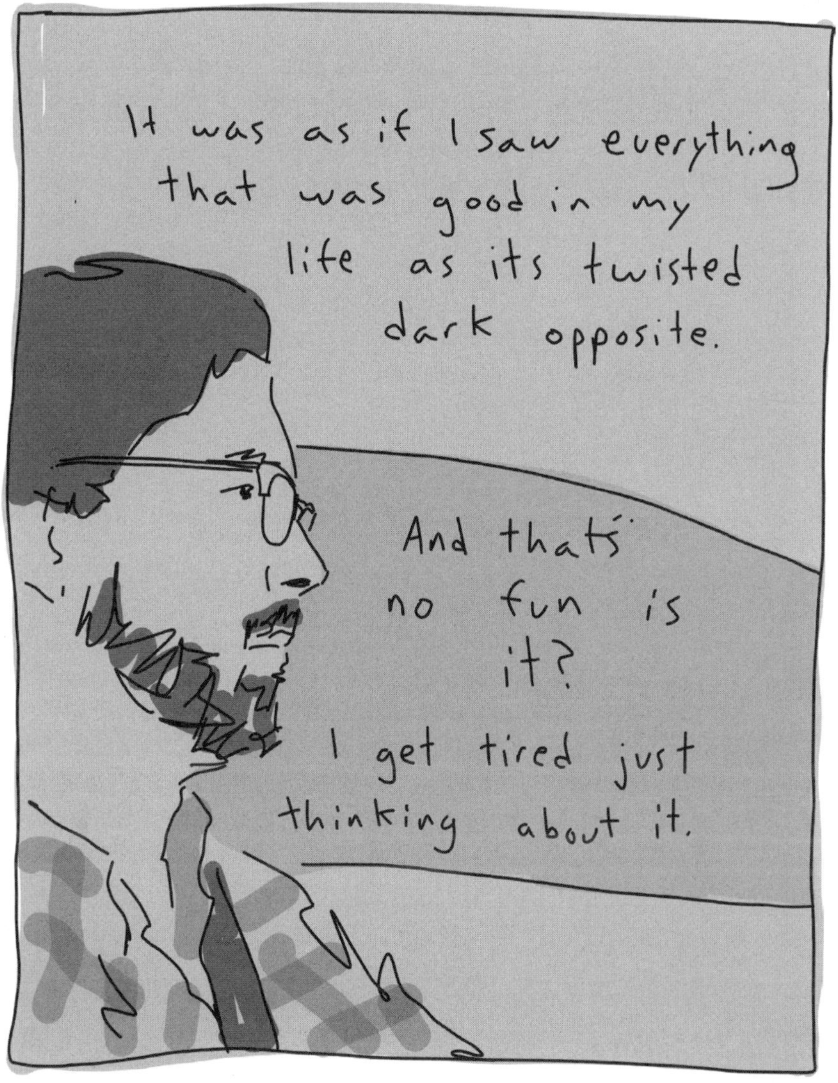
It was as if I saw everything that was good in my life as its twisted dark opposite.
And that's no fun is it?
I get tired just thinking about it.

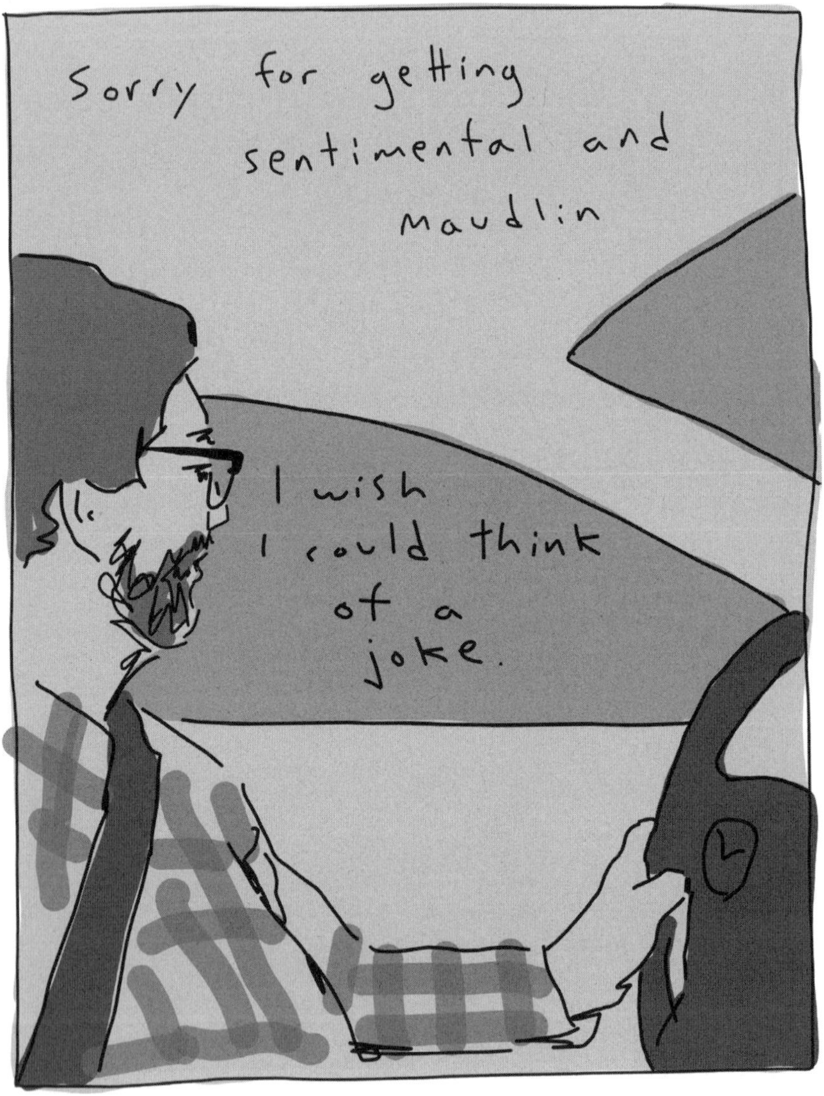
Sorry for getting sentimental and maudlin
I wish I could think of a joke.

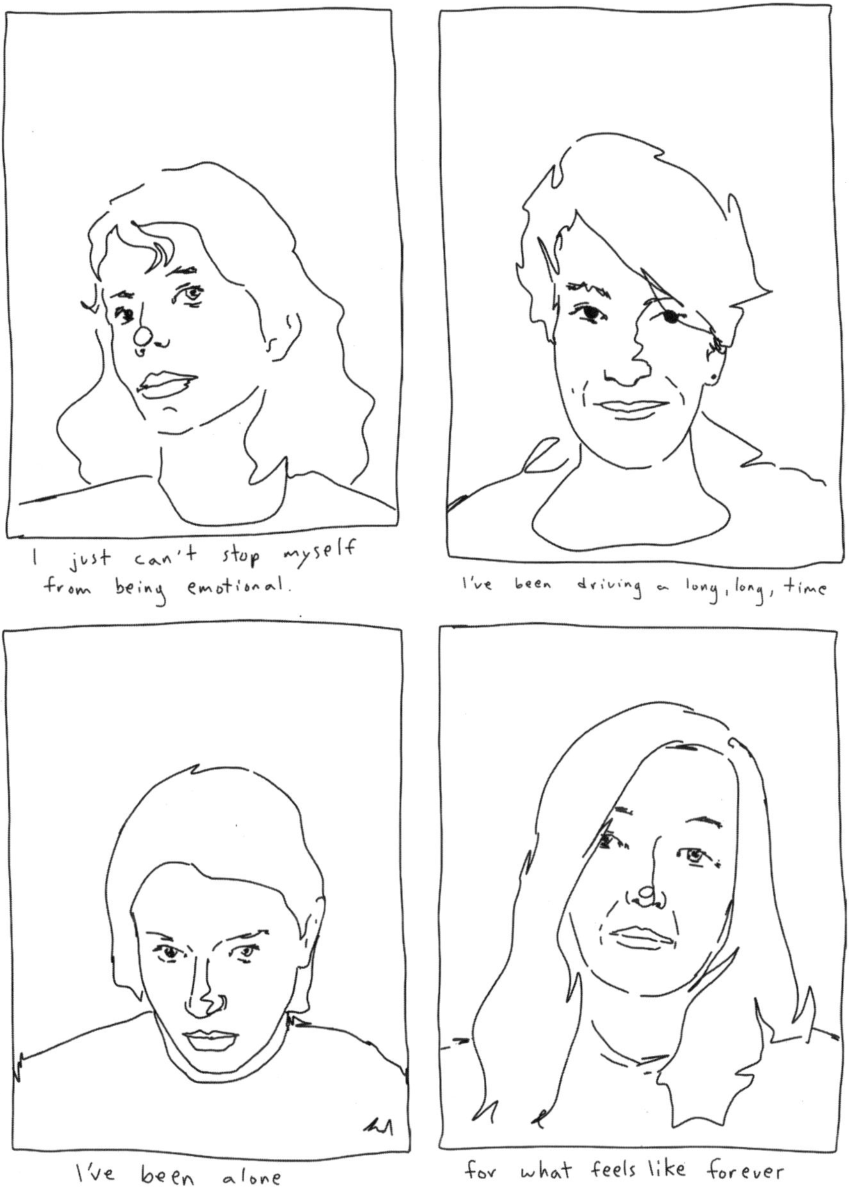
I just can't stop myself from being emotional.
I've been driving a long, long, time
I've been alone
for what feels like forever

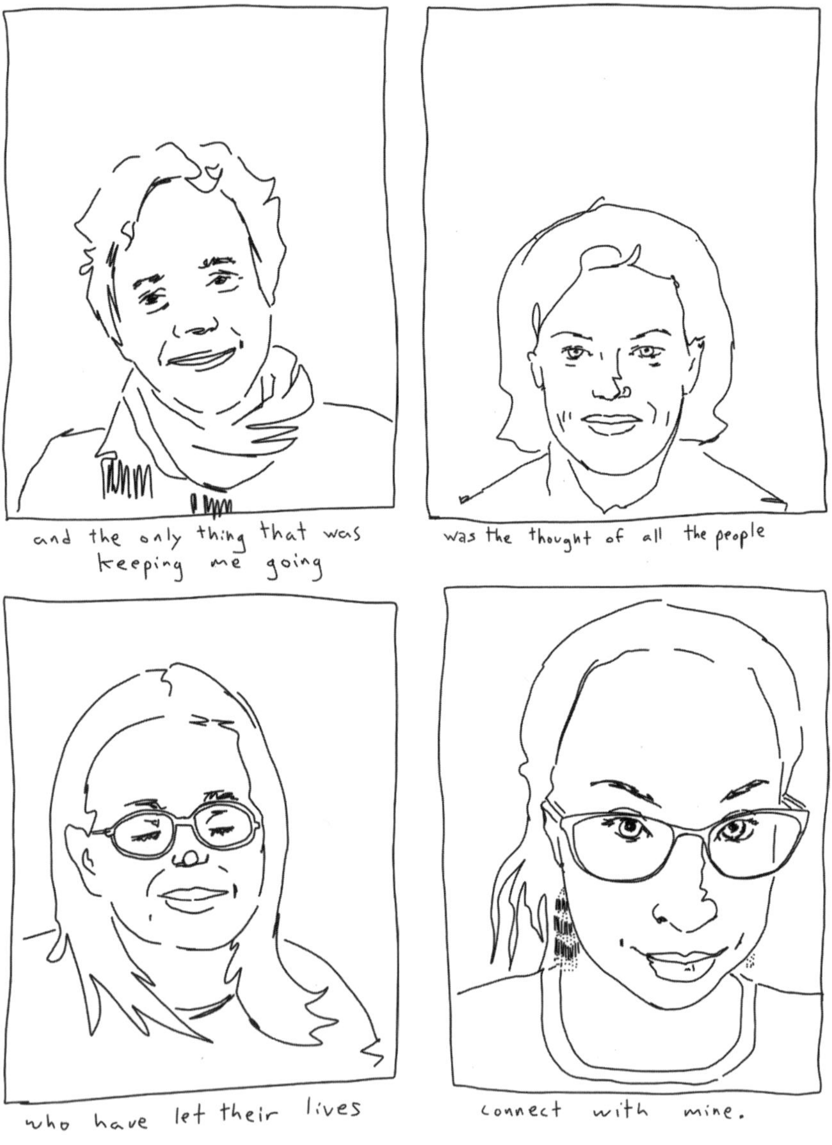
and the only thing that was keeping me going
was the thought of all the people
who have let their lives
connect with mine.

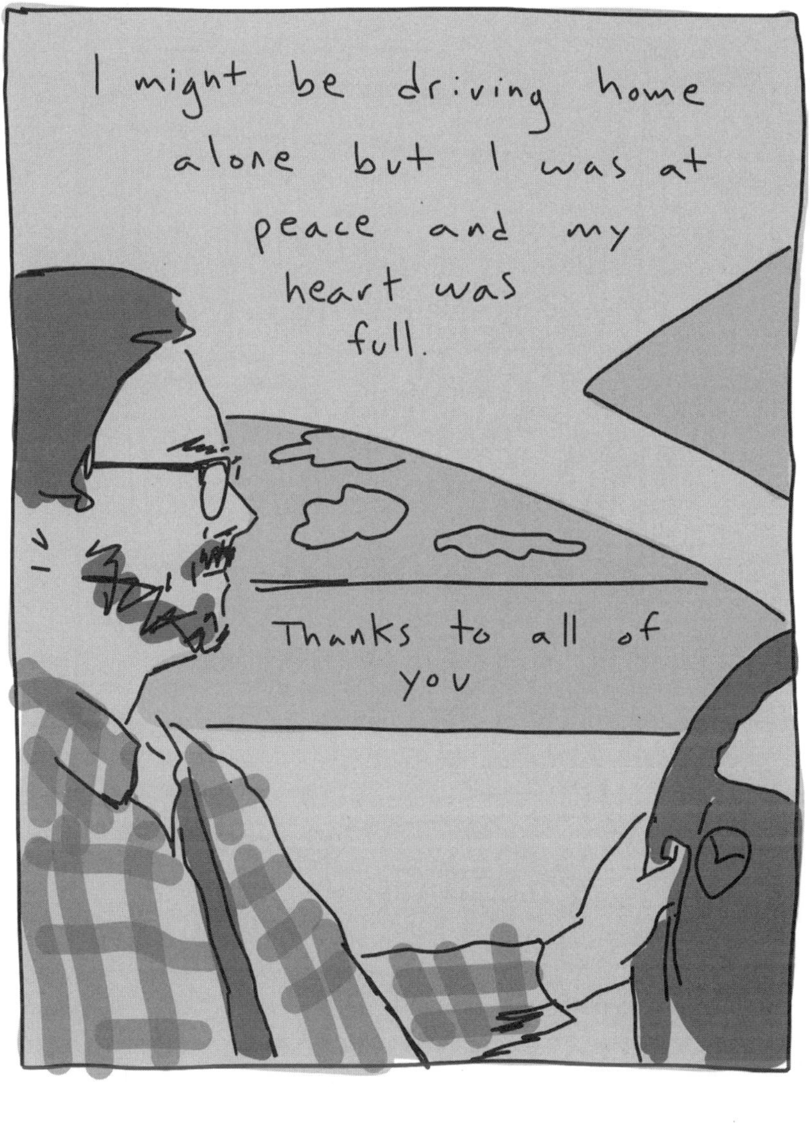
I might be driving home alone but I was at peace and my heart was full.
Thanks to all of you

54

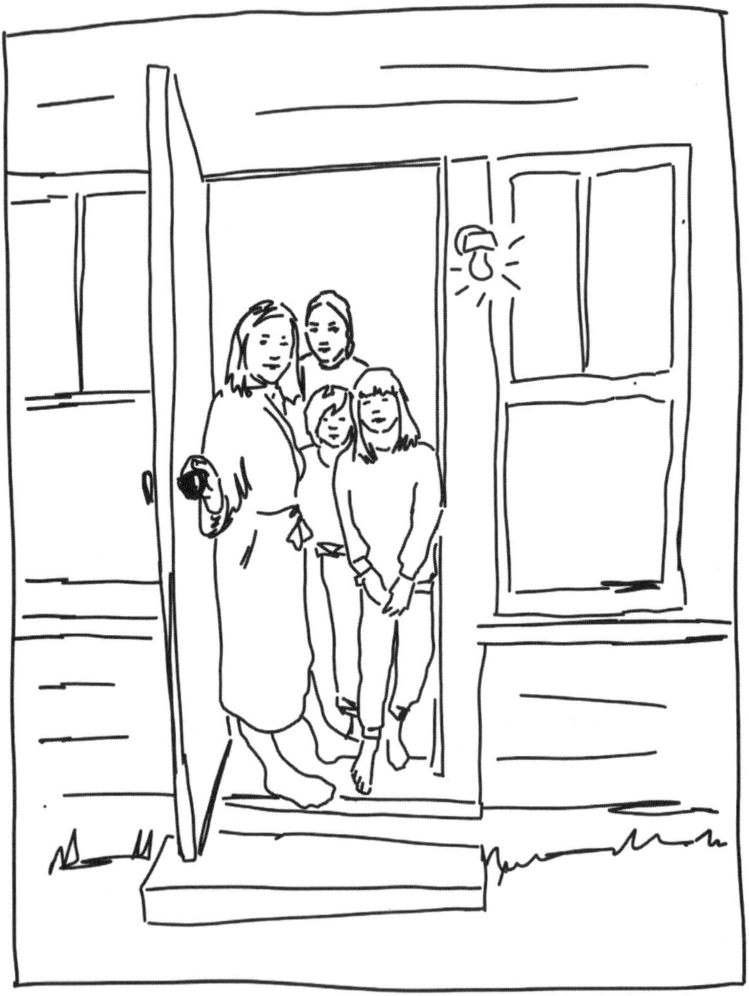

When I arrived in Sackville I went straight to pick up Rose and Stella. The twins were just getting ready for bed.

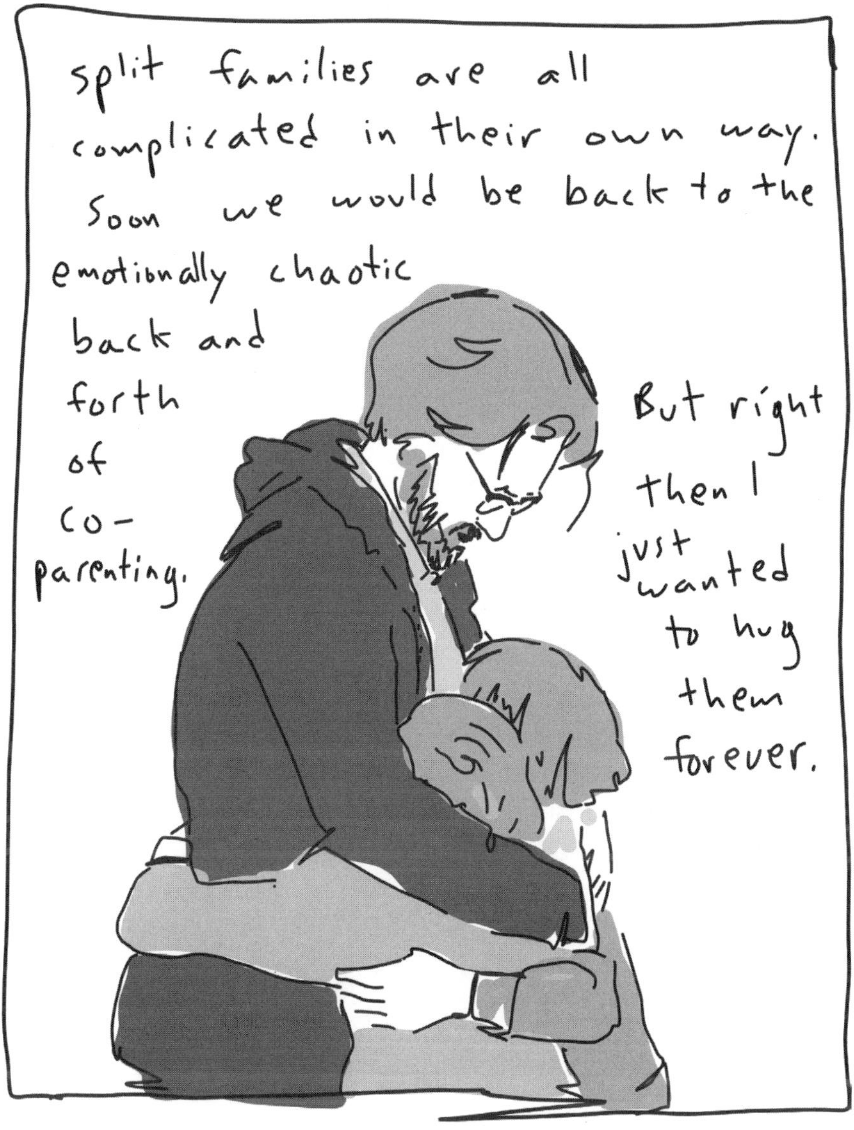
split families are all complicated in their own way. Soon we would be back to the emotionally chaotic back and forth of co-parenting.
But right then I just wanted to hug them forever.

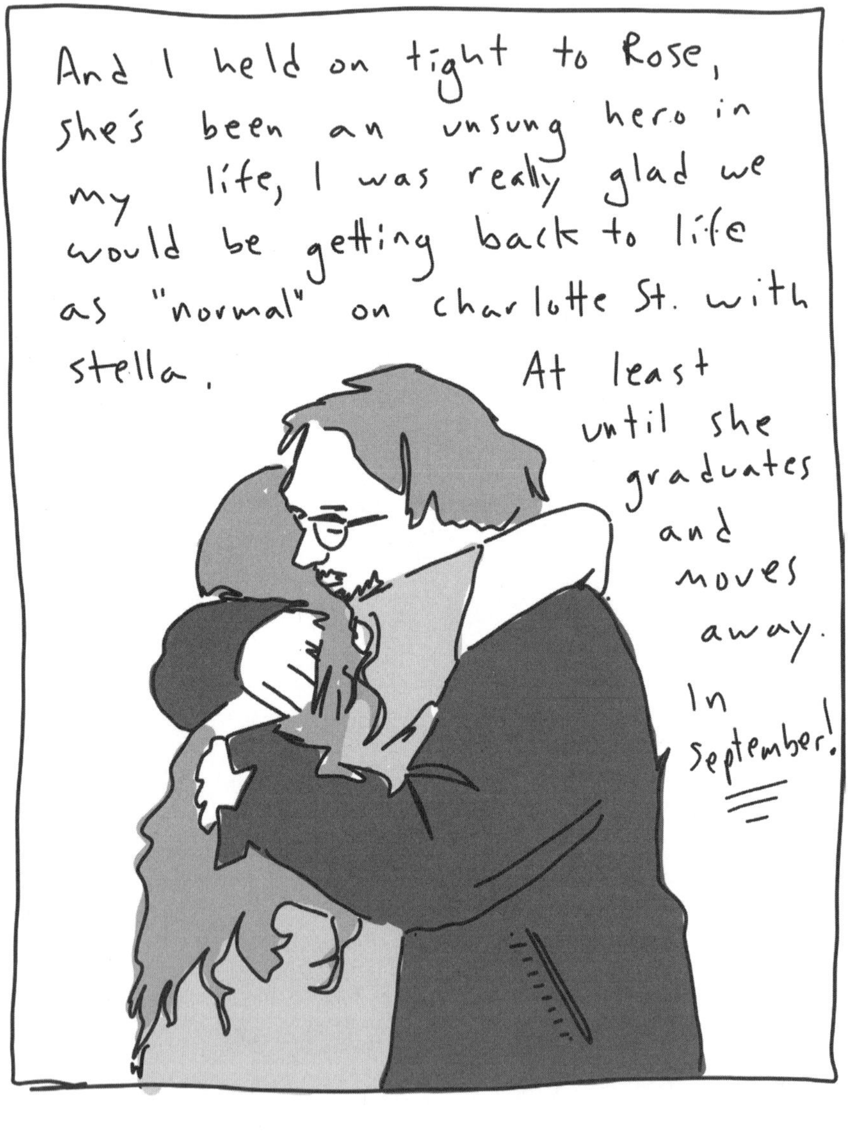
And I held on tight to Rose, she's been an unsung hero in my life, I was really glad we would be getting back to life as "normal" on Charlotte St. with stella.
At least until she graduates and moves away.
In September!

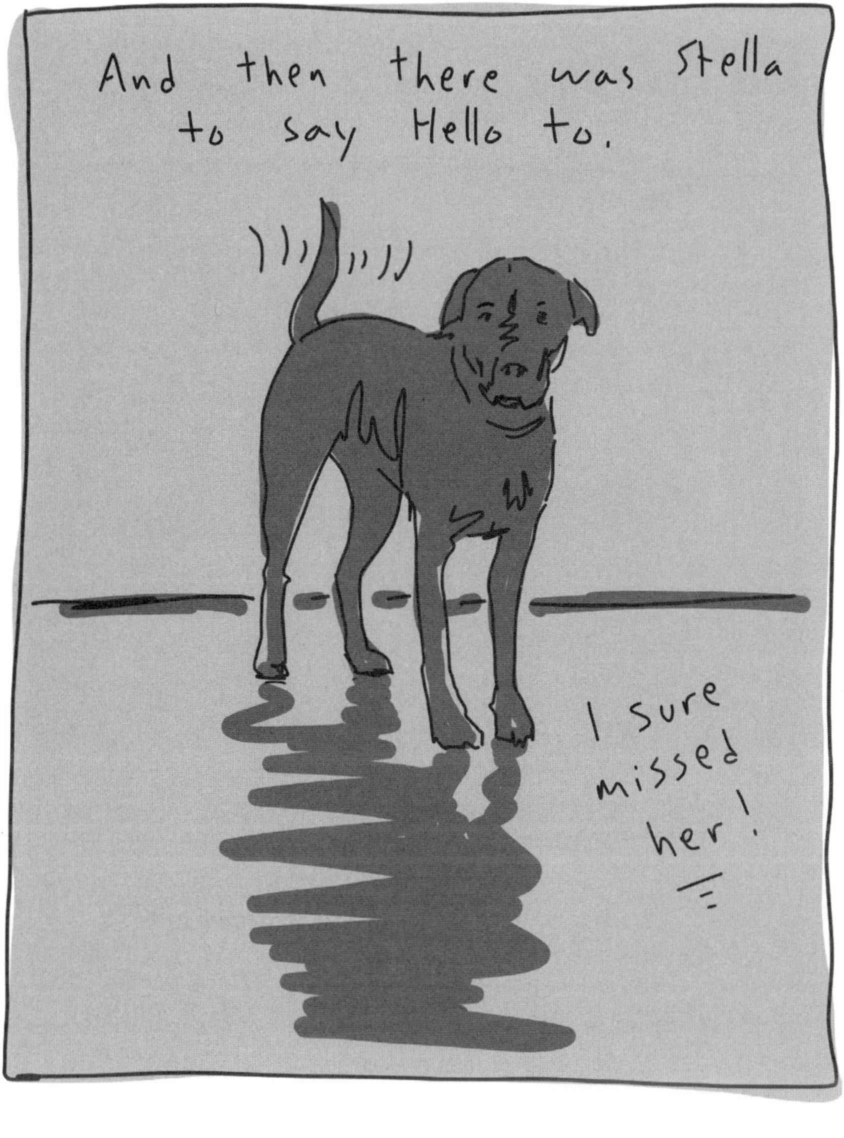
And then there was Stella to say Hello to.
I sure missed her!

After saying goodnight to the twins,

Rose, Stella and I drove through town before going home. Rose drove of course.

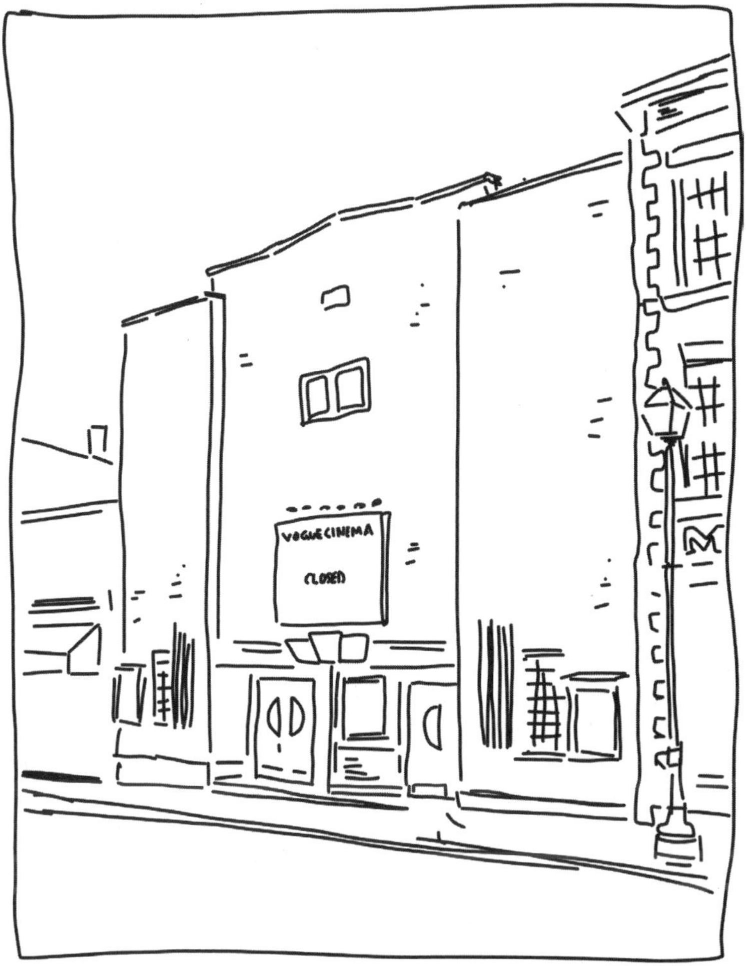
VOGUE CINEMA
CLOSED

Rose had been missing her driving lessons and her endless rambling tours of the town.

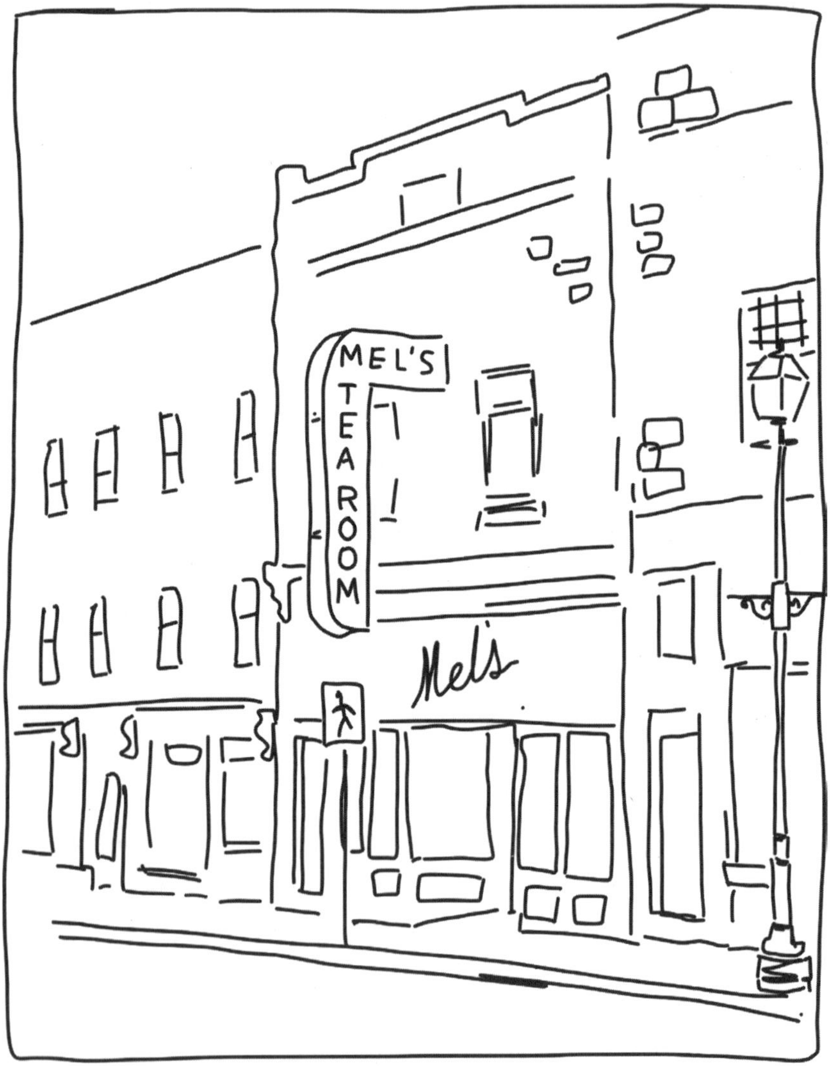
MEL'S
TEA ROOM
Mel's

We drove down Main St. three times

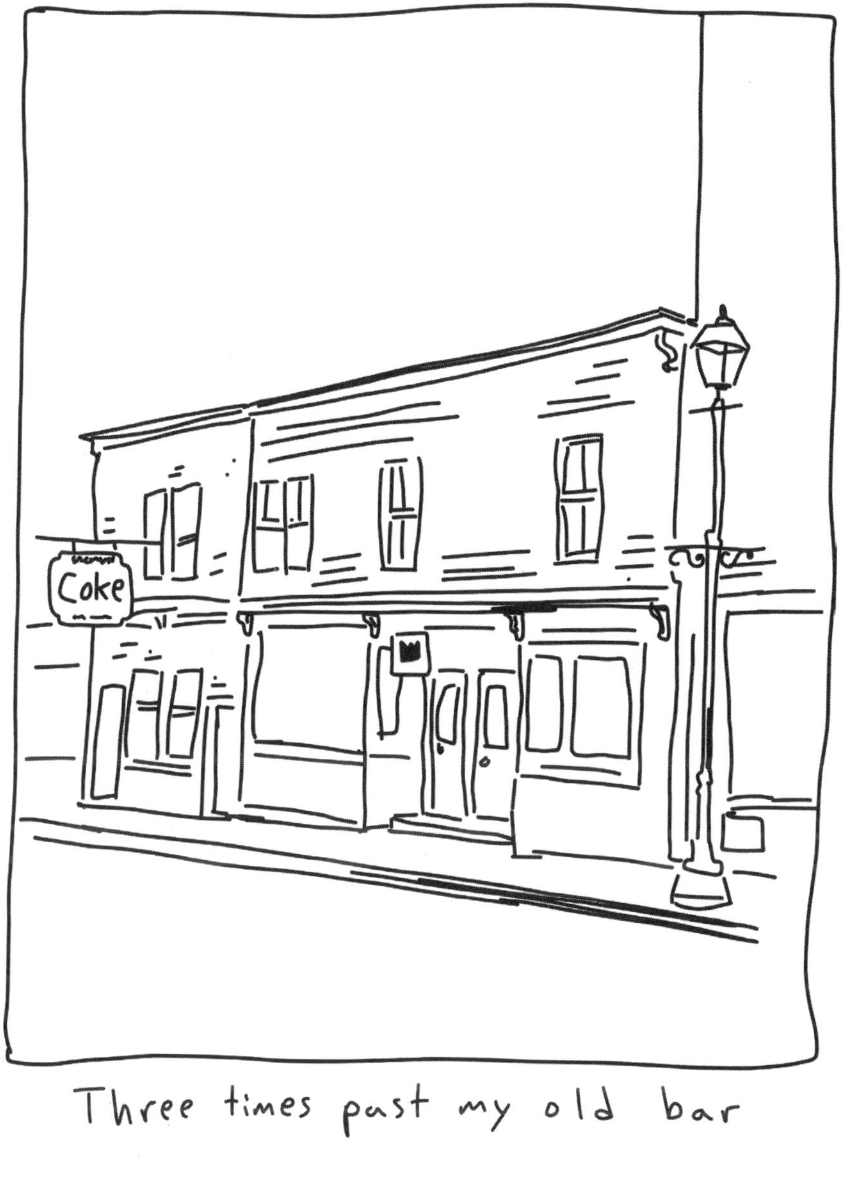
Coke

Three times past my old bar

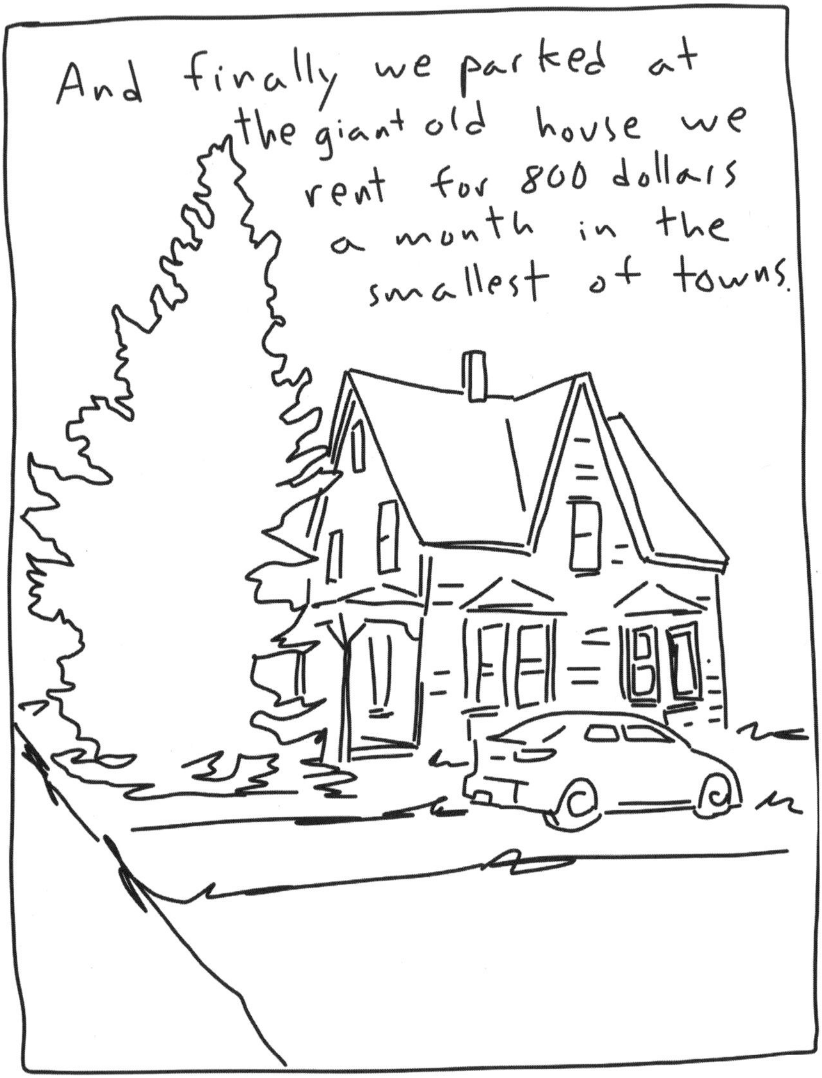
And finally we parked at the giant old house we rent for 800 dollars a month in the smallest of towns.

we were home for now

55

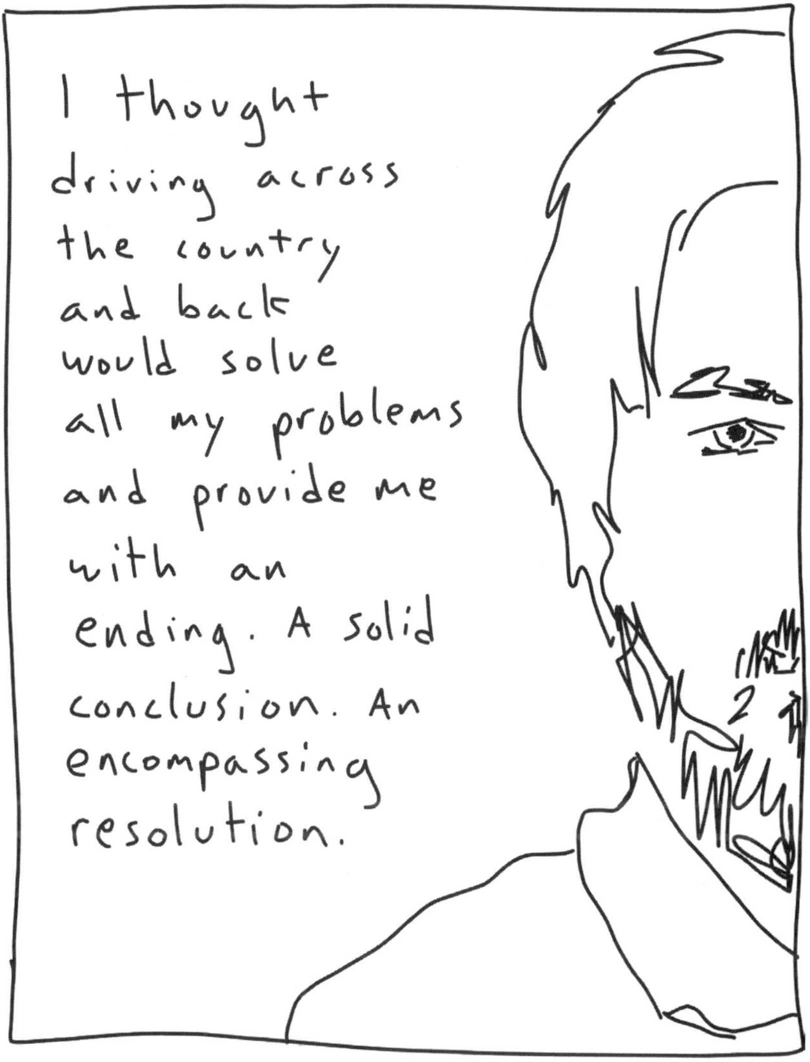
I thought driving across the country and back would solve all my problems and provide me with an ending. A solid conclusion. An encompassing resolution.

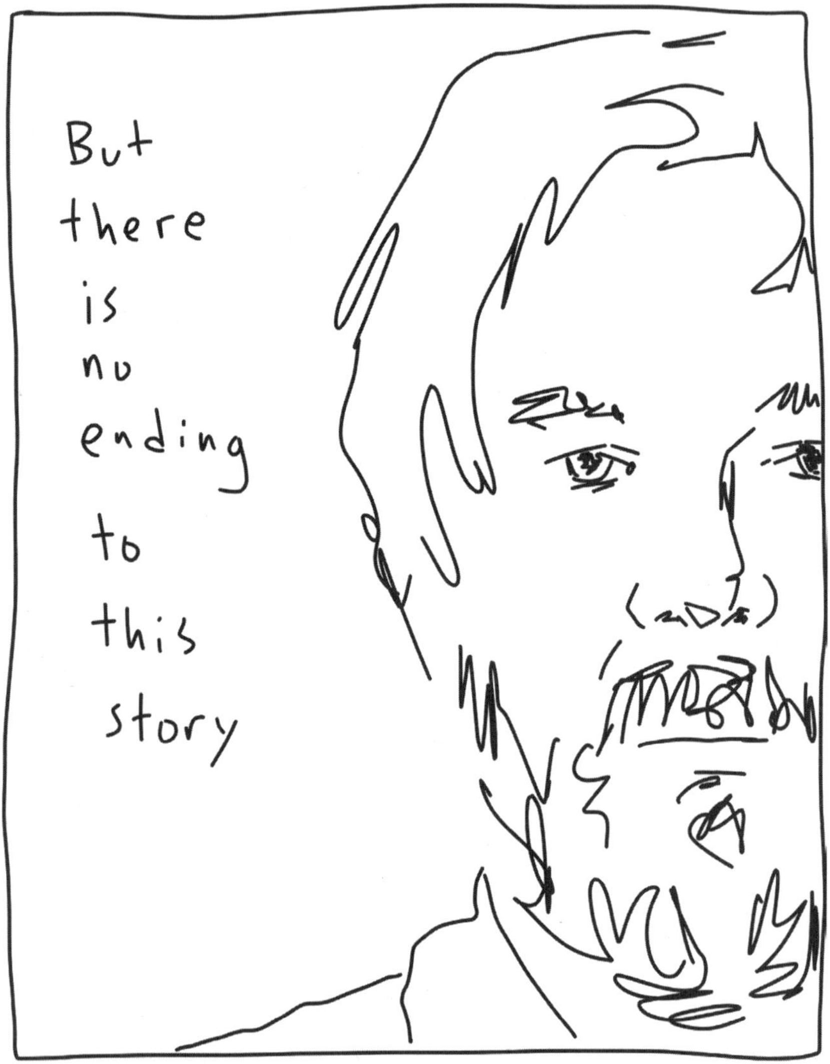
But there is no ending to this story

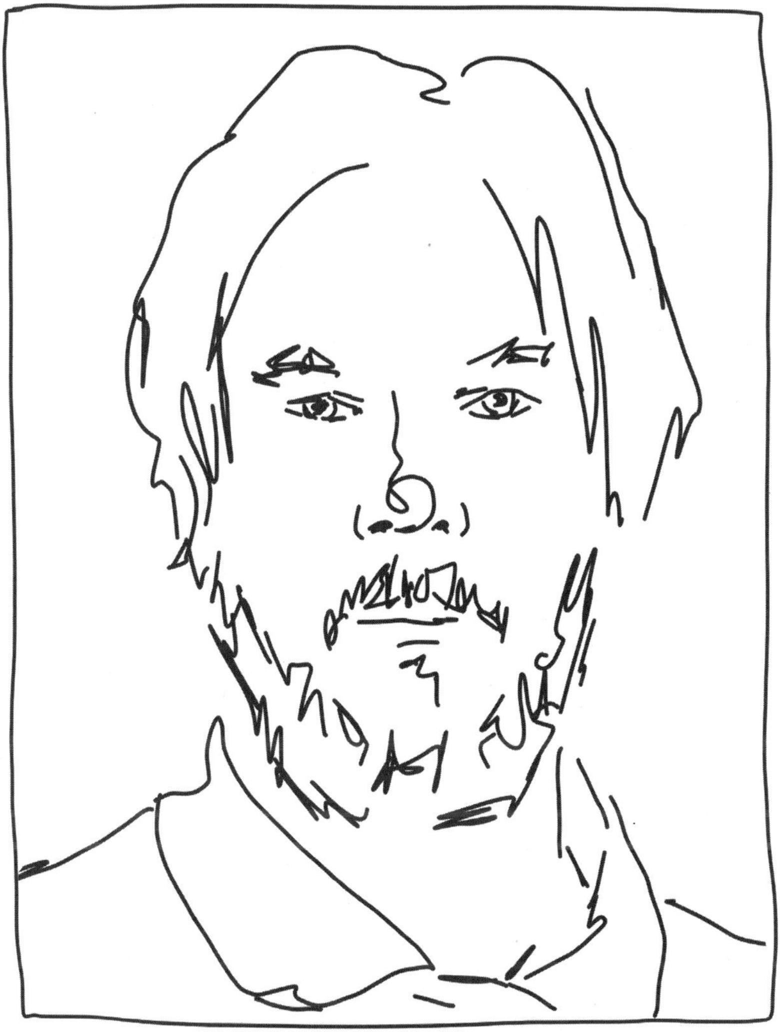

It is only the middle.

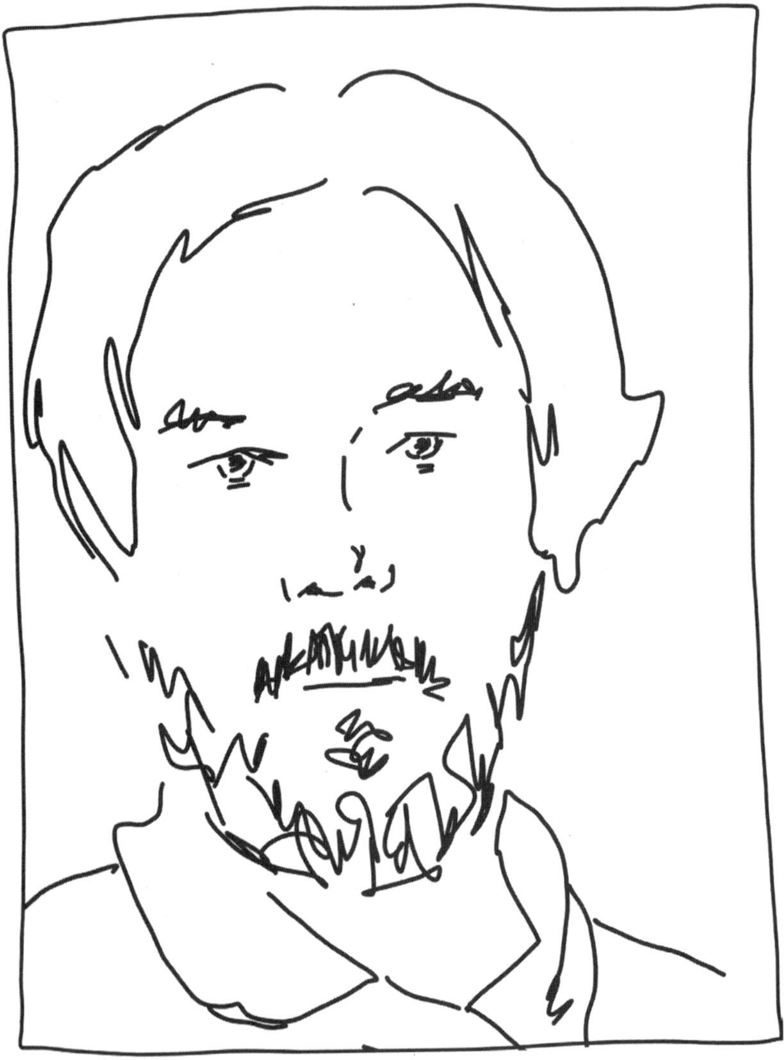

But maybe that's the best part of life

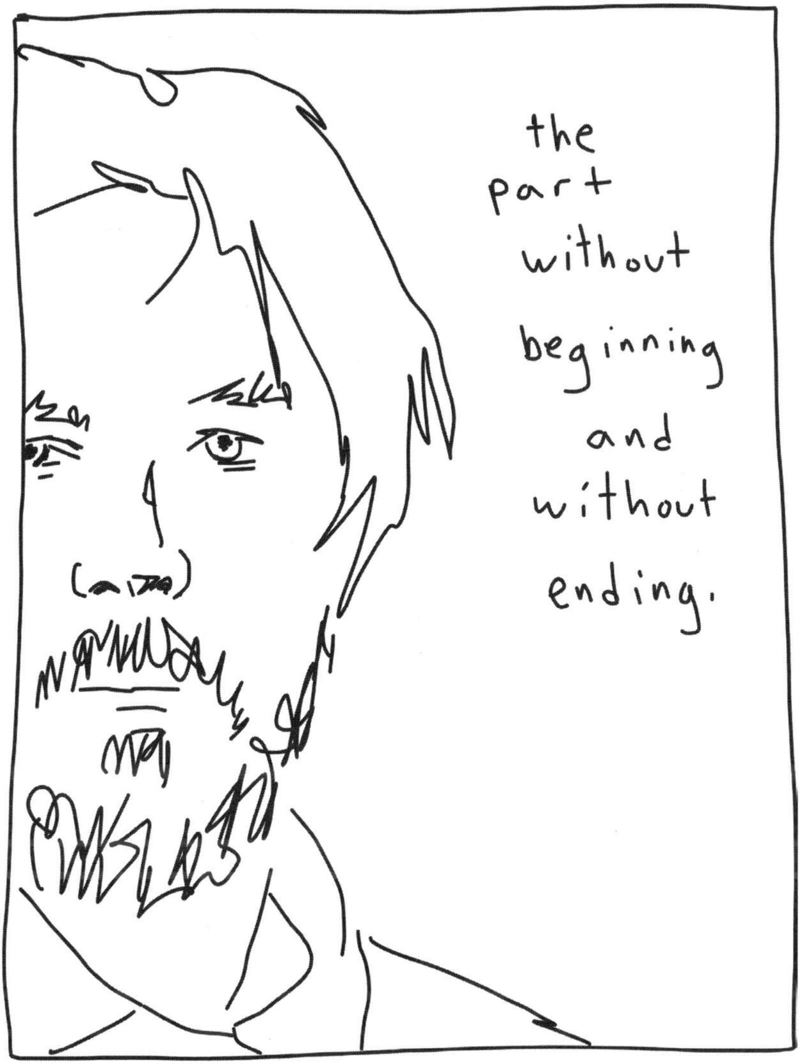
the part without beginning and without ending.

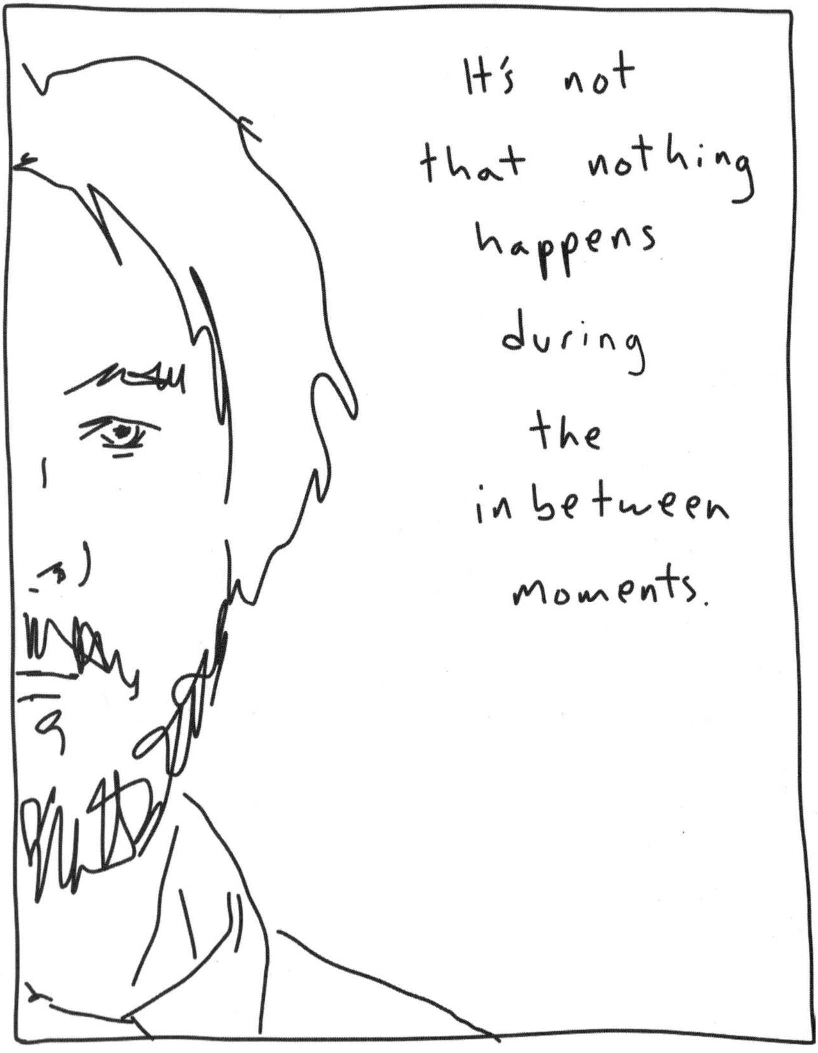
It's not that nothing happens during the in between moments.

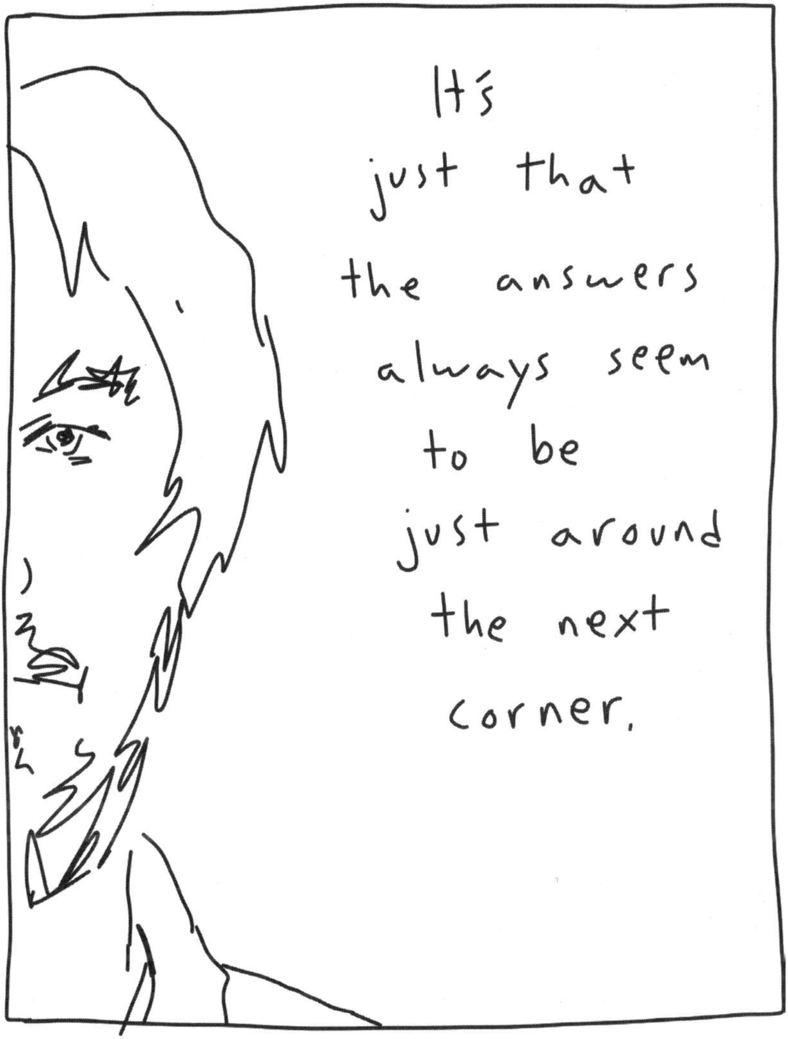
It's just that the answers always seem to be just around the next corner.

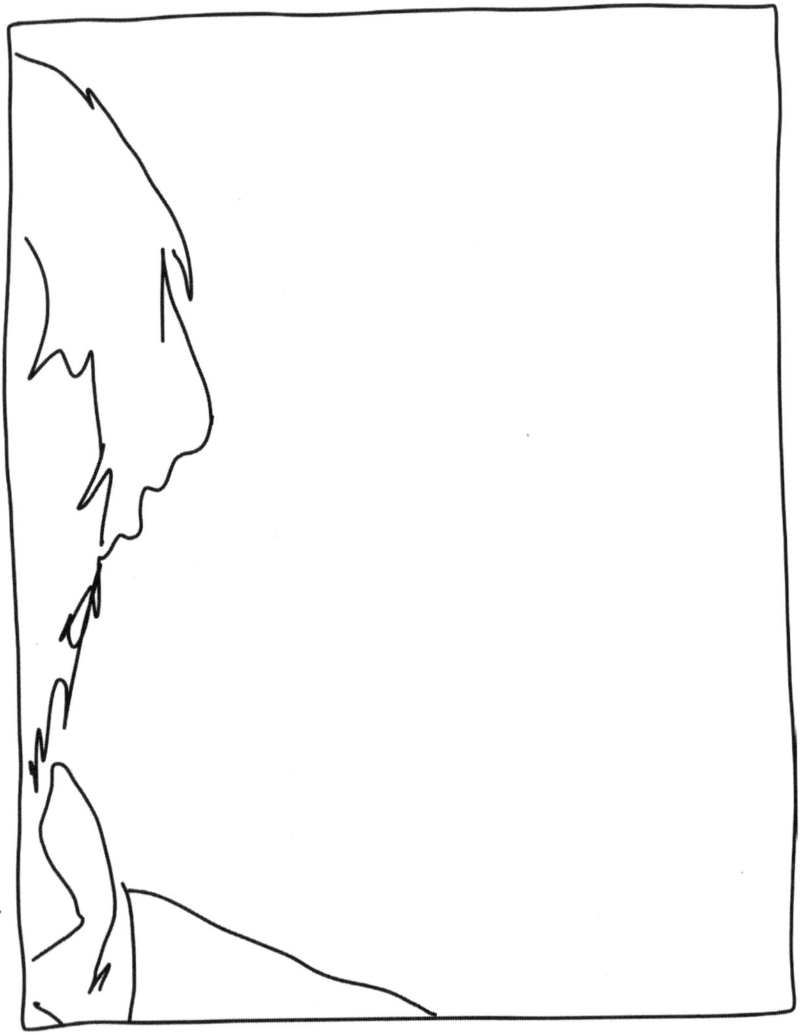

THE
END

A temporary epilogue

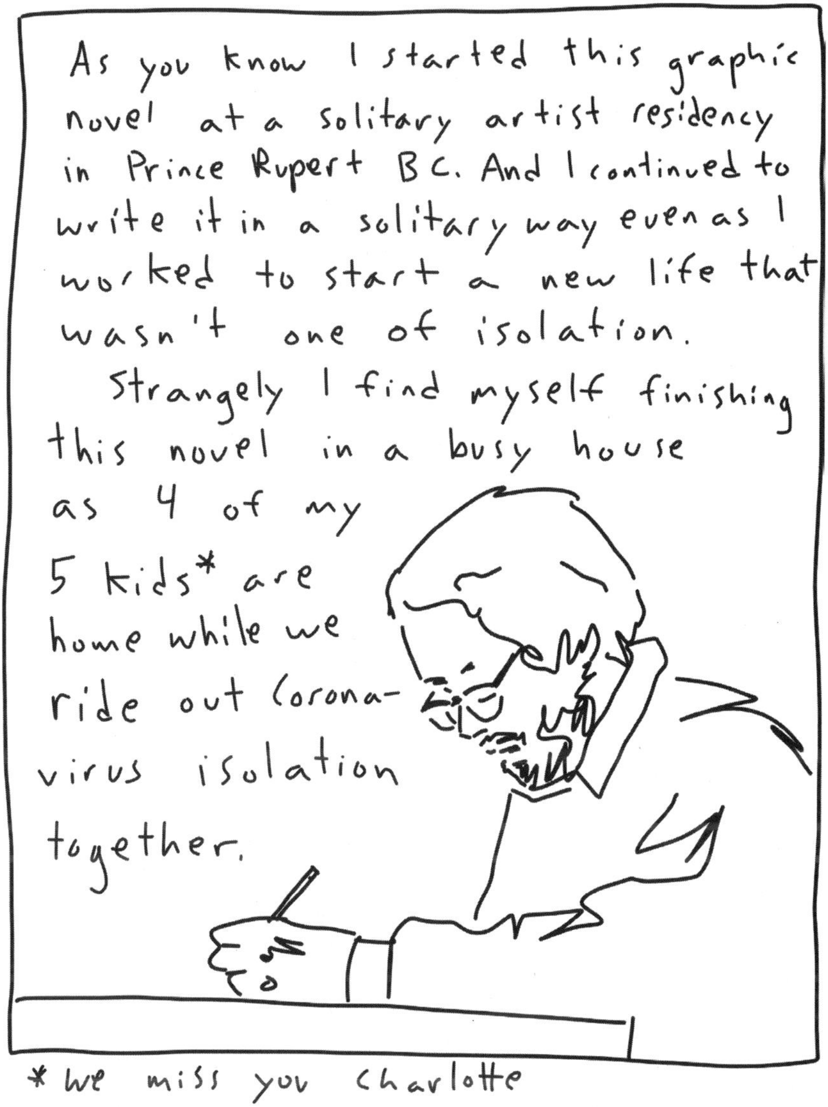
As you know I started this graphic novel at a solitary artist residency in Prince Rupert BC. And I continued to write it in a solitary way even as I worked to start a new life that wasn't one of isolation.
Strangely I find myself finishing this novel in a busy house as 4 of my 5 kids* are home while we ride out Corona-virus isolation together.

* we miss you Charlotte

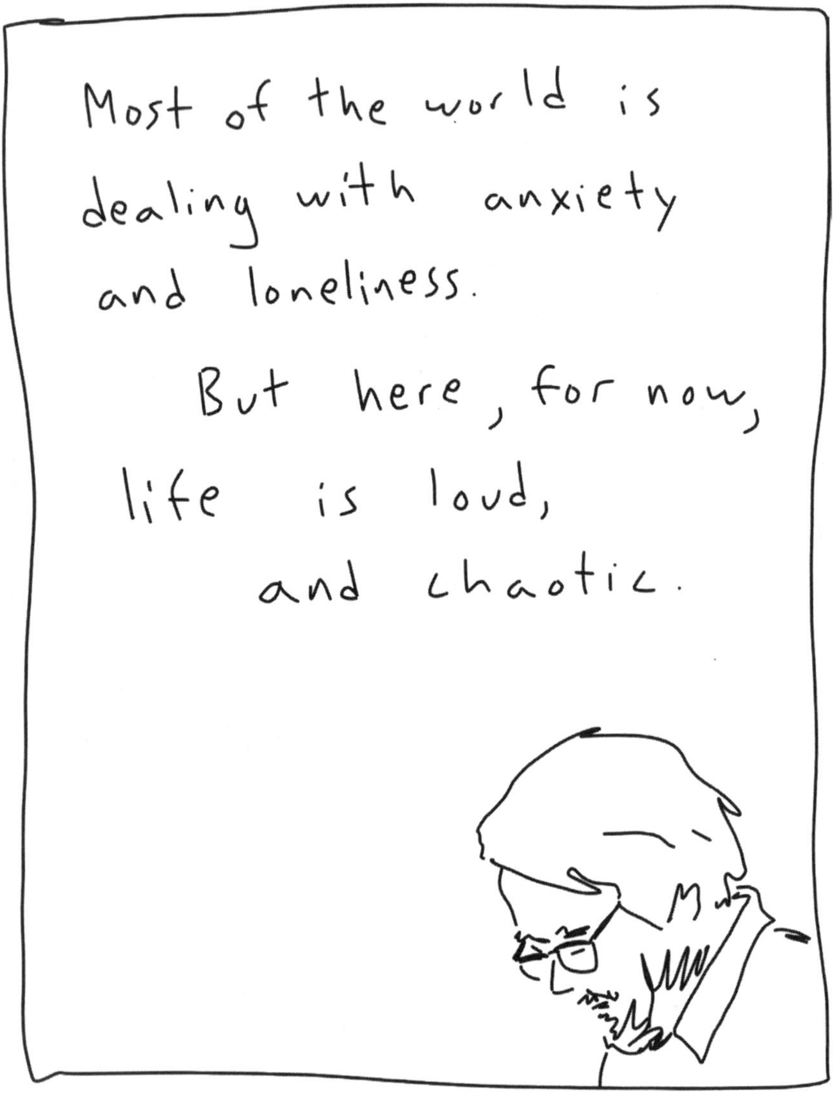
Most of the world is dealing with anxiety and loneliness.
But here, for now, life is loud, and chaotic.

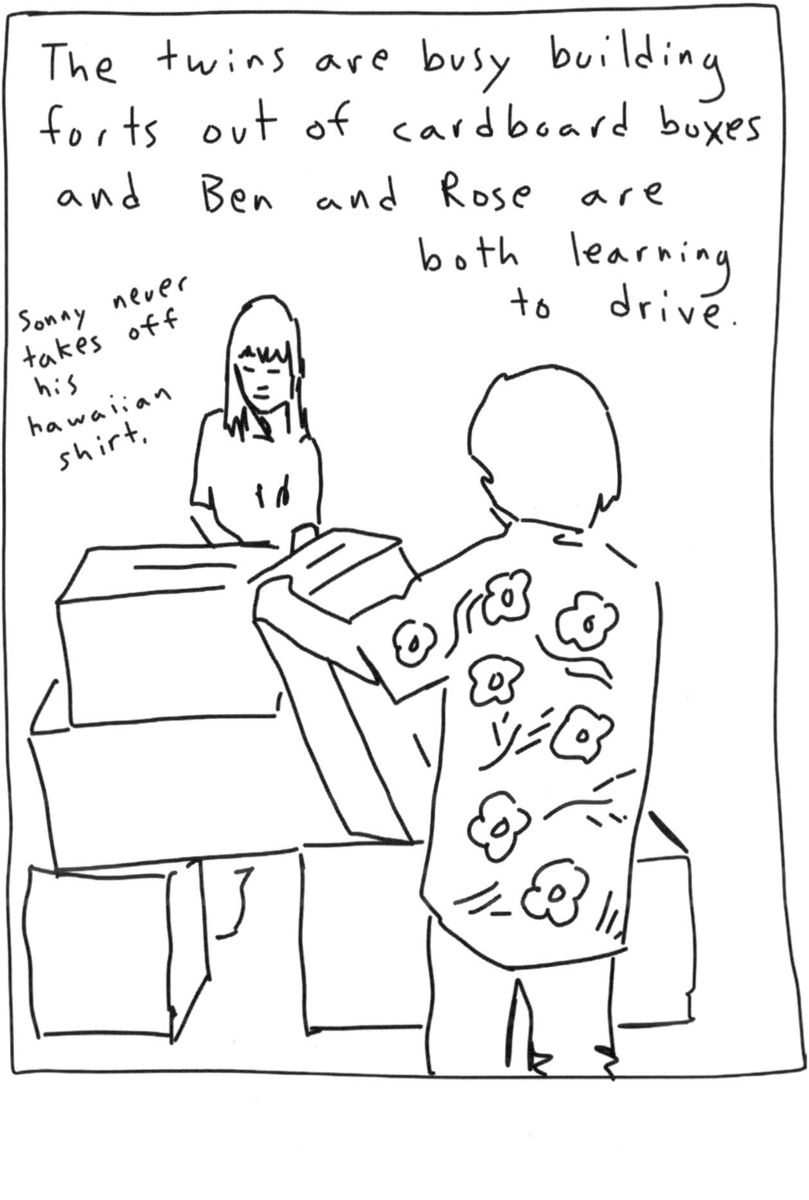
The twins are busy building forts out of cardboard boxes and Ben and Rose are both learning to drive.
Sonny never takes off his hawaiian shirt.

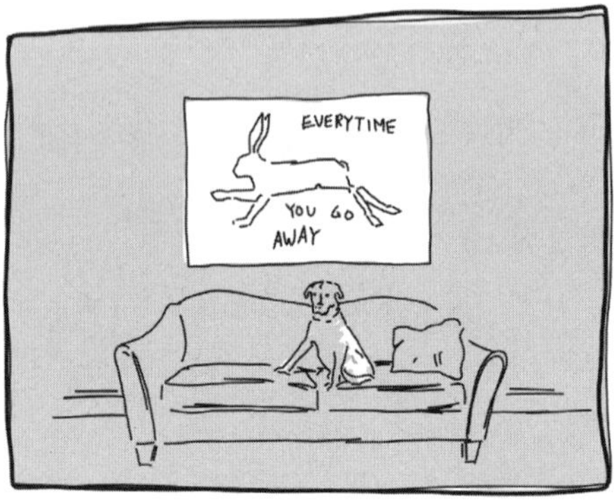
EVERYTIME
YOU GO
AWAY

stella is happy

and I'm busy

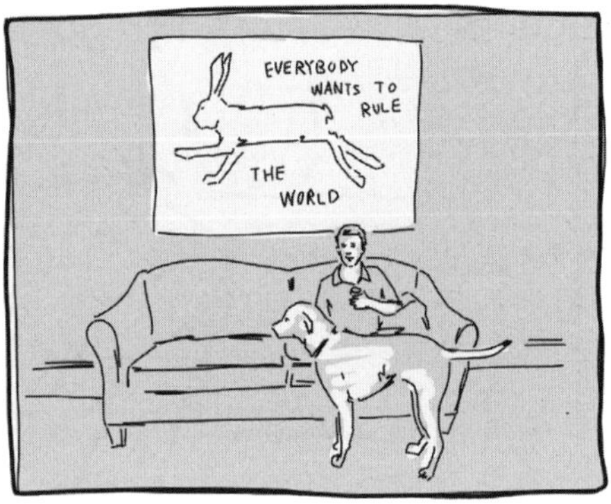
EVERYBODY
WANTS TO
RULE
THE
WORLD

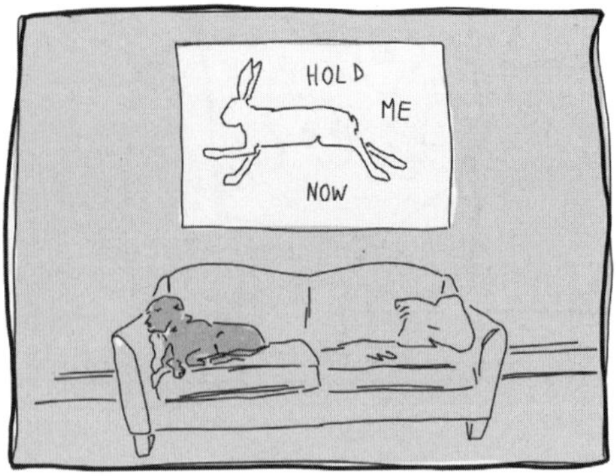
HOLD
ME
NOW

writing and painting rabbits

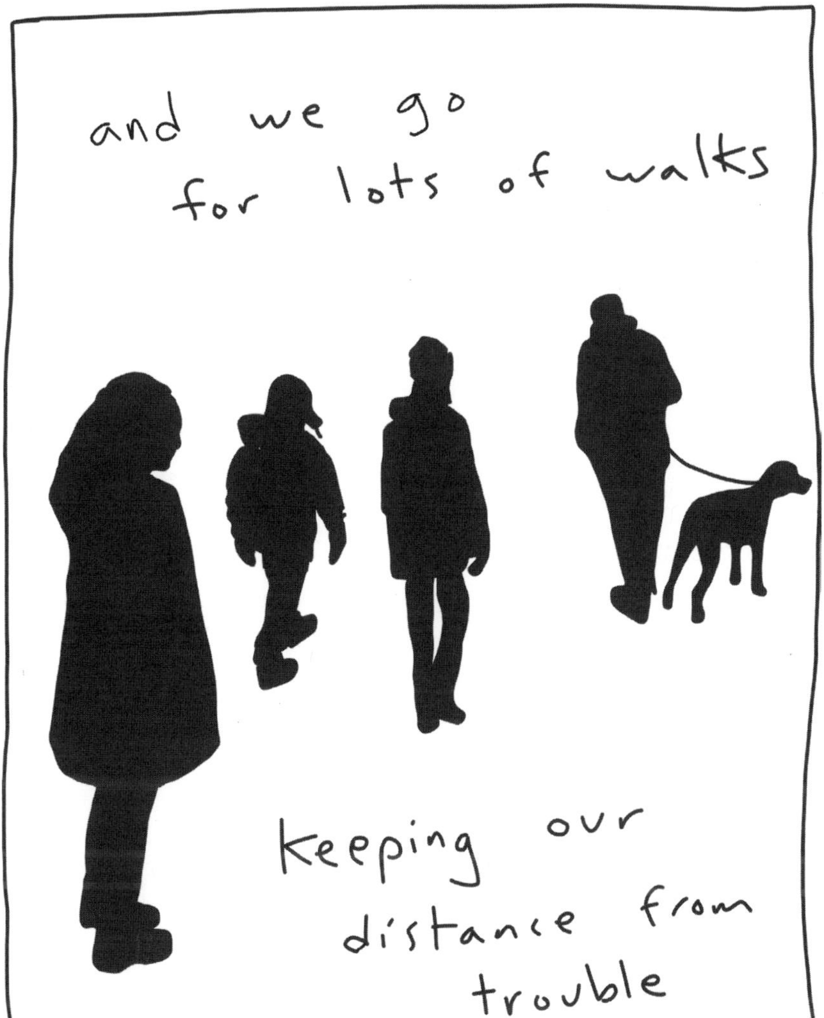
and we go
for lots of walks
keeping our
distance from
trouble

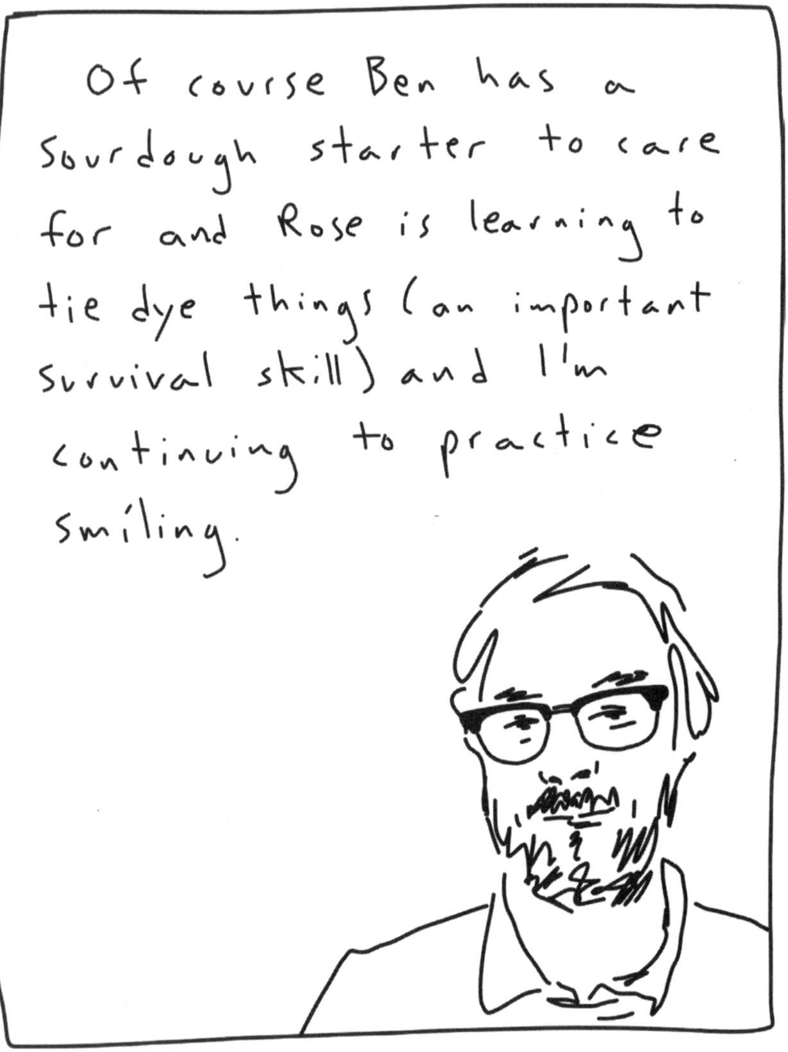
Of course Ben has a sourdough starter to care for and Rose is learning to tie dye things (an important survival skill) and I'm continuing to practice smiling.

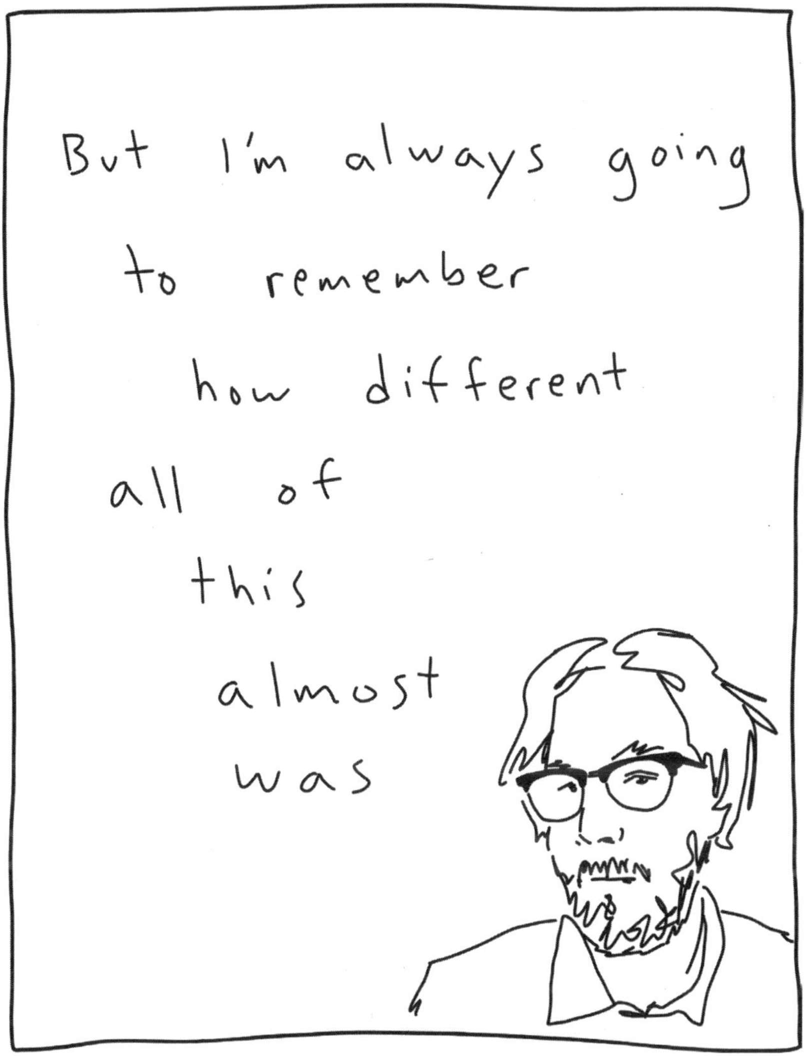
But I'm always going
to remember
how different
all of
this
almost
was

And the feeling of what could have been and of what might happen leaves me at a loss for words.

Or maybe just the right words.

I love you all, I love you all.

and

thank you.

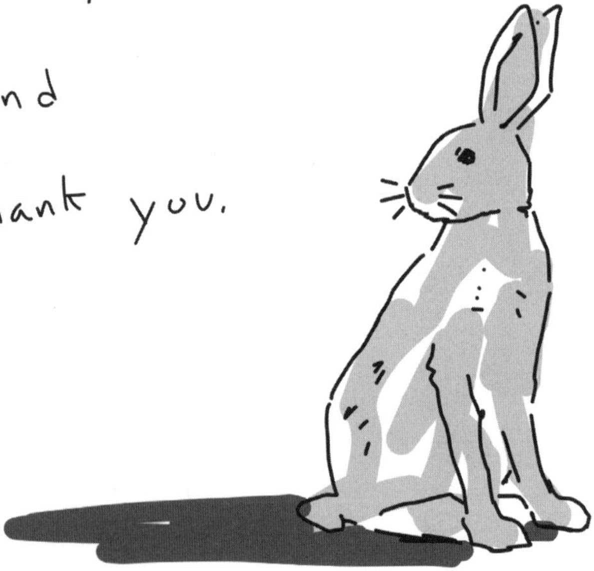

Jon Claytor is a Maritime-based artist, painter, and writer. He is a co-founder of SappyFest, an independent music and arts festival and was a bartender and co-owner at Thunder & Lightning Ideas Ltd. in Sackville, New Brunswick. Jon is a father to five children and, for him, being a father is the biggest part of being an artist.

Jon Claytor's work ranges from oil painting and watercolour to filmmaking, and he recently became a comic-writer. He worked with Ingram Gallery in Toronto and exhibited his paintings in Los Angeles. Jon holds an MFA from York University (2012), attended Nova Scotia College of Art and Design University (1991), and holds a BFA from Mount Allison University (1998).